Learning and the Brain

Advisors

Marilee Sprenger, Ph.D.
Pat Wolfe, Ed.D.

Learning and the Brain

A Comprehensive Guide for Educators, Parents, and Teachers

Edited by Sheryl Feinstein

Rowman & Littlefield Education
Lanham, Maryland • Toronto • Plymouth, UK
2007

3 1257 01848 6604

Published in the United States of America
by Rowman & Littlefield Education
A Division of Rowman & Littlefield Publishers, Inc.
A wholly owned subsidiary of The Rowman & Littlefield Publishing Group, Inc.
4501 Forbes Boulevard, Suite 200, Lanham, Maryland 20706
www.rowmaneducation.com

Estover Road
Plymouth PL6 7PY
United Kingdom

British Library Cataloguing in Publication Information Available

Library of Congress Cataloging-in-Publication Data

Learning and the brain : a comprehensive guide for educators, parents, and
teachers / Sheryl Feinstein.   p. cm.
  Includes bibliographical references.
  ISBN-13: 978-1-57886-615-1 (pbk. : alk. paper)
  ISBN-10: 1-57886-615-4 (pbk. : alk. paper)
  1. Learning—Encyclopedias. 2. Brain—Encyclopedias. I. Feinstein, Sheryl.
II. Praeger handbook of learning and the brain.
  LB1060.P683 2007
  370.15'2303—dc22   2007015176

To Mom, Dad, and my sister Susan

Contents

List of A–Z Entries

Guide to Related Topics

Adolescent
Adolescent Addiction
Adolescent Cognitive Development
Adolescent Social and Emotional Development
Anorexia
At-Risk Behavior
Legal Culpability and Correctional Facilities
Sexual Learning
Sleep

At-Risk
Addiction
Adolescent Addiction
Anorexia
At-Risk Behavior
Legal Culpability and Correctional Facilities
Obesity
Poverty

Brain Development
Adolescent Cognitive Development
Adolescent Social and Emotional Development
Adult Brain
Aging Brain
Critical Periods (Sensitive Periods)
Early Childhood Brain
Infant Brain
Prenatal Brain

Classroom Management
Classroom Management
Handling Specific Classroom Management Problems
Motivation
Proactive Classroom Management Strategies
Visual Strategies for Classroom Management

Complex Cognitive Processes
Creativity
Critical Thinking
Mastery
Transfer

Culture
Gender Differences
Poverty
At-Risk Behavior

Curriculm and Instruction
Art
Bilingualism
Drama
Math
Mozart Effect
Multimedia Technology
Music
Reading and Comprehension
Reading and Fluency
Reading in the Content Areas
Reading Vocabulary and Word Recognition
Writing

Emotion
Aggression
Anger
Animal Studies
Depression
Emotion
Emotional Intelligence
Pleasure
Stress

Emotional or Behehavioral Issues
ADD and ADHD
Emotionally and Behaviorally Challenged
Emotionally and Behaviorally Disturbed

Foods
Aroma and Learning
Beverages
Nutrition

Learning and Instruction
Assessment
Attention
Challenge and Enrichment
Communication
Feedback
Forgetting
Motivation
Nature of Knowledge
Patterns and Programs
Pedagogy
Processing Time
Social Context of Learning
Teaching Model for the Brain

Learning Challenges
ADD and ADHD
Autism Spectrum Disorders
Blindness
Cognitive Disabilities
Deaf and Hard of Hearing
Emotionally and Behaviorally Challenged
Emotionally Behaviorally Disturbed
Fetal Alcohol Syndrome
Gifted
Language Acquisition and Disorders
Learning Disabilities
Schizophrenia
Trauma

Learning Environments
Classroom Environment
Classroom Management
Motivation
Physical Environment
Social Context of Learning
Visual Strategies for Classroom Management

Learning Styles
Auditory Development and Learning
Learning Cycles
Learning Styles
Multiple Intelligences
Suggestopedia and Accelerated Learning
Visual Images and Learning

Learning Theories
Behaviorism
Constructivism
Distributed Intelligence
Episodic Memory
Information-Processing Model
Procedural Memory
Semantic Memory

Physical Movement
Early Childhood Brain and Physical Movement
Physical Movement
Play

Reading
Reading and Comprehension
Reading and Fluency
Reading in the Content Areas
Reading Vocabulary and Word Recognition

Senses
Auditory Development and Learning
Blindness
Deaf and Hard of Hearing
Language Acquisition and Disorders
Visual Images and Learning

Social, Emotional and Moral Development
Self-Efficacy
Self Esteem
Moral Development
Spirituality

Preface

Study of the brain holds promise and fascination for almost every educator and parent. Recent strides in the field of neuroscience are impacting and changing the quality and quantity of information on the brain. Modern medical technology and brain scans enable us to view the brain while it's alive and functioning. We can literally see which areas of the brain are involved in various thought processes. Observing the brain while in action provides rich information on attention, making meaning, memory, and social/emotional development; confirming many things we're already doing in education and giving insight into meaningful changes. The field of cognitive neuroscience opens the doors to understanding the brain, adding to medical findings, pedagogy and child rearing.

The purpose of this handbook is to provide practical and informative explanations of the most important issues and Best Practice in education. Best practice refers to exemplary instructional strategies and curricula for students. This book provides through coverage of each topic. The themes for the entries are wide-ranging, offering a comprehensive look at teaching and learning. I began by tapping into my own long-term memory storage and from there expanded to journal articles, textbooks, the Internet, classroom teachers, and leading authorities in education, psychology and cognitive neuroscience. The entry topics fall under three main areas: student characteristics, classroom instructional topics, and learning challenges. It would be difficult to imagine more fertile soil than the brain for understanding the development and learning processes of students.

Selecting authors was done in a purposeful manner. Cognitive neuroscience is an interdisciplinary field involving neuroscientists, psychologists and educationists. Their joint purpose is to understand the mind, brain, and behavior. Authors came from all three disciplines. After reading their books, journal articles, and/or research endeavors authors with an expertise in a subject area were invited to participate. I contacted them and invited them to be part of this project. Most authors were leaders in their field; others were junior faculty at universities, graduate students, and classroom teachers. This book gave them an opportunity to grow and contribute to the body of knowledge in their chosen profession. I believe it is a testament to the field that almost everyone contacted chose to participate in the book. I found their generosity and commitment to education personally inspiring.

Educational topics are covered systematically and comprehensively. Each entry provides enough information to enable the serious reader to grasp the fundamental concepts and instructional strategies to take directly into their classroom. The entries are organized with an extensive connection to the latest discoveries in cognitive neuroscience, an overview of the educational topic, and then classroom instructional strategies. The book combines a justification of how the brain works, why a strategy is brain-compatible, followed by practical applications.

Three unusual features of this encyclopedia deserve mention. First, is the "See Also" listing and in-text items in BOLD included with each entry. They refer to cross-references in the book; entries are extensively cross-referenced in the book. For example, the entry on Adolescent Social & Emotional Development is cross referenced with Adolescent Cognitive Development and At-Risk. The purpose of the cross-references is to enable a reader who has looked up a topic to obtain additional information that is either directly or indirectly relevant to it. This aids the reader in serious scholarship. Secondly, a Further Readings section is included with each entry. Further Readings are suggested books, journals, and Internet sites that the individual authors recommended in order to learn more about their specific topic. They are current and practical in nature. In Addition, a glossary of terms exclusively dedicated to brain structure and function is provided.

Acknowledgements

A special thank you to the following individuals: Susan Jordan for her unwavering capacity to listen and offer valuable advice; my children, Jennifer, Scott, Rachel, and James Feinstein for their patience and encouragement; Belinda Kaffar for her perspective and assistance; Jyl Baartman, Michelle Buboltz, Laura S. Anderson, Cory Sweet, Sarah Hanna, and Annmarie Kowalczyk for their help and initiative; Bob Wood for being my first mentor; Bob Kiner for his support and vision; and to the Augustana College community, and in particular the library staff for their expertise and support of scholarship.

I would also like to thank my acquisition and copy editors, Marie Ellen Larcada, who conceived and shepherd the project, Sarah Colwell who supported and saw the book to completion and Bharath Parthasarathy who's attention to detail was a necessary pleasure.

Introduction

How does emotion impact learning? What is plasticity's role in fostering lifelong learners? Are there sensitive periods in brain development? What is the importance of the first five years in future learning? Are there differences between the male and female brain? These are intriguing questions facing educators and they are all questions this book will answer.

Educators are becoming increasingly aware of the advances in neuroscience and what it can offer to improve educational Best Practice. Developments within neuroscience have provided new ways of examining the mind and brain. In the past, an autopsy or an examination of brain-damaged individuals was the only way to gather information. Studying an inactive brain was a severe limitation to educators whose purpose was to actively engage the brain. The invention of functional neuroimaging such as functional magnetic resonance imaging (fMRI) and positron emission tomography (PET) changed the landscape. With these new technological advances, the U.S. scientific community declared the 1990's the Decade of the Brain. This has resulted in study focused on areas such as perception, memory, and emotion and added support to a new discipline called cognitive neuroscience.

Cognitive neuroscience integrates scholarship from neuroscientists, psychologists and educationists. The structure and function of the brain plays an integral role in their research. The purpose is to better understand how the brain processes, stores, and retrieves information and how this then impacts behavior. Universities across the country are endorsing this area of study. Many programs include a combination of understanding content areas of learning (language, science, reading, and math) and the cognitive neuroscience of learning (transfer, lateralization, social aspects, and brain development) in their global objectives.

There's no magic bullet to solve all of education and society's challenges. Some over zealous educators have stepped over the line connecting neuroscience to education, creating a prickly feud between educators and neuroscientists. In some instances this may be true, box it is equally irresponsible to ignore what is being learned about the brain. A synthesis of what neuroscience, psychology and education have to offer is important in offering a quality educational experience. Knowledge helps us make better decisions. While we must be cautious when interpreting research, it holds the potential to inform our teaching and increase students' academic achievement.

Classroom teachers will find this book helpful because it not only validates much of their teaching through research-based instructional strategies, but also adds to their stockpile of strategies. It provides a rich rationale for why we structure educational experiences the way we do. Teachers, principals, and parents (children's first teachers) will find substantial options to select and deliver instruction. As we understand more how the brain is structured and functions the greater is our ability to unleash brain power.

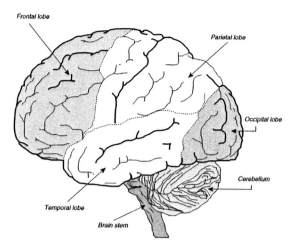

The structure of the brain.

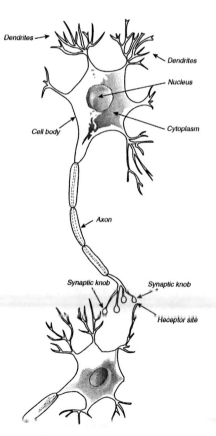

The structure of a neuron.

A

ADD and ADHD

Attention deficit/hyperactivity disorder (ADHD) is defined as a pattern of inattention and/or hyperactivity/impulsivity that is persistent and unusually frequent and severe, given a person's level of development. While the term "attention deficit disorder" (ADD) was used in a previous edition of the *Diagnostic and Statistical Manual of Mental Disorders* (*DSM-IIIR*), "ADHD" is used in the current edition (*DSM-IV-TR*). Although the two terms have been used interchangeably, the latter represents the fact that hyperactivity is a commonly occurring symptom of this disorder.

ADHD is characterized by poor sustained attention and hyperactivity-impulsiveness, across three subtypes: predominantly inattentive, predominantly hyperactive-impulsive, and combination types. The general symptoms include: (1) being inattentive, (2) not listening or following directions, (3) having problems with organization and/or losing items, (4) being distracted, (5) moving or talking excessively, (6) acting impulsively, (7) interrupting, and (8) not taking turns in play or conversation. To be diagnosed with ADHD, a person must exhibit several of these behaviors, which must have emerged before age seven, impede performance (social, educational, and occupational) in at least two settings, and not stem from other health conditions. ADHD often occurs along with a conduct, anxiety, or learning problem, often remains after puberty, and is currently the most commonly diagnosed neurobehavioral disorder among children. Treatment may be through medication, behavioral therapy, or a combination of both.

The diagnosis of ADHD is controversial because the scientific community has been unable to establish how common it is and because, as stated above, it often coexists with other disorders, which makes isolating it difficult. Research, however, has begun to shed some light on the involvement of the brain. Studies, for instance, have confirmed that the prefrontal cortex, the basal ganglia, and the cerebellum (areas that help regulate attention, motor activity, inhibition, and impulsive behavior) are less active in people with ADHD and that the neurotransmitters dopamine and norepinephrine (responsible for carrying nerve impulses) are involved in some way.

According to brain imaging research that examined how water moves along the fibers that form a signal network among brain components, such motion is abnormal in children with ADHD. This abnormality was detected in the fiber network in the frontal cortex, basal ganglia, brain stem, and cerebellum, suggesting that there may be a breakdown in the brain's communication system.

Brain imaging studies have also begun to reveal how ADHD-related chemical and electrical irregularities can be corrected through medication. Some critics of medications to treat ADHD have voiced a concern that such drugs might reduce brain size. While one study indeed established that the brains of children with ADHD were on average 3–4 percent smaller than those of a control group (a difference that apparently occurs early in development), the children examined were not taking such drugs. Nevertheless, critics still contend that children with ADHD are often over-medicated and not receiving adequate behavioral training. Many if not all of the strategies that follow may address the call for behavioral intervention while helping to compensate for the related brain-specific issues mentioned above.

As long as the disorder adversely impacts their academic performance, students with ADHD may receive special education services. They may also receive services if the disorder co-occurs with another disability that is covered under the Individuals with Disabilities Education Act. Students with ADHD who do not qualify for special education services may receive educational accommodations through Section 504 of the Rehabilitation Act.

To determine if a student has ADHD, a functional behavioral assessment (FBA) may be conducted. This measure collects student behavior data, determines the reasons for particular behaviors, and identifies variables that trigger and maintain them. The FBA can help the teacher decide how to implement educational strategies.

A comprehensive approach to working with students with ADHD involves academic instruction, behavioral interventions, and classroom accommodations. To engage these students more effectively, instructors should teach within contexts that are personally relevant to them, incorporate physical movement into lessons, allow students to use response cards, and allow them to choose from a menu of instructional activities. Teachers should use advanced organizers and graphic organizers, check for comprehension, break down work into manageable units, increase quiz and test time, and use cooperative learning. Moreover, they need to schedule cognitively challenging content during the morning hours and hands-on activities in the afternoon. Research indicates that the behavior of students with ADHD commonly deteriorates throughout the day.

Other instructional strategies include getting students' attention before giving directions; keeping the directions clear, concise, and specific with regard to expectations for performance; avoiding multi-step directions; and giving directions three times. To ensure that students understand assignment instructions, teachers can have them respond to questions that call on them to state (1) what they are being asked to do, (2) what steps they need to follow, (3) what materials they will need,

(4) whom they should ask for help, (5) how much time they have to complete the assignment, (6) how their work will be graded, (7) what they may do if they finish early, and (8) what questions they have about the assignment. Instructors also need to encourage efficient transitions by informing students that they will have excess transition time deducted from their free time and ensure that students attain 90 percent accuracy before working independently.

Additional steps that teachers can take include providing students with a job card that displays step-by-step instructions on how to complete a particular task and having students use an assistance card when they need help. When instructors see the card, if they are busy at the moment, they can flip the card to the "continue working" side to acknowledge the request. They can also use peer tutoring and immediate feedback, highlight important task features with color variation, and allow the students who struggle with handwriting to use word processors.

To respond effectively to behavioral issues, teachers may define appropriate behaviors, use praise, ignore inappropriate behavior selectively, use proximity control, provide tangible rewards, and implement token economies. They may also provide frequent feedback and have peers ignore inappropriate behavior.

The classroom environment is another factor to consider. To make it more conducive to learning for students with ADHD, instructors may seat the children near their desk or the board—whatever location the teacher will frequent—and surround them with peer role models. They should seat the student away from high-traffic areas and potential distractions (e.g., doorway, window, or pencil sharpener), and they can provide a stand-up desk that the students can move to when they need a location/physical change. Instructors may also make a study carrel available; arrange the desks in rows; and use student mailboxes, storage bins, and color-coded folders to help students organize their materials. Finally, they should reduce noise to the degree at which it is not interfering with academic performance.

What can be most useful to students with ADHD is learning how to monitor and manage their own behavior and academic performance. Students can be taught to analyze how they arrive at successes and failures and how their learning is affected by their effort and motivation. Students can also learn to set behavior goals and to reinforce those behaviors that they wish to increase.

Self-management training, however, needs to be supplemented with the development of appropriate social skills. A program of social skills instruction should call on teachers to (1) assess students' social skill mastery; (2) model respectful and inclusive social behaviors; (3) teach appropriate behavior through children's literature and videos; (4) facilitate peer interaction through academic assignments; (5) promote effective interpersonal strategies by offering rewards, (6) de-emphasize competition, especially in games; (7) teach students how to recognize nonverbal communication and how to respond appropriately; (8) clarify the rules of various social situations; and (9) teach students to examine both the positive and negative outcomes of their social encounters and to evaluate the effectiveness of the strategies they used. Teachers may also promote friendship and class cohesion through the use of games, songs, art activities, and group exercises.

Much of the focus on ADHD strategies has applied to K-12 students. Some research is now aimed at postsecondary education, including the transition from high school to higher education and the world of work. Relatively few **adults** with ADHD obtain a professional job, but high school counselors can help students prepare for the world beyond graduation in a number of ways. For instance, they can involve students in preparing a file in which they organize the information they need for the transition to post-secondary education and help them research what accommodations are available at a particular campus. They can assist teachers and parents in developing mnemonic strategies for students and help students develop skills of articulation, especially language specific to the target work environment.

Counselors may also role-play potential real-life job situations with students and teach them how to self-regulate their communication. They can do the latter by teaching students to encourage others to evaluate their conversational ability and to ask their listeners clarifying questions. They should teach them how to process large amounts of information through listing, audio-recording, and flowcharting, and help them to become more adept at relationships by having them take part in counseling groups. Additionally, they can teach them other memory strategies, such as the use of a daily calendar, electronic reminders, visual prompts, and routines, and having back-ups for important items and information.

Counselors can even further help their students by teaching them daily living strategies and how to avoid over- and under-stimulation. For example, with regard to daily living, they can teach students to (1) frequently ask themselves what they should be doing at a given moment, (2) regularly examine how intrusive thoughts impede their productivity, (3) take frequent breaks, (4) repeat difficult material they hear to themselves and restate it in their own words, and (5) create incentives for sustained periods of concentration. Concerning over- and under-stimulation, counselors may teach students how to (1) designate space for periodic isolation, both at home and at work; (2) avoid traffic jams, shopping malls, crowds, and noisy locations; (3) alternate between lower- and higher-interest activities; (4) seek interpersonal contact; (5) be physically active; (6) seek challenging situations; and (7) pursue an intrinsically rewarding career.

Finally, researchers have found that massage therapy may help students with ADHD. In a study in which special education students between the ages of seven and eighteen received a massage for twenty minutes, twice per week, for a month, the therapy appeared to improve their short-term mood and reduce their ADHD-related behaviors. While the relationship between the therapy and the apparent benefits is unclear, researchers stress its potential value in a multimodal approach to managing the disorder.

Educators can assist students with ADHD in many ways. With the benefit of a variety of strategies, tailored to their individual needs, these students can manage the often-frenetic pace of their mental activity and lead lives of achievement as contributing members of their world.

See also: **Attention; Feedback; Patterns and Programs; Physical Environment; Social Context of Learning.**

Further Readings

Barkley, R.A. (1998). *Attention-Deficit Hyperactivity Disorder: A Handbook for Diagnosis and Treatment* (2nd ed.). New York, NY: Guilford Press.

Honos-Webb, L. (2005). *The Gift of ADHD: How to Transform Your Child's Problems into Strengths.* Oakland, CA: New Harbinger Publisher.

Jensen, E. (2003). *A New View of AD/HD: Success Strategies for Teaching the Impulsive Learner.* San Diego, CA: The Brain Store, Inc.

Minskoff, E., Allsopp, D. (2002). *Academic Success Strategies for Adolescents with Learning Disabilities and ADHD.* Baltimore, MD: Paul H. Brookes.

National Resource Center on AD/HD (2005). Home page. Retrieved on February 11, 2005 from http://www.help4adhd.org/

CRAIG A. DAVIS, M.ED. AND
LINDA S. BEHAR-HORENSTEIN, PH.D.

Addiction

Addiction is a disorder of the brain characterized by an impaired ability to refrain from using a psychoactive substance despite serious negative consequences. Such substances include some that are legal, such as alcohol and certain prescription medications, as well as others that are illegal, such as heroin, cocaine, marijuana, and methamphetamine. Addiction afflicts people from all ethnic groups, and all walks of life. According to the National Institutes of Health, more than a third of American adults report having a family member affected by this disease. The widespread nature of this illness coupled with its negative impact on those around the addict make this disease a major social problem.

While addiction is a problem that no group is immune from, much evidence suggests that both biological and environmental risk factors contribute to the expression of addictive behavior. In addition, neuroscientists have learned a great deal about the neural circuitry involved in addictive behavior. However, despite this knowledge, few treatment options are yet available. This lack of treatment options highlights the current importance of prevention strategies.

For people suffering from this illness, the compulsion to continue using the substance they are addicted to is often stronger than any other motivation. Under normal conditions, hunger, thirst, and a healthy fear of death or bodily harm are so powerful that they ensure that our most basic needs for food, water and physical safety are met. The needs for emotional companionship, financial security, and sexual gratification are also normally potent motivating forces guiding our actions. However, for the addict, some or all of these drives become secondary to obtaining their abused substance. This misdirection of motivation can lead to physical damage to the body, loss of vital relationships, loss of employment, and loss of shelter. Observing addictive behavior can be frightening and puzzling.

Why do addicts risk such harm? The answer seems to be that in the throes of addiction, certain circuits in the brain that normally guide goal-directed behavior are malfunctioning. Evidence for this comes mainly from studies of animal models of addiction, although more recent studies in humans also support this hypothesis. Although addiction is generally viewed as a uniquely human disorder, animals can become addicted to all of the substances that humans become addicted to. Thus, it may be simply our unique access to concentrated forms of these substances that selectively precipitates the disease in our species. Animals also demonstrate similar risk factors for susceptibility to addiction. This fact allows scientists to study in detail the relative contribution of each of these risk factors, how they interact, and how they may be remedied or counteracted. These risk factors will be discussed in more detail below.

Animal studies have been instrumental in furthering our understanding of addiction. Such studies have determined which circuits in the brain play a role in addictive behavior. Important components of these circuits include a brainstem site called the ventral tegmental area (VTA), the prefrontal cortex, and two areas located deep in the brain, the amygdala and the nucleus accumbens. The VTA neurons produce a neurotransmitter called dopamine, which they release into the other three brain areas listed above. Such dopamine release normally occurs in response to natural rewards like food, water, and sex, but it also occurs in response to all drugs of abuse. These circuits are affected by learning, with the result being that cues associated with rewards also trigger dopamine release. Chronic intake of drugs of abuse results in an intensified version of such learning, producing extreme hypersensitivity to drug-related cues.

This knowledge gathered in animal studies has enabled scientists to take a more educated approach to studies of addiction in humans. In addition to clinical trials of therapeutic interventions, developing laboratory measures for pre-clinical testing of potential treatments in humans is essential. This area of research, which falls generally into the domain of cognitive neuroscience, has focused primarily on three aspects of cognition impacted by addiction. First, a great deal of this work has focused on conditioned sensory responses elicited by drug-related sensory cues. Second, a growing area of investigation encompasses different aspects of decision-making. Third, some work has focused on behavioral inhibition, or impulse control. By combining careful studies in these areas with neuroimaging and pharmacology, a great deal of progress toward improved treatment options is anticipated in coming decades. Already, results have confirmed that the same neural circuits are similarly impacted in human addicts.

However, given the few currently available treatments, understanding risk factors for addiction is an important element in prevention. Known risk factors include both biological and environmental types. Among biological factors, genetic risks for addiction have been repeatedly demonstrated. However, as with other complex neuropsychiatric disorders, such as schizophrenia, there is no single gene that causes the illness. On the contrary, there are clearly a whole host of genes in which particular forms, or "alleles," increase one's susceptibility to developing a serious problem with alcohol or other drugs of abuse. Also important are "epigenetic" biological factors, such as exposure to hormones and other chemicals in the womb. For example, maternal nicotine ingestion increases the likelihood of later substance abuse in the exposed offspring.

It is vital to note that these biological predispositions are not equivalent to predetermination. As with diseases like adult-onset diabetes, or heart disease, one's behavior and environment interact with one's biological makeup to determine whether the disease will be expressed. In the case of addiction, an obvious necessity is exposure to the substances of abuse. Other important environmental factors include attitudes within the family and the larger social group toward drug and alcohol use and abuse. Another critical factor is the age of initiation. The earlier that one is exposed to alcohol or other drugs, the more likely it will be that addiction manifests. Moreover, those who started using earlier find it more difficult to stop abusing drugs or alcohol. Though not yet proven, this is thought to be due to the immaturity of the frontal lobes until relatively late in life. This area of the brain, which helps us to control our behavior and to plan for the future, generally does not mature completely until the late teens to the early twenties. This area, also referred to as the prefrontal cortex, is the brain's "executive control" center, and is strongly impacted by both acute and chronic abuse of drugs and alcohol. Moreover, much evidence suggests that the prefrontal cortex is under functioning in the setting of addiction.

When addiction does surface, what can be done about it? The available treatment options can be broadly classified as psychotherapeutic or medication based. Within the psychotherapeutic realms, there are two main divisions. Perhaps the most well known are mutual support group methods based on the Twelve Steps of Alcoholics Anonymous; however, other more recently established organizations based on approaches such as cognitive behavioral therapy are also available. Another commonly employed option is one-on-one therapy with a mental health professional specializing in addictive disorders. Many states currently provide certification for this specialty, both for medical doctors and for clinical psychologists. Medications are also currently available for treating some forms of addiction, especially nicotine, opiates, and alcohol.

All of these forms of treatment are designed to attack the problem using one (or a combination) of three basic approaches. The first is to try and remedy the underlying biopsychological cause of the disease. This assumes that there is a psychological problem or chemical imbalance that causes the addict to "self-medicate" with drugs or alcohol. Some examples include **depression, anger, anxiety, and stress**. This approach tends to focus on treating the presumed underlying cause rather than the addiction per se, with the assumption that the addiction will resolve itself when the root problem is alleviated.

The ideas behind the other main treatment options are designed to more directly address the addiction problem itself. These approaches are generally designed to either eliminate craving, or to block the pleasurable, or "hedonic," effects of the drugs. The first approach assumes that overwhelming drug cravings are responsible for maintaining the addiction, and if these cravings can be effectively quelled, the addiction can be cured. This can be accomplished with either aversion or replacement therapy. In prophylactic aversion therapy, patients are given a medication that will cause severe sickness if combined with the drug of abuse. Currently, this approach is only available for alcohol. Another form of aversion therapy involves sessions in a treatment center where the substance in question, as well as associated items, is paired with aversive stimulation such as electric shock or chemically induced nausea. Unfortunately, this approach may only be effective for those individuals who have not yet experienced severe negative side-effects as a result of their addiction.

The second tactic for craving prevention involves substituting a non-addictive substance that stimulates the same target sites in the brain. The most commonly known treatment of this sort is methadone, which is used primarily to treat heroin addiction. The so-called substitution therapy has a twofold method of action. First, by stimulating the drug target sites, withdrawal symptoms are prevented. Second, by occupying drug target sites, "getting high" becomes impossible. The success of methadone therapy in treating heroin addiction has motivated scientists to actively pursue similar medications for other classes of drugs of abuse. This approach has also included providing the drug itself in an alternative form. In the case of nicotine, replacement therapy has effectively helped many people conquer their addiction to tobacco products.

The final common therapeutic approach, hedonic effect blockade, is designed to prevent the "high" produced by the drug. By eliminating the pleasurable effects of the substance, presumably the motivation for using it is also abolished. While this approach has proved successful for opiate addiction, the side effects of medications that block other classes of drugs of abuse are too severe to be suitable for addiction treatment. A surprising development, however, is that medications that block the action of opiates in the brain also reduce the compulsion to drink alcohol. These results indicate that blocking the initial action of the drug is not the only effective route for hedonic blockade. Moreover, it highlights that common circuitry is being engaged by addictions to substances with differing primary sites of action. Interestingly, opiate receptor blockers are also effective for treating compulsive gambling and **eating disorders**, lending credence to the idea that these are true addictions with shared underlying mechanisms in the brain.

The limited range of current treatment options emphasizes the importance of addiction prevention. Children should be educated about the risks of drug and alcohol use with particular emphasis on the increased risks associated with use in the teens or earlier. Young people should also be alerted to the increased risks linked to a family history of drug or alcohol abuse. The fact that addressing addiction problems in earlier stages tends to predict better outcomes, calls for education regarding the warning signs of a problem in one's self and others. Finally, given the prevalence of data suggesting that difficulty coping with negative emotions contributes to addiction problems, society would be well served by expanding and improving early training for handling of negative emotions, thereby reducing the need for people to "self-medicate."

Much progress remains to be made in understanding the underlying causes of addiction and in developing new treatments. A crucial step, however, has been the acknowledgement that addiction is a brain disease, like **depression** or **schizophrenia**. This acknowledgment is reducing the stigma of the disease and promoting the expansion of research aimed at finding a cure. Emerging scientific fields, such as cognitive neuroscience, show particular promise for contributing to our understanding of the problem by taking new approaches to it.

See also: **At-risk Behavior; Adolescent Addiction; Fetal Alcohol Syndrome.**

Further Readings

Cardinal, R.N., Everitt, B.J. (2004). Neural and psychological mechanisms underlying appetitive learning: links to drug addiction. *Current Opinion in Neurobiology* 14:156–162.

Helmuth, L. (2001). ADDICTION: Beyond the pleasure principle. *Science* 294:983–984.

Nestler, E.J., Malenka, R.C. (2004). The addicted brain. *Scientific American* 290(3):78–85.

National Institute on Drug Abuse: www.nida.nih.gov

CHARLOTTE A. BOETTIGER, PH.D. AND
MARK D'ESPOSITO, MD.

Adolescent Addiction

Experimentation with drug use typically occurs during adolescence, a critical period for continuing brain development. Repeated exposure to alcohol and other drugs during adolescence can alter the course of brain development, with potentially profound effects on brain integrity and cognitive functioning. Most adolescents who experiment with drugs do not progress to addiction. Addiction involves compulsive drug seeking and use, and sometimes uncontrollable craving for a drug, despite recurrent, serious problems caused by continued drug use. Adolescents may be at particular risk for addiction once substance use begins due to higher levels of sensation-seeking and risk-taking during this developmental period, less developed problem-solving and coping skills, as well as the need to manage stress associated with physical changes brought on by puberty, increasing independence from the family, and transition to adult roles (e.g., work, marriage).

During adolescence, experimentation with alcohol and other drugs typically occurs out of curiosity regarding a drug's effects, desire for excitement and sensation-seeking, as well as for social reasons, such as wanting to fit in with peers and feeling pressured by peers to engage in drug use. The drugs most commonly used by adolescents include alcohol, tobacco, and marijuana. Adolescents who increase their involvement with alcohol and other drugs tend to report a mix of social (e.g., partying with friends) and coping reasons for drug use (e.g., drinking to relax or escape from problems). Teens who spend time with deviant peers or use drugs to cope with problems appear to be especially vulnerable to increasing drug use and addiction.

For some individuals, drug use produces temporary feelings of pleasure (feeling "high") and well-being. One way in which drugs produce these pleasurable effects is by acting on the brain's "reward system," the limbic system. In response to the drug, the limbic system increases the release of the neurotransmitter dopamine in the brain, which is associated with feelings of pleasure. To maintain these pleasurable feelings, the individual may engage in repeated drug use. As a result of continuing drug use and the high levels of dopamine that it produces, neurons in the brain may begin to reduce the amount of dopamine that is available either by reducing the number of dopamine receptors or making less dopamine. The individual may then feel the need to use a drug to maintain normal levels of dopamine in the brain. In addition, the individual may feel the need to increase the amount of drug consumed to raise dopamine levels to the point of feeling "high." When a heavy drug user stops or cuts down on drug use, withdrawal symptoms in the form of negative mood (e.g., irritability, depression), and physical symptoms (e.g., hand tremor, sweating) may occur. To keep withdrawal from occurring, or to make it go away, an individual may feel compelled to continue drug use, despite repeated serious problems caused by drug use (e.g., poor school or work performance), and a strong desire to quit or cut down on use. Thus, prolonged and heavy drug use affects brain functioning and behavior, resulting in a compulsive pattern of drug seeking and drug use behavior.

By the senior year in high school, the majority (60 percent) of adolescents have "been drunk," and about half have tried cigarettes (53 percent) and marijuana (46 percent). According to the 2003 National Survey on Drug Use and Health, 6 percent of adolescents, aged twelve to seventeen, had recurrent problems related to alcohol use in the past year, while 5 percent reported repeated problems due to illicit drug use, most often because of marijuana use. The course of substance-related problems varies. Some individuals experience drug problems that are limited to adolescence or young adulthood, while others experience drug addiction as a chronic, relapsing illness that requires continuing care even after sustained periods of abstinence.

Among adolescents who experiment with a drug, it is difficult to predict who will and will not become addicted. However, certain risk factors have been associated with greater likelihood of addiction. These risk factors include: drug use in the family, parental neglect or abuse of the child, family discord, conduct problems, early age of first drug use, and spending time with friends who engage in substance use and delinquent activities. Risk factors represent psychological and social challenges that may differentially impact pathways leading to substance use depending on their timing, duration, and severity. Protective factors that reduce the likelihood of problematic drug use include: consistent parental supervision, cohesive family relations, positive adult and peer role models, feelings of success in school and extracurricular activities (e.g., youth groups), positive peer relationships, and normative beliefs about drug use.

Treatment for adolescent drug use ranges from brief interventions that enhance a teen's motivation to change alcohol and drug use, to formal counseling, and self-help groups (e.g., Alcoholics Anonymous). Counseling typically involves developing skills to refuse drugs, strengthening coping and problem-solving skills, and increasing non-drug related recreational activities and relationships. Family involvement in treatment also plays an important role in helping a teen to maintain a healthy lifestyle. Ideally, treatment programs for adolescents provide a combination of counseling and social services to meet the needs of the individual, with special attention to how cultural values, history of physical and sexual abuse, and other mental health issues (e.g., depression) may inform the content of treatment. Treatment for adolescent substance users generally results in reduced levels of use for many youth. Longer time spent in treatment has consistently been associated with better outcomes for adolescents in areas of school and work performance, and in relationships with family and friends, particularly for youth with more severe substance-related and other mental health problems.

Heavy alcohol and other drug use during adolescence appear to alter the normal course of brain development. Important developments occur in the brain during adolescence (that is, roughly from ages twelve to eighteen) that help make the brain an efficient processing organ by adulthood. The brain is full-sized by the start of adolescence, but white matter increases, especially the myelin (fatty coating) around neuron (brain cell) axons, which help make electrical signals between brain cells transmit more rapidly. At the same time, gray matter decreases, as redundant or unneeded synapses (connections) between brain cells are eliminated, which helps information transfer within the brain to be more efficient.

Chronic, heavy alcohol and other drug use appear to affect brain structure and brain function. Adolescents, compared to adults, appear to be more vulnerable to the negative effects of alcohol on the brain, specifically on tasks involving memory and learning. While it is difficult to directly compare the effects of alcohol on adolescent humans versus adult humans, a series of studies on rodents has provided strong evidence for the heightened susceptibility of the brain and cognitive functioning to heavy alcohol exposure during adolescence. The typical pattern of alcohol use for many teens, which involves heavy episodic drinking (such as drinking five or more drinks at a weekend party), may have particularly detrimental effects on the developing brain. Chronic heavy drinking during adolescence has been associated with reduction in the size of the hippocampus, a brain structure involved in learning and memory. As the duration of adolescent heavy drinking increases, hippocampal volume tends to decrease. White matter, which is key for relaying signals between brain cells, appears less healthy in adolescents who have histories of heavy drinking.

Importantly, changes in brain structure due to substance use translate into deficits in cognitive performance. Adolescent drinkers demonstrate poorer performance than non-drinkers on tasks involving learning, memory, and visuospatial functioning. Heavy alcohol use by adolescents, particularly alcohol use that includes symptoms of hangover or withdrawal, has a negative impact on memory and attention. These deficits remain after several weeks of detoxification and appear to persist into adulthood. Studies of brain function during thinking and memory tasks suggest that adolescents with one to two years of heavy alcohol use require *more* brain effort to complete a task. With two to three additional years of heavy drinking, the brain may no longer be able to compensate for subtle alcohol-related problems, and some individuals may not be able to perform as well on challenging thinking and memory tasks. In summary, drinking to the point that unpleasant effects are noticed the following day appears linked to a risk for adversely affecting thinking and memory abilities, and some studies suggest this could be as much as a 10 percent decline, similar to the difference between an "A" and a "B" grade.

Use of other addictive substances has also been associated with deleterious effects on brain functioning during adolescence. Some studies have suggested that chronic heavy marijuana use may be associated with greater commission of errors on tests of attention, and difficulty in learning new verbal material with just a single exposure to the information. Moderate to heavy use of ecstasy (MDMA, methylenedioxymethamphetamine) has been linked to problems with verbal learning as well as impulsivity, sleep, and mood problems due to its effects on the neurotransmitter (brain chemical) serotonin. Other illicit stimulant drugs such as methamphetamine ("speed," "crystal") and cocaine have also been linked to some problems with attention, organization, and planning. Repeated use of inhalants (such as sniffing glue, paint, or gasoline) to get high is associated with serious motor, sensory, and cognitive problems that may be permanent. Some studies have suggested subtle neural abnormalities in adolescent smokers (i.e., nicotine), although further research is needed to confirm whether or not nicotine, alcohol, marijuana, and other drugs cause the cognitive problems observed in these studies, and how long after abstinence these problems persist.

Images of addictive compounds and associated items may produce different brain responses and cognitive reactions among adolescents with addictive disorders than among teens without addiction problems. Using functional magnetic resonance (fMRI) imaging, adolescents with one to two year histories of drinking problems showed dramatically greater brain response while looking at alcohol advertisements compared to non-alcohol beverage ads, while nondrinkers did not show many brain response differences to the two types of pictures. This might suggest that adolescent heavy drinkers could be more sensitive to alcohol advertising efforts. Differences were particularly notable in the left frontal brain regions, visual cortex, and brain regions involved with reward, such as the nucleus accumbens.

The frontal lobes and hippocampus, in particular, appear to be susceptible to the toxic effects of alcohol and other drug use during adolescence, perhaps because these brain structures continue to develop prominently well into adolescence. In summary, addiction in adolescence results in deficits in certain cognitive abilities that may persist through young adulthood, resulting in delays in development of problem-solving skills and successful transition to adult roles.

See also: **Addiction; Adolescent Cognitive Development; Adolescent Social and Emotional Development.**

Further Readings

Galanter, M. (Ed.) (2005). *Recent Developments in Alcoholism: Alcohol Problems in Adolescents and Young Adults,* Vol. 17. New York: Plenum Press.

Kaminer, Y. (1994). *Adolescent Substance Abuse: A Comprehensive Guide to Theory and Practice.* New York: Plenum Press.

Monti, P.M., Colby, S.M., O'Leary, T.A. (Eds.) (2001). *Adolescents, Alcohol, and Substance Abuse: Reaching Teens through Brief Interventions.* New York: Guilford Press.

National Institute on Alcohol Abuse and Alcoholism for teens: http://www.thecoolspot.gov/

National Institute on Drug Abuse: http://www.nida.nih.gov/

TAMMY CHUNG, PH.D. AND
SUSAN TAPERT, PH.D.

Adolescent Cognitive Development

The turbulence of adolescence echoes explosive development in body and brain. Despite their sometimes volatile moods and behavior, most teens gradually gain deeper understanding of themselves, their emotions, and their social world. This time of rapid growth is a time when the brain is primed to learn, and when it is important for adults to nurture this potential.

Science is gaining new understanding of the dramatic developmental changes the brain makes in these years. A long-range study by researchers at the National Institute of Mental Health, UCLA, Harvard Medical School, and several other institutions is mapping the development of the brain from childhood to adulthood (about ages ten to twenty-five). Using magnetic resonance imaging, which does not use radiation, they discovered to their initial surprise that the brain undergoes massive physical changes during this time.

The frontal lobes, the last to develop, undergo the most change during adolescence. They include the prefrontal lobes, located behind the forehead, the CEO of the brain and the seat of voluntary action and abstract thought. When mature, it allows us to plan, set priorities, consider different perspectives, and anticipate consequences. Its immaturity forces early teens to respond to social situations with the gut instincts of the amygdala and the other emotional centers of their brains without the moderating influence of reason. When teens appear unreasonable, it may be that their brains are not yet able to reason.

At about the age of nine or ten the frontal lobes have a period of rapid growth of dendrites and synapses, or connections, which reaches its peak at about the age of eleven in girls and twelve in boys. The other period of rapid growth for the brain occurs in early childhood. A massive pruning of these synapses, reducing the gray matter by 15 percent, follows; this compares to a 1–2 percent pruning rate annually through the lifespan. Accompanying these changes is an ongoing process of myelination, which gradually insulates nerve connections and helps the various parts of the brain to work together more efficiently. The result is fewer but more effective connections. Short-term, or working, memory improves, allowing more thoughts to be held at once. Abstract thinking develops, with the ability to plan, dream, and develop a core identity.

How the developing brain is used is critical to the final outcome. The brain follows a "use it or lose it" principle in its development. A brain that watches TV and plays video games will grow to be different than the same brain used to play sports, learn an instrument, and conduct science investigations. As the brain at this time is so susceptible to the influence of experience, it is particularly vulnerable to damage from drugs and alcohol, but equally open to positive experiences. It is empowering to students to learn about the biology of their brains and to realize they can choose how their brain will develop.

By age fifteen or sixteen the emotional centers of the brain come under the moderating influence of the frontal lobes. These teens can read facial expressions more accurately and can respond to social situations more appropriately than their amygdala—gut response—suggests to them. They develop impulse control, the ability to see consequences, defuse anger, and delay gratification. Their growth in making judgments and decisions and in understanding the consequences of their behavior continues to mature until their early twenties. Understanding this biological process has led the American Bar Association to recommend banning capital punishment for juveniles.

Many other developments during adolescence affect cognition. Neuroscientists are just beginning to investigate the role of glial cells, for example. We have about ten times as many glial cells as neurons in our brains. While it was thought for years that they served only a supporting function, it now appears that they may have a communication system of their own and might contribute in some way to the thinking process. The cerebellum as well was thought to function mainly for the coordination and control of fine muscle movement. Now, scientists are studying its role in the coordination of complex thought sequences, spatial reasoning, reading, writing, and problem-solving.

The anterior cingulate gyrus, which matures in the mid-teens, controls the process of shifting and maintaining attention. Its development may account for the teens' new ability to focus thoughts more sharply and for longer periods of time, allowing for the development of more complex thoughts, consideration of multiple points of view, and anticipation of future outcomes. The hippocampus, important in memory, continues to grow in volume up till at least age eighteen. Its growth may help in the ability to remember complex social situations for future decision-making.

The structures and technologies of modern society may be inadvertently interfering with the normal development of adolescents' brains. The "use it or lose it" principle means our brains will be changed physically by a society that over encourages quick responses and mental multi-tasking. Teens are at a developmental stage when they need to learn how to plan, set goals, think through choices, and anticipate consequences. They are at the stage where they need to develop judgment and maturity. Talking with one friend while on a cell phone with another and simultaneously searching the Internet for an answer to an instant message from a third, if a consistent pattern of behavior, will affect the brain. The outcome is unknown, but intuitively it would not help the maturing brain develop thoughtfulness.

A developing social issue concerns the earlier onset of puberty in recent years. The role of hormones in brain development is not completely clear, but it appears that the brain develops on a timeline that is not completely tied to puberty. One result of our modern environment is that teens reach sexual maturity and develop an interest in romance and sex years earlier than older generations, while their brains continue to mature according to the older, genetically driven, time schedule. The result is several years without impulse control, judgment, or a stable self-image, being buffeted by surges of hormones, before their frontal lobes finally develop the ability to control their emotions and behavior.

In addition to developing physically, emotionally, and intellectually, teens are also programmed to develop socially. Early teens, before about age fifteen, defy authority and long to be popular, to belong. Older teens gain a more comfortable acceptance of who they are—they can be themselves. Teens' intense interest in their peers and their need to develop the complex skills of social interactions give educators an opportunity. They can help teens navigate this important passage, while capitalizing on their intrinsic motivation to succeed in their peer group, by using small groups as effective learning structures.

Strategies

Educators finally have the opportunity to move beyond choosing teaching strategies based on personal philosophies or tradition. Neuroscience can help choose and design more effective teaching models. Although the incredible complexity of the brain means that much of how it perceives, learns, and thinks remains mysterious to neuroscientists, much is known, and scientists can make educated guesses about much of the rest. Teachers can test the hints emerging from neuroscience against the knowledge gained from cognitive psychology and educational research—and especially through results in their own classrooms—their action research "laboratories."

We know some things about the learning brain. Classrooms need to be physically and psychologically safe, or the "fight or flight" syndrome will shut down the learning capability of the cortex. Conversely, we know that emotionally flat classrooms produce little learning. Instead, we must engage students' emotions to ignite their motivation and to mark their learning memories with extra vividness.

We need to be mindful of the varieties of memories in the brain. Rote learning, repetition, is good for facts that need to become automatic, like the multiplication tables. Concepts like vocabulary words, on the other hand, need elaborative rehearsal to enter long-term memory. Using imagery—associating mental images or symbols with new vocabulary—for example, produces gains 35 percent higher than rote memorization.

It is also clear that the memory of a fact, event, or concept is not stored in a single location in the brain, but instead is distributed, for example, across the visual, auditory, and motor cortices. The more ways students have the memory stored, the more ways they have to reconstruct it. Telling students that Cortez landed in Yucatan in 1519 uses few neural systems. The mnemonic, which ends "Columbus sailed the ocean blue," uses more. Stories about the colonialists' conflicts with indigenous populations use more yet, including the emotional centers of the brain, which make memories especially vivid. Having students compare these events from European and native perspectives makes the learning even richer.

Another observation supported by research is that more is learned by doing than by watching or listening. Television viewing is no substitute for reading to preschoolers or for facilitating inquiry discussions for adolescents. We know that the most skilled musicians and athletes begin to practice very early in life, often before they begin school. They have had more years of practice, during a time when their brains are particularly plastic, to develop skills that someone starting at twenty cannot make up. The **critical period** for learning another language accent-free shuts at about puberty. It is possible that learning other academic skills and concepts will be most effective if they are also learned through active participation and as early as possible. Even algebra should be accessible to younger students if it is presented in terms of the brain's natural, concrete thinking.

A seemingly simple, commonsense observation about the brain has important implications for education. Research shows that we use the same regions of the brain to think about going to the kitchen for a cup of coffee as we would if we physically went there. In fact, the "motor brain," the frontal and parietal lobes, is crucial to memory, emotion, language, and learning.

All students can be helped to think more complexly if encouraged to use this natural ability to think about the physical world. Using objects to explore and play with, having time and freedom to inquire, and being encouraged to imagine and to use analogy and metaphor can help students recognize the tools they have for thinking. These tools are the same, whether thinking about concrete objects or "abstract" entities.

A meta-analysis of research on instructional strategies by the Mid-continent Research for Education and Learning (McREL) found that a powerful strategy was comparing, classifying, and creating metaphors and analogies. These are effective tools for learning because their mental operations are fundamental to the workings of the human brain. Other strategies identified by McREL that capitalize on the brain's facility with motion, maps, and metaphors include nonlinguistic representations such as graphic organizers, note taking (especially webbing), and narrative or visual advance organizers.

The developing adolescent brain is also trying to navigate its social world. A powerful way to use this intrinsic interest in each other is to engage students in group inquiry discussions, or "Socratic Seminars." As students problem-solve together, they gain control of the tools for thinking. While students explain a line of reasoning, they become more consciously aware of their own thinking process. As others listen and follow their thinking steps, they also learn how to use that strategy in the future.

Other types of cooperative learning have powerful impacts in the classroom. Group Investigation, for example, organizes the classroom into groups to investigate the curriculum topic, beginning with students' questions and being conducted according to student plans. The power of the democratically organized group process leads to some of the largest gains in the learning of any model of teaching. By working together, problem-solving, creating presentations, negotiating, and investigating, students are practicing the skills, and training the neurons, that they will need in their future lives.

Other effective teaching models that stimulate the adolescent's developing ability to think abstractly and complexly include problem-based learning; inquiry methods in science; analysis of complex, authentic data; community-based projects; creative and persuasive writing; reciprocal teaching; and simulations.

See also: **Adolescent Social and Emotional Development; Adolescent Addiction; At-risk Behavior.**

Further Readings

Giedd, J.N., Blumenthal, J., Jefferies, N.O., Castellanos, F.X., Liu, H., Zijdenbos, A., Paus, T., Evans, A.C., Rapoport, J.L. (1999). Brain development during childhood and adolescence: a longitudinal MRI study. *Nature Neuroscience* 2:861–863.

Park, A. (2004, May 10). What makes teens tick. *Time* 163:56–65.

Ratey, J.J. (2001). *A User's Guide to the Brain.* New York: Vintage Books.

National Institute of Mental Health Publications: http://www.nimh.nih.gov/publicat/

JACK HUHTALA, M.A.

Adolescent Social and Emotional Development

Teenage behavior is often unpredictable and volatile in nature. "Why can't they act like adults?" is a question that resonates with teachers and parents. This perpelexing, moody, and defiant creature has perplexed and frustrated adults for ages. With new technology we're now looking beyond hormones and growth spurts to the field of cognitive neuroscience for enlightenment on their erractic and often incomprehensible behavior. Neuroscience confirms what we've always thought; the adolescent brain is a brain in transition. The teenage brain is transforming as neural growth occurs promoting abstract thought and logical thinking. Growth in the adolescents' cognitive development parallels dramatic changes in their social and emotional development.

Traditionally, the heart has been the organ associated with emotions and feelings while the brain has been considered the organ involved in thought, logic, and rational decision-making. Upon closer scientific examination the heart may have an aesthetic connection to **emotion**, but the brain is the organ in control of our emotions.

Recently, there has been an increase in the studies conducted on two parts of the brain and their connection to emotion: the frontal lobes and the amygdala. These two areas of the brain differ greatly in their structure and function. The amygdala is one inch long, shaped like an almond, and is part of the unconscious brain. It is the area of the brain most closely associated with emotion, in charge of identifying danger and self-preservation. It allows us to feel fear and anxiety by alerting us to danger and enabling us to react with the fight or flight response. Survival is the primary role of emotion, so it is no shock that information arrives at the amygdala much quicker than it does to the cortex. Speed is imperative when safety is concerned. Interestingly, the adolescent brain has twice the activity level as the adult brain in all areas and an even higher level of activity in the amygdala.

The frontal lobes are part of our conscious brain, processing information rationally and determining appropriate action. There are many more circuits from the amygdala to the frontal lobes than from the frontal lobes to the amygdala, putting the amygdala in a firm position of power. It is very difficult for the conscious, rational area of the brain to overtake an emotionally charged brain.

When confronted with information the adolescent brain reacts quite differently from the adult brain. Adults dependent more on the frontal lobes of their brain and less on the amygdala, thereby responding logically to information. Adolescents, on the other hand, tend to rely more on the amygdala than the frontal lobes when responding to emotional stimuli. This is particularly true of younger adolescents; there is substantial difference between the immature brain of a sixteen-year-old and the more adult like eighteen-year-old brain.

As the adolescent's frontal lobes do not function fully, the adolescent's reaction to information tends to be considerably more emotional than the adult's and often more impulsive. This leads to conversations such as the following: The parents make what they believe is an innocent and logical statement, "Be home by 11:00." The adolescent responds with, "You don't trust me! I hate you!" and leaves the room in a fury, feet stomping and arms flailing, an emotionally charged response to a calmly stated comment.

A study by Deborah Yergelun-Todd confirmed the adolescent's dependency on the amygdala. MRI scans were used to record and compare adult and teenage brain responses. Each individual was asked to identify the emotion on the face of a woman. Adults were able to identify the emotion as fear 100 percent of the time, but only 50 percent of the adolescents were able to identify the emotion correctly, instead they identified shock or anger as the emotion represented. This discovery fascinated researchers and they began to delve deeper into the adolescent brain. MRIs revealed the difference between the adolescent's amygdala lighting up when they responded to the photograph compared to adults' frontal lobes lighting up with the same information.

Not only were adolescents' responses more emotional, but Yurgelun-Todd also theorized that reading body language and facial expressions was something that was learned, not inherently known. Teenagers had not yet mastered the ability to read others' emotions. The face is the area of the body with the greatest number of neurons and where feelings are most obviously exhibited. Adolescents were in the process of learning how to interpret others' facial expressions. In the meantime, misunderstandings and misinterpretations were common occurrences resulting in moodiness, hostility, and other negative behavior.

The inaccurate interpretation of others' intent makes it difficult for teenagers to navigate important **social** situations. The teacher that asks a student if their work is complete is interpreted as saying, "You're stupid" or the peer innocently staring at them in the lunchroom is thought to be conveying the message, "You're not wanted at our lunch table."

Neuroscientists believe adolescent behavior is further complicated because the adolescents feel things before they can regulate or articulate the feeling. They feel an emotion, but don't have the ability to express it in a socially appropriate way. This propensity to communicate in emotionally laden words causes further frustration between the adolescent and those sharing their world.

In a confrontation between a college student and professor the college student's frontal lobes may determine that fear and anger are the emotions appearing, but they may logically say, this is your teacher, it is not appropriate to fight with your teacher, calm down and speak appropriately. The adolescent, on the other hand, with his/her immature frontal lobes, too often responds with un-carefully chosen remarks.

Yurgelun-Todd believes there are also implications for **at risk** behavior. She believes that teenagers' frontal lobes are not always functioning fully, making it difficult for them to think through the consequences of their behaviors. The imbalance in their brain may explain drunken driving, drug addiction, and unprotected sex. They believe bad things happen to other people, not them. This inability to determine the consequences of their behavior contributes to their delusion that they are indestructible.

Jay Geidd of the National Institute of Mental Health began doing MRIs on the brains of 145 healthy children, aged four to twenty-one, in the early 1990s. The children selected for the study were scanned every two years to monitor possible anatomical changes occurring with maturation. Neuroscience discoveries revealed an over-production of dendrites and synapse happens twice in the human life span. The first time is in early childhood and the second time is during early adolescence.

MRIs show that as the teenage brain experiences a surge of dendrite and synapse (gray matter) growth organization and function in the frontal lobes change substantially. This process peaks at about the age of eleven in girls and twelve in boys, coincidentally, about the same time as the onset of puberty.

Just as important as the creation of additional gray matter to the adolescent, is the process of pruning that follows. The prominent theory in memory studies is *use it or lose it.* The neural connections that endure last a lifetime, but the connections that don't will be lost, just as they are in early childhood. It is hypothesized that pruning at this age permits the adolescent brain to organize its circuitry, refining the thinking processes. White matter is created in the adolescent brain along with gray matter. After synapses are generated in the brain, myelin, a fatty substance made of glial is sent to insulate the neurons. This mylenated tissue is referred to as white matter. Myelin's job is to cover the axons of neurons enabling information to travel efficiently. The more myelin that is distributed, the more potential there is for mastery of information.

It is theorized that the brain does not release myelin to all neurons at the same time, but instead releases it in stages. Different areas of the brain receive myelin at different times. The timing of the release of myelin appears to be dependent upon the developmental age of the individual. The last part of the brain to receive myelin is the frontal cortex, the area responsible for higher-order thinking skills and decision making. The frontal lobes appear to become fine-tuned during adolescence prompting the ability to think abstractly and rationally.

All experiences, positive and negative, cause emotional reactions in the amygdala. Positive emotions are remembered by the amygdala and it craves more of them. Negative emotions, such as anger and fear, are also remembered. When an educational experience is associated with a negative emotion the amygdala closes the gate to learning. The student that continually experiences school failure will continue to be unsuccessful because the amygdala will emit emotions preventing the brain from relaxing and learning the information. Instead of trying new instructional strategies, educators often need to get to the root of the problem and change the students' emotional outlook toward the subject area.

The impact of emotion on academics indirectly affects a student's **self-concept**. Self-concept is shaped by our past experiences. The strong correlation between a student's academic achievement and self-concept puts them in either an upward spin or downward spiral in school. Succeeding in school, having friends, and living up to family expectations help build a positive self-concept. Failing in school, being bullied and ignored by peers, or neglected at home reinforce a negative self-concept. Students with negative self-concepts are more at risk of dropping out of school, becoming pregnant or using drugs—scary realities for too many adolescents.

Egocentrism is a common characteristic seen in the adolescent. Egocentrism appears to accompany the ability of the adolescent to think abstractly. This new capability in their brains to think abstractly allows them to become acutely aware of themselves to the point of being self-centered. Egocentrism expresses itself in self-conscious and self-absorbed beliefs and behaviors. The adolescent believes that everyone is as interested in them as they are in themselves so everyone is constantly watching them. They are on stage playing to an imaginary audience. It is easy to become exasperated when they actively avoid their parents, too embarrassed to be seen with them, or obsessed over minor indiscretions such as wearing jeans when everyone else wore khakis. As they adjust to their new mental abilities this behavior declines.

Teenagers are particularly sensitive to **stress**. The amygdala starts the process by sending information concerning emotion to the cortex. If stress persists cortisol is released into the body. Cortisol is the hormone most associated with stress. It is released when there is physical, academic, emotional, or environmental danger and it stays in the body a long time. Higher levels of progesterone in teenage girls seem to allow cortisol to run rampant, accentuating the feelings of stress.

Adolescent stress usually does not revolve around survival issues; instead it is associated with peers, grades or unhealthy family situations. A prime time for adolescents to experience stress is during semester tests. They are concerned about their grades, are deprived of sleep, and eat unhealthy and irregularly. When students feel stress the brain downshifts with an overwhelming need to protect itself. This is accompanied by feelings of helplessness making it hard to remember the correct answer. Positive risk taking is out the window and creativity is absent.

Classroom Strategies that Support the Social/Emotional Development of the Adolescent

Classrooms that support emotional and social growth are instrumental in the transformation from childhood to adulthood. Due to discoveries by neuroscientists educators are rethinking the role of emotion and acknowledging emotion as not just a piece of life, but a critical part of learning and memory. Emotions stimulate all areas of the brain; they focus our attention and help give meaning to information.

Many teaching strategies and testing options have a great deal of difficulty keeping attention and arousing emotion. Activities, like worksheets, require students to pay attention to something that evolution says is not relevant. Lecture is an efficient way to convey large amounts of information in a concise and controlled manner, but it is rarely emotionally charged. Objective tests, such as multiple choice and true/false, don't spark emotion and are difficult for students to apply to the real world. Overuse of strategies that neglect our emotional constitution miss an academic opportunity.

Teachers can make a difference in reducing negative emotion and enhancing positive emotion. A positive classroom climate is deeply dependent upon a sense of belonging, a basic human need. Respect each student and expect the same in return. Get to know each individual in the classroom with his or her own strengths and weaknesses. Be consistent and fair; let students know your expectations. Allow students to have input in the classroom and when appropriate allow them to make decisions. Give up some of the control.

Create a sense of comfort and happiness in the classroom. Be available to students; assist them individually with their schoolwork when needed. Allow them to ask a neighbor for clarification when appropriate. Enhance memory of the subject matter by combining emotion and instruction. Bring music into the classroom, it can calm or energize. Be a positive role model; let students see your love of learning. Celebrate important accomplishments of your students that occur within and outside school. Last, but not least, understand and be tolerant of the transformations going on in the teenage brain.

Teenagers are sculpting the brain they will take into adulthood. They enjoy and rely more on their families and significant adults then is commonly thought. There is a unique adult opportunity to assist them in this challenging passage in life.

See also: Adolescent Cognitive Development; At-Risk Behavior Sleep.

Further Readings

Crawford, G.B. (2004). *Managing the Adolescent Classroom.* San Diego, CA: The Brain Store, Inc.

Feinstein, S. (2004). *Secrets of the Teenage Brain.* Corwin press. San Diego, CA: The Brain Store Inc.

Giedd, J.N., Blumenthal, J., Jeffried, O., Rajapakse, J., Vaituzis, A., Liu, H., Berry, Y., Tobin, M., Nelson, J., Castellanos, F. (1999). Development of the human corpus callosum during childhood and adolescence; a longitudinal MRI study. *Progress in Neuro-Psychopharmacology & Biological Psychiatry* 23:578–588.

Sousa, D. (2001). *How the Brain Learns* (2nd ed.). Thousand Oaks, CA: Corwin Press.

Yergelun-Todd, D. (February, 2002). *Interviews inside the teenage brain: interviews: deborah yurgelun-todd/PBS.* Retrieved June 12, 2002 from Public Broadcasting Systems Teenage Brain Interviews http://www.pbs.org/wgbh/p...ne/shows/teenbrain/interviews/todd.html. Secrets of the Teenage Brain www.theteenagebrain.com

SHERYL FEINSTEIN, ED.D.

Adult Brain

Learning is a dynamic and fluid process that cannot be confined to the classroom setting. Human beings are perpetual learners from infancy throughout the twilight years. From high school graduates to seasoned and mature learners with previous degrees, teaching adults can be both a challenging and rewarding experience for educators.

Adults live multidimensional lives, and often experience conflicts trying to balance family, work, and social responsibilities while learning. Stress and normal age-related memory loss may contribute to the challenge of learning new information. This chapter highlights the physical and psychological differences between the brains of adult and child learners, examines the effects of aging upon the brain, and validates the use of a brain-compatible approach to overcome the inevitable cognitive decline of the adult learner.

Physical Differences in the Brain of Adult and Child Learners

Anatomically, the brains of children were thought to be similar to the brains of adults. Over the last three decades however, neuroscientists have studied how the synaptic density of the brain evolves over the life cycle in both animals and humans. Synaptic density refers to the number of synaptic connections per volume of brain tissue. Greater synaptic connections ensure greater speed and accuracy in communication between brain cells. Memory and recall of information is enhanced with greater synaptic connections.

Although newborns start off with levels far below the average adult, they increase the number of synapses as they absorb the world around them until they actually develop far greater synaptic densities in all brain areas than adults! However, the natural pruning process kicks in around puberty, decreasing synaptic densities to about the same level as the average adult.

Despite this natural pruning process, researchers have determined through animal and human studies that the adult brain is highly plastic and able to restructure connections and reorganize itself as a result of exposure to new learning environments. Therefore, even though humans have greater synaptic densities early in life, most mature learning occurs when synaptic densities are pruned to adult levels.

Over the years, adults may notice some impairment in memory and recall as a result of normal, age-related changes. Fortunately, neural research suggests that, barring structural damage or illness, adults have the ability to recall previously learned factual information (explicit memories) and processes and skills (implicit memories) from their long-term memory with sufficient mental stimulation. Younger learners tend to exhibit quicker recall of both explicit and implicit memories than adult learners. Activating nerve cells in several areas of the brain through stimulating multisensory learning activities is one way to promote retrieval of memories in adult learners. Educators can help adult learners activate their memories through mind stimulating multisensory learning activities. The more novel and challenging the stimulation, the more the brain thrives and grows.

Neural research reveals that new connections are produced in the hippocampus of adults in response to the challenge of learning. This research certainly validates that the brain not only creates new cells throughout a lifetime, but that the new cells live longer and grow stronger when the brain is actively engaged in new learning. This research is particularly exciting in terms of adult learning and supports the need for promoting learning activities that naturally engage adult's motivation, interest, and attention by drawing upon personal experiences.

Psychological Differences Between Adult and Child Learners

Despite the physical differences in synaptic density, adults tend to be much more psychologically prepared to learn than children. When adults set out to learn a new skill, they approach the task with much greater independence and sense of purpose than a child does. Adults require less supervision, direction, and structure in meeting their learning objectives. Adults have a broader life experience base to draw upon than children have. Although they may have less synaptic connections, they certainly have the potential to draw upon their own personal experiences and relate them to new learning. This experiential base influences their overall attitude toward learning. For example, based upon successful past work, organizational, or social experiences, adults tend to have greater motivation and interest in learning than children do.

Children are influenced by positive and successful learning experiences as well, but are less likely to relate them to the current learning situation, because they lack the maturity and self-awareness that adults bring into the learning environment. However, negative past learning experiences affect children and adults in very much the same way. Both the adult and child's brain tend to downshift to a primitive survival mode when self-integrity and ability to learn are threatened. Fortunately, the adult has the cognitive skills to analyze and evaluate the negative experience, counterbalancing it with positive affirmations about themselves as current learners.

Both adults and children tend to learn best by becoming actively involved in the learning process. Active engagement in the learning process is one of the key principles of brain-compatible learning and is absolutely essential in both formal and informal learning sessions. While this is not an exhaustive list of characteristics of adult and child learners, the following matrix synthesizes the distinguishing characteristics (see Table 1).

Physical Effects of Aging Upon the Brain

Conventional wisdom has it that as a person starts to age, senility is inevitable. That certainly is a grim prospect for any adult who is investing time and energy into their education! While some older adults do become senile, the majority of adults are able to maintain their mental capacities until the day they die. Most cases of senility are the result of hardening of the arteries, causing diminished cerebral blood flow, or neurological diseases, such as stroke, which cause physical damage to

Table 1. Distinguishing characteristics of adult and child learners

	Child learner	Adult learner
Memory/Recall of information	Tends to be faster	May slow with age
Emotional/Physical maturity	Developing	Greater level
Self-awareness	Developing	Greater level
Past negative experiences	Influences greatly	Influences slightly
Past positive experiences	Influences slightly	Influences greatly
Motivation and interest	Developing	Greater level
Level of independence	Dependent learner	Independent learner
Need for structure	Requires more	Requires less
Need for direction/guidance	Requires more step by step	Requires less...stand-by guidance preferred
Need for involvement	Great	Great

the brain. Elderly people who are in good physical health generally remain cognitively intact throughout life.

The healthy human brain does go through some normal physical changes; however, the most noticeable effect is upon short-term memory. Long-term memory recall declines slightly as the adult ages, along with the ability to problem solve and pay attention to multiple stimuli at the same time.

As previously stated, by the time a person reaches young adulthood, in the early twenties, they have lost approximately half of their synaptic connections. Granted, most of those connections have withered away from lack of use. Positron emission tomography (PET) scans reveal that at the age of thirty, the brain begins to shrink noticeably, causing slight cognitive decline. Fortunately, because of the brain's amazing plasticity, new synaptic connections are formed, so the cognitive decline is not that pronounced.

By about the age of forty, however, there is a 2 percent decrease in brain weight with every decade of life. Although this may not sound like much, the brain areas that are affected the most are those primary areas associated with memory. The hippocampus and the amygdala, located in the limbic system of the cerebrum, shrink 25 percent by the time a person reaches seventy years of age. These two structures are responsible for storing short-term memories and sending memories into long-term storage within the neocortex. The hippocampus is responsible for the storage of semantic memory (book-learning), while the amygdala is responsible for the processing of emotional memories. As a person ages, the hippocampus loses the ability to transfer short-term memories into long-term storage. That is why short-term memory is more susceptible to effects of aging. Persons tend to recall long-term memories more efficiently because they are safely stored within the neocortex.

Because of these age-related biological changes, adults tend to become stressed while trying to learn new information. This becomes a vicious cycle. Enduring long periods of **stress** causes the release of cortisol, which further affects the ability of the hippocampus to transfer long-term memories. Cortisol decreases glucose supply to the brain, which is needed to power up the brain. As a result, new concepts are difficult to remember and existing memories are more difficult to recall. Excess cortisol levels further interfere with neurotransmitter function, thus reducing synaptic transfer between cells. Attention and focus are impaired as well as creativity and cognitive processing. Cortisol has been implicated with free-radical production as well, which cause severe dysfunction of brain cells. The memory centers in the hippocampus and amygdala regions are most susceptible to free-radical destruction.

In addition, the myelin sheath, the protective covering that insulates each axon, declines more in the limbic areas than other parts of the brain, thus decreasing the speed of impulse transmission between neurons.

The result of these changes is a noticeably slower ability to process, transfer, and retrieve information as efficiently as the younger brain.

Another primary cause of age-related memory impairment is the gradual decline of the neurotransmitter, acetylcholine, which is the primary carrier of memory. Studies of Alzheimer's patients have shown a decrease in acetycholine, especially in the temporal region of the neocortex, where most long-term memories are stored. Memories are stored in not one cell but in several cells throughout the brain. Acetylcholine triggers the thought process between cells. Without sufficient acetylcholine on board, brain cells cannot communicate as efficiently with each other as a person tries to recall a memory. Concentration and focus in older adult learners is diminished as well with declining production of acetylcholine.

At around the age of fifty, people are less able to multitask and learn new complex skills. Memory continues to decline, especially auditory and visual memory, while kinesthetic memory seems to remain intact. The reason for that is kinesthetic memory is stored in the cerebellum, which is less vulnerable to degenerative changes than the neocortex and the hippocampus, where most visual and auditory learning is processed. As memory begins to decline, an individual's creativity also begins to wither. This may be in part because creativity requires the ability to recall and focus on memories in an inventive way.

By the time a person reaches their sixties, there is a significant decline in cognitive function as well as memory. The ability to memorize new facts and to focus and concentrate is affected dramatically. Older learners may experience difficulty in matching names to faces, remembering phone numbers, and in learning new information. The nervous system also begins to slow down, thus decreasing speed and agility in performing tasks.

Although these changes may seem quite dismal and frustrating, adults can learn to activate neural connections and build upon previously learned information using the following brain-compatible strategies tailored to the adult brain.

Brain-Compatible Approaches to Teaching Adults

A brain-compatible philosophy for teaching adults encompasses recognition of learning styles; positive affirmations; brain nutrition; use of music, breathing, and movement exercises to promote whole brain processing; and use of graphic organizers to activate memory and facilitate optimal processing of information. Following is a brief summary of how such a brain-compatible approach can be used in adult education.

Learning Styles

Whether teaching a semester-long class or a short study session, it is imperative to promote understanding among students of their unique blend of **learning styles.** There are many surveys available on the market to assist educators in assessing the learning styles of students. From the website studygs.net, a variety of on-line learning style inventories can be accessed and scored upon completion. Once learners understand their dominant learning style (auditory, visual, or kinesthetic), they can tap into strategies most appropriate for each style. Ideally, learners can use this information to build upon less dominant learning styles to become a multisensory learner. For example, the learner who depends upon visual techniques to learn begins to incorporate auditory and kinesthetic techniques to ensure a more successful learning experience.

Having an awareness of what natural learning talents a learner possesses is beneficial as well in promoting an understanding of personal learning attributes. Howard Gardner has developed a total of 8½ unique learning intelligences, of which a learner may be dominant in one to three areas. For example, having knowledge of the combination intelligences of naturalistic, bodily/physical, and intrapersonal, might prompt a learner to take a hike in the woods while reflecting deeply upon a lesson plan or assignment.

Positive Affirmations

As previously mentioned, negative learning experiences can adversely affect anyone's ability to learn. Developing positive affirmations about your own ability to learn is an empowering technique indeed. By encouraging adult learners to come up with a list of positive attributes about their unique ability to learn, the learner becomes empowered to take charge of their own emotional responses. These affirmations become their personal mantras as they experience highs and lows throughout the learning process. Among the many positive affirmations that students have shared over the years are the following:

- I am an independent and inquiring learner.
- I will focus and finish.
- I can do whatever I set out to do.
- I am a competent and knowledgeable learner.
- I will use my creative potential to discover my world.

A well-developed affirmation that a student becomes committed to can counterbalance negative experiences from the past and promote an even greater sense of purpose for current and future learning.

Brain Nutrition and Learning

There is a distinct relationship between **nutrition** and learning. Educators can predict with a fair degree of accuracy that students who enter the lecture hall with a can of pop and a candy bar are sure to fall into a lethargic sugar slump within thirty minutes. The brain requires a balanced intake of glucose throughout the day to function properly. The best balance of glucose comes from a blend of protein, carbohydrates, and fats. Unfortunately, the typical diet of an adult student who is trying to balance work, home, and school responsibilities is often far from balanced.

Every time a person makes choices about what to eat, he/she is also choosing how effectively he/she learns. Proteins, carbohydrates, vitamins, and minerals are transformed into membranes and chemicals that are used by the brain to remember, think, and feel. The amino acids tyrosine and tryptophan often compete with each other for the brain's full attention. Tyrosine is used by the brain to make dopamine and norepinephrine, which in turn provide the brain with the ability to think quickly and alertly, react fast, and access long-term memory. Tryptophan, which the brain uses to make serotonin, tends to slow reaction times down, impair concentration, and make learners sleepy.

If tyrosine gets to the brain first, it will stimulate production of those neurotransmitters that accelerate mental capacity. However, if tryptophan gets into the brain before tyrosine, serotonin will go to work slowing mental productivity down to a halt. Wurtman suggests eating protein foods that are naturally higher in tyrosine during the first few bites of a meal and saving the carbohydrates for the last part of the meal. By selecting a high protein snack food (meat, peanuts, cheese, or yogurt) rather than a high carbohydrate snack (potato chips, candy bar, or soda pop), learners can boost their natural production of dopamine and norepinephrine to optimize the learning potential.

The B-complex of vitamins (1, 2, 3, 6, and 12), found in food sources such as fish, chicken, pork, eggs, soybeans, oats, whole wheat breads and cereals, leafy green vegetables, and peanuts are recommended as well to convert carbohydrates and protein into pure mental energy.

Vitamin C is another vitamin that uses protein to produce the necessary neurotransmitters to enhance memory. Good sources of Vitamin C include citrus fruits, green peppers, and broccoli...all best eaten when raw for the maximum effect. Minerals are just as important as vitamins in boosting mental performance. In particular, insufficient amounts of boron, copper, and iron have been linked to impaired memory, thought, and mood. Raisins and apples are especially rich in boron, while copper is abundant in fresh fruits, vegetables, and seafood; and meat sources are high in iron. While research continues in the area of nutrition and mental function, scientists recommend eating a well-balanced diet, paying particular attention to the vitamin and mineral sources discussed in this section.

Fats are especially important nutrients for the brain, as brain cells are made up primarily of fat. Although we need fat in our diets to maintain our brain cells, the type of fat that is taken does matter. Diets rich in saturated fats, such as those in animal protein and palm oil have a negative effect upon thinking, while diets rich in polyunsaturated fats, such as safflower, sunflower, and soybean oils have a positive effect upon thinking. As our need for protein is equally important, nutritionists suggest getting primary protein sources from leaner cuts of red meat, chicken, pork and fish, while avoiding highly marbled and fatty cuts of red meat.

The need for water in the human body is absolutely vital. The human body is 90 percent water, the brain is 75 percent water, and total body weight is 70 percent water. We rely upon water for all sorts of bodily processes, including circulation of nutrients and oxygen to the brain. When blood flow to the brain is increased, learners are naturally able to process information more efficiently. Fresh water is the ultimate brain beverage.

One of the easiest and most inexpensive ways to get the most out of students' learning potential is to BYOB (bring your own bottle of water)! Even the strictest establishments will allow for water to be brought in and consumed by learners. Fresh water is naturally packed with minerals and both sugar and fat-free...appropriate for any diet! Feedback from students indicates that drinking water during learning sessions keeps minds sharp and focused. Drink at least 8 oz. of fresh water every hour while attempting to learn new and complex material.

It may be beneficial to address nutritional intake over the course of the day to ensure an even balance of nutrients for optimal brain processing. Staring with breakfast, take in a balance of protein, complex carbohydrates (such as fruit, vegetables, grains) and unsaturated fat at least every four to five hours.

Music and Learning

Music can also be used to set the stage for learning, especially if the tempo is slightly lower than the heart rate, as in baroque and classical music. This type of music slows down the autonomic nervous system, which induces active relaxation. Not only does this music have an impact on the heart, it lowers blood pressure temporarily, dilates the blood vessels in the brain, and allows more blood and oxygen to be available for brain activity. These combined relaxation effects of baroque and classical music actually prime the brain for learning by synchronizing the beta and alpha brain waves.

Following are a number of suggested baroque and classical artists:

Georg-Friedrich Handel	Johann Sebastian Bach
Georg-Phillip Telemann	Antonio Vivaldi
Tomaso Albinoni	Wolfgang Mozart

Play the music while students are filing into a classroom and then turn it down to a barely audible pitch while presenting content. During group work, turn the music up again to stimulate creativity. The ironic thing about this type of music is that students don't even have to like the music to benefit from its effects. Encourage students to listen to this same type of music while studying to increase brain processing.

Using music as a background for collaborative group work is also beneficial. The effect of the music continues to balance brain waves while learners process information collaboratively. The cerebral cortex is responsible for conscious and unconscious thought processes. Researchers found that the non-conscious mind actually acts before the conscious mind directs the body to act. In other words, before the brain is even consciously aware of thinking about an activity, the non-conscious mind is already acting upon that activity. More than 99 percent of all learning is non-conscious. Implications for education are profound...learners are unconsciously absorbing, interpreting, and acting upon environmental cues, such as music, over and above the actual lesson presented to their conscious minds.

Breathing Exercises and Learning

The brain requires a continuous supply of oxygen to function at optimal learning capacity. While the process of breathing is natural and automatic, breathing patterns change with certain behaviors. The shallow type of breathing that learners engage in while passively sitting through a lecture is not at all conducive to optimal learning. Breathing deeply and rhythmically will assist in relaxing both the mind and the body. Oxygen is needed by every cell, muscle, bone, and organ. When any part of the body is tense, the whole system is thrown off balance.

Stressful and negative emotional states can often be overcome by a change in breathing patterns. As oxygen provides the energy needed to center and focus, start a learning session with some form of breathing exercise. Breathing exercises are also effective study strategies that can easily be incorporated into any learner's study routine. Following are three basic exercises that can be adapted into any learning environment.

Diaphragmatic Breathing

To fully oxygenate the brain and charge the cells fully, encourage learners to do deep diaphragmatic breathing at least once an hour. At the start of every presentation, lead learners through a cycle of five diaphragmatic breathing exercises to get their brains primed for learning. Schedule a brain break halfway through the presentation if it is longer than one hour. In addition, empower learners to give themselves a brain break when they start to feel sluggish (under oxygenated) during the presentation.

Diaphragmatic breathing exercises can be done rather subtly and without distracting other learners. This type of breathing quickly calms an anxious mind and centers the body for learning. Directions: Stand with feet about a foot apart, or sit straight up in a chair with hands placed over diaphragm (upper abdomen). Breathe in deeply through the nose and out through the mouth, concentrating on raising the diaphragm with every inhalation. After a few practice breaths, close your eyes and continue to breathe for a cycle of five breaths.

Ratio Breathing

Ratio breathing increases the ratio of parasympathetic to sympathetic nervous-system activity, thereby decreasing internal anxiety and producing more harmonious functioning of the circulatory and digestive system. As blood supply is enhanced, greater amounts of oxygen are circulated to the brain, which increases the brain's overall efficiency. This exercise is especially beneficial for learners who tend to have test-taking anxiety. Start with a few cycles of diaphragmatic breathing before beginning the ratio breathing as follows: Directions:

Breathe in deeply through the nose, raising diaphragmatic muscles to one count (3), hold breath to four counts (12) and exhale through pursed lips to two counts (6). A deep cleansing breath is recommended between each breathing cycle. Repeat five times and end with a deep cleansing breath. Follow with Alternate Nostril Breathing exercise.

Alternate Nostril Breathing

This particular breathing exercise helps to balance the supply of oxygen to both hemispheres of the brain. When both hemispheres are fully stimulated and ready to learn, the whole brain is engaged. Naturally, when the logical left hemisphere and the creative right hemisphere are both involved, the learning experience is whole-brain enhanced. Directions:

Begin by completely exhaling through both nostrils, as in blowing the nose. Close off the left nostril by pressing the thumb or forefinger against the opening and breathe in slowly and deeply through the right nostril. Hold the breath for five seconds and then breathe out through the right nostril while holding the left nostril closed. Next inhale deeply and slowly through the left nostril while holding the right nostril closed. Hold the breath five seconds and then breathe out through the left nostril while holding the right nostril closed. Continue alternating nostrils for five cycles. End exercise by breathing slowly and deeply through both nostrils and clearing secretions away with a tissue if necessary.

Movement Exercises and Learning

Education kinesiology (edu-k) is a series of simple and fun movement exercises developed by Dennison and Dennison to enhance whole-brain learning. The word kinesiology is derived from the Greek root kinesis, which means motion, and is the study of the movement of the human body. Edu-k is a proven system for empowering learners by using movement activities to tap into hidden potential.

These are exercises to integrate and balance the right and left hemispheres of the brain, brainstem and frontal lobes, and the limbic system, and cerebral cortex. In other words, all parts of the brain are merged to work together for optimal processing of new information. Edu-K is composed of exercises to promote the lateral, focus, and centering dimensions of the learning process.

The lateral dimension (right and left hemispheres) ensures that linear and symbolic information can be processed from right to left and left to right. Inability to process in the lateral dimension has been related to problems such as dyslexia.

The focus dimension (brainstem and frontal lobes) promotes the ability to express, participate with others, and generally attend and comprehend new information. Inability to process in the focus dimension has been related to hyperactivity, language delay, comprehension, and attention problems.

The centering dimension (limbic and cerebral cortex) promotes a state of relaxed alertness allowing students to take in information and process it without feeling threatened emotionally. Once students are emotionally balanced, they begin to attach meaning to what they are learning. Inability to process in the centering dimension has been related to problems such as inability to express emotions appropriately, irrational fears, and over stimulated fight or flight response.

Following are a few exercises designed to promote learning in each dimension:

A. Lateral Dimension:

Cross Crawl: Start by taking right hand and placing on left shoulder, then left hand on right shoulder...right hand to left elbow and left hand to right elbow...right hand to left wrist and left hand to right wrist, and so on down to the feet and then back up to the shoulders. For fun, these can be done to music and with a bounce in the step!

B. Focus Dimension:

Arm Stretch: Start with arms outstretched above head, while standing on tiptoes. Come down flat on feet and outstretch arms to sides and point middle finger up toward ceiling. Bring back above head and stand on tiptoes again, then twist torso while outstretching arms first to the front and then to the back with fingers pointed up toward ceiling.

C. Centering Dimension:

Neck Rolls: Have student breathe deeply while slowly rolling the neck forward and around, then backward and around, as if it was a heavy ball. Do with eyes closed, then with eyes open.

Dennison and Dennison offer edu-k as a solution to stuck learning states. In other words, when the learner switches off the brain mechanisms required for learning, information becomes unavailable to all parts of the brain. Through movement and repatterning activities, learners are able to access all parts of the brain for a complete learning experience.

Energizing Exercises

Dennison and Dennison's energy exercises assist in re-establishing neural connections between body and brain to promote the flow of electromagnetic energy throughout the body. During periods of increased stress, adrenaline levels rise, forcing electrical energy away from the neocortex and toward the sympathetic nervous system. Energy exercises activate the neocortex, thereby redirecting electrical energy back to the thinking part of the brain. In turn, the parasympathetic system is stimulated and the relaxation response is initiated. One exercise that is helpful in redirecting students before a test is the thinking cap.

Thinking Cap

The thinking cap exercise promotes focused attention on auditory stimuli as it relaxes tension in the cranial bones. As a result, students have greater listening comprehension and ability to concentrate as they filter out distractions and tune into meaningful learning. The student uses thumb and index fingers to gently pull the ears back and unroll the creases. Beginning at the top of the ear, instruct the student to gently massage down and around to the lobe and back up again for three to four cycles.

The Use of Graphic Organizers

There are a variety of brain-compatible learning strategies that can enhance the learner's ability to acquire, consolidate, and retrieve information in a more meaningful way. Graphic organizers are an excellent tool to use for organizing complex information into meaningful patterns of association. The brain thinks in pictures and sorts information into patterns that can be easily accessed by the learner. New information is filed into an existing mental map of associated concepts. Using a graphic organizer is an extremely brain-compatible technique as it complements this natural learning process!

Hart (1999) maintains that the structures within the cerebral cortex work together to detect and make patterns of meaning out of incoming information. It is here that raw information is deciphered, reorganized into patterns and relationships, and indexed for future reference. This, in fact, is one of the foundational principles of brain-based learning…the natural ability and propensity of the brain to elicit patterns of meaning. Everyone brings their own personal experiences into the learning environment and the brain depends heavily upon these experiences or perceptions in developing patterns of association. Once new information is patterned and associated with personal experiences, learners are able to relate this information from one area to another and truly derive meaning or knowledge from the information.

Information processed graphically is much easier to recall than the same concepts processed in a linear fashion. Graphic organizers also engage the attention, getting learners actively involved in constructing knowledge. Better yet, graphic organizers reinforce concepts to strengthen learning every time the concepts are reviewed by the learner.

Knowledge acquired in a meaningful way, such as through the use of graphic organizers is retained much longer, enhances subsequent learning of related material, and can be applied to a wide variety of new problems or contexts, thus increasing transferability of knowledge. The ability to transfer concepts and learning further enhances higher levels of critical and creative thinking as well as meaningful learning.

By using graphic organizers, learners gain control of the incoming information by organizing and processing separate and unrelated facts, eventually turning this raw information into meaningful knowledge. Likewise, graphic organizers visually demonstrate linkages and connections that are faulty, allowing learners the opportunity to rethink and correct misconceptions before building upon them. Misconceptions in knowledge are more difficult for learners to see using traditional, linear methods of processing information, and may never be realized by the learner until years later.

Adult learning principles are supported using metacognitive learning strategies such as graphic organizers. Learners are free to relate new concepts to their prior knowledge and experiences, thus reinforcing and validating their own conceptual knowledge base. The very nature of graphic organizers promotes active learning and higher-level cognitive skills, such as analysis, synthesis, and evaluation. The use of graphic organizers as a schematic study strategy tool further promotes autonomy and control over knowledge acquisition and learning outcomes.

Graphic organizers can be used as a method for presenting new material by introducing a partially constructed graphic organizer at the beginning of a unit. Students can be given copies of the same graphic so that they can modify their understanding as new concepts are presented and added to the master graphic. As concepts are introduced, encourage students to supply the rationale to support the relationships between concepts. Encourage learners to make their graphic organizers unique to their understanding by color-coding the concepts and linkages in a way that makes sense to them.

Adult learners want to get involved in the process of learning every step of the way. In addition to getting them involved, help them understand how the strategies work from a brain-based perspective. Using any of the brain-compatible strategies featured in this book will promote success in learning. Using several of the strategies, however, is a sure recipe for academic success!

See also: Beverages; Physical Movement.

Further Readings

Holtmaat, A.J., Van Someren, E.J., Vergraagen, J., Swaab, D.F., Hofman, M.A. (2002). *Plasticity in the Adult Brain: From Genes to Neurotherapy.* London, UK: Elsevier, Inc.

Knowles, M.S. (2005). *The Adult Learner 6th Ed.: The Definitive Classic in Adult Education and Human Resource Development.* London, UK: Elsevier, Inc.

Merriam, S.B., Caffarella, R.S. (1999). *Learning in Adulthood: A Comprehensive Guide* 2nd Ed. San Francisco, CA: Jossey Bass, Inc.
American Association for Adult and Continuing Education www.aaace.org

LAURIE MATERNA, PH.D., RN.

Aggression

Violent behavior in the United States has significantly declined in the last few years. Despite this progress, the victim-producing and fear-provoking nature of aggressive behavior makes it an issue that continues to disturb most citizens. Who can explain the behavior of Charles Whitman, the sniper who in 1966 stood on the University Tower in Texas and randomly shot and killed innocent bystanders? Interestingly, Whitman left a note before he died begging people to examine his brain to find out what was wrong. His suspicions were correct; an autopsy showed he had a tumor pressing into his amygdala, the part of the brain associated with **emotion**.

Aggression is more complicated to define in humans than in non-humans. Animals generally become aggressive to eat, gain territory, or protect their young when reacting to everyday situations. Due to the factor of intent, humans are more complex in their behavior. Essentially, there are three categories of human aggression: (1) predatory, (2) social—gaining dominance, and (3) defensive.

Psychology, sociology, education, and biology all bring separate evidence to unravel this complex emotion. Most scientists agree that there is a genetic component to aggression. Due to the fact that violence tends to run in families, a great deal of research has been done to try to identify the aggression gene. As yet, nothing has crystallized. This research is complicated by the fact that it is difficult to separate genetics and environment.

Beyond the evidence found in Whitman's brain, research supports the fact that the amygdala is heavily involved in aggressive behavior. A study of monkeys whose amygdalas were removed found them to be quite docile. Other studies showed that when the amygdala was electrically stimulated, the animal became more violent. Adrian Raine, Professor of Psychology at the University of Southern California, studied violent behavior at the far end of the spectrum, criminals convicted of heinous crimes. He found these individuals had a lack of activity in their prefrontal cortex and higher activity in the limbic region.

Similar findings were found among adolescents that played violent video and computer games. Neuroscientists discovered games stimulated the amygdala and neutralized the frontal lobes. Teens that engaged in excessive violent video play had under-active frontal lobes, the part of the brain responsible for reflective logical reasoning. This inactivity persisted long after the person had stopped playing the game, leaving the emotionally charged amygdala in control. In addition, games that were violent in nature triggered more testosterone to be released into the system, further agitating the amygdala.

A lack of impulse control and subsequent aggressive behavior may also be the result of an imbalance of chemicals in the brain. Research in the area of serotonin levels, a neurotransmitter that provides a feeling of well being and calmness, in the brain indicates that children who feel successful and have high self-esteem have higher levels of serotonin in their brain than children who are reprimanded for poor behavior on a regular basis. Social feedback from a significant adult that is positive has also shown to result in an increase in serotonin levels in the brain. Violent criminals and individuals with a history of hostile, impulsive behavior have low levels of serotonin in their cerebral spinal fluid.

Testosterone has also been linked to aggression. Males with higher testosterone levels tend to be more socially aggressive, but not more violent. While this aggressive pre-disposition is usually destructive, it can be directed in a positive manner. Proof is seen in individuals such as CEOs, professional athletes, and high ranking politicians who often have elevated levels of testosterone.

The environment plays a significant function in aggressive behavior. Children who are not supported in a positive environment or who do not bond with an adult, either a parent or any other designated care provider, tend to exhibit aggressive behaviors and poor social skills. Another cause of aggressive behavior in young children is learned through observation. Children who consistently view or are the object of violence are more aggressive in their actions. Exposure to violence in the media has also been linked to aggressive behavior.

There appears to be gender differences with aggression. Research studies have noted a male child is six times more likely than a female child to be identified as having aggressive behavior that is disruptive to his life. Aggressive behaviors exhibited by boys can be attributed to several issues, including biology, cultural differences, learning style, the structure of the classroom, and the acceptance of the nurturing adult. Language development may also be a determinant of aggression. Studies have shown that young boys do not develop language as early as young girls. This may result in frustration and acting out.

The physical and emotional environment of a child has a dramatic impact on the level of aggressive behaviors. Environments that are not crowded with furniture and that have space for children to get away by themselves help reduce anxiety and frustration in children. The emotional environment must be positive, encouraging children to explore, take risks, and problem solve in a manner that is developmentally appropriate.

Treatment for aggressive behavior may involve a medical prescription. Serotonin-boosting medication may be used to increase the child's feeling of well-being. Other medications may be prescribed to reduce impulsive acts. These medications are stimulants that encourage the brain to respond before the child acts. Some children's aggressive behavior can be redirected and supported in an environment that nurtures the child.

Regardless of the cause of the aggressive behavior in young children, the need for nurturing adults, a flexible learning environment, and early intervention is clear. If the child is treated with medication, additional supports and interventions will be needed within the classroom. Teachers need specific training and support to be able to understand the typical development of young children and to adequately support children with aggressive behaviors.

See also: **Anger; Emotion; At-Risk Behavior.**

Further Readings

Anders, M.P. (2001). ACT against violence. *Young Children* MRIs revealed the difference between the adolescent's amygdala lighting up when they responded to the photograph compared to adults' frontal lobes lighting up with the same information. 56(4):60–61.

Lipelt, K., Bonilla, C.A. (2001). *Brainworks: Birth to Kindergarten—the Aggression Component. A Question/Answer Workbook.* U.S.; California: ICA. Retrieved November 27, 2005, from ERIC database.

International Brain Research Organization: http://www.ibro.info

SUSAN CATAPANO. ED.D.

Aging Brain

We now live longer than ever before in the history of mankind. During the last century, life expectancy at birth increased dramatically in developed countries, rising from about forty-eight years to about seventy-six years for men and from fifty-one years to almost eighty-one years for women. This trend is expected to continue due to better understanding and management of age-associated diseases. Thus, the percentage of people over eighty years of age is predicted to quadruple over the next twenty years, raising the question: Is "aging," or the perception of what constitutes aging, changing? The common dogma about aging is that it is characterized by inevitable decline, with widespread and noticeable physical and mental changes. With senescence, signs of "wear and tear" in the body become increasingly evident. Clearly, older individuals do not display the same physical strength or the same mental agility as their younger counterparts. Aging, however, is not a single process that takes place in a uniform fashion. It has many facets and metrics within and between individuals that are influenced by a large number of variables.

Structural Brain Changes in Aging

Even to the naked eye, an eighty-year-old brain differs from a twenty year-old brain. The sulci (grooves) and gyri (ridges) making up the foldings of the brain are more apparent and more pronounced in the older brain. As we age, some neurons (nerve cells) shrink and some die resulting in a decline in neuronal integrity and neuronal density. Shrinkage also occurs in the white matter, which consists of long and shorter fibers (axons) connecting neurons within a brain region and between brain regions. Axons are typically encased in a sheath of fat called myelin and are responsible for transmitting messages among neurons. With aging, the thickness of this myelin decreases resulting in reduced white matter density, which is apparent under the microscope. Reduction in white matter integrity with aging can be observed on magnetic resonance imaging (MRI). Alterations are visible around the brain ventricles (openings within the brain filled with cerebrospinal fluid) and in deep white matter. Other abnormalities apparent with aging include gliosis (scarring), neuritic plaques, and neurofibrillary tangles, which, when numerous, are diagnostic of Alzheimer's disease.

Brain structural changes, however, are not limited to old age and do not solely reflect loss or damage. During childhood and adolescence, the brain undergoes significant alterations characterized by an explosion of new connections among neurons called dendritic arborizations. This process is particularly pronounced in the frontal lobes of the adolescent brain, which is the last brain region to reach adult maturation. Simultaneously, a large number of connections are discarded because they are redundant and unnecessary. Suzanne Corkin and her colleagues at the Massachusetts Institute of Technology have recently shown that reduction in gray matter thickness already takes place in individuals in their twenties. Of particular interest is that these changes in cortical thickness were observed in numerous brain areas, including primary visual, somatosensory, and motor cortices, in addition to those multimodal cortices (parietal and prefrontal regions) that had been reported.

Sprouting and pruning of connections among networks of neurons is not restricted to early development, but is present throughout life. In addition, contrary to the general belief until recently, new neurons continue to emerge during adulthood. These new neurons have been observed in rodents and in monkeys; evidence suggests that they may also be found in humans. They originate in specific brain areas (hippocampus and olfactory bulbs) and then migrate to other brain regions. The role and life span of these new neurons remain to be fully understood.

Environmental and Genetic Contributions to Aging

Environmental variables influence brain aging, with dramatic consequences in some instances. For example, a 30 percent reduction in caloric intake results in an increased lifespan by up to 50 percent in mice, delaying the onset of signs of aging. Variations in the diet may also have short- or long-term effects in humans; for example, severe vitamin deficiency (C or B12), fat intake, and alcohol consumption are known to have deleterious effects on health. A diet high in saturated fat results in elevated cholesterol level and high blood pressure, which increase the risk of cardiovascular and cerebrovascular disease in later life. These conditions, if untreated, can disrupt normal brain function and accelerate aging processes. Exposure to certain chemicals (e.g., mercury) and acquired brain injury have also been associated with short- and long-term deleterious effects on the brain.

Not all variables have a negative impact, however. Formal education, professional attainment, general lifestyle, including level of social involvement and hobbies, significantly modify aging processes in a protective way. Animal and human studies confirm the importance of the environment and social interactions. Increased brain weight, reflecting increased neuronal size and increasing neuron connectivity, has been observed in rats and monkeys who had been exposed to enriched environments compared to animals without such exposure. Similarly in humans, exercise is reported to promote brain health, with smaller age-related brain loss in people who exercise regularly compared to those who do not.

Our genetic makeup also influences how and how quickly we age, in the same way that height and weight are partly determined by our parents' genes. One extreme example is that of Werner's syndrome. This rare inherited disorder results in accelerated aging, with early signs of aging starting soon after puberty, and death generally occurring before age fifty. An explosion of research in genetics has led to the identification of a number of genes that are linked to pathological aging and neurodegenerative diseases. The early 1990s saw the first report of an association between Alzheimer's disease and a gene located on chromosome 19: the apolipoprotein E (APOE) gene. Three alleles of APOE are present in the general population (ε2, ε3, and ε4), and each individual receives two copies of the gene, one from each parent. Having one or two copies of the ε4 allele of the gene is associated with an increased risk of developing the disease. Importantly, however, APOE is only a susceptibility gene: Not all individuals carrying the ε4 allele will develop Alzheimer's disease, and fewer than half of Alzheimer's disease patients have the ε4 allele. Since then, other genes have been implicated in Alzheimer's disease (e.g., amyloid precursor protein, presenilin-1, and presenilin-2), as well as in frontotemporal dementia (tau) and in Parkinson's disease (α-synuclein, parkin, and DJ-1). In general, the presence of specific pathogenic mutations in these genes results in an earlier age of disease onset and a more rapid progression, leading to an earlier death. Unlike the APOE gene, known mutations on these genes trigger the disease in over 99 percent of the mutation-carrying individuals. Genes, however, remain only one piece of this complex puzzle. Currently, causal genetic mutations account for less than 5 percent of all cases of dementia. Familial factors (i.e., genetic, environmental, or both) play a role in Alzheimer's disease and Parkinson's disease.

Cognitive Changes in Aging: The Case of Memory

Cognitive abilities show different courses and patterns of change with aging. Importantly, not all cognitive abilities decline and not all decline at the same rate. In addition, changes may not affect all aspects of a particular domain. To illustrate these points, we investigate the cognitive domain associated with one universally voiced complaint of loss with aging: memory.

Declarative Memory

A complaint of poor memory generally refers to a difficulty in consciously remembering specific pieces of information. This kind of memory, called declarative memory, has been shown to be sensitive to the effects of aging. Declarative memory can be divided into memory for specific facts called **semantic memory** (e.g., What is the capital of France?), and memory for events called **episodic memory** (e.g., What did you have for dinner last night?). Within declarative memory, a greater difference in performance between young and older adults is observed on tasks of episodic memory compared to tasks of semantic memory.

Studies have shown that older individuals' ability to encode (i.e., learn) novel information is impaired. This impairment probably reflects an inability to use effective mnemonic strategies spontaneously. As these higher-level cognitive processes rely on prefrontal circuits, older adults' deficits likely reflect the age-related cortical and subcortical changes in the prefrontal region. Interestingly, once learned, retention of the information over time is unimpaired. Retrieval of information is also affected, particularly in situations requiring spontaneous recollection, generally referred to as "free recall." Performance improves with the provision of cues (i.e., cued recall) and even more so when using a recognition format (e.g., "Did you see this word before?"). Thus, it appears that for declarative memory, older adults experience difficulty whenever there is a greater need for self-initiated strategies and whenever environmental support decreases, either during encoding or retrieval operations. A striking example is the impaired ability of older adults to remember names. Underuse of cognitive control processes is also reflected in a difficulty with prospective memory (i.e., the ability to plan ahead) and with certain aspects of working memory (i.e., the ability to retain information on-line while operating on it).

Nondeclarative Memory

Nondeclarative memory encompasses implicit knowledge and learning, such as driving a car or touch typing, as well as classical conditioning and repetition priming. Priming reflects a bias (e.g., increase in speed, or accuracy) when naming or recognizing words or pictures presented previously. It reflects the nonconscious aspects of memory, or learning without awareness. In marked contrast to declarative memory, most aspects of nondeclarative memory are more resilient to the effects of aging, with little or no change in performance observed across decades. One exception is classical eyeblink conditioning where older adults show greater variability in learning to associate a neutral stimulus (e.g., a sound) with a relevant noxious stimulus (e.g., a puff of air on the eye) compared to younger adults. This variability in performance likely reflects the integrity of the cerebellum, a structure known to support classical conditioning in animals.

Emotional Memory

Memory performance is also contingent upon the content of the information being processed. In general, negative or positive information is better retained than neutral information, a phenomenon called "emotional memory enhancement." In recent studies, Elizabeth Kensinger, Corkin, and colleagues have shown that some, but not all, aspects of emotional enhancement are preserved in older individuals. For example, older adults, just like their young counterparts, recalled more negative and positive than neutral words. In contrast, this mechanism was absent in patients with mild Alzheimer's disease. The investigators showed, however, that older individuals were inferior to young individuals in retrieving neutral information that was embedded in an emotional context, likely due to impaired cognitive control processes. Thus, these researchers demonstrated that aspects of emotional memory are dissociable and are differently affected by age-related processes.

Nonmnemonic Cognitive Changes

Other cognitive domains differ in their patterns of change. For example, speed of information processing, which denotes how quickly one manipulates pieces of information and responds to presented cues, peaks in late adolescence followed by a steady decline over time. On tests measuring this ability, for example the Digit Symbol subtest of the Wechsler Intelligence Scales, one observes a steady decline in performance with each decade. This change is not trivial in that an eighty-nine-year-old person needs to perform at only 40 percent of the level achieved by an eighteen-year-old person to earn the same age-adjusted score.

In contrast, other cognitive abilities remain stable across adulthood, and show decline only late in life. Verbal memory span, which reflects the amount of information that can be held simultaneously within immediate memory (e.g., strings of digits, such as phone numbers), remains remarkably stable, and shows minimal decline even in very old individuals. Similarly, general knowledge continues to improve during life. These abilities reach their peak during the sixth decade of life and remain stable before showing some decline in the ninth decade.

In the Seattle Longitudinal Study, K. Werner Schaie and his colleagues have examined age-related cognitive changes in six ability dimensions (inductive reasoning, spatial orientation, perceptual speed, numeric ability, verbal ability, and verbal memory). Groups of individuals of different ages have been tested every seven years, with a new cohort recruited at each time point. Several important findings emerged from this complex study. First, when investigating differences between groups of different ages (cross-sectional differences), they showed that younger age groups performed better on all cognitive tasks compared to older age groups, with the exception of numeric ability (i.e., number manipulations and operations). Second, they showed that, at the same age, younger cohorts (i.e., cohorts more recently enrolled in the study) performed better than the older cohorts, particularly on inductive reasoning and verbal memory, but not on perceptual speed or numeric and verbal abilities. These differences likely reflect the younger cohorts' access to more years of education and more diverse curricula. Third, for each mental ability, the changes from one testing session to the next within each age group (longitudinal differences) were not as pronounced as the cross-sectional changes, indicating stable performance across time within each cohort. Schaie also demonstrated that as participants became older, they showed larger spreads of possible scores on testing and a decrease in the consistency of their performance across abilities. This final finding reflects individual differences in sensitivity to the effects of aging as well as possible signs of neurodegenerative processes and other illnesses of aging.

Neuroimaging Yields Insights about Aging

Functional neuroimaging (fMRI) has opened the door to the investigation of the neurological correlates underlying behavioral test performance. During the past decade, an exponential number of studies has used functional MRI to investigate the neural substrates of changes in cognition with aging. This technique measures changes in oxygen level and blood flow in discrete brain areas during task performance, thereby identifying the regions that participate in a particular cognitive ability. Several findings have emerged from fMRI studies. In general, older individuals show patterns of activation that are similar to those seen in young adults on a wide range of tasks, but they show decreased amplitude of activation and increased interindividual variability. Another general finding is one of increased symmetrical activation in older individuals. For example, on a word encoding task, young individuals showed activation limited to the posterior frontal region in the left hemisphere, whereas older adults showed, in addition, activation in the same region in the right hemisphere. The meaning of these changes in patterns and levels of activation in aging remains open for debate. The observed under-activation of brain regions appears to reflect an inability for older individuals to spontaneously engage brain regions fully compared to their younger counterparts. The recruitment of additional brain regions, which has been labeled "nonselective recruitment," may reflect a compensatory mechanism to meet task demands accompanied, possibly, by the use of alternative strategies. What remains unclear is whether changes in strategies lead to changes in activation or vice versa. Another view suggests that nonselective recruitment may not be a compensatory mechanism but rather reflects a breakdown in appropriate activation reflecting age-related physiological changes, such as the neuronal and white matter changes described previously.

Combating Age-Related Cognitive Impairment

Fortunately, aging does not denote an ineluctable decline in brain function. As has been demonstrated, not all cognitive functions are susceptible to the aging process. Further, although there is suggestive evidence that the spontaneous use of efficient strategies declines with age, we know that this tendency can be reversed with the use of external support and explicit rules. For example, when encouraged to use "deep" encoding strategies, such as actively linking items together, older individuals' performance on episodic memory tasks improves dramatically. Findings from fMRI research also suggest that, as we get older, we may compensate by recruiting additional brain regions that are appropriate for the task. Recovery of function was also reported in the Seattle Longitudinal Study where the investigators showed that intellectual decline could be reversed with targeted educational interventions. They demonstrated that two-thirds of individuals who had shown a decline over the two previous testing sessions benefited from a cognitive training program, and 40 percent reached their pre-decline level (i.e., fourteen years previously). Importantly, the benefits were long-term and could be observed even after seven years.

In summary, the brain, just like other parts of the body, is continually changing throughout life, in response to environmental, endogenous, and genetic variables. Brain aging is evident at different levels: structural, behavioral, and functional. Age-related changes, however, are not limited to the later years of life: Changes occur in early adulthood and in middle age as well. Further, brain plasticity and adaptive responses are seen well into senescence. At the cellular level, new neurons may continue to develop in the hippocampus and surrounding neocortex in adulthood. Behavioral and functional neuroimaging studies indicate that older adults benefit from appropriate training programs, allowing gains to be made; patterns of activations seen on fMRI can become similar between young and older adults after appropriate training.

See also: **Procedural Memory and Emotion.**

Further Readings

Buckner, R.L. (2003). Functional-anatomic correlates of control processes in memory. *Journal of Neuroscience* 23:3999–4004.

Kensinger, E.A., Brierley, B., Medford, N., Growdon, J.H., Corkin, S. (2002). Effects of normal aging and Alzheimer's disease on emotional memory. *Emotion* 2:118–134.

Schaie, K.W. (1994). The course of adult intellectual development. *American Psychologist* 49:304–313.

Corkin's Behavioral Neuroscience Laboratory website: http://web.mit.edu/bnl

OLIVIER PIGUET, PH.D. AND
SUZANNE CORKIN, PH.D.

Anger

Anger is a defensive, emotional response, evoked when something is viewed as a threat to one's physical or psychological well-being. This threat or annoyance may be real or perceived. Anger, like fear, causes the limbic area to generate strong emotional responses that the frontal cortex may not be able to manage or at least not control fully.

The brain works on a system of checks and balances. An analogy could be made to a disaster at a nuclear power station, when the external control system is unable to manage the large amounts of energy produced by the nuclear core. It is noteworthy that expressions like "meltdown," "out of control," and "running amok" are used when describing both nuclear power station disasters and people who are experiencing major anger episodes. To carry the analogy one step further, a "superheated" limbic area can overpower the frontal cortex and render it unresponsive.

The analogy ends, however, when we begin to understand the integrative and developmental nature of the brain. Unlike the highly technical but rigid structures of the power station the limbic and frontal cortex areas of the brain are extremely plastic and interactive. Both, experience change and continual growth. The cognitive and emotional development of every brain is unique. Hence, every brain has its own anger response/management system that is more likely to initiate a "fight" rather than to "take flight or freeze."

Genetics, pre and postnatal environments, conscious and nonconscious learning are all critical contributing factors to brain development. Genetics determine, among other things, the level of the enzyme monoamine oxidase MAO(A), which metabolizes norepinephrine and serotonin. Low levels of these neurotransmitters lead to a propensity for violence and anger. A predisposition to **depression** and **Attention Deficit Hyperactive Disorder (ADHD)** is also a genetic trait.

An underdeveloped cerebral cortex or hyper vigilant fetal brain may be caused by prenatal exposure to nicotine, street drugs, high stress level, or poor diet, while the prenatal influence of alcohol may result in **Fetal Alcohol Syndrome**. These brains may be temporarily or permanently unable to maintain the cognitive/emotional equilibrium necessary for normal living.

Postnatal environments that feature inconsistent, often harsh discipline, and low levels of emotional attachment negatively impact children's brains. The overpowering stress can inhibit brain growth resulting in an underdeveloped frontal cortex, an oversensitive amygdale, and a less efficient "neural corridor" between the two. As a result the cognitive/emotional appraisal and control systems of these brains are less effective, often confused, and at times seriously dysfunctional.

Example: Girls who have been sexually abused often impulsively display intense anger and engage in physical violence.

Cognitive and emotional neural networks are constantly being formed and re-formed in response to internal and external stimuli. This growth can either be a help or a hindrance in determining a person's propensity for anger. For example, racism is cognitively learned by example and conscious instruction; the resulting memories however, become part of both the frontal cortex and the amygdala.

The frontal cortex is the least developed region of the brain at birth, but with active exposure to a safe, stimulating, and challenging environment the frontal cortex grows to become the center for complex memory, abstract thought, and advanced social skills. Unfortunately, not all children experience such favorable environments, resulting in a great variation in the cognitive and emotive capacities of the general population to manage anger and other emotions.

The principal interactive brain components involved in anger are the amygdala, the anterior cingulate, and an area of the frontal cortex, the orbital frontal cortex (OFC). The amygdala, considered to be part of the limbic area, is one of the first brain components to assess all incoming messages. It is here primary decisions are made on the degree of "uncertainty," such as the level of danger, intimidation, annoyance, pleasurable excitement, and the nature of the response. The amygdala's response speed is three to five times faster than that of the frontal cortex.

The OFC, located behind the eyes, operates as the interface between the amygdala and the remaining frontal cortex. Both the OFC and the amygdala are involved in creating and evaluating the messages that flow between them; these messages affect both cognitive memories in the frontal cortex and emotional memories within the amygdala. The OFC is more than an on/off switch.

The anterior cingulate is located near the adjacent inner surfaces of the frontal hemispheres. Its purpose is to enable the brain to shift from idea to idea and to let new ideas enter the thought process. An under-performing cingulate may become "stuck" or "over focused" resulting in the following, from an anger perspective:

(1) Obsessing on one or more anger irritants. Anger irritants are individual and the possibilities are endless. An anger irritant could stem from a minuscule speck of dust, the sound of a person's voice, or the presence of an undesirable person.

(2) Oppositional Defiant Disorder (ODD). Many children and a slightly smaller percentage of adults become verbally or physically violent when confronted by authority figures. Their defensive anger outbursts are spontaneously generated, supported in part, by genetic traits but largely due to living or having lived in a stressful, hostile environment.

(3) Road rage is similar to ODD in that the actions of one driver cause another driver to "explode" into anger. This "road raged"

anger includes swearing, gesticulating, chasing the other driver, forcing the other driver off the road, damaging the car or physically attacking the other driver. The nature of the anger is impulsive, intense and extremely over focused.

Examples of anger triggers may include:

- Bigoted reactions to persons of another race, color, creed, sex, or sexual orientation.
- Intense impatience such as: waiting in line, having someone cut in front of you, failing to get service or failing to find someone who can help or who appears to care about your concern.
- Losing a game, being fired or not hired, being cheated, experiencing vandalization of your property, being hit or insulted, feeling negative discrimination and being unable to perform a task.
- Refusal to accept responsibility and being angry with: God, political leaders, the boss, parents, spouse, children, neighbors, coworkers.
- Impulsiveness as presented by children afflicted with ADHD, Fetal Alcohol Syndrome, brain injury, and neural underdevelopment. The impulsive nature of such individuals often leads to bouts of frustration and inappropriate behavior often resulting in frequent and harsh discipline. Both the impulsiveness and the discipline can serve as future triggers for anger.

Anger, as does fear, affects not only the brain but also the body by increasing the levels of norepinephrine in the brain and epinephrine in the body with corresponding increases in heart rate, blood pressure and levels of glucocorticoids. Sections of the brain and body either shut down or function at lower levels while other parts become more efficient allowing the brain-body to move into survival mode.

Angry people are unable to enter into rational conversations or make quick, appropriate decisions, but are far more likely to make rash decisions with drastic consequences. They also have difficulty forming or recalling long-term memories.

The angry brain is less specific and more global. The left hemisphere that is largely responsible for analytical reasoning, tends to be "turned off" but the more global right hemisphere continues to operate, in a fashion. For example, the ranting of an angry person usually includes a variety of expletives and a range of generalities such as, "You *never* get it right," You *always* take me for granted." You seldom, if ever, hear "*seven of eleven* times you mess up."

There is a relationship between one's mental wellness and one's propensity for anger. For example, persons suffering from depression routinely experience anger. The combination of reduced capacity in the frontal cortex and intense internal messaging can cause these individuals to become angry over even minor inconveniences and fixate on certain irritating thoughts.

The stress experienced when suffering from poor physical health often leaves people angry about their condition. Brain injury, especially to the frontal cortex (control center) or temporal lobe (mood management) may also contribute to anger. Persons who have suffered concussion due to falls, playing contact sports, being in car crashes or physically abused, or who suffer from brain tumors/cysts are all candidates for anger problems.

Poor diet, sleep deprivation, and low blood sugar change the neurochemical balance within the brain resulting in either an overactive amygdala and an underactive frontal cortex or both and hence a propensity for anger. Alcohol anaesthetizes regions in the cerebral cortex including the frontal cortex. This not only reduces the inhibitory capability of the brain but also negatively affects a person's ability to manage anger impulses. Moreover, there is a strong correlation between alcoholism and depression.

Lindqvist *et al.* discovered that anabolic androgenic steroid (induced) animals had significantly lower levels of serotonin in basal forebrain and dorsal striatum compared to controls. The net effects are increased levels of aggression. The level of aggression existed not only during time of usage but a considerable time afterward depending upon intensity of abuse.

Anger Management

Anger is a complex mental condition and the roots of an individual's anger lie largely within the person's implicit memory systems. Therefore, it is difficult for an outsider to fully understand the unique nature of another's anger. Also there are no simple solutions to most anger problems.

Anger management is more than controlling anger outbursts. It must work at changing the brain's reaction to specific stimuli. Change of this behavior is difficult and time consuming because of the complex cognitive/emotional nature of the issue.

Background on Anger

Anger:

Is a natural emotional response.

Is supported, in part, by cognitive input.

Occurs when a situation is deemed threatening and the emotional response overpowers the frontal cortex.

Is dependent upon the influences of genetic, environmental, and learned inputs upon brain development.

May be the result of a brain injury or brain dysfunction.

May require pharmaceutical as well as psychotherapy treatment.

Management Processes

Step One: Acceptance of anger management needs
    Some of your anger is legitimate and healthy.
    Some of your anger is out of control and could lead to serious trouble.

Step Two: Knowledge
    Learn about the nature of anger.
    Make a list of irritants that cause your anger.
    Analyze your background, understand why you have specific anger triggers.

Step Three: Developing an Action Plan
    Determine who or what is to blame.
    Take responsibility for your actions.
    Recognize and evaluate anger triggers.
    Accept the emotive memories that are triggering anger.

Note: The implicit memories that form emotive memory do not have a language base. It is necessary to use therapy processes that may involve role-play, art, distraction, neuro feedback, and controlled interaction with "anger triggers." Steinberg proposes that future neuro research may lead to pharmaceutical treatments to help interrupt specific, harmful emotional memories.

    Acknowledge that physical behaviors are the outputs of anger and not the sources of anger.

Note: Learn how to manage the physical aspects of anger from the perspectives of safety for self and others and for personal health reasons.

    Accept that your anger response pattern is unique, complex, and will take concentrated effort over time to achieve change.
    Seek professional help.

Step Four: Develop strategies to lower anger level.
    Prepare one's self when entering "anger zones."

Note: It is virtually impossible to avoid all stress/anger-creating zones at home, work, or at play. It is possible, however, to make mental and physical preparations. Examples include: Plan ahead, physically reduce stress, avoid caffeine and high levels of sugar in food or drink, be prepared for meetings, avoid being annoyed by snide innuendo, set a personal objective for the event, become appropriately distracted, determine what is important, use self-talk, if possible, take a bathroom break, assess the role others are playing in terms of their own self-esteem.

    Find an anger mentor.
    Use distractions to help manage anger causing obsessions.

Note: Impatience may be solved in some situations by reading a book, doing crossword puzzles, and the like.

Note: Counting to ten before taking action does two things. It provides time to think of alternatives plus it provides the brain with a distraction.

Step Five: Things to avoid.

Self-medicating with alcohol or other drugs.

"Hitting a punching bag." Too often angry people, especially men are unable to distinguish between their girlfriend or spouse's head and a punching bag.

Repressing the anger. The amygdala continues to generate emotive anger responses that may be augmented by cognitive thoughts thus keeping the brain-body anger responses highly energized. The resulting angry outbursts are often directed at innocent third parties.

Personally using anger to manage or control other people.

Committing yourself to a self-help program that promises instantaneous results.

See also: **Trauma.**

Further Readings

Amen, D.G. (1998). *Change your Brain, Change your Life* (1st ed.) New York, NY: Times Books.

LeDoux, J. (2002). *Synaptic Self* (1st.ed.) Toronto, ON: Viking-Penguin Books.

Lindqvist, A.S., Johansson-Steensland, P., Nyberg, F., Fahlke, C. (2002). Anabolic androgenic steroid affects competitive behaviour, behavioural response to ethanol and brain serotonin levels. *Behavioural Brain Research* 133(1):21–29.

Steinberg, D. (2004). Possible PTSD Treatment. *The Scientist* 18:22.

American Psychological Association www.apa.org/pubinfo/anger.html

DAVID HALSTEAD, M.ED.

Animal Studies

Animal studies have contributed to a better understanding of human behavior, how and why the human brain works, and possible treatments for disorders and extreme activities for many decades. The following studies highlight some important findings about how mammals learn and what scientists have observed using Functional Magnetic Reasoning Images (fMRI) and other recent technology to understand the effects of specific learning experiences on various parts of the brain. Observation of mammals in their natural habitat also reveals emotional responses to ordinary and extreme situations that are common to the human experience.

Sex Differences in Learning

Sampson, a young male, and Schweini, a young female, sit with their mother as she fishes. Schweini fishes with a technique resembling that of her mother. She chooses a fishing tool that is similar in length to the one her mother uses and spends a significant amount of time watching her mother fish. Sampson has spent much less time observing his mother fish and chooses a fishing tool and a technique that are not consistent with those used by his mother. Schweini becomes proficient at fishing by age 3 1/2 years and Sampson becomes proficient at age 5 1/2 years.

Sampson, Schweini, and their mother represent a family of wild chimpanzees in Gombe National Park, Tanzania. The director of Field Conservation for the Lincoln Park Zoo, Dr. Elizabeth Lonsdorf (2004), investigated sex differences exhibited by young chimpanzees in learning to termite-fish in a four-year longitudinal field study. The community's offspring were observed to find the learning pattern of this cultural behavior. Fourteen wild chimpanzees under the age of eleven years were videotaped, along with their mothers, while they fished for termites.

Lonsdorf found that even though young males and females spend similar amounts of time with their mothers, females begin termite-fishing at a younger age, spend more time observing their mothers fish, use techniques consistent with their mothers and were more successful at termite fishing once the skill was acquired than males.

All females studied could termite-fish by age 3 1/2 years, while all males were able to fish by age 5 1/2 years. Once learned, the time spent on this activity was not significantly different between the males and females.

The vast difference between males' and females' ability to successfully and consistently termite-fish may appear surprising, however, several possible explanations exist. Young male chimps may not spend long periods of time learning this small motor task because they do not have the patience for it and they spend more time playing. Similarly, according to Dr. Margot Prior (1993), University of Melbourne, Australia, human boys lack in motor skills until the ages three to four. Prior also found hyperactive and aggressive types of behavior were seen in boys significantly more often than in girls at all ages.

A study done by Marian Diamond (1988), Professor of Anatomy, Berkley, focused on gender differences in rats with regard to differences in the male and female when placed in an enriched condition. Diamond found that when exposed to the same type of enriched condition the female neocortex responded differently than the male neocortex. Significant changes in cortical thickness in the occipital cortex were seen in the male, but no significant changes in the somatosensory cortex were seen. The thickness of the occipital cortex in the female was significantly increased in response to enrichment. According to Diamond, the findings indicate that testosterone is not involved in the observed increase in cortical thickness in rat brains when the rats are living in an enriched environment. Significant changes were found in both male and female rats exposed to even a short period of enrichment, described as forty minutes. The longer the rats were in the enriched environment, the longer the cortex in both male and female rats retained its increased thickness after being returned to its normal environment.

Christophe Boesch, Director of the Max Planck Institute for Evolutionary Anthropology, and Hedwige Boesch-Achermann (2000) studied Tai chimpanzees and recorded observations of **gender differences** in learning to crack nuts. Boesch reports females more frequently crack nuts in trees and are more proficient cracking nuts on the ground. These differences begin to emerge in late adolescence. They also observed females becoming independent earlier and using more effort to open nuts by themselves than the males. Surprisingly, males between the ages of four and thirteen years are more efficient at cracking Panda nuts than females. Later, however, during adulthood, females become more efficient Panda nut crackers. Observations by Boesch also revealed young males may have better access to their mother's tools while young females get less support from their mothers.

Similar patterns are seen in humans. It has been shown that there are general sex differences in the corpus callosum, cerebellum, hypothalamus, and white and gray matter in the human brain. This has been attributed to evolution and natural selection for specific survival skills in many species. According to Dr. Sheryl Feinstein (2004), Augustana College Sioux Falls, the division of labor may have been essential to the survival of the species. These specialties of the sexes during natural selection, males hunting and females gathering food and caring for their young, may have led to gender differences in their brains.

Humans and rhesus monkeys share approximately 95 percent of their genes. Apes and gorillas share around 98 percent of human DNA. According to Steve Suomi (1999), National Institutes of Health animal center in Maryland, although adolescence in rhesus monkeys is earlier and shorter than humans, it has many similarities. Rhesus monkeys go through a period of time when they have a significant growth spurt, much like human teenagers. As with humans, their cognitive growth and abstract thinking skills progress at this time. Due to these close similarities, the study of primates, as well as other mammals, such as rats, are considered particularly significant in understanding human behavior and the inner workings of the human mind.

Male and female rhesus monkeys reach puberty at ages four and three, respectively. At this age the female monkeys begin learning to care for babies and groom them. During the teenage years, male monkeys fight, forage for food, form gangs, and join other bands, reports Suomi. The shy male monkeys sometimes fare better than the aggressive males. They may be less annoying or more mature and therefore less likely to be ousted by the older females.

The hypothalamus, which is larger in men, leads to their more aggressive behavior and increased sexual desire, while females are more passive. Girls who are overly nurtured can become more dependent, according to Feinstein. Girls should be encouraged to be hands-on in their learning activities, much like the mothers of the chimpanzees of Gombe and the Tai Forest have been shown to be. The male chimpanzees, with increased levels of testosterone, are more likely to spend time fighting for tools and playing than spending quiet time observing and practicing skills. Similarly, boys are more likely to be behavior problems in school and show hyperactive, "rough play" behavior considered inappropriate in most learning situations. Boys are more likely to be ousted from the classroom as their chimp counterparts are to be ousted from their pack, for aggressive, testosterone-driven behavior.

Memory

Humans depend on their memories to navigate everyday activities, recognize familiar events, make plans, assess situations, and make decisions. Nonhumans also depend on and utilize memory. The Grand Central Station of memory is the hippocampus. It changes incoming short-term memory messages into long-term memory when it decides the information is important and should be saved. Ronald Kotulak (1996), author of *Inside the Brain; Revolutionary Discoveries of how the Mind Works*, reports on man-made ampakines, a chemical compound that was devised at the University of California and Santa Barbara by Gary Lynch and Gary Rogers. Understanding how the NMDA receptor works, they were able to develop and fit discreetly in this key receptor, a member of a family of compounds they labeled ampakines. Young, healthy rats that were given ampakines learned tasks significantly faster, in half the time, compared to the other rats. This finding is potentially significant for the **aging brain** and for younger people with memory problems affecting their ability to learn.

Sleep deprivation has also been shown to affect memory. Physicists at Indiana University have studied the memory of rats running a particular route and then studied their memory of the route after a night of sleep interruption. A rat's ability to repeat the same route the next day was compromised when its dreams were interrupted. According to Phillip Schewe, the results of this study are significant in determining that dreaming and uninterrupted sleep help preserve memory.

Tetsuro Matsuzawa (2001), Professor at the Primate Research Institute Kyoto University, Japan, has conducted research in the area of working memory, described as holding information for only a short period of time, in chimpanzees. In two of his trial research projects the chimpanzees had to retrieve items which then had to be memorized. The chimpanzees' reproductive memory processes, not recognition, were being studied.

When studying the human working memory, two common ways of assessing retention are using a delay interval or testing memory span using numerical ordering. Matsuzawa applied both these techniques to chimpanzees.

The delay interval task, "constructive matching-to-sample" required the chimpanzee, Ai, to observe a lexigram that consisted of nine basic elements and then recreate the samples using the nine elements. If all elements were correctly completed the chimpanzee was rewarded with food. However, if an incorrect choice was made at any time during the trial, the activity was suspended immediately. Constructing meaningful lexigrams, ones that Ai could match with colors and actual items, was learned more quickly than meaningless ones. These same results have been replicated in human memory, as well, according to Fergus IM Craik and Endel Tulving (1975) of the University of Toronto, Canada.

Matsuzawa also performed numerical ordering trials using a masking experiment with the chimpanzee, Ai. The numbers zero to nine represented the use of Arabic numerals that had already been learned by Ai. Before responding in the masking trial Ai had to memorize all numbers presented and their respective positions. She was tested in the varying set sizes of 3-item, 4-item, and 5-item conditions. According to Matsuzawa, Ai's performance was comparable to human preschool children, with a 90 percent accuracy rate in the 4-item set size and 65 percent accuracy in the 5-item set. These test results indicate that when given a random set of five numbers Ai can memorize them and retain the memory for a certain amount of time.

Although controversial, recent research by Nelson Cowan (2001), a professor at the University of Missouri, Columbia, of humans suggests that memorizing four items may be their capacity. Four has been referred to as the magical number in humans. Based on Ai's performance, Matsuzawa spoke of the magical number of five in chimpanzees, equating the chimpanzee's memory capacity to that of humans, allowing for further research.

In a study by neuroscientists Patricia Goldman-Rakic, Yale University School of Medicine, and Adele Diamond, University of Massachusetts Medical School (1989), humans and monkeys took similar versions of tests. A reward, such as a toy or food was hidden in a particular receptacle. Then, all receptacles were hidden from the subjects' view. A few seconds later, the receptacles were revealed and it was recorded if the children and animals remembered which one contained the reward. Although the infants and young monkeys failed the tests, as they became older they could maintain the information in their brains for increasingly longer periods of time. Later studies done by Lisa Parr (2001) showed this skill improved through late adolescence, which is consistent with the delayed prefrontal cortexes refinement.

MRI studies of chimps have been done measuring the anatomy of the hippocampus and amygdala by Hani D. Freeman, Claudio Cantalupo, and William D. Hopkins (2004) of the Yerkes National Primate Research Center. The hippocampus of the chimp was found to be asymmetrical, the right half being much larger than the left half, and bigger in males, which is consistent with the human hippocampus. The anatomy of the amygdalas of chimpanzees, similar to that of humans, was symmetrical.

Emotional Awareness

Created through millions of years of evolution, the nervous system's general design is thought to be a factor in the emotional processes of evolution, for example, empathy. Stephanie D. Preston, of the University of California Berkeley (2001), states that the primate society and community is complex. It requires individuals to be able to perceive gestures, sounds, body language, and facial expressions accurately and respond accordingly. These findings were confirmed in research done by Psychiatrist,

Leslie Brothers, Professor Richard W. Byrne, and Andrew Whiten of the Scottish Primate Research Group, Scotland.

One of the most critical factors in evaluating social interactions among primates is the ability to recognize and comprehend other's **emotions**. This awareness is necessary when forming relationships, interacting in groups and in working together toward a common goal.

Affective resonance, known as emotional contagion, is an important way in which humans evaluate and understand others' emotional state. Observed facial expressions, verbalizations and posture, or body language, can cause an observer to experience physiological changes leading to a like emotional state. This emotional contagion, states Lisa Parr, of the Yerkes Regional Primate Research Center and Living Links, can be very powerful in facilitating shared actions and feelings in mammals and may lead species closely related to humans to experience empathy.

Carroll E. Izard, (1971) author of *The Psychology of Emotions,* reported on six emotions: anger, disgust, fear, happiness, sadness ,and surprise, that have been documented in humans by researchers and have been determined to be universally recognizable and are biologically determined facial expressions. Parr studied chimpanzees' transmission of emotion using two basic mechanisms. First, changes in skin temperature were measured as chimpanzee subjects viewed a video containing emotional scenes. Next, the chimpanzees were required to match similar negative and positive facial expressions and categorize emotional scenes emitted on a computer monitor, requiring them to exhibit awareness of the stimuli presented and the emotional similarity. Parr referred to this as matching-to-meaning (MTM).

Three adult chimpanzees that had been raised by humans in peer groups until age four years were observed to collect data. All testing was voluntary and there was no deprivation of food. Jan ARAM van Hooff (1995), Professor of Ethology and Socio-ecology, University of Utrecht, Netherlands, showed photographs and videos depicting expressions to chimpanzees that they were reportedly able to discriminate. Bared-teeth face, scream face, pant-hooting, relaxed lip face, neutral portraits, relaxed open mouth expression (play face), and the whimper were the facial expressions used.

Each subject's physiological measurements were made as they viewed videos. The chimpanzees were shown several scenes depicting positive and negative social scenes that were matched to recognizable facial expressions. Control scenes were also shown. An example of a negative scene would be scenes of a veterinarian threatening chimpanzees with a dart gun. The chimpanzees could correctly pair this scene with the scream face or bared-teeth expressions in photos. A positive scene, which would be correctly matched to the play face, or relaxed-lip face, would, for example, be a scene of their favorite foods.

Parr's findings indicate chimpanzees gather emotional information through affective sharing. Significantly greater decreases in skin temperature were shown while viewing negative scenes than while viewing neutral scenes. Similarly, in humans, Dr. Paul Ekman and colleagues (1983), at the University of California at San Francisco, reported that decreased skin temperatures had been recorded when sadness and fear were elicited in subjects.

Parr also concluded chimpanzees have some awareness, or understanding of the emotional meaning of facial expressions. They were able to categorize positive and negative video scenes using facial expressions. The study indicates the discriminatory cue used by the chimpanzees was an emotional valence.

Although chimpanzees show patterns of physiological arousal and data of the chimpanzees' physiology as they viewed negative scenes showed a degree of personal arousal, thus supporting the conclusion that it is similar to that of humans, Parr felt it was too early to draw the conclusion that the chimpanzees' emotions are qualitatively like those experienced by humans, or that the chimpanzees were aware of their categorization process. However, according to Gene P. Sackett (1966), Professor Emeritus, University of Washington, past experience has been shown to be critical for learning social and emotional signals in both humans and nonhuman primates.

Similarly, results of several studies, including one by the director of neuropsychology and cognitive neuroimaging at McLean Hospital in Belmont, Massachusetts, Deborah Yurgelun-Todd (1999), (have revealed that the human adolescent brain has a very different way of interpreting emotional expressions than the human adult brain. David Walsh (2004), president of the National Institute on Media and the Family, reported on a study wherein subjects were asked to look at a series of photographs of people in a variety of emotional states, including anger, sadness, surprise, and fear. Then the subjects were asked to identify the depicted emotion while brain scans were being performed. It was indicated that adults, using the prefrontal cortex area of the brain, correctly identified the emotional signals. Surprisingly, adolescents misread the emotional states quite often. The adolescents were found to rely on the amygdala, or primitive, part of the brain, frequently misinterpreting the pictures. These wrong interpretations can lead to serious problems with human teens, as they seem to with chimpanzees.

Jane Goodall is legendary in the study of the chimpanzees of Gombe. She has studied chimpanzees for forty years and founded the Gombe Stream Research Center in Gombe National Park, Tanzania, and the Jane Goodall Institute for Wildlife Research Education and Conservation. Her book, *In the Shadow of Man* (2000), is an account of her early observations at Gombe Stream Reserve. Goodall reports that most knowledge chimpanzees acquire is through a complicated system of trial and error, observational learning, and perception. Increasingly, a sound or a particular object will become significant to a chimpanzee. Rewards and punishments play an important role in their learning process. Noted researcher, E.W. Menzel, Jr. (1964) states that a chimpanzee must learn, through experience in a social setting, the proper contexts and sequences in which a specific communication should be performed.

Depression

Among a multitude of behaviors Goodall observed in the Gombe were actions consistent with depression. One example of **depression** is Goodall's observations of three-year-old Merlin. Merlin is observed traveling away from the camp with his mother, Marina, and they are gone for approximately three months. Merlin returns alone and it is surmised that his mother has died of a polio outbreak as she is never again seen. Merlin is then adopted by his older sister, Miff, who grooms him and lets him sleep in her nest. However, Miff does not take Merlin on her back after a few days and is unable to care for him as his mother did. No other adult female makes an attempt to adopt Merlin. After a few weeks, Merlin becomes emaciated, his eyes sinking into their sockets, his hair becoming dull. He is lethargic and he plays less and less with the other youngsters. Merlin appears to have regressed in his ability to properly read signs of aggression from others and responds inappropriately. He becomes overly submissive or hits out aggressively in ordinary social situations where he had not done these actions prior to his mother's death. Although he had previously been able to read others' signals and respond appropriately, he regresses and is not able to properly interact socially with the other chimps.

Another chimpanzee observed by Goodall was Cindy, whose mother died when she was three years old. Typically, a female of this age would begin traveling with an adult female that had been her mother's companion. However, Cindy moves about alone or follows groups indiscriminately. She shows signs of depression immediately following her mother's death. For example, she stops visiting the feeding area, spends a significant amount of time alone and then disappears. This young chimp appears to not be able to function due to her loss.

The National Longitudinal Study of Adolescent Health began in 1995. Robert Blum, along with Ann Masten, have reported that a human teenager's success can be attributed to something as simple as having one significant adult who cares about them in their life. A study at the National Center of Addiction and Substance Abuse at Columbia University, indicates that teenagers with parents who are active in their lives are significantly less likely to use drugs, smoke, and drink.

In a report regarding depression in children and adolescents, the National Institute of Mental Health (NIMH) lists the third leading cause of teen death as suicide, following car accidents and homicide. Teens are likely to overreact to many stresses and are at excessively high risk for depression. The neurotransmitter serotonin can make an adolescent feel blue, while it gives adults a peaceful feeling. Seemingly irrational feelings of despair and rejection can be overwhelming. Depression in humans, as in primates, often leads to isolation and suicide, or death.

Focusing on cortisol, the stress hormone that gives us extra energy in emergency situations, experiments with rat pups have revealed that they have extreme stress responses in follow-up tests when they have been separated from their mothers for extended periods of time, for example, neglected. This response lasted into their adulthood, according to the NIMH.

Addiction

Scientists have long studied what occurs in the brains of animals that makes them behave in a manner that will lead them to some form of pleasure. Specifically, cocaine-addicted rats have been studied, recording their dopamine levels when given visual cues. Paul Phillips and his coworkers (2003), at the University of Washington Seattle, trained rats to associate flashes of light and noise while pressing a lever when obtaining a hit of cocaine, considered a pleasure to the addicted rats. The elevation in their dopamine levels spiked instantaneously as they pressed on the lever for a hit, before the cocaine could have reached the brain. This led Phillips to believe this measured an anticipatory signal. The researchers further tested this theory by continuing to flash light and sound without the cocaine reward. Dopamine levels were again measured and were shown to rise with the visual and auditory cues alone. This change in neurochemistry indicates there is a signal in the brain that is influential in addictive behavior.

According to Claire O'Brien (1996) at the Centre for Clinical Informatics, in the journal Science, even a small dose of cocaine primes the reward system of the brain. The craving for more of the drug is increased and environmental cues that the addict associates with accessing the drug may be triggered. The amount of dopamine sending messages to the brain increases with cocaine use. O'Brien reports on a team at Yale University that has been conducting research to help understand the neurobiology behind the environmental or social cues an addict associates with getting and taking a drug, the reward-priming mechanism. The team gave rats, addicted to cocaine, a shot of compounds known to stimulate one of the two types of neural receptors. The rats' craving for cocaine subsequently increased. However, when given a compound known to stimulate only the other receptor, the rats showed no craving for cocaine. This suggests that different biological routes add to drug-seeking behavior, within dopamine pathways, as well as other dimensions of cocaine addiction. Dopamine is one brain chemical blamed for cocaine addiction. However, recent studies of animals done by Leah Ariniello have shown that glutamate, a chemical known to aid memory, may be as or more important.

Barbara Strauch (2003), a medical science and health editor of *The New York Times* and author of *The Primal Teen*, notes that between childhood and adulthood levels of dopamine measured in humans decreases. Dopamine levels in teenagers are significantly higher than those levels found in adults. A neuroscientist at Brookhaven National Laboratory in New York, Nora Volkow, MD, believes a possible reason that adolescents are involved in taking drugs, drinking, and other risky behavior is that they may have a built-in susceptibility to taking risks and have a greater range of stimulation leading to behavior that is on the edge. Volkow says that an increase in dopamine levels in the pleasure areas of the brain are seen in almost all drug addicts.

Aggression

Aggression plays a key role in the chimpanzee's social structure, reports Goodall. Their relationships are complex; friendly behavior, as well as antagonistic behavior, establishes their community. Testoterone has been found to increase levels of aggression in most primates and it has been established that this had led to more aggressive behavior in males than females. Arriving in camp alone, Goodall observes Goliath, a male chimpanzee, who frequently stands upright to stare behind himself. He startles at every sound, seemingly stressed. Soon after, Goliath disappears into some bushes as three adult males charge toward him. The next day Hugh, along with the other two adult males who had charged Goliath, returns. Goliath, dragging a large branch, attacks Hugh and Hugh gives up. During their fight another adult male chimp, David Greybeard, makes deep pant-hoots, and, although he doesn't join Goliath in the fight, his presence seems to provide him with the moral support he needs to attack Hugh.

The quest for domination among adult male chimpanzees is one of the most common causes of aggression. Males, having higher levels of testosterone than females show aggressive behaviors much more often and with more damaging results. As Plato (428–348 BC) said, "Of all the animals, the boy is the most unmanageable."

Fighting over food, mating, and a reaction to fear are also common causes of aggressive behavior. Communities of males, or gangs, sometimes join in a fight for no obvious reason, piling up on one individual and, at times, causing serious harm for no apparent reason. The antagonistic behaviors used to describe aggression in chimpanzees are attack, threat, and defense, according to Goodall. Generally, aggression in chimpanzees is used to increase or maintain distance between individuals and communities through avoidance or flight.

Female chimpanzees infrequently compete for social rank. It is possible that aggressive physical fighting would not be in the better interest of their young, who cling to their bodies for years. Goodall notes two situations, feeding and protection, as appearing to elicit aggressive behavior in females. When female rhesus monkeys received injections of testosterone during their pregnancies, the youth showed higher levels of aggression than their counterparts. Their lower testosterone levels may also keep them from having a pronounced will to attack overtly.

The hypothalamus, which produces hormones, is the area of the brain that appears to be significant in regulating aggressive behavior. It receives and integrates messages, then sends out messages through the midbrain that then produces patterns of aggression. Adrian A. Perachio (1978), University of Texas Medical Branch Galveston, studied the role of the hypothalamus in rhesus monkeys during brain stimulation experiments, confirming its importance. According to Goodall, a male rhesus fetus begins to produce testosterone around the forty-fifth day of fetal life. This exposure to testosterone in utero is seen to be a cause of male infants having higher levels of aggression, reports Harry Frederick Harlow (1965), Professor at the University of Wisconsin Madison. Androgens have been shown to play an important role in the initial difference between male and female aggression and has been shown to last through adolescence.

Behavioral neuroscientists, using male rats, conducted experiments measuring responses to stimulation of the brain's aggression center, recording whether blood levels of a stress hormone were increased and if higher levels of that hormone led to aggression. A fast-acting feedback loop was shown. One variable appeared to raise the other variable in both directions. This supports the belief that stress and aggression reinforce each other. During the study, the rats' hypothalamus was stimulated, releasing corticosterone. Humans similarly release cortisol when under stress. Generally, rats only release corticosterone when facing an opponent or some other major stressor.

Understanding the human brain and its workings has been enhanced by the study of animals, both in and outside the laboratory. As technology becomes increasingly sophisticated in researching animals, these studies will continue to become even more valuable and important in the study of the human animal.

See also: Emotional Intelligence; Adolescent Social and Emotional Development.

Further Readings

Baird, A.A., Gruber, S.A., Fein, D.A., Maas, L.C., Steingard, R.J., Renshaw, P.F., Cohen, B.M., Yurgelun-Todd, D.A. (1999, Feb). Functional magnetic resonance imaging of facial affect recognition in children and adolescents. *Journal of the American Academy of Child and Adolescent Psychiatry*, 38(2), 195–9.

Craik, F.I.M., Tulving, E. (1975) Depth of processing the retention of words in episodic memory. *Journal of Experimental Psychology Gen* 104:268–294.

Ekman, P., Levenson, R.W., Friesen, W.V. (1983). Autonomic nervous system activity distinguishes among emotions. *Science* 221: 1208–1210.

Goodall, J. (2000). *In the Shadow of Man*, First Mariner Books revised edition, Houghton Mifflin Company.

Izard, C.E. (1971). *The face of emotion* Appleton-Century-Crofts, New York.

Lonsdorf, E. (2004). Sex differences in learning in chimpanzees. *Nature* 428:715.

Matsuzawa, T. (2001). Reproductive memory processes in chimpanzees: homologous approaches to research on human working memory, *Primate Origins of Human Cognition and Behavior*. Tokyo:Springer-Verlag.

Menzel, E.W., Jr. (1964). Patterns of responsiveness in chimpanzees reared through infancy under conditions of environmental restriction. *Psychol. Forsch.*, 27:337–365, as seen in Goodall (1986).

O'Brien, C. (1996). Rat Study Sheds Light on Cocaine Craving", *Science, Vol.* 271,

Preston, S.D. & deWaal, F.B.M. (2001). Empathy: Its ultimate and proximate bases, *Behavioral and Brain Sciences*, 25(1), 1–71.

Preuschoft, S. & vanHooff, J.A.R.A.M. (1995). Homologizing primate facial displays: A critical review of methods. *Folia Primatologica*, 65, 121–137.

Strauch, B. (2003). *The Primal Teen: What the New Discoveries about the Teenage Brain Tell us about our Kids.* Anchor Books.

Volkow, N.D. *Changes In Human Brain Systems After Long-Term Cocaine Use; Cocaine And the Changing Brain.* www.nida.nih.gov/MeetSum/ccb/volkow.html

Walsh, D., Ph.D. (2004), *Why Do They Act That Way?, A Survival Guid to the Adolescent.*

Yurgelun-Todd, D., MD. *Brain for You and Your Teen,* Free Press. "Inside the Teenage Brain. One Reason Teens Respond Differently to the World: Immature Brain Circuitry," http://www.pbs.org/wgby/pages/frontline/shows/teenbrain/work/onereason.html

The Jane Goodall Institute www.janegoodall.org

SUSAN GIBBONS, M..^.

Anorexia

Diagnostic Definitions

Persons diagnosed with anorexia typically have a morbid fear of weight gain, restrict their food intake, have body weight at least 15 percent below normal body weight for their height, and have missed their period for at least three consecutive menstrual cycles. They have a distorted body image and remain convinced that they are overweight ("too fat") even though they are starved and look emaciated. There are two types of anorexia. Restricting type is characterized by dieting, fasting, and/or excessive exercise alone, whereas the binge-purge type is characterized by caloric restriction plus binge eating and some sort of purge behavior such as self-induced vomiting, laxatives abuse, excessive exercise, using diet pills, and/or diuretics. Although the exact causes of eating disorders remain unclear, research suggests that anorexia is caused by multiple factors, stemming from individual, familial, and cultural influences.

Biological Influences

We know less about biological influences on anorexia than we do for almost any other psychological disorder. A summary of research on the heritability of anorexia found that the heritability of anorexia may be as high as 50 percent, although it is unclear how exactly genetics contribute to the development of the problem. What we do know for certain is that genetics play a significant role in determining body shape and size. In fact, many men and women with body and weight concerns are striving for an ideal physique, which is physically impossible given their inherited bone structure and body type. It is important for such people to take note of these basic genetic facts and not fight their biological makeup to the point of starvation. The fight against biology is also common when weight gain and psychosexual changes occur during puberty.

There is also no clear understanding how puberty with its dramatic psychosexual and hormonal changes may function as a risk factor for anorexia. As with other individual characteristics, puberty interacts with other risk factors and is neither a necessary nor a sufficient condition for the development of anorexia.

Brain imaging techniques have been used to determine any damage to the brain as the result of a pattern of starvation and extreme nutritional deficiency that is characteristic of anorexia. The documented problems anorexic people experience with attention, concentration, memory, and visuospatial ability could be related to structural neural changes caused by severe starvation. Specifically, studies have found enlargements of the lateral ventricles as well as reductions in gray and white matter volume in the brain. Some individuals with anorexia have serotonin deficits, a chemical in the brain, which helps regulate mood and behavior. Interestingly, serotonin is the same neurotransmitter that plays a role in chronic anxiety, obsessions, and perfectionism, which also characterize anorexia. Some of these changes (e.g., white matter volume deficits) return to normal after weight gain. There is evidence, however, that some damage, such as gray matter volume deficits and serotonin abnormalities, may be more long-lasting. Likewise, some cognitive impairments (e.g., concentration, attention, and memory deficits) resolve with weight gain, whereas others do not. The results of most studies are not conclusive because it has usually not been possible to study the brain *before* the onset of the eating disorder.

Traumatic Events

Studies show environmental events such as exposure to trauma may increase risk for developing abnormal eating behavior. Research has found higher rates of sexual abuse for women with eating disorders than for women without eating disorders. Some experts argue individuals restrict eating to regain a sense of control resulting from the traumatic loss of control and associated feelings of helplessness and victimization. These notions support the more general theory that dieting functions as an avoidance strategy to cope with negative unwanted thoughts and feelings.

Familial Influences

Much research has focused on exploring the relation between eating disorders and family dynamics. Some of the earliest eating disorder theorists cast blame on parents, especially mothers. Current research has found families of anorexic clients to be hard driven, concerned about success and appearances, and over-involved yet unsupportive. Studies also describe families as having difficulty resolving conflict and eager to maintain harmony by denying or ignoring problems.

Research findings suggest eating disorders may develop as a way of coping with familial pressure to be good enough and thin enough. For instance, parents, especially mothers, who express dissatisfaction with their own weight, use extreme weight loss techniques, and comment on their daughter's weight, are likely to have a daughter who diets. Additionally, mothers of daughters with eating disorders were more likely to rate their daughter as less attractive than the daughter rated herself.

Cultural Influences

Eating disorders are the most culturally specific psychological disorders. The impact of social context on psychological disorders is nowhere as powerful and destructive as in the case of eating disorders. Sociocultural factors such as media glamorization of thinness appear to have a significant impact on the development of eating disorders. One study found exposure to fifteen issues of a fashion magazine led teenage girls with social support deficits to experience increased body dissatisfaction, dieting, and bulimic symptoms. Similarly, college women who viewed slides of fashion models reported more anger and depression relative to women who viewed slides without human figures.

The ideal body image as portrayed by the media has changed dramatically in less than forty years. For instance, data collected from the *Playboy* magazine centerfolds and from *Miss America* contestants from 1959 to 1988 show substantial decreases in weight and size measures. This change was accompanied by a striking increase of articles in major women magazines on exercise and diet in the same time period. One of the most disturbing findings of the study was that 69 percent of the *Playboy* centerfolds and 60 percent of Miss America contestants weighed 15 percent or less than normal for their age and height and thereby met one of the current diagnostic criteria for anorexia. By associating slenderness with success and high approval, the media sends the message that behavior designed to lose weight is likely to lead to positively valued outcomes. The "glorification of slenderness" is pervasive and difficult to break free from. Eating disorders are most prevalent in affluent Western culture, which tend to equate being thin with being successful. Eating disorders are less prevalent in non-Western societies and become more common with increasing exposure to Western media and values. For instance, Pakistani researchers found exposure to Western culture positively correlated with the occurrence of eating disorders in Pakistani women.

Current Conceptual Models

Behavioral Models

Eating disorders cause significant personal and family distress and may have potentially fatal consequences. Yet, these problems are persistent and often difficult to change. Eating disorders may be maintained because the reinforcing consequences of dieting, purging, and binging outweigh the punishing effects.

Social praise may positively reinforce weight loss. The increased attention and compliments regarding physical appearance may play a role in the early stages of anorexia. Yet, praise alone is not a sufficient maintaining variable, especially when people reach a weight that is lower than socially acceptable and face criticism for being "too thin." A more crucial positive reinforcer is a sense of control or success resulting from achievement of calorie limits or weight goals. When individuals experience failure and/or lack of control in important areas of life (e.g., work, school, etc.), they may resort to restrictive eating to control their diet to compensate for such loss of control. Unlike other areas of life, which are influenced by other people, eating is under the sole control of the individual.

Excessive dieting, weight loss, or purging can also be maintained through the process of negative reinforcement. This occurs when these behaviors help to avoid or reduce negative feelings or thoughts about oneself.

Cognitive Models

Cognitive models view cognitive distortions, negative core beliefs, and appraisal deficits as possible causes of eating disorders. These cognitions include irrational thoughts related to eating and body weight and shape, as well as the meaning associated with being thin (e.g., high self-worth, beauty) and with being fat (e.g., being flawed, being a failure, being alone). These cognitions are "implicit": they occur automatically and are not under conscious control of the individual. Research has shown women with anorexia, compared to other dieters and a control group, report more negative beliefs about themselves and hold more distorted assumptions about weight and body shape. These women also show biased attention to food and body-shape-related information. Such cognitive activities, automatic thoughts, and rigidly held beliefs are highly resistant to change.

Role of Experiential Avoidance in Anorexia

Experiential avoidance refers to an individual's attempts to avoid, suppress, or otherwise control painful private events such as bodily sensations, emotions, thoughts, worries, and memories. The function of experiential avoidance is to control or minimize the impact of such aversive experiences. Experiential avoidance can produce immediate, short-term relief from negatively evaluated thoughts and emotions that reinforce such behavior. In the long run, however, experiential avoidance strategies do not work and produce more suffering. For example, although purging may successfully reduce feelings of anxiety and guilt after eating, it will eventually lead to more guilt and shame and medical problems.

The ability of humans to engage in experiential avoidance is greatly facilitated by language, which permits humans to evaluate themselves and contemplate the past and future. For instance, people with anorexia often use dieting as a way to cope with negatively evaluated thoughts and emotions triggered by reflecting on past situations (e.g., "I am worthless because I failed my exam") and worrying about future events (e.g., "I will never be accepted if I stay so fat"). Language also leads to cognitive and emotional fusion, in which the private events individuals experience become fused with the evaluations of their experience. For example, when a woman thinks or says, "I am fat and worthless" rather than "I am having the thought that I am fat and worthless," she connects worthlessness both with fatness and her as a person. Fatness, worthlessness, are fused together—they become one and the same. Thinking and saying it in this way brings the feeling of worthlessness alive in her. At that point, fat and worthless are no longer just two words. The person reacts to the words or the thought as if she is the embodiment of fatness and worthlessness.

There is growing evidence pointing to the issue of control as a central problem in people with eating disorders. For instance, a recent study involving extensive interviews with hundreds of women with anorexia found two recurring themes in the statements women made. The first theme was that women used dieting and weight control to gain or regain control over their lives and as a way of coping with stressful situations and bad feelings about themselves. Dieting served to gain a sense of empowerment, achievement, and was a way to cope with difficult life events.

The second theme was a realistic assessment of the long-term failure of this approach of coping. Many women noted dieting did not lead to lasting control over painful thoughts. Dieting was also causing them to suffer physically because they felt weak and unable to do things they wanted to do. So the women's attempts to change how they feel by changing how they look were not only unsuccessful in producing the desired outcomes, but these attempts also led to further problems and life restrictions. Nonetheless, they had become caught in a vicious cycle of continuously managing their weight as a way of managing their feelings.

People with anorexia starve themselves to change or reduce their unwanted thoughts and feelings about themselves. This strategy may indeed produce short-term relief. Yet, in the long term, thoughts like "I am a failure" or "I am ugly and fat" always seem to resurface no matter how much weight loss is achieved. This can become a vicious cycle in which problematic behaviors such as restricting and purging are used to get rid of painful thoughts and feelings. Such rigid and inflexible patterns of emotional and experiential avoidance are common to all eating disorders. The problem is not the presence of particular thoughts, emotions, or urges. The problem is the constriction of a human life, which occurs when people desperately try to run away from their unwanted experience.

Treatment of Anorexia

Cognitive Behavior Therapy and Interpersonal Psychotherapy

Cognitive behavior therapy (CBT) and interpersonal psychotherapy (IPT) remain the most established treatment approaches. CBT includes self-monitoring, exposure to feared stimuli and situations, cognitive restructuring techniques, and attempts to change eating behavior directly. IPT does not address eating behavior directly, and focuses instead on the identification and improvement of interpersonal problems. Even though these approaches have been the most effective treatments for eating disorders, they frequently fall short, have high relapse rates, and often fail to produce clinically meaningful change.

The need for an improved treatment approach is emphasized by the mortality associated with eating disorders. Anorexia is the most lethal condition of all psychological disorders with a death rate that is five times greater than for same-age and same-gender peers in the general population. Many anorexia-related fatalities are attributed to physical complications secondary to malnutrition (e.g., multiple organ failure). Suicide is another major cause of death associated with anorexia: individuals diagnosed with anorexia are thirty-three times more likely to commit suicide than their same-age and same-gender peers in the general population.

One of the main problems with traditional interventions has been their over-reliance on re-establishing normal eating as the primary treatment goal while at the same time not sufficiently addressing the functions of restrictive and other types of abnormal eating.

Acceptance and Commitment Therapy

Acceptance and Commitment Therapy (ACT) is a contemporary behavior therapy that directly targets the function of restrictive eating, experiential avoidance, and the individuals' efforts to control aversive experiences. As the development and maintenance of abnormal eating behavior stems from rigid and unworkable control and avoidance strategies, ACT seeks to undermine such strategies and thereby reduce the unnecessary suffering caused by experiential avoidance. The ultimate goal of ACT is to help people focus on what they really want their lives to be about.

ACT encourages people give up their struggle of changing and accept what cannot be changed—their thoughts and feelings—for the sake of promoting change in valued areas of their life where change is possible. The basic idea is to let go of ineffective and unworkable change strategies to open the door for genuine, fundamental change to occur. ACT utilizes metaphors, mindful techniques, and other experiential exercises to teach clients to respond less literally to their thoughts and emotions, and separate themselves from their thoughts and feelings. Metaphors are stories and allow clients to make contact with unwanted and frightening aspects of their experience. They help create distance between the client and how they approach their discomfort opening the door for new solutions to emerge. Studies have shown symbolic metaphorical language is emotionally more meaningful, and hence more likely to impact a person's overt behavior than straightforward rational-logical talk.

Advice for Teachers

Teachers are in a unique position. A teacher may be the first person who notices anorexic behavior or a student may confide in a teacher about their behavior. At other times, families are already aware of their child's struggle with anorexia, and teachers simply want to do something extra to help the student. It is important for teachers to remember they cannot change the behavior of the person with anorexia. Teachers should avoid getting drawn into the battle. Some examples would be monitoring the students' eating habits, making sure the student does not go to the bathroom after eating, or getting too involved with the family of an anorexic student.

Many times the person with anorexia has been engaged in a battle for some time against the people who try to get her to eat more. A teacher who tries to get her to eat more will just become one more person to beat in that battle. A student's anorexia may actually worsen if she feels a sense of achievement for "beating" efforts to get her to eat. Each time someone pulls for eating, she will pull back harder to diet. If a student talks about their struggle with anorexia, it is important to simply listen to them rather than argue ("You're thin enough"), challenge ("You don't need to lose weight"), or question them ("Don't you know what you're doing to yourself?"). This will put the student on the defensive and place the teacher alongside the people the student is already fighting against. Many times a student just needs someone who is outside of their family to talk to and support them. A teacher can be that person.

When teachers become aware of a student's struggle with anorexia it would be helpful to find out if the student is currently receiving treatment. If yes, teachers can show support and that they care about the student without trying to solve the problem themselves. If the student is not receiving treatment, teachers can speak with the student and the family about their concern. It would be helpful to be aware of local resources to give referrals and to know what kind of treatment is available for anorexia. Common treatment options include individual and family therapy, group therapy, support groups, and in severe cases, inpatient hospitalization. Determining the right kind of treatment depends on the specific needs of the individual and whether or not their immediate health is at risk.

See also: **Behaviorism; Beverages; Nutrition; Obesity.**

Further Readings

Barlow, D.H., Durand, V.M. (2005). *Essentials of Abnormal Psychology* (5th ed.; Chapter 10). New York, NY: Wadsworth.

Brain theory of Eating Disorders: http://news.bbc.co.uk/2/hi/health/4144755.stm

Fairburn, C.G., Harrison, P.J. (2003). Eating disorders. *The Lancet* 361: 407–416.

Hayes, S.C., Smith, S. (2005) *Get Out of Your Mind and Into Your Life: The New Acceptance and Commitment Therapy Guide.* Oakland, CA: New Harbinger Publications.

Heffner, M., Eifert, G.H. (2004). *The Anorexia Workbook: How to Accept Yourself, Heal Suffering, and Reclaim Your Life.* Oakland, CA: New Harbinger Publications.

National Eating Disorders Association: www.edap.org

**GEORG H. EIFERT, PH.D. AND
KIMBERLY CORNIA, M.A. (MFT)**

Aroma and Learning

Our sense of smell is likely the most primitive of our senses. Life originated in the sea and saline fluids are essential to our bodies. Blood, tears, and even the nasal fluids that dissolve odor molecules are connections to the beginning of life. Limbic structures in the brains of modern men developed from the rhinencephalon or "nose-brain" in our genetic past. Smells perceived as safe or to be avoided prolonged survival in primordial life. Today, humans do not depend on the sense of smell to the same degree as other beings, but emotional-odor-associated memory is just as important to modern man. Emotions help us perceive what is safe and what to avoid in our survival too. Researchers are finding that aroma, as well as emotion, is not only important to learning for survival, but all learning.

Emotion is mediated by many different brain networks, as is smell. The amygdala is responsible for emotional state and reaction to incoming stimuli, including smells. Activation of the amygdala converts an experience into an emotional experience and therefore is important to motivation and memory. Our emotional states are changed by odorants even before we are aware of them and even when we are not aware of them.

From what we know about the gene pool, genes coding olfactory receptors constitute the largest known gene family, in fact, the largest family contributing to a single physiological function. Unlike the other senses, the perception of a smell is "hard-wired" to the mid-brain areas of the brain rather than the cortex. We perceive with our other senses by neuronal impulses passing through the thalamus and then to other areas of the cortex. In smell, however, each odorant has a specific chemical identity that our receptor repertoire must recognize. Brain scans have shown as many as thirty-four structures and fifty-three pathways affected by smell. Smell is so important to our brain formation that babies born with *anencephaly*, a defect in which the brain fails to develop, are often born without a nose.

The first cranial nerve is the olfactory nerve. It consists of about twenty actual fibers, bundles of cilia ending neurons. These fibers descend to the olfactory lobes and from there to the mid-brain areas, which include the amygdaloid complex and the hippocampus. Next, impulses may be sent to the medial dorsal nucleus of the thalamus. The cilia ending neurons, and those of the sense of taste, must be replaced every thirty days because these neurons have receptors that actually have physical contact with the outside environment. Our other senses are mediated by skin, eyeballs, or eardrums.

There are actually three kinds of olfactory discrimination cells within the cilia lining our noses. They are involved in three different brain processes: **episodic-memory**, odor intensity, and aroma quality. Structures in the medial temporal lobe play critical roles in quality discrimination and odor identification. The prefrontal cortex is a major area of activation in tasks tapping working memory, whether odors are similar or dissimilar; skills needed by perfumers. Educators are interested in the passive smelling of single odors that activate the amygdala, episodic memory events.

When the olfactory bulb receives its stimulation, emotions and or memories can be immediate and powerful. Scientists have found that projections from the amygdala to the cortex are denser than from the cortex to the amygdala. Many of these projections carry messages of smell and aroma and can reinforce long-term memory.

In the 1990s, researchers suggested that thalamic nuclei such as the polviner area, where the perception of smell is "hard wired," have attentional functions. Excitation of this region affects the function of looping, reasoning, memory, and cognition. In other words, olfactory perception is closely linked to **attention.** In 1999, researches found that subjects exposed to unconscious odor exposure subsequently exhibited behaviors that were influenced by their exposure to those odors. When subjects were engaged in a demanding cognitive task, they were not aware of the olfactory stimulation, but later introduction of the same olfactory stimulation affected their cognitive performance on a similar task. Perfumers take advantage of this phenomenon and educators can use it too. Aroma therapists have long known the power of aroma.

The use of certain essential oils to stimulate memory and concentration can be traced back to the first century AD. In the last fifteen years, however, brain imaging equipment has advanced studies on the influence of odor on cognition, attitudes, performances, and perceptions of health. Psychologists have long known that Pavlovian conditioning is when something is remembered when a pair of stimuli are presented together. Aroma is proving to be a powerful paired-stimulus. Odor–emotion associations have been used therapeutically to train subjects to associate an odor with muscle-relaxation exercise and it was found that later, odor alone could elicit the relaxation responses. Odor and taste have been used to condition patients from high doses of potentially lethal medications.

Smell can decrease stress and increase alertness. Researchers at Yale's Psychophysiology Center are working on how smell can reduce blood pressure in stress situations, avert panic attacks, and make one more alert. Lavender affected mood positively in a stressful arithmetic task. Student performance was not as high as with clove aroma, but less stressful. Lavender also helped students score better in proofreading efficiency. It is interesting that men improved more with peppermint, women with lavender.

As the environment has such a powerful impact on student learning, teachers might try different aromas to see the reactions with their students. Cognitive studies are just starting on the various essences that aroma therapists suggest might affect learning. We do know, however, that essential oils work differently than synthetic aromas. The chemical structure of synthetics do not match neural receptors in the same way as essential oils. Also, many students are allergic to synthetic odorants. There is ongoing research suggesting brain antagonistic results with synthetic odorants. Shopping mall developers use real essences to their advantage. Scientists found that cinnamon calms a crowd and makes people friendly toward strangers. It also engenders a feeling of comfort and nurture. Statistically, shoppers are freer buyers when they smell cinnamon. Notice the Cinnabun when you enter a mall. This is not a coincidence.

Natural odorants in the classroom should be changed for different memory events. Research suggests that aroma can be used for long-term results, matching explicit memory with episodic aroma events. The aroma does not have to be at a conscious level, and because pleasant odors gain a deeper access to our nervous systems, flowers and herbs are most effective. Lemon has been shown to focus attention and stimulate the central nervous system. Orange oils may help with anxiety states. Some researchers have shown that orange can calm and focus attention in students with **ADD and ADHD**. These studies have been limited. They have been based on psychology and observation rather than neural imaging.

Research by diverse groups has shown specific small sample results. Ambient smell of chocolate or baby powder caused people to look longer at photographic slides and reported better moods compared to no-odor subjects. Photograph recognition on subsequent recognition tests showed equal results for odor and no-odor subjects. Peppermint presented in very low concentration significantly improved student performance in word-dictation spelling and arithmetic dictation.

Robert Tisserand from Warwick University, United Kingdom, has encouraged research in aroma and feels that because of the ways in which olfaction and memory are related, aroma may have the capacity to stimulate memory and concentration. He notes that basil, peppermint, and rosemary are among the most potent essences in these connections. Rosemary is not a commonly recognized fragrance to many students, and therefore might be used as a link to memory pathways. Common aromas may call up emotional memories rather than the semantic memory desired. An aroma that is unfamiliar, but pleasant enough to associate positively with the semantic material presented is the perfect choice. As mentioned before, each learning event should have its specific aroma. Every school population will respond differently to certain aromas because aroma response is learned.

The human nose protrudes like an antenna. Even unconscious natural aromas affect our emotions and the way we feel about our environment. Aroma can be used to form associative memories. Just like the bulletin board removed during the test is "looked at" for answers, memory can also be stimulated by aroma. We believe that implicit and episodic memory can be tied by specific aromas for certain learning events.

See also: **Information Processing Model.**

Further Readings

Degel, J., Koster, E.P. (1999). Odors: implicit memory and performance effects. *Chemical Senses* 24:317–325.

Rougy, C., Schaal, B., Dubois, D., Gervais, R., Holley, A. (2002). *Olfaction, Taste, and Cognition*. Cambridge, United Kingdom.

Smith, A. (2004). *The Brain's Behind It*. Stafford: Network Educational Press Ltd.

Springer, M. (1999). *Learning & Memory, the Brain in Action*. Alexandria,VA.:ASCD.

DONNA STARR

Art

According to art therapists art gives children a chance to play in an emotionally and psychologically safe place. Richard Riley, Secretary of the Department of Education said that through engagement with the arts, young people can better begin lifelong journeys of developing their capabilities and contributing to the world around them. The arts teach young people how to learn by giving them the first step: the desire to learn.

Painting, drawing, and sculpturing, all of the visual arts, have a positive relationship on brain functioning. The brain is more than a soft, grayish, and whitish mass of nerve cells and nerve fibers enclosed in the skull; it is virtually an electronic system that guides all thinking and body functions. The arts provide learners with opportunities to simultaneously develop and mature multiple brain systems.

The visual arts are linked to our ability to think abstractly and critically. A piece of art enters the brain through the retina and optic nerves. Vision is two-dimensional, but the brain is able to comprehend a three-dimensional world, leaving room for interpretation and appreciation. Once visual information enters the brain it is directed to the temporal lobes, parietal lobes, and occipital lobes. Temporal lobes process names and memory, while the parietal lobes process spatial layout, and the occipital lobes process color, movement, contrast, and form. The frontal lobes also play a role in visual information. They determine how long you will pay attention to the piece of art; if it is intriguing and interesting your attention will focus on the work.

The brain doesn't simply view the visual art. The more complicated the piece the more the brain will engage in feedback and reconstruction of the piece, involving more and more neurons in the process. The more complex the piece of art, the more interaction that occurs in the brain.

There is strong evidence that the visual arts are a way to express and reconcile our emotions. The thalamus and amygdala, emotional centers of the brain, are involved in creating and interpreting visual arts. Visual art that is familiar to us is recognized by the hippocampus; we pay attention to it because we can easily relate to it. The unusual visual art engages the thalamus and parietal lobes as they try to make sense of the piece.

Preferences in symmetry, shape, spatial orientation, and abstraction may be found in the right and left hemispheres of the brain. Left brain dominant individuals prefer subject matter found on the right of a work and right brain dominant individuals prefer the subject matter to be on the left. Left hemisphere individuals prefer the known and expected, preferring realism in their visual arts, while those with right hemisphere dominance prefer the novel and unusual, thus preferring abstract art. This correlates with brain research that found the left hemisphere was more conservative and stable, seeking to organize material while the right hemisphere was more spontaneous and integrative. This explains why art appreciation is not only in the eye of the beholder, but in the brain of the beholder. What may be beautiful to one person is dreadful to another.

Color is also processed in the brain. For most individuals different colors evoke different emotions. For example, red is arousing, passionate, exciting and intense—many dining rooms are done in this color to encourage a healthy appetite; black signifies power, sexuality, anger, and sophistication—symbolized by wearing a black suit to an executive meeting; and blue is related to peace, tranquility, and truth—no wonder campers love to relax in front of an open sky or near water.

A differentiation should be made between artistic **creativity** and artistic preference. Creating art requires active participation and art preference is a passive activity. The visual arts are a whole brain experience. New research shows that brain laterality plays a role in creating art. Both the dominant and non-dominant part of each individual's brain is involved in creating a visual art, suggesting bilateral brain activity. The dominant side of the brain, which in the visual arts is primarily the right hemisphere, enables the left hand to play the active role and the right, non-dominant hand to help shape and provide a stabilizing force while creating the work of art.

Research Linking the Visual Arts and Brain Functioning

There is substantive research connecting brain processes and the visual arts. The visual arts develop visual processes needed for reading, interpreting visual images, and visually organizing abstract thoughts and concepts. All of the arts play a valuable role in the process of intellectual development and enhance brain functioning.

A groundbreaking study found higher Scholastic Achievement Test (SAT,) scores of pre-college aged students who had a background in the visual arts. The scores of visual arts students scored an average of 47 points higher on the math and 31 points higher on the verbal section of the SAT. Howard Gardner (1991), perhaps the most insightful current observer of children's creative development, describes the relationship between academic achievement and the visual arts in a younger group of students. Gardner relates how reading and math scores were significantly higher for 96 students in eight visual-art-enrichment first grades. The students scored an average of 77 percent at grade level, as compared to 55 percent for the control group.

Several research studies support the linkage between involvement in the visual arts and cognitive/intellectual ability. A study in 1996 conducted by researchers from the Center for Arts Education Research, Teachers College, Columbia University found significant relationships between rich in-school arts programs and creative, cognitive, and personal competencies needed for academic success. They also reported that more students who received high levels for arts instruction earned high scores on measures of creative thinking compared to those students with the lowest levels of arts instruction. Evidence from the brain sciences and evolutionary psychology increasingly suggests that the arts (along with such functions as language and math) play an important role in brain development and maintenance.

Components of an Effective Art Program

The following are elements found in exemplary art programs:

- Change the environment to one of discovery. This can re-ignite the love of learning in students tired of being filled up with facts.
- Provide challenges to students at all levels from the delayed to the gifted.
- Develop abilities to learn to be sustained, self-directed learners. Learners are not a repository of facts from direct instruction for the next high-stakes test.
- Provide opportunities for students from the lower socioeconomic strata to gain as much or more from arts instruction than those from the higher socioeconomic strata.

Implications for Life-Long Learning

The link between the visual arts and brain functioning has implications for lifelong learning. Skill requirements for all workers are increasing, including those in production and support jobs. These attributes can be nurtured and honed through studying the arts. In the future, life-skills, such as, being a positive team member, a creative decision maker, and the skills to present information in digitally novel forms, will be essential to sustain employment. Making art is a highly cognitive process that involves problem-solving, critical thinking, and creative thinking. When art is integrated into the curriculum the competency scores in other subjects increase.

Arts education is important as a means of giving our young people a sense of civilization. The arts provide individuals with a universal language that cuts across the disciplines and helps to bring more coherent meaning to our world.

See also: **Drama; Music; Play.**

Further Readings

The Definition of the Brain & Learning. (n.d.). Retrieved January 11, 2005 from http://www.ascd.org/portal/site/ascd/menuitem.12471550933c56bddeb3ffd6218a0c/

Eloquent Evidence: Arts at the Core of Learning. (1996). Retrieved January 11, 2005 from http://www.nasaaarts.org/nasaanews/ee.pdf

How Can Research on the Brain Inform Education? (n.d.). Retrieved December 28, 2004 from http://www.sedl.org/scimath/compass/v03n02/1.html

Wardle, F. (October 2004). Art across the curriculum. *Early Childhood News.* 16(5):36–42.

2005, from http://www.newhorizons.org/neuro/caine.htm

JUDITH LYNNE MCCONNELL, ED.D. AND LINDA REIMOND, M.S.

Assessment

Assessment is the process of gathering information about students…what they know, understand, and can apply. Ideally, assessment should be the central aspect of classroom practices that links curriculum, instruction, and learning rather than something added on after a unit has been taught.

Recent brain research using functional Magnetic Resonance Imaging (fMRI) is revolutionizing our understanding of how the human brain learns. Such research suggests that while the human quest for meaning is innate, this quest occurs via a search for patterns that help the brain to process and store information for later retrieval. Traditional instructional methodologies appear to work in opposition to this natural way of increasing the brain's knowledge base. Similarly, traditional assessment methodologies fail to measure authentic learning, knowledge, or any level of deeper understanding.

Educators today need background information to make sense of current research in the brain sciences, and its implications for instruction and assessment. Current research suggests that an integrated and connected approach to learning is most in alignment with the way the brain naturally processes and internalizes new information.

Most neuroscientists believe it is best to wait at least twenty-four hours after information has been learned before testing to see if it has been stored in long-term memory. Working memory usually fades within seconds or hours. For instance, remembering a telephone number while you dial, and then quickly forgetting the number is an example of working memory. Long-term memory is relatively permanent. As educators, essential knowledge needs to be stored in long-term memory, waiting the twenty-four-hour period before testing will alert us to successes and problems in the learning process. A warning, reviewing just prior to a test is not a good measure of what has been stored in long-term memory; working memory is being activated that will conceal the true location of the information.

Retrieving information from working memory takes less than a second to achieve. Retrieval from long-term memory takes much longer and is not determined by intelligence. The **gifted** person learns material quickly, but that does not mean that they will retrieve material faster than the student of average intelligence. This has implications for class discussions (wait time) and un-timed testing.

How do students retrieve information during assessments? When information is retrieved from long-term memory neurons fire all along the path to where the memory of the information is stored and then return back to working memory. The more frequently information is used, the more quickly and efficiently it can be retrieved and the less brain energy required. Interestingly, the brain stores information by connecting new information to information that has already been learned, it looks for similarities. But to retrieve information, the brain differentiates information that has been stored. When trying to remember the mathematical problem 9×7, the brain scrutinizes how this answer differs from all the other numbers stored in the brain. Testing over material that is very similar will be very challenging until it is firmly established in long-term memory.

While assessment should be used for the purpose of providing lesson focus for the teacher and the students as well as feedback for the students (which aspects of the learning need modification) and the teacher (which aspects of the unit need re-teaching or additional instruction), evaluation is the process of interpreting and making judgments about assessment information...are the students learning what we want them to learn? In addition, testing, when used with the many assessment tools comprising a valid student profile, provides one measuring instrument to document student learning.

Most standardized tests fall into two main categories: norm-referenced and criterion-referenced. *Norm-referenced* standardized test scores alone give authentic numbers that reflect achievement and performance of isolated skills at a particular moment in time. This norm-referenced perspective views testing as a means of ascertaining an individual's performance in relation to the performance of other individuals on the same measurement device (a test, constructed to spread scores along some form of the normal distribution curve). Such a test is designed to show how a given student or group of students rank when compared with other test takers of the same age and grade. With this method of evaluation, a certain percent of the tested population *must* fail to establish the *norm* against which all the other students are measured. The typical questions on this type of test are not selected to demonstrate what the student knows or can do, but rather how well that student performs when compared to his or her peers nationwide. These, in fact, are the tests that give rise to the statistical comparisons often found in newspaper headlines.

A *criterion-referenced* test, on the other hand, views testing as a way to measure an individual's performance against established criteria or expected standards (what a student should know at a given point in his or her education). With this view, the goal is to help all students attain at least the minimum level of mastery. Items chosen for these kinds of tests are intended to reveal a student's strengths and weaknesses in terms of knowledge or skills. Examples of such tests would be competency tests and achievement tests. While both these test types have different purposes, they have traditionally favored a multiple-choice format.

A third testing perspective is one referred to as the *self-referenced* approach. Such an assessment evaluates a student's cognitive growth based on comparisons of pre-test and post-test performances. This view takes into account the wide range of individual abilities students possess, and allows the testing to be modified for each individual. Such a self-referenced approach helps to individualize the testing process.

Some of the criticisms of test use as an evaluation strategy are that tests often address student comprehension and understanding on only a limited basis. In addition, when tests are constructed, a variety of subjective decisions must be made such as the format of the test, the number of items or questions, and the point value of each. A test will reflects the developer's bias in terms of which concepts are considered important, and therefore, how many items for each concept or skill are to be included on each test. Whenever tests are used, it is best if teachers use a variety of different test formats such as short answer, fill-in-the blanks, matching, multiple-choice, or open-ended questions based on the information taught, so that students have the opportunity to demonstrate their strengths as well as weaknesses.

A criticism raised about standardized tests is that they measure meaningful learning and critical thinking skills on a somewhat limited basis. Standardized tests (even those of specific subject areas) often neglect the assessment of depth of understanding and the integration of knowledge. In addition, such testing neglects the vital aspect of emotion in assessment. If a student typically learns in a classroom and then is tested in a media center or an auditorium, that student is more likely to under perform. Similarly, if a student learns in a particular emotional state, he or she will most readily recall that learning when in that same state. It is the job of the assessor to match the memory mechanism at assessment time or the student may not be as successful as he or she might be in the demonstration of that knowledge.

Extensive use of these kinds of tests has perpetuated the misleading impression that every problem has only one correct solution and has turned students into passive learners who need only recognize information rather than construct their own answers and solutions. The end result of all this testing is that teachers are pressured to focus more on what can be tested easily than on what is important for students to learn.

According to current research, such practices appear to be in opposition to the natural progression of the learning process. To be compatible with brain function, educational practices would instead need to encourage students to learn through the search for patterns and connections rather than memorization of facts. Students would be encouraged to search for multiple solutions to problems, using varied and different strategies suited to each student's individual learning style. They would actively participate in their own learning and "meaning-making" while being encouraged to connect emotionally, physically, and intellectually with curriculum topics. Most importantly, they would be afforded the opportunity to work in an environment that provides ample challenge with a minimum of stress.

While assessment should be the link between curriculum, instruction, and learning, it is still primarily being used at the end of instructional units to both assign grades and differentiate the successful students from the unsuccessful.

The term alternative assessment refers to any and all assessments other than the traditional test-type assessments. By listening to, observing, and talking with students, by asking students questions to help reveal their reasoning, by examining students' individual or group written and/or problem-solving work, teachers are able to develop a more accurate and valid picture of what students know and can do. When conceived of and used in such a non-threatening manner, assessment provides the teacher with the best way to gain valid insights into their students' thinking and reasoning abilities. In addition, assessment becomes a powerful tool to help teachers monitor the effectiveness of their own instruction, judge the validity of the learning tasks, and consider when and where next to go with the instruction.

Authentic Assessment

One of the major forms of alternative assessment is the "authentic" assessment. An assessment is considered to be "authentic" when it involves students in tasks that are worthwhile, significant, and meaningful. Such assessments involve higher order thinking skills along with the use of a broad range of content knowledge. In addition, authentic assessment demonstrates to the student exactly what excellence looks like by making explicit those standards by which that work will be judged. In this sense, authentic assessments are *standard-setting* assessment tools rather than *standardized* assessment tools.

Authentic assessments are most valid when they emphasize learning and thinking, especially those higher order thinking skills involved in problem-solving. They are most compelling when they are comprised of meaningful tasks that reflect real-life, interdisciplinary challenges, present students with complex, ambiguous, open-ended problems and tasks that integrate their knowledge and skills. In fact, the strongest neural connections are those made through real life, hands-on, minds-on experiences. Such assessments usually culminate in student products or performances that recognize and value each student's multiple abilities, varied learning styles, and diverse backgrounds.

Some of the characteristics of authentic assessment include the following:

Assessment Structure

- usually involves an audience (performance-based)
- is not dependent upon arbitrary or unrealistic time constraints
- employs questions or tasks that are known beforehand rather than developed 'in secret'
- involves multiple opportunities for demonstration of growth (i.e., portfolios) rather than single, stressful experiences
- is done in collaboration with others rather than individually
- does allow for a significant degree of student choice

Assessment Design Features

- involve more sophisticated uses of knowledge and skills (i.e., critical-thinking skills)
- are contextualized (tasks not isolated from the outcomes)
- assess thinking processes rather than bits and pieces of isolated information
- involve ambiguous or "messy" tasks and/or problems
- involve student's own research or use of knowledge
- designed as a challenge emphasizing depth of knowledge and understanding

Assessment Evaluation

- scored using clearly articulated criteria/performance standards rather than a curve or norm
- employs performance indicators that exemplify excellence for students at the outset of the project
- includes metacognitive activities such as self-assessment and self-reflection in total assessment process
- uses a multifaceted scoring system rather than a single numerical grade

Equity in Assessment

- identifies hidden strengths rather than weaknesses
- de-emphasizes competitive comparisons between students
- allows for different learning styles, abilities and interests.

Authentic assessment changes the traditional model of the teacher-centered classroom to one of a more student-centered approach. In the authentic assessment model, the teacher's main role is to *assist* students in taking responsibility for their own learning and in helping them become accomplished self-evaluators. Authentic assessment also provides teachers with the ongoing feedback they need to monitor their students' progress as well as evaluate their own instructional strategies.

When most people think about assessment, they think of the traditional "end-of-unit" test. In authentic assessment, however, tests are just one of the many different tools in the teacher's repertoire. The different authentic assessment designs can be grouped into three basic categories based on the kind of information they provide about students:

- *Observations*: these consist of information gathered mainly by teachers in their day-to-day classroom encounters with the students. Well-designed developmental checklists and interview sheets can be used to record information efficiently and on a regular basis.

- *Performance samples*: tangible products that serve as evidence of student achievement.

- The performance assessment approach that has generated the most interest is the one borrowed from artists and designers: the creation of a **portfolio** that demonstrates the range and quality of an individual's work.

- The *open-ended task* (similar in concept to the free-response question) is another example of performance assessment. Well-designed open-ended tasks present students with situations that encourage those of differing abilities and backgrounds to approach tasks in different ways, and to follow multiple paths in the framing of their responses.

- *Extended tasks* are long-term, multiple goal projects that might be assigned at the beginning of a term or unit of study. Such long-term projects often serve as the focal point for a unit of study. They create a real-world context for learning and assessment by connecting content to a challenging and interesting task.

- *Tests* and test-like procedures measure student achievement at a particular time and place. Many states throughout the country have been redesigning their standardized test formats to better reflect authentic assessment by including some free-response type questions and using questions.

The Rubric

For years our test-obsessed society has relied on machines to attach numbers to large-scale assessments. Newer assessment models, those based on observations, portfolios, and performance tasks cannot be scored in the same way as standardized tests. As our educational focus shifts away from the mechanistic factory-school paradigm, and more toward a more valid, authentic assessment, humans will need to perform more of the evaluation process. This reliance on human evaluators raises the question about cost and the time involved in scoring such authentic assessments. It also raises concerns about the reliability and consistency of scores based on human judgment. In an effort to deal with these concerns, scoring tools and methods are constantly being improved and developed to go along with the more "authentic" assessments. The new tools and methods must be based on clearly articulated standards. A scoring rubric is one way of communicating these articulated standards.

A *rubric* is an established set of criteria used for scoring or rating student tests, portfolios, or performances. A scoring rubric describes the levels of performance a student might be expected to attain relative to a desired standard of achievement. These *descriptors,* or performance descriptions, tell the evaluator what characteristics or signs to look for in a student's work, and then how to place that work on a predetermined scale or continuum.

Rubric scales may also be based on a numerical continuum, with a number such as zero to four, or zero to five, being assigned to the differing levels of achievement. Rubrics are effective because they allow for a clear communication of the desired standard of achievement. Rubrics help to create scoring systems that are easy to learn and use. They help students to assess their place on the achievement scale and indicate what is needed to improve their performance. The same rubric can be used repeatedly throughout the year to document a pattern of performance and progress.

Scoring rubrics are often supplemented with *benchmarks,* or performance samples that serve as concrete standards against which other samples may be judged. Benchmarks are generally provided for each achievement level in a scoring rubric.

Evaluators can score student work in one of two ways, holistically or analytically. *Holistic* scoring refers to an evaluation system based on the overall impression of a sample of student work viewed as a whole. This system produces a single number, typically based on a 4–6 point scale, and is used when a relatively quick yet consistent scoring method is needed.

Analytic scoring involves the apportioning of separate scores for different qualities or traits of a student's work. This type of scoring, while much more time-consuming than holistic scoring, provides more detailed information. Analytic scoring is often used for diagnostic purposes, curriculum evaluation, or evaluation of instructional programs as it is the best scoring type to pinpoint areas in need of improvement.

Critics of authentic assessment often express concern about the "human" factor, claiming that people cannot be as reliable as machines. The fact of the matter is that no test can give perfectly reliable results regardless of how it is scored. Another concern of authentic assessment critics is that of objectivity. Test companies promote machine scoring as a means of ensuring objective results. This assurance, however, does not address the question of whether the tests themselves are bias-free in their designs.

See also: **Emotion.**

Further Readings

Caulfield, J., Kidd, S., Kocher, T. (2000). Brain-based instruction in action. *Educational Leadership* 58(3):62–65.

D'Arcangelo, M. (2000). How does the brain develop? A conversation with Steven Peterson. *Educational Leadership* 58(3):68–71.

Goldberg, M. (2004). The test mess. *Phi Delta Kappan* 85(3):361–366.

Holloway, J.H. (2000). How does the brain learn science. *Educational Leadership* 58(3):85–86.

Popham, J. (2002). *Classroom Assessment: What Teachers Need to Know* (3rd ed). Boston, MA: Allyn and Bacon.

Ronis, D. (2000). *Brain-Compatible Assessments.* Glenview, IL: Skylight Professional Development.

Slavkin, M. (2002). Brain science in the classroom. *Principal Leadership* 2(8):21–23.

Stiggins, R. (2002). Assessment crisis: "The Absence of Assessment For Learning." *Phi Delta Kappan* 83(10):758–765.

Walsh, P. (2000). A hands-on approach to understanding the brain. *Educational Leadership* 58(3):76–78.

No Child Left Behind – Ed.gov www.edgov/nclb/landing.jhtml

DIANE RONIS, PH.D.

At-Risk Behavior

Brain research opens new frontiers in understanding young persons experiencing problems in school and community. Blending this knowledge with findings from resilience science provides a roadmap for reclaiming young persons identified as being "at risk."

The Concept of Risk

Risk is a synonym for *danger.* Terms like *children at risk* and *youth at risk* first came into wide use in the 1980s. Originally, these described *dangers in the environment* of children, such as poverty or alcoholic parents. Designations like *at-risk youth* and *high risk behavior* shifted the focus from how to build supportive environments to casting the child as deviant or defective.

The *deficit mindset* has dominated traditional approaches to troubled youth. The *Diagnostic and Statistical Manual* (DSM) catalogues hundreds of psychiatric labels for *mental disorders*. Problem checklists tick off *behavior disorders*. *Risk assessments* profile persons presumed to pose a danger. *Zero-tolerance discipline* calls for automatic punishment or exclusion. Such pessimistic, reactive approaches are now being challenged by a "strength-based" revolution.

Most developmental psychologists view risk as resulting from interaction of a child in the ecology of family, school, peers, and community. In a healthy ecology, children develop their strengths. If they display behavioral problems, this usually is a symptom of "dis-ease" in the ecology rather than "disease" in the child. All young persons have strengths and with positive support can change the course of their lives. Their resilient brains can be "rewired" by positive learning experiences.

The Concept of Resilience

Resilience is the ability to thrive in spite of adversity. The term came from physics: a resilient object bends under stress but then springs back rather than breaks. To extend the analogy, a resilient youth not only endures adversity but can become stronger in the process, like tempered steel.

Each child has a checkerboard of strengths and limitations. Children are also endowed with unique temperaments which, depending on the match with persons in their ecology, can contribute to harmony or conflict.

Initially, researchers thought resilience was a rare personality trait of a few *invulnerable* super-kids. However, no person is invulnerable to extreme levels of stress. Still, regardless of external risk factors, by age thirty, a majority of persons are able to achieve successful life outcomes. Resilience turns out to be a natural trait of all humans. Our brains are wired to surmount life's problems.

Resilience is a combination of inner strengths and external supports, called *developmental assets*. A shortage of these assets places youth "at risk" for poor life outcomes. Such youngsters need supportive communities, schools, and mentors to develop their assets. Schools can build assets or magnify problems. The most "dangerous" and "high risk" schools are those with negative climates marked by disrespect among both peers and adults.

The Resilient Brain

Resilience is universal across all cultures and encoded in human DNA. Our brains are intelligently designed to cope with challenges that have confronted all persons in history. New imaging techniques are providing a better understanding of key brain-based processes impacting risk and resilience.

The Brain under Stress

The starting point for any problem is **stress**, a state of physical and psychological arousal that signals some challenge or difficulty. Sensory cues are first processed by the amygdala, the sentry of the emotional brain. When it detects possible danger or opportunity, stress is triggered:

Danger produces distress (negative stress) activating painful emotions like fear and shame.

Opportunity produces eustress (positive stress) activating pleasurable emotions like curiosity and affection.

The same stressful situation is interpreted differently by various individuals; one person's threat is another person's thrill. Whether a situation is a threat depends on one's coping strengths and outside support. Humans handle stress better when supported by others than when alone.

The brain operates selectively to keep a permanent record in memory of highly stressful events. Learning tied to negative emotions is more enduring, and painful memories can last a lifetime. A crisis presents a potent learning opportunity, as the outcome will likely be long remembered.

Youth at risk widely report that they experience deep inner pain. These first-person accounts are borne out by brain scans: experiences like social rejection activate pain centers in the brain just as physical distress does. The term *pain-based behavior* refers to destructive or defensive reactions triggered by negative emotional states. Thus, a rejected youngster might act out, retreat in depression, or avoid love to avoid the pain of further rejection.

Many young persons daily navigate environments of severe physical, emotional, and social stress. Those unable to cope with this stress are in a state of crisis. The last thing they need is more pain and distress, but that is precisely what punishment is designed to do. *Punishment* comes from the Latin word *poena* or *pain*. By design, punishment produces physical, emotional, or social pain. Stripped of any euphemism, punishment is using pain to try to change the behavior of youngsters who are acting out of pain.

Emotions as Motivators

The word **emotion** comes from the same root word as *motivation*. Emotions motivate specific patterns of behavior. Thus, fear preps us for flight and anger girds us for battle. Emotions are like colors: primary tones, like anger, fear, disgust, affection, and joy, can combine to create a full spectrum of hues.

Our emotions signal to others how we are feeling and what our intentions might be so they know how to act toward us. Charles Darwin first discovered that humans have inborn capacities to express and interpret emotions. Facial expressions are a universal language across cultures. Emotions more truly reveal our intentions as words are easily falsified.

The amygdala reads emotions from facial expressions, tone of voice, and gestures. Most of the data a distrustful youngster uses to decide whether to connect or disengage from a person comes from these subtle emotional cues. Only those who can make the youth feel safe, respected, and liked can build strong positive connections.

With extreme emotion, the brain's center for rational thinking shuts down. Thus, the first priority when working with a youth in crisis is to create a safe environment and calm chaotic feelings. Young persons need to develop the ability to reflect on their emotions instead of acting them out impulsively. By thinking and talking about feelings, the brain begins to manage them.

Coping with Problems

The human mind is intelligently designed to "solve" the important problems all persons face for survival and well-being. In fact, our brains don't seek a totally stress-free state, but actively search for problems to solve. When not facing problems, we invent them through puzzles, games, or solving conflicts vicariously through novels or movies. The brain cannot let go of unsolved problems but is driven to keep hunting for solutions. This is called the Zeigarnik effect. Even when we dream, our brain is scanning for solutions. This Zeigarnik effect provides intrinsic motivation for youth in conflict to find better coping strategies.

The problem-solving brain is less like a computer than a *resilience library*. It selects and stores information bearing on our survival and well-being and discards less important stuff. The brain catalogues memories of important life events. Once these episodes are archived in memory, they are preserved unless reprogrammed by the verbal brain. Among the most significant contributions an adult can make is to help a youth gain new perspectives on important life events, including those causing pain.

Conflict and Trauma

While conflict is normal among all social animals, the human brain is unique in its ability to spot threat, not just physically but in subtle social encounters. We are disposed to respond positively to those who treat us well, but turn negative when others show hostility. Psychologists call this the Tit for Tat rule:

On the first encounter with another person, be cooperative.

Then, reciprocate the friendly or hostile reaction encountered.

Humans are by nature friendly, but at the first sign of danger or disrespect, we are hard-wired to quit being nice. Tit for Tat hostility is the prototype of a conflict cycle. Most conflicts start small and escalate in a series of hostile barbs. Before one spike of anger dissipates, another is triggered, fueling a surge of intense feelings. When a youth shows hostile behavior, adults in authority are in a double bind: coercive discipline mirrors the youth's behavior; backing down might reinforce a youth's coercive tactics.

Punitive discipline sparks brain programs that motivate fight or flight behavior. Young persons need behavioral limits, but a tone of rancor renders correction ineffective. *Rancor* is an emotionally charged communication conveying bitterness and malice. It is the prime symptom of discord in relationships. The first step in calming agitated brains is to remove any tone of rancor from the interaction. If children experience chronic hostility or traumatic treatment, they can develop serious patterns of self-destructive and self-defeating behavior.

Most explanations for childhood emotional and behavior problems are **trauma** theories whether using the word or not. Basically, something went wrong in the developmental process that had a damaging effect on emotional and behavioral adjustment. In trauma, some highly distressing experience produces very painful feelings and the individual adopts defensive coping behaviors to protect against a recurrence. These may be conscious or unconscious.

A key task of the brain is recognizing and dealing with danger. The brain initially treats unfamiliar persons or stimuli as potentially threatening, sending a low level alarm of possible danger. Throughout history, the most serious threat to human survival has been other humans. When our brains sense a person, group, or situation is unfamiliar, they are judged to be dangerous unless proven otherwise by opportunities for unthreatening or positive interactions.

Our brains go on high alert if we encounter a situation similar to previous unpleasant or painful events. An abused youngster who faces an angry authority figure may experience painful emotional reactions similar to the original abuse. When children tap into past trauma, their reactions may range from low level alarm to feeling overwhelmed by panic, fear, anger, or terror.

Intense emotional experiences, both pleasurable and painful, are etched, perhaps indelibly, in a child's emotional storehouse. Traumatized children are "at risk" because their brains become less plastic—less likely to face new experiences in an unguarded and positive way. A child who is chronically maltreated may live in a persistent state of low to high levels of alarm, and may respond to these feelings through aggression (fight), withdrawal (flight), or strategies to numb or block out the pain (freeze).

Five million children in the U.S. each year experience some trauma, and over two million are victims of physical or sexual abuse. These children have tremendous capacity for positive growth and development, but trauma can stunt their ability to reach their potentials. Past painful experiences become the dark lens through which future experiences are filtered. If painful memories are triggered by new situations, the brain acts as before, replaying the past or using defensive strategies to avoid further pain.

Psychiatrist Bruce Perry has found that children traumatized by neglect and abuse overuse more primitive brain systems. Their survival brains are chronically stimulated and they are at high risk of engaging in behaviors that hurt themselves or others. These destructive emotional impulses can only be regulated by mature capacity in the higher brain centers. But many of these youngsters have not had the nurturance and learning experiences to fully develop brain pathways for self-control. Thus, their heightened impulsivity, frustration, and motor hyperactivity combine with an underdeveloped capacity to accurately perceive situations and problem-solve. This unfortunate combination severely limits the child's ability to maximize his or her potential.

Prolonged alarm responses can alter the brain's neural systems. Some pathways are strengthened (e.g., strike out, retreat). Others are weakened (e.g., stay calm, problem-solve). Brains rigidly organized in this way are less responsive to the environment. Rather than learning new behaviors, a child's emotional energy is diverted to avoiding pain. Traumatized children cannot optimally perform in the classroom if in a persistent state of arousal. The brain that should be focusing on learning is instead preoccupied with survival and safety.

The Resilience Code

We have inherited from our ancestors a resilient brain equipped with bio-behavioral programs for survival and well-being. For each of the universal problems humans have faced throughout their history, specific brain circuits motivate patterns of action. Once these circuits are triggered in the brain, we are strongly motivated, often unconsciously, to follow a particular course of action.

Beyond physical and survival needs, children have *growth needs* that enable them to develop their potential strength and resilience. A mass of resilience research suggests that four growth needs are universal in all children and across all cultures: attachment, achievement, autonomy, and altruism. In effect, these are the brain-based instructions in the human resilience code:

Attachment: Developing Belonging

Children are biologically programmed to find other humans as the most interesting and important objects in their world. From birth, infants attend with great interest to the human face and the human voice. They do not form attachments randomly, but connect with persons who treat them with sensitivity and meet their needs. Children's brains are also primed to seek trusted attachment figures in times of trouble.

The brain has programs to decide who can be trusted and who cannot. The amazing amygdala serves as a trust detector in deciding if someone is "safe" or "dangerous." Before the logical brain can make a judgment about a person, the amygdala scans facial expressions and tone of voice to spot the slightest cue of deception or dislike. When the amygdala detects facial cues that someone likes and trusts us, it releases the chemical oxytocin in the brain; this substance stimulates close social bonding and care-giving behavior in mammals.

The brain very rapidly processes cues of rancor or respect to determine whether to connect or disengage. In effect it decides, "Is this friend or foe?" Children who have been subjected to mistreatment are hypervigilant for cues of hostility; even casual eye contact can be misconstrued as a threat. Youngsters who have learned to fear adults may try to avoid close relationships, even though they are starving for love. Building connections is a prerequisite to being able to teach these individuals.

Achievement: Developing Mastery

The human brain solves problems necessary for social and personal competence. Without opportunities for mastery and achievement, the child experiences confusion and frustration. Children acquire a mass of knowledge, including an entire language code, without formal instruction. But the strengths and abilities of young persons can only fully develop with guidance from adult mentors or more skillful peers.

Problem-solving has been studied for a century since John Dewey first suggested that all goal-directed behavior begins with some "felt difficulty." The brain works best with tasks that are challenging but not boring or overwhelming. This is called "Just Manageable Difficulty." By mastering new skills, children are better equipped to face future challenges. *Task motivation,* the joy of accomplishment, is preferable to *egoistic motivation* where the youth are preoccupied with how they stack up in comparison to others.

Resilience involves practical intelligence, which is not closely related to high IQ scores. Practical intelligence is the ability to creatively solve problems and meet one's goals by capitalizing on strengths and overcoming weaknesses. Resilient youth learn to overcome negative expectations and pursue their goals in the face of setbacks. Resilient youth seek out role models for success, and they carefully observe people who fail so they can do things differently.

Autonomy: Developing Independence

Like animals, humans are born to be free and are endowed with brain programs that trigger alarm if deprived of control over their bodies by restraint, confinement, or coercion. The desire for freedom and independence is seen even in very small children. Positive growth requires balancing the need to attach and the need to be free.

Children not securely attached to adults have great difficulty becoming securely autonomous and self-directed Youth who lack a sense of control over their destiny often display one of two broad patterns of problems: *Rebellion* is seen in youth who declare "nobody is going to tell me what to do"; *Helplessness* is the mindset of youth who feel "what's the use, nothing I do will make a difference." Obedience training discipline applies external controls but fails to foster the self-control necessary for successful independence.

Resilient children develop a sense of self-efficacy, learning to take responsibility for their behavior. They are no longer victims of lousy life experiences but surmount these difficulties and thrive. Even if one can't erase past pain, traumatic memories can be transformed into "survivor's pride." Then, no longer prisoners of their past, young persons are pilots of their future destiny.

Altruism: Developing Generosity

Altruism is behavior motivated by concern for others. For decades, psychology operated as if all human behavior were selfishly motivated. Now, research on altruism has shown that concern for others is central to human nature and is even tied to particular brain programs. While humans are predisposed to show concern for others, this innate altruism is only activated by experiencing caring treatment from others.

Precursors of altruism are present in infancy. Babies in a nursery will cry and show signs of distress at the sound of another baby crying. Remarkably, recordings of their own cries do not produce this effect. As soon as they develop coping skills, children often try to console another child in distress. As they mature, altruism is motivated not solely by distress cues, but by a genuine desire to be generous with fellow humans.

Neuroscientists are beginning to map the brain circuits dedicated to empathy and altruism. When we experience empathy, our brains register patterns of emotional activity matching those being experienced by the other individual. Helping others releases chemicals in the brain that produce feelings of pleasure and well-being. Being generous also strengthens the immune system. Pioneering stress researcher Hans Selye saw altruism as the ultimate antidote to distress.

The human brain seeks to make meaning out of life, not only by solving practical problems but by finding a spiritual purpose for being. Humans function best when part of a community of mutual social support. As they fulfill obligations to others, they discover that they are valued and esteemed. This gives life meaning and contributes to well-being reflected by positive changes in brain chemistry.

In sum, meeting needs for attachment, achievement, autonomy, and altruism develops strength and resilience in children and youth. Frustrating these universal growth needs interferes with positive growth and development.

Brain-Friendly Strategies for Turning Risk into Resilience

Blending brain science, resilience research, and best practices with youth at risk suggests practical strategies for turning problems into opportunities to develop their strength and resilience. These involve disengaging from destructive conflict and creating positive bonds.

Disengage from Destructive Conflict

Before we can help, we must "do no harm." A basic foundation skill for working with all youth, and particularly those who have been traumatized, is to avoid getting into destructive conflict cycles. Here are steps to defuse conflict in the brain of young persons and adults:

1. Never take anger personally.

Conflict is a mirror image: both parties feel threatened and believe they have been violated. The sooner empathy can crowd out anger, fear, or blaming thoughts, the easier it is to de-escalate. Tell yourself that this is a kid in pain and don't add to it or let the young person's pain become yours.

2. Monitor and defuse your own emotional arousal.

This requires awareness of internal cues that anger or fear is reaching disruptive levels. If you are unable to manage your feelings, it is usually better to disengage for a time until you are no longer telegraphing rancor.

3. Monitor and defuse a youth's agitation.

In a brewing conflict, an alert adult carefully tracks a youth's emotional arousal to avoid explosive outcomes. This involves reading cues in facial expression and tone of voice as well as listening with empathy to what the youth is saying.

4. Allow sufficient time for cooling down.

In a natural course, intense emotion spikes and then decays. Time is our ally if we don't do something to rekindle the fires. In talking with a youth, a calm and concerned tone of voice can often quiet turbulent emotions. Sometimes you may need a bit of separation, but never disengage with a tone of rancor or rejection.

5. Model a generous spirit.

There is no greater act of giving than forgiving. Small acts of kindness can have powerful restorative effects as they communicate benevolence instead of malevolence. We are also modeling for the young person how to rebuild damaged relationships.

Build an Alliance with Challenging Youth

These strategies enable one to build positive connections with youth at risk so they can solve problems and develop strength and resilience.

1. Reach out to guarded youth.

Rather than wait for problems, one practices "pre-emptive connecting" with wary youth. This should be unobtrusive so as not to create impressions of favoritism. Connecting does not require a major investment of time; bonds can be built in natural moment-by-moment interactions. Small doses of connecting behavior are most effective. Forcing intimacy only frightens away youth who already are in an approach-avoidance conflict with adults. Those with histories of negative encounters with adults are strongly influenced by small cues of respect, humor, and goodwill. The emotional brain signals, "This person is safe."

2. Avoid a judgmental tone.

Two centuries ago, pioneering educator Johann Pestalozzi suggested that the crowning achievement of education was being able to correct a student while at the same time communicating positive regard. We don't ignore problems, but criticism conveying anger or disgust only drives youth away. To be effective, criticism must be delivered in tandem with empathy and positive concern. To avoid adversarial encounters, one responds to needs and searches for strengths.

3. Connect in times of conflict.

All children have natural brain programs motivating them to attach to trusted persons when they are upset or in trouble. Thus, crisis offers a unique opportunity to connect with young persons who are wary of adults because of past trauma or mistreatment. In crisis, the child's brain is signaling "find somebody who is safe" but traditional discipline by punishment or exclusion only creates further threat. A crisis presents unparalleled opportunities to build trust, respect, and understanding. There are now specific training programs that provide mentors the ability to connect with youth in conflict and develop their strength and resilience. For example, Life Space Crisis Intervention (LSCI) and Response Ability Pathways (RAP), both use problems as teaching opportunities.

4. Clarify challenging problems.

The human brain is designed to make meaning out of chaos and confusion. This usually does not require formal counseling strategies but rather an understanding mentor who can help a youth sort out "what happened." By using the brain's natural inclination to try to find meaning in events, we help a youth learn from problems. By exploring what happened in some challenging event, such as getting kicked out of class, we help a youth develop more effective coping strategies. After connecting with a youth, we explore what actually happened, what started this problem, and what the youth was thinking and feeling. This gives us a window on the youth's private logic and goals. The youth examines how this behavior serves to meet his or her goals, and how others are affected by these actions. By resolving problems, youth develop foundations for resilience.

5. Restore harmony and respect.

Inner conflict and interpersonal discord trigger painful emotions in the brain. We help youth resolve problems and restore harmony. This entails building internal strengths and providing external supports. Examples of *internal strengths* are self-control and empathy for others. Examples of *external supports* are an engaging curriculum, respectful relationships, and positive expectations. Traditional discipline uses pain-based methods to motivate change. Restorative methods seek to restore broken bonds and build a climate of mutual respect.

See also: **Episodic Memory; Adolescent Social and Emotional Development; Adolescent Addiction; Legal Culpability and Correctional Facilities.**

Further Readings

Brendtro, L. Brokenleg, M., VanBockern, S. (2002). *Reclaiming Youth at Risk.* Seattle, WA: New Horizons for Learning.

Feinstein, S. (2004). *Secrets of the Teenage Brain.* San Diego, CA: The Brain Store.

Reclaiming Youth Network http://www.reclaiming.com/news/

**LARRY K. BRENDTRO, PH.D. AND
JAMES E. LONGHURST, ED.D.**

Attention

"Listen up, class" were the words heard coming from the classroom. Upon further investigation it was clear that the teacher not only wanted the students to hear the morning announcements that were broadcast throughout the school at 8:05 a.m., but the teacher also wanted to help focus the students' attention on the information that they would need for the events of the week. This teacher understood and realized that for learning to occur, the students' attention needed to be gained and then directed toward the task at hand.

Attention

Attention is usually defined as focus on a stimulus. An individual is bombarded with countless pieces of information each minute that the brain must analyze and process making decisions about what should be attended to and what can and should be ignored. Even in a well-managed classroom there can be unplanned distractions. A student dropping a pencil, sneezing and coughing, sharpening a pencil, or asking an unrelated question are all spontaneous events that happen in classrooms. Each of these distractions can cause a student to focus their attention on the distracting event instead of focusing their attention on their learning.

Brain Development and Attention

It is the reticular activating system, which is located near the brainstem in a human being that acts as the gatekeeper, allowing specified stimuli to enter the brain and be relayed to the appropriate area. Stimuli may include sounds, words, as well as actions of people around them. Typically, if the incoming information has meaning to a person or they see that it may be useful information, they pay closer attention to the information. If it is information that an individual does not recognize or for which they see little use, their net doesn't catch it and they will not attend to it. So, how do we help an individual realize that information that they may not recognize or know yet, is essential information for them to learn?

The limbic system is responsible for some of what catches our attention. The limbic system is the area of the brain in charge of emotions. After an individual is alerted that information may be important the limbic system processes the information. This system weeds out the survival and emotional aspects. If incoming stimuli indicates that the individual is in danger or there is threat of potential danger, it is the limbic system, specifically the amygdale, that deciphers this and puts the individual on alert.

The frontal lobes are also critical in the attention process. Individuals process information that enters through their senses. After stimuli moves from an individual's senses to the brain stem and then on through the limbic system, the stimuli moves to the executive control center located in the frontal lobes, which is sometimes referred to as the executive control center. The front lobes in an individual mature rather slowly so the problem-solving, higher order thinking, and inquisitiveness that aids an individual in attending and beginning to make sense of the stimuli may not be in full working condition. Researchers believe that the frontal lobe does not develop fully until sometime during late **adolescence** or even early adulthood. Hence, information is dealt with by the teenager at the emotional level instead of moving on to the frontal lobes for more logical reasoning.

If a student looks out the window and sees something that alarms them (stimuli entering their reticular activating system and moving into the limbic system) that student may continue to function at the emotional level for a period of time until the student feels it is safe to focus on the lesson and not on the stimulus in the hallway. Students can be easily distracted by the sight of a person walking down the hall, or students talking or laughing outside the classroom (stimulus entering the reticular activating system being processed by the limbic system). If a teacher is continually competing with the distractions coming from the hallway a simple solution is to close the door. If a conversation between peers in a classroom (stimuli entering the reticular activating system) begins to take on an emotional tone (being processed by the limbic system), it may be that neither of them will actually be attending to their instructional lessons (stimuli can't move past the "emotional center" of the limbic system) until one or both realize that the information that they are learning (higher level processing or reasoning conducted in the frontal lobe) has some meaning to them.

Emotion and Attention

Many factors impact a person's ability to attend to a task. If a child comes to school fearful of being bullied, that child is attending to their physical needs and has a very difficult time attending to any learning tasks. Consequently, a safe environment is necessary to aid in attention which ultimately impacts the learning process in a positive manner. Similarly, if a child comes to school angry, upset, or frustrated about an argument that occurred with a family member or peer, their emotional system is in control and they will have great difficulty focusing their attention on any learning activity.

Food and Attention

A student who eats sugary sweets for breakfast or even lunch such as donuts, cookies, and candy then drinks a soda to wash it down is consuming a high level of simple carbohydrates and sugar. Children operate at an optimum level when their breakfast consists of high levels of protein followed by a balanced diet with complex carbohydrates. This high protein food at breakfast time allows the brain to be fed. Some high protein options might include an egg, cheese, peanut butter, or lean bacon. It is important for attention that a well-balanced diet includes a breakfast, lunch, dinner, and snacks that follow the appropriate nutritional guidelines for each child.

Three Aspects of Attention

Although attention is complex, Lerner suggests there are essentially three aspects of attention; coming to attention, selecting or focusing attention, and sustaining or maintaining attention. Coming to attention involves the individual's alertness. Selecting or focusing attention involves focusing on relevant information and ignoring distractions. Sustaining or maintaining attention involves the individual's ability to attend to the task for a period of time that is long enough for the individual to understand what they have heard, read, or learned. During this time the individual will also need to filter out unnecessary information or noise that does not specifically apply or impact the information that they are attempting to acquire.

Maintenance of Attention

Several techniques aid an individual in the attention process and ultimately help maintain attention on the task being presented. They include study guides, feedback, questioning, wait time, and lecture pauses. These techniques that are rooted in research help to focus the learner's attention to the task at hand. Strategies that work include:

1. Place a student at or near the front of the room to help them focus their attention on the task. The teacher can also attend to a student if they are placed in a location in the classroom that is within "eye shot" of their teaching location.

2. Keep routines simple so the student is able to maintain their attention to the task.

3. Make the task more interesting. Some tasks or concepts are more easily made interesting than others.

4. Note information that you are presenting which is important by saying something like, "Please write these points in your notes, they are very important." Or "Pay attention, please, this is very important for you to remember."

Additional techniques that will assist in gaining, focusing as well as maintaining an individual's attention include:

1. The use of an overhead projector in a classroom to focus the attention of the student.
2. The use of multi-sensory techniques.
3. The use of graphic organizers such as a Venn diagram, concept maps, or other visual frameworks that will allow the student to follow the instruction of the teacher.
4. Use of demonstrations by the teacher to better understand how the task is to be accomplished.
5. Use of hands-on activities to allow those students who need the manipulation of objects to aid them in their learning.
6. Eliminate sounds in the learning environment that may distract the attention of the learner from the task at hand.

Maintaining attention is a complex task for the learner as well as the teacher. There are many factors that must be considered when attempting to focus an individual's attention on learning a task or concept. Some of those factors include the child's emotional well-being, physical and nutritional well-being, and their developmental levels. Helping an individual focus upon the incoming stimuli, working the stimuli to move it from the emotional center (limbic system) to the processing and problem-solving center (frontal lobes) are complex, but essential for attention, the first step in learning.

See also: **Adolescent Social and Emotional Development; Aroma and Learning; Beverages; Information Processing Model; Nutrition.**

Further Readings

Given, B.K. (2000). Theaters of the mind. *Educational Leadership* 58(3):72–75.

Lerner, J. (2002). *Learning Disabilities: Theories, Diagnosis, and Teaching Strategies.* (9th ed.). Boston, MA: Houghton Mifflin.

Lyons, C.A. (2003). *Teaching Struggling Readers: How to Use Brain-Based Research to Maximize Learning.* Portsmouth, NH: Heinemann.

Philp, R. (2005). *The Engaged Brain.* San Diego, CA: The Brain Store, Inc.

Slavin, R.E. (2003). *Educational Psychology: Theory and Practice.* (7th ed.). Boston, MA: Allyn & Bacon.

Sylwester, R. (1995). *A Celebration of Neurons: An Educator's Guide to the Human Brain.* Alexandria, VA: Association for Supervision and Curriculum Development.

GLORIA A. DYE

Auditory Development and Learning

Auditory learning begins in the womb. The **prenatal brain** develops familiarity with environmental sounds and voices. Maternal heartbeat, walking rhythms, volumes and patterns produce sound and voice discrimination abilities that are observable at birth. Over time, the infant brain discriminates tonally and recognizes repeated sounds, including voices, instrumental music, inflection, timbre, intonation, rhythms, and intensity.

As the neurons in the brainstem receive myelin (insulation that allows the brain to function efficiently) it produces the ability to discriminate alarming sounds that provoke avoidance and fear responses. Midbrain/limbic centers decipher emotional content in vocal inflections communicating at a pre-language level. While some connections to cerebral hemispheres and cortical cells occur early, language begins to be understood from about fourteen months. Teaching sign language during this pre-verbal stage helps prevent frustration in communication.

During ages two to four, significant vocabulary acquisition is paralleled by brain maturation. Vocabulary acquisition is accelerated by exposure to others repeatedly verbalizing names and defining the environment. Throughout childhood, enrichment consists of activating neurons by experiencing an expanding variety of sounds that are eventually named and described to indicate increasingly complex cognitive discrimination.

Interference

Outer, middle, and inner ears are all involved in sending auditory information through the brain stem to the midbrain. Obstruction with auditory development involves blockage from the ears to the temporal lobes which is the destination of the message.

Deficient experience with sound fails to inhibit the auditory startle reflex and the Moro startle reflex. The startle reflex is involuntary muscle response to loud, sudden sound and the Moro startle reflex is a sudden embracing movement of the arms and drawing up of the legs of infants and small children in response to sudden loud sounds. This contributes to immature sound sensitivity (blinking at repeated stimuli), defensiveness (hands over the ears), and distractibility. Middle ear congestion, especially common with allergies, can restrict sound experience and deprive cells of needed activation. Allergies, therefore, need to be avoided or controlled.

Deprivation also occurs through fatiguing continuous sound, such as radio or television, in which the brain turns off sounds as unwanted noise or habituates irregular brain waves. Environmentally, listening only to local dialect and language deprives the brain of flexibility in relating to others in both inflection and vocabulary.

Auditory Learning Strategies

The sequence of auditory skills proceeds along parallel paths of sound sense, music, and languages. Automatic brainstem abilities (A) maturing in early childhood, consist of reflexes and discrimination abilities. Musical (M) listening usually registers in the right cerebral hemisphere and later links to associations in the left hemisphere in trained musicians. Language listening (L) is usually registered more in the left hemisphere. Persons with left-hemisphere language dominance demonstrate a slight advantage for hearing language in the right ear and a similar advantage for perception of music in the left ear.

Auditory learning demonstrates the need for repeated activation of neurons through affector (receptive) inputs to the brain to facilitate memory acquisition and fluent recall and retention. Requesting outputs (questioning, quizzing, testing) teaches nothing new, but merely indicates what is already in the brain through effector (expressive) output. Stimulation involves daily modeling activation by an enthusiastic adult. By repeating patterns often and loudly auditory abilities will expand. The following are strategies to engage automatic brainstem abilities (A), musical (M), and language listening (L) skills:

- Auditory startle and Moro reflexes (A): Adult gives ten repetitions of short/loud/sharp stimuli at regular or irregular two-second intervals; ten Moro supine sudden dropping repetitions with associated sounds and arm extension.

- Tone/sound perception (A): Adult repeats infant vocalizations; child makes and controls sounds; playing recorded and live music; early repeated pure tone and music lessons before age 6 develop perfect pitch.

- Vital threat perception/interpretation (A): Spontaneous cry of infant at threatening sound.

- Emotion inflection perception/interpretation of adult vocal intonations (A): Adult intensifies positive emotion through exclamations, "Wheeeeeeee!" while sliding or swinging, and laughing with infants.

- Associated environmental and animal sound perception (L): Adult repeatedly models animal/object/action sounds related to pictures.

- Music perception (M): Adult repeatedly models toy sounds, pitch, timbre, melody, rhythm, beat, harmony, songs, instruments (and with recordings).

- Rhythm perception (M) in associated sound/kinesthetic movement/balance: walking, dancing, jumping, clapping, swaying, marching, tapping, drumming to music.

- Perfect pitch (M): music lessons before age six; listening to tape of a repeated pure tone.

- Figure-ground perception (A) of particular sound/voice amid background sounds: Person with persisting startle reflex will be distractible or confused. Play a tape containing background noise, such as lunchroom noise while giving two and three step directions. Increase background noise level and/or number of directions given as figure-ground perception increases.
- Songs (M): Adult presents model for listening many times prior to singing along.
- Foreign languages (L): play tapes for early familiarity of sounds of target languages. Europeans sequence child-care givers speaking target languages, or, each parent speaks a different language to the child.
- Auditory memory (A): Beginning first-graders carry out three unrelated commands given once by the teacher. Some students may need to hear directions/commands and content many times to acquire/register, retrieve, and apply the message. Memory for mastery performance is facilitated by listening to a tape of the recitation for twenty to eighty times, or until the performer can automatically deliver the content with feeling and spontaneity.
- Phonemic Awareness listening readiness abilities for phonetic word analysis in reading are as follows:

  > Beginning sounds (A) in words: adult models b-b-b-b-bear, ch-ch-ch-ch-chair.
  > Rhyming words (A): adult models sequences of three to ten rhyming words daily.

- Auditory closure (A) for missing sounds in words: Adult repeats model, "Listen, ilk is milk, ilk is milk. What is ilk? (Child answers, "Milk"). "Yes, ilk is milk." "Listen, ool us is school bus; ool us is school bus. What is ool us?" (Child: "School Bus") "Yes, ..."
- Auditory discrimination of words (A): Adult calls attention to similar sounding words with different meanings: sip-ship, book-took, pup-puck, weather-whether. Auditory discrimination immaturity produces misunderstandings and malapropisms.
- Word sound segmentation (A): Adult repeats model, "Listen for the sounds in dog, Dog is d-o-g, dog is d-o-g. Say the sounds in dog." (Child: Dog is "d-o-g") "Yes, dog is d-o-g." Review previous words and model new word daily.
- Letter-sound association (A): Adult models sound and names letter. "Sssssss is es (S). Sssssss is es (S). What letter says Sssssss?" Show letter for shape association later.
- Reception of language (L): Language is a medium that activates mental images, and vocabulary and general information are the highest correlates to intelligence. Adult names and defines meanings of words repeatedly as encountered: vocabulary, concepts, phrases,

idioms, and sentences. Adult defines reasons, causes, and consequences for comprehension ability. Name pictures and actions in books and magazines. Listening comprehension ability is the foundation for reading comprehension and oral expression. The expanding reading vocabulary also expands listening comprehension.

- Language association (L): Adult explains concepts of likenesses, differences, opposites, analogies, and symbolism. Simile is used beginning in early childhood.

- Math language association: Adult models counting, skip-counting, naming, attaching language to everything: time, quantity, sequence, pattern, calculation, relationships.

- Poetry (L): Adult repeatedly models rhythm, inflection, rhyme, intonation, humor.

- Emotion recognition (L): Adult states emotion word to describe child's emotion: "You are excited/happy/glad/delighted/overjoyed/satisfied/feeling great/good. Negative sequence through surface, anger to fear levels: You are annoyed, aggravated, disgusted/intimidated. You are angry/mad/enraged. You are feeling scared/afraid/fearful/terrified. You are afraid it might happen again."

- Self-talk recognition (L): Listening to the voice inside the head and noticing the content as a form of meta-cognition. Conscious awareness allows cancellation of negative and self-hypnotic messages and substitution of positive content. Teachers tell students to clear their minds for the brain to take in content without judgmental, distracting, or confusing interference.

- Social listening (L): Giving total attention to the cognitive/intellectual and affective/emotional content of the speaker rather than thinking about what to say.

Auditory Learning Style

Auditory learners learn through listening to explanation, discussion, and argument. Some auditory learners may prefer background music while studying, although others may be distracted by music, sounds or visual action. Some learners may be unable to understand speech without their eyeglasses or with eyes closed if the auditory temporal lobe is activated by the organized signals from the visual occipital lobe. Others receive content better with eyes closed to avoid visual distraction. Auditory learners tend to speak at a particular steady frequency and pitch all the way to the end of their sentences, according to Neuro-Linguistic Programming. This is in contrast to descending and ascending sentence endings for kinesthetic and visual learners, respectively.

Auditory and visual information are the two primary methods the brain uses to gather information. Master teachers learn to present content and directions using all learning style intonations to engage all students.

See also: **Bilingualism; Language Acquisition and Disorders; Learning Styles; Music.**

Further Readings

Armstrong, T. (2001). *Multiple Intelligences in the Classroom.* (2nd ed.) Alexandria, VA: ASCD.

Devinsky, O., D'Esposito M. (2004). *Neurology of Cognitive and Behavioral Disorders.* University Press: Oxford.

Staso, W.H. (1997). *What Stimulation Your Baby Needs to Become Smart.* Orcutt, CA: Great Beginnings Press.

Sternberg, R.J., Zhang, L.F. (2001). *Perspectives on Thinking, Learning and Cognitive Styles.* Mahwah, NJ: Lawrence Erlbaum Associates, Inc.

Multiple Intelligences, www.thomasarmstrong.com/multiple_intelligences.htm

LYELLE L. PALMER, PH.D.

Autism Spectrum Disorders

A number of studies suggest that the frequency of Autism Spectrum Disorders (ASDs) is significantly on the rise. A teacher with an average of twenty-five children per class has gone from the likelihood ten years ago of never meeting a student with an ASD label during her entire career to being likely today to encounter one in as few as every seven classes. ASDs include "classic autism," "autistic syndrome," Asperger Syndrome, Pervasive Developmental Disorder – Not Otherwise Specified (PDD-NOS), Rett's Syndrome, and several other conditions meeting specific diagnostic criteria. The long-term functional implications of ASD labels range from mild (i.e., difficulty with language and social pragmatics) to severe enough to require full support in the areas of community living, employment, and communication. While the theory that ASDs are due to cold mothering has long been abandoned by the preponderance of evidence as to their physiological basis, the extent to which genetics plays a direct or indirect role in causing or predisposing an individual to develop ASD remains uncertain.

The number of laboratories, clinical settings, and research centers currently pursuing brain-based research on ASD has grown substantially in response to the increased prevalence and incidence of ASDs. Some of the more noted names in neuroscientific research related to ASDs are Ralph Maurer, M.D., and colleagues at the University of Florida, Gainesville; Gene Blatt, Ph.D., Margaret Bauman, M.D., and their colleagues at the Boston University School of Medicine; and Eric Courchesne, Ph.D., and colleagues at the University of California, San Diego. Most of the work of these neuroscientists and others resulting in our present knowledge about the brain-based range of behavioral deficits and excesses associated with ASDs is grounded in four areas of study: (1) comparisons of people with ASDs to people with conditions induced by illness or injury (e.g., Parkinson's Disease) that have established connections to lesions in specific parts of the brain; (2) procedures that induce or otherwise draw from autistic-like behavior in **animal studies;** (3) known relationships between various brain structures and their functions in typical human control groups as compared to brain differences in study participants with ASD labels; and (4) post-mortem investigations comparing the brains and brain tissue of people who had diagnoses of ASDs with those who did not. Neuroimaging methodologies used to explore ASDs have included functional techniques (e.g., fMRIs, PET and SPECT scans, magnetic stimulation techniques such as MEG and TMS, Auditory Brainstem Response tests, and EEGs) as well as structural techniques (e.g., sMRIs and CAT scans). Laboratory analyses of the composition of blood and the cerebrospinal fluid have provided information about differences in brain chemicals in people with ASD labels.

Neuroscientists using these various methods have found significant brain differences in both the structures and functions of many parts of the brain responsible for movement including both voluntary and involuntary motor activity, anxiety, communication, and cognition at both language-based and nonverbal levels such as involved in the reading of social cues and varying levels of **reading comprehension,** as well as sensory perception. The acronym MACS (Movement, Anxiety, Communication/Cognition, and Sensory) is a useful frame for understanding the brain structures and functions involved in ASDs and for sorting and interpreting the plethora of information on this topic.

The Basis in the Brain of Movement Differences in ASDs

Donnellan and Leary have well-documented the challenges people with ASD labels face when environmental experiences (e.g., social demands, transitions, and speech production) require movement-based responses. More than sixty studies confirm that differences in the cerebellum, which is primarily involved in motor control, occur in approximately 95 percent of all people diagnosed with ASD. These differences include smaller overall size, smaller but more densely packed neurons, and inefficient functioning. The loss of or decrease in the number of Purkinje neurons, specialized cells concentrated in the middle layer of the cerebellar cortex that have the greatest number of branches and long distance connections to other areas of the brain, occurs in some people with ASD. This may account for their delayed processing and/or responding as well as lost or skewed messages between various parts of their brains. As significant generation, branching, and myelination of these neurons occur during early childhood, abnormal Purkinje cell development may also explain the loss of previously developed skills in those individuals who are asymptomatic of ASD during infancy and toddlerhood.

Other brain-based movement differences associated with ASDs have been attributed to smaller portions of the basal ganglia that helps coordinate motor activity, thinning of pyramidal cells in the cortex related to coordination of movement and other brain functions such as emotional regulation and memory, dysfunction of the motor cortex (both as the recipient of faulty messages from other parts of the brain and the sender of faulty messages to the motor neurons), and abnormalities in the cingulate gyrus as the "gear-shifter" of the brain. Smaller and more densely packed cells in the frontal lobes (which, along with the thalamus, are also the sites of decreased serotonin synthesis among people with ASDs) may account for seizure-like behaviors. Involuntary tic-like motions exhibited by some people with ASD labels may result from abnormalities in the extrapyramidal system and their cingulate gyrus may be a contributor to compulsive behaviors. Increased levels of the neurotransmitters dopamine and oxytocin may explain the Parkinsonian-like movements and other unusual motor behaviors exhibited by some people with ASDs. Research also suggests that motor challenges may be due to problems with the superior temporal sulci and other brain structures related to detecting and mirroring biological movement.

Anxiety in ASDs

The amygdala, the site of primary (i.e., survival-related) emotional memory, sets into motion the release of hormones such as adrenaline in emotionally charged settings involving stress or threat that results in arousal of the parasympathetic nervous system to facilitate fight or flight. Research suggests that, in people with ASD labels, the on-off switch of the amygdala may not function as well as in neurotypical people, resulting in a heightened state of anxiety that in turn leads to either aggression or withdrawal. Suppressed functioning of the amygdala given certain sensory input or lowered cortisol levels may be responsible for the "fearless" behaviors demonstrated by some individuals with ASD labels whereas a learned reliance may develop on either self-injurious or calming behaviors such as rocking to release b-endorphins, tryptophan, and other neurotransmitters that exhibit an inhibitory effect on adrenaline surges resulting from overactivity in the amygdala. As the locus of post-traumatic stress disorder reaction in neurotypical people, the amygdala also may be responsible for the heightened negative emotional responses exhibited in some circumstances by some individuals with ASD labels who have been subjected to trauma in the name of treatment.

Brain Links to Communication and Cognitive Differences Experienced by People with ASDs

In addition to its function in the motoric aspects of speech production, the cerebellum plays a role in overall language generation. The basis in the brain for communication differences exhibited by people with ASDs (ranging from those who are nonverbal but able to type independently to those who are highly verbal but may have problems with the rhythm or flow of speech resulting expressively, e.g., in a monotone) includes the previously described cerebellar differences and reliably less activation in Broca's area rendering oral language dysfluent. Decreased levels of norepinephrine are associated with decreased communication.

In contrast, the reliably greater activation of Wernicke's area, the site of language comprehension, as compared to neurotypical people is probably the strongest evidence that ASD (including "classic autism") is not a variant of cognitive impairment *per se* even though cognition among people with ASD labels and in comparison to others not so labeled may differ. Rapid growth of the cortex from smaller than average to above 90th percentile between the ages of two and five years also has been found in some people with ASD, particularly in the frontal lobes. Such growth may result in hyperlexia (early and untaught ability to read) or other areas of impressive strength such as the *Rainman*-like facility with calendar dates. This phenomenon may be related to the discovery that various brain proteins (e.g., BDNF, VIP, CGRP, NGF, and NT4) involved in regulation of brain growth are at higher levels at birth, and overall brain volume and head circumference tends to be greater, in people who acquire a diagnosis of an ASD.

Cortical hemispheric differences such as suppressed blood flow to the left hemisphere and increased right brain activity found in some studies may explain other cognitive differences such as why some people with ASDs can't seem to comprehend certain "big picture" qualities of objects or concepts. Brain-based gender differences have been found to be more extreme in some people with ASDs (e.g., significantly smaller or absent anterior commissures and less dense cellular composition of the corpus callosum in general) and may explain the decreased empathy and increased tendencies to be rigidly rule-based about one's world, including interpersonal relationships, commonly ascribed to people with ASD labels. There is an idiosyncratic reliance on so-called "lower brain" structures such as the fusiform gyrus for certain memory tasks as well as idiosyncratic convolutions, likely related to abnormal cell migration during development, throughout all four lobes of the cortex.

Differences in the cerebellum described previously, as well as the combination of differences in brain structures and functions related to anxiety, communication, and sensory processing may also result in the difficulties many people with ASDs have concerning complex problem-solving and concept formation (strengths in literal comprehension/rote memory do not align with weaknesses in inferential comprehension), paired-associate and working memory, and learning novel skills.

The Basis in the Brain for Sensory Processing Differences in ASDs

Cerebellar differences also affect sensory discrimination and visual spatial perception, and sequencing. Other brain-based sensory differences among people with ASDs have been well-documented. Decreased blood flow to the auditory cortex may make it difficult for some individuals with ASDs to make sense out of auditory input. The more numerous but smaller and less compact cellular columns in the overall temporal lobes may result in too rapid a transmission of sensory input and subsequent overload. In the parietal cortex, loss of cell volume may be linked to differences in sensation of pain, pressure, temperature, and touch while smaller brain waves in the parietal lobes have been shown to be related to shifting attention between various auditory and visual stimuli. The sensory cortex has been implicated in hypo- or hyper-sensitivity to certain stimuli in some people with ASD that may be so extreme as to cause discomfort or pain. It may contribute to overreactions of the amygdala and account for "mis-perceptions" reported by many people with ASD.

Overall deficiencies in the neuronal pathways from the limbic system leading to, and more numerous but smaller and less compact cells comprising, the prefrontal cortex may explain why the expression of emotions in people with ASD sometimes appears atypical (e.g., laughter instead of becoming upset) and why some emotions—e.g., anxiety, rage, fear—are overwhelming. All of these structures and functions, both subcortical and cortical, are also involved in social interactions that are by definition compromised in people with ASD.

Poor metabolism of neurotransmitters functionally impairs the hypothalamus that specifically has been linked to difficulties people with ASDs have with regulation of sleep, hunger, thirst, and body temperature. Their thinner-celled hippocampuses may result in their seemingly greater difficulty transferring some of that information into long-term memory "as is" such that long-term memory is then skewed. This may account for the over-reliance some people have on "extraneous" stimuli (i.e., things MUST be a certain way) to perform routines and/or "over-programming" or over-learned responses (e.g., to the sight of videos regardless of the setting). Difficulties interpreting sensations from the face and sense organs of the head (eyes, ears, nose, mouth) have been attributed to the fact that the pons division of the brainstem does not increase with age in people with ASDs as compared to those who are neurotypically developing. Overall hyper- or hypo-arousal may be explained by fewer receptors for certain neurotransmitters such as acetylcholine, variations at different ages in the size and number of cholinergic neurons in the basal forebrain.

Implications for Teaching People with ASDs

Despite what appears to be a confusing onslaught of information, we can conclude three things at this time. (1) The involvement of multiple brain systems, working both independently and in concert with other brain systems, leads to the ASD diagnosis. (2) The same brain systems may not be involved for different people with ASD who manifest similar movement, anxiety, communication/cognitive, and sensory perception-based behavioral deficits or excesses because functional differences are not yet causatively linked in a comprehensive manner to structural differences. (3) Manifestations across individuals, even when neuroimaging and other methodologies suggest comparable systems are involved, are so varied and intriguing that no one theory as to the origins and mechanics of ASDs fits all. Yet, for each individual student with ASD, an understanding of possible brain differences yields more possibilities for effective interventions.

Effective brain-based strategies to facilitate learning among students with autism spectrum disorders included accommodating movement differences, minimizing anxiety, providing access to multiple but universally understood communication options, being respectful of cognitive differences and teaching alternative strategies as needed, and supporting sensory differences.

Accommodate movement differences through provision of extended wait time, nonverbal prompting to "jump start" desired behavior, visual supports to aid memory and provide step-by-step expectations for transitions, start-to-finish practice executing required movements so that automaticity through **episodic memory** is achieved, and minimization of movement requirements (e.g., allow dictation for verbal students and typing instead of handwriting). Don't call attention to extraneous movements so as not to increase anxiety and exacerbate the difficulty the student has performing the required task.

Use functional behavioral assessment strategies to determine whether undesired behaviors are important enough to require intervention at the moment and, if they are (i.e., for **aggression** but not necessarily for occasional inappropriate expression of emotion), to determine the appropriate intervention(s). These may include a referral from the school nurse to the student's doctor for medication to alleviate anxiety, social stories to allow internalized practice of applying appropriate social skills in social situations, scripts to eliminate the need to mirror others' behaviors, and planned orchestration/application of any of the other teaching methods discussed in this entry.

Provide extra support in learning environments to minimize anxiety and avoid inadvertently creating a post-traumatic **stress** response set. Extra supports may include a 1:1 paraprofessional to allow for supervised "break-taking" in sensorily overwhelming situations, access to appropriate sensory activities *in situ* (e.g., a weighted vest; opportunities to jump hard, do push-ups, or run; fidget toys; permission to walk around the room; access to a rocking chair or swing) to modulate arousal level; rest, healthy snacks, and opportunities to regulate one's own temperature with cool surfaces or body wraps; and calm, predictable activities and environment to the extent possible. Again, social stories and social scripts that provide both explanations of human behavior and behavioral expectations, as well as "how to" directions to the person with ASD, are important tools for managing less predictable social situations.

Communication supports are essential, especially for students whose speech is echolalic or who get stuck saying something that is not what they intend to say. Such supports can range from laminated, icon-based word and phrase cards (maintained on key rings) that can be used "in a pinch" to high tech augmentative communication systems involving voice output (e.g., a Lightwriter). Audio or video taping of the individual engaged in communicative activities as well as of peers engaging appropriately in the same activities can be an important teaching approach to address such issues as prosody of speech, acceptable personal space, and friendly actions (provided the student's attention is kindly but explicitly directed to the behaviors of concern).

One of the most important strategies for teaching students with ASDs is to apply the Criterion of the Least Dangerous Assumption concerning their competence—that is, to adopt the assumption that, if proven false, is least dangerous to the individual. For people with ASDs, this translates into assuming competence regardless of the intensity of supports the individual needs. While some people with ASD labels can demonstrate competence easily (especially in selected academic areas), MACS issues get in the way of others being able to demonstrate their intelligence. The Criteria of the Least Dangerous Assumption also applies to behavior—that is, the individual student would be good if he could. Maintain high expectations but modify performance demands according to the individual student's strengths and challenges.

Employ more "right-brained" strategies such as picture schedules, other visuals, and music to cue behavior because these can be more successful than language-based cues alone. Where difficulties in pragmatics occur, tell the individual with ASD what the speaker, author, artist, etc., is likely to be "saying" so the individual can adopt that interpretation as his own rather than trying to infer meaning from an assortment of potentially confusing input. Provide algorithms for math problems and calculators or number fact charts for those students who have difficulty with rote memorization. Facilitate generalization of these higher order thinking skills by providing multiple opportunities to learn them across multiple and varied situations.

Expect that each individual with ASD will respond to a different configuration of teaching and support strategies because each individual's MACS profile is unique. Slow down your presentation style and, when multimodal instruction is used, provide choices as to which modality or combination of modalities works best for the specific student. Be wary of the individual "mis-learning" a task and be prepared to re-teach it as needed. Programs such as the Alert Program (see http://www.alertprogram.com/) can be helpful in teaching the individual how to regulate his own arousal level.

See also: Reading Comprehension; Language Acquisition and Disorders; Information Processing Model.

Further Readings

Autism Research Institute (1987–2003). *Autism Research Review International* 1–17 San Diego.

Bauman, M.L., Kemper, T.L. (Eds.) (2004). *Neurobiology of Autism* (2nd ed.) Baltimore: The Johns Hopkins University Press.

Donnellan, A., Leary, M. (1995). *Movement Differences and Diversity in Autism/Mental Retardation: Appreciating and Accommodating People with Communication and Behavior Challenges*. Madison, WI: DRI Press. http://www.courchesneautismlab.org

Volkmar, F.R., Paul, R., Klin, A., Cohen, D.J. (Eds.) (2005). *Handbook of Autism and Pervasive Developmental Disorders, Volume One, Diagnosis, Development, Neurobiology, and Behavior* (3rd ed.). Indianapolis: John Wiley & Sons.

The National Autistic Society www.nas.org.uk

LINDA H. RAMMLER, M.ED., PH.D.

B

Behaviorism

Behavior modification is now recognized as the single most effective way to learn behavior. Yet, just a few decades ago, its practice was considered by many people to be unethical and superficial.

B.F. Skinner was the first to demonstrate how behavior modification was a natural outgrowth of social interactions and how it shaped behavior almost without fail. Consider these everyday events:

- A waiter gives excellent service and, as a consequence, the diners leave a twenty-five percent tip.
- As a woman enters a public building, she notices that the man behind her is carrying a large package; she holds the door open for him. He thanks her.
- A mother asks her teenager to help clear the table and he promptly does. She thanks him.

These and similar behaviors from everyday life demonstrate what B.F. Skinner considered operant conditioning. Through tightly designed research, he showed that organisms operate on the environment and, through their interactions, discover stimuli that may be rewarding, punishing, or of no consequence. Those events that are rewarding increase behavior and those that are punishing decrease behavior and those that do neither have no effect on the behavior. Skinner's work generally forms the basis of those applications that we now call "behavior modification." These include, but are not limited to, contingency contracting, behavior shaping, cognitive behavior modification, and social modeling.

By the 1960s, behavior modification was used successfully in hospitals, prisons, special education classes, and ultimately with normally developing school children. In the early 1980s, research evidence in favor of behavior modification dispelled questions of effectiveness. But, issues of an ethical nature continued. These have been effectively addressed through informed consent, human subject guidelines, and tightly regulated practices through the licensing of psychologists and related professionals who use behavior modification.

Psychologists and other behaviorists subscribe to a few basic principles that have been well documented in research studies. These are: a behavior followed by a reinforcing stimulus increases the probability of that behavior reoccurring; a behavior not followed by a reinforcer decreases the probability of that behavior reoccurring; and a behavior followed by an aversive stimulus will over time extinguish that behavior.

Of utmost importance is that reinforcing and aversive stimuli are relative to the preferences, or reinforcement histories, of individuals. Obvious examples are that of a masochist who finds physical punishment rewarding and an ascetic who finds acquisitions repulsive. Behaviorism is rooted in the belief that all behaviors, except the autonomic ones, are learned as a result of a person's environment and not his genetic makeup.

The Brain and Behaviorism

Skinner's radical behaviorism considered the brain to be a "black box," and it did not need to be studied for purposes of behavior change. But, cognition does have a central role in behavior modification by providing the necessary connections for people to associate their behavior with the consequences of that behavior. Thus, they learn how to behave to achieve specific outcomes such as higher academic achievement, more consumer power, and improved social experiences to cite a few examples.

The brain stores predictive patterns. Through neural processes memories are stored that share certain attributes. We organize and recognize activities, thoughts, and individuals through patterns. For instance, when we walk into a room and see desks, a teacher, and bulletin boards we know we are in a classroom. Our brain recognizes this structure and behaves accordingly. This ability to form patterns allows us to have programmed responses to stimuli.

Dopamine is the neurotransmitter that plays the greatest role in activating the reward system. The brain's function, in this regard, is to help the learner's neurons send electrical impulses that will release neurotransmitters in the medial forebrain system. These transmitters make the associations that result in the decision-making through which behaviors are likely to facilitate desired outcomes. If the brain is rewarded for an activity it is likely to replicate that behavior. Activation of brain reward systems can be considered a natural component of normal behavior that is instrumental in motivation.

The power of dopamine and the reward system can be seen in research done with laboratory rats. Rats were connected to electrodes emitting dopamine as a reward for scampering across a hot griddle. All rats were willing to endure the pain to receive the dopamine reward. In fact, when given a choice between food and the pleasure of dopamine, they chose to starve themselves. Research on humans has equated a dopamine rush to a sexual orgasm. Because of ethical issues, research on humans has been limited.

Researchers have found separate but interactive neural pathways arbitrate reward and punishment. Punishment activates the amygdala, the site of emotional control. Punishment is interpreted as a threat to survival by the brain. The reticular activating system propels adrenaline through the body which directs all attention to the stimuli. The individual wants the punishment to stop and so learns to change their behavior. During this period the amygdala overrides the higher level thinking areas of the brain and academic learning ceases. It is generally understood that punishment is not as effective at changing behavior as positive and negative reinforcement.

Classroom Application

The application of behavioral principles has been studied under differing conditions and with various sample populations. These studies have generated numerous technologies that are used in schools, clinics, and hospitals. They are used to facilitate academic learning; improve social behavior; change body weight; extinguish tobacco use, alcohol and other addictions; correct sexual dysfunctions; and treat a host of other problems of daily living.

Procedures for behavior modification, whether self applied or administered by others, follow similar patterns. First, target behaviors are selected and identified. Second, incentives (rewards) are determined. Third, conditions for changing behavior are established. Fourth, an evaluation system is set up to chart behavior improvement, and to change treatment as needed.

Behavior modification has had a great influence on classroom instruction, particularly in **feedback** in elementary and high schools. The simple act of providing immediate feedback, be it correction or accolades, is widely recognized as a way to maintain and correct responses and to control group behavior. Timing of reinforcement is critical in Skinnerian instruction. Schedules of reinforcement are used as a means to extinguish, strengthen, and maintain behavior.

When teaching, the frequency of rewards is of utmost importance. Issuing rewards may be an encouragement and a guide; it can help learners know that they are on the right track. Ideally, reinforcement should occur simultaneously with the desired response or as closely following the behavior as possible.

One offshoot of behaviorism is programmed instruction. The instructional delivery may take the form of a textbook, a computer, or even a teacher. But regardless of the form the common characteristic is that, through a series of successive approximations, subject matter is taught by eliciting responses and systematically reinforcing only the correct responses. Corrective feedback is also an integral part of programmed instruction.

The nature of rewards must also be considered. For example, an untrained behaviorist may rely heavily on edibles as rewards. This practice is not uncommon in classrooms where candy and other snacks are given. But, in addition to dietary issues, edibles are not very desirable as rewards because they rapidly satiate and the responses are weakened over time.

Experienced behavior therapists and teachers observe students and clients and then establish a hierarchy of reinforcers using the most subtle ones first, gradually moving toward the more obvious rewards until one is found that is of sufficient strength to maintain the desired response.

In classrooms, the most powerful rewards over time are those that tend to be social, such as: positive feedback, verbal praise, and other support.

Behaviorism assumes that all behavior can be considered as a set of responses that have been learned through interactions with the environment. In that sense, behavior is neither good nor bad, correct or incorrect; it may be valued only within the context that it occurs. Thus, it is either adaptive or maladaptive with respect to a specific environment. Teachers, parents, and other caregivers can help students and others in their care adapt to their environments by setting conditions through which they will learn controlled responses that are conducive for success within that particular environment.

Behaviorists do not deny the importance of cognition. Rather, they believe that the reinforcers occur as a result of individuals' interactions with their environments. As a result of this belief, they are able to objectify how behavior is learned and how it can be changed.

See also: **Constructivism; Motivation; Transfer.**

Further Readings

Cooper, J.O., Heron, T.E., Heward, W.L. (2006). *Applied Behavior Analysis* (2nd ed.). Upper Saddle River, NJ: Merrill/Prentice Hall.

Malott, R.W., Suarez, E.W. (2004). *Principles of Behavior* (5th ed.). Upper Saddle River, NJ: Merrill/Prentice Hall.

Michael, J.L. (2004). *Concepts and Principles of Behavior Analysis* (rev. ed.) Kalamazoo, MI: Society for the Advance of Behavior Analysis.

Skinner, B.F. (1974). *About Behaviorism.* New York: Knopf.

THOMAS M. STEPHENS, PH.D.

Beverages

As the brain is estimated to be 75–85 percent water, it needs adequate hydration for optimal function. Water moves oxygen and nutrients into the brain, maintains blood volume, and carries electrical impulses from sensory organs, like the eyes and ears, to the brain to be converted into memory and learning. Next to oxygen, water is the second most important nutrient for brain performance. Symptoms of brain dehydration include mental fatigue, slight memory problems, and confusion. Therefore, choosing beverages that hydrate the brain enhances learning and memory. Unfortunately, people frequently select beverages that hinder brain function.

Water

As little as 2 percent dehydration decreases brain performance. By the time someone feels thirsty, the body and brain are mildly dehydrated. Therefore, hydration requires drinking water regularly. A common guideline for water intake is one ounce water for every two pounds of body weight. Thus a 50 lb child should aim for 25 oz (about three cups) of water daily, while a 150 lb adult would need 75 oz (about nine cups) per day. Students who regularly eat fruits and vegetables absorb water from these sources, while students who avoid them have to drink more water. As temperature increases and humidity decreases, need for water escalates. Using the Water Intake Tool calculator at the Apollo Life website of the Apollo Hospitals Group, students can determine their personal water consumption guideline, based on their height, weight, age, gender, and level of activity.

When the body does not get enough water, it sustains blood volume by removing water from the respiratory tract, digestive tract, and fluid in the joints. Reducing water in these areas also affects the brain. Dehydration in the digestive tract often results in constipation, which increases intestinal absorption of ammonia. Excess ammonia may lead to encephalopathy (abnormal brain function) with such symptoms as foggy thinking and sleepiness. Dehydration of the respiratory tract increases risk for sinus infection, which reduces oxygen flow to the brain. Finally, withdrawing water from synovial fluid produces joint pain, which distracts from mental concentration. Other symptoms of dehydration include fatigue, dry mouth, dark yellow urine, and sinus congestion.

To check hydration status, students can evaluate urine or skin. If their urine is the color of either pale lemonade or a yellow legal pad, hydration is adequate. They can also pinch the skin on top of one hand. If the skin snaps back completely in one second, the body and brain have sufficient water at that time. These tests are very important for persons who train or work outdoors in hot weather, engage in vigorous activities, or ingest a lot of caffeine. To restore hydration, every pound of weight lost during hot weather or vigorous physical activity should be replaced with two cups of water.

Students can regularly hydrate their brains by keeping a water bottle on their desks, drinking at water fountains, and having water available before and during physical activities. For electrolyte balance, sipping water throughout the day is better than gulping a large amount at one time. Individuals with kidney problems should ask their physician before increasing water consumption.

Good Beverages for Hydration

Plain or bottled water is the best way to hydrate the brain and body. Use a filter to remove chlorine from tap water before drinking it; chlorine interferes with the absorption of iodine needed for thyroid function. If chlorinated drinking water hinders thyroid function, the resulting hypothyroidism affects the brain, producing such brain symptoms as difficulty concentrating and remembering, depression, fatigue, and sleepiness. The chlorine issue is especially important in the American Midwest, which was once called the Goiter Belt because the thyroid glands of its residents enlarged to compensate for lack of iodine in the soil.

Fruit juices (100 percent juice), vegetable juices, and broth soups made from vegetables not only provide hydration, they also contain valuable antioxidants, vitamins, and minerals that nourish the brain. Note that drinking either pure fruit juice or sweetened juice drinks on an empty stomach can stimulate a rush of sugar to the brain, leading to excess insulin release, followed by hypoglycemia (low blood sugar) and lack of concentration.

Milk and soy beverages are other popular drinks, particularly because of their effects on bones. The protein in these beverages increases the flow of tyrosine and phenylalanine into the brain to make the neurotransmitters norepinephrine and dopamine, which improve attention and concentration. Consuming too many soy beverages, however, may lower thyroid function and lead to mineral deficiencies that affect brain function.

Caffeinated Drinks

Beverages that decrease hydration, such as those that contain caffeine, may diminish brain performance. Many popular beverages contain caffeine, including coffee, tea, soft drinks, and hot chocolate.

Limits for Daily Caffeine

Brain researchers offer different views about caffeine consumption. Dharma Singh Khalsa, M.D., suggests no more than 100 mg caffeine per day for adults, while Gary Small, M.D., recommends one caffeinated drink per day without specifying the amount of caffeine. Yet another guideline is 1 mg caffeine for every 2 lb body weight, so that the maximum caffeine for an 80-lb student would be 40 mg caffeine daily. Most students, parents, and educators however, do not know how much caffeine they ingest. Table 1 lists the caffeine content of popular beverages. For comparison, a 12-oz beverage is a can of soft drink or an average mug of coffee. Students may determine their daily caffeine totals using the comprehensive Caffeine Calculator at the website of Caffeine Awareness Alliance.

Table 1. Caffeine content of popular beverages (12 oz portions)

Beverage	Caffeine mg	Beverage	Caffeine mg
Brewed coffee	202	Sunkist Orange	40
Tea (hot or iced)	75	Pepsi	37
Diet Coke	70	Barq's Root beer	23
Mountain Dew	55	Decaf Coffee	7–12
Coca Cola	45	Hot chocolate	12
Green tea	45	Herbal tea	0

Table reprinted with permission of Sandy Baumann. M.S., from *Feed Your Brain for Learning,* page 10.

Decaffeinated coffees and teas are less hazardous to the brain, as they only contain about 1 mg caffeine per ounce of beverage. Simple ways to cut caffeine ingested from beverages include drinking fewer colas, mixing 1/4 cup regular coffee or tea with 3/4 cup decaffeinated, or slowly switching from caffeinated to decaffeinated drinks. Tapering caffeine consumption slowly is necessary to avoid headaches. In the presence of caffeine, blood flow to the brain is constricted. When caffeine is reduced, blood flow increases, causing withdrawal headaches.

Caffeine's Effects on Health

Caffeine is a diuretic, which causes the body to excrete water, B vitamins, and Vitamin C. Students can learn how caffeine affects them personally by consulting a chart of common B-vitamin deficiency symptoms. These include: aggression, anemia, anxiety, apathy, depression, extreme sleepiness, fatigue, fear, headaches, insomnia, irritability, mood swings, nervousness, poor concentration, restlessness, slow learning, sullenness, withdrawal, and worry—all of which aggravate interpersonal relations and increase personal stress.

As caffeine promotes wakefulness, it may hinder **sleep.** Ohio State researchers recorded for two weeks the sleep patterns and caffeinated soft-drink consumption of 191 teens aged fourteen to sixteen. Teens who drank more of these beverages were more likely to wake up during the night, be fatigued during the day, and sleep fewer hours than those who drank less.

Persons challenged with anemia and its negative effect on memory and energy need to lower caffeine intake, as a 12-oz mug of coffee (202 mgs caffeine) can reduce iron absorption from a meal by 39 percent. Caffeine also causes headaches. The journal *Cephalgia* reported a study of therty six children and teens, ranging in ages from six to eightden, who complained of almost daily headaches and also drank up to 1.5 liters of caffeinated soft drinks daily. After withdrawing from soft drinks over a two-week period, all but three participants stopped having headaches and remained headache-free for twenty four weeks after the end of the study.

Student groups can research the health effects of caffeine by keeping a daily diary about sleep and fatigue issues compared to cola and caffeine intake, correlating headache occurrence with caffeine consumption, and observing whether intentionally decreasing caffeine ingestion reduces irritability, mood swings, or anxiety. Working in groups to compare data promotes honest discussion while preserving personal anonymity.

Sweetened Beverages

Beverages with Sugar

When students consume a 12-oz soft drink, they ingest up to 1/4 cup pure sugar. All sugared beverages (juice boxes, soft drinks, iced tea) cause blood sugar to rise when they enter the stomach. Excess blood sugar in the brain raises serotonin and produces extreme sleepiness. (In young children, sugar overload from beverages may lead to hyperactivity.) Meanwhile, the body releases insulin to move excess sugar from the bloodstream into cells. If too much insulin is released, blood sugar drops too low, producing irritability, anxiety, shakiness, and extreme hunger, thereby diminishing concentration and attention.

Artificially Sweetened Drinks

Beverage producers currently offer flavored waters and soft drinks containing the artificial chemical sweeteners sucralose (Splenda) and aspartame (Nutrasweet, Equal), which affect the brain. Sucralose is chlorinated table sugar; the chlorine in this sweetener can negatively affect the thyroid, just like chlorinated water does.

Drinks sweetened with aspartame release in the body the excitatory chemicals phenylalanine, aspartic acid, and methanol. Phenylalanine enhances the production of dopamine, which may result in headaches and anxiety. Methanol is toxic to the brain. Aspartame is also associated with increased appetite and more risk for seizures.

To observe the brain effects of soft drinks, students can deliberately drink a sweetened (non-caffeinated) beverage on an empty stomach and then record how they feel (hungry, sleepy, irritable, etc.) one, two, and three hours after consuming it.

Alcoholic Beverages

No discussion of beverages would be complete without describing the harmful effects of alcoholic beverages on the brain. They cause dehydration, deplete water-soluble vitamins, decrease blood flow to the whole brain, prevent absorption of minerals, and may destroy brain cells. By acting to depress the central nervous system, excessive alcohol use can produce anxiety, depression, memory loss, lack of coordination, accidents, and even death. As alcohol relaxes inhibitions through its effect on the prefrontal cortex and the temporal lobes, alcohol abuse can cause aggression and antisocial behavior.

For compelling pictures of the brain on alcohol and other drugs, students can investigate the website www.brainplace.com. In the "Brain SPECT Atlas" at that site, psychiatrist Dr. Daniel Amen presents "Images of Alcohol and Substance Abuse." Students can view a brain scan of a person who abused alcohol, compare it with a normal brain scan, and see hope for recovery in scans of the same brain taken after the person quit alcohol. There is also a brain scan of a person who used excess nicotine and caffeine.

See also: **Addiction; Adolescent Cognitive Development; Adolescent Social and Emotional Development.**

Further Readings

Amen, D. Images of Alcohol and Drug Abuse. Retrieved April 26, 2005 from http://www.brainplace.com/bp/atlas/default.asp

Batmanghelidj, F. (1997). Your Body's Many Cries for Water. Vienna, VA: Global Health Solutions.

Hering-Hanit, Gadoth, N. (2003). Cutting caffeine may reduce headaches in some children and teens. *Cephalgia* 23:332–335.

Pollak, C.P., Bright, D. (2003). Caffeine consumption and weekly sleep patterns in US seventh-, eighth-, and ninth-graders. *Pediatrics* 111:42–46.

Small, G., Vorgan, G. (2004). The Memory Prescription. New York, NY: Hyperion.

"Caffeine Calculator." Retrieved on April 26, 2005 from http://www.caffeineawareness.org/calcu.php

"Water Intake Tool." Retrieved on April 26, 2005 from http://tools.apollolife.com/water/water1.asp

SANDY BAUMANN, M.S.

Bilingualism

Among the most innovative models in second-language education in the past four decades have been the French immersion programs developed in Canada. In the predominately French-speaking province of Québec in the mid-sixties, a group of English-speaking parents in the town of St. Lambert were anxious for their children to become highly proficient in French. At that time, there were two public school systems drawn along confessional lines: Protestant and Catholic.

The Protestant schools were English, almost without exception, and the Catholic schools mostly French. The parents were aware of Dr. Wilder Penfield of the Montreal Neurological Institute, and his views on the advantage of early bilingualism. When they discovered that their local French schools did not accept English-speaking children, they were determined to find another solution. They contacted other parents and enlisted the support of Dr. Wallace E. Lambert, an expert in the cognitive aspects of bilingualism, at McGill University. Together they persuaded the local School Board to open a kindergarten class for children with English as their mother tongue, to be taught completely in French by a native French speaker. Lambert would monitor the progress of these students.

The success of that class and evidence from subsequent elementary grades convinced both educators and parents that French immersion was an effective way to achieve a high level of proficiency in a second language, without negative effects on language and literacy in the first language. The findings provide what has become the best-documented teaching project to this day and has laid the foundation for the collaboration in the areas of cognition, language and perception, the field of behavioral neuroscience, and developmental psychology.

Neuroscience and Bilingualism

With the rise in sophisticated and noninvasive technology, there is ongoing research using neuroimaging including positron emission tomography (PET) that measures localized brain activation, functional magnetic resonance imaging (fMRI) that assesses cognitive activity, and magnetoencephalography (MEG) that records electromagnetic activity. These techniques identify neural networks associated with phonological processing and word recognition skills. There is considerable controversy as to how specifically language is represented in the brain. Are cognitive functions processed by separate areas of the brain or in overlapping areas? The question still remains on how the brain becomes bilingual.

New evidence suggests that the brain is more malleable than we thought: flexible, adaptable, and compensatory. We also know that the specialized functions of specific regions of the brain are shaped by experiences and learning, not fixed at birth. Researchers can study language breakdown through MRI and PET scans but this does not help us truly understand how the brain stores and processes language. Researchers have relied on the study of the effects on language of neurological disease in humans through post-mortem analyses. Experiments with animals have proven helpful but there are no animals that have symbol systems as rich as the language of human beings. Young and aging rats exhibit enhanced synaptic growth in complex environments. Studies in the ways zebra finches develop their characteristic songs helped researchers understand that in humans, just as in songbirds, the sounds produced by individuals themselves are essential for normal vocal development

Brain systems in humans and in other higher vertebrates interact together as a whole brain through neuro-chemical and electrical connections between neurons. With time, once neural networks are formed, less input is required to activate established connections. There is converging evidence that the inferior frontal and superior temporal areas in the left hemisphere are crucial for language processing in most individuals. Parts of the brain specialize in language with lateralization of language to the left hemisphere with differentiation in males and females. Scientists do not agree on where exactly particular language operations are carried out in this language region. Some believe that the language region works as a unit, while others believe that language operators are localized in specific parts of the brain. This knowledge enables researchers to continue their search for a better understanding about how language is processed in the brain.

Joy Hirsch and her colleagues at the Cornell University used fMRI to determine how multiple languages are represented in the human brain. They found that native and second languages are spatially separated in Broca's area, a region in the frontal lobe of the brain that is responsible for the motor parts of language movement of the mouth, tongue, and palate. Two languages, however, show very little separation in the activation of Wernicke's area, a region of the brain in the posterior part of the temporal lobe that is responsible for language comprehension. This study suggests that adults learning a second language may not have difficulty in understanding the words of the second language but rather with the motor skills of forming the words with the tongue and mouth. The implication for learners is to focus on methods related to speaking more than on reading and listening.

The Cornell researchers studied the brains of early beginners in second language acquisition and discovered that these learners showed no spatial separating in either Broca's or Wernicke's areas for the two languages. This demonstrated that in terms of brain activation, the same regions of the brain controlled their ability to process both languages. Researchers at UCLA also reported that the language areas of the brain seem to go through the most dynamic period of growth between the ages of six and thirteen.

Neuroscientists found the brain of infants and children to be more plastic and, therefore, more open to language acquisition. The high density of dendritic branching of a child's brain enhanced the child's general cognitive abilities. The young child possesses openness to new learning through creativity and play. Their affective social attitudes are positive and have not been marred by prejudice and/or years of experience. The younger the child learns a second language increases the probability of speaking the second language fluently. In addition, the window of optimal language learning all played a part in setting up the early or total immersion programs.

Research and empirical evidence acknowledge that there may be a time when learning a second language is optimal but there is no critical period as once believed. The window never closes but declines progressively with age. An early start may be desirable but not strictly imperative given so many variables in second language acquisition. The emphasis in recent years has been on how learning a second language might best occur rather than on when it should begin. Researchers do agree that in second language acquisition, the younger the learner, the better the learning, in the long run. Certain features of the language system and the way language is processed may be more related to distinct **critical periods** than others.

Late immersion programs, whereby students were totally immersed in the second language at the 7th grade level, demonstrated that the students achieved the same levels of proficiency in most aspects of second language learning as those in the early total immersion programs. This was due to the general cognitive maturity and learning efficiency of older learners. Although the older beginners showed an initial advantage, with time they were overtaken by the younger learners. The age factor is an important one, not to be undermined or discounted, but it is only one of the determinants in attaining an ultimate level of second language proficiency. The older one learns a second language, the more difficult the learning as the brain loses some of its plasticity and the number of brain connections or synapses is greatly reduced. On average, there is a continuous decline in ability as one ages.

Immersion

Immersion is intense and comprehensive programs whereby two-language competence is developed through two separate monolingual instructional routes. The premise is that people learn a foreign or second language in much the same way as they learn their first, and that languages are best learned in contexts where the person is socially stimulated to acquire the language and is exposed to it in its natural setting.

The consistent findings of twenty-five years of longitudinal research in Canada are impressive. The students were tested for reading and listening comprehension in French, analysis of oral and written production skills, creativity, concept formation, and other cognitive gains, and to determine advantages in cognitive and conceptual processing and controlled attention skills. These results bear linguistic as well as psychological and social consequences.

First, immersion students taught by monolingual teachers reached a level of functional bilingualism that could not be duplicated in any other fashion save that of living and being schooled in a foreign setting. Second, students achieved that level of competence without any detriment to home language skill development. Third, students do not fall behind in the all-important content areas of the curriculum, demonstrating that the incidental acquisition of French does not prevent or distract the students from learning new and complex ideas through French. Fourth, immersion pupils do not experience any form of mental confusion or loss of normal cognitive growth. Fifth, students do not experience any loss of identity or appreciation for their own ethnic background. Lastly, and perhaps most importantly, students know and appreciate French Canadians by having learned about them and their culture through their teachers, through their developing skill with language, through familiarity with literature and value of French Canadians.

In addition to the educational and cognitive impact of these results, the study highlights the distinct realization and possibility of peaceful democratic co-existence with other ethnolinguistic groups. Second language learning is, indeed, more than the sum of its parts. It is more than just learning another language. The children with immersion experience, compared to control groups, learned that both ethnic groups of young people need to interact socially on an equitable basis, a high order perceptual insight often not attained even by adults. Immersion is an effective means of developing a functionally bilingual Canada and the United States depending on the intensity of the experience and on when the other language or languages are introduced.

There is evidence that documents a marked enhancement of English language skills at the upper grade levels when Anglo students are immersed in total French schools, even when there is relatively little time allotted to instruction through English or about English culture. This development of English fluency and competence is derived, through transfer, from the high level development of French. In a similar manner, mathematics taught through French was also strengthened whether students were tested through English or through French.

Advantages of Bilingualism

Bilingualism has been shown to foster classification skills, concept formation, analogical reasoning, visual-spacial skills, creativity, and other cognitive gains. All this to be based on a certain level of competence before the positive effects of bilingualism can occur. Bilingual individuals may possess an added cognitive flexibility by knowing two or more words for one object or idea. Bilingual children have also demonstrated superior story-telling skills because they are adept at navigating two languages. Proficiency in two languages brings awareness in thinking about language itself rather than just as a means of communication. This enhanced metalinguistic awareness is considered a key factor in reading development in younger children, including sensitivity to detail, to the structure of language, early-word recognition, understanding of ambiguities, control of language processing, and correction of ungrammatical sentences. Due to the influence of English grammar, immersion students exhibit limitations in oral and production skills. In addition, immersion students' French use of speech proves to be mainly nonidiomatic. Their lexical and syntactical usage deviates from that of native speakers and although the findings suggest their productive language skills to be linguistically truncated, they are functionally effective. Even among children with lower cognitive ability, testing (I.Q.) has demonstrated that there seems to be no significant difference in performance between immersion programs and regular English programs.

In the spring of 2004, researchers in the field initiated an ongoing dialogue on the current status and future directions of childhood bilingualism. The researchers at this symposium, sponsored by the U.S.

Department of Education and the U.S. Department of Health and Human Services and other organizations, reached a consensus. Based on the results of empirical evidence, they agreed that having a command of more than one language is an asset. There is still, however, the need for further research in the areas of bilingualism that focuses on cross-linguistic fluency, second language processing, vocabulary, neuroimaging, effects of age and proficiency, and competence vs. performance. This dialogue will continue well into the twenty-first century.

See also: **Animal Studies; Language Acquisition and Disorders.**

Further Readings

Baker, C. (2000). *A Parent and Teacher's Guide to Bilingualism.* London, UK: WBC Book Manufacturers, Ltd.

Bialystok, E. (2001). *Bilingualism in Development; Language, Literacy, and Cognition.* New York, NY: Cambridge University Press.

Mechellie, A., Crinion, J.T., Noppeney, U., O'Doherty, J., Ashburner, J. et al. (2004, October). Neurolinguistics: Structural plasticity in the bilingual brain. *Nature* 431:757.

JEAN SEVILLE SUFFIELD

Blindness

Vision is a fundamental way to obtain information about our environment. It requires the interdependence of intact neurological and physical systems. The occipital lobes of the brain are the center of our visual perceptual system. One of its primary functions is to process visual data delivered from the eyes by way of the optic nerves. The eyes start developing at eighteen days gestation and appear as "Bulges." The neurological pathways as well as the physical structure (i.e. macula, fovea) of the eye are still underdeveloped in the newborn infant. At birth, the infant eyesight is so underdeveloped that they can only discern light, gross shapes, and movement. Infants spend their first twelve to thirty months learning how to see; this includes focusing, determining preferred eye, coordinating eye movement, coordinating eye–hand movement, recognizing depth and making spatial judgments, and refining visual acuity.

There are multiple reasons a child could be blind that may involve either the neurological or physical structure. Unfortunately, there are many chances to develop problems within the visual cortex, some of which are linked with other neurological conditions such as Neurofibromatosis. Even during birth, a perfectly healthy fetus can suffer oxygen deprivation that results in damage to the neurological or physical structures affecting vision. The etiologies of vision loss can be attributed to genetic/hereditary conditions, pregnancy based issues, pre/peri/post birth related conditions, physical injury and, in some cases, unknown. Therefore, it is possible to have a perfectly healthy occipital lobe or a perfectly intact physical system but possess no vision.

Vision is not a separate function in the developing child. It is an integral part of the total sensory system and plays a vital role in cognitive development. Vision is a powerful way to obtain information about the environment and contributes to physical accomplishments in the infant such as rolling over, sitting, crawling, and walking. All of these behaviors contribute to normal cognitive development.

Cognitive development in blind children is often different than that of sighted children. Early development is greatly affected by information gathered through the sense of vision. Vision is thought to be the most important modality for knowledge acquisition. Properties of objects such as color, shape, size, and motion are almost immediately accessible through vision. Other senses gather information from objects but typically do not possess, on their own, the most discrete properties of objects. Sound is fleeting, and touch can be limited to objects only within reach or only parts of an object at a time. The development of complex cognitive skills is dependent on the acquisition of comprehensive information. The child who is blind needs access to and considerable guidance from a multitude of experiences to understand information that is available to the sighted child at a glance.

Due to a reduction or loss of visual input, the attainment of information is not always intact. Patterns and rates of development are influenced by these altered interactions with the environment. Incidental learning through the use of vision is limited or non-existent. A variety of learning methods are needed to compensate for this reduced mode of obtaining information. A blind child must replace visual insight with a combination of sensory inputs from the remaining senses. The blind child must demonstrate, at an early age, flexibility to obtaining new information that is not required of the sighted child. Visual impairment in and of itself does not affect what a child is able to learn cognitively. It does, however, affect how these children learn.

To determine normal cognitive development, standardized assessments can be administered. There are measures for developing infants that are norm or criterion referenced. They rely on observation of the infant and parent report. Unfortunately, cognitive development is very difficult to measure with infants who are visually impaired or blind because most of the assessments rely on vision. Some behaviors typically used to measure cognitive development of infants are duration of eye contact, visual tracking of objects, and facial response to familiar and unfamiliar visual stimuli. Access to the environment through movement or touch may be limited in an environment due to a parent's fear of injury, lack of information, or lack of knowledge in how to increase the interaction and learning of the blind infant.

Jean Piaget proposed that the development of thought processes in children occurs between the ages of birth to two and is known as the sensorimotor period. It is during this time that the infant develops the concepts of object permanence, object constancy, and cause and effect.

Cause and effect, the next significant cognitive factor, is largely a visual experience. The child with vision sees a door being opened, milk spilling from a cup, a plate falling and hitting the floor. The blind child experiences only a small portion of this incidental learning. Incidental learning is reduced as well as the totality of the interaction or experience. The blind child may hear the plate falling or feel the food that splatters from the plate. They may feel the cold from the refrigerator or freezer but will not immediately know its content or typical placement of items.

This important period is when ample opportunities and structured experiences must be provided for infants to act upon the environment to provide equal understanding. These opportunities provide stimulation and intentional/non intentional feedback. This is fundamentally necessary for infants who are blind. Activities such as pushing a door closed, feeling water come out of a faucet, and dropping a plastic plate or cup to the floor to experience the actions are necessary to make the connection to events and outcomes. Increased effort and attention is essential and must be actively and consistently given to these infants to provide the needed input, stimulation, and experience. Parents and caregivers must be vigilant during this important sensorimotor period to provide what is needed for normal cognitive development to occur. These comprehensive learning experiences are fundamental for the development of a strong cognitive foundation.

The six general areas or domains of growth in infants and children is generally agreed to include cognition, communication, motor skills, self-help, sensory, and social development. The domains are interrelated and lack of development or opportunity in one area can significantly affect other areas. The ability of the adult to analyze the aspects of learning in these six domains is essential to provide the blind child with comprehensive learning experiences.

Cognitive development in blind and visually impaired children is intimately tied to the acquisition of fine and gross motor skills needed for interaction with the environment. One of the first events to occur in infant development is the engagement in exploratory behavior. This behavior is an important means by which infants obtain information about their environment and develop cognitive skills. These behaviors include mouthing, rotating, shaking, and looking. The use of active touch and movement of objects in this exploratory mode is referred to as haptic learning. Infants are able to adapt their behavior according to the characteristics of the objects they are examining. It is agreed that by these actions, infants perceive characteristics of objects such as size, temperature, hardness, texture, and shape. All of these behaviors are noted in blind and visually impaired infants. In one study congenitally blind children performed as well as, if not better than, blindfolded subjects on simple 2-dimensional tactual processing tasks. The acquisition of complex cognitive reasoning is more difficult but is achievable in blind and visually impaired children. The lack of vision in the acquisition of cognitive skills can be a challenge in the development of more intricate perceptual concepts and abstract reasoning. Although the congenitally blind children performed well on simple 2-dimensional tactual processing tasks, they did less well on more complex tasks requiring them to store, compare, and label objects. This poorer sensory coding ability is directly related to more limited experience with pictures and the representation of objects. Visual impairment and blindness significantly reduce input, interaction, and experience with the environment. This reduces incidental learning and a comprehensive understanding and opportunity to build more complex cognitive skills. Interaction with the environment is fractured and incomplete. It becomes more difficult to build upon previous learning when the totality of the event cannot be experienced.

For the blind or visually impaired child to develop more complex cognitive skills, the missing elements of the event or experience must be provided. The orchestration of the child's environment is essential for cognitive development to occur at a similar rate and pattern. A variety of techniques must be employed by parents and caregivers to make concept and perceptual development as expansive and dynamic as possible. When connections between new information and old information can occur, more effective and permanent learning will occur. Learning for the visual impaired or blind child must also be as interactive as possible. Introduction and interaction with the environment must consider the six general areas or domains of growth including communication, motor, self-help, sensory, and social development. The opportunity to experience an event for the visually impaired or blind child must be closely equivalent to their sighted peer. This requires the implementation of a variety of methods of exposure and interaction. In addition, the reinforcement of skill acquisition must occur, a number of times, after the event to ensure comprehensive understanding and incorporation into the child's knowledge base.

It is evident that active touch is an important aspect of learning for the blind child. Exploratory behavior does occur with the blind infant and is an effective way to obtain information about the environment and contribute to the acquisition of complex cognitive skills. The active interaction with an object through kinesthetic movement and tactile perception is a significant means to meaningful and sustainable learning. In the educational setting, the involvement of students in the active investigation of the properties of objects is a powerful motivator and increases attention to learning. This allows the blind child to be able to control actions, learning, and even the speed of exploration. This control has been found to be an important part of intrinsic **motivation** and is a tremendous key to engagement in the educational process and retention of new information and skills.

Researchers view haptic learning as playing an important role in the complex cognitive development. The kinesthetic and tactile processes provide meaning to objects that are unique to learning. From a purely physiological point of view, haptic perception involves sensors in the skin as well as the hand and arm. The movements that accompany hands-on exploration involve different types of mechanoreceptors in the skin (involving deformation, thermo-reception, and vibration of the skin), as well as receptors in the muscles, tendons, and joints involved in the movement of the object. These receptors contribute to a neural synthesis that interprets position, movement, and mechanical skin inputs. It is argued that this combination of kinesthetic and sensory perception creates particularly strong neural pathways in the brain.

Based on the information presented, it is essential to consider the impact of such a loss on the processing of information for school-aged students who are visually impaired or blind. When introducing new materials or concepts, time to explore the new materials is essential. When introducing a new concept, information must be presented to an array of sensory channels; some of the sensory channels for consideration should include olfactory, tactual, kinesthetic, proprioceptive, and auditory. For example, when studying photosynthesis in a science class, the teacher may want to use tactual drawings, real leaves, and 3-dimensional models. In addition, taking the class outside and searching for different types of leaves and plants would give all the students the opportunity to learn in a natural environment; which is often considered optimal for students who are visually impaired or blind.

The acquisition of complex cognitive skills in the blind child is attainable. The challenge for the parent and educator is to consider all of those discrete aspects of learning critical for the development of intricate perceptual concepts and abstract reasoning needed for optimal learning to occur. At all times, the blind child must be actively involved in the learning process and be allowed frequent opportunities to ask, explore, and evaluate in expansive and dynamic learning experiences.

See also: **Multiple Intelligences; Visual Brain.**

Further Readings

Bradley-Johnson, S., Johnson, C.M., Swanson, J., Jackson, A. (August 2004). Exploratory Behavior: A comparison of infants who are congenitally blind and infants who are sighted. *Journal of Visual Impairment and Blindness.* 98(8):496–502.

Csibra, G. (2003, March 25). *Electrophysiological studies on the neural bases of visual cognitive development in infancy.* Paper presented during the Center for Cognitive Science Spring 2003 Colloquia series. Abstract retrieved January 28, 2005, from http://www.cogsci.umn.edu/OLD/calendar/colloquia/abstracts.html

Lueck, A.H., Chen, D., Kekelis, L.S. (1997). *Developmental Guidelines for Infants with Visual Impairment: A Manual for Early Intervention.* Louisville: American Printing House for the Blind, Inc.

Sutton, A. (Summer 1996). The basis for visual development from prenatal through infancy. *Journal of Optometric Vision Development* 27:80–86. Article retrieved April 18, 2005, from http://braincenteronline.org/content/pdf/basisforvisualdevelopment.pdf

Verry, R. (1998). Don't take touch for granted: An interview with Susan Lederman. *Teaching Psychology* 25(1):64–67.

**DORIS SEÑOR WOLTMAN, ED.S. AND
LISA M. JACKSON, PH.D.**

C

Challenge and Enrichment

All students benefit by learning in an enriched environment, especially when simultaneously challenged to expand their processing. There are many valuable strategies we can utilize to encourage both challenge and enrichment. This was dramatically emphasized by Marion Diamond's landmark study in 1988 at the University of California, Berkeley. Rats in an enriched environment with stimulation and plenty to do, increased the number of connections in their brain by 25 percent, compared to rats raised in a more mundane environment. The rats with increased environmental enrichment developed larger and heavier brains, with increased dendritic branching. Their nerve cells communicated better with each other and the junction between the cells, the synapse, increased in dimension. These highly significant effects of differential experience also apply to humans.

Enrichment and challenge are inherently linked in an efficient teaching environment. The students feel safe and their brains learn more and become enhanced. Students who are bored, unchallenged, and feel threatened, flood their midbrain (our survival subcortex) with electrochemical activity and survival takes precedence over school learning. Students experiencing **stress** tend to shift energy from the reflective to the reactive part of their brains.

Students who feel challenged while in a safe environment energize the reflective parts of their brains and learn most efficiently. Teach students to valiantly welcome new challenges by insuring that the classroom atmosphere celebrates creativity and sincere attempts at performance. Include positive expressions of celebration and cheer, along with pleasant classroom rituals that encourage a sense of fairness, predictability, and enjoyment.

It is prudent for all those in a teaching position to be cognizant of the importance of enrichment on students' developing brains. Our brains operate by a series of rules and three of the important brain rules related to enrichment are *belonging, meaningful learning,* and *empowerment*.

Belonging

All humans need to belong somewhere and to be accepted. Students need to feel safe and accepted. We accomplish this by creating a sense of togetherness, giving students tools they need to be successful, and the opportunity to fulfill that success.

Meaningful Learning

Students become more involved when they feel the learning is meaningful. This involves providing connections to their experiences, choices, and using rituals to adjust mind–body states.

Empowerment

We tend to feel uncomfortable when powerless. A positive climate in the classroom involves students in class rules; rituals and choices in assignments give them a sense of power and self-control. Students who feel empowerment are more motivated and challenged to learn.

High Sensory Stimulation

Learners do best when presented with novel stimulation (something out of the ordinary) and with sensory-motor stimulation. When not engaged, our thinking cortex goes into a passive waiting mode, similar to a computer screensaver. Our reticular activating system within the brain (the RAS) becomes stimulated when presented with sensory-motor activity and the RAS turns on the thinking cortex. We stimulate the RAS by incorporating movement, altering our voice, changing a location, or adding a novel component to our lesson.

Physical movement and exercise develop more connections (synapses) between neurons and the actual nerve cell connectors (dendrites). Repetitive gross motor activities like walking, swimming, and running increase dopamine production, (one of the brain's reward chemicals) and modulate our serotonin levels (mood stabilizer). Secondary effects occur when students gain more control and mastery over their body, resulting in improved **self-esteem.**

The cerebellum, the cauliflower-shaped tissue at the base of our brain, contains more than one half of all our neurons and about forty million nerve fibers. This is forty times more than even the highly complex optical tract. The nerve fibers feed information from the cortex to the cerebellum and from the cerebellum to the cortex, creating communication between these two critical brain areas. This process is comparable to a two-way highway system.

We enhance students' learning by integrating movement activities into everyday activities: hands-on activities, stretching, walk and talk, role playing, and movement games. Our internal communications system greatly influences learning and 98 percent of this system takes place in the body. Sensory-motor stimulation produces neurochemicals that open neurons (the way a key opens a lock) passing along information. Our moods, enzymes, and body peptide chemicals travel in the bloodstream throughout our entire body/brain and greatly influence thoughts, feelings, behaviors, and our processing.

As an example, when we use only logical thinking and worksheets in math class, we are ignoring current brain research. Rather, we should weave together the logic of math, movement, visual organizers, social skills, analogies, and role playing. If we are able to further integrate math with geography, social science, science, or literature, so much the better.

Different Types of Memory

The traditional modes of memory include short-term, long-term, and auditory/visual. There are many more ways in which we process and recall information including declarative memory (**semantic** and **episodic**) and non-declarative memory (**procedural,** classical, and priming). Typical lectures, worksheets, discussions, and quizzes build word-based **semantic** memories that are generally less permanent. Sensory-motor activities build episodic and procedural memories that grab attention, boost memory, and enrich students' learning.

Each of these memory modes involves the brain differently. Retrieval memory is reconstructive: to retrieve information we reactivate elements of our experiences that reside all over our brain. Each student comes to our classroom with different preferences for memory input and retrieval and we can accommodate these by providing choices within our learning and assignments.

Important commonalities relating to all memory modes involve the need for rehearsal and breaks. We firm up the connection along the axon/synapse/dendrites pathway by providing substantial rehearsal, especially if students review information using different modes and modalities. The synapse periodically needs time to settle to help students consolidate information. Too much information at once interferes with synaptic adhesion. As learning involves establishing new circuits, the process is easier by taking in smaller amounts of information at a time and chunking the information into logical groups.

Music

Music makes the neural networks more receptive for learning and improves memory, cognition, concentration, and creativity. Many books are commercially available to explore using music judiciously to enhance challenge and provide enrichment and depth to students' learning. Even clapping games, singing, sounds, and simple rhythms alter physiological states and create more receptivity for learning.

One example of using music is for students to generate their own songs by writing lyrics to a familiar tune, incorporating the lesson's words/concepts. Examples include *Jingle Bells, Happy Birthday,* or simple folk songs. Singing the songs multiple times creates a memory pattern for students, who may also review information by singing outside of class.

Attention

Emotions direct conscious **attention** and we cannot isolate the cognitive from the affective. The almond-shaped amygdala (located in the midbrain) records pleasure and reward, and stores intense feelings in long-term memory.

We need to attend to the physical and emotional state of our learning environment. New experiences release electrochemical messages sent from neuron to neuron, creating new circuits that results in expanded learning and memory. However, students must attend to receive these experiences. Attention, energy, and enthusiasm are contagious within the classroom environment. Incorporate a variety of positive and consistent rituals while also incorporating novelty to help grab your students' attention.

Uniqueness

Our brains continually change: they are plastic and develop and integrate every experience in a way that is unique to itself. Theories such as **multiple intelligences** emphasize the variety we find among our students.

Neuroscience has discovered that all external behaviors correlate to the brain's internal processes. All states of consciousness, sleeping, imagining, hoping, dreaming, thinking, are results of electrical and chemical activity in our brain. These states are like "weather conditions" in our brains: they can change frequently. Acknowledging states that our students might be experiencing and also working to encourage shifts to appropriate states matching our curriculum goals, greatly increases our students' sense of belonging, meaningfulness, and empowerment.

Meaning

The search for meaning is innate: our brains thrive on meaning and dislike randomness. Once we are engaged in a learning endeavor, we cannot stop our brain from searching for some meaning and connectedness to past learning. Learning takes place at both conscious and unconscious levels and motivation accelerates once the student incorporates a positive, personal learning goal. This generates greater empowerment and enriches students' experiences.

As teachers, we can help our students' hippocampus (a seahorse-shaped structure in the midbrain that holds memory of the immediate past and sends memory to the cortex) encode new memories by creating connectedness for our students to real-life experiences. Connect new ideas to a time, place, and event, integrated with emotions. Two excellent strategies are frames and stories.

Frames create meaning. Framing a picture provides a structure and organizes meaning around the picture. A frame is also the perspective that people take concerning experiences in their lives. A learning activity can vary from being excellent to being meaningless depending upon the frame provided. Create a reason for the learning so that students perceive greater value. This will greatly enrich the connectedness they perceive between new information and their own lives.

Storytellers in early history were considered the most revered and venerated among tribe members. Stories create links and tie information together in a cohesive manner. Stories including exaggerated sensory images increase visualization, connections, and hence, recall of the information. Furthermore, stories and metaphors used to communicate basic concepts help our students learn by example. Stories challenge students to think about a concept in greater depth, which enhances and enriches their overall learning.

Synergy between the Left and Right Hemispheres

There are differences in how each hemisphere of our brain prefers to process information. The hemispheres also engage in simultaneous parallel processing that creates a synergy between wide ranges of processing styles. Encourage students to create visual organizers to integrate visual learning with the semantic or verbal learning.

We help our students enhance this synergy by providing choices, presenting information and reviews using a variety of modalities that focus on varied processing styles, and being cognizant of diverse **learning styles** and multiple intelligences.

Low Threat

Students benefit from challenge and enrichment when the threat level is low so that they feel safe and secure. We need favorable physical, mental, emotional, and social states for higher level thinking tasks.

Decrease stress by increasing predictability. Provide students with a roadmap or framework for the new learning to give them an overall picture of where they are and where they are going. Doing so decreases stress and enhances understanding. Challenge your students to perform at higher levels while also ensuring the output is realistic.

Higher Order Thinking Skills

Higher order thinking skills (HOTS) are essential to enrich students and make learning more challenging. Simultaneously energizing the activity with sensory motor involvement (toe-tapping, cheers) helps solidify the learning and body/brain growth.

HOTS lead students to create quality products. Our expectations shape the outcomes and if we expect more creativity and higher order thinking and problem-solving, our students will challenge themselves to move to those more complex levels. At the highest level, the products should benefit not only the student, but others as well.

Our students require predictability about the outcome and we need to provide clear parameters for the finished product. Such parameters will ensure quality but we must also teach the process skills and set benchmarks along the way. Bloom's taxonomy includes six areas of thinking (knowledge, comprehension, application, analysis, synthesis, and evaluation).

To exemplify using HOTS with naturalist activities, the level of information analysis and processing might include using formal systems for classifying the natural world or classifying natural phenomena in groupings by features derived from observations of unusual patterns. To increase the **HOTS** complexity level, encourage students to discern new relationships and connections between the natural and human-created

Table.1 Levels of bloom's taxonomy

Level	Definition	Example
Evaluation	Appraise, assess, Judge	Determining the value or utility of information using a set of standards
Synthesis	Imagine, compose, design, infer	Weaving together component parts into a coherent whole
Analysis	Analyze, contrast, distinguish, deduce	Discovering in differentiating the component parts of a larger whole
Application	Practice, calculate, apply	The capacity to transfer knowledge from one setting to another
Comprehension	Summarize, discuss, explain	The ability to translate, paraphrase, interpret, or extrapolate material
Knowledge	Define, label, recall	Rote memory skills: knowing facts, terms, procedures, classification systems

© 2003 LinguiSystems, Inc.
The Source for Learning and Memory by Regina G. Richards, Page 56.

world and or reveal personal connections to the natural world for abstract, symbolic, or metaphoric representations.

Feedback

The brain thrives on immediacy of feedback, on diversity, and on choice. Consistent feedback helps students improve the quality of their understanding and observe their own progress.

To enable the brain to learn from challenging, novel stimuli, feedback is essential. For example, if you are learning to walk a tightrope and you make a mistake, you fall: that is feedback. If you press a lever and you get food or you don't: that is feedback. The more consistent, specific, timely, and learner controlled the feedback is, the better.

A learning environment consciously attuned to how students' brains learn is one where the students' curiosities are piqued. Potential anxiety or confusion are diminished. Students have a sense of anticipation and curiosity because they are confident about knowing what is ahead. They are well-informed about the agenda, engaged in the process of learning,

interested in the topic, and feel safe enough to take learning risks. This is how we challenge students and provide an enriched environment.
See also: **Communication and Processing Time.**

Further Readings

Allen, R.H. (2002). *Impact Teaching: Ideas and Strategies for Teachers to Maximize Student Learning*. Boston, MA: Allyn and Bacon.

DePorter, B., Reardon, M., Singer-Nourie, S. (1999). *Quantum Teaching: Orchestrating Student Success*. Boston, MA: Allyn and Bacon.

Jensen, E. (2003). *Tools For Engagement: Managing Emotional States for Learner Success*. San Diego, CA: The Brain Store.

Lazaer, D. (2004). *Higher Order Thinking The Multiple Intelligence Way*. Chicago, IL: Zephyr Press.

Richards, Regina G. (2001). *The Source for Learning and Memory*. East Moline, IL: Lingui Systems.

REGINA G. RICHARDS, M.A.

Classroom Environment

Learning establishes new memory. Memories are sequenced patterns stored in the human brain. We gain them through experience in our world, which causes brain nerve cells (neurons) to fire in response to incoming environmental stimuli. Voila! We learn. And if we could peer inside a brain, we would detect subtle changes in its architecture. The pattern or network of brain communication would be altered, physically. New connections would have grown between neurons that never before communicated, or old neural connections would expand in size and complexity. It would be much like building a new highway to connect two towns, or putting in a new exit along a freeway. Learning brings change to the brain's communication networks much like building new roads brings a change to a map. It forms a network of ever-expanding pathways.

Learning is quite different from *practicing*, however, which re-fires and reinforces already-established memory circuits. Such retracing of circuits eventually creates a near default communication pathway in the brain, making recall or behavior automatic. If we practice Mamba dance steps enough, the memory networks controlling movement of our body and feet become so automatic that we no longer must concentrate to get the moves "right" when we're dancing. But when a new, unfamiliar dance is introduced to us (like the waltz), we must learn anew. We watch, experience, and experiment to reproduce the subtle sequences of movement involved in waltzing. And in our brains, neurons that never before communicated, now do—in *new* sequenced patterns—establishing new communication networks. Quite simply, brain wiring changes as a new memory is established.

Learning, therefore, is change—doing something new. Because change means doing things differently, it removes us from the predictable (comfort zone) and transports us to the uncertain and unpredictable (discomfort zone). We are unsure of the process, and unsure of the expectations. So it is risky to choose to learn and not just do things the "same old way." And risk implies danger.

Trying things for the first time almost always results in imperfection. Think of the first time you rode a bicycle, or the first time you tried to recite the Pledge of Allegiance, or the first room you painted. So when perfection is expected from the get-go, it can be pretty stressful. It is no different when "firsts" involve academic learning.

Educators have long recognized the importance of safety in formal learning environments. Educators Geoffrey Caine and Renate Caine popularized the notion that stress "downshifted" the brain into a primitive fight-flight mode, too caught up in self-preservation to focus on school curriculum. A student who fails in early attempts at change (learning) and earns humiliation (or a seat on the dunce chair in the corner!) is far from eager to set himself up for another risk at failure. He is too worried about avoiding failure to take the risk to learn.

Learning, however, demands attention and motivation on the part of the student: otherwise, it just isn't going to occur. When humiliation, failure, or social survival is at stake, one is not likely to care much about the importance of keeping number columns straight before subtracting, or care much about the three causes of the Boston Tea Party. The brain is bound up in preventing embarrassment (or worse). Brains pay attention to information deemed to be essential for their well being, and the brain automatically wires and "learns" in response to such experiences.

School subjects and projects aren't always viewed as essential to a learner (regardless of what culture and society says). They are "secondary" experiences, or experiences to which the brain is not naturally inspired to attend. They are not sought by a brain, and may draw little interest. They often appear irrelevant, and learning them might be very difficult. So why try a difficult task that is (1) tough, and (2) irrelevant. It might bring, "(yawn...) Who cares?" Or "Whoa Rudy, I'm not doing THAT." Oh, no. A brain must first *pay* attention (Hey – what's in it for me?), and then be convinced that trying or learning the new concept—is *worth the risk of failure*. Because anything done the first time is likely to need tweaking. Lots of it. Michael Jordon missed the basket the first time he threw the ball.

All humans, you see, have two fears that keep us from taking unnecessary risks: fear of failure and fear of peer disapproval. They grow more intense every year of a youngster's life until about age sixteen, when they level off and begin to lessen. So students in schools find themselves in very public places (classrooms full of their peers) being asked to take public risks to master content or learn behavior that could end in failure or humiliation. So how *does* this effect learning?

Fear causes **stress,** and stress causes the adrenal gland to release the hormone cortisol into the bloodstream. Cortisol causes the brain and body to revert to fight/flight status and *bypass* the portion of the brain essential for planting and retrieving memory, the *hippocampus.* As learning requires the formation of new and retrieval of old memories to construct meaning, full involvement of the hippocampus is needed. Fear, in essence, inhibits learning by stressing the brain to cause a bypass of the hippocampus. So what can educators do to prevent it?

As learning is change and is risky, learning *environments* either make risk-taking dangerous (where falling short results in failure and disapproval of individuals) or safe (imperfections on the road to mastery are expected and retries are invited). Safe environments make risk-taking attractive, reducing stress and allowing full function of the hippocampus in learning tasks. Such safe environments *welcome* stutter steps toward refinement, as well as trial and error to achieve change (learning). Making mistakes is not a problem (although endless repeating them is!). So safe learning environments provide feedback to illuminate problems that need remedying. Polishing skills enroute to mastery.

Several strategies provide such safety, including establishment of rituals and setting parameters. Learners must know exactly what is expected and what mastery looks like. With clear expectations, they are capable of altering behavior to reach a goal. There must be consistency in expectations, dependable enough that students can gauge reactions and consequences for their behavior. Providing models, rubrics, checklists, rules, and exemplars allows learners to measure and self-evaluate their responses/products/behavior before laying it out for public scrutiny. Such self-assessment is a great motivator, and a key to self-confidence in one's actions. Set a target and let them go—as General George S. Patton (1885–1945) said years ago, "Don't tell people how to do things. Tell them what to do and let them surprise you with their results," and with their sense of confidence and security in knowing how their product "measures up."

A safe environment provides more than targets and clear pictures of mastery, however; it provides continual feedback to keep learners aware of their progress toward mastery. To know when they are on track, as well as when to refine, re-do, re-think, re-try, and correct before going forward again. Feedback, ongoing and clear, guides the student. It reduces risk in the learning process, because the learner never strays too far off the path that leads to their destination. Safety!

Yet there are bound to be errors. So, safe environments provide opportunity for anonymity in student demonstrations of progress during the learning stage of instruction. For example, a forum for sharing "answers without ownership" invites full learner participation. Students might record ideas on paper and exchange them multiple times before opening them to discussion or evaluation; by then, no one knows which idea belongs to whom, and a judgment regarding the merit of an answer is limited to its content, not its author. Or the responses of many students might be charted/listed before evaluating individual ideas against some pre-determined criteria. If an idea is doomed weak, no one has ownership; if the idea is strong, the owner can take private—or public—credit. It is up to the student!

To eliminate peer disapproval, it is best to use tasks that force consensus among two or three students to produce "best" answers. After lectures, students turn to a neighbor and summarize what they have heard—and agree on a summary of key points. Not only is failure eliminated (everyone will have *some* answer), but disapproval is also wiped out; no one constructed the answer alone. At least one other person agrees with each student. Welcome "think tanks" (two to three person reflection teams) for reaching an answer or solving a problem; prize group work and discussion during the march toward mastery. Avoid situations where a learner must produce, perform, or express as a solo act. Ask for the *group* to produce and to practice for public expression. Cheating? No. Full participation is a *safe process* of learning. Solo performances are for final, summative assessments, not for the *process* of learning.

Modifications for students who struggle also can make learning safer:

- Invite students to write their answers on scrap paper, and not try to hold them in their heads until they are called upon. Then they can give full attention to other student responses and to classroom discussion, yet return to their ideas without losing their "train of thought" and looking foolish. The paper scraps become a sort of script to refresh memories or sequence ideas.

- When teachers record brainstormed ideas, each answer is acknowledged with "Thank you" rather than an evaluative response. Even if a teacher gives all positive responses to students, they are not inherently equal; "Why did she get, 'Great idea!' and I only got 'Good thinking?'" Varied teacher responses sort students, and sorting implies relative failure—at least to a student. Remember: fear of failure is a cause of stress—and a cause of brain communication bypass of the hippocampus. (Note: Use this strategy only when you seek divergent, creative thinking—not when you are looking for a single, correct idea. Then, you must be discriminating.)

- Provide adequate time for students to form ideas and respond. Doing so eliminates traps that increase or highlight student failure. Classic dyslexics process slowly, as they must rely on higher level reasoning and the context of the learning activity to jell their thoughts. Dyslexics also do poorly when expected to respond orally in a quick and spontaneous way. Time allows them to successfully prepare for an oral task. Language learning impaired children may process at a slower pace. The truth? Too fast often means error—error often means disapproval or failure. Disapproval or failure means stress—and stress diminishes learning.

Safety in learning tasks is not only essential, it is achievable. And it is a brain-friendly feature in achievement-rich environments!

See also: **Attention; Classroom Management; Self-Esteem; Semantic Memory; Stress.**

Further Readings

Jensen, E. (2003). *Environments for Learning.* San Diego, CA: The Brain Store, Inc.

Jones, S.J. (2005). *Backstage Pass for Trainers, Facilitators and Public Speakers.* Thousand Oaks, CA: Corwin Press.

Jones, S.J. (2003). *Blueprint for Student Success: A Guide to Research-Based Teaching Practices K-12.* Thousand Oaks, CA: Corwin Press.

Shaywitz, S. (2003). *Overcoming Dyslexia: A New and Complete Science-Based Program for Reading Problems at Any Level.* New York: Alfred A. Knopf.

Sylwester, R. (2003). *A Biological Brain in a Cultural Classroom.* Thousand Oaks, CA: Corwin Press.

Sylwester, R. (2005). *How to Explain a Brain.* Thousand Oaks, CA: Corwin Press.

SUSAN J. JONES, M.A.

Classroom Management

Classroom management has been a prime concern for educators since the origin of the profession. It is the second reason, after low pay, for teachers to leave the field. The beliefs, feelings, and actions a teacher demonstrates in managing the classroom create a classroom culture. Research about brain function shows that the culture teachers create through their classroom management system will enhance or impede students' learning. It will also determine the resiliency of students who enter the classroom with maladaptive life strategies. Brain research points the way for educators to create a classroom management system that fosters both increased social-emotional skills and academic learning. Such a system, based upon elements of safety, connection, and problem-solving, can help us to manage our selves, our children, and our classrooms more effectively.

Research over the past thirty years confirms teachers' trepidation toward classroom management, naming it a critical ingredient in effective teaching. The strongest evidence of this came from Margaret Wang, Geneva Haertel, and Herbert Walberg in 1993. They combined the results of eighty-six chapters from annual research reviews, forty-four handbook chapters, eleven journal articles, twenty government and commissioned reports, and ninty-one major research syntheses to conclude that classroom management was rated number one in terms of its impact on student achievement. Classroom management is critical because the environment it fosters directly impacts the brain function of both teacher and student.

The brain itself is physically altered by experience. The lives we live shape the brains we develop. This is called neuroplasticity, and is central to teaching and learning. Neuroplasticity is the ability of neurons to forge new connections. It allows us to adapt neural systems to address environmental demands faced in daily life. Research shows that large doses of stress hormones inhibit new learning in favor of strengthening survival strategies. These survival strategies trigger the brain into reactive mode, equating life's inconveniences with life-threatening events. Every person has experienced this short-fuse reacting instead of responding. Students who spend time defending instead of engaging in the learning process do not have the necessary behaviors, brain chemistry, or neural wiring for success. The key to encouraging neuroplasticity in these, and all students, is **attention**. Research shows that attention produces real and powerful physical changes, directing the wiring of the brain.

Both individually and collectively, the question becomes, "Where do we place our attention?" The brain, being pattern-seeking and survival-oriented, diverts attention depending on the type of sensory stimuli that is registered. Information or experiences that pose a threat are processed immediately. Threats include perceived issues from arriving late, to getting one's name on the board, to not knowing an answer. Upon registering threat, a rush of adrenalin courses through the brain, shuts down unnecessary activity and throws the student into a survival state. When experiencing a survival state, attention shifts from higher thinking skills to reactive, fight or flight skills. Emotional data takes high priority and the threat information is processed ahead of new data for cognitive learning. To be successful classroom managers, teachers must know how to use emotions intelligently.

Alternately, when classroom management provides a safe and emotionally secure environment, students' attention can shift from coping to engagement. Students must feel physically safe and emotionally connected before they can turn their attention to cognitive learning (the curriculum), because attention directs the wiring of the brain. Educators have the ability to wire students' brains to be defensive, aggressive, self-centered, or hopeless. Or, educators can help wire students' brains for problem-solving, cooperation, responsibility, and achievement. The choice is ours.

From Control to Connection: The Paradigm Shift

Historically, classroom management has focused on controlling unproductive student behavior and keeping students on task. Discipline was something the teacher did to the student after misbehavior occurred. The goal was order and compliance, with coercion and threat as the motivating weapons of choice. The most common threats used included loss of privilege, detention, lowered grades, humiliation, and removal. When the threat system proved ineffective, the strategy shifted to competition for rewards as another method of control. Competition creates a threat through the fear of failure.

The traditional classroom management system is counterproductive to learning because attention is placed on threat and emotional insecurity. With the students' attention focused on threat, their brains are wired for fight or flight reactions, not the higher order thinking skills that wire their brains for continued learning and problem-solving.

Fear and control-based systems of management also attempt to eliminate social-emotional issues from the classroom. Students and teachers must leave their emotional and social selves outside the room, and arrive prepared to learn or teach. The belief system behind this culture of control is not brain-compatible. It implies that emotions and rational thought are separate entities, that emotions impede learning, and that controlling others is possible and predictable. We now know that perception exists between stimulus and response. It is the perception dictated by the attention that controls behavior, not the stimulus itself. Research shows that **emotions** are integral to all learning because they direct attention. Today, attempts are still made to teach social-emotional and academic skills with separate curriculum, even though these skills are integrated within the brain. Current research indicates that in brain-compatible classrooms, the classroom management system *is* your social and emotional curriculum.

In the traditional culture of control-based classroom management, the goal was to control outside events and behaviors to regulate internal states. Teachers attempted to manage their emotions by controlling student behavior. Students attempted to control their emotions by controlling who or what was encroaching on them. Control of one's own emotions was achieved through controlling another. When we shift from a culture of control to a culture of connection, self-regulation becomes paramount to all. With self-regulation, students and teachers have "response-ability," the ability to respond instead of react to life events. Brain-compatible classroom management must shift attention from a focus on controlling others' behaviors to a focus on each person regulating his/her own internal state to more effectively learn, problem solve, adapt, and resolve conflict.

Paradigm shifts happen when we stop looking for new answers to old questions and start asking new questions. Creating a brain-compatible classroom demands that we ask new questions, changing from "How can we *make* students behave and succeed?" to "How do we create safe, connected, problem-solving classrooms to support the neuroplasticity necessary for emotional and academic learning?" Once we shift to thinking in terms of connection, we ask, "How can we learn to perceive and respond to conflicts as opportunities to teach life skills, as opposed to viewing them as disruptions to order?" New questions like these require teachers to shift attention from attempting to control unproductive student behavior to creating learning environments that encourage social-emotional health.

Creating Safe Classrooms

Effective, brain-compatible classroom management programs provide safety, connection, and problem solving opportunities for students and staff. Learning occurs more easily in environments free from threat. When a student or teacher detects a threat, thoughtful processing yields to emotional or survival reactions. As perception exists between stimulus and response, we know that perception of threat is constructed by the individual. Some teachers perceive students "talking back" as a threat to authority. Other teachers see these students as having experienced a trigger that shifted them into a survival state. Similarly, some students perceive math or an accidental bump by a classmate as a threat, while others view these events as normal occurrences. The perception of threat creates an internal state of survival with a limited repertoire of skills like blaming, attacking, and withdrawing. To create safe classrooms that lessen the perception of threat, we need:

- Emotionally intelligent teachers
- Self-regulating classroom strategies
- Predictable classrooms with well-taught routines
- A culture of safety.

Emotionally Intelligent Teachers

Classrooms managed by a culture of control require the teacher to design rules, administer consequences and complete paper work. Classrooms managed by a culture of connection require teachers to become emotionally intelligent members of that culture. Robert Marzano, in his meta-analysis of more than one hundred research studies, concluded that the most important factor in effective classroom management is the mindset of the teacher. A mindset is similar to the "mindfulness" in psychology literature popularized by Ellen Langer and "**emotional intelligence**" made popular by Daniel Goleman. Mindfulness and emotional intelligence involve situational awareness and conscious control over one's thoughts, feelings, and behavior relative to a situation. In neuroscience, this would be equated to optimal neuroplasticity and integrated functioning of the prefrontal lobes of the brain. The prefrontal lobes manage impulse control, empathy, problem-solving, conflict resolution, time management, motivation, and other executive activities. Emotion and cognition merge in the prefrontal lobes to allow each person conscious choice and free will. This union frees us from past habitual actions so we can respond with creative options instead of pre-determined strategies that may or may not be effective.

As mindfulness and emotional intelligence grow, people tend to stop blaming forces "out there" for determining how they act or feel. Safe classrooms require that both students and teachers own their own upset instead of projecting their distress onto others. How we manage and discipline ourselves internally is how we will manage and discipline students. Teachers are asked to teach students conflict resolution when 60 percent of marriages fail. It takes reflective insight for teachers to realize that they motivate themselves ineffectively. We often control ourselves with an internal voice of threat believing this type of self-discipline keeps us in line. In the classroom, this translates to being afraid of relinquishing control strategies in fear that our students will erupt in chaos. Yet, these control strategies are ineffective in developing healthy relationships in our personal lives as well as the key to brain development. Unless teachers learn to shift from motivating themselves with fear to generating optimal internal states to achieve personal goals, the shift in the classroom cannot occur. Teachers must make the internal shift of becoming emotional managers of themselves before the classrooms can experience the paradigm shift from fear and control to connection and problem-solving.

Self-Regulating Classroom Strategies

With mindfulness and emotional intelligence, self-regulation increases. Self-regulation involves the conscious recognition of an upset internal state, identification of the triggers that produced it, knowledge of how to change it into a more productive state for learning, and the willingness to actually change. We can call our emotional states "action sets" because they prepare us to act in certain ways. Internal states precede behavior. They provide a pool of choices from which all behaviors emerge. If your internal state is "sleepy," you are more likely to rest. If it is "grumpy," you are less likely to do a favor for a friend. Eric Jensen in his book, *Tools for Engagement,* provides an excellent understanding of states.

Effective classroom managers can regulate their own emotional states, teach their students how to regulate their states, and are responsive and attuned to the emotional state of the collective classroom. Educators can help to create a composed internal state with elements such as deep breathing, caring rituals, stretching, relaxation, music and movement, the arts, touch, humor, and anger management classroom structures such as the safe place promoted by the program *Conscious Discipline.* All of these components are essential to the classroom management plan. Paradoxically, as we increasingly focus on achievement scores, we are also stripping classrooms of the very processes that improve scores and create thriving classrooms.

Predictable Classrooms with Well-Taught Routines

Teachers can utilize daily routines to increase the predictability of the classroom to enhance the perception of safety. Routines are socially shared procedures of sequenced behavior in the classroom. The classroom contains many routines such as arrival, dismissal, hygiene, eating, transitions, homework, asking questions, obtaining partners and "what do you do when you finish early" routines. These routines must be taught in multiple ways, including posting visual representations, role-playing, and establishing prompts. At the beginning of the year, routines are novel. They take up working memory space for new information. As routines become habitual, the working memory is freed up and students are better able to focus on curricular activities.

A Culture of Safety

To build a culture of connection based on safety, a shift must occur at the job description level. Teachers have been told their job is to *make* children behave and to *get* them to learn. Making others do anything against their will creates power struggles and generates a culture based on fear and coercion, not cooperation. Teachers need to adopt a new job description that focuses the classroom on safety, both physical and psychological. A brain-compatible job description for teachers is,

"My job is to keep the classroom safe. Your (the students') job is to help keep it that way." With this job description, the school year starts with a discussion about safety. "What helps students feel safe; safe enough to ask questions, risk a new behavior or assertively speak up to classmates?" As the students have the job of helping to keep the classroom safe enough for all to learn, the discussion extends to behaviors that are considered helpful. From these discussions come a class mission statement, song, or chant. Together, teachers and students draw up principles and from these principals rules are established. By focusing on safety and helpfulness instead of what will happen if you break a rule, we positively focus our attention on elements that support learning.

Stressful **physical environments** are linked to student failure. Crowded schools, fluorescent lighting, and poor nutrition can impede classroom management effectiveness. On an individual level, brain cells consume oxygen and glucose for fuel. The more challenging the brain's task, the more fuel it consumes. Water is essential to move neuron signals through the brain and keep the lungs sufficiently moist to transfer oxygen into the bloodstream. The current recommendation for water consumption is eight ounces per day for each twenty-five pounds of body weight. For these reason, children need healthy diets and plenty of water for optimal self-regulation.

Creating Emotionally Connected Classrooms

When emotions are strong, they can be detected in the changing pattern of our heart rhythms. When people feel frustrated, worried, scared, or upset, their heart rhythms are uneven and irregular. These incoherent heart rhythms signal the brain, impede thinking, and hinder decision-making. Coherent heart rhythms are associated with a sincere sense of appreciation, feeling cared for, and confidence. Coherent heart patterns facilitate long-term improvements in self-control and cognitive performance. Therefore, learning starts in the heart not the brain.

Positive emotions that optimize learning and create a sense of belonging, connection, and contribution for all in the classroom are cultivated with the following:

- A felt sense of interconnectedness
- Recognition through celebrations, not rewards
- Problem-solving.

A Felt Sense of Interconnectedness

Newtonian physics once defined the world as matter consisting of predictable governing laws of matter. Behaviorism then took a strong hold, offering the notion of rewards and punishments as reliable ways of governing others. Quantum physics redefined reality as a world of energy instead of matter. In the world of energy, everything is interconnected and we influence each other in profound ways that we are just beginning to understand. Schools, classrooms, and families operate better when people perceive they are interconnected to one another, rather than separate individuals. This can be achieved by using a family model of classroom management. Establishing a school family philosophy will help shift attention from "what do I get if I'm good" to "what can I give to help others." It will also provide the necessary bridge to link the home family with the school family, increasing communication. The underlying premise is "what we offer to others we strengthen within ourselves." The school family philosophy can be achieved through caring rituals, contributing class jobs for all students, and specific feedback with a focus on class values such as caring and helpfulness.

Caring rituals are designed to create a sense of connection; they provide the heart of the classroom. Life-change rituals such as birthdays or losing a tooth are common in elementary grades. Over the years, these rituals have become more about cupcakes then about honoring others. Heart-brain research says these rituals must be revisited and expanded for all grade levels. Rituals can be incorporated into any classroom at any age. For example, assign a morning message writer to write an inspirational quote on the board daily, or conduct an absent student ritual in which the class offers returning students a warm welcome back note or song. These rituals generate the notion that school is an extension of home.

Classroom routines and rituals can be effectively managed by assigning a class job to every student. Historically, this position of value has been reserved for a handful of "good" students. We now know that being a contributing member is essential for the positive states that optimize learning. Every person is reassured by feeling they contribute and have value. A job for every student helps accomplish this goal. Meaningful class jobs fulfill classroom management functions and are determined by the needs of the class. Sample jobs include material manager, morning message writer, absent student committee, media specialist, door holder, attention helper, and line leader.

The brain is exquisitely designed to operate on **feedback**, both internal and external. Feedback is brain food. It reduces uncertainty by increasing coping abilities and lowering the pituitary-adrenal stress response. Several conditions, including specificity, immediacy, and being reflective in nature, make feedback more effective. Sadly, classroom management is more likely to meet these conditions with negative feedback than with positive feedback. For example, "You have repeatedly interrupted me. I asked you to be quiet several times, but you continue to talk, disrupting the learning of others. You know the rules. By continuing to talk, you have chosen to be removed from my classroom." Positive feedback, on the other hand, is usually a generic judgment such as, "good job," "excellent," or even "thank you for listening."

A classroom management system can promote neuroplasticity by providing effective positive feedback with noticing. The starter sentence for noticing is, "You _____ so _____. That was _____." Begin with "you" and then state specifically what the student has done that was positive. Follow up with "so" and describe how the behavior contributes to. End the statement with a tag that defines the action as kind, thoughtful, considerate or helpful. For example, "You straightened up the book area so the class could find the reading materials. That was helpful." This focus of attention on caring acts is key to neuroplasticity, a sense of safety, connection, and emotional security.

Recognition through Celebrations, Not Rewards

Historically, rewards have been systematically tied to classroom management. The popularity of **behaviorism** inspired generations of teachers to embrace rewards as a classroom management strategy. At the time, little was known about the brain, and rewards seemed harmless, were easy to administer, and often appeared effective. According to behaviorists, learning was dependent on a reward. With modern brain research, we see this assumption is false. Humans consistently seek novel experiences with no perceivable reward.

Neuroscience takes a different approach. It sees the brain as a pharmacy that makes its own rewards, the general name for which are "opiates." They act to regulate stress and pain, and produce natural highs similar to cocaine, alcohol, and morphine. The pleasure system in the brain stimulates certain neurotransmitters that let us enjoy behaviors. Simple, brain-compatible strategies include replacing rewards with authentic rituals, recognition, meaningful learning, and celebrations in the classroom.

The external reward system fails because it is not a brain-compatible approach to classroom management. Humans construct meaning from the inside out, so it is impossible to build an external system that would be fair and meaningful to everyone. External systems rely on personal judgment and perception. The "reward" of extra recess could be a feel-good experience for some and a threatening experience to others.

Schools based on rewards and consequences miss essential learning opportunities. If one child pushes another, the name goes on the board or a privilege is lost. In a brain-compatible classroom, these conflict moments are opportunities to transform hurtful behavior into helpful interactions called "teaching moments." In the above situation, a pushing student gives the teacher an opportunity to teach assertiveness skills to the victim and socially acceptable verbal skills to the aggressor. If the problem persists, problem-solving through class meetings and consequences are options. Empowering students to resolve their own social conflicts appears to be intrinsically motivating.

Managing classrooms using principles of intrinsic **motivation,** positive climates, clear expectations, problem-solving approaches to conflict and meaningful learning experiences allow each child to respond favorably in their own unique biological way.

Traditional strategies teachers employ to manage classrooms and deter problems often contribute to and exacerbate the problems. Brain research shows us how to become more effective managers of our children, our classrooms, and ourselves. In order for children to realize academic achievement, personal fulfillment and self-control, they must first learn how to accept responsibility for their behavior, how to respect the rights of others, how to solve problems, and how to make choices that are in the best interest of themselves and others. Teachers who maintain well-managed, brain-compatible classrooms empower themselves and their students to attain these goals.

Often the teacher is presumed to have one role in the classroom: Instruction. This role demands specific subject and skill knowledge, however, to successfully teach students, the teacher must cope with the social system of the classroom and the emotional needs of the individuals. The traditionally perceived role of "instructor" does not adequately address new information about the brain's integration of social-emotional and academic function. Brain research tells us that to effectively provide instruction, teachers must possess the emotional intelligence skills needed to design safe, emotionally connected, problem-solving environments. Emotional intelligence asks teachers to undertake the great task of becoming reflective about their own behavior first. The payoff is that emotional intelligence puts the heart back into schools. Teachers often choose their field by following their hearts on a mission to make a difference. Brain research, ironically, puts the heart back in education.

See also: Classroom Environment; Proactive Classroom Management Strategies.

Further Readings

Bailey, B.A. (2000). *Easy to love, Difficult to Discipline.* New York, NY: HarperCollins.

Bailey, B.A. (2000). *I Love You Rituals.* New York, NY: Quill.

Bailey, B.A. (2001). *Conscious Discipline: 7 Basic Skills for Brain Smart Classroom Management.* Oviedo, FL: Loving Guidance.

Bailey, B.A. (2003). *There's Got to Be a Better Way: Discipline that Works* Oviedo, FL: Loving Guidance.

Jensen, E. (2003) *Tools for Engagement: Managing Emotional States for Learner Success* San Diego, CA: The Brain Store.

Marzano, R.J. (2003). *Classroom Management that Works: Research-based Strategies for Every Teacher.* Alexandria, VA: Association for Supervision and Curriculum Development.

Schwartz, J.M., Begley, S. (2002). *The Mind and the Brain: Neuroplasticity and the Power of Mental Force.* New York, NY: ReganBooks.

Sousa, D.A. (2001). *How the Brain Learns.* Thousand Oaks, CA: Corwin Press, Inc.

BECKY A. BAILEY, PH.D.

Cognitive Disabilities

Cognition is the psychological outcome of complex human brain processes. Neuroscientists, psychologists and educationists view cognitive processes as including memory, emotion, attention, language, planning, judgment, thought, and insight. Cognitive disabilities can affect any of these processes in isolation or in combination. For example, some individuals who have trouble learning language exhibit other cognitive problems such as problems with certain kinds of auditory memory. Yet others may show problems with understanding or use of language with little apparent difficulty in other cognitive areas. There are individuals with reading disturbances, for example, who when tested carefully show problems with certain types of auditory memory and perception. But there are others who might just have problems using certain speech sounds or learning vocabulary with no other cognitive limitations.

In recent years, new brain imaging technologies such as functional magnetic resonance imaging (fMRI) have allowed neuroscientists to peer into the working brain, to better understand the brain mechanisms that underlie cognition. Whereas several years ago researchers thought that many cognitive functions could be localized to discrete regions of the brain, they now believe that cognitive processing occurs in networks of cells distributed across the brain that become wired together over time. These processing networks allow brain cells to multitask so that one region of the brain may be involved in such different tasks as mathematical computation, language and same/different discrimination. Apparently, cognitive networks are plastic and can change over time. This permits humans to learn new information throughout their lifespan. It also enables individuals with cognitive disabilities to increase their brain capacity and efficiency by building new networks and, in effect, "rerouting" information through new pathways.

There are several cognitive networks that are currently under study. Researchers are especially interested in attentional networks as attentional disturbances affect children as well as adults with a variety of cognitive problems. **Attention,** like most cognitive processes, does not appear to occur in a specific area of the brain, rather there are attentional networks that involve portions of the brain stem, the emotional centers of the brain in the limbic system, and the pre-frontal cortex. Attention is modulated by neurotransmitters that enable a person to stay alert, focus on behaviorally relevant tasks, and follow-through. Neurotransmitters now seen as important to attention include acetylcholine and dopamine.

Memory, like attention, requires a wide distribution of neurons throughout the brain. The hippocampus, a small horseshoe shaped region of the limbic system, is important for learning new information and effortful retrieval of information. The hippocampus appears to allow us to search our brains for details of experience that can be put together into a cohesive memory. Information associated with very negative experiences appears to require activation of the amygdala, an almond shaped region just adjacent to the hippocampus. But, easily accessed memories do not require the hippocampus or amygdala and can be activated directly through various regions of the cortex.

Brain researchers have known for many years that language is largely localized to the left hemisphere, specifically the regions of the left hemisphere that surround the sylvian fissure. Although some communication skills such as modulation of tone of voice and use of gestures are processed in the right hemisphere, formal properties of language such as phonology, syntax, and semantics, are lateralized to the left hemisphere in most people. Mathematical and musical skills share the right and left hemisphere regions of the parietal and temporal lobes, respectively. Executive function, the ability to plan, organize, and anticipate consequences of actions, is attributed to regions of the pre-frontal lobes, especially the dorsolateral pre-frontal regions.

Children and adults can exhibit cognitive disabilities for a variety of reasons. Strokes or other brain injuries can occur at any time of life and affect cognitive skills. Cognitive skills, which develop during childhood and adolescence along fairly consistent and predicable timetables, can be also be delayed or interrupted. The etiology of developmental cognitive disabilities is an area of intense investigation. Limitations in cognitive development can occur as a result of a generalized developmental delay but are also evident in individuals without any known neurological illness or injury. To some extent cognitive aptitudes may be inherited but cognition is also affected by environmental exposure and experience. As cognition covers almost all higher human intellectual processes, any learning problem could be considered a cognitive disability.

This chapter will describe four types of cognitive disabilities commonly identified in educational settings that are likely to affect academic success: attentional problems, language/communication problems, nonverbal learning disabilities, and executive function disorders. It should be noted that there are several more pervasive disabilities that broadly affect cognitive skills and learning such as generalized developmental delay and autistic spectrum disorders that are beyond the scope of this chapter.

Attentional Disturbances

There are several attentional networks in the brain that can easily be disrupted by mechanisms that strain or block blood flow to the brain. As a result, attentional problems are frequently a residual of traumatic brain injury. Attentional problems are also a component of other cognitive disabilities. When an individual exhibits attentional problems in the absence of neurological illness or injury and without other specific cognitive impairment, it is referred to as ADHD (attention deficit hyperactivity disorder.) *The Diagnostic and Statistical Manual of Developmental Disorders* (DSM IV) breaks **ADHD** down into three types:

- ADHD—predominantly inattentive type with at least six symptoms of inattention

- ADHD—predominantly hyperactive/ impulsive type with at least six symptoms of hyperactivity or impulsivity
- ADHD combined type—six or more symptoms of both inattention and hyperactivity-impulsivity that have persisted for at least six months.

According to the DSM IV a child must exhibit a preponderance of (six or more) symptoms in a given category both at home and in school to be diagnosed with ADHD. Symptoms of inattention may include failure to attend to details, frequent careless mistakes, difficulty sustaining attention, failure to listen, inability to follow through on instructions or finish work, problems with organization, avoidance of tasks that require sustained mental effort, forgetfulness, and distractibility. Symptoms of hyperactivity may include fidgeting or squirming, leaving the seat when remaining seated is expected, running about or climbing excessively, difficulty engaging in leisure activities quietly, or excessive talking. And, symptoms of impulsivity may include interrupting or intruding on others, blurting out answers before questions have been completed, and difficulty awaiting turns.

Children or adults can be diagnosed with ADHD by a physician or psychologist and are usually treated using behavioral modification techniques and/or with medications that improve attentional focus and quiet hyperactivity. A fourteen month multimodal treatment study of ADHD conducted in 1992 by the National Institute for Mental Health randomly assigned 579 children to four conditions: medication only, medication and behavioral treatment, behavioral treatment only, and community care. The results revealed that children who received a combination of behavioral treatment and medication showed the most robust improvement. Re-evaluation of the children after twenty-four months showed that 68 percent of the combined group, 56 percent in the medical management only group, and 34 percent in the behavioral treatment group continued to show improvement.

Language/Communication Problems

Language encompasses several symbolic abilities that enable an individual to share information as well as communicate ideas and needs. Language includes auditory and verbal symbol systems as well as written symbol systems. Language impairments can result from neurological illness or injury to the left or dominant hemisphere and are usually called aphasia or alexia. Language problems can also be part of pervasive cognitive disturbances. However, as with other cognitive disabilities language disabilities can occur developmentally in relative isolation. Variously called specific language impairment (SLI) or developmental language disorder (DLD) the cause(s) are largely unknown. Etiologic factors may include: inherited genetic traits, problems with auditory processing of the rapid elements of speech problems with development of certain language regions in the brain, the myelination of brain path-ways, or other as yet unidentified environmental or physiological factors. Speech Language Pathologists diagnose language problems that affect auditory-verbal language comprehension and usage. Psychologists and **learning disability** specialists may diagnose dyslexia, a language problem that specifically affects reading, the comprehension of written language.

Language problems may specifically affect development or use of: the sound system (phonology) of language, grammatical formulation and word order (syntax), and the ability to understand or use words and word-endings meaningfully (semantics.) These are often referred to by linguists as the formal properties of language. Children and adults can also demonstrate problems learning or using language to communicate effectively in social contexts. These communication impairments, some-times referred to as social learning or pragmatic language impairment, may be seen in association with other language problems or be part of a syndrome of nonverbal learning disabilities (NVLD).

Treatment of language disorders falls under the domain of the speech-language pathologist and may effectively involve a combination of individual language intervention, teacher collaboration, and technologi-cal interventions such as the Fast ForWord Products. Treatment of dyslexia usually falls under the domain of the learning disability specialist.

Nonverbal Learning Disabilities

First described in 1967 by Mykelbust and Johnson, disorders of nonver-bal learning often include problems with visual-spatial skills, mathematical concepts and social skill learning. Like other cognitive impairments, nonverbal disabilities can occur as a result of neurological illness or injury; usually caused by damage to the right, or nondominant, cerebral hemi-sphere. Often this is referred to as right-hemisphere dysfunction. Psychol-ogists and speech-language pathologists may diagnose NVLD when it occurs in children, although psychologists are usually better able to specify the visual-spatial, constructional, and mathematical components of the disorder. Children with nonverbal learning disabilities often show subtle problems that are not obvious until school-age years. The children may appear as "loaners" when young children but as they progress in school may develop specific problems learning mathematical concepts and devel-oping other performance skills like drawing, construction, and the ability to complete jigsaw puzzles. Because the social and visual spatial aspects of their disability are not routinely or systematically assessed or taught in school, the child may not be diagnosed unless a parent or educator requests a special assessment.

Treatment of NVLD usually consists of addressing the specific cogni-tive impairments through a combination of learning disability interven-tion for the mathematical and visual-spatial components and speech-language pathology or social work for social skill development. Occupational therapy may also treat the visual-motor components.

Executive Function Disorder

Executive function refers to the higher cognitive skills of planning, organization, judgment, and insight. They are necessary for appropriate behavior, social responsibility and self-regulation. Executive function is generally attributed to areas of the prefrontal cortex, the very front of the human brain. The prefrontal cortex is the last area of the human brain to mature so executive functions are thought to begin emerging around four years of age and continue to develop for many years, perhaps into the fourth decade. Executive function disorders are often associated with traumatic brain injuries but can occur developmentally. Executive function disabilities are diagnosed by psychologists or neuropsychologists through testing of volition, planning, purposive action, effective performance, and working memory. In academic environments, students with executive function disorders may seem impulsive, socially inappropriate or insensitive, and disorganized. Some researchers have asserted that executive function disorders are a component of ADHD, so children with executive function disorders may seem similar to children with ADHD, although weaknesses on executive function assessment can occur in the absence of attentional difficulties.

Treatment of various components of executive function disorder may fall under the domain of the learning disability specialist, speech-language pathologist, social worker, or psychologist. The learning disability specialist might work with a student to develop learning strategies for planning and organization. The speech-language pathologist might address working memory skills and language organization. A psychologist or social worker might help the teacher or family with strategies for enhancing self-regulation and socially appropriate behavior.

See also: **Language Acquisition and Disorders; Learning Disabilities; Trauma; Social Context of Learning.**

Further Readings

Devinsky, O., D'Esposito, M. (2004). *Neurology of Cognitive and Behavioral Disorders.* Oxford: Oxford University Press.

Stuss, D., Knight, R. (2002). *Principles of Frontal Lobe Function.* Oxford: Oxford University Press.

MARTHA S. BURNS, PH.D., CCC-SLP

Communication

Most people have memories of talking in class during school. These memories usually involve two types of talking: answering the teacher's questions and talking to your neighbor. The latter conversations may have been motivated by a lack of interest in the work or a keen interest in the work and the desire to share thoughts with someone. This suggests that many of the latter conversations led to some form of negative intervention from the teacher because student conversations were not seen as a productive use of time in relation to the teacher's objectives. It does not take long before the student realizes that the teacher dominates the talking in the classroom and the students tolerate the listening.

In her book "Raising Life Long Learners" Lucy Calkins states that talking is the foundation of literacy. She cites the research of Gorden Wells regarding the talk of children from a variety of socioeconomic backgrounds engaged in conversation at home and at school. Wells found that even in the most "linguistically deprived" homes children received far more support for oral language development than they did at school. Wells believes children do not have sufficient opportunities to discuss their ideas in the classroom. They are at the mercy of the teacher, passive followers.

Talking has an important role in the development of literacy. Developing students' literacy knowledge and skills is a primary goal of education. The brain is equipped to speak and listen. It seems reasonable then for educators to bring a more balanced approach for students to speak and listen in the classroom and make this natural communication process an integral part of the learning process at all grade levels. The development of literacy is not confined to the primary classroom. It is a life-long pursuit.

Before Reading and Writing there is Listening and Speaking

Language is something humans are wired to do. We are born with an innate ability to develop language. It is unique to the human species and is a marvelous accomplishment for a number of reasons. At the very least, it gives form to our memories and words to express our thoughts. The ability to listen to the environment and convey to others whether or not it is safe is seen by neuroscience as the brain's first job, ensuring survival of the individual and the species. Communication is also a matter of social survival. People with poor communication skills generally do not succeed in their personal and professional lives.

Spoken language is the pathway from the concrete world to the world of abstract thought and consciousness. Language is the vehicle that opens up a universe of endless possibilities. Once you can label the things around you, your brain will develop a filing system where you store these representations of your world. The potential for pulling the files forward at will, juggling them, juxtaposing them, and in the process creating new ideas is vast. When you combine the communicating of these ideas with others, you create social constructs, giving practical expression to your notions.

Language lives in the brain. The job of supporting language is not, however, evenly distributed across the whole brain; rather it is concentrated in the left hemisphere. Language initially develops in both sides of the brain but by the age of five, shifts to lodge in the left hemisphere for 95 percent of people. Individual and sex-related differences contribute to the fact that everyone's brain is different. Although the standard description of the left hemisphere as the seat of language is true for 95 percent of the population, it is not true for everyone and the degree of dominance is not always the same. People who are left handed (but still left hemisphere dominant) and even people who are right handed but have left handed family members may show more bilateral participation in language. Interestingly, women show more bilateral participation in language than men.

The two main language structures in the left hemisphere are Broca's area and Wernicke's area. Broca's area stores vocabulary, grammar, and orchestrates articulation. Broca's area allows us to speak with expression. It is located next to the part of the motor cortex that controls the muscles of the mouth and lips. Wernicke's area is the receptive language area, registering incoming words. Analysis of word meaning is carried out either in or very close to Wernicke's area. Wernicke's area is located near the auditory cortex.

Language is not exclusively a left-hemisphere function. The right hemisphere shares language functions with the left hemisphere. It appears that the right hemisphere does more for some individuals than others, and on average more in women than in men. A study of what the right hemisphere contributes to language, given the left hemisphere is intact, indicates that the right hemisphere is involved in semantics and pragmatics but syntax is the province of the left hemisphere.

The advancement of technology now allows us to look inside the living brain. Using PET scans, neuroscientists report that spoken language production is a highly complex process. Before we can utter a word, the brain must first assemble appropriate words in Wernicke's area and then relay them to Broca's area for transshipment to the motor cortex that controls speech production. When preparing to produce a spoken sentence the brain uses not only Broca's and Wernicke's areas but also calls on several other neural networks scattered throughout the left hemisphere. Nouns are processed through one set of patterns; verbs are processed by separate neural networks. The more complex the sentence, the more areas in the brain that are activated in both hemispheres of the brain.

Research into sign language supports the concept that we are born to communicate. Research has demonstrated that sign language is not just a loose connection of hand gestures thrown together at the whim of the signer. Sign languages are highly structured linguistic systems with all of the grammatical complexity of spoken languages.

Reading and **writing** are critical communication skills in our society. Both require the development of oral language if they are to be learned effectively. Reading, as noted above, seems to be particularly dependent on the foundation of strong oral skills of spoken language.

Skill in decontextualized oral language (words stand on their own) may provide a bridge from oral language to literacy. The ability to produce decontextualized speech—a narrative—emerges first in conversation and receives significant support from children's interactions with others. The process of becoming skilled in decontexualized language begins early in language development, but the process continues throughout childhood and beyond. School requires the skill of decontexualized language use, oral and written, and it is important for teachers to provide scaffolding to children's talk in school to enable their development of writing skills.

But Students are Supposed to be Quiet in School

There are a variety of reasons why teachers do most of the talking in the classroom. First, there is a long-standing belief that the teacher is the expert and the students are empty vessels to be filled. This view has dominated all levels of education since the beginning of public schooling in North America. The problem is not confined to the school classroom. The federal government talks while the state listens; the state talks while the Superintendents listen; the Superintendent talks while the school-based administration listens; and school-based administration talks while the teachers listen. This is not the case for all local systems but there are enough who perpetuate the idea that those below are empty vessels to be filled that the attitude permeates the education scene in North America.

A second reason for curtailing student conversation in the classroom seems to be located in the teacher's mandate to cover vast amounts of curriculum, and perform numerous duties not pertaining to classroom instruction—collecting pizza money—and deal with the constant waves of reform. Evidence that it is critical to the depth of learning to engage students in talk about what they are learning is buried beneath an overcrowded desk.

Third, keeping students quiet in the classroom is a long-standing management strategy. The quiet student is the working student and is therefore the one learning the material. The concept of focused, structured conversations is often seen as beneficial to educators during workshops, but just as quickly questioned with students. The problem is the solution.

Human beings quickly lose interest in learning when it does not involve them in an active way. Sitting and listening, even doing hands-on activities does not always sustain the interest of the human brain if the mind is not engaged at the same time. The thinking part of the human brain works in concert with the emotional part of the brain and the emotional part of the brain demands a more meaningful, purposeful approach to learning, one that fully engages the brain in the learning process. Talking about important ideas and sharing insights in a subject area is a powerful way to get the brain to sit up and take notice of the material at any age.

Ideas to Get Students Structured and Focused for Meaningful Conversation

Invite people to begin talking with each other within five minutes of opening the class. The sooner learners have an opportunity to engage with the material and each other, the sooner they are hooked into the work and the realization that they will not be passive receivers of information. Through carefully structured and thoughtfully focused questions and/or a task, people of all ages will quickly "dig into" the work and remain engaged for long periods of time.

Research on the human brain demonstrates that the emotional regions of the brain are more powerful than the thinking and reasoning regions of the brain. That is, emotional considerations in any situation will be the first order of business for a brain, learning is second. It is therefore important to organize conversations between learners in an emotionally safe environment. Many learners have had difficult experiences with teachers, facilitators and classmates judging their thinking and are not comfortable in settings where they are expected to talk to the whole group.

People are much more likely to engage in early conversations in pairs. This conversation format is called "A/B Partners." At first allow partners to be friends, it will remove some of the stress. Decide who is A and who is B in the space of ten seconds. The next set of instruction outlines the process or structure for the conversation. This includes the focus question or task, the time they have to complete the task, and other details for the question or task. Invite people to take a moment to think about the process, have a twenty second conversation regarding: "Do we get it?" and then an opportunity to ask clarifying questions. Reduce the number of questions by putting the instructions on an overhead or on chart paper. The time constraint signals boundaries around the conversation—students cannot talk for as long as they want. It may take three to four times before people believe that you really mean "ten seconds." This will be irritating for learners who are used to having several reminders before actually settling down.

The brain needs time to recall any previous information that may be needed for the task at hand. It is important therefore to provide between thirty seconds to two minutes (depending on the work) for learners to think alone—generate ideas, connect to prior knowledge—before engaging with their partner. It may take some learners Zlonger before they are comfortable with the idea that they need to be working with the question or task.

The next step provides both people "the floor." The amount of time each person has for talking about their ideas depends on the age of the learners, their experience with focused structured conversation. Fifteen to thirty seconds is ample time for primary students. As they become more skilled in listening and speaking, they will require more time. For later elementary students it would require thirty to forty-five seconds in the beginning. Middle school students may only handle thirty to forty-five seconds in the early stages. High school students usually need sixty to ninty seconds.

For time efficiency it is helpful for the teacher to control who speaks first. As students become familiar with the process they can decide among themselves who speaks first.

Most learners will be irritated with the time constraints, however, as you teach them how to organize and support their thinking and then articulate their thinking to someone else, the time lines will increase.

Many children have very weak speaking skills, using only utterances or clipped sentences to communicate. You may find you need to spend time increasing their vocabulary, organize and support their thinking, and help them clearly articulate their thinking to others.

Accountability

As part of the process, there needs to be some accountability for having the conversation. There are several ways to know whether or not students are focused.

Reporting out from each group signals to students that every partnership will have to share their thinking with the whole group. Students are more inclined to report out when they are not solely responsible for the response. The accountability process is enhanced when the teacher records the responses on chart paper and posts the list. The most important aspect of recording the thinking is the information it provides for all the students and it can be used as a reference point later in the lesson or unit. Learners of all ages begin to take pride in their thinking being recorded and posted.

Reporting out a task provides the opportunity for diversifying the work. Provide learners with a list of ways they can organize their product to ensure all major learning styles are included in the list. When there are several learning styles in one group, the product is particularly rich.

From the A/B Partner format move into trios then quads. If table groups are larger than four (hold the size to eight) structure conversations that include everyone at the table. Invite people to report out to the whole class, ask for volunteers in the beginning stages. As the learners become more comfortable with sharing their thinking with others, randomly call on people. Over time teach learners the skills of active listening and speaking so they are understood.

Peer assessment becomes a natural process when learners are used to engaging in meaningful conversations. Each has skills for speaking clearly and supporting their thinking and each has skills for listening and helping the speaker to clarify their thinking.

Cognitive Strategies

The focused structured conversations can be used with the many learning strategies available to staff developers and classroom teachers. For example, "Reciprocal Teaching" may be organized in the following manner:

- Organize students into A/B Partners.
- Alert them to the fact they will be teaching the information you are teaching to their partner.
- At the end of the teaching sequence or in the middle of it, provide one minute for students to organize their notes and thinking in preparation for teaching.

- Provide two to three minutes for each person to teach, remind listeners to be listening carefully for new ideas or content they missed.
- Have pairs report out their experience, their learning of the content.

Many regions of the brain are engaged in communication processes and not every brain uses the regions in quite the same way. The differences between male and female brains in the language speaking centers are particularly noticeable. It is important therefore that there needs to be a balance in the types of strategies, the conversation formats, the tasks and questions and the time lines to accommodate all learners.

See also: **Language Acquisition and Disorders; Classroom Environment. Deaf and Hard of Hearing.**

Further Readings

Davis, B., Sumara, D., Luce-Kapler, R. (2000). *Engaging Minds*. Mahway, NJ: Lawrence Erlbaum Associates, Publishers.

Gallas, K. (1994). *The Language of Learning*. New York: Teachers' College, Columbia University.

Nelson, J. (2001). *The Art of Focused Conversation for Schools*. Gabriola Island, BC: New Society Publishers.

SUSAN CLAYTON AND SUE ELLIOTT

Constructivism

According to constructivists, we learn by connecting new knowledge to the knowledge we already have. Twigs on a tree cannot grow out of nothing but must grow on an already existing twig or branch. In the same way, each higher, more complex, more sophisticated level of knowledge must be connected to, constructed from, a pre-existing foundation of knowledge. Jean Piaget, the widely recognized seminal thinker about constructivism as the architecture of knowledge, said that our initial learning as infants starts from what is innate, such as the sucking reflex.

For each new object of learning, we must construct, from the ground up, a "tree" of knowledge (a knowledge network or cognitive schema). These trees of knowledge or networks are specifically constructed for what the learner is actively experiencing and processing (exploring, practicing, figuring out, creatively and critically thinking about). **Transfer** is problematic because the twigs or branches of one tree cannot magically become the twigs or branches of a different tree. Similarly, one kind of knowledge (knowledge network) cannot magically become a different one. However, if the kinds of knowledge are very similar, one network can suffice. For example, a student can transfer basic knowledge of how to do addition to different addition problems and perhaps even to simple addition-based word problems but not to complex word problems without first having constructed knowledge of (learned) how to solve such problems.

Synthesis, on the other hand, occurs when two or more different knowledge networks are comparably well developed enough to connect, thereby constructing an inter-network that is richer and more complex than the component networks. A student takes Art History of the Renaissance one term and, during that term, constructs a relatively high level of knowledge for the subject. Then, the next term, the student takes History of the Renaissance. Perhaps halfway through that term, only after having constructed a more-than-basic level of knowledge of the religious, cultural, scientific history of the Renaissance, will that student be able to have an "aha" experience about Renaissance art: "Now I see why those artists were painting those subjects and in those ways!" What has happened is that the two networks have connected, constructing a complex inter-network.

The constructivist teacher's goal is to help students construct their knowledge networks and inter-networks. The image of branch- and twig-like structures growing and then inter-connecting in complex networks is, in fact, an accurate picture of the neurophysiological creation and structure of knowledge in the brain.

Neuroscientists say that the brain is the most complex entity in the known universe. However, as information about the brain and how it functions is voluminous, possibly arcane, and ever-increasing, we will focus here only on the least we need to know to understand how the brain constructs networks and inter-networks of knowledge (learns) and how to use that information in the classroom to help students learn.

To begin, the brain has more than one hundred billion nerve cells (neurons); each neuron has one body and tens of thousands of branches and twigs (dendrites) growing from its body. If you want to see what a neuron looks like, observe the leafless branches and twigs of a tree in the winter. Further, there are communication connections (synapses) between neurons, which create the networks and inter-networks for remembering and thinking. Each neuron might have ten thousand receiving and sending synaptic connections with other neurons, creating immeasurably complex neural networks and inter-networks.

Both trees and neurons are organic, living structures. They grow in a nourishing environment and wither or die when deprived of it. What environment nourishes the construction of neural networks so that we can increase and enrich our knowledge, and what environment does not? The answers to these questions are found in the converging neuro-scientific, Pigetian, and classroom/field research, discussed below.

Marion Diamond is the pioneering brain-and-learning researcher who, in 1967, found that dendrites grow when subjects are experiencing and interacting with novel and challenging environments. Since then, other researchers have corroborated her findings. For example, in 1993, Bob Jacobs, Matthew Schall, and Arnold B. Scheibel discovered that dendrite growth reflects the learner's educational and vocational experiences. They also found that the dendrites furthest from the neuron's body, those grown on the highest level of the knowledge structure, are the most capable of responding to complex stimuli in the environment. This research suggests that as and because we are actively experiencing, exploring, practicing, figuring out, creatively and critically thinking about specific objects of learning, the specific networks, which *are* our learning, are growing, physiologically constructing the new knowledge. Thus, the more we actively experience and process an object of learning, the more highly grown are the resultant networks and, commensurately, the more refined, in-depth, and sophisticated is our understanding of this object of learning. The constructivist view is that the more we grow, the more we know.

Additionally, the more a person experiences and processes a specific object of learning, the more abundant and stronger are the synaptic connections in that network. The result is a greater ability to do **creative** and **critical thinking** within that network (about that object of learning) and also to construct syntheses or inter-networks between networks of comparable development for even more complex creative and critical thinking.

Moreover, **motivation** increases when learners have the opportunity to construct new knowledge by their own active processing because the brain produces endorphins, the so-called pleasure hormone, when the brain is thus actively engaged. The brain is born knowing how to construct new knowledge and feels pleasure when constructing both new and higher levels of knowledge.

Teachers, then, invite students to learn by giving them opportunities to construct new knowledge networks, which the brain is innately motivated and able to do. Students start learning something new by making a connection with something they already know because, like twigs on a tree, dendrites cannot grow from nothing; they must be constructed on something that is already there. Students also need opportunities to work cooperatively with others, to get and give feedback, to hear other points of view, and to reflect with self-awareness, all of which contribute to the construction of richer and more complex neural networks than what one person might be able to construct alone.

How does this apply to a classroom when the object of learning is a complex academic subject? Classroom and field research conducted with more than six thousand subjects from different cultures, from second graders to graduate students to educators, finds that human beings learn a new skill or concept in sequential stages. This process corresponds with the process Piaget found in his research as the one by which infants from birth to two years learn new skills and concepts. This process also corresponds with the research on the brain's constructive learning process. These three converging areas of research find that learning starts with what the learner already knows and then is constructed, through experiencing and processing, stage upon stage, to higher and higher levels of knowledge, skill, and understanding.

What kind of environment nourishes the construction of neural networks? Learners' active and inter-active experiencing and processing of an object of learning is the nourishing environment. On the other hand, an environment that does not include these opportunities is not conducive to the construction of complex networks of deep and rich knowledge and understanding. Also, when a learner ceases to use an area of knowledge, its neurophysiological structure, its neural network, is in danger of withering away: a rule of the brain is "use it or lose it."

The converging brain, Piagetian, and classroom/field research provides guidelines for how to develop and implement constructivist curriculum and pedagogy.

Constructivist educators might start by identifying what students should know and be able to do at the end of the unit, lesson, course, or multi-course program. Then they would identify what knowledge students need as the foundation upon which to construct that highest level and ask, "Will they be able to see and do *that* if they do not first know and can do *this?*" They would continue this de-constructing process until they identify a task that will allow each student to construct the critical first connection with the unique and idiosyncratic knowledge networks in each student's brain. For example, this is a successful constructivist assignment that invites students to construct a personal connection that will prepare them to read *Hamlet:* "A young college student accidentally finds out that his new stepfather, the most powerful businessman in the city, had killed the student's father and then married the student's mother. However, the student has no physical proof of the murder. How does he feel? What should he do?"

Students think about it by themselves. Then, in small groups, they discuss their ideas. Finally, as a whole class, they talk and think together about all their ideas. Everyone now has a foundation upon which to construct the next higher level of understanding. These students are prepared to read *Hamlet,* to personally and thoughtfully connect to, and understand it.

It is implicit in the theory and practice of constructivism that when students have the opportunity to be active and inter-active constructive learners, they are motivated and capable learners.

See also: **Nature of Knowledge: Teaching Model for the Brain.**

Further Readings

Brooks, J.G., Brooks, M.G. (1999). *In Search of Understanding: The Case for Constructivist Classrooms.* Alexandria, VA: ASCD.

Diamond, M. (1967). Extensive cortical depth measurements and neuron size increases in the cortex of environmentally enriched rats. *Journal of Comparative Neurology* 131:357–364.

Jacobs, B., Schall, M., Scheibel, A.B. (1993). A quantitative dendritic analysis of Wernicke's area in humans. II. Gender, hemispheric, and environmental factors. *Journal of Comparative Neurology* 327:97–111.

Lambert, L., Walker, D., Zimmerman, D.P., Cooper, J.E., Lambert, M.D., Gardner, M.E., Szabo, M. (2002). *The Constructivist Leader* (2nd ed.). NY: Teachers College Press.

Smilkstein, R. (2002). *We're Born to Learn: Using the Brain's Natural Learning Process to Create Today's Curriculum*. Thousand Oaks, CA: Corwin Press.

RITA SMILKSTEIN, PH.D.

Creativity

Creativity has long been the province of psychologists, describing at a high level of speculation what goes on in the mind during creative thought. Psychologists suspect that the brains of creative people make stronger associations between seemingly unrelated ideas. In other words, when one node of the memory network is activated, distant nodes are more likely to be activated as well. This allows the mind to bring together seemingly unrelated components, which is the essential ingredient in novelty and creativity.

Creativity is a fundamental activity of human information processing. It is generally agreed to include two defining characteristics: The ability to produce work that is (1) original or unexpected, and (2) useful or adaptive. While much has been written about creativity from social, psychological, developmental, cognitive, and historical perspectives, less had been known about the brain mechanisms that underlie creative thinking.

Sensible Neuroanatomy

Now, inevitably, neurobiologists—scientists that study the brain—are entering the fray, hauling along their favorite tool: brain-imaging technologies that measure *the where* and *the how* of the brain during creative thinking.

The capacity to identify the brain areas that are recruited during information processing has been enhanced by brain imaging technologies that identify where the brain structures and processes information. Modern brain research conceptualizes cognitive function as hierarchically ordered. The cerebral cortex, and in particular the prefrontal cortex, is at the top of that hierarchy, representing the neural basis of higher cognitive functions. The data suggests that creative thinking is the result of common mental processes. Brain function conceptualizes information processing as hierarchically structured. The brain functions localize the most sophisticated mental abilities in the prefrontal cortex. This is to say that the prefrontal cortex contributes highly integrative functions to the conscious experience, enabling novel combinations of information.

Consciousness is defined as the selection of various attributes such as self-reflection, memory, attention, and perception, which were ordered in a functional hierarchy with the frontal lobe. The brain has developed two different types of neural systems, each designed to extract a different kind of information from the environment.

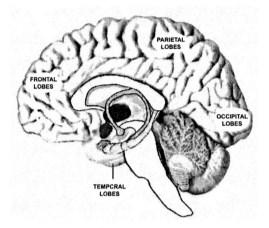

The figure shows the locations of the four main lobes involved in the creative process and the prefrontal cortex lies in the most front of the frontal lobe.

The prefrontal cortex region is involved in executive function; that is, it further integrates already highly processed information, formulates plans and strategies for behavior in a given situation and instructs the adjacent motor cortices to perform their roles. At all levels of the functional hierarchy, neural structures have direct access to activating the motor system, but behavior that is based on prefrontal activation is sophisticated.

The frontal lobe does not receive direct sensory input nor store long-term memory. The prefrontal cortex, which comprises approximately half of the frontal lobe, integrates highly processed information to enable still higher cognitive functions such as a social charge, abstract thinking, planning, and determined action to provide the communications to exercise these complex cognitive functions. Creativity requires cognitive abilities, such as working memory, continuous attention, cognitive flexibility, and judgment of propriety, that are typically ascribed to the prefrontal cortex. Not surprisingly, the prefrontal cortex must play a central role in creativity.

The first step in converting novel combinations of information into creative work is gaining an insight. Once an insight occurs, the prefrontal cortex can bring together the higher cognitive functions to the problem, including central processes such as directing continuous attention, retrieving relevant memories, buffering that information, and ordering it in space and time. All at the same time thinking abstractly and calculating consequences and suitability. Innumerous insights turn out to be incorrect, incomplete, or trivial, so judging which insight to pursue and which to discard requires prefrontal cortex integration.

The prefrontal cortex engages highly processed information to enable still higher cognitive functions, such as self-construct, self-reflective consciousness, complex social function, abstract thinking, and cognitive flexibility.

To understand the role of the frontal lobe in the creative process it is valuable to provide a more detailed view of how the prefrontal cortex relates to the later posterior cortices—the temporal lobe, the parietal, and the occipital lobes. The function of the posterior lobes is primarily devoted to perception and long-term memory. Working memory that is processed in the prefrontal cortex is described as the ability to process information in action. It is a monitoring system of ongoing events that temporarily keeps the mind informed of that which is important to the situation. As the working memory has limited capacity, it access a *'buffering filter'* that appears to be a prerequisite for cognitive flexibility, abstract thinking, strategic planning, and access to long-term memory. The immediate conscious experience of the here and now are made possible by the sustained buffering of information in working memory. It is therefore suggested that a working memory buffer is critical, indeed a prerequisite for creative thinking.

It would be neglectful to not address the power of knowledge. Facts and novel combinations of stored knowledge are implemented in two distinct neural structures. The prefrontal cortex and the lateral cortices, temporal, parietal and occipital lobes house knowledge.

To claim that scientists are on the verge of mapping out, neuron–by-neuron and synapse-by-synapse, the brain processes that generate creative ideas, would be naïve and irresponsible.

Creativity is a function of mental and emotional flexibility. And, most important, these attributes can be learned and enhanced throughout life. Though some would argue that intelligence is genetically controlled, it is believed that no one is restricted solely to one's genetic, cultural, or educational heritage. It is the spirit of an individual that determines how intelligent, emotionally or mentally, one aspires to be. No genetic endowment or environmental influence has precedence over the human spirit.

Promoting Creative Thinking

The most powerful way to develop creativity in students is not only in the telling of and showing creative thinking, but also in planning set-up time to allow the creative process to evolve. Although there is no unique personality associated with creativity, creative people tend to tolerate ambiguity, be open to varied experiences, be attracted to complexity and novelty, and display broad interests. They are more likely to have a tendency toward introversion than extroversion. As well they tend to be independent, enthusiastic, and hard working. People with a wide range of interests are likely to have knowledge from many different fields, providing a wide range of elements that are the raw ingredients for novel ideas. By being open to ambiguity and complexity, a person is less likely to reject a novel idea before it has risen to the level of consciousness— the mark of low latent inhibition. Introverts are more likely to tolerate the long hours of solitary thought necessary for creativity.

Based on what scientists are learning about the creative process, it seems safe to say that cultivating creativity begins with acquiring knowledge and experience. Read widely, live life fully, engage with as many knowledgeable people as possible, and increase the number of facts and memories available to be recombined into novel thoughts and ideas. Allow the mind to consider seemingly ridiculous juxtapositions; open new neural pathways to what creative people seem to do effortlessly.

By all indications of research narrowing the creative process these hallmarks are a very good beginning to preserve the creative thinking process: (1) acquire knowledge—developing long-term memory storage is highly correlated, (2) perseverance in the face of failure—several bad ideas must be sifted through to find the best combination, (3) risk taking—willingness to try something new, (4) open minded, and (5) tolerance for ambiguity, these traits seem to require the use of new neural pathways, thus breaking through the habituation of precedent neural pathways.

Compatible Instructional Strategies

- *Open Ended Questioning Techniques—open-ended questions* are useful for encouraging creative thinking because they rarely have one answer and they stimulate further inquiry. They ask for clarification, probe for assumptions, search for reasons and evidence while searching for implications and consequences.

- *Discovery Learning*—problem-based learning activities are usually labor intensive and time consuming. Look to collaborate with other teachers.

  - Identify some complex issues or problem situations selecting a local issue, such as environmental preservation or city planning to add relevancy to the process.

  - Regional and national issues can be found in books, newspapers, magazines and television news, and documentary programs.

  - State the problem in a way this is interesting for students and that puts the situation in an intriguing context. The statement should suggest avenues they can pursue but should not provide all the information and resources they will need.

- *Metaphors*—Teach through metaphors—students can understand many new and complicated concepts when the concepts are compared to dissimilar ones that the student already knows and understands. People who think metaphorically can see connections where others cannot. Therefore, successful teachers can stretch creativity by assisting the students to interpret or create metaphors.

- *Reflection*—provide plenty of time for personal and/or written reflection. Leave the perplexing issue alone to allow for pondering potential outcomes.

- *Walk Away*—build time into the learning problem to walk away and begin another task. Thus allowing students time for processing and internal brainstorming. Approach the dilemma with a fresh start at a later time. Most creative solutions are reported to transpire when one is doing something else. The brain needs **processing time.**

Note on Aging and Creativity

The tendency to adhere to outdated rules might be compounded by the fact that mental states that enable the spontaneous processing mode, such as day-dreaming go dramatically down with age. It seems that, as we age, a certain version of reality becomes *hardwired* through decades of reinforcement. The result is that the continuously diminishing ability for cognitive flexibility is overpowered. As we age we must continuously seek new ideas and solutions to vitalize the development of new neural pathways keeping the creative process effervescent.

See also: **Aging Brain; Art; Critical Thinking; Gifted; Play.**

Further Readings

Andreasen, N.C. (2005). *The Creating Brain, The Neuroscience of Genius.* New York, N.Y.: Dana Press.

Kraft, U. (2005, April). Unleashing Creativity. *Scientific American* 16(1):16–24.

Personality and Biological Markers of Creativity. *European Journal of Personality.* 19:83–95. http://www.uwsp.edu/education/lwilson/links/Brainbasedlinks.htm

CRISTAL L. MCGILL, PH.D.

Critical Periods (Sensitive Periods)

The research on brain development gave the early care and education field the theoretical basis for what teachers and others in the field have always known, a child's brain begins developing before birth and the early years are important productive learning years. Some brain scientists (neurologists) agree that there are critical periods of brain development during a child's life to support optimal learning opportunities. Some scientist argue that it is impossible to know how much a child's brain develops, at what rate, and whether or not there are critical periods of development without observing the brain as it develops. There is limited opportunity to do that because to do so would require the child to submit to invasive testing on their brain to answer the questions. Developmental psychologists agree that it is important to provide children with developmentally appropriate stimulus at critical periods of physical, cognitive, and social development. The age for critical periods of development and learning vary among children; however, there are typical age ranges that can be attributed to different milestones of learning.

Prior to Birth

The fetal brain is developing billions of brain cells before birth. The cells that develop the brain begin to form and migrate to the place where they belong in developing a baby's brain. Any interruption in this development and migration can cause both physical and mental challenges for the developing child. Interruptions can be caused by the mother's use of alcohol, drugs (both prescription, recreational, and over-the-counter), and illnesses or infections contracted by the mother during the pregnancy.

First Year of Life

During the first few months of life, the baby's brain is very active developing connections that are called synapses that develop pathways for learning. The development of language is constant and infants can utter every sound of every language known to man at birth. The sounds of the baby's native language will be the sounds that are supported with interactions by the adults in the baby's world. The other sounds will not be supported and will disappear thus making the child a native language speaker of one specific language. Later in life, if the growing child learns a foreign language, the early sounds may be supported and connections made with the language that the child is learning. For this reason, the earlier additional languages are introduced to children the more likely the child will become fluent in the language. There is a particular advantage of learning a second language before puberty.

After the initial phase of a baby's life where eating and sleeping take up most of the day, the baby will gradually start staying awake longer and become more socially interactive with the world around them. The brain is continuing to develop, cells are sending out synapses to connect to other cells. The baby's vision is developing and making connections with the things he or she sees regularly in the environment. He or she begins to recognize the adults who care for them and respond to the person. This connection is made allowing the baby to store knowledge in their brain. They think, "This is someone who takes care of me and feeds me." As a result, every time the person approaches the baby, he or she responds positively, even if the child is not hungry. The most fundamental reaction to something that brings pleasure is called a conditioned response. Babies have conditioned responses to many things, such as, people they connect with food, their bottle, or a favorite toy.

Language is continuing to develop at this time and exposure to sound and words is critical at this time. Children that don't develop phonemic awareness during this time will struggle. The typically developing child will start to use words to communicate. It is important to support language development by repeating back to the child what they are saying or attempting to say. Key aspects of language development are both auditory (hearing) and visual (seeing) stimulation. This also supports the social and emotional development of the child. Appropriate attachment to key adults in the child' life helps the child with social and emotional development, a key in overall brain development.

Two-to-Five Years Old

The child's brain is continuing to develop and the neurological pathways look like a large, tangled, mass of yarn. Most of the connections, or synapses for learning, are created in the first three years of a child's life. The child is curious about their world, asking many questions, and adding connections to the things they observed as a young infant and began to explore as a toddler. They begin to make conclusions, commenting on things they have never been taught, which, however, they have figured out. It is important at this stage to make sure to have many open-ended materials for children to explore, test out, and discuss. Adults are the child's source for information and must take the time to discuss what the child is thinking about, being careful to recognize *how* the child is thinking about his or her world, not just what the child is thinking. The processes of thought, if supported by the adult, will provide the child the tools he or she needs when they enter formal education settings and begin to understand the cognitive processes of reading, writing, and computation.

Six-to-Eleven Years Old

The formal school years can be broken down into two periods of learning for brain development. In the first three years, kindergarten through second grade, children are exposed to and develop skills that they need in later grades. They connect the letter sounds of their language to the alphabet code that names them; they learn to recognize numerals and attach value to them, and they begin to combine both letter sounds and value to develop reading and computation skills. Children are developing their procedural or implicit memory which is the ability to use memorized information fluently, without stopping to try to consciously recall the information. Use of multiplication tables, after they are memorized, is a good example of learning that uses implicit memory.

By third grade, implicitly memorized learning is used to think more critically, compute problems that require inference recognition, and look for the meaning in what is read. Now information is memorized using explicit or declarative memory which is the ability to take information and apply it to different situations to expand knowledge. A good example of this type of knowledge would be the understanding of how a multiplication problem is solved, using the multiplication tables. It goes further than just using implicit memory in that the learner can describe how the problem is solved rather than just recalling memorized answers. The process that the learner recalls in solving and describing how the problem was solved is learning using information in the explicit memory.

Also, by this time, the synapses are beginning to thin out. All of the things that a child has been exposed to, from birth until this time, will have caused the cells through the synapses to make connection, weaving an intricate pattern within the brain. The synapses that were not used to make additional connections will begin to disappear. As the child continues to think more and more critically, the synapses that are being used become more intricately connected. Humans continue to learn throughout childhood and adulthood. As children enter adolescence, new learning is connected to prior knowledge.

See also: **Adolescent Cognitive Development; Adolescent Social and Emotional Development; Childhood Brain; Infant Brain; Language Acquisition and Disorders.**

Further Readings

D'Arcangelo, M. (2000). How does the brain develop? A conversation with Steven Peterson. *Educational Leadership* 58(3):68–71.

Davis, S.M. (Winter 2000/01). Look before you leap: Concerns about "brain-based" products and approaches. *Childhood Education* 77(2):100–101.

Hakuta, K. (2001). A critical period for second language acquisition? In Bailey, Jr., D.B, Bruer, J.T., Symons, F.J., Lichtman, J.W. *Critical Thinking About Critical Periods,* 193–208. Baltimore, Maryland: Paul H. Brookes Publishing Co.

Horton, J.C. (2001). Critical periods in the development of the visual system. In Bailey, Jr., D.B, Bruer, J.T., Symons, F.J., Lichtman, J.W. *Critical Thinking About Critical Periods,* 45–66. Baltimore, Maryland: Paul H. Brookes Publishing Co.

Logue, ME. (2000). Implications of brain development research for Even Start Family Literacy Programs. Look at Even Start. Office of Compensatory Education, Washington, D.C., Even Start Program.

Thompson, R A. (2001). Sensitive periods in attachment? In Bailey, Jr., D.B, Bruer, J.T., Symons, F.J., Lichtman, J.W. *Critical Thinking About Critical Periods,* 83–106. Baltimore, Maryland: Paul H. Brookes Publishing Co.

Dana.org http://www.dana.org/

SUSAN CATAPANO, ED.D.

Critical Thinking

Critical thinking can be defined as the process of thinking about any subject matter and the ability to analyze and evaluate an outcome that is meaningful and well reasoned. Critical thinking is considered a "higher order skill" as it is a skill that is built upon other cognitive "lower level" skills, such as language development, information processing, and comprehension. These lower and higher level skills develop systematically as an individual matures biologically.

The prefrontal cortex is considered the "thinking" region of the brain—responsible for judgment, problem-solving, and critical thinking. The prefrontal cortex is essential to critical thinking and to the development of the lower level skills. The development of these skills is, in large part, impacted by the physical and social environment of the individual and can change based on these experiences.

Jean Piaget, a leading cognitive theorist posits that the final stage of cognitive development is when humans can move from concrete thinking to more logical and abstract thinking. To be an accomplished critical thinker, one must effectively master lower level skills. Some cognitive theorists believe that only 30–35 percent of the population master Piaget's final stage of cognitive development. This makes it difficult for these individuals to develop critical thinking skills. Other theorists speculate that critical thinking is innate. As the brain develops, critical thinking skills develop, and this occurs very early in infancy. To understand this construct one must have a primary understanding of how the human brain develops from conception through the gestation period. Millions of neurons develop during a pregnancy and these neurons connect to the fetus. Once a mother gives birth, neuron connections occur rapidly. This happens as the baby interacts with its environment. The key is brain stimulation—neuron stimulation is based on specific environmental stimulation.

The level of interaction will also determine the amount of neuron connections made. Basic critical thinking occurs in the form of language development. As early as two months, infants can discern aspects of speech, which helps them make sense of their environment. Some theorists believe that infants are not taught this skill, but instead are hotwired for such activity enabling all humans to have the ability to be critical thinkers. If this is the case, why is there a common belief that individuals need to be taught these skills? An answer to this is perhaps how an individual is "taught" to process information contradicts how the brain naturally develops and learns.

A major component of critical thinking is that it is not focused as much on the answers of a particular dogma but on the questions that are generated. Paramount to critical thinking is the ability to ask pertinent questions and interpret important data—data that is either congruent or in opposition with the answer at hand. A critical thinker examines opposing viewpoints with an open mind and is willing to be challenged on personal assumptions and beliefs. Through this process, the critical thinker comes to a well-thought out conclusion based on solid facts.

Dr. Richard Paul and Dr. Linda Elder, leading researchers in critical thinking, posit that impediments to critical thinking are egocentric and sociocentric thinking, or the self-centered manner in which an individual views and understands phenomena. Couched in egocentric thinking is the belief that something is innately true because the thinker believes it to be. This belief is often times grounded in the personal experiences of the person. For example, an individual may believe that a particular group is more prone to illegal drug use, based on the individual's interaction with the group or what is viewed in the media regarding this group.

Parallel to egocentric thinking is sociocentric thinking or the belief that phenomena must be true because a group of people believe it to be true. An example of this would be accepting something as fact because society accepts it as a fact. History is replete with examples of how faulty this logic can be, such as the once pervasive belief that the world was flat. In both egocentric and sociocentric thinking, individuals usually embrace information that corroborates their thinking, while ignoring or downplaying information that challenge their truths. In the afore-mentioned example regarding illegal drug use among groups of people, research data might indicate that illegal drug use among a cer-tain group of people is no higher than other groups. However, some individuals have the "truth" of drug use so deeply imbedded in their set of core beliefs that they will criticize the research data as being faulty or ignore it altogether.

Two areas of the brain that assist in critical thinking are the basal gan-glia and the cerebellum. These areas coordinate thinking processes such as being inquisitive, skeptical, reflective, and the ability to discern opinions from facts—characteristics that are analogous to a critical thinker. Additionally, the left hemisphere of the brain, or the logical hemisphere assesses information rationally, while the right hemisphere, or the intuitive hemisphere, interprets data through context. Both work in concert when processing information. Many individuals lean either to the left or the right hemisphere. This does, in many ways, determine how information is processed; however, both hemispheres are impor-tant in effective critical thinking. As an example, let's examine the fol-lowing passage on crime in the U.S. to see how the left and right hemispheres process the information critically:

> The U.S. has witnessed a dramatic increase in crime within the last several years. One cannot turn on the television or read the newspapers without seeing or reading about a violent crime. This particularly holds true for murders, with most of the lead news coverage centered on a murder. This extensive coverage is indicative of the increase in murders in our society. Moreover, the media fuels this increase through the glorification of violence. Movies and television shows are replete with examples of gratuitous violence. As a result, our society has numbed itself to acts of violence and it has encouraged many to imitate what they view in these mediums. This certainly explains why the crime rate in the U.S. has increased.

Together, both hemispheres work simultaneously to make sense of the passage, utilizing logic, word cognition, and language (left hemisphere) and interpretation, internal and abstract processing (right hemisphere). While the passage appears to be logical, through the lens of the critical thinker, the weakness in the passage becomes evident. The critical thinker would begin by asking pertinent questions such as, "How does one define crime?" "Are television and newspaper reports an accurate barometer to measure crime in America?" "Would other data, such as F.B.I. crime statis-tics be more credible?" "What evidence supports the notion that the media fuels violence?" "Is violence and crime synonymous?" and "What is the percentage of non-violent crimes such as shoplifting and embezzle-ment and how does it impact the increase in crime?"

Second, the critical thinker would seek to determine the accuracy of the passage. The reader is to presuppose that there is an increase in crime in the U.S. Statistics will show that this is partly true. While there is an increase in certain crimes, such as white-collar crime, there has been a decrease over the years in violent crimes.

Third, the critical thinker would examine the passage rationally. Are the ideas presented in the passage logical? For example, can an argument on the increase in crime be substantiated based purely on crime reporting on television and in newspapers?

Fourth, the critical thinker would look at alternative theories or perspectives in understanding the passage. For example, if it is true that violent crimes, particularly murder, are decreasing, what can the increase in violent crime reporting in the media be attributed to? A plausible explanation could be that perhaps the reporting of crimes, particularly violent or sensationalistic ones, garners higher ratings and an increase in readership. Thus, the increase in crime reporting is not due to an increase in crime per se, but the public's interest and fascination with violent crime stories.

Fifth, the critical thinker tests the original passage against new information and makes a conclusion to either accept the passage as is; accept the passage amended; or soundly reject it altogether.

Paul and Elder surmise that there are eight criteria for evaluating reasoning. These are (1) Purpose—is the purpose of the reasoning evident? (2) Question—is the question understood and free of bias? Is the question and purpose strongly related? (3) Information—is there strong evidence to support reasoning? Is there an understanding of the issue? (4) Concepts—are key concepts clarified? (5) Assumptions—are there questionable assumptions made that are not adequately addressed? (6) Interferences—is there a line of reasoning that describes how a conclusion was made? (7) Point of View—does the reasoning take into consideration other points of views or reasoning? and (8) Implications—is there sensitivity to the implications in taking a particular position?

As humans gain a clearer understanding on how the brain functions in processing and interpreting information, particularly as it relates to hemispheric preferences, critical thinking will evolve.

See also: Adolescent Cognitive Development; Challenge and Enrichment.

Further Readings

Kincheloe, J.S., Weil, D. (2004). *Critical Thinking and Learning: An Encyclopedia for Parents and Teachers.* Westport, CT: Greenwood Publishing Group.

Sousa, D.A. (2001). *How the Brain Learns* (2nd ed.). Corwin Press, Inc: Thousand Oaks, CA.

The Critical Thinking Community. (n.d). Retrieved January 10, 2005 from www.criticalthinking.org

DWAYNE SMITH, PH.D.

D

Deaf and Hard of Hearing

All children, deaf and hearing, possess the potential for developing cognitive skills. The extent to which this potential develops may depend on a variety of factors within a child's environment such as the experiences that a child encounters in his or her environment and the ability to comprehend these experiences in the environment. Language is a crucial component of a child's ability to comprehend an experience in the environment. Therefore, it is very important to provide a deaf and hard of hearing child full access to language to ensure comprehension of the environment and to ensure optimal development of cognitive skills and academic success.

For deaf and hard of hearing children to maximize the development of their native language, language must be introduced very early in life. Studies have demonstrated that the earlier a deaf child is exposed to American Sign Language (ASL), the greater the likelihood that the deaf child will develop superior cognitive and linguistic skills. It is well-documented in research that deaf children of deaf parents possess better cognitive and linguistic skills than deaf children of hearing parents. Deaf children of deaf parents, who have a strong foundation in ASL, are able to achieve the same language developmental milestones as hearing children. In addition, a strong foundation in ASL can assist deaf children in developing proficiency in the development of the English language. A strong foundation in one's native language serves as a bridge in acquiring skills in another language. Deaf children of deaf parents achieve these linguistic skills using visual strategies instead of using auditory and oral strategies. Additional studies of how native ASL users process language demonstrate that the brain is capable of processing language using visual as well as auditory modes. Therefore, focusing solely on auditory strategies to develop language may not ensure optimal language development of a deaf child.

A study compared the brain responses of hearing and deaf individuals while they read English words and watched American Sign Language. The hearing subjects in this study showed that all four language areas in the left hemisphere were utilized while reading English words. However, the deaf subjects in the study used one of the four language areas in the left hemisphere, Wernicke's area, and two areas in the right hemisphere while reading English words. When processing ASL, the deaf subjects in this study utilized all four of the language areas of the left hemisphere, similar to the manner in which the hearing subjects processed English. The findings of this study demonstrated that regardless of the modality of language, there seems to be specific areas of the brain that all individuals use to process one's native language. Therefore, the processing of linguistic information in the brain occurs in a similar manner for all individuals.

Although the left hemisphere is the dominant area of the brain that processes sign language, studies have shown that deaf individuals who use sign language do use the right hemisphere to process ASL as well as the left hemisphere. The processing of sign language occurs in both hemispheres of the brain as a result of the simultaneous use of visuospatial and linguistic information. As ASL is a visual spatial language, more areas of the brain are used to process visual, spatial, and kinesthetic input.

Researchers have demonstrated that deaf individuals are comparable to hearing individuals with spatial memory. Sign language exposure may help to improve the development of visual attention, visual memory, and visual spatial skills. When comparing individuals who use ASL and individuals who do not use ASL, a difference in visual spatial skills was noted. Individuals who use ASL demonstrated that they were better able to recognize facial expressions than individuals who did not sign and performed better on mental imagery tasks, thus confirming sign language enhances visual spatial skills.

Deaf and hard of hearing children who are proficient in their native language also demonstrate better memory of sequential information. When a child is proficient in their native language, they are able to develop automaticity skills that make it easier to use rehearsal strategies that allow one's short-term memory to be more efficient when recalling sequential information. Automaticity also helps individuals to retrieve words and basic syntax structures that are stored in memory that are needed while reading.

Deaf and hearing individuals process short-term memory information differently. Hearing individuals use a speech-based code while deaf individuals use a visual spatial code. There is conflicting evidence regarding the short-term memory of deaf individuals. Some studies have demonstrated that deaf individuals do not perform as well as hearing individuals in memory tasks that require verbal encoding of sequential information because short-term memory seems to work best with speech-based codes. One study revealed that there was no significant difference between the short-term recall of sequential verbal information of signing deaf individuals, oral deaf individuals, and hearing individuals. Thus, studies in which deaf individuals were found to possess limited short-term memory are not the result of not using a phonological code but rather the result of limited general and linguistic knowledge.

As a strong foundation in one's native language promotes good cognitive development, parents and teachers need to consider strategies that will promote language development. Although language needs to be introduced to a child very early in life, parents and teachers need to consider the quality of communicative interactions with deaf and hard of hearing children. Studies demonstrate that deaf parents are better communicators with their deaf children. In addition to being fluent in their child's native language, they understand how and when to clarify and expand on concepts. The communicative interaction between deaf parents and deaf children occurs in a natural manner. Due to limited skills in signing, hearing parents will often engage their child in dialogue in which the parents determine the topic and provide responses to their children that are unrelated to comments made by the child. In addition, hearing parents tend to use more commands during their interaction with their deaf child.

When studying the interaction between deaf mothers and deaf infants, it was noted that deaf mothers will determine the focal point of their child's attention to establish the topic of their dialogue. Deaf mothers tend to provide their infants with time to view the item of interest and then, wait for their child's eye gaze to return to them before providing the child with language input. It was also noted that the deaf mothers were willing to wait longer for their child to respond, thus taking less control of the interaction and providing their child with more autonomy.

Teachers may also dominate the classroom conversations by asking questions that only require short responses rather than allowing students to expand on topics that may be brought up in classroom discussion. Often, parents and teachers will dominate conversations when they are not fluent in communicating in the child's native language. Deaf and hard of hearing children need to be given the opportunity to engage in meaningful and relevant conversations that allow them to be true participants of the conversation. Such conversations give deaf and hard of hearing children the opportunity to be creative, bargain, and make inferences. These skills are not only necessary for academic tasks but they are also important skills that are necessary for social interaction. In addition, allowing deaf and hard of hearing children to engage in meaningful and relevant conversations in which they can determine the topic of the conversation gives them the opportunity to become assertive and independent.

Language skills of deaf children are developed through fluent communicative interactions with their parents. Fluent communicative interactions also allow deaf children to acquire general knowledge. This general knowledge allows deaf children to comprehend academic information. Often teachers of deaf and hard of hearing students find that deaf students are not able to comprehend academic information because they do not have background knowledge. As a result, teachers must determine the extent of their students' background knowledge of a topic before presenting new information to their students. Deaf and hard of hearing students need background knowledge to acquire new information that is taught in content areas such as science and social studies but they also need background knowledge to comprehend reading material. Reading material is more meaningful and easier to comprehend when students have the background knowledge regarding the topic of the reading material.

The quality and quantity of experiences in one's environment and the ability to comprehend these experiences, also impacts a child's ability to develop cognitive skills such as problem-solving. Problem-solving means that one is able to draw on previous experience, knowledge, and skills to address an unfamiliar situation. Problem-solving skills are necessary for a variety of situations that individuals must address in daily experiences and can range from simple to complex tasks. Thus, children who have been able to access the information in their environment and comprehend their experiences will have the background knowledge and skills that are necessary to problem solve situations that they may encounter.

Another cognitive skill, Theory of Mind, is the ability to judge and describe the feelings and thoughts of another person. Based on this judgment, one can also predict the future actions of another person. Children develop Theory of Mind skills through interactions with adults in their environment. Interactions with adults provide children with opportunities to use language to explain their own feelings as well as the thoughts and feelings of others. Deaf children of deaf parents are able to perform Theory of Mind tasks like hearing children. Deaf children, who do not have adults in their environment who can interact with them and explain their world to them, will be delayed in developing Theory of Mind skills. Parents with limited sign language skills or parents who are unfamiliar with strategies to expand their child's language will not be able to involve their children in discussion that will help their children to develop Theory of Mind skills.

Theory of Mind skills are important skills for deaf children to acquire because they are skills that are necessary for developing skills for social interaction and reading comprehension. Theory of Mind skills are required for understanding narratives and creating narratives which are skills that are needed for reading comprehension. Teachers and parents can use literature to help deaf children develop skills in narratives. In addition, literature can be used to discuss the thoughts and feelings of the characters in stories and predict the future actions of the characters. Teachers and parents can also involve their children in discussions about current and past events. This discussion can help children develop Theory of Mind skills by helping them to consider the feelings and thoughts of individuals involved in these events and the future actions that were taken by these individuals. Through this discussion children can make a connection between the feelings and thoughts of these individuals to the actions taken by these individuals. Teachers and parents can also discuss opinions, personal feelings, and perspectives that are presented in various situations that are presented in books and real-life occurrences.

Educators need to understand the relationship between cognition and language to develop appropriate instructional strategies and educational programming that will benefit deaf children and help them to develop their linguistic, cognitive, and academic skills. Educators and professionals, who work with parents of deaf and hard of hearing children, must also help parents to understand the relationship of cognition and language and help parents to understand the importance of providing their child with a strong foundation in language by communicating and interacting with their child. Language must be introduced very early in a child's life to ensure that a child will develop their cognitive and linguistic potential to the greatest degree possible.

Deaf children, who are proficient in their native language, also demonstrate better memory of sequential information which may help deaf children to develop skills that will help them to become better readers. The quality and quantity of experiences in a child's environment and the ability of the child to comprehend these experiences, also impacts their ability to acquire general knowledge and their ability to develop cognitive skills. Providing deaf children with full access to language within their environment will promote their development of linguistic, cognitive, and academic skills.

See also: **Bilingualism, Critical Periods (Sensitive Periods); Language Acquisition and Disorders.**

Further Readings

Marschark, M., Lang, H.G., Albertini, J.A. (2002). *Educating Deaf Students: From Research to Practice*. New York, NY: Oxford University Press.

Miller, P. (2002). Another look at the STM capacity of prelingually deafened individuals and its relation to reading comprehension. *American Annals of the Deaf* 147(5):56–69.

Schick, B., De Villers, J., De Villers, P., Hoffmeister, B. (2002). Theory of mind: Language and cognition in deaf children. Retrieved August 20, 2004 from http://www.asha.org/about/publications/leaderonline/archives/2002/q4/f02 1203.htm

Wood, D. (1991). Communication and cognition: How the communication styles of hearing adults may hinder-rather than help-deaf learners. *American Annals of the Deaf* 136(3):247–251.

MONICA SOUKUP, ED.D.

Depression

Depression is a disorder of mood that renders one sad, lethargic, and disinterested in life. It is perhaps the most significant health risk of all emotional disorders. The presence of ideas to harm or kill oneself or others is not a characteristic of other mental disorders except psychotic problems. Suicidal and homicidal ideas can lead to death, physical harm to oneself, or physical harm to others. If interventions can be delivered early enough all the associated costs of death and harm can be prevented. Approximately 80–90 percent of individuals suffering from depression can be helped.

Brain-Related Factors in Depression

There are a number of indications that brain-based factors are associated with, and likely cause, depression. It is well known that when a stroke occurs in the forward parts of the left side of the brain, an individual will experience what is often thought of as depression. The individual will experience sadness, depressed mood, anhedonia, and social disinterest along with crying. In contrast, when a stroke occurs in the forward part of the right side of the brain, the individual will express hopelessness and helplessness, and may appear angry and somewhat hyperactive. Clearly the depression's characteristics are associated with the location of the brain damage from the stroke.

There are indications that certain abnormalities in the structures of the brain can be associated with different types of depression. Injuries and reduced amount of brain tissue on the surface of the brain (cortex) in the frontal area of the brain have been shown to be associated with depression. Further, reduced amounts of tissue in a structure inside the brain (known as sub-cortical), called the hippocampus, have been associated with depression as well. It is not clear if the reduction is a cause of the depression or a by-product of the depression, but clearly the association between the brain's tissue and depression exists.

Another indication of the role of the brain in depression is the effect of chemicals in the brain on the mood of the individual. Generally speaking, chemicals known as monoamines are related to depression and mood. These substances are released by one neuron into the gap between it and the next neuron. The gap is referred to as the synapse, and the chemicals are known as synaptic transmitter substances. Monoamines such as dopamine, serotonin, adrenaline, and noradrenaline are known to be associated with depression, so that drugs that affect the levels of these chemicals in the synapse, predominately increasing these levels, improve mood, and reduce depression.

One way in which the brain is manipulated to reduce depression is to slow down a process known as re-uptake. When a neuron places a monoamine into the synapse, some of the chemical is taken back up by the sending neuron through the process of re-uptake. Some medications inhibit the re-uptake process leaving larger amounts of the monoamines in the synapse, presumably allowing for more of the chemical to promote its specific type of communication to the other neurons. This process in the brain appears to improve depression. More recently, there is evidence that the release of the monoamines affects not only the neuron on the other side of the synapse, but also neurons further away.

Another brain abnormality found in depressed patients has to do with unusual flows of blood to parts of the front area of the brain. The flow of blood can be associated with the brain's use of the blood in an activity. Lower blood flow can suggest reduced activity in these areas of the brain associated with depression. Further, when some areas of the brain are affected in this manner, the probability of the depression being accompanied by psychotic symptoms is greater. Again, the presence of depression and associated features are closely tied to how typical or atypical the brain's areas are functioning.

Along with brain-related factors it is important to consider a combination of historical factors, physical problems, and other emotional disorders that are often associated with negative mood. Historical factors often are considered factors that predispose an individual to depression. Family history, sexual and physical abuse appear to play a significant historical role in the likelihood of experiencing depression.

Signs of Depression

Generally speaking, there are signs of depression that break down into specific categories of symptoms: cognitive symptoms, physical symptoms, mood symptoms, and behavioral symptoms. Cognitive symptoms represent depressive ways of thinking; physical symptoms are those that affect health-related factors; mood symptoms reflect changes in the way one feels emotionally; and behavioral symptoms represent changes in ones actions.

The cognitive symptoms are usually thought of within three subcategories: thoughts about the future, thoughts about the self, and thoughts about the world and others. These categories are sometimes referred to as the cognitive triad. Thoughts about the future usually represent hopeless ideas, while thoughts about the self include ideas that one is worthless, helpless, or guilty. Thoughts about the world include ideas that the world is no longer interesting or fun, and others would be better off without you in their life. The ideas within the triad often produce the most serious ideas if help is not obtained, namely thoughts of suicide. Below are samples of these kinds of thoughts.

Future Thoughts—"Things will never get better." "I will never feel happy again."

Self Thoughts—"I am worthless and don't deserve to live." "It's all my fault."

World/Other Thoughts—"Life has no meaning." "My family hates me."

Suicidal Thoughts—"I can't take the pain anymore, the only way out is to die." "If I don't wake up tomorrow, the world would be better off."

Physical symptoms of depression can be found in neurological functioning primarily, although sometimes other symptoms are also present.

The primary physical symptoms are difficulty in concentrating, problems with memory, reduced sex drive, loss of or increased appetite, and insomnia or over-sleeping. Other physical symptoms can include a sense of heaviness in the arms or legs, and frequent crying without any reason.

Emotional symptoms are sometimes referred to as subjective symptoms. Often depression is expressed as sadness, but sometimes it is more a feeling of emptiness accompanied with tension. This latter feeling can be described as "keyed-up" or "agitation." Another typical feeling in depression is the loss of interest in life, particularly interest in things that were previously found to be enjoyable. This experience is called anhedonia. Finally, the loss of a sense of purpose in life, which is sometimes described as a feeling of being lost or alone, can be described as the existential feeling of depression. When existential feelings are at their worst, it is usually referred to as anaclitic depression.

The behavioral signs of depression can be seen both in everyday activities and social behaviors. When depressed, one often reduces overall levels of activity, becoming lethargic about life. Usually self-care reduces, leaving the individual disheveled and unkempt. Daily activities diminish, with fewer chores being done and truancy and grades suffer. Often the reduction in these behaviors feeds the ideas of worthlessness or helplessness. It is common for schedules to no longer be kept and routines to be discarded. Social behaviors change as well, leaving the individual withdrawn and socially isolated.

Incidence and Prevalence of Depression

According to studies of depression in the United States population, it is estimated that about 15 percent of the population will experience a major depressive episode at least once in their life, about 3 percent will experience dysthymia in their lives, and about 0.5 percent will experience bi-polar disorder with depressed mood features.

Studies of the manifestation of depression over history have found that one is at most risk of having a major depressive episode between the ages of sixteen and twenty-five years, and more at risk if one is a female rather than a male. The occurrence of depression in children is somewhat different. Between the ages of eight and twelve, boys are often more likely to experience depression than girls, or the rates are the same for both genders. But at age thirteen, the frequency of depression appears more like that in adults, with girls experiencing depression over two-times more often than boys.

Studies of suicidal attempts reveal that when consideration is given to racial background, whites are more likely to experience depression at some point in their lives, but are no more likely than other groups to make a suicide attempt, when compared to blacks and Hispanics. However, when suicide attempts and depression are evaluated in various sub-types of the Hispanic population, those from Puerto Rico are more likely than those from Mexico and Cuba to experience depression and to make suicide attempts.

Treatments for Depression

Many major studies and reviews of studies have shown that depression is treatable, and that if the treatment is effective, the depression can be reduced for long periods of time. For example, studies have shown that the use of medications for typical major depression disorder (MDD) (without agitation, for example) produce reductions in depression that persist after a removal of the medication. The drugs usually used in these studies are medications that affect serotonin and adrenal systems. These medications usually inhibit the re-uptake of the monoamines.

Other studies have shown that the method of non-medication treatment effective on depression is the application of cognitive-behavioral therapy (CBT). CBT targets specifically the ways in which the brain thinks its thoughts, and the ways the person behaves. CBT was developed as a treatment for depression in the 1960s by the pioneering psychiatrist Aaron T. Beck at the University of Pennsylvania. Since the 1970s, CBT has been shown to be largely successful in the treatment of major depression, as well as with other disorders, at least as effective as medication. The CBT treatment approach is considered an educational and skill-oriented psychotherapy that intends to prevent relapse when treatment is over through transference of skills to manage depression from the therapist to the patient.

Cognitive Therapy and Behavior Therapy Strategies

Cognitive Therapy Techniques

1. Educate the individual about the role of unhealthy thinking patterns in depression.
2. Teach the individual how to monitor one's thoughts, learning to rate the believability of one's thoughts.
3. Describe and rate the intensity of the depression and observe how the feelings are related to the unhealthy thinking patterns.
4. Examine the evidence in real-life that supports or is contrary to the unhealthy thinking patterns.
5. Create new thoughts that are based on the real-life evidence.
6. Re-rate the believability of the unhealthy thoughts, rate the believability of the new thoughts, and re-rate the intensity of the depressive feelings.

Behavior Therapy Techniques

1. Educate the individual with depression about the role of unhealthy behaviors in depression.
2. Teach the individual how to record what one does throughout the day, and how to rate the feelings of accomplishment and pleasure associated with each activity.

3. Create routines of activities to be done each day.

4. Identify and schedule pleasurable activities into one's life.

Studies that compare medication therapy with CBT typically find that CBT is equally as effective for improving mood and reducing depression, and superior when considering reduced likelihood of a return of the depression after treatment. When adolescents are reviewed, findings are somewhat different. In one study, approximately two-thirds of the adolescents who received the medication improved, while less than half of the teens receiving CBT alone saw a reduction in depression. However, when the medication and the CBT were combined, the adolescents improved at a higher rate than did those who were treated with medication alone (above 70 percent improved). However, when teens who were both depressed and displayed anti-social behaviors were exposed to CBT alone, they revealed immediate and sustained benefits.

What Can Teachers Do?

Often the last place a depressed student wants to be is school. Academics and relationships with teachers and peers seem meaningless. The following are suggestions for educators:

1. Be patient. It takes a long time to overcome depression, do not expect them to snap out of it.

2. Don't ignore the depressed student. This will only result in them crawling further into their shell. Make a concerted effort to talk with them and engage them in the class.

3. Show you care. Offer extra help, study time, and study groups, allow them to make up a late assignment—this is the time to make accommodations.

4. Let them know you have confidence that they'll get better, don't give up on them.

5. Refer them to proper individuals in the school or agencies outside the school for support.

See also: Adolescent Social and Emotional Development; Emotion.

Further Readings

Clark, D.A., Beck, A.T., Alford, B.A. (1999). *Scientific Foundations of Cognitive Theory and Therapy of Depression.* New York: John Wiley.

Klosko, J.S., Sanderson, W.C. (1999). *Cognitive-Behavioral Treatment of Depression.* New York: Aronson.

Depression Alliance www.depressionalliance.org

Mental Health Foundation www.mentalhealth.org.uk

KEVIN D. ARNOLD, PH.D. ABPP

Distributed Intelligence

The 1990s were "The Decade of the Brain" and while we learned a great deal, many unanswered questions remain. Precisely because we have focused on analyzing thinking and problem-solving, the promise of Artificial Intelligence (AI), while still on the horizon, seems a bit further from reality. IBM's "Deep Blue" defeated the world's champion, Boris Kasparov, at chess, but we realize that successfully playing at a board game, even one as complex as chess, is a limited operation. Deep Blue didn't think or create; it responded, powerfully, to its programming. The more we know about how the brain functions, the more we also know what we do not know.

Cognitive neuroscience is important in our quest to understand how the brain functions and how we learn, but in understanding learning we should not limit our focus to what happens inside the brain. Instead, we should also look at how the brain capitalizes on its context.

Intelligence used to be conceived narrowly, as an endogenous quality that could be accurately captured by a two- or three-digit number obtained on a standardized test. We have come to realize that while such tests are reliable, there is much to question about their validity, whether they truly measure *intelligence*. It is clear that traditional intelligence tests are limited and typically ascertain proficiency in only one or two areas of intelligence.

This realization is due to the fact that we have become far more pragmatic about the definition of intelligence. We now understand that intelligence is the ability to solve problems. Further, we recognize that problems are not limited to paper and pencil multiple-choice items. Indeed, real-world problems come in many different forms and are situated in a range of contexts. The genesis for looking more broadly at how intelligence is defined stems from Howard Gardner, who set out the theory of **multiple intelligences.** Breaking the paradigm that intelligence is a single entity (the "g factor") and that individuals have more or less of this quality, Gardner defined intelligence as solving a problem or creating a product that is valued in a culture. The Distributed Intelligence shares Gardner's pragmatic focus on solving problems and creating products, but it is quite different from the biopsychological potential inherent in each of us that he described. The Distributed Intelligence extends our definition of intelligence by looking outward.

Distributed Intelligence is the notion that our intelligence is not limited to what is inside our skin. Our intelligence—our ability to solve problems and to create products—is not only in our head (although it is there) any more than it is only in our hands (although it is also there). Rather, our intelligence is also a function of our ability to access the relevant resources that are around us. When we solve complex, real-world problems, we rely upon and draw from tools, symbols, forms, calculators, computers, and, perhaps most important, from other individuals. Knowing the resources that are distributed in our environment and knowing which resources are helpful in what situations, increases the likelihood that we will be able to successfully solve problems. (The term "distributed intelligence" initially referred to the increased power that becomes available when a series of computers are linked together. Vice-President Al Gore used the term as a metaphor for human collaboration resulting in increased problem-solving power.)

Distributed Intelligence has always been used by "smart" people (indeed, they were often "smart" because of their Distributed Intelligence) even though the resources from which they drew changed over time and by context. For example, hundreds of years ago the sailors who could understand clouds to predict weather patterns were more likely to make it safely to the next seaport. Their ability to draw inferences from the skies, knowing which cloud formations gave a meaningful message and which did not, was a use of their Distributed Intelligence. In 1455, when Gutenberg invented the printing press and books proliferated, reading became an even more important skill. Those who could read had an advantage because they were able to draw information from many more books. While the ability to read was beneficial in any case, a strong Distributed Intelligence meant that one knew which books needed to be read because they were relevant to the problem or situation.

When machines were invented to supplement and supplant physical labor, those who could use and work with the machinery appropriately—whether a cotton gin, a jack-hammer or a typewriter—held an advantage over those who could not. Today, simply having an ample tool box (whether filled with hand-tools or as a metaphor for conceptual skills) does not guarantee success. Success stems from knowing which tools are appropriate for what situation, and then knowing when and how to use the tools. These patterns, that knowledge, come from using one's Distributed Intelligence.

Distributed Intelligence enables individuals to be smarter because of their ability to draw from their environment. This is captured by Harvard Professor David Perkins' terms, "person-plus" and "person-solo." "Person-plus" is an individual supplemented by the resources in the environment; "person-solo" only can draw upon what is in her head. Similarly, in illustrating how the group is typically smarter than the individual, there is the wisdom of the crowd.

It may seem obvious that Distributed Intelligence is even more important today because of advances in technology. A PDA (Personal Digital Assistant), small enough to be easily placed in a pocket, can hold far more data than any of us can commit to memory. Access to the Internet means that a few keystrokes can open pathways to a wealth of information. Likewise, the ability to use PowerPoint can enable one to organize and present information in a persuasive way.

But these sorts of technological advances do not necessarily result in better thinking and problem-solving; indeed, they can be deleterious. Access to too much information can overwhelm, and the availability of too many bells and whistles can distract. Students need to be taught to use their Distributed Intelligence, to be aware of not only what resources are available, but which ones are relevant to solving particular problems.

Teaching for Distributed Intelligence is a three-step process. First, it begins with analyzing the task: what, exactly, is the problem? Second, students must have a sense of their own talents and skills so that they can know the areas in which they are strong and weak, and how that relates to the problem at hand. With that self-knowledge, they can begin to supplement their own intelligence profile by drawing from other resources. Third, students must be taught to identify the resources, including other people, around them and determine how they can become part of solving the problem.

Unfortunately, too often educators give little, if any, attention to this process. Often, the problem is taken as a given, and the first step, analyzing it, is overlooked. Rarely do we cause students to reflect on their own strengths and weaknesses in thinking about how to proceed. Seldom do we take the time to teach them to inventory the resources that are available and to then consider which ones are relevant to solve the problem.

As this three-step process is essential if we are to help students become effective problem-solvers who use their Distributed Intelligence, it should periodically be incorporated into student assessment. We need to judge students on both the solution to the problem and the process that they followed in arriving at their answer. The point is to not only assess students on how well they use just what is in their heads, but also on how well they are able to identify and use the relevant resources in their environment. The goal is to help students become better problem-solvers by causing them to become aware of their Distributed Intelligence and how it can be used.

In thinking about the educational implications of Distributed Intelligence, it is most important to focus on human relationships and interactions. This begins with developing what Howard Gardner identifies as their "intrapersonal and interpersonal intelligences," termed their "**emotional intelligence**" by David Goleman. The "intrapersonal intelligence" is the students' sense of self, their knowledge of their own strengths and weaknesses. The "interpersonal intelligence" is their ability to understand others, to identify and appreciate their talents, and to be able to work with them. Regardless of the subject matter or the age of children that they teach, educators have an obligation to focus on developing these understandings in their students. In virtually any role and with virtually any problem, the probability for success is increased when one can work with and learn from others. A strong Distributed Intelligence stems from well-developed intrapersonal and interpersonal intelligences coupled with an awareness of the relevant resources in an environment.

See also: **IQ.**

Further Readings

Goleman, D. (1995). *Emotional Intelligence: Why It Can Matter More Than IQ.* New York: Bantam Books.

Gore, A. (1996, April). The metaphor of distributed intelligence. *Science* 272: 177–180.

Hawkins, J. (2004). *On Intelligence.* New York: Henry Holt & Company.

Hoerr, T. (2003). Distributed intelligence and why schools need to foster it. *Independent School* 63(1):76–83.

Salomon, G., Brown, J.S., Pea, R. (1996). *Distributed Cognitions.* Cambridge University Press: Cambridge, UK.

Surowiecki, J. (2004). *The Wisdom of Crowds.* New York: Doubleday.

THOMAS R. HOERR, PH.D.

Drama

In the United Kingdom, Australia, Canada, and increasingly in the United States, classroom teachers have been drawing upon drama techniques to support learning in other academic content areas. Rather than present staged productions for an audience, these *drama in education* practitioners involve the entire class in improvised role playing within an imagined context. Though research is growing in this area of teaching, there is no neuroimaging research that directly studies student learning during drama in education activities. This is due in part to the difficulty of reducing the complexity of drama in education activities to a form that lends itself to the current limitations of neuroimaging research methodology. As a result, any neurological research insight concerning learning during drama in education activities must be inferred tentatively from neuroimaging studies in other areas.

For example, a concern of using drama in education is whether pretending to do an activity is cognitively comparable to actually doing the activity. Though neuroimaging research has not addressed this issue in activities comparable to the complexity of drama in education, studies have shown that some forms of simulated activity, such as pantomiming of tool use activate the same areas of the brain as the actual action, adding evidence to the argument that using drama as a teaching technique is more than "just pretending."

As with other arts, part of drama's artistic strength is derived from its ability to invoke emotion and to use that emotion to provoke thought. For the audience member watching Shakespeare, Lady Macbeth's guilt and madness may raise emotions, centered in the amygdala, that not only make the experience memorable, involving long-term memory function of the hippocampus, but also promote thoughtful consideration of her plight, which is processed in the prefrontal cortex. Cognitive research of drama performances has shown that the emotional content of the work can affect not only audiences' later recall of the performance but also facilitate the higher order processing of the performance to appreciate the aesthetics and themes of the work.

Theaters of the Mind

As a subset of the field of drama and theater, drama in education also takes advantage of emotional content to facilitate memory and higher order thought. In addition, drama in education draws heavily on the active involvement of participants, in contrast with the passive role of audience members during a performance. This active involvement is designed to tap into intelligence beyond the methods employed in traditional classroom instruction as in the views of **multiple intelligences** by Howard Gardner, Robert Sternberg, and others. Through the use of movement, which involves the cerebellum, basal ganglia, and motor cortex, communication with others, involves the frontal lobes, temporal lobes, and limbic system, and other modes.

Instead of relying on neuroimaging studies, educators looking for brain-based research on drama in education practice have drawn upon the findings from cognitive psychology. The success of these drama techniques in furthering classroom learning has been attributed to their ability to tap into an area of cognitive psychology that has been previously neglected by traditional education: *situated learning*.

Situated Learning

Public education is frequently criticized for not linking its learning to the world outside the classroom. Ideally, students would learn academic content in the context of a "cognitive apprenticeship," much as craftspeople learned in the past. The apprentice is immersed in the culture and practices of the craft and, as a result, acquires new knowledge within the context of real problems that arise. In this model of education, students would learn science under the tutelage of professional scientists in laboratories and learn history alongside historians. However, the pragmatics of mass education preclude an approach like this. Instead, educators work to make learning more authentic by introducing elements of the real world into classroom instruction.

The notion of embedding classroom instruction within authentic contexts is not new—John Dewey championed the idea at the start of the twentieth century. But it is only within the last twenty years that cognitive science has developed a research base to support our understanding of situated learning. A long-standing concern of both cognitive scientists and classroom teachers is the difficulty that students have in the **transfer** of learning to new contexts. Two reasons are often cited for the difficulty in transferring learning. First, learners do not always acquire sufficient knowledge due either to shortcomings in the learning environment or to lack of **motivation** to engage and learn. Second, even if learners have acquired the knowledge, they may not see the connection between that knowledge and new contexts.

By situating learning in authentic contexts, these difficulties are overcome in several ways. First, though traditional classroom instruction can convey a great deal of information on a topic, the application of that knowledge often involves implicit knowledge and habits of mind that is difficult to teach out of context. Second, because knowledge acquired in a classroom context is often abstracted and disconnected from the "real world," students often question its applicability. However, when new knowledge arises from within an authentic context, this skepticism is reduced and learning is perceived as more meaningful. Finally, learners have a tendency to "compartmentalize" their knowledge, separating school-acquired knowledge from everyday application, for example. By situating learning within a context that is similar to that in which it later will be applied, the knowledge avoids being isolated with school-acquired knowledge and becomes accessible for solving real-world problems.

Drama in Education Strategies

The use of drama techniques to support classroom learning has a variety of labels in addition to drama in education, including developmental drama, creative dramatics, educational drama, mantle of the expert, informal drama, process drama, and framed expertise. Drama in education differs from theater that is performed as scripted dialogue on a set in front of an audience. Instead, drama in education often involves the entire class in improvised *roles* within an imagined context, or *frame*. As a result, these dramas do not sharply distinguish between actor and audience; the learner is both participant and observer, playing a role while interacting with others in the role. The drama is facilitated by the classroom teacher, who builds on the actions and reactions of students-in-role to change, or *reframe,* the imagined context to create an episodic sequence of dramatic action.

For those of us with an image of drama as skits and scripts, the practice of drama in education can be difficult to grasp. To help explain their approach, practitioners of drama in education often point out their emphasis of process over product. In a staged theater production, there is often more of a focus on rehearsal as a means to an end (that end being the performance). In drama in education, the process is the end in itself. The learning emerges out of the choices and decisions made during the development or improvisation.

An important goal of role playing during simulation methods, such as drama in education, is to experience, and therefore understand, different points of view. Neuroimaging studies of conceptual perspective-taking, though not in the context of drama activities, have shown that taking perspectives different from one's own is associated with activation of different brain areas, the medial portion of the superior frontal gyrus, in the left superior temporal sulcus and left temporal pole, and in the right inferior parietal lobe, compared to thinking about one's own perspective. It may be that perspective-taking portions of drama in education activities activate the same areas identified in the perspective-taking tasks. Neuroimaging findings in related areas may provide some guidance to the interested practitioner.

The methods of drama in education have the potential to create "as-if" worlds within the classroom that can foster situated learning. For example, drama frames can be constructed with essential elements of authentic contexts, thereby bringing the laboratory (or studio, archeological dig, etc.) to the classroom. Though obviously not identical to its real-life referent, the frame's inclusion of essential elements from the authentic context may be a sufficiently effective simulation that situated learning is supported.

As the drama frame is a simulation, its effectiveness in promoting situated learning depends in part on the learners setting aside disbelief and "buying in" to the simulation. Part of the teacher's job in the drama is to build students' belief in the context and their improvised role within the drama.

However, situating learning in an authentic context does not necessarily mean expecting learners to shoulder the full expectations and responsibilities of a professional. Instead, the learner needs to be able to be involved in "real" (i.e., socially valued) work at a developmentally appropriate level, *legitimate peripheral participation*. By structuring the nature of the frame and roles, the teacher allows learners to make a valued, legitimate contribution at their own level, peripheral. It is not enough simply to frame learners as scientists in an as-if laboratory; the frame must provide enough cognitive structure and support to permit learners to engage in meaningful roles.

One goal of situating learning within a real-world context is to allow learners to think not as students, but as professionals within that context world. Within a laboratory, the learner has the opportunity to think as a scientist, while in a studio, as an artist or dancer. Thus, the benefits are caused not only by simply being situated in an authentic context, but also by working and thinking as a professional within that authentic context.

Similarly, educators can use drama techniques to not only create as-if worlds that serve as authentic contexts for situated learning, but they also can use these contexts to allow learners to work and think within meaningful roles. As a learner negotiates a dramatic role, two sets of skills are employed. First, by assuming a role, the learner adopts the thinking of that role. From an educational point of view, this allows the learner-in-role to think as a scientist (or historian, etc.) would, exploring scientific knowledge and thinking from the perspective of a scientist rather than the perspective of a student. The learner-in-role thus experiences this thinking firsthand.

When learners assume a role, much of the learner in role's attention may be devoted not only to thinking *as* a scientist, but also to thinking *about* what a scientist would think. This second set of skills, *metacognition,* can be thought of as a monitor of the first set. As learners engage in cognitive tasks (thinking as), they employ metacognition (thinking about) to guide the execution of the task.

Learners-in-role are constantly oscillating between the cognitive (thinking as) and the metacognitive (thinking about). Metacognitive knowledge guides and monitors the use of cognitive abilities, thereby strengthening and refining their application. Similarly, the success or failure of a cognitive ability provides feedback to modify the guidance provided by metacognition. The use of role is a particularly powerful method for fostering the cognitive/metacognitive interaction needed for effective learning to occur.

Cognitive research has shown that the challenge of education lies not so much in teaching a strategy as it does in acquiring the metacognitive knowledge about that strategy so that it is used when appropriate. Though this metacognitive knowledge is critical for learning, it is rarely addressed in the classroom. Students often are taught only *how* to do something and not metacognitive knowledge of when or why. For example, in a traditional mathematics classroom, much time is spent memorizing and practicing computational formulas without sufficient explanation of when one formula is more appropriate than another. In contrast, learners-in-role benefit from the cognitive and metacognitive benefits of thinking as and thinking about a role, respectively. It is the interaction between the cognitive and the metacognitive that produces learning; metacognition (thinking about) guides and refines the execution of cognitive functions (thinking as), while the successes and failures of cognition change the nature of the guidance provided by metacognition.

See also: **Creativity; Social Context of Learning; Moral Development; Music; Play.**

Further Readings

Andersen, C. (2004). Learning in "as-if" worlds: Cognition in drama in education. *Theory Into Practice* 43:281–286.

Courtney, R. (1989). *Play, Drama & Thought: The Intellectual Background to Dramatic Education.* Toronto: Simon & Pierre.

Heathcote, D., Bolton, G. (1994). *Drama for Learning: Dorothy Heathcote's Mantle of the Expert Approach to Education.* Portsmouth, NH: Heinemann.

O'Neill, C. (1995). *Drama Worlds.* Portsmouth, NH: Heinemann.

Ruby, P., Decety, J. (2003). What you believe versus what you think they believe: A neuroimaging study of conceptual perspective-taking. *European Journal of Neuroscience* 17:2475–2480.

Toga, A.W., Thompson, P.M. (2005). Genetics of brain structure and intelligence. *Annual Review of Neuroscience* 28s:1–23. (doi: 10.1146/annurev.neuro. 28.061604.135655)

American Alliance for Theatre and Education http://www.aate.com/

CHRISTOPHER ANDERSEN, PH.D.

E

Early Childhood Brain

The age group from three to eight, usually called early childhood, is an extremely important one for brain development. In this age period, development of neuronal connections (synaptogenesis) is at its peak in the frontal lobe and myelination (insulation of axons with fatty glial cells) and pruning (elimination of synaptic overproduction) in cortical structures begin in earnest. Frontal lobe maturation is necessary for the development of executive functions such as self-regulation, impulse control, attention monitoring, decision making, problem-solving, planning, long-term memory, and metacognition; and while these functions continue to develop after age eight, they are evident by the end of the early childhood age period. The increased myelination and pruning contribute to the faster and more efficient thinking of the eight-year-old, compared to the three-year-old. The changes in the brain that occur over this time period are related to many social-emotional and academic learning abilities essential for children's effectiveness in formal education settings; that is, for school success. By the age of six the child's brain is 90 percent of its adult weight, due to both synaptogenesis and myelination. Cerebral size begins to level off during this age period. Synaptic density in the frontal lobe peaks at about seven years, in comparison to the visual cortex, which has its synaptic peak at one year.

Researchers who have studied brain development report blood flow and metabolic changes during the early childhood period. For example, cerebral blood flow levels increase in the sensorimotor and parieto-temporal areas of the brain at about age three, signaling further refinements in fine motor, sensory, and gross motor skills, and increases in cerebral hemispheres are evident by age five, when memory and language skills are developing greatly. At age four, the cerebral metabolic rate of glucose utilization (which indicates synaptogenisis is occurring) is about twice the adult level. The levels of dopamine, a neurotransmitter that improves functioning of brain circuits, also rise gradually in the frontal lobe during this age period. There is an improvement in children's ability to narrow their attentional focus which accompanies changes in noradrenaline release. By age six or seven, children begin to achieve adult level performance on tasks requiring attention and inhibition. Another important brain processing feature that increases over this age period is the P300 wave, which is thought to signal children's ability to be conscious of their mental experiences. From age four to eight these P300 responses increase rapidly. Source memory, which is awareness of where and when something was learned, is evident by age seven or eight, indicating further maturation of the frontal lobe. Researchers have also found that during the early childhood years children gain the ability to understand that other people may think differently than they do. This move from egocentric thought to "theory of mind" is usually accomplished by age five and is further evidence of maturation of the frontal lobe. Brain imaging experiments have also shown that less glucose (the energy source) is burned as tasks are mastered. During this entire age period children process information more slowly but use more energy than adults. Brain processing speed shows large gains between ages five and eleven.

The structures of the brain continue to mature as well. Speech discrimination and language skills increase greatly due to development of these brain areas, and researchers have found that early exposure to sign language or second languages results in native speaker ability at adult age. The early childhood age period is considered a sensitive period for language learning as language learners at later ages may learn the language but still show variations from native speakers. The size of the corpus callosum, which integrates brain activity of the cerebral hemispheres, increases during the latter part of this age period, and there is a decrease in signal intensity, reflecting movement toward maturation of this structure. Studies of left and right hemisphere functioning in children who have had brain injury indicate that brain plasticity is still great enough during this age period for one hemisphere to take over functions of the damaged hemisphere.

Although research has not yet shown a direct link with cognitive developmental theories, these brain processing changes appear congruent with cognitive theories that describe stage changes in thought processes. Researchers have related neo-Piagetian levels of cognitive development to emerging brain research evidence of cortical cycles related to electrical energy activity in the brain. They suggest that new discoveries about brain functioning have provided evidence that there are cortical cycles parallel with the cognitive developmental cycles. As yet there has been little empirical validation of these theoretical relationships; however, this hypothesis is a promising area for further study.

The age period from three to eight involves increasing individualization in brain structures and functions. Although genetic factors play a role as well, the interaction of children's environmental experiences with their brain development during early childhood is important. While brain development during the prenatal and first few years of life is especially vulnerable to nutritional deficits, teratogens, and neglect/abuse, these environmental factors are still crucial for brain development throughout the early childhood years. Enriched environmental experiences are also likely to be a factor in brain development during early childhood because a number of vital cognitive functions that occur at this age period, such as vocabulary development, grow at astounding rates if encouraged by environmental factors. For example, during early childhood, when the language areas of the brain become active, the types of words children speak and their general vocabulary growth appear to be related to the quantity and variations of words spoken by their mothers. Studies have also shown that mothers of different socioeconomic classes differ in the amount and complexity of speech to their children and these differences show up in their children's speech. Research on literacy indicates that there is a positive relationship between having a large vocabulary at school entry and later reading ability, so the early language environment can be influential in children's later school success. Schooling itself appears to have an effect on brain development because it may assist children in gaining "meta" skills that enable them to think about their memory strategies and learning strengths. There is presently debate over how much of the brain's plasticity can overcome the absence of rich experiences at these sensitive time periods. While the brain continues to change during all of childhood, by age eight or nine, extensive opportunities for expansion of the synaptic system in some areas of the brain do appear to become more limited. As early as age six, individual brain differences may become relatively stable, and these differences may be reflected in individual children's talents and in some children's problems with skills such as phonological awareness, vocabulary richness, and other abilities that may affect academic success. More studies of brain activation areas in children of age six to eight are needed to confirm specific hypotheses about the effects of environment on differences in brain functioning. However, it is likely that environmental stresses during children's early childhood years can negatively affect neuronal complexity and brain functioning, especially if they occur during more sensitive periods of brain development. Neuroscientists believe that there is a window of opportunity for growth under normal circumstances, but the brain is particularly vulnerable to adverse conditions during the early childhood years.

As the executive functioning skills only show their presence during the latter part of this age period when the frontal lobe is gaining maturity, problems in brain development are often not identified until age seven or eight when children's success in school-related activities require these skills. Two disabilities that are often diagnosed in the latter part of this age period are dyslexia and attention deficit disorders. There is therefore much interest in studying whether brain processing patterns differ in young children with these behaviors. Presently, most research related to brain patterns in dyslexic individuals has been conducted with older subjects. In these studies, atypical cortical patterns of blood flow in the left temporal and parietal regions have been observed when reading disabled individuals perform literacy tasks, and some neuroimaging studies of reading and early sensory processing do implicate sites in the left hemisphere. Brain differences in children who exhibit attention problems in this age period are also being explored by many researchers. There may be a genetic component in which gene variants may interfere with transmission of biochemical messages or there may be abnormalities in the maturation of areas associated with the motor cortex. The behaviors of these children appear to be related to problems in executive functioning and working memory, which are sited in the frontal lobe.

Environmental deprivation and stress during this early period may also alter neuronal, hormonal, and immune systems. Although, due to ethical reasons, experimental research is not possible, some "natural experiments" involving children in neglect situations (e.g., low adult-ratio orphanages) show correlations between stressful early environments, cortisol levels, brain synaptic density, and developmental delays. Caution is needed in interpreting these findings, however, because many additional hazards may be present in the non-random samples studied; thus, no cause/effect conclusions can be drawn. In addition to frontal lobe differences, poor early experiences may affect other areas of the brain. For example, abnormal development of the hippocampus, the site of some types of memory, may affect memory development; and injury to the amygdala, the site of emotional processing, may affect emotional regulation and theory of mind development. Abused children may show a different pattern of electrical activity in the frontal and temporal lobes and even differences in brain activity in the midbrain and brainstem, which may make them have strong physiological responses even to minimal stress conditions. The impulsivity, hyperactivity, and poor affect regulation often seen in children aged three to eight from abusive environments may be evidence of this distortion in brain development. Another area being explored extensively in research is the possible brain correlates of **autism**, which often becomes evident in the early part of this age period. Although many brain structures and functions have been investigated and some seem to be implicated, definite conclusions cannot be drawn at this time.

Due to the sparseness of brain research with children in the early childhood age period, strategies that parents and educators can use to foster optimum brain development are still highly speculative. While many strategies have been suggested, at present there are no definitive studies that show direct linkages between environmental factors and improvement of specific brain structures or functions. There are also no "brain-based" curricula that are clearly derived from brain research. However, there are some general strategies that parents and educators can use that will be likely to foster optimum brain development during this age period.

First, adults can provide environments that include many opportunities for children to exercise all of their capabilities, including social-emotional, physical-sensory-motor, and language-cognition. As early childhood is a period in which synaptogenesis is occurring rapidly, especially in higher brain centers, opportunities for children to use all of their skills and abilities can encourage synaptic growth. It is at least likely that the richer the synapses, the more opportunities exist for children to create and maintain a "learning" brain. In particular during the latter part of this age period, experiences that give children opportunities to exercise executive functioning skills to develop a plethora of synapses and strong synaptic connections in the brain's frontal lobe should be provided. The development of a mature and elaborated frontal lobe is essential for later overall success in social and academic learning.

Mere exposure to many experiences is not sufficient, however. In early childhood, mastery of experiences that allow children to use their emerging skills in repetitive games, attention-focused activities, and meaningful "real-world" tasks will also assist them in strengthening synaptic connections, especially in cognitive areas that will improve later educational success (e.g., language, memory). It may be the case that the stronger such brain networks are, the less likely they are to be pruned during this age period. Playful repetition of skills, time to focus attention on pretense and rule-based games, and adult efforts to help children connect their learning to the real world can all assist in this development. Self-regulation skills should also be practiced because these are vital for effective use of other executive functioning skills. As the myelinizaton process is also proceeding rapidly, children's efficiency of thinking should increase; therefore cognitive challenges can also increase. During this age period, adults should also monitor the development of children who do not seem to be exhibiting progress in executive functioning because these children may need to have additional assistance while brain plasticity is still high.

In addition to stimulating overall brain development, at the later ages in this period adults can identify the particular specialized skills and talents of individual children and provide interesting experiences that encourage practice of these abilities. It is then likely that such abilities (e.g., artistic or mathematical talent, interest in history or science, sports-related skills) may be further strengthened through mastery-focused practice. Although, at present, the triggers for the pruning process are not clearly understood, it seems likely that stronger synaptic connections are retained and weaker ones pruned during the latter part of this age period and beyond. Enabling children to exercise their unique abilities allows them also to develop their unique brains.

See also: **Autism–Spectrum Disorders; Bilingualism; Critical Periods (Sensitive Periods).**

Further Readings

Bergen, D., Coscia, J. (2001). *Brain Research and Childhood Education: Implications for Educators.* Olney, MD: Association for Childhood Education International.

Fischer, K.W., Rose, S.P. (1998). Growth cycles of brain and mind. *Educational Leadership.* 56(3):56–60.

Nelson, C.A., Carver, L. (1998). The effects of stress and trauma on brain and memory: A view from developmental cognitive neuroscience. *Development and Psychopathology* 10(4):793–809.

Paciorek, K.M., Muro, J.H. (2005). *Annual Editions: Early Childhood Education 04/05.* Hightstown, NJ: Dushkin/McGraw-Hill. www.sciencedirect.com. (for journal *Brain and Cognition*)

DORIS BERGEN, PH.D.

Early Childhood Brain and Physical Movement

Control over the body occurs from top (head) to bottom (toes) and from the middle (trunk) to the outside (extremities). Not only do children grow considerably during the first three years of life, but they also gain considerable mastery over their bodies. They become more coordinated, more stable, and more determined to explore every bit of space available to them. This determination, combined with the drive toward independence and their inexhaustible energy, makes motor development one of the most important aspects of their young lives.

Thanks to new insights in brain research, we now know that early movement experiences are beneficial to optimal brain development. In fact, early movement experiences are considered essential to the neural stimulation (the "use-it-or-lose-it" principle involved in the keeping or pruning of neurons) needed for healthy brain development.

Not long ago, neuroscientists believed that the structure of a human brain was genetically determined at birth. They now realize that, although the main "circuits" are "prewired" for such functions as breathing and the beating of the heart, the experiences that fill each child's days are what actually determine the brain's ultimate design and, consequently, the nature and extent of that child's adult capabilities.

The brain of an infant has an abundance of brain cells (neurons) at birth, which have been "hardwired" for movement. During the first month of life, motor activity is primarily reflexive, with such reflexes as sucking, swallowing, yawning, blinking, and eliminating present at birth. As the central nervous system matures, intentional, purposeful behavior begins, and the infant becomes able to lift the head and upper body on the arms when lying face down. When lying face up, the infant can hold the head up at about four months of age.

Other significant physical milestones between the ages of four and eight months include the ability to sit with only arms propped in front for support, getting into a creeping position by raising up on arms and drawing the knees up under the body, and rolling over from front to back and the reverse. Perhaps the most noteworthy development between six and twelve months is the onset of crawling (moving on the belly) and then creeping (moving on hands and knees), the child's first real form of locomotion. Also during this period the baby begins to pull up to a standing position and eventually stands alone while using the furniture for support. Then, between twelve and eighteen months the baby finally walks unassisted.

Although it has not been clearly determined that such early movements as kicking, waving the arms, and rocking on hands and knees are practice for later, more advanced motor skills, it is believed they are a part of a process of neurological maturation needed for the control of motor skills. In other words, these spontaneous actions prepare the child, both physically and neurologically, to later perform more complex, voluntary actions.

Then, once the child is performing voluntary actions (e.g., rolling over, creeping, and walking), these movements impact brain development, as they provide both glucose (the brain's primary source of energy) and blood flow ("food") to the brain, in all likelihood increasing neuronal connections.

The theory of **critical periods** contends that nature provides certain times when children's experiences can have the greatest impact on various aspects of their development. These windows of opportunity begin opening before birth but shrink as the child gets older. For basic motor skills the critical period—the time during which experience can have the most influence—seems to extend from the prenatal stage to about age five.

This does not mean that the physical development of a child who does not take full advantage of this critical period will be stunted for life. However, it can mean that, without enough appropriate movement experiences from birth to age five, the child will miss out on the opportunity to achieve the best possible motor skill development. Scientists believe that, for certain skills, there is definitely a "too late." The brain's motor neurons must be trained between the ages of two and eleven, or they won't be "plastic" enough to be rewired later in life.

Unfortunately, most people believe children automatically acquire motor skills as their bodies develop—that it is a natural, "programmed" process that occurs along with maturation. A study involving parents and teachers in fifteen countries found that the majority of them consider the development of motor skills important for children. However, neither the parents nor the teachers felt it was their responsibility to promote it. Nor did they feel it was the responsibility of the other group.

The assumption is that motor skill development takes place without adult intervention. As described earlier, it appears that motor skills miraculously occur and simply take care of themselves. However, maturation takes care of only part of the process—the part that allows a child to execute most movement skills at an immature level.

As evidence of this, an Australian study of 1200 students between the ages of five and twelve found a surprisingly low level of ability in basic motor skills. The researchers discovered, among other things, that fewer than 10 percent of the children were able to run correctly; and only

45 percent of the elementary students could catch with correct form. Additionally, although the eleven-year-old boys demonstrated they were best able to perform a vertical jump, only 11 percent of them could do it properly.

If children are to achieve correct form and technique in their motor skills, both gross (large muscle) and fine (small muscle) movements must be taught and practiced. The repetition of practice not only allows for greater confidence and skill development, it also creates specific patterns in the brain, helping movement skills advance from an immature to a mature level.

As concerned as they are with children's cognitive and social/emotional development, the proper development of motor skills often sinks to the bottom of the list of priorities for most early childhood professionals. It is important to remember, however, that the domains of child development—physical, social/emotional, and cognitive—do not mature separately from one another. Also, young children do not differentiate among thinking, feeling, and moving; when they learn something in one domain, it impacts the others.

For example, studies show that physical skill is positively associated with peer acceptance and leadership. Even among five- and six-year-olds, those with the highest levels of motor skills were more popular than those with the lowest levels, particularly among the boys. Simply put, the more skilled children are, the more they engage in physical play, which grants them greater opportunities for social interaction. Along with it come more confidence and higher levels of self-esteem. Thus, movement influences the social/emotional domain.

Similarly, movement impacts cognitive development. Not only does it affect the creation of synapses and stimulate the brain with glucose and oxygen; but numerous studies have also demonstrated a connection between the cerebellum (the part of the brain previously associated with motor control only) and such cognitive functions as memory, spatial orientation, attention, language, and decision making, among others. Furthermore, we now know that most of the brain is activated during physical activity—much more so than when doing seat work. Additionally, young children must physically experience concepts to best understand them.

Early childhood professionals working with infants must ensure that babies do not spend the majority of their time in such things as high chairs, baby bouncers, and play pens. "Tummy time" is particularly important, in that it allows opportunities for rolling over and for creeping and crawling. The cross-lateral movement associated with these motor skills has been shown to activate both hemispheres of the brain and to increase communication across the corpus callosum, which can increase ease of learning, especially as it relates to reading and writing.

With toddlers and preschoolers, early childhood professionals should ensure the children have the time, space, and opportunity to experience both small and large motor skills. They must also provide instruction in the correct execution of these skills, beginning with the basics (e.g., walking and running) and progressing in a developmental order through the more challenging skills (like hopping and skipping), as children will not automatically acquire the ability to perform them well. Additionally, bad habits acquired early in life are likely to persist throughout an entire lifetime.

Educators should also take every opportunity to employ movement across the curriculum. Research shows that movement is young children's preferred mode of learning because they best understand concepts that are experienced physically. For example, children need to get into high and low, small and large, wide and narrow body shapes to truly understand these quantitative concepts. They need to act out simple computation problems (for instance, demonstrating the nursery rhyme "Three Little Monkeys" to discover that three minus one equals two) to comprehend subtraction. They need to move in slow motion to Bach's "Air on the G String" and rapidly to Rimsky-Korsakov's "Flight of the Bumblebee" to learn the direct relationship between the movement element of time and the musical element of tempo, and to understand the abstract ideas of slow and fast. They have to take on the straight and curving lines of the letters of the alphabet to fully grasp the way in which the letters should be printed.

Given all the information provided by recent brain research, early childhood professionals need to be aware that whenever children are learning to move, they are also moving to learn.

See also: **Physical Movement; Play.**

Further Readings

Jensen, E. (2000). *Learning with the Brain in Mind: The Scientific Basis for Energizers, Movement, Play, Games, and Physical Education.* San Diego: The Brain Store.

McCall, R.M., Craft, D. (2004). *Purposeful Play: Early Childhood Movement Activities on a Budget.* Champaign, IL: Human Kinetics.

Pica, R. (2004). *Experiences in Movement: Birth to Age eight.* Clifton Park, NY: Delmar Learning.

PBS Teacher Source www.pbs.org/teachersource/prek2/issues/202issue.shtm

RAE PICA

Emotion

The emotional brain is the part of the brain that is responsible for receiving, interpreting, and acting upon the emotional content of incoming information. Emotion plays a key role in memory. For example, consider the following questions:

- Where were you when JFK was shot or the World Trade Center crashed to the ground?
- The last time you went to dinner with friends, what reason(s) caused you to say yes to the invitation?

- Remembering back to grade one or two—was one of your first memories a negative experience?

The above are examples of the brain remembering and interpreting an event that the emotional brain perceived to be important. Neither remembering nor interpreting is possible without emotional memory.

The brain's priority and purpose is to ensure the survival of the individual. This function is mediated by the emotional brain. It is commonly thought there are six universal emotions: surprise, happiness, anger, fear, disgust, and sadness. The emotion of "love" is often added and so it has been included here. The biological reactions are described as:

- *anger* increases heart rate and therefore blood flow to the appendages while increasing adrenaline, generating an increase in strength and aggression.
- *fear* begins with the "freeze" response, allowing the brain to determine the best course of action. An increase in blood to large skeletal muscles devoted to mobility makes it easier to flee imminent danger, while diverting blood from the face and brain makes the face region turn pale. Higher cognitive skills are somewhat limited as the brain fixates on the danger at hand.
- *disgust* raises the nose as though to escape an obnoxious odor or to spit out a bad taste.
- *surprise* causes the eyebrows to rise allowing the eyes to gather more visual information.
- *happiness* is seen as a time of rest while energy stores are allowed to build up. Negative thoughts are inhibited and enthusiasm for new tasks increases.
- *sadness* produces a decided lack of energy. Its effect depresses the metabolism allowing time for reflection or reassessment of one's goals or dreams.
- *love* produces the "relaxation response" that is a direct contrast to the "fight or flight response" produced by fear. Calm, contentment, and commitment best describe this emotional state.

The emotional brain is certainly not limited to six or seven basic emotions. If each emotion can be thought of as a continuum from less intense to extremely intense, emotions can be categorized into families. For example, fear might range from anxiety to terror, while love might range from acceptance to devotion. Blends of emotions produce still more possibilities.

Researchers such as Antonio Damasio (2004) point out the involvement of the emotional brain in our daily decision making. Damasio was asked to examine patients with dysfunctional emotional systems, either as a result of tumors or of strokes. One of these patients, a man was asked to pick one of two dates for his next appointment. The individual engaged in fruitless comparisons of his options, and was never able to come to a decision. Tests of the patient's intellectual skills proved to be normal. Yet, his and their lives were anything but normal; they lost their jobs, their families, and their ability to make daily decisions. The problem was traced to damage in the emotional brain. Without a fully functioning emotional brain, reason is held captive to its own devices and is unable to make a decision.

Such work illustrates the importance of the emotional brain functioning in conjunction with the thinking "cognitive" brain. The thinking brain acts like a ship without a rudder when the emotional brain is impaired.

Technology and aggressive research techniques are challenging old assumptions, such as the long regarded importance of the "limbic system" as the seat of emotions. Current research questions if it is the seat of emotion or a system. Using his research on fear, Joseph LeDoux (1996) proposes the amygdala as the hub that mediates fear as well as other emotions.

LeDoux further proposes that each emotion probably evolved separately, rather than as a group, to respond to some biological need of the evolving organism. Therefore, we should not expect to find all emotions located in one central structure; and individual emotions would need to be studied separately. It is speculated that each will be found in groups of circuits acting in concert to produce what is termed an emotion.

Pathway

Information from the senses passes through the brainstem which is associated with attention. Information that is perceived by the brain to deserve its attention is passed on to the thalamus that distributes the information to the appropriate part of the cortex, for example, visual information would be sent to the visual cortex located at the back of the brain. The only exception would be the sense of smell that has a direct pathway to the olfactory center without passing through the thalamus.

Before 1992, it was believed the sensory projections of the thalamus extended mainly to the sensory areas of the cortex. The cortex then sent projections to the amygdala and an emotion would then be experienced. Neuroscientists discovered an additional shorter parallel circuit from the thalamus to the amygdala, allowing the cortex to be bypassed.

Why Does the Brain Maintain Two Circuits?

The cortical pathway may be characterized as precise but slow. However, the amygdala and thalamus are separated by only a short distance and only one synapse. This translates into a signal arriving at the emotional brain a split second before reaching the cognitive brain. As the emotional brain is hardwired to respond to strong emotional stimuli and the thinking brain is wired to compare, contrast, and generally analyze, it is reasonable to expect an emotional response before a cognitive response. This is why some students act in an irrational manner when they perceive strong emotional messages.

Emotions travel the brain's quickest neural routes. Examination of the sheer numbers of fibers entering or leaving the amygdala shows there are far more fibers from the amygdala to the cortical brain than the reverse. In an emergency, the emotional brain is wired to dominate brain output. An "emotional hijack" is the norm under conditions of a perceived threat. Individuals often conceive of the best responses about twenty minutes after a heated debate, this is because the brain requires that amount of time to diffuse the caustic chemicals of a hijack.

The good news for educators and parents is that a circuit also extends from the prefrontal cortex back to the amygdala! The important function of this circuit was alluded to by Damasio's work with patients who severed this circuit and were experiencing life without emotions. The prefrontal cortex sends back messages that enhance or inhibit the role of the amygdala.

Neuroscience can differentiate the roles played by the left and right prefrontal cortexes in regulating emotions. The left prefrontal cortex is involved in keeping the emotions in the positive register, sending out good feelings and taming frustration. It is the optimistic side. The right prefrontal keeps the amygdala agitated and in the negative register. It is active during periods of stress or emotional hijack; it keeps the brain fixated upon the source of distress. It is our pessimistic side.

Social Role of the Emotional Brain

One of the emotional brain's more important jobs is assessing the emotional states of those around it. Careful observation of facing another individual in silence for a two-minute period will usually result in the following observations: that each person *transmits* emotional messages; that emotional messages can be *read* by the observing individual; that the emotions are *contagious* and that we can even change the *physiology* of other individuals. This receptive state of the emotional brain was paramount to a brain that had not yet evolved language.

Implications for Teaching/Learning

A group of nuclei within the brainstem work together to focus attention. Their job is to rid the brain of tasks as mundane as how our shoes feel. Teachers and consequently learners need to get past this barrier into the brain by giving their work some emotional importance. Copying notes will likely send the information to the same part of the brain that indicates how our shoes feel. The following are suggested ways to bring emotion into the classroom:

- *Role playing* involves students and their amygdalas. For example, in a literature class, the teacher reads a poignant passage, then asks student volunteers to play the roles of the characters in the story as a "freeze frame." They then interview each character to personalize the learning. In a biology or chemistry class, students are asked to become the carbon atoms in one of the energy reactions, using only their interlocked arms to form or break bonds.

- *Emotional hooks*—Many teachers use these to introduce topics. Imagine a chemistry class that began with a demonstration of changing "water" to "wine" and finally to "milk." Give student's brains a question that their brains would like to solve. The emotional brain will open up a floodgate into the student's attentional system.

- *Trips* to the zoo to see the animals pictured in the text is emotionally stronger and more meaningful than looking at pictures or even watching a film. Trips show that learning is a life-long activity and is not reserved for the confines of the school setting.

- *Mind maps or concept maps* that allow the student to express their feelings (good or bad) for the topic involves the students' emotional brain and therefore their attention.

- *Class discussions or debates* that involve the students choosing and/or defending sides are particularly interesting if the students must switch sides halfway through the debate.

- *Cooperative learning strategies* that emphasize emotional intelligence skills equip students with the employability skills that fewer parents are able to provide at home. Most failures of this strategy tend to focus on cognitive learning strategies. The emotional brain is programmed not in lectures but in modeling and in practicing appropriate behaviors.

- *Safe emotional environment* or threatening emotional environment; emotions are a double-edged sword. Engaging students' emotional brain system has to take place in a safe environment. If the student's brain perceives threat during the learning process, their brain will focus on the threat rather than on the learning.

Students' emotional brains perceive almost instantly the emotional state of the teacher as they walk into the classroom. They are more apt to catch their emotional state than vice versa as they are in authority. Administrators can be true leaders in establishing the emotional mood of the day. Personal attacks at any level that flood the brain with caustic chemical cause the brain to downshift and have an effect not only on the individual involved.

Passion for what is being taught is probably the first step to turning on the emotional brains of learners. The necessity to make a good mark is not a compelling reason for many students to learn.

Finally, the other axiom in applied neuroscience—"use it or lose it"—is as applicable to the programming of the emotional brain as to the sensory brain. Jay Giedd of the National Mental Health Institute found that the emotional circuits that give feedback to the emotional brain, the prefrontal–amygdala circuit is not mature till about twenty years of age. That means for parents and educators that modeling, patience, and guidance are required to mold the teenage brain. Do not hesitate to bring emotion into your classroom; it will enhance remembering and interpreting information.

See also: **Adolescent Social and Emotional Development; Emotional Intelligence; Depression.**

Further Readings

Damasio, A. ed. Johnson, S. (2004). Theory of thinking faster and faster. *Discover* 25(5):44–49.

Giedd, J. (2002) Frontline: *Interviews Inside the Teenage Brain.* http://www.pbs.org

Goleman, D. (2002). *Primal Leadership, Realizing the Power of Emotional Intelligence.* Boston, MA: Harvard Business School Publishing.

Ledoux, J. (1996). *The Emotional Brain, the Mysterious Underpinnings of Emotional Life.* New York, NY: Simon and Schuster.

Wolfe, P. (2001). *Brain Matters, Translating Research into Classroom Practice.* Alexandria, VA: ASCD.

ALLISON MAXWELL

Emotional Intelligence

The first scientific definition of the term emotional intelligence appeared in a 1990 article by Peter Salovey and John D. Mayer in the journal, *Imagination, Cognition, and Personality.* Salovey and Mayer defined emotional intelligence as, "The ability to monitor one's own and others' feelings, to discriminate among them, and to use this information to guide one's thinking and action." The concept of emotional intelligence stemmed from two converging trends in psychology: changing views about the functionality of **emotions** and broadening definitions of what it means to be intelligent. Although Western psychology has historically considered emotions as interfering with rational thought, Salovey and Mayer emphasized how emotions can be adaptive. In the spirit of Charles Darwin, who viewed emotions as necessary for survival across many species, Salovey and Mayer believed that emotions provided people with important information they could use to navigate their social environment.

Popular and Scientific Definitions

After the publication of the bestselling book *Emotional Intelligence* by New York Times science writer Daniel Goleman in 1995, the concept of emotional intelligence gained enormous popular appeal and received intense media attention. Subsequently, the term emotional intelligence has been used very broadly. For example, the term has motivated the writing of self-help books and the designing of programs to improve workplace performance. The present discussion is restricted to the scientific study of emotional intelligence, which abides by a formal definition of the concept as encompassing a set of specific abilities.

These abilities, often referred to as the four branches of emotional intelligence, were described as the following: (a) the ability to accurately perceive and express emotions; (b) the ability to access and generate feelings when they facilitate cognitive activities; (c) the ability to understand emotion-related information and make use of emotional knowledge; (d) the ability to manage emotions optimally in both the self and in others.

The first branch of emotional intelligence, perceiving emotions, is the ability to recognize emotions in faces, voices, pictures, and other stimuli. The second branch of emotional intelligence, using emotions, is the ability to use emotions to facilitate thinking (e.g., reasoning, problem-solving). The third branch, understanding emotions, involves the ability to correctly label different emotions and make complex associations between emotions. For example, it would include understanding how irritation can lead to rage if not properly attended to. The fourth branch of emotional intelligence, managing emotions, is the ability to regulate one's own emotions as well as the emotions of others. Managing emotions includes the ability to change one's mood from good to bad (or vice versa) as well as the ability to help change or stabilize the emotions of others in social situations.

Measuring Emotional Intelligence

As emotional intelligence garnered attention from both scientists and the general public, demand for emotional intelligence tests grew rapidly. Self-report tests of emotional intelligence gained in popularity due to the ease with which they can be designed and administered. Two commonly used self-report tests of emotional intelligence are the Emotional Quotient Inventory (EQI) and the Self-Report Emotional Intelligence Test (SREIT). Salovey and Mayer also constructed a self-report scale that examines the meta- or reflective, experience of mood. This scale is the 30-item Trait Meta-Mood Scale (TMMS), which taps into a person's beliefs about how much they commonly attend to and label their own mood states as well as repair their more negative emotion. Sample items from this measure include *I pay a lot of attention to how I feel* (Attention to feelings), *I can never tell how I feel* (Clarity of feelings), and

I try to think good thoughts no matter how badly I feel (Repair of feelings). Like the EQI and the SREIT, the TMMS depends on a person's willingness and ability to report on whether or not they have various competencies and experiences consistent with being emotionally intelligent; it does not require individuals to demonstrate their emotional competencies. A more valid measure of emotional intelligence requires objective tasks rather than self-assessments.

To address this need for an ability-based test of emotional intelligence, the Multifactor Emotional Intelligence Scale (MEIS) was created. The test demonstrated good reliability and administering the test to a wide sample of people showed that emotional intelligence seems to increase with age which is an appropriate finding for something worthy of being called intelligence. A few years later, the MEIS was improved upon in the form of the Mayer, Salovey, and Caruso Emotional Intelligence Test. The MSCEIT consists of eight different tasks, two for each of the four branches, or abilities, of emotional intelligence. The MSCEIT has demonstrated good reliability as well as appropriate discriminate validity with respect to measures of personality and analytical intelligence. Specifically, scores on the MSCEIT tend to overlap very little with commonly used measures of personality and only moderately with measures of analytical intelligence. Both these findings suggest that the test taps into emotional skills and abilities, rather than personality traits, and measures something distinct from traditional IQ tests.

One of the more difficult issues involved with emotional intelligence is the question of how to score ability-based measures. Unlike tests of analytical intelligence, the questions associated with emotional intelligence tests lack clear right and wrong answers. This problem of how to score emotional intelligence tests has been addressed through two methods: consensus and expert scoring. With consensus scoring, an individual's answers on the MSCEIT are statistically compared to the answers that were provided by a normative sample of five thousand people. A higher degree of overlap would indicate a higher score and thus, higher emotional intelligence. With expert scoring, an individual's answers are compared to those that were provided by a group of leading emotions researchers. However, it is important to note that consensus and expert scores are highly correlated and therefore, both scoring procedures generate very similar scores for the same individual.

Research Using the MSCEIT

Since its publication in 2002, the MSCEIT has been used by investigators interested in studying relationships between emotional intelligence and important, real-world outcomes. One such outcome that has already yielded substantial empirical evidence has been the quality of personal relationships at home, school, and at work. Higher scores on the MSCEIT have been found to be associated with positive self-ratings of relationships with parents, roommates, and friends. People who score higher on the MSCEIT were rated by their friends as being more emotionally supportive than people who score lower. In one study, employees at an insurance company completed the MSCEIT and evaluated their peers on a variety of social and emotional competencies. They were also rated by their supervisors on these same competencies. Employees who scored higher on branch four of the MSCEIT, managing emotions, were rated more positively by both their peers and supervisors. They also tended to have attained higher positions and salaries than their lower scoring colleagues.

Future Directions and Ongoing Issues

Although promising so far, empirical research on emotional intelligence lags far behind popular claims that have been made in the media about the importance of emotional intelligence in everyday life. The term emotional intelligence has been popularly used to represent many different aspects of emotional life. Scientific researchers interested in studying emotional intelligence prefer to focus on the specific abilities involved in appraising, using, understanding, and regulating emotions as outlined in the Mayer and Salovey model. The use of ability-based measures, such as the MSCEIT, represents a promising approach to reliably and accurately assessing these abilities and examining how they relate to important, real-world outcomes. Research in the coming years should continue to address how best to measure the skills associated with emotional intelligence and in addition, how they manifest themselves in the different contexts and situations that require them.

Although the MSCEIT has demonstrated adequate psychometric properties and good predictive validity, much more research is needed to examine how people apply the skills of emotional intelligence in their everyday lives. It is likely that additional research will reveal that the skills associated with emotional intelligence are to some degree context-specific. For example, some individuals might be quite skilled at handling their emotions at work while having great difficulty dealing with the emotions of their loved ones. Future research should focus on an individual's strengths and weaknesses in using their emotional skills in different situations. Doing so would give us an even better understanding of how emotional intelligence accounts for behavior not predicted by traditional, analytical intelligence.

See also. Aggression; Anger; Depression; Emotion; Pleasure; Stress.

Further Readings

Lopes, P.N., Salovey, P. (2003). Toward a broader education: Social, emotional, and practical skills. In J.E. Zins, R.P. Weissberg, M.C. Wang, H.J. Walberg (Eds.), *Building School Success on Social and Emotional Learning*. New York: Teachers College Press.

Mayer, J.D., Salovey, P., Caruso, D.R. (2000). Emotional intelligence as Zeitgeist, as personality, and as a mental ability. In R. Bar-On, J.D.A. Parker (Eds.), *The Handbook of Emotional Intelligence* (pp. 92–117). San Francisco, CA: Jossey-Bass.

Mayer, J.D., Salovey, P., Caruso, D.R., Sitarenios, G. (2003). Measuring emotional intelligence with the MSCEIT V2.0. *Emotion* 3:97–105.

Salovey, P., Mayer, J.D., Caruso, D.R. (2002). The positive psychology of emotional intelligence. In C.R. Snyder, S.J. Lopez (Eds.), *Handbook of Positive Psychology* (pp. 159–171). New York: Oxford University Press.

DAISY GREWAL, M.S. AND
PETER SALOVEY, PH.D.

Emotionally and Behaviorally Challenged

One of the greatest challenges faced by educators today is balancing the complex and varied needs of students who exhibit behavioral and emotional challenges (BECs) in school settings with the needs of others. Some BECs may not disrupt the learning of others but certainly affect the individual student's availability for learning. Neuroscience refutes the long-standing assumption that BECs are due to characterological flaws and provides insights into why various BECs occur, the brain differences they represent, and what educators and other practitioners can do about them.

Diagnostic and Statistical Diversity

BECs may stand alone as diagnoses (e.g., Tourette's Syndrome; **anorexia** and other eating disorders; intermittent explosive, oppositional, or conduct disorders); contribute to the definitions of specific psychiatric conditions (e.g., **schizophrenia,** mood disorders such as **depression** and bipolar disorder, or various anxiety disorders); or be secondary to other developmental disabilities (e.g., **autism spectrum disorders, learning disabilities, language acquisition and disorders,** or sensory integration dysfunction).

Etiologies of BECs may be primarily experiential (as with post-traumatic **stress** disorder, reactive attachment disorder, or learned helplessness) or linked to other environmental factors such as exposure to brain toxins (e.g., **fetal alcohol syndrome** or adolescent substance abuse that may actually reflect an effort to self-medicate). Disease (e.g., brain tumor) or acquired brain injury (such as due to excessive cerebrospinal fluid or accident) can also play a causative role for some individuals who display BECs. The genetic basis for some BECs is strongly suspected (e.g., in **ADD/ADHD** or panic attacks) and research into genetic susceptibility to other BECs (e.g., eating disorders) is currently underway. Most researchers agree that it is the interaction of nature v. nurture that results in the manifestation of BECs in some individuals but not in others.

Observable characteristics of BECs may involve excess behaviors (e.g., **aggression** to self or others, **at risk behavior,** or outbursts of **anger**); difficulty in learning, demonstrating **mastery,** or forming relationships with others or withdrawal/flight. Long standing histories of

BECs adversely affect **self-concept/self-esteem** and, in some cases, the individual's overall health and well-being.

Not all students who exhibit BECs are currently considered eligible for special education although the argument has been made that all are in need of specialized treatment. The number of students newly identified as eligible for special education each year because of "emotional disturbance" (which includes those who present behavior challenges) has remained at just under 1 percent of all students. Estimates of the prevalence of BECs range from 2 to 6 percent of all students. The prevalence rates for BECs differ according to specific diagnoses and are difficult to interpret because of variations in identification criteria as well as significant co-morbidity. However, girls appear to be underrepresented whereas African-Americans tend to be overrepresented in most statistics.

Contributions from Neuroscience in Understanding BECs

A number of areas of the brain have been linked to BECs through neuroimaging alone and in concert with studies of the effects of pharmacological interventions. Family and **animal studies** have contributed to the knowledge base.

Research has shown, for example, that the combined structures of the limbic system act as a "screener" for all incoming sensory information to the brain such that threat messages (actual or perceived) are sent directly to the amygdala and other "lower brain" areas for action without thought. Threats in an educational setting can be obvious as is the case with bullying or subtle such as when a student feels incompetent as a learner. Initial interpretation of sensory input also sets the individual's mood states (e.g., negative outlook, irritability, or hostile attitude) and regulates primary and secondary emotional responses (e.g., anger, frustration, sadness, guilt and embarrassment/shame or lack thereof). In some students, emotional responses are chronic whereas other students may appear stable for an extended period of time but then exhibit acute episodes or emotional turmoil or behavioral outbursts. Overactivation of the emotional regulation system can lead to behaviors consistent with bipolar disorder, often likened to an emotional rollercoaster.

Hemispheric differences in limbic activation may account for differential expression of behavior, with more outer directed behaviors (e.g., fighting, verbal aggression) associated with the left side and more internalizing behaviors (e.g., withdrawal, anxiety) associated with the right hemisphere.

Differences in the overall limbic system structures also can account for differences in **motivation** between individuals and explain why some students (especially those with BECs) don't seem to care about doing well in school or what others think. The limbic system as a whole also modulates the ability or inability to delay gratification (contributing to impulsivity and demands that one's own needs be met immediately), affects bonding (e.g., by promoting it with inappropriate peer models and impeding it with adults and positive peer models), and affects patterns of **sleep** and appetite. Problems with sleep and appetite have themselves been linked to BECs.

Through brain imaging studies, two deep structures of the limbic system—the hypothalamus and the amygdala—have been specifically associated with many types of BECs. Overactivity in either or both of these structures results in a heightened probability of autonomic nervous system arousal that stimulates fight or flight responses (e.g., aggression, storming out of a classroom without permission, or refusing to do work or comply with directions). Heightened fear and anxiety responses linked to differences in the structure and function of the amygdala have been associated with various phobias (ranging from general school phobia to shutting down during certain classes or for tests). The amygdalas of students who have repeatedly gotten into trouble in school may cause them to respond without thinking when negative emotional memories are triggered. Chronic stress related to impoverished or violent home environments, a history of school failure, or lack of social connections may exacerbate this effect.

Other structures of the limbic system that have been implicated in BECs are the basal ganglia and the cingulate gyrus. Dysfunctions in the basal ganglia and its striatum (notably in two substructures called the caudate nucleus and the putamen) affect some students' ability to sustain attention constructively, to make smooth transitions between classes, activities, or learning states, and/or to "let go" of a perceived insult or other event experienced as negative by the individual. An overactive cingulate gyrus has been linked to repetitive thinking and behavior as well as depressive symptoms.

The pathways connecting the limbic structures of the brain to each other as well as to the cortex, and the various neurotransmitters involved, have varied roles in BECs. Deficient levels of the neurotransmitter gamma-aminobutyric acid (GABA) are related to heightened anxiety, phobias, and depression. Deficiencies in another neurotransmitter, Substance P, may increase impulsivity and at-risk behaviors because suppression of pain signals normally transmitted reduces the inhibition of learned responses resulting from pain avoidance. Differences in the metabolism of glucose, the major "food of the brain," has been documented in individuals with attention deficits. Overall high levels of the neurotransmitter, serotonin, in brain synapses can result in irrational behavior (e.g., symptomatic of schizophrenia) whereas too little resulting from excessive reuptake by the sending neuron is linked to depression.

Non-threatening information received through the limbic system goes to the cortex for processing, understanding, recognition, and other higher order thinking processes. The prefrontal cortex has been linked to numerous adaptive human behaviors and thought processes cumulatively referred to as "executive function."

Differences in the structure and function of the prefrontal cortex are linked to "executive dysfunction." Such differences have been found in individuals who (1) have short attention spans, poor organization, and poor planning skills; (2) are highly distractible, hyperactive, and impulsive; (3) lack the ability to persevere and manage time well; (4) experience high levels of anxiety; and (5) procrastinate, misrepresent the truth by omission or commission, tend to misperceive other's intentions, and exercise poor judgment. For example, in individuals who exhibit antisocial and violent behaviors, the prefrontal cortex is smaller, there is a decrease in gray matter, and brain wave activity is less robust. For those with behaviors characteristic of depression (e.g., refusal to participate in activities that were previously enjoyable) and schizophrenia, there is also a decrease in prefrontal cortical activity. Increased activity, however, appears to be associated with obsessive–compulsive behaviors.

Decreased activity in the temporal lobes has been found in individuals exhibiting behavioral symptoms of depression. Similar decreased activity has been found in the specific areas of the temporal lobes related to auditory information processing in individuals with conduct and attention deficit disorder. In contrast, Daniel Amen's SPECT studies of individuals with a range of other BECs have revealed excessive cortical activity in the frontal, parietal, and occipital lobes resembling a "ring of fire."

The onset of some BECs during late adolescence/young adulthood appears related to the well-documented developmental changes that typically occur in the adolescent brain. Abnormal cell development and inefficient pruning may play a role in causing brain differences that result in the onset of BECs and may account for changes in the manifestations of certain BECs (e.g., depression in childhood may be exhibited as anger and aggression toward others whereas, in adulthood, it is more typically characterized as pervasive sadness and withdrawal from others). The increased hormones associated with puberty also have an impact on brain functions involved in BECs by affecting the transmission of neuronal messages from one brain cell to another. Certain societal structures imposed on adolescents (such as increased stress from working, maintaining good grades, and having a social life as well as the poor match between changes in the circadian rhythm of adolescents and the early start times of many secondary schools) can exacerbate BECs.

Brain-Based Intervention Strategies

Punishment intended to decrease BECs and artificial positive reinforcement intended to increase appropriate behavior have been shown to be ineffective in managing BECs. Similarly, calling attention to BECs can exacerbate them. Instead, proactive classroom management strategies in concert with brain compatible strategies for handling specific problems are essential to effectively educating students with BECs and their classmates who are challenged themselves when their learning environment is disrupted. Proactive, brain-compatible strategies emphasize preventive tactics (e.g., building on individual strengths and removing, minimizing, or ameliorating the effects of environmental barriers to success), educative approaches that effectively re-wire the brain, and positive interpersonal relationships/social connections.

To determine which particular strategies will be most effective in dealing with individual students, practitioners must conduct comprehensive functional behavioral analyses (FBAs). The most effective FBAs are developed by a team (the student, selected peers, his parents, teachers, and others) who know and care about the individual student. FBAs must objectively specify the behaviors of concern in terms of the severity of impact each has on the individual's and other's learning. The frequency, intensity, duration, and other patterns of occurrence (e.g., whether more problems occur on specific days of the week, how escalation progresses) should be data-based.

Most importantly, known antecedent events or triggers should be identified and the team should also generate other hypotheses about both the functions the behaviors potentially serve and what the underlying brain-based causes may be. Examples may include diagnoses or undiagnosed psychiatric conditions, failure to accommodate **learning styles** or **learning disabilities,** sensory integration dysfunction, and one or more structural or functional brain differences.

Strategies that have had demonstrated success (and those known not to result in positive behavior change) should be identified. New strategies that systematically address antecedents and hypotheses should be articulated. Results must be incorporated into an individualized behavior support/intervention plan (BS/IP) that requires adults involved to collectively "pick their battles." This occurs when the BS/IP targets behaviors of greatest concern for intervention while refraining from placing demands on the student to refrain from other, less serious behaviors to occur *for now.* This enables the student to develop appropriate coping strategies and concentrate on meeting non-negotiable demands. Strategies known not to work with a particular student should be conscientiously avoided.

Effective interventions range from using collaborative problem-solving strategies (i.e., empathy, reflective listening, reassurance, problem definition, and invitation to problem-solve) to providing appropriate sensory diets and outlets for success. For more extreme BECs, BS/IPs may need to include individualized consequation strategies through the time-limited use of external motivators that are meaningful to the specific student and restitution that "fits the crime" to repair and restore interpersonal relationships with peers and adults.

For some students, classroom-based strategies may need to be supplemented by the provision of "safe places" outside the classroom for them to regroup, therapeutic interventions involving cognitive-behavioral or similar techniques, wrap-around services to families (e.g., parent training, sibling support groups, respite, and crisis intervention), and administration of such medications as stimulants, anti-depressants, anti-anxiety agents, or anti-psychotics. Particularly with adolescents, research has shown that a single positive and unconditionally accepting relationship with one adult can make the difference between the student ultimately being successful or continuing to exhibit significant BECs into adulthood.

Adult attitudes and behaviors play major roles in managing BECs. Often, BECs "are in the eyes of the beholder." Adults with a low tolerance for kinesthetic learning styles and a lack of appreciation for typical **gender differences** in activity level and social skills (with boys generally being more active and less socially connected than girls) are more inclined to mislabel behavioral differences as behavioral or emotional problems. When willful lack of self-control rather than hardwired brain differences are assumed to cause BECs, interventions tend to be overly simplistic. They can exacerbate the BECs because rewards are either undesirable or not attainable (leading to increased frustration) and punishments disrupt already tenuous interpersonal relationships involving trust and respect. Neither primes the brain for learning. BECs don't develop overnight and a genuine commitment by the team of both time and resources is necessary to overcome them.

"Good education for all" is the final ingredient for effectively addressing BECs in the classroom. When students are constructively engaged in learning activities that provide choices and balance novelty with familiar routines; when the content is meaningful, built on prior knowledge, and their brains can recognize patterns; when threat is absent and the environment is enriching; when skills in collaboration and cooperation are taught and expected, behavioral and emotional challenges have been shown either to decrease significantly or to disappear altogether.

See also: **Adolescent Cognitive Development; Adolescent Social and Emotional Development; Classroom Management; Language Acquisition and Disorders.**

Further Readings

Sapolsky, R. (2004). *Why Zebras Don't Get Ulcers: The Acclaimed Guide to Stress, Stress-Related Diseases, and Coping.* (3rd ed.) New York, NY: Henry Holt & Co.

Jensen, E. (2000). *Different Brains, Different Learners: How to Reach the Hard to Reach.* San Diego, CA: The Brain Store.

Center for Effective Collaboration and Practice. http://www.air.org/cecp/ http://www.brainplace.com

LINDA H. RAMMLER, M.ED., PH.D.

Emotionally and Behaviorally Disturbed

Rebecca was just completing kindergarten; she'd been a model student and a pleasure to have in class. The second week of May, for no apparent reason, everything suddenly changed. Rebecca began screaming hateful remarks and tearing up the house. Her mother attempted to calm her, but with every effort Rebecca's behavior worsened. She fought her mother, screaming that she was going to kill her and herself. She was wisely taken to the emergency room. A psychiatrist was called in; after an evaluation and observation Rebecca was sent to her home with instructions "hide all knives in the house and make an appointment with the Children's Counseling Center next week." With the out of control behaviors continuing her mother contacted the family doctor asking for some brain imaging and neurological tests but was told "we have to wait until her behaviors are under control."

Every day educators experience the backlash of behaviors that disrupt learning. Students who exhibit emotional and behavioral difficulties seriously disrupt the climate of a class and building, and crush their self-esteem and sense of self worth each time they experience difficulties. Educators sit through student conferences frequently hearing one of two scenarios: "The behaviors in question are learned, therefore no special services may be provided"; or, "This child's problems are emotionally based and he's eligible for services for "**emotionally disturbed"** students. What seldom, if ever, is heard is that a child should be evaluated for possible brain dysfunctions.

Specific brain dysfunctions cause identifiable clusters of behavioral symptoms. Many of these symptoms are characteristic of the special education classification known as "emotionally disturbed." Examples of such behaviors that may need medical attention include difficulties with almost all relationships across multiple settings, aggression toward self and/or others, mood swings, anxieties, confusion, learning problems, depression, oppositional behaviors, and inappropriate affect. Serious behavior problems are also often labeled as a "Conduct Disorder," which is thought to be due to learned behaviors without any consideration that such patterns of behavior may indicate specific brain dysfunctions. Therefore, educational professionals should be front and center in recognizing possible brain dysfunctions and refer these children and parents to physicians that understand that a "broken brain creates broken behavior." The difficulties these children experience require a multifaceted approach that includes proper educational, behavioral, and medical expertise.

Knowledgeable educators could become the first qualified person to recognize that specific problems may be related to brain function. Specific symptoms may indicate serious and often correctable neurological problems. Many problems that are correctly noted by teachers could be diagnosed through the use of single photon emission computed tomography (SPECT) scans.

The SPECT scan is a diagnostic tool utilizing nuclear medicine that measures the blood flow and brain metabolism. It reveals information related to the physiological activity of the brain—the activity of the brain at work. SPECT scans reveal which areas of the brain function normally and which are overactive and underactive. Years of research have resulted in understanding behavior patterns (symptoms) that correlate with specific levels of activity in various areas of the brain. Debra Hughes reported that recent improvements in brain imaging techniques provided information regarding neurobiologic and genetic factors related to neuropsychiatric and mental disorders. Not every student exhibiting behavior problems or emotional disturbances needs a SPECT scan; that would be impractical. But what is practical and necessary is for those who work with children to become knowledgeable about the clusters of behaviors that may indicate the possibility of brain dysfunctions. Looking at some of the most common behavior problems noted in the schools will bring to the fore the desperate need for educators, school psychologists, school social workers and others working with children to understand the relationship between the brain and behavior.

Based on research from tens of thousands of SPECT scans by physicians and researchers many patterns of behavior, exhibited by both children and adults, have been identified as resulting from specific brain dysfunctions. The correlation of behaviors to specific areas of the brain has led researchers and practitioners to treatment plans that are highly effective and manageable. Based on the results of over 22,000 SPECT scans, Dr. Daniel G. Amen, of the Amen Clinics, describes patterns of behaviors related to brain functions and dysfunctions. A brief summary will elucidate the need to understand the relationship between the behaviors observed in schools and their possible indication of problems in brain function.

The basal ganglia regulates the brain's anxiety and "idling" levels as well as integrates movement, emotions, and thinking. Overactive basal ganglia may create anxieties that look like and create serious emotional problems. Such anxieties include excessive shyness, low or excessive motivation, poor handwriting, tendency to freeze in situations when others their age react adaptively, low tolerance for embarrassment, negative thinking, phobias, nervousness, headaches, and stomach aches.

The temporal lobes play an important part in memory and emotional stability. The right and left lobes serve different functions. Dysfunctional temporal lobes produce behavioral characteristics such as aggression (to self and/or others), thinking that others are talking about or laughing at them, learning problems, language problems, violent behavior (provoked and unprovoked), irritability, dark thoughts, word find problems, memory problems, and difficulty reading facial expressions and/or vocal intonations.

The cingulate system is designed to correctly govern transitions and accommodate change. Amen refers to this system as the brain's "gear shift." Consider for a moment these behavior patterns: argumentative, oppositional behavior, inability to move on to another topic and/or alternative behaviors due to being preoccupied and almost controlled by the thoughts or behaviors of self/others. When you see these and other behaviors it may well be due to increased activity in the cingulate system.

The prefrontal cortex is designed to help people stop and think, use appropriate judgment, control aggression and focus. A dysfunctional prefrontal cortex may result in behaviors such as impulsivity, aggression, violence, inattentiveness, hyperactivity, poor judgment, distractibility, disorganization, misperceptions, disruption in access to emotions, and short-term memory difficulties.

Co-morbidity, or overlapping disorders, adds to the need for proper diagnosis and treatment, as some medications will exacerbate the behavioral symptoms created by dysfunctions in different areas of the brain. Therefore, it is important that the treating physicians be knowledgeable of the work of researchers and practitioners in the field of neuropsychiatry.

Interventions that address specific brain dysfunction vary according to the cause of the abnormalities. For example, nutritional needs and medications differ depending on which brain systems are not functioning optimally. The scope of this article does not permit listing specific strategies for each system dysfunction, therefore global recommendations are given.

Knowledgeable medical intervention is the first step in addressing neurological problems. It is imperative that the family, school, and medical personnel work together to coordinate treatment plans that ensure consistent delivery across all settings.

Teachers and other school personnel should collaborate in developing a climate that is safe, secure, and presents appropriately high expectations. Rules and procedures need to be taught to students through a **multiple intelligence** approach to maximize understanding. Clear expectations should be developed and implemented by everyone in the school. Consistency is not possible unless all people respond similarly to maintain stated expectations.

Strategies that increase students' feeling of self-worth are imperative. Positive attention, meaningful relationships, successful experiences, developing talents, and increasing a sense of belonging help encourage students to continue their effort to improve brain functioning. Children need a sense of hope to give them the will to persevere.

Teach students to see things in a positive light by facilitating awareness of their negative perceptions. Knowing what negative comments and thoughts sound like and feel like will help students become aware of their negative thinking. Teach them what positive and alternative points of view feel and sound like. This teaching process should be integrated throughout the school. Many students with brain dysfunctions have experienced negative interpersonal relationships, therefore social skills should also be taught using a multisensory approach.

Movement and exercise are beneficial for students with brain dysfunction. They increase levels of dopamine, a neurotransmitter in the brain that enhances abilities to focus and feel better emotionally and physically. Movement may be integrated into many lessons, recess, and activities. Permitting students to move rhythmically, do cross-laterals and stand next to their desks adds stimulation, interest, and improves brain functioning.

Many students with brain dysfunctions experience confusion and chaos in their lives. It is important not to reinforce chaos by arguing or ignoring inappropriate behaviors. Students experiencing these problems often react negatively, yet such behavior literally makes them feel better. Their reactions cause the brain to produce specific chemicals that actually improves the way they feel and function. Inappropriate adult responses may reinforce behaviors that are related to the dysfunction. Remain calm, positive, and consistent. Take deep breaths, redirect the student to your expectations, and alter the environment to decrease anxieties, distractions, and factors that cause frustration. Setting short- and long-term goals aids students in refocusing and decreasing confusion.

Abnormal brain activity levels may also adversely affect memory and communication skills. Directions, conversations and classroom activities should be presented in a concise, clear, multisensory manner to enhance understanding. Check to see if the student understands what is expected in a way that avoids embarrassment.

The difficulties and frustrations that are inherent with brain dysfunctions are very real and may cause emotional difficulties secondary to those created by the neurological problem itself. Remembering that no child would elect to have these problems helps educators to maintain calm and work diligently to find effective interventions. The more educators know about how the brain functions, the more understanding and effective they become when dealing with dysfunctions that are not the fault of the individual. Through professional development educators will become knowledgeable, involved, and invaluable advocates for students with brain dysfunctions.

See also: **At-Risk Behavior; Emotionally and Behaviorally Challenged; Multiple Intelligences.**

Further Readings

Amen, D. (2002). *Healing ADD: The Breakthrough Program That Allows You to See and Heal the Six Types of ADD.* New York, NY. G.P. Putnam's Sons.

Brooks, R. (1994). Children at risk: fostering resilience and hope. *American Journal of Orthopsychiatry* 64:266–278.

Honos-Webb, L. (2005). *The Gift of ADHD: How to Transform Your Child's Problems Into Strengths.* Oakland, CA: New Harbinger Publications.

Niehoff, D. (1999). *The Biology of Violence: How Understanding the Brain, Behavior, and Environment Can Break the Vicious Circle of Aggression.* New York, NY: The Free Press.

http://www.brainplace.com

LINDA WEISBAUM SELTZER, PH.D.

Episodic Memory

Psychologists predicted that long-term memories could be distinguished according to what the memories were about. They proposed that episodic memory is autobiographical memory for the events in one's life. Episodic memory is an explicit, or declarative type of memory, so it stores information that can be put into words or declared. The other explicit memory is called semantic, and it deals with factual knowledge about places, objects, and concepts. **Semantic memory** is timeless. There are certain facts that we remember that will be forever with us. Episodic memory relies on events. It appears that episodic and semantic memories develop in an interactive manner. Episodic memory stores spatial and temporal information that categorize particular times and places where events occur. Like semantic memory, it relies on the hippocampus, a structure found in the medial temporal lobe of the brain, but the frontal lobes are also involved in maintaining the consistency of the memory.

Although semantic memories are also stored through the hippocampus, it appears that the areas for each type of memory are exclusive of each other. This fact was elucidated in a study of London cabdrivers. To become a cabbie in London, one must complete a test on an enormous amount of information regarding maps and directions. Thought to be perfect subjects to determine where our mental maps are located, eleven cabbies were given positron emission tomography (PET) scans. The PET images, which highlight neural activity by measuring changes in brain blood flow, indicated the right hippocampus was activated significantly when the taxi drivers recalled complex routes, but not during other types of complex memory recall. In other research published in the Proceedings of the National Academy of Sciences, cabbies were given brain scans and compared with non-cabbie controls. The cabbies were found to have a larger hippocampus. Those with the most experience had more gray matter in this area than others.

Episodic memory is the memory of specific times, places, and contexts. Your first date, first interview, and what you had for dinner last night are all stored through the episodic pathway. According to Rusiko Bourtchouladze (2002), all memories begin as episodic, but only those with distinctive characteristics survive in our brains. Other episodes may contain factual information that we will retain as semantic memories, but we may forget the episode itself. Episodic memories are thought to require cortical storage sites, the hippocampus, and the frontal lobes to store where and when an experience transpired. Ken Kosick (2000) of Harvard University suggests that our brains automatically create maps of our surroundings. We have brain cells called "place" cells that create connections. As the brain is first interested in survival, the hippocampus maps the exits and other vital places, like the restroom.

Flashbulb memory is an episodic memory that has been emotionally charged. Knowing where you were when you heard about the 9/11 terrorist attacks brings forth memories that will be preserved. This very detailed and vivid memory was stored on one occasion and will last a lifetime. Personal autobiographical memories may also be recorded in this way. Squire and Zola (1996) from Emory University remind us that vivid memories are not always valid memories. Our episodic memories are not always accurate in every respect.

Episodic memory has often been referred to as "source" memory. The source of a memory may be the basis or foundation of it. Source memory can be easily confused. Both children and older adults confuse their sources of information. Usually this problem is not grounds for concern, but in a school situation it may cause confusion on a test. For instance, an English class is studying the work of Shakespeare. The teacher has given the students biographical information on the bard. She shares with them the theory that Shakespeare's plays were written by others is very weak. That, indeed, there may have been one play with which he received help, but it seems likely that he wrote the others. One of the students watches a biography of famous playwrights on television. The commentator shares the view that in all probability Sir Francis Bacon wrote some of Shakespeare's work. The day of the assessment in English class there is a true/false question: It is likely that others wrote Shakespeare's plays. The student who also saw the television program mistakenly remembers that information coming from his teacher. He answers the question with True. His source memory is inaccurate.

One of the interesting aspects of episodic memory is the ability the brain has to transport you to the event or location you are thinking about. It does this through the process of visualization. When asked what you had for dinner last night, your mind takes you to the place where you ate. You have the ability to visualize the location, the people present, and also the activity that took place. Most helpful memory books suggest that we notice more of the things that go on around us. In other words, if we attend more to our surroundings we can strengthen the episodic memories.

When utilizing episodic memory strategies, it is most productive to create a unique environment for every unit being taught. Numerous studies have been conducted on the power of location and events. Some have suggested that retrieval of memory is more successful when the cues and the context of the experience at the time of learning are the same at the time of recall. Words learned underwater were recalled better when the learners were underwater. Those who learned words on a beach best recalled the words when they were again on the beach.

Creating an attractive and interesting classroom containing information that will be studied and learned is a constructive practice. Bulletin boards should be changed after each unit of study to make the classroom novel and unique once again. Most teachers have watched students working on an assessment look at a blank bulletin board or chalkboard and then quickly write down an answer. These students are visualizing the material that was once there. This invisible information has been accessed through the episodic memory pathway. For standardized testing, many schools have posters containing content removed from the walls, yet students look at the areas where the information was hanging and can visualize the information.

Another useful strategy is through the careful consideration of seating charts. Creating new seating charts is a way to separate some students who don't work well together or who spend too much time conversing, but changing at the wrong time can cause interference with episodic memory. Some students remember better the information they have encountered in one area of the room when they remain in that spot. Therefore, it may be best to maintain a seating chart until the unit is concluded and the assessment given. For the next topic to be studied, make some creative changes in the seating arrangements, such as putting students in triads or dyads. A geometric shape may also give a new look to the room and prepare students for new learning.

Students often recall accessories easily. A social studies instructor who dresses as a famous military general creates a memorable experience. If that uniform is worn again, information learned at the first encounter is more easily recalled. Pupils may also enjoy wearing accessories that enhance their experience and thus their learning. Role-playing an historical battle with or without costumes may create an episode worth remembering.

Taking students to an entirely new learning environment may augment memory. Field trips that include interactive experiences and hands-on learning are more dynamic and interesting than a rote lesson in the classroom. Debriefing is necessary after such an experience, particularly if the information learned at the new location will be formally assessed. Take the time to bring the essence of the trip back to the classroom and discuss the important concepts. On a classroom assessment that includes the field trip information mention the trip and help students visualize the experience. Taking students outdoors for a lesson also provides a unique environment and may enhance interest and memory.

Episodic memory techniques may do more than help students remember. They may also make learning more interesting and exciting. Students may be motivated by a change of scenery or a new face and attend to new learning for a longer period of time. Guest speakers can create a distinctive atmosphere and add to learning. Other teachers in your building, parents, administrators, and community members may be wonderful sources for creating new episodes.

See also: **Constructivism; Information Processing Model; Procedural Memory.**

Further Readings

Bourtchouladze, R. (2002). *Memories Are Made of This.* London: Columbia University Press.

Kosick, K. (2000). Speaker. Designing schools based on brain research. Using brain research to reshape classroom practice. Cambridge, MA.

Squire, L.R., Zola, S.M. (1996). Structure and function of declarative and nondeclarative memory systems. *Proceedings of the National Academy of Sciences* 93:13515–13522.

Terrazas, A., McNaughton, B. (2000). Brain growth and the cognitive map. *Proceedings of the National Academy of Sciences* 97:4414–4416.

MARILEE SPRENGER

F

Feedback

Teacher feedback is the reaction a teacher has to a student's work, that then helps shape their future efforts. It holds the potential of changing the learning landscape. The primary purpose behind feedback is to bolster academic progress. By defining specifically what needs to be improved on or by reinforcing competency, it acts as a motivator and guide to students. Simply sending out a positive statement does little to impact learning. To be useful feedback needs to be specific. A balance of supportive and corrective comments is most effective in creating high-quality learning.

Feedback is an instructional strategy that has been well researched in the fields of education and psychology. There is a general consensus that if carried out properly it produces positive academic results. Neuroscience is adding its voice to the findings of educators and psychologists. The more feedback students receive, the faster and more accurate their learning.

Brain and Feedback

Learning creates a physical change in the brain. The brain is continually being bombarded with thoughts and emotions and from that information is able to construct knowledge. The human brain contains approximately 100 billion neurons. Neurons communicate information through dendrites and axons. Dendrites are small hair-like structures that are produced from neurons when new learning or experiences occur. One neuron may have as many as 100,000 dendrites emerging from it. Their job is to receive information from other neurons. Each neuron has only one axon, it sends information between neurons. When a dendrite from one neuron communicates with an axon of another neuron a synaptic connection is made. Each neuron is capable of making between 5,000 and 10,000 synapses, further proof that the human brain is continually generating, bursting, and exploding with thought.

Information enters the brain through existing networks of neurons. We learn by attaching the new to the old. Every time new information is gleaned the brain organizes, modifies, and adjusts it either into its stored memories of a concept or by creating a new concept. This procedure may modify the old beyond recognition, but the brain is always building on prior knowledge.

The more often a neural network is fired in response to a stimulus, the stronger the synaptic connection. Synapse that are continually used, such as those engaged in math facts or sight words, become automatic. This enables the individual to easily recall facts such as, $9 \times 6 = 54$ or the word "yes." Once information becomes hardwired it may be difficult, but not impossible to alter.

The brain has the ability to constantly change its structure and function in response to experiences and new information. This attribute is referred to as plasticity. Plasticity allows the brain to acquire new skills and knowledge throughout the lifespan. It works in two main ways. First, it permits the brain to increase the number of synapses between neurons and second, it modifies existing synapses. Both these processes are important when the brain receives feedback. The switch can be turned on to activate a connection or turned off to deactivate a connection.

When a student receives positive feedback confirming an answer is correct, synaptic connections are strengthened, increasing the likelihood of the same response being elicited in the future. On the other hand, feedback that indicates an incorrect response hopefully disengages the synapse and the brain is rewired to the correct response. Changing the brain's firing patterns through repeated thought and action is what happens when students receive feedback.

Plasticity has implications not only for the student receiving the feedback, but for all students in the classroom. As Albert Bandura's (1994) research on social learning has indicated, one way students learn is through vicarious experiences. During a class discussion, if a teacher does not correct a student when they respond incorrectly in front of the class, the entire class is likely to wire their brain to an incorrect response. Teachers need to verbalize correct and incorrect responses in a kind and caring manner so that students can hardwire correct information.

Instructional Strategies

Feedback comes in a variety of forms. It can be done in a group, individually, informally, or formally. Informal feedback is done through class discussions or casual remarks as a teacher circulates throughout a classroom. Formal feedback takes the form of checklists, written comments, and tests.

Feedback is best when it is corrective. Students need to know what they are doing right and what needs to be improved. In this process teachers are defining for students what is important in the learning activity or skill. Rubrics are particularly helpful in establishing a specific criterion for proficiency. They aid in communication, making it clear to students the need for revision and strengths in their work.

Timing is everything. This adage is particularly true with feedback. If possible, students should receive feedback within 24 hours of completing an assignment. While this is not always realistic with larger classroom size, added responsibilities, and other pressures facing teachers today, an effort should be made to return work as soon as possible. If weeks elapse before students receive feedback on work, the impact is diminished.

Students should not be left out of the loop. They can participate in their own self-feedback. A combination of teacher and student feedback is important in developing self-reflection strategies and facilitating student responsibility for their own learning.

See also: **Constructivism; Teaching Model for the Brain.**

Further Readings

Jensen, E. (2004). *Brain-Compatible Strategies* (2nd ed.) San Diego, CO: The Brain Store, Inc.

Marzano, R.J., Pickering, D.J., Pollock, J.E. (2004) *Research-Based Instructional Strategies that Work.* Upper Saddle River, NJ: Prentice Hall.

Neuroscience for Kids. http://faculty.washington.edu/chudler/neurok.html

SHERYL FEINSTEIN, ED.D.

Fetal Alcohol Syndrome

Since early times, people have thought that alcohol could harm a developing fetus. Both in art and oral tradition, references to the potential damage of an unborn child from a mother that imbibed alcohol were found. In the early 1960s, literature was distributed that warned expectant mothers of the potential harm if alcohol was consumed during pregnancy. It was not until 1973 that the first research paper confirming the characteristic pattern on abnormalities resulting from exposure of a human fetus to alcohol was released in the journal, *Lancet.* University of Washington professor David W. Smith and his student Kenneth Jones defined fetal alcohol syndrome (FAS) and they made the first concerted effort to educate expectant mothers about the hazardous behavior of drinking during their pregnancies.

When FAS was first described as a birth defect in 1973, the patients were very young children. No one knew exactly how they would develop mentally or physically, however, since that time science has devoted a great deal of time and money to determine the impact of this totally preventable condition. Unfortunately, many children were yet to be born that suffered from FAS or other debilitating conditions. It was not until nine years later, in 1981, that the Surgeon General of the United States recommended not drinking alcohol during pregnancy or when planning a pregnancy.

In the United States, the prevalence of FAS is between 0.5 to 2 cases per 1,000 births. It is estimated that for every child born with FAS, three additional children are born who may not have the physical characteristics of FAS but still experience neurobehavioral deficits resulting from prenatal alcohol exposure that affect learning and behavior.

Diagnostic Criteria

We are now beginning to understand the mechanism by which alcohol can damage the fetal brain. The brain is thought to be most sensitive to the effects of alcohol during the period called synaptogenesis where the brain develops rapidly during the third trimester of pregnancy; however, research also suggests that damage from alcohol can begin even before a woman is aware that she is pregnant. This fact demands that women are made aware of the embryo's sensitivity to the teratogenic (material that causes malformations in the fetus) effects of alcohol.

Many labels have been used to describe the effects of alcohol on the unborn baby since Jones and Smith first defined a pattern of facial and other deformities in 1973. The diagnosis of FAS however only identifies a small portion of children affected by their mothers drinking alcohol during gestation. The term FAS does not include children born with a variety of variant disorders resulting from alcohol ingestion.

To describe alcohol-related birth defects that focused on the physical anomalies rather than brain defects the term "alcohol related birth defects" (ARBD) has been used since the late 1980s. The term "fetal alcohol effects" (FAE) describes children victimized by their mother's alcohol consumption who do not have the recognizable craniofacial features associated with FAS. These FAE children suffer from brain deficiencies, however, may appear to be in the normal range of development physically. The term, "alcohol-related neurodevelopmental disorder" (ARND) is now being used to describe the same condition as FAE and the terms are both found in the literature to describe the same or similar patients. It would be incorrect to define the disorders along a continuum, although, patients with FAS have more apparent physical abnormalities such as craniofacial identification, heart malformations, and slow growth patterns. There is very good evidence that the brain disorders of people with FAE/ARND are often as severe as FAS patients. The extent of disability for people with FAS or FAE/ARND can vary greatly.

A term used by the Surgeon General in a report released in February of 2005 poses an umbrella term for all of these disorders. The term is fetal alcohol spectrum disorders (FASD). FASD is the full spectrum of birth defects caused by prenatal alcohol exposure. The spectrum may include mild and subtle changes, such as a slight learning disability and physical abnormality, through full-blown FAS.

The Human Face of FAS

Children suffering from FAS have characteristic craniofacial features that are quite recognizable and very obvious. The eyes and eyelids are the most common and consistent sign in the facial features of children with FAS. Children often appear to have widely spaced eyes but measurements

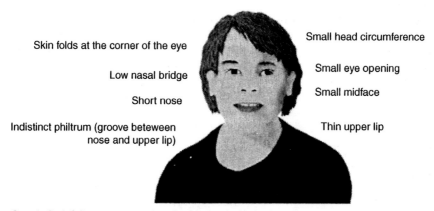

Skin folds at the corner of the eye

Low nasal bridge

Short nose

Indistinct philtrum (groove beteween nose and upper lip)

Small head circumference

Small eye opening

Small midface

Thin upper lip

Craniofacial features associated with fetal alcohol syndrome.

reveal that they are spaced normally. This appearance is caused by short eye openings. The next common feature in these children is the slow growth of the center of the face. This produces an underdeveloped midface and the zone between the eye and the mouth appears to be flattened. Subtle, but still characteristic is the area between the nose and the mouth, called the philtrum. In the FAS child, it is smooth and flat without ridges, and forms a thin upper lip.

The Tools of Research for FASD

Research on the physical and nervous system abnormalities of FASD have provided scientists and the lay public with a great deal of information in the past decade. Scientists have relied heavily on experimental animals to help them determine the molecular and cellular events affected by exposure of embryonic tissue to alcohol. Animal models have demonstrated widespread damage following relatively high prenatal exposure to alcohol as well as moderate usage. Although animal models have been helpful in understanding how animals metabolize alcohol, humans do not digest alcohol exactly like their animal counterparts. One of the key factors recognized by researchers in their quest for how alcohol affects the human embryo and fetus is the absence of confounding factors such as malnutrition, disease, and concomitant abuse of other drugs when using animal models.

With the proliferation of magnetic resonance imaging (MRI) in the past 10 years, researchers have been able to look non-evasively at the living brains of children, adolescents, and adults with FASD and compare their brains with normal controls. Detailed analysis has shown significant differences in the brains of FASD patients when compared to normal brains.

Structural Abnormalities in the Brain

Problems occur in a number of important areas of the brain. The end result includes deficits in intelligence, memory, motor coordination, complex problem-solving, and abstract thinking. With more effective measurement and the advent of MRI technology, researchers have looked for differences between normal brains and those of FASD patients. Some of the differences even surprised experts by their significance. The corpus callosum (the pathway that connects the two hemispheres of the brain) was drastically different in FASD patients. Research reported by noted FAS expert, Ann Streisguth from the University of Washington, illustrated that some patients showed incomplete development of the corpus callosum while others possessed thicker or thinner structures. There was no specific difference between those subjects with craniofacial features and those without. In other words, all subjects with FASD had an irregular corpus callosum. Interestingly, those subjects with a thinner callosum demonstrated deficits in motor coordination but had relatively normal executive function abilities while those subjects with thicker callosum had the reverse.

Similar studies have been conducted to determine that the size of the basal ganglia (a structure lying in the midbrain that is thought to be partially responsible for helping regulate, manage, and translate emotions into thinking.) is significantly reduced in children with FAE. The volume of the location of the cerebellum (located at the base of the brain and responsible for procedural and reflexive learning.) in general showed marked reduction in size in FAE children. Many of these children exhibit poor coordination and fine muscular movements. The hippocampus (a critical structure that plays a key role in memory formation and intellectual function located in the midbrain) has also been shown to be highly sensitive to alcohol. Children with FASD have shown mild to severe deficits in this area of the brain. Some of the cognitive deficiencies and **learning disabilities** may be related to hippocampal damage produced during fetal alcohol exposure.

The overall size of the brain is decreased in many of these children. The diminution in the thickness of the outer layers of the cortex (most complex part of the brain of which the frontal portions are uniquely human.) indicates the reduced size is due to the decrease in the total numbers of cells. During brain development, certain types of cells are programmed to move to precise locations so they can serve a specific role in the coordination of the brain. In many of these FASD children, these nerve cells have failed to migrate to their appropriate sites. It appears the misplaced neurons do not fulfill their roles thus adding to the mental deficiencies associated with this spectrum of disease.

Brain Imaging Analysis

New methods of image analysis are being developed to provide a better picture of the brains in FASD children as compared to normal brains. With the ability to precisely measure the relative position points on the brain, researchers can detect lack of growth or overgrowth of many important structures like the corpus callosum. By comparing the average sizes of the identified structures with average sizes of normal structures, researchers are beginning to be more effective in their diagnostic strategies.

This is helping to develop tools that may identify biomarkers associated with FASD and provide attending physicians and parents with courses of action in treating these children. Correlating brain anomalies with specific cognitive and behavioral problems caused by prenatal alcohol exposure could help provide diagnostic services for people with FASD.

Physiological, Behavioral, and Sociological Deficiencies

Besides the craniofacial changes exhibited in children identified with full-blown FAS, many other deficiencies are known in children born with FASD. It is not uncommon to see these children have abnormalities or deformities of their limbs, hands, and feet. Heart, liver, and kidney problems are also common, as well as vision and hearing problems. Children with FASD can experience low birth weight, slow growth, and poor coordination.

Research suggests that people exposed to alcohol during development may exhibit striking changes in social behavior that can be attributed to the embryonic and fetal association with alcohol and not the external environment. Behaviorally, children with FASD tend to have greater problems adjusting to school and peers. Evidence suggests that many of these children are not raised by their biological families. Without early diagnosis and the appropriate support and intervention many develop poor relationships in school society. A higher percentage of disrupted school experience, fatigue, frustration, and many other antisocial behaviors have been observed in children with FASD.

Unfortunately, children do not outgrow FASD and its serious consequences. Unlike the facial features of FAS children, which tend to become more normal as the affected child grows to adulthood, the cognitive deficits persist, creating long-term problems in many aspects of life. In adulthood, people with FASD show higher rates of trouble with the law, inappropriate sexual behavior, depression, suicide, and failure to care for children. As many of the infants that were first diagnosed in the early 1970s are now adults there needs to be further study on how to address their cognitive and emotional problems.

The Risk Factors for FASD

It is clear that not every woman who drinks during her pregnancy will give birth to a FASD child. It has been estimated that 4.3 percent of heavy drinkers give birth to a FAS child and that one-half of heavy drinking women will give birth to healthy babies. The converse of this finding indicates that approximately one-half of what are considered heavy drinking mothers will give birth to a child that has FASD. Other risk factors include maternal age, socioeconomic status, ethnicity, and genetic factors. Different drinking patterns tend to be associated to risk also. Studies indicate that it is not so much the total amount of alcohol consumed, but rather, the high number of drinks consumed at one occasion. This produces a high peak of blood alcohol concentration that appears to be the greatest risk factor for prenatal injury from alcohol.

It is obvious that no single mechanism is responsible for the full range of disorders called FASD. Research suggests that women who drink in the early part of their pregnancies cause excessive cell death in a special population of embryonic cells that give rise to facial structures and certain peripheral nerves. It appears that women who drink later in their pregnancies initiate the mechanisms that kill specific brain cells in the cerebellum. Although a great deal is known about these mechanisms in both the normal and FASD fetus, scientists are actively reviewing new theories on how the fetus is affected by prenatal alcohol exposure.

Preventing Prenatal Alcohol Use

It is obvious to parents, educators, and all responsible parties that if a woman drinks alcohol anytime during a pregnancy they are at high risk for giving birth to a child with birth defects. In spite of this knowledge and the preventative efforts at all levels, reports indicate a disturbing trend in recent years toward women drinking during pregnancy. Some are unaware of the problem while some alcohol-dependent women are unable to abstain. Still another group of women who intend to abstain from alcohol during pregnancy may have consumed alcohol in the first trimester of their pregnancy before they realize that they are pregnant.

Treatment Strategies

Parents report that an early diagnosis has been helpful in setting reasonable expectations for a FASD child's performance in school. Although there are no systematic studies that have shown benefits from early intervention, it is generally agreed that interventions must include the entire family, and parents must be made aware of the behavioral and cognitive problems that can arise as the result of a diagnosis of FASD.

It is hoped that new strategies will be developed to address the neurodevelopmental and learning problems of children with FASD including the use of appropriate behavioral and cognitive therapies. Medication is another avenue of intervention, particularly in FASD children that have attentional problems and significant levels of **depression** in adolescents and adults suffering from FASD. Interventions that include making families aware of gaining access to special education and vocational services have been helpful and so have parent support groups and organizations. These groups have shared effective behavioral strategies with parents, written guides along with support from

other families saddled with the responsibility of raising children with mental and physical challenges.

What Educators Need to Know

It is important to reinforce the abstinence from alcohol message for young women who are sexually active and not using birth control methods. Some of the messages could include: "When a pregnant woman drinks, so does her baby." "The baby's growth from consuming alcohol can be altered or slowed." "The baby may suffer lifelong damage as the result of a mother drinking." We know that FASD babies are not only born to women who abuse alcohol or are heavy drinkers. Evidence suggests that it only takes a few drinks in early pregnancy or a binge episode (four or five drinks at one sitting) to kill developing brain cells.

FASD students are highly susceptible to sensory overload. A backdrop that is stimulating and exciting for most students is agitating for these students. Minimizing loud noises, bright lights, and distracting displays (posters, mobiles) creates a calm, productive learning environment. Headphones are an effective way to limit and focus noise. Small group work and individualized attention are also ways to reduce stimulation and attend to specific academic needs.

Short assignments are more effective than long assignments. If it is necessary to have long- term assignments, numerous checkpoints along the way will help them stay organized and track their progress. Direct instruction on social skills and self-management skills is a proven strategy. Often social skills and self-control are a high priority and must be achieved before the emphasis can be on reading, writing, and arithmetic. Repetition and practice are key elements in essential information to be retained.

A classroom that is consistent, offering specific routines and procedures increases the FASD student's ability to manage their behavior. Routines for starting and ending the day, along with procedures for other activities such as walking down the hallway and going to the restroom, need to be established. Playing slow, soothing music during transitions prevents this time from becoming one of chaos. Setting up clearly defined personal spaces by taping the designated area, study carrels, or a cushion planted in the right spot help regulate and communicate classroom expectations.

Fathers, family, and friends all have important roles to play by encouraging and supporting a woman's decision to be abstinent from alcohol during her pregnancy. They can avoid placing the expectant mother in a situation where alcohol is the only option and can avoid alcohol themselves to set an example.

Perhaps one day new insights from ongoing FASD research will provide ways to ameliorate the birth defects associated with a woman consuming alcohol during gestation. That time may be measured in years, if not decades. There will always exist a risk because of the lack of knowledge and the potentially disastrous behavior of mothers to be. Continued efforts must be made to provide the knowledge every expectant mother needs to help make informed decisions regarding her baby's health.

See also: **Addiction; Adolescent Addiction; Cognitive Disabilities.**

Further Readings

Kulp, L., Kulp, J. (2000). *The Best I Can Be: Living with Fetal Alcohol Syndrome – Effect.* Brooklyn Park, MN: Better Endings New Beginnings.

Streissguth, A. (1997). *Fetal Alcohol Syndrome: A Guide for Families and Communities.* Baltimore, MD: Brookes Publishing Company.

U.S. Surgeon General Releases Advisory on Alcohol Use in Pregnancy, Monday, February 21, 2005. http://www.hhs.gov/surgeongeneral/pressreleases/sg02222005.html

Warren, K., Foudin, L. (2001). Alcohol –Related Birth Defects—The Past, Present, and Future. *Alcohol Research and Health* 25:3.

National Institute on Alcohol Abuse and Alcoholism http://www.niaaa.nih.gov/publications/aharw.htm

RALEIGH PHILP

Forgetting

Ask teachers how long they want their students to remember what they were taught, and the answer is a resounding, "forever." Yet, that is rarely the case. Much of what is taught in school is forgotten over time, usually within a few days. Forgetting is often viewed as the enemy of learning. But, on the contrary, forgetting plays an important role in promoting learning and facilitating recall.

The human brain processes an enormous amount of incoming information every day. Much of that information remains in temporary memory sites and soon fades. For example, the name of a person that one has just met may remain in memory for just a few minutes. Yet, the name of one's best friend is turned into a long-term memory and lasts a lifetime. Why do we forget so much and preserve so little? Forgetting manifests itself in two major ways: the process of discarding newly acquired information, and the decay that occurs with memories already in long-term storage.

Forgetting New Information

The first major studies on forgetting were conducted by Hermann Ebbinghaus, a German psychologist, *Über das Gedächtnis* (1885; *Memory*) whose work led to the development of a forgetting curve. The curve was a mathematical representation of how quickly new experiences were forgotten. Subsequent studies have somewhat modified his findings. When the brain is exposed to new information, the greatest amount of forgetting occurs shortly after the learning task is completed, and continues rapidly throughout the first day. Items that do not make sense to the learner are usually forgotten first. Conversely, traumatic and vivid experiences are rarely forgotten. But for most information, forgetting slows down after two weeks when there is not much left to forget.

Forgetting new material can occur as a result of interference from earlier learning. Sometimes, old learnings can interfere with the processing of new learnings, a situation referred to as *proactive interference*. This can happen when learning a new language. Words from a person's native language get mixed up with similar words in the new language, making it difficult to learn the new vocabulary. *Retroactive interference* occurs when new learnings interfere with the recall of old learnings. Generally, the recall of related old learning can help in the acquisition of new learning—a process called **transfer**. But if the new learning, for example, is excessively complicated, such as trying to understand the maze of codes for using a new digital notebook, then frustration may prevent the old technological skills and feelings of confidence from mastering the complex new device. Whenever new information stirs up negative feelings or attitudes, these emotions can interfere with the acquisition of the new material. This is known as *reactive interference*. A person strongly opposed to capital punishment, for instance, is not likely to learn about and remember more humane methods of execution.

Even *how* one acquires new learning can affect forgetting. It is easier to forget what is heard than what is read. When listening to new information, extraneous sounds can divert the attention of the brain. But reading is a much more focused activity, thereby reducing the effect of distractions. **Stress** and lack of **sleep** also contribute to forgetting.

Forgetting has some definite advantages. When the brain is presented with a large amount of information, forgetting prevents irrelevant information from interfering with the acquisition, remembering, and recall of relevant information. By screening out the unimportant, the essential data and experiences have a chance to be fully consolidated into long-term memories. Teachers, of course, believe that the material they present in class is relevant. Why doesn't the student's brain perceive it that way, too?

To answer that question, studies have shown that sense and meaning (relevancy) are key factors that affect the remembering and forgetting of new information. When processing new information, the brain relies heavily on previously stored learnings to determine whether the item makes sense and is meaningful to the learner. The brain rarely devotes much attention to what it perceives as nonsense. Those items are quickly discarded. Meaning, of course, is a very personal thing and is greatly influenced by the learner's individual experiences. The same item can have great meaning for one student and none for another. Questions like "Why do I have to know this?" or "When will I ever use this?" indicate that the student has not, for whatever reason, accepted this learning as meaningful.

A good example of the importance of meaning is to think of all the television programs that people have watched and soon forgotten, even though they spent hours viewing the program. The show's content or storyline made sense, but if meaning was absent, the brain just did not save it. It was entertainment and no learning resulted from it. One might remember a summary of the show or whether it was enjoyable or boring, but not the details. On the other hand, if the story reminded the viewer of a vivid personal experience, then meaning was present and the brain more likely consolidated details of the program into long-term memory.

Now think of this process in the classroom. Students may diligently follow the teacher's instructions to perform a task repeatedly, and may even get the correct answers. But if they have not found meaning after the learning episode, there is a high probability that the information will be soon forgotten. Mathematics teachers are often frustrated by this. They see students using a certain formula to solve problems correctly one day, but they cannot remember how to do it the next day. If the process was not stored in long-term memory, the information is treated as brand new once again. Sometimes, when students ask why they need to know something, the teacher's response is, "Because it's going to be on the test." This response adds little meaning to learning. Students resort to jotting the learning into a notebook so that it is preserved in writing, but not in memory. Alternatively, students can memorize information through repetition of the new information, a process called *rote rehearsal*. This process enables the brain to remember something even though it may lack meaning.

Teachers spend about 90 percent of their planning time devising lessons so that students will understand the learning objective, that is, make sense of it. But to convince a learner's brain to persist with that objective, teachers need to help establish meaning, primarily by making connections to their students' experiences. Furthermore, teachers should remember that what was meaningful for them as children may not be necessarily meaningful for their students today. Helping students to make connections between subject areas by integrating the curriculum increases meaning and retention, especially when students recognize a future use for the new learning. Brain imaging scans have shown that when new learning can be connected to past experiences, there is substantially more cerebral activity followed by dramatically improved retention.

Forgetting Past Memories

Imagine if the brain remembered everything for a lifetime. Just trying to recall the name of a childhood friend would be a significant challenge. The brain would have to search though thousands of names scattered among the long-term memory sites. At best, the name would take a long time to find; at worst, the result could be confusion, resulting in the recall of the wrong name. By gradually forgetting the names that are not important, the recall process becomes more efficient. Forgetting also helps to update obsolete information. As one changes jobs and relocates, for example, new data, such as addresses and telephone numbers, overwrite the old data. The old data may still reside in long-term memory, but if it is not recalled and rehearsed, it will eventually become less accessible.

Exactly what happens in the brain to old memories over time is still an open question. Some researchers suggest that memory loss of a specific experience can occur if the memory has not been recalled for a long time. They believe that this leads to the slow but steady disassociation of the network of brain cells that form the memory, making retrieval increasingly difficult. Eventually, the integrity of the network fails and the memory is lost, perhaps forever. Such a process, the researchers say, frees up memory resources so that they become available for new information.

Other researchers contend that old memories remain intact, though other factors somehow block access to them. These factors can include medications, drugs, vivid new experiences, stroke, and Alzheimer's disease. Recent studies have also found that some people can voluntarily block an unwanted past experience with such persistence that it results in forgetting.

More research is needed before scientists can draw any conclusion about the mechanisms that result in the forgetting of old memories. Meanwhile, teachers can take advantage of what *is* known. Namely, that important information that students have already learned is more likely to be accurately and firmly consolidated in long-term memory if it is recalled and rehearsed periodically as the students progress through grade levels. Too often, information deemed important is taught just once, and the students are expected to remember it for a lifetime. They may even be tested on it years after they initially learned it. Something worth remembering is worth repeating. If important information is purposefully revisited throughout a student's entire school experience, then firmly consolidated and robust memories will be available for a long time to come.

See also: **Mastery; Teaching Model for the Brain.**

Further Readings

Fleck, D.E., Berch, D.B., Shear, P.K., Strakowski, S.M. (Spring 2001). Directed forgetting in explicit and implicit memory: The role of encoding and retrieval mechanisms. *The Psychological Record* 51:207–221.

Schacter, D.L. (2001). *The Seven Sins of Memory.* New York: Houghton Mifflin.

Sousa, D.A. (2001). *How the Brain Learns* (2nd ed.). Thousand Oaks, CA: Corwin Press.

Wixted, J.T. (2004). The psychology and neuroscience of forgetting. *Annual Review of Psychology* 55:235–269.

DAVID A. SOUSA, PH.D.

G

Gender Differences

Men and women differ on average in their cognitive strengths. Men are superior in certain spatial tasks, especially those requiring imaginary rotation or manipulation of complex visual forms. Women, in contrast, do better in recall of the location of objects presented in an array, though not in location-memory *per se*, independent of objects. Consistent with this is the tendency of women to use landmarks (unique objects) in their environment to find their way, whereas males tend to use geometric cues such as distance or direction.

Men have higher scores on mathematical reasoning tests, though women have a slight advantage on calculation tests. Even though grades on math tests in school (achievement tests) may not differ, or girls may even do better, boys still outperform girls on aptitude tests that generally sample relatively unrehearsed problems. Males are over-represented at the high end of difficult tests like SAT-Math or the Putnam competition.

Women tend to be better at tests of perceptual speed, in which designated items must be quickly found or matched. They also do better on verbal fluency where the task is to generate words containing specified letters. A large female advantage is found for verbal memory—recall of words from a list or short paragraph. Women are not, however, better at all verbal skills. For example, on vocabulary tests there is usually no difference between the sexes or men may be slightly better.

In the motor sphere, women do best on fine motor skills emphasizing dexterity, whereas men do far better on throwing accuracy—hitting a target with a missile.

Although the differences described above are found quite reliable across many studies, there is always overlap in the scores of males and females. We measure the overlap indirectly by something called "effect size," which is roughly a ratio of the average difference between groups to a measure of the dispersal of scores around the means. The wider the scatter of scores, the more overlap there will be, and the smaller the effect size. Imaginal rotation and throwing accuracy show large effect sizes favoring males (averaging approximately 1.0), indicating less overlap between the sexes, whereas most of the other differences have smaller effect sizes, considerably less than 1.0, indicating more overlap than on rotation and throwing.

These cognitive sex differences will necessarily translate into differences in ease of learning various kinds of material, though there are actually very few studies comparing the *learning* process itself.

The Role of Experience in Cognitive Sex Differences

Social scientists have tended to consider cognitive sex differences almost entirely as products of the social milieu in which men and women were reared. It is true that in Western societies until the 1950s, there was limited opportunity for men and women to engage in equivalent occupations and activities. Most of the research on cognitive sex differences has been conducted on Western populations and Caucasian subjects, but we do have limited information on other ethnic groups as well, where social division of the sexes is generally even more marked. Asian (mainly Japanese and Chinese) subjects show similar patterns of sex differences as Caucasians, on imaginal rotation and math reasoning favoring males, and on verbal memory favoring females. Evidence from other cultural sources is only slowly being accumulated, but it does appear that a similar pattern of abilities may emerge. The *size* of the sex difference may vary, but contrary to socialization predictions, the differences do not appear to be consistently larger in more traditional Asian cultures.

If cognitive sex differences were due primarily to the different life experiences of men and women, one might expect that they would have diminished over the last few decades, as their life experiences became more similar. It had been suggested that such differences were declining, based on some standardized tests on large numbers of American high school students between 1947 and 1980; but this claim was later modified somewhat. Our own and others' research has indicated that no systematic change over the last three decades has been found on a widely used imaginal rotation test administered primarily to college students. Mathematical reasoning tests also appear to show a fairly constant male advantage (effect size approximately 0.40) in US high school students since about 1940. Tests that show a large female advantage, such as verbal memory, have not been studied long enough to admit or comment on possible changes over time.

If sex differences in cognition were due entirely to different exposure to certain tasks, one might expect that giving intensive practice would reduce the sex difference. A number of studies employing spatial tests, in which such practice was given, have shown that the scores of both sexes do improve. However, the differences do not become smaller, that is, the scores of men and women do not converge. So it appears that intensive practice in adult life does not reverse the picture.

Other studies bearing on the role of experience have sometimes shown a relation between people's past experience and their current scores on certain spatial tasks. People who report a greater childhood interest in mechanical activities and computer games, for example, do somewhat better on spatial tests as adults. The inference usually made, that the experience has determined the current ability, is unfortunately not valid. Simply showing a correlation between two things does not allow us to decide the direction of causality. Without more information we cannot conclude that the experiential differences between men and women determine the cognitive differences. We might equally well argue the reverse—that better native spatial ability results in greater participation in activities more demanding of spatial ability. To judge the contribution of experience to specific abilities, we need to know more than that the two are related.

It used to be thought that sex differences on cognitive tasks did not appear until after puberty. Such claims were supposed to demonstrate the major role of experience in the appearance of cognitive sex differences. It could however be argued that, like other sex differences, cognitive differences might be influenced by physiological factors pre- or peri-natally, yet not be manifest until adolescence. Moreover, recent research has shown cognitive sex differences to be present well before puberty. This has been especially well established for the male advantage on spatial tasks, which may appear as early as age four.

Origins of Cognitive Sex Differences

Most researchers who study sex differences regard them as natural outcomes of a sexual division of labor throughout our evolutionary history. According to the "hunter-gatherer" schema, women were the child-bearers, were smaller and physically weaker than men. Men filled the role of hunters, scavengers, and defenders, using weapons and travelling farther from the home base, whereas women's overarching contribution would be the care and sustenance of infants, and their contribution to the food supply was primarily as gatherers of local provisions. This would result in the selection of slightly different problem-solving traits in the two sexes, with women, for example, using navigational strategies dependent more on local landmarks and men using strategies dependent on geometric cues. Women in their role as chief caregivers might be expected to be more sensitive to facial cues than men, and so on.

While this is a hypothetical schema difficult to confirm for past history, surviving simple societies show similar divisions of labor. Moreover, the schema generates testable predictions about current sex differences, giving us insights about how these arise. However, we need not infer that cultural practices therefore have no role. Assuming that there are innate differences between men and women, societies would be expected to develop cultural norms that are consistent with such differences, and which therefore contribute to the maintenance of different gender roles.

Hormonal Influences on Cognition

It is not widely realized that having a male (XY) or female (XX) genetic makeup is just the beginning of the story of sexual differentiation. Becoming a male is a complex process that has the potential to allow for more variation than forming a female. The most potent influence on male sexual differentiation is exercised by sex hormones. However, if something goes awry and either male or female hormones are lacking or ineffective, the female form will emerge. So a simple view would be that in mammals at least, the female is the basic or default form.

The primary source of sex hormones in the human body are the gonads—ovaries in females, testes in males. Testes develop by about eight weeks of fetal life, earlier than ovaries, and they set to work soon after that to finish the job of making a male, by producing an androgen called testosterone (T). A derivative of testosterone (DHT) is necessary for male genitals to form, and for either of these hormones to take effect there must be receptors in the body's cells to respond to the hormones. So it can happen that we have genetic males who have apparent female genitals at birth but may develop male genitals at puberty when androgens are produced in larger quantities; and sometimes we have genetic males who never develop male genitals, who have breasts, and who look and act like females all their lives, because they have no androgen receptors.

However, the influence of sex hormones is not limited to the physical appearance of the body. There is a wealth of evidence from the nonhuman animal literature that much of the behavior that differentiates males and females is also dependent on male sex hormones or their derivatives. For behavior to be affected, the hormones must be acting on the brain. This effect holds not only for reproductive behavior, but for activities like rough-and-tumble play in juvenile males, and for solutions to spatial maze problems. Male rats, for example, use primarily geometric cues in a maze, whereas female rats prefer the use of landmark cues, and these "strategies" can be reversed by early manipulation of sex hormones.

Given these findings in nonhumans, we might expect that early exposure to sex hormones would also affect spatial and possibly other cognitive functions in humans. In a condition called congenital adrenal hyperplasia (CAH), individuals are exposed before birth to excess androgens from the adrenal glands. Affected girls may have male-like genitals at birth, which are surgically corrected. The androgen imbalance is restored by administration of appropriate hormones. Nevertheless there seem to be permanent irreversible effects of such early exposure. CAH girls grow up to have more masculine interests and activities than do unaffected girls, and they show less interest in infants. They also have better spatial ability than unaffected girls. So it is reasonable to think that sex hormones early in life also contribute substantially to the normal differences between men and women.

In CAH boys, the additional androgenic influence does not enhance spatial ability; it may in fact slightly reduce it compared to unaffected boys. That would be consistent with suggestions (see below) that there is an optimum level of androgens for the appearance of spatial ability, so "the more androgens the better" is not an accurate depiction of the relation between them.

The CAH research and other studies also suggest very strongly that, even apart from sex differences, much of the variation in specific cognitive skills from person to person should be related to levels of sex hormones. Most such research has focussed on the role of testosterone (T) in spatial abilities, and several studies have found that in normal men, those who have lower (but normal) levels of T do better on spatial tasks than those who have higher levels. So the "optimum" level of T for spatial ability appears to be in the lower range of normal males. In women, those who have higher levels of T do better than the low-T women. There is very little overlap of testosterone levels in adult men and women, so the high-T women, although approaching the male levels, are still very significantly lower in T.

It appears then that not only are the cognitive differences between men and women strongly influenced by sex hormones, but so also are the differences *within* each sex.

So sex hormones early in life influence our adult cognitive pattern, but adult levels of hormones also continue to do so. Men and women both experience natural fluctuations in hormone levels—in women over the menstrual cycle, and in men across seasons and even time of day. Such natural fluctuations, regardless of whatever other functions they serve, have also been related to changes in cognitive pattern.

In women, testosterone levels change very little across the menstrual cycle, but estrogen varies greatly. When estrogen levels are high (late follicular and midluteal phases), women perform better on some tasks at which women excel—verbal fluency and manual dexterity—than they do in the low estrogen phases. However, the reverse is true of spatial tasks at which men usually excel—scores on such tasks are worse in the high-estrogen phases than in low estrogen phases in normally menstruating women.

In men, testosterone levels are higher in autumn than in spring, and also higher early in the day than later. [Recall that low-T men perform better at spatial tasks than high-T men.] Men tested in the spring (when T levels are lower) do better than those tested in the fall, but only on spatial, not other tasks; and men tested later in the day do better than those tested early in the morning.

Brain Mechanisms

Many anatomical differences between human male and female brains have been demonstrated, but so far, none of these has been convincingly related to the cognitive differences. Parts of basic structures such as the hypothalamus, which among other things mediates reproductive behavior, are larger in males than in females. But there are also differences in the overall size of the brain (men's are larger), in size or relative size of commissural systems connecting the two hemispheres (larger in women), in degree of asymmetry of certain brain regions, and so on. It has also been proposed that the *functional* asymmetry of the brain, that is, the dependence of certain functions on one or the other hemisphere is different, being greater in men.

Nonetheless, relating such differences to performance on sex-diferentiated tests has so far been relatively unproductive. For example, the cross-sectional area of portions of the corpus callosum, a major structure connecting the two hemispheres, was found in one study to be larger in women, and in women also was related to scores on sex-differentiated tasks such as verbal memory and a spatial rotation test. In men, however, there was no relation of callosal areas to the same test. Other researchers have claimed that basic speech functions, known to be dependent on the left hemisphere in both sexes, are *more* tied to the left hemisphere in men than in women; but subsequent research has suggested that the major difference may be between dependence on front and back portions of the left hemisphere.

Of course, reliable differences in cognition between men and women *must* in some way be mediated by differences in brain function, and this is the subject of intensive investigation. These need not be reflected in gross structural differences, but might be due to differing organizational features not visible simply by viewing the brain. We would also expect sex hormones to play a role in shaping the brain mechanisms.

Occupational Choice

It is obvious that men and women are to some extent fitted for different work roles because of their substantial physical differences. Men are on average taller and stronger than women, which means that they are more likely to fill jobs that require extra strength, and to be superior in many athletic fields. However, the cognitive differences would also be expected to result in different proportions of men and women in a variety of occupations. Men's better spatial ability and their stronger representation at the high end of mathematical reasoning tasks may influence them to choose and excel in the physical sciences, which focus on inanimate objects; whereas women are increasingly drawn to biological sciences as a field of study where the focus is on living organisms. Women's superior perceptual speed and verbal memory probably gives them an edge in clerical and perhaps copy editing jobs; and in some fields of teaching. Men's superior mechanical ability may fit them better for automobile and computer repair jobs, and so on. Even with equal opportunity, it is unreasonable to expect men and women to be equally represented in every occupation, given the cognitive differences between the sexes and, equally important, their differing interests and lifestyle preferences. However, we must keep in mind that the cognitive differences are *average* differences, and that any one man or woman may not fit the average pattern. So some women will indeed choose and excel in engineering, and some men will adapt readily to secretarial work.

See also: **Animal Studies.**

Further Readings

Estrich, S. (2001). *Sex and Power.* New York, NY: Berkley Publishing.

Goy, R.W., McEwen, B.S. (1980). *Sexual Differentiation of the Brain.* Cambridge, Mass: MIT Press.

Halpern, D.F. (1992). *Sex Differences in Cognitive Abilities.* (2nd ed.) Hillsdale NJ: Erlbaum.

Hampson, E. (2002). Sex differences in human brain and cognition: The influence of sex steroids in early and adult life. In J.B. Becker, S.M. Breedlove, D. Crews, M.M. McCarthy (Eds.), *Behavioral Endocrinology* (2nd ed.). Cambridge, Mass: MIT Press, pp. 579–628.

Kimura, D. (1999) *Sex and Cognition.* Cambridge Mass: MIT Press.

Lee R.B., DeVore, I. (Eds.) (1968). *Man the Hunter.* Chicago: Aldine.

Pipher, M.B. (1994). *Reviving Ophelia: Saving the Selves of Adolescent Girls.* New York, NY: Random House.

Pollack, W. (1999). *Real Boys: Rescuing Our Sons from The Myths of Boyhood.* New York, NY: Random House.

DOREEN KIMURA, PH.D.

Gifted

Giftedness is a blend of intelligence, creativity, self-confidence, intrinsic motivation, and interpersonal skills. Gifted children have a thirst for knowledge and a potential to improve our world. It is our responsibility as educators to challenge them and support them in their academic endeavors.

Too often our aim for gifted students is too low. Rarely are gifted learners truly challenged by the academic content, product expectations, or learning processes of their school years. As a group, gifted students make less academic progress during the school year than do average and below average learners. Identified gifted students are capable of working through curriculum at least two years above grade level, yet research shows that 84 percent of the instructional time in a regular classroom is spent on whole-class/one level learning activities that are typically at or below grade level. No Child Left Behind (NCLB) require ments for public schools have likely increased this practice and lowered the level of instruction. As professionals we advocate that our schools must provide educational experiences appropriate to the needs of all students and that the gifted student should not be left out or left behind.

The brains of highly able students function differently in both quantitative and qualitative ways. Functional brain magnetic resonance imaging (fMRI) scans of gifted students are exploding with action, the screens blaze with the intense and dispersed connections being made between neurons. The "g" intelligence, measured by **IQ** tests, indicate that gray matter (created by dendrites and synaptic connections) in certain regions of the brain determine an individual's level of intelligence. Gifted students have more neural connections and those connections are more complex and active than an individual of average intelligence.

This increased gray matter is located throughout the brain. No one area, such as the frontal lobes, is responsible for giftedness. However, the location of gray matter appears to determine the areas of giftedness. That is why individuals of identical IQ's can have different strengths and weaknesses. Two individuals may both have IQ's of 135 and yet one is strong in math and the other in language skills. Not all gray matter is created equal, only 6 percent is related to IQ. It should be noted that more gray matter does not increase the size of the brain, or in other words a larger brain does not equate to a more intelligent person.

Gifted brains are capable of coordinating information between diverse areas of the brain, including the verbal, auditory, and visual-spatial modules. They are multi-mode thinkers; rarely do they just use one mode when learning. They store memories in many different ways, which not only makes it easier to retrieve information, but also aids in making connections that the average person would not make.

Mathematically gifted adolescents did better than average-ability adolescents on tests that required communication between the left and right hemispheres of the brain. A study published by the American Psychological Association and conducted by a joint effort of the U.S. Army Research Institute for the Behavioral and Social Sciences at Fort Benning, Georgia and the University of Melbourne, Australia discovered that mathematically gifted boys were better at relaying and integrating information between the two hemispheres. Average ability teens relied on either their left hemisphere or the right hemisphere depending upon the task. This study further supported the theory that the functional organization of the brain is a factor in intelligence, not the structural composition.

Testosterone in boys seems to play a role in mathematical abilities. Scientists speculate that a prenatal wash of testosterone in the right half of the brain increases math abilities. It should be noted that taking testosterone as an adolescent or adult will not enhance math abilities, this only occurs in vitro.

The hippocampus, an area of the brain clearly involved in memory, and the parietal lobes, linked with visual-spatial skills and math, appear to be unique in the gifted brain. The hippocampus of the gifted was found to be less compartmentalized than those of lower achieving students. They have increased memory capacity and efficiency. Information is easily stored in their brain and they do not require frequent repetition to learn. The parietal lobe, which is normally folded, was larger than normal and un-folded in the gifted student. While it does appear that there are significant distinctions between the gifted and normal intelligent brain, more research is necessary to firmly establish why some children are gifted.

The highly qualitative and quantitative nature of the gifted brain causes them to often see the complex as simple and the simple as complex. When presented with a simple task or problem they can see so many possible answers that narrowing it down to one seems impossible. Likewise a seemingly sophisticated process seems like a "given understanding." For example, gifted students "see" or intuit patterns that develop in math, such as inverse operations, without being instructed. They are then able to transfer this knowledge from addition and subtraction to multiplication, division, and fractions with no instruction. Gifted brains also demonstrate an intense need for perfection and exactness. They expect a logical answer and may argue, challenge, or correct those who answer in generalities. Preschoolers asked to identify basic shapes on a diagnostic tool may understand a square to be a polygon or a rectangle because its four sides are not exactly the same. The ability to think abstractly, long before their age mates, is also a cognitive skill associated with gifted learners.

They understand humor involving metaphors; they are able to determine meaning of proverbs and they are able to make connections across disciplines. A fifth grader when asked to develop a metaphor for multicultural education shared the following. *Multicultural education is like recycling because some do it willingly and others avoid it at all costs.* The brain of a gifted learner often shows early insight into social and moral issues and related causes and effects. For example, a fourth grader reading about poverty in America develops a proposal to end poverty by asking that all the wealth in America be pooled and then redistributed to each family evenly; thereby, eliminating the need for poverty programs and allowing all families approximately $140,000 to live on each year. This fourth grader demonstrates an atypical depth of moral understanding and the ability to connect cause and effect.

The gifted brain is able to process information nearly eight times as fast as the average learner. They absorb information like a sponge and need very little repetition due to high memory capacity. This learning trait is described as the "velcro" mind. Learn it once and it sticks forever. Gifted students do, indeed, think differently and the differences call for modifications in the classrooms and curriculums of our schools.

Fewer than 20 percent of gifted students are enrolled in schools with programs specifically designed to meet their academic needs. Gifted students respond to rigorous content and need comprehensive and advanced high-level learning experiences at school. Aiming too low for gifted students is a problem educators, parents, and policymakers can and must address. Research offers several options that public schools can modify and combine as they work to effectively meet the needs of students with gifted brains. Aiming high will enable these learners to avoid the danger in Michelangelo's warning.

For gifted students achieving the mark of an unworthy aim does nothing to build **self-efficacy**, academic work ethic, or one's realistic vision of what they can do with their academic skills. Michelangelo warns that the danger is not in setting the aim too high and falling short. If gifted students typically know at least 50 percent of the curriculum to be offered in the five basic subjects before the school year begins then our aim for them must be set substantially higher. Schools can set the aim higher by adopting a menu of options that allow for an optimal match to student needs. These options are not discrete entities and in practice they overlap. Options to explore include differentiation (of content, process, and product), subject-based acceleration, grade-based acceleration, compacted/telescoped curriculum, and full-time gifted classes centered on acceleration of content.

Differentiation is a practice that asks classroom teachers to intentionally modify content, learning processes, and assessments to better meet the needs of the learners in their current group. Teachers, who differentiate effectively, know the students well and make informed decisions about what to change in the *one-size fits all* standard grade level framed curriculum. This option is effective when student needs for acceleration are not extreme and when the teachers are knowledgeable and have the necessary materials and time to implement the differentiated curriculum in most subject areas.

Subject-based acceleration invites the highly able student to join another class or a small group that is working through the curriculum at a higher grade level and at a faster pace. Gifted students learn rapidly and classes that repeat information or tasks more than twice actually impede gifted students' learning of information. Gifted students with one or more particular strengths would benefit from this design option.

Grade-based acceleration (i.e. skipping a grade or two or more) is the oftentimes spurned option for meeting the needs of gifted learners. For years educators, administrators, and those in higher education have contended that this practice is harmful. However, acceleration is the most effective curriculum intervention for high-able learners and it has positive effects both socially and academically. Current studies negate the myth that acceleration is injurious.

Employing a compacted/telescoped curriculum allows the learner to test out of known materials and move on to work that is either accelerated and an extension of the regular classroom curriculum. Like differentiation, this option is effective for gifted students with mild to moderate needs and calls for teachers with sufficient time, skill, and resources to implement it successfully.

Full-time classes centered on the acceleration of content produce substantial academic gains for gifted learners. For the highly gifted student this setting is thought to be their *least restrictive environment*! A highly gifted student in middle-school can absorb a year's worth of high school content in three weeks. Gifted students attending full-time programs with accelerated content perform better on academic achievement measures than their gifted peers not in full-time programs.

All of these options are research-based practices that promote the academic achievement of gifted students and do nothing to harm the achievement of other students in the regular classroom. Regardless of which option(s) a school elects it is critical that gifted students be given the opportunity and support necessary to aim high and advance at a rate and pace that matches the way their brain learns and truly challenges their abilities.

See also: **Creativity; Critical Thinking.**

Further Readings

O'Boyle, M.W. (2005). Some Current Findings on Brain characteristics of the Mathematically Gifted Adolescent. *International Education Journal.* 6(2):247–251.

Rogers, K. (2002). *Re-forming Gifted Education.* Scottsdale, Arizona: Great Potential Press.

Sousa, D. (2001). *How the Gifted Brain Learns.* Thousand Oaks, CA: Corwin Press.

Tomlinson, C. (1996). *Differentiating Instruction in Mixed Ability Classrooms.* VA: ASCD.

Council for Exceptional Children www/cec/sped.org.

LAURIE WENGER, ED.D.

H

Handling Specific Problems in Classroom Management

A happy, respectful, organized classroom is one where students are well behaved, teachers can teach, and learning can flourish. Time spent in creating this environment during the beginning weeks of a school year results in additional time during the year dedicated to instruction rather than solving behavioral problems. Effective, brain-compatible classroom management is described by three general characteristics: it establishes and maintains clear expectations and consequences for the students, it fosters responsibility in the students, and it is considerate of the social-emotional needs of the students.

Clear Expectations and Logical Consequences

The human brain seeks out patterns and routines; a person feels security in being able to predict cause and effect. Therefore, to be brain-compatible and student-focused, a classroom management plan should have clear, predetermined rules or expectations as well as predictable positive and negative consequences. A lengthy list of detailed rules is difficult for students of any age to understand and remember. More valuable is the use of five or less simple, consistent expectations that students can easily remember and internalize. For instance, respect people and property, follow directions, put forth your best effort, use good manners, and move silently and slowly through hallways are five simple rules that could apply to all students in any grade level. These expectations are general enough to encompass virtually any situation or behavior within a classroom or school setting. Also brain-compatible is the fact that the rules are stated in a positive manner describing the desired behaviors and not in a negative, punitive fashion such as no running, no swearing, or no teasing.

Although the posted rules are general and few in number, the details of desired behaviors included within each rule are taught in a lengthy, specific manner at the onset of the school year. The teacher may use multi-sensory methods to teach the expectations such as discussion, posters, or role-playing. This helps to ensure every student in the class understands both the appropriate and inappropriate behaviors encompassed within each rule. In the classroom, or preferably throughout the entire school, these same few rules are enforced consistently during the entire school year. School staff using the exact same terminology of the posted rules during each and every discipline interchange ensures a constant, easy to remember message to the students.

Similar to an academic rubric wherein the students know exactly what level of work will yield each possible grade or score, students should realize in advance the consequences of their behaviors within the classroom or school environment. The consequences should be prompt and specifically related to the behavior so the students learn the cause and effect of their actions. For instance, if students make the poor choice of scribbling on a desk, one logical consequence is a discussion with the teacher about respecting property and then spending recesses or time after school cleaning up the mess. The students learn cause and effect; if they make a mess, they will lose personal free time to clean up the mess or perhaps need to pay for replacement of the damaged object.

Instances do arise when misbehavior is chronic and typical, logical consequences are not effective in permanently halting the behavior. The most difficult students likely will require more intensive, specific expectations and consequences. These may be established through an individualized behavior plan that allows the teacher to provide and document structured interventions for the student. The first step in developing an individualized behavior plan is to pin-point the one or two specific behaviors that are most detrimental to the success of the student and the rest of the class. The related proper behavior/expectation is listed. For instance, "you will remain quiet unless called on by the teacher." It is important to determine what internal need of the difficult student is being satisfied by his or her misbehaviors so that appropriate positive and negative consequences are chosen. For instance, if the purpose of the actions seems to be to gain attention from adults, then a consequence of an immediate, private discussion with the teacher will only promote more of the same misbehavior. In addition to the target behavior/behaviors, the plan also denotes the support and positive consequences the teacher or other adults will give the student for choosing the proper way to behave. Also identified in the behavior plan are the corrective actions or negative consequences that will result each time the student chooses inappropriate actions associated with the target behavior. The teacher must consistently adhere to all portions of the behavior plan to see a long-lasting change in the student's conduct. When implementing an individualized behavior plan, it is usually advantageous to solicit the support of the student's parents/guardians in establishing long-range goals and rewards for the student as the misbehaviors diminish.

Whether dealing with a very difficult student, or the typically well-behaved child, teachers must not forget to use positive consequences for properly following the expectations. Positive consequences or reinforcement is effective because success breeds success. For instance, when students study long hours for a test, and then are rewarded with a high score and a compliment from the teacher, it reinforces in their brains that hard work pays off so they will likely repeat this positive cycle. Often teachers find it effective to reward students with external incentives like positive notes, points, stickers, words of praise, and the like to foster a sense of accomplishment and pride in the students. Typically, the ultimate goal in rewarding desired behavior is to eventually have the students intrinsically feel good about their actions so they continue to do the right thing simply because it is the right thing to do.

Student Ownership and Responsibility

An important skill for students to learn, for the classroom and for life in general, is to take responsibility for their own actions. Brain and learning research tells us that students benefit from choices and decision making power within the school setting. It is more likely for students to feel ownership of and responsibility for the classroom expectations if they have some power in establishing those guidelines. The development of a classroom social contract during the first few days of each new school year is an effective course of action. This process of discussing and recording how people in the class should be treated and why, allows the teacher to lead the formulation of behavioral expectations for the class with substantial input from the students. Building the social contract helps to establish a classroom environment of teamwork and mutual respect. By signing the completed social contract, every student and the teacher agree to abide by the document and feel ownership of those parameters as all opinions were taken into account during its development.

Although a healthy climate of mutual respect may be present in a classroom, some infractions of the rules or social contract are inevitable. When this occurs, in addition to the logical consequences previously discussed, students will learn from taking responsibility for their action through problem-solving. Neuroscience studies of learning indicate that complex problem-solving is enriching for the brain. In fact, reaching a solution during problem-solving is not nearly as valuable to the brain as the process itself. This intricate thinking process allows new ideas to be developed and then contemplated through comparing, contrasting, and evaluating each thought. These high-level thinking skills spark the growth of new dendrite connections between neurons and this is how the brain "grows" intelligence.

Despite the fact the brain may not particularly benefit if a solution is reached at the end of a problem-solving session, a classroom teacher certainly wants or needs to reach a solution to a discipline problem. After an infraction of the rules, the following questions will steer the students through a problem situation to understand the mistake made, empathize with the person affected, understand future ramifications, and determine how to prevent the same behavior in the future: What are you doing? What are you supposed to be doing? Why is this a problem? How will you solve this problem to make sure it does not happen anymore? What will happen if you do it again? These questions are best answered during a discussion with the teacher. However, they may be answered in writing if time or circumstances do not permit a discussion. These written responses may prove useful as a reminder to the student during a similar situation down the road or for documentation for parents or administration. When a teacher finds that these questions are being asked time and time again of the same student without a change in behavior, it is either time to increase the consequences, such as implementing an individualized behavior plan described previously, or it is time to provide the student with detailed training related to the misbehavior. The student may not be comprehending or internalizing his or her responsibility for the misbehavior and the need for improvement. Seeking out the help of an expert such as a counselor, social worker, special education teacher, or psychologist may be beneficial.

Social-Emotional Needs of Students

A nurturing, stimulating environment is the best kind of classroom for the human brain. Studies of the physical brain reveal that the same structures in the limbic system area of the brain that assist in learning and long-term memory are also actively involved with **emotions** and reactions to **stress**. Both scientific research and instinctual knowledge tell us that students who are under significant stress are not in peak form for learning new information. The physical and mental well being of a person, managed in the brain stem and limbic system areas, take precedence for brain activity over the cortex, or the conscious thinking area, of the brain. For instance, a student sitting through a math class fretting about the upcoming walk home due to daily harassment from the class bully, is likely not to recall much about the process to find the lowest common denominator for two fractions taught during that class period. Teachers who cause or allow stressful, threatening situations in the classroom are building memories of those negative experiences rather than the academic concepts.

Often times, the most difficult students in classrooms have social-emotional needs that are at the root of misbehavior and are, therefore, interfering with learning. Ideally, such a student will have a close, trusting relationship with an adult in the school so she/he can open up and discuss the problems and prevent misbehaviors from increasing. One of the most critical things for a teacher to remember is to control his/her own reactions during a student's behavioral outburst. Yelling back, using sarcasm, returning dirty looks, criticizing, and the like will only serve to spark a power struggle or, worse yet, crush the student's self-esteem. More effective will be to defuse the immediate situation and eventually address the behavior in a calm, problem-solving manner. For instance, suppose a student repeatedly yells at a teacher, "I am not going to do this test!" The student is likely expecting the teacher to react in a harsh manner. It may be effective to react in the opposite manner expected such as very quietly sympathizing with the students by saying, "I can see you don't want to take the test. They are not fun. But, I want you to do well in my class. You did well on that quiz a week ago and I would hate to see your grade drop if you bomb this test. I hear you. It is clear to me you don't want to take this test. However, it is your job to take the test right now." Acting in this manner, the teacher is providing the message that the test must be completed, yet is still responding to the student in a caring manner. If the student were to continue to act in a disruptive manner, ideally the teacher would find another adult to sit in with the rest of the class so they can complete the test in a non-stressful environment. The teacher and disruptive student would further discuss the problem away from the classmates.

Students' **self-esteem,** participation, and effort are strengthened when they feel a part of a group, are accepted for who they are, and cared for by the teacher. Therefore, teachers bear a crucial responsibility to treat students kindly and to establish, model, and maintain a respectful environment among all participants in the classroom. The topics reviewed previously of setting clear expectations and consequences as well as implementing a social contract are two ways for teachers to reduce stress and build a sense of acceptance and teamwork within a classroom. Additional components of a classroom management system that take students' social-emotional needs into account may include class meetings to solve problems, peer mediation, anti-bullying programs, and positive teacher behaviors such as personally getting to know each student, establishing a trusting relationship with each student, calling parents with good news rather than purely the bad news, frequent smiling and use of appropriate humor, handling discipline issues privately, never embarrassing a student with sarcasm, never giving up on even the toughest students, and genuinely listening to and expressing concern for the students.

See also: Aggression; At-Risk Behavior; Classroom Management and the Brain; Proactive Classroom Management Strategies.

Further Readings

Canter, L., Canter, M. (1993). *Succeeding with Difficult Students.* Los Angeles, CA: Canter and Associates, Inc.

Erlauer, L. (2003). *The Brain-Compatible Classroom: Using What We Know About Learning to Improve Teaching.* Alexandria, VA: Association for Supervision and Curriculum Development.

Flippen Group (2003). *Capturing Kids' Hearts.* College Station, TX: The Flippen Group.

Howard, P.J. (2000). *The Owner's Manual for the Brain.* Austin, TX: Bard Press.

Sergiovanni, T.J. (1992). *Moral Leadership: Getting to the Heart of School Improvement.* San Francisco, CA: Jossey-Bass, Inc.

LAURA ERLAUER

I

Infant Brain

The first year of life marks a period of tremendous growth in children's brains and mental abilities. Babies progress from largely reflexive behavior at birth to willful, creative thinking by the end of the first year. As in all development, this progress reflects the intricate interaction of "nature," or innately programmed brain maturation with "nurture," the molding of a child's growing neurons and synapses by his or her environment and interactions.

At birth, the brain is a mere one-quarter of its adult size. The two soft-spots, or *fontanels,* in the front and back of a newborn's skull are literal gaps between the bones that permit a rapid increase in brain size after birth. An infant's brain grows incredibly in the first year, nearly tripling in size, to reach about three-quarters of its average adult weight of about three pounds. Just as larger computers are capable of faster, more complex processing, so do babies' rapidly growing brains provide them with the machinery to perceive, move, think, and interact with increasing sophistication throughout this first year and beyond.

What fuels this rapid brain growth? Surprisingly, it is not the addition of new brain cells, or *neurons*. Babies produce their total complement of neurons—some 100 billion cable-like cells—well before birth. Although scientists recently discovered that some neurons, known as *neural stem cells,* can continue to divide into adulthood, the number of these is relatively small (sufficient only to replace any dying neurons) and does not increase the total population of neurons in the brain.

Rather, the brain grows as a result of the massive growth of each of these individual neurons. Neurons have a shape unlike most other cells of the body. They are often compared to trees, with one group of branches, the *dendrites,* that receive input from thousands of other neurons, and a second branching domain, the *axon,* that sends electrical output to thousands more neurons. And just like trees, whose roots and branches sprout from sapling size to towering oaks or redwoods, the growth of dendrites and axons adds up to an enormous increase in the overall size of a neuron, most of which takes place over the first few years of life.

Unlike the trees in a forest, however, babies' growing neurons do more than stretch out their branches. Their elongating axons and dendrites literally reach out and start communicating with each other, forming the trillions of synaptic connections that literally turn on the circuits responsible for babies' many emerging abilities.

Vision, for example, is quite poor in newborn babies, because neurons in the visual part of the brain, located at the back of the head, have very few synapses and short, unconnected dendrites. During the first six months, however, as their branches grow out and the number of synapses explodes, the visual brain starts working: babies progress from blurry, two-dimensional vision to full-color, sharp, 3D acuity, all within the space of a few months. You can see this change in their visual behavior. While newborns have difficulty focusing, four-month-olds are looking machines, intently interested in any high-contrast or bright visual stimulus, often staring for many minutes at a time. There are even hints of this growth in the shape of babies' heads, which protrude a prominent occipital bulge long before they expand in the forehead area. This sweet, baby-shaped head reflects the more rapid growth of the visual and other sensory circuits at the back of the brain, as compared to the more slowly maturing frontal lobe that underlies the cognitive and emotional advances of later childhood and adolescence.

Myelination

While the number of neurons does not increase after birth, babies' brain growth is fueled by an increase in the number of neural supporting cells, known as *glia*. These cells, which actually outnumber neurons in the brain, carry out many important metabolic and structural jobs. Among these is to manufacture *myelin*, a dense, fatty insulating material that wraps around long axon cables and prevents their electrical current from leaking out. Axons run along each other inside nerves much like the thin wires inside a fat computer printer cable. And just as each of these printer wires is encased in plastic, so adjacent wires don't short out each other, so are each of our axons wrapped in myelin to prevent cross-talk, for example, between a sensory neuron and motor neuron that run within the same nerve.

Another critical benefit of myelin is to massively increase the speed at which axons transmit information. In some axons, the addition of myelin accelerates their signaling by more than tenfold. Internet users can appreciate the significance of faster information flow, but the consequences for our mental function are even more dramatic. Patients with demyelinating diseases, such as multiple sclerosis, may lose their vision or ability to walk because their axons are unable to transmit fast, coherent information to the next relay in a sensory or motor circuit.

Considering the importance of myelin to normal brain function, one of the more startling facts about the infant brain is that it has very little myelin. Myelination begins before birth, but it is a very gradual, uneven process. By birth, only the spinal cord and lower part of the brain, the *brain stem*, are substantially myelinated. This lower brain maturation permits babies the many reflexes—such as breathing, sucking, swallowing, and coughing—that they need to survive outside the womb. However, newborns are capable of very few voluntary and conscious behaviors, because the highest part of the brain, the *cerebral cortex,* has virtually no myelin at birth. Put another way, myelin is the white matter of the brain, and newborns, unlike adults and even older children, have only gray matter in their cerebral cortex.

Myelination of the cerebral cortex does kick off immediately after birth. By the end of the first year, all areas of the cerebral cortex have begun myelinating in some measure. Areas devoted to sensory perception, especially touch, vision, and hearing, myelinate first, along with the primary motor area, involved in controlling voluntary movement. These areas are located mostly in the rear half of the brain, and their myelination (along with synaptic and dendritic growth), permits babies' rapidly improving sensory and movement abilities. Much slower to myelinate, however, are the cognitive and emotional centers in the frontal and temporal lobes. Although these areas begin to add some white matter in the first year, their myelination continues throughout childhood, into adolescence, and, by some measures, well into our early twenties.

Experience and Synaptic Pruning

Myelination and synapse formation are largely programmed events. Although they can be disrupted by disease or other insults, such as severe malnutrition, both these processes appear to be largely controlled by genes. The next major phase of brain development, by contrast, is crucially influenced by nurture, or experience. This is the "pruning phase," when babies select among their trillions of newly formed synapses to preserve only those connections that are most useful for getting along in their newfound environment.

One of the more surprising facts about brain development is that neurons don't merely connect up and start working; they actually form an *excess* number of synaptic connections in early life. Such synaptic exuberance serves as the basic substrate for all of early learning. Instead of a mere *one* trillion synapses in the visual cortex, the number present in adults, infants produce *two* trillion by just eight months of age. They then spend the next eight years or so whittling this number down to only those connections that are most useful for the job of seeing. The same over-production and subsequent pruning occurs in all parts of the cerebral cortex, though once again, things are slower in the frontal and temporal lobes, where pruning is thought to last into late adolescence.

How does a baby "decide" which synapses to preserve and which to prune? Just as in Darwinian natural selection, synapse selection depends on utility. And usefulness, in the nervous system, is measured in volts—that is, in amount of electrical activity. Those synapses that interconnect two neurons more effectively—that cause a greater amount of electrical firing in both partners—will be preserved, while those that more weakly connect their partners will be pruned. Neuroscientists abbreviate this relationship as "Cells that fire together, wire together." The flip-side is the more familiar "use it or lose it" expression we all use to describe the effects of practice and experience on our repertoire of abilities.

These rules apply, to an even harsher degree, in infancy and early childhood. Babies whose vision is in any way perturbed (the most common causes are crossed eyes or congenital cataracts) are in danger of permanently losing visual acuity if the problem is not corrected during the period of peak synaptic exuberance, which lasts until about two years of age. (Fortunately, highly effective medical treatment is available to treat such congenital visual problems and preserve most of the vision in affected babies.)

On the positive side, synaptic exuberance also represents a time of great opportunity for infants: every sight, sound, and loving touch will help to strengthen—in some cases, permanently—the synapses and neural circuits it activates. This flexibility is perhaps most evident in the language skills of babies adopted early in life. No matter where they were born, or what language their biological parents spoke, babies adopted into a different culture effortlessly learn to speak the language of their adoptive parents, without any hint of an accent. In babies and young children, the simple act of hearing a language preserves the neural connections that optimally perceive and produce those specific speech sounds. The same synaptic plasticity, alas, is not available in adults' brains, which have already pruned away their excess synapses. Many researchers believe this is the reason why older individuals never learn to speak a second language as fluently as children do.

Strategies

Thanks to their rapidly growing brains, as well as their postnatal explosion of myelin and new synapses, babies learn incredibly quickly. They absorb immense quantities of information about the world around them, tuning their brains to best perceive and respond to whatever environment they happen to be growing up in. Based on what is known about the developing brain and its sensitivity to a child's early experience, babies need the following for optimal brain wiring in the first year of life:

- First and foremost, loving, sensitive parents and other caregivers. Babies are utterly dependent on the adults in their life to feed, care for, and teach them the basics of communication and social interaction. Warm, responsive caregiving models this positive social interaction and promotes a baby's security and confidence that his or her needs will be met. An emotionally healthy baby is in the best position to advance his or her other sensory, motor, social, and cognitive skills.

- Language stimulation. A simple equation describes the relationship between babies' language exposure and later verbal abilities: "Language In = Language Out." Beginning at birth, babies who are talked to, sung to, read to, and generally conversed with more by their parents and other caregivers develop larger vocabularies, higher verbal IQs, and may even have an easier time learning how to read, compared to babies not immersed in such a verbally rich environment.

- Opportunity for movement and physical challenge. Motor milestones may seem automatic, but each depends on many hours of diligent practice, to strengthen the muscles and hone the neural circuits necessary to carry out smooth, coordinated movement. These days, babies have less and less opportunity for gross motor play, as they are increasingly confined in car seats, strollers, and "exersaucers."

- Varied sensory diet. Babies thrive on novelty. They quickly get bored with the same old rattle, mobile, or jar of pureed peas. Although familiar routines are important to develop a sense of security, babies seek out and will learn more if there is some variety in their playthings, their morning stroll, or the words to a favorite lullaby.

- "Down time" to rest, recoup, and learn to occupy themselves. While social and sensory stimulation are important to optimal development, babies should not be entertained during every waking hour. They also need to take their time, explore on their own, and learn to prolong their own attention span. "Over-stimulation" is as much a danger as understimulation, particularly in our complex, fast-paced modern world.

See also: **Blindness; Bilingualism; Critical Periods (Sensitive Periods); Prenatal Brain.**

Further Readings

Brody, B.A, Kinney, H.C., Kloman, A.S., Gilles, F.H. (1987) Sequence of central nervous system myelination in human infancy. I. An autopsy study of myelination. *Journal of Neuropathology and Experimental Neurology* 46:283–301.

Committee on Integrating the Science of Early Childhood Development, National Research Council and the Institute of Medicine (2000) "The developing brain," Chapter 8, in Shonkoff, J.P. and Phillips, D.A., *From Neurons to Neighborhoods*, Washington DC: National Academy Press, pp. 182–217. Available online at: http://books.nap.edu/books/0309069882/html/R1.html

Eliot, L. (2000). *What's Going On in There? How the Brain and Mind Develop in the First Five Years of Lifes*. New York: Bantam.

Huttenlocher, P.R. (1990). Morphometric study of human cerebral cortex development. *Neuropsychologia* 28:517–527.

"BrainWonders": Information about the brain and early learning written through a collaboration between Zero-to-Three, Boston University School of Medicine, and the Erikson Institute. http://www.zerotothree.org/brainwonders/ index.html

LISE ELIOT, PH.D.

Information-Processing Model

The degree to which all learners understand ideas and disciplines depends, in part, on prior understandings and the levels at which the information is processed. The ability to make sense out of this paragraph may depend on one's experience with teaching or educational psychology. Similarly, when learners turn their attention to new information, they attempt to attach meaning to the ideas by searching their memory for related or previously experienced information. No one model of cognition is sufficient to express what really happens in the mind of a learner, but one thing is for sure: not much learning occurs without attention to a stimulus or synaptic connections. Thus, the information-processing theory posits that learners perceive, attend to, dispose of, attach meaning to, and store information.

An Information Explosion: Attached or Trashed

The information explosion of the last twenty years increasingly demands that learners have the capacity to attend to many stimuli and to determine what to process and what to disregard. Take for example any of the mega-electronics stores in any shopping mall in America. Upon entering such a place, one is bombarded with stimuli from every direction. One can imagine what it must be like for the brain to perceive and process information. Immediately, for someone who is electronically challenged, the store is a trip to the unknown. For those with more expertise, the store becomes a playground of new equipment with all the latest bells and whistles.

For the electronics novice, the experience is a sensory explosion. The visual and auditory registers of the brain are inundated with a cacophony of sound and a kaleidoscopic of images. Music blaring from every corner of the store enters the brain, and patterns of meaning are created for new devices by using established templates, prototypes, feature analyses, or structural descriptions of known electronics equipment. If one has a lot of experience with the electronics equipment, the capacity for processing the myriad stimuli is much greater than the attenuated processing abilities of those less experienced. So it is with all learners. Our classrooms are not dissimilar from the electronics store: students must use their information-processing abilities to make sense of the ideas shared on a daily basis. To more fully understand the information-processing model it is necessary to describe the sensory memory, encoding, and retrieval processes students use and that we must understand to effectively induce meaningful learning.

Sensory Memory

As we sense stimuli from our environment, whether it is smell, taste, touch, sound, or sight, we begin to temporarily store the information for milliseconds of time to begin processing it. Each of the senses has its own sensory register that is used to begin the process of assigning meaning to the new information. Most of the past and current research is focused on the visual and auditory senses, but more recently a growing body of knowledge has emerged regarding the other senses as well. Additionally, a significant body of literature exists regarding how humans process multiple stimuli that may be interfering with each other for our attention. While teachers may include all the senses in the learning experience, the vast majority of inputs occur through auditory and visual means. Our detection and interpretation of sensory information is called perception.

Visual Perception

Recent neuroscience research has revealed that different parts of our brain are used to perceive different types of visual stimuli. For example, when we perceive recognizable materials the inferior temporal cortex is used, and when novel stimuli are involved we use the left hippocampal/parahippocampal region of our brain. Early researchers focused on how we perceive briefly presented visual information, how long visual images (letters) were retained in our visual register, and how much of the visual information was registered. The research revealed several important findings and concluded that we are able to perceive more visual information than we can recall.

Auditory Perception

A number of studies have been done on the concept of auditory interference and its impact on auditory sensory processing. Interestingly, much like visual icons, auditory (echo) registers hold information while processing starts. Auditory input results in the production of an echo that preserves the essence of the stimulus and may remain in temporary storage for as long as ten seconds. The critical components of the auditory modality are alertness, discrimination, memory, sequencing, figure-ground, and the ability to relate sound–symbol relationships.

Students must be able to hold auditory inputs long enough to discriminate a consonant from a vowel or to put together a prefix with a suffix. Students must be able to hear a letter such as "A" and put it together with its symbolic form. Students must be able to cue into sounds, put them in order, and remember them if they are going to be successful readers, listeners, computers, and learners.

These research findings suggest to teachers that the oral presentation of information may help students perceive and understand when it is coupled with visual stimuli. Furthermore, it is critical that teachers organize and present visual and auditory information in modalities consistent with auditory and visual processing theories for students to attach meaning to the stimuli presented in the classroom. For a student to perceive information they must attend to it. However, human attention abilities are more complex than simply listening, or seeing a stimulus.

Attention

Unless you are dead asleep, you are always attending to what is going on in your environment. People can make choices as to what they attend to. We can direct our attention, and even divide our attention. We might, for example, be able to keep track of multiple baseball games while watching a television with the capabilities of showing several games at once. Many current television programs have scrolling information across the bottom or top of the screen that provides additional information to the viewer other than what is seen through the main images being telecast. In classrooms, teachers continually divide their attention among their students. You may be watching one student while talking to another and still be able to monitor the entire class all at the same time. More demanding tasks such as driving a car in a snowstorm while trying to talk on a cellular phone may take all of one's attention to accomplish. While a number of theories have been offered regarding how people select what stimuli to attend to, in all of the models various cognitive tasks are influenced by the quality and quantity of the data available to perform the task. Some tasks will improve if more of our attention is shifted to them, and still others will improve if the quality of the input is improved. For example, students are better able to process information if it is emphasized, organized, contextualized, and focused. Listening to music, while watching television, and studying for a mathematics test would not result in better test performance. However, if the student focused solely on a study guide for the mathematics test that showed examples, and included strategies or algorithms for solving various problem types, it is more likely that the student would process more information relevant to the test

Learners with limited attention capacity must develop their abilities to focus on what is most important, and be able to recognize and ignore irrelevant information. Selective attention studies show that older children develop greater abilities to "filter" the wheat from the chaff. Older students, have the capability of ignoring extraneous stimuli while focusing on task relevant stimuli. While our ability to monitor and regulate our heart rate and other physiological functions is innate and quite developed at birth, our abilities to selectively adjust and shift our attention appears to develop as children grow into young adults. As teachers we must realize that students' perceptions and their abilities to attend to them are partially dependent on how we present information. The novelty of a stimulus can influence students' attention to the subject matter. The intensity with which the stimulus is presented, and whether or not the stimuli are moving significantly impacts students' attention. Strategies that create emotional and episodic memories are also powerful and lasting for students.

Working and Long-Term Memory

Once a learner has perceived and attended to information, the information-processing model posits that both long-term and working memory are used to attach meaning to it. Working memory thinks about the information, repeats the information, and connects it to prior knowledge enabling it to be stored in long-term memory. It is important to note that some sensory information is also discarded in our conscious processing of it.

The distinction between long-term and working memory is a central tenet of most information processing models. However, recent findings from neurobiology memory research emphasize that working memory and long-term memory are interrelated in a holistic process. Issues of primacy, recency, maintenance rehearsal (repeating information), elaborative rehearsal (connecting new information to prior knowledge), and the way information is organized influence how information in working memory gets stored in long-term memory. Memory can, therefore, be a function of how often or how recently one has processed information, and the level at which the information is rehearsed and organized when encountered.

When the brain encounters the world, it can encode and store the information for later retrieval. Most importantly, new information shapes the way the brain encodes in the future. The brain responds to experience by altering synaptic strengths and creating new synaptic connections.

Memory is therefore, the firing of newly created circuits of neurons that then alter the probabilities of certain patterns firing in the future. Memory is enhanced if similar patterns have been activated in the past, or if the pattern is fired repeatedly. When focused, emphasized, and organized information is repeatedly processed; students can begin to make some operations automatic.

For example, some mathematics operations, if repeatedly accomplished, can become more automatized. Just as one doesn't consciously think about all the mechanics of driving a car, one can do some cognitive tasks with very little mental effort. Skilled athletes are able to use the concept of automaticity to play their sports without thinking about how to do each and every procedure of the activity. Take for example Kevin Garnett's ability to dunk a basketball. If he had to think about each step of the process of dunking, he would be unable to perform his magic. As a young musician learns to play the trombone, the slide positions are awkwardly found by trial and error. After significant amounts of practice, the slide positions are found without even thinking about the process. Similarly, students who have proceduralized the reading process do not need to decode individual letters to make sense of letters in combination with others. A very recent functional magnetic resonance imaging (fMRI) research study has revealed that reading disabled children taught with a phonics-based intervention demonstrated increased activation in the brain area responsible for making meaning of written language. In other words, the students' brains are capable of being rewired in ways that their neural systems for reading are changed by a teaching intervention, and become comparable to those of good readers with similar automaticity abilities.

In addition to the general memory theories, other theories suggest there are two types of memory storage: declarative memory—our ability to recall information about people, places, and things; and **procedural memory**—our ability to move, and sense without having to think about it. For example, as you type words into a word-processor, you do not need to think about how to move your fingers on the keyboard.

Most information processing theories posit that information that is stored isn't readily accessible despite the fact that a memory trace in long-term memory is permanent and that long-term memory appears to have almost unlimited storage capacity. Very recent research theories suggest that short-term working memory must also include a long-term working memory that can be accessed by retrieval cues in short-term working memory. Skilled activities such as text comprehension and mental calculation are examples of how information stored in long-term memory is kept accessible by means of retrieval cues in short-term working memory. If a student is able to proceduralize an algorithm or a decoding process related to reading, their long-term memories are cued and directly accessible. The process by which students encode and retrieve memories can be enhanced by our understanding of its dimensions, and by our application of specific teaching strategies related to them.

Dimensions of Encoding and Retrieval

As students are exposed to new material, the depth at which they process information can influence how well they remember it. If teachers provide opportunities for elaboration, rehearsal, organization, and contextualization, the research is clear that students will not only encode information better, but also be able to recall it better. The more meaning a student makes of stimuli the greater his/her depth of processing. When a student processes at shallow levels the memory trace in long-term memory may be quite superficial. Students may be able to remember basic characteristics of an idea, but not much meaning. However, if a student is able to make meaning of an idea by creating associations with prior knowledge, and by connecting the new information to other related ideas, they are likely to leave lasting memory traces that can be recalled.

Researchers have identified two main ways by which students attempt to put ideas to memory. First, students may simply repeat a new idea over and over without connecting it to prior knowledge. This shallow processing is called maintenance rehearsal. In contrast, when students process material at a deeper level their processing is more elaborative. For example, if a student attempts to learn the concept of planetary motion by imagining him or herself on a large merry-go-round, or on the "scrambler" carnival ride, they begin to make connections between prior experiences and planetary motion. The more distinct and connected the student can make the concept, the greater their chances of creating lasting memory traces. If better memory results from greater depths of processing, teachers must provide multiple opportunities for students to maximize their elaborative rehearsal processes.

Teaching Strategies

There are many teaching strategies and techniques that teachers can use to enrich students' elaborative processes. The use of note taking techniques promote elaborative processing when they focus students' attention on the most important text material through the use of previewing, questioning, reading, reciting, reviewing, reflecting. Some research suggests that when students formulate questions for themselves about the reading they process it at deeper levels.

Another useful elaborative strategy is referred to as visual imagery. Making connections between what one knows and what is to be learned can be strengthened by using visualization techniques. Because images are the products of imagination, they can represent concepts, feelings, and sensory experiences. If students can make connections between concrete images and concepts to be learned, there is a high likelihood that they will remember it better. For example, abstract mathematics concepts can be visualized through the use of images of Islamic tilings. Recent technological advances enable teachers and students to visualize complex calculus concepts with an inexpensive, but powerful handheld calculator. When students can actually visualize a complex equation, they are better able to learn it.

When students attempt to encode and store information, research suggests that the use of self-referent encoding also enhances the probability that a student will remember the information. In other words, if a student can make the information personally relevant or meaningful they will encode it better. Teachers who can give students multiple examples, or explain how the information is relevant allow students opportunities to make those same meaningful connections for themselves.

How often have teachers heard students say, "I learned it but I can't remember it?" One cannot discuss encoding and storage without mentioning issues of retrieval. How can teachers best help students to recall information? There is little doubt that how one learns the material directly impacts one's ability to recall it. To help students encode and subsequently recall information, teachers need to include three critical elements in their lessons: elaboration, organization, and context.

As mentioned earlier elaboration causes students to process information at deeper levels. Teachers who use questioning and discussion to facilitate students' thinking about such things as cause and effect, consequences, similarities and differences, and analysis produce elaborative learning environments.

Research also suggests that organizing materials to be encoded will enhance students' abilities to remember it later. For example, the use of non-linguistic representations, concept maps, flow charts, and outlines helps students produce frameworks for recall. Additionally, teaching students how to cluster information, or to create conceptual hierarchies such as classification also helps students to remember large amounts of information. Teaching mnemonic strategies such as loci improves students' capabilities of remembering information by associating it with locations familiar to them.

The context in which students learn new material directly impacts how they will retrieve the information. Most people have experienced memories associated with a place, a person, or a specific experience. Remembering where one was when they first heard of the events surrounding 9/11 is not difficult for most people. The power of physical and emotional contexts in learning environments should not be overlooked. Even simple things like bulletin boards can impact students' memories. Teaching with music, creative dramatics, or role-plays creates contexts for learning and remembering.

In an era when teachers are expected to teach to standards and to teach more material than ever, it is increasingly important to use brain-compatible teaching strategies that induce long-term memories not rote learning. The more fully we have students process information the better they will be able to retain and retrieve meaningful information that has been connected to prior knowledge. In addition to creating learning environments that include elaboration, organization of information, and contextualized learning, teachers who model, develop analogies and metaphors, clearly communicate learning outcomes, use cues, and reduce learning anxiety will markedly improve student achievement.

See also: **Episodic Memory; Semantic Memory.**

Further Readings

Siegel, D.J. (2001). Memory: an overview, with emphasis on developmental, interpersonal, and neurobiological aspects. *Journal of the American Academy of Child and Adolescent Psychiatry.* September 40(9):997–1011.

Sylwester, R. (2005). *How to Explain a Brain: An Educator's Handbook of Brain Terms and Cognitive Processes.* Thousand Oaks, CA: Corwin Press.

Visualizing Mathematics: Imagery Techniques for Learning Abstract Concepts. http://www.mupad.com/mathpad/2004_1/visual_maths/#intro.

JOHN J. CLEMENTSON, PH.D.

IQ

The relationship between IQ and the brain is one of the great puzzles of biology, social science, and education. In the everyday world, IQ is important because it has predictive value for academic and career success, social outcomes that matter greatly. IQ represents intelligence insofar as it summarizes performance on tests of cognitive skill and relates that performance to population norms. While IQ is an imperfect indicator of intelligence, it is the best-established indicator available. The distinction between *mind* and *brain* is important when considering IQ. The mind is an abstraction responsible for cognitive ability—thinking, reasoning, and problem-solving—the skills that IQ quantifies. The brain, however, is a physical organ composed largely of nerve cells. Although the precise relationships between the brain and IQ form an enduring scientific puzzle; research has revealed many associations between IQ and the brain's size, structure, and function, and some of these have applications to education.

Brain Size and IQ

There is a moderate correlation, or relationship, between larger brain size and higher IQ. That said, there is no evidence that people who are particularly creative or accomplished inevitably have larger brains than less distinguished individuals. Einstein is a vivid example of the imprecise relationship between brain size and intelligence. Einstein's brain, which was preserved after his death, weighed less than the average brain for similarly-aged males. His brain was distinctive in other ways, however. Research showed that Einstein's brain had more glial cells than eleven other male brains. Glial cells support the nerve cells, or neurons, that are responsible for all mental activity. Of course, findings on Einstein's brain cannot be considered representative of the brains of all intelligent people. However, these findings imply that intelligence is imperfectly related to brain size. They also suggest that intelligence and IQ may have correlates in other brain qualities, including glial cell density.

Male/female differences in brain size also pertain here. Women, on average, have smaller brain sizes than men, but there is no significant difference in IQ between men and women. One plausible explanation is that the larger bodies of men require more brain mass for somatic control, a correlation that applies broadly across species. In humans, though, the correlation between brain volume and body size is only marginally significant. Hence, the brain size difference can only be partly explained by the proportional brain/body weight differences between men and women. An alternative explanation for similar IQ scores between men and women is the factor of brain cell density. In the area of the brain associated with higher order functioning, women have a higher density of neurons than do men. Like the research on Einstein's brain, research on men's and women's brains have suggested that there is much more to IQ than brain size.

The topic of brain size and IQ has yet another, more sinister, face. Stephen Jay Gould, a Harvard professor and evolutionary biologist, has made the case that, historically, anatomists have sought to detect average differences in cranial volume across racial groups. The goal of this research may have been to justify a theory of racial superiority favoring, most often, northern Europeans. Indeed, the study of intelligence has sometimes been associated with an agenda—covert or blatant—of proving the intellectual inferiority of some races and the superiority of others. Gould argued that this agenda was not necessarily malicious on the part of the investigators because it may have been subconscious, but the racist motives were active nonetheless in guiding their selection and interpretation of data. Gould revealed the theory of race differences in cranial capacity to be an unproductive hypothesis, and yet one that beguiled science for many decades.

Brain Structure and IQ

While the meaningfulness of any correlation between brain size and IQ has been challenged, more successful efforts have been made to link intelligence and IQ with brain structure. Research on brain structure, especially on neurons and synapses, has illuminated the biological foundations for IQ. Synaptic connections between neurons are the anatomical counterparts of cognitive activity—learning, thinking, wishing, and feeling. The number of synapses in the brain changes radically over a life span. An infant's brain experiences prolific growth in the number of synapses, a process called "blooming." The number of synapses reaches a maximum at about the age of two years. Strangely, from that point onward, the number of synapses decreases significantly. This reduction in the number of synapses has been called "pruning," evoking the image of a gardener pruning a shrub, reducing its overall volume while increasing its cohesive shape and definition. Different parts of the brain undergo this pruning process at different times. Additionally, learning can result in entirely new synapses, and existing synapses can become more active or less active in response to experience. In many ways, then, learning alters brain structure at the level of neurons. In fact, the pattern of synaptic connections in the brain is the best current physical model for accumulated learning and intelligent functioning.

One factor that seems to promote brain development is a complex environment. Rats raised in complex environments, as opposed to simple caged environments, have increased blood supply to the brain and have larger cerebral cortices, both of which increase the efficiency and effectiveness of brain function. In addition to these biological effects, research has shown that environmentally stimulated rats are better problem solvers. Marion Diamond conducted a study with two groups of rats, one group raised in an environment supporting play and exploration activities and the other group raised in a barren cage. The rats raised in the complex environment were not only better problem solvers, but also had 20 percent more synapses in their visual cortices than did rats raised in plain cage.

The established link between learning and synaptic growth is an important scientific discovery, even if the specific learning experiences that promote neural development are not yet well understood. As early as the 1960s, there was a widespread belief in human neural plasticity, or the potential of the brain to develop in a way that improves IQ. This belief inspired programmatic efforts to boost intelligence and, therefore, the potential for academic and life success. These efforts have produced some, mostly moderate, positive results. Head Start, a program designed to increase the chances of academic success for economically disadvantaged children, was shown to raise children's IQ scores by an average of nine points. While the IQ advantage did not persist past the first year of schooling, other indicators of academic success did extend into adolescence. Other programs, including the Abecedarian Project and the Milwaukee Project, produced impressive, though sometimes controversial, results.

On a level less microscopic than neurons and synapses, scientists have long had insights into the associations between brain structure and cognition. It is well known, for example, that the brain's cortex is vital for higher-order cognition. The cortex, which is unusually large in humans, is the outer layer of the two cerebral hemispheres. It mediates reasoning, perception, and language—indeed virtually all forms of complex cognition. Pictures of brains illustrate the folded surface of the cortex, its bumps (gyri), and its dips (sulci). Interestingly, the thickness of the cortex does not vary much between mammals. However, cortex folding does vary across species, and humans have more of it. More folding means greater cortex volume, and greater volume implies that humans have more potential for development of higher-order cognitive functioning. The frontal cortex, in particular, is responsible for the general functions of planning, goal monitoring, and problem-solving. There is some evidence for a correlation between more gray matter in the frontal cortex and higher IQ. Skills as specific as identifying nouns and verbs have been isolated as a function of the frontal cortex.

Damage to the cortex often results in negative effects on cognitive abilities, lending further evidence to the dependence of IQ on cortex functioning. Diseases that affect the frontal cortex, such as multiple sclerosis, have demonstrable adverse effects on higher-order cognition. Likewise, localized injury to the cortex often has specific, definable cognitive effects. Studies of limited impairment have had great importance in neuroscience, from the identification of the brain region responsible for speech disruption (aphasia) by Paul Broca in 1862, to the advancement of **multiple intelligences** theory by Howard Gardner in 1983. Traumatic brain injury can also have direct general, and negative effects on IQ.

Toxins and nutrients can also affect IQ. As the brain is a material structure, it is not surprising that its molecular constituents can impede or facilitate its development and functioning. Pre-natal exposure to lead, methylmercury, and polychlorinated biphenyls (PCBs) all show adverse effects on brain development. Lead and insecticides, in particular, have been linked to lower IQ scores. Both can cross the placenta and affect fetuses in utero. Research on low-dose exposure is less conclusive, but no "safe" level of exposure has been determined. The greatest societal impact of toxins on brain development is surely caused by prenatal exposure to alcohol. **Fetal alcohol syndrome**, with its manifestations in facial abnormalities, affects thousands of children annually. Children with clinically identified fetal alcohol syndrome have a 35-point disadvantage in IQ. A far greater number of children have significant prenatal exposure to alcohol but do not manifest the syndrome phenotype, the facial abnormalities. Even these children have an average IQ decrement of about 25 points.

Another toxin, actually manufactured by the brain, may result in deficits of cognitive function. Alzheimer's disease involves progressive dementia caused by the degeneration of neurons. People with Alzheimer's gradually lose functions of memory and learning; processes supported largely by the brain's cortex and associated with IQ. A likely cause of Alzheimer's disease is an abnormal accumulation of B-amyloid, a plaque made up of proteins and polysaccharides.

Of course, not all substances are toxins. Breastfeeding may have a positive influence on IQ. Data suggest a 4-point advantage in IQ for children who had been breastfed. Other findings have suggested that the IQ advantage associated with breastfeeding might actually be a result of correlated factors, such as the mother's IQ. While the relationship between higher IQ and breastfeeding is not conclusive, there is a biological explanation for a cognitive advantage resulting from breast milk. The connection between breastfeeding and cognitive ability may lie in docosahexaenoic acid (DHA). DHA is a fatty acid that is needed for neural development. The human body does not make DHA, except as a component in breast milk, and American infant formula does not normally contain it.

Brain Function and IQ

Research on brain function has revealed fascinating connections between the brain and IQ, especially in relationship to brain efficiency. Exercise seems to have a surprisingly important role in brain development and the maintenance of cognitive functioning. Among the elderly, several studies have supported the positive effects of exercise on higher-order cognitive functioning. The mechanism for cognitive enhancement appears to be increased production of neurotrophins. Neurotrophins are important molecules in brain development. They can stimulate the growth of neurons and increase brain vascularization. Elevated levels of neurotrophins can lead, therefore, to more profuse synaptic connections and to more efficient delivery of nutrients to neurons. The presence of neurotrophins increases with both cognitive activity and physical activity.

Another important discovery of brain efficiency relates to glucose consumption. The brain expends energy during mental activity, and that energy is supplied in the form of a simple sugar, glucose. During cognitive activity, all individuals metabolize glucose—but at different rates. Somewhat surprisingly, people with higher performance levels on cognitive tasks appear to consume *less* glucose during mental activity—their brains are more efficient. For example, as students become proficient at writing essays, their brains may actually become metabolically more efficient while they engage in writing essays. These findings do not diminish the importance of glucose, however. Even if neurons become more efficient with experience, the availability of glucose for cognitive processing is now known to be quite important. Research has shown that the availability of glucose to the brain is a particularly potent nutritive predictor of cognitive functioning. The conventional wisdom that regular meals are important to a child's readiness to learn seems to some have scientific support.

Brain-Based Theories of Intelligence

Brain imaging technologies, especially positron emission tomography (PET) and magnetic resonance imaging (MRI), have both extended and challenged theories of intelligence. Studies using brain imaging have revealed that cognition, and therefore IQ, is not a function of a single brain area. Rather, intelligent thought almost always involves several areas of the brain acting in concert—what neuroscientists call circuits. What is the relevance of neural circuitry to intelligence theories? To answer, we can consider Howard Gardner's theory of **multiple intelligences.** According to Gardner, each of the eight intelligences is housed in a different area of the brain. His theory has broadened research on intelligence and practices of education. However, his assertion that the intelligences operate semi-autonomously is questionable. Correlations among three of the intelligences—logical-mathematical, linguistic, and spatial—have been confirmed repeatedly over decades of research. Brain imaging seems consistent with this interconnectivity: when complex tasks are performed, the usual pattern is that several brain areas become active. The accumulated evidence that general intelligence is a meaningful construct might relate to the brain's ability to coordinate activities in different regions of the cortex. Consistent with this proposal, general intelligence, *g*, is most closely related to one of Gardner's proposed intelligences: logical-mathematical intelligence, which is not localizable but is distributed widely over the brain's cortex.

J. P. Das has also posited a multidimensional theory of intelligence known as the PASS theory. The P stands for planning, the A for attention, the S for simultaneous processing, and the S for successive processing. Using neuroimaging data and a framework of brain function developed by Luria, Das located these four dimensions of intelligence in specific areas of the brain. The Das-Naglieri Cognitive Assessment System (CAS) was developed to assess the cognitive competence of individuals. There are twelve measures in the CAS, three for each of the four dimensions of mental functioning. Measures of the planning dimension have proved particularly useful in developing interventions for students with mathematical difficulties.

Das's work is a tentative step in the direction of linking educational interventions with brain-based theories of cognitive ability. However, as John Bruer cautions in his article "A Bridge Too Far," what we know about the brain at this time can inform, but cannot yet prescribe, educational practice. Direct and definite applications of neuroscience to education are usually not possible, or prudent, with our current state of knowledge about the brain development and learning—it is a bridge too far. Certainly, findings in cognitive science can and should inform educational practice, but indirectly. Bruer suggests that cognitive science be thought of as the middle island between neuroscience and education. In other words, neuroscience can inform cognitive science, and then cognitive science can inform educational practice. Bruer's metaphor can help educators and others maintain a healthy skepticism of claims that discoveries in brain science have immediate applications to educational practice.

For the last half-century, education practice has benefited significantly from theories of cognition that focus on the functional abstraction called the mind. Cognitive scientists have long known that the mind must depend on the physical structure of the brain. However, the mind–brain cross-mapping has proved to be a very difficult scientific problem, just as it was for Descartes a perplexing philosophical problem. The last two decades have clarified the functional relationships between mind and brain and have hinted that more exciting scientific discoveries lie ahead. As research extends its reach, scientists and educators can expect a greater theoretical correspondence between the brain and intelligent thought, as well as more direct and powerful applications to teaching and learning.

See also: **Aging Brain; Gender Differences; Nutrition; Physical Movement.**

Further Readings

Bruer, J.T. (1997). Education and the brain: A bridge too far. *Educational Researcher* 26:4–16.

Huttenlocher, P.R. (2002). *Neural Plasticity*. Cambridge, MA: Harvard University Press.

Martinez, M.E. (2000). *Education as the Cultivation of Intelligence*. Mahwah, NJ: Lawrence Erlbaum Associates.

National Research Council. (2000). *How People Learn: Brain, Mind, Experience, and School*. Washington, D.C.: National Academy Press.

**MICHAEL E. MARTINEZ, PH.D. AND
DIANNA TOWNSEND**

L

Language Acquisition and Disorders

Language is a conventional or socially shared system for representing thoughts through a set of rule-based symbols (words). It is also considered to be part of the bigger picture of communication. While language acquisition lasts through early adulthood, the majority of language is acquired during the preschool years, which is a time of tremendous brain growth and organization. Neural organization and efficiency are necessary for language acquisition and the general processes through which this organization is acquired are somewhat predictable. Failure to develop organized, efficient, synchronous neural pathways, can lead to language disorders. Neural plasticity is dependent on experience; therefore the processing and production issues demonstrated by children with language disorders can be resolved through systematic intervention.

Language acquisition is highly correlated to brain maturation and specialization. Functional brain imaging techniques have shown that language functions are distributed throughout the cortical areas of the brain in both hemispheres during infancy (bihemispheric language representation). From infancy through adulthood, language tasks that are more complex require more cerebral area and more energy. Typically as the child learns language, smaller areas of the cortex are needed to process language tasks, which lead to an increase in speed of processing and greater linguistic efficiency. These smaller areas lateralize to the left hemisphere and are known as Broca's and Wernicke's areas. This synaptogenesis or pruning process typically occurs from early childhood through mid-adolescence and is experience driven.

In addition to the pruning process, the brain also goes through a progressive myelination process. Myelin is a fatty sheath that insulates nerve fibers and allows for rapid, efficient conduction of impulses. Myelination occurs in a caudal to rostal direction, and occurs in nerves serving the primary sensory and motor areas of the brain before the association areas used for language. The myelination process is important for the simultaneous processing of sensory, motor, and linguistic information, as well as the ability to make the rapid, refined movements needed for verbal language production.

Language is considered to be a rule-based, generative system. During language acquisition, the child must learn the rules governing the language to generate or produce language. Lois Bloom, (1078) has organized these language rules into three major components: content, form, and use. Content refers to development of words (vocabulary) and word meanings. Form includes rules regarding syntax (word order), morphology (appropriate words and word beginning and endings), and phonology (appropriate speech sounds). Use (pragmatics) concerns the social and discourse rules of language. Acquisition of these rules, like other development, is predictable, orderly, dependent on experience, and highly individualized.

Infants and toddlers spend their energies learning speech sounds, the social intentions of language, and semantic rules. Newborns can discriminate universal speech sounds but experience with a specific language triggers the neural pruning process and over time their speech perception becomes refined to the speech sounds of their native language. At the same time, infants are playing with speech sound production. It is also during this time that children figure out they can get their wants and needs met using vocalizations, gestures, and words. As children reach the age of twelve to twenty-four months, they use the same one and two-word utterances to convey many different semantic meanings (e.g. "shoe" can be used to name an object, but it is also used to direct a person to "get the shoe").

During the preschool years, children learn language form or the rules regarding word order. By the age of five, they have mastered about 90 percent of the rules regarding language form, and sound adult-like. It is during the preschool years that child's work is play. **Play** is the perfect medium for language acquisition. Play is fun and it provides a no pressure avenue for learning. During play, like conversations, the children are focused on the same topic and share attention. Games offer children the opportunity to practice turn-taking and reciprocity; both are integral to the social rules of language.

During the school years, children focus on the pragmatic and semantic language rules that reflect subtle meanings or language use. Children learn to understand and use irony, sarcasm, metaphors, idioms, and the like. It is during these years that children refine their metalinguistic skills and can make judgments about language as well as use it to learn to read and write.

There is a correlation between activity within specific neurological areas of the brain and the cognitive functions that reside within those areas. For instance, children need perceptual and memory skills to process speech-sound sequences. The exact relationship between language acquisition and cognitive skills is not known; however, during early childhood, children talk about what they know. When children exhibit cognitive delays, they usually follow the typical sequence for language acquisition, but at a slowed rate. Cognitive delays result in problems with neural organization that can affect information processing abilities.

A language disorder can be described as impaired comprehension and production of spoken and written language content, form, and use. The language deficit is developmental and may be the result of the child's inability to process the brief components of information that are presented in rapid sequences (speech) along with deficiencies in organizing rapid and sequential motor output (speech). This delay can have a negative impact on the child's ability to discriminate speech sounds which then affects reading abilities.

Alan Baddeley, (1996) proposes a working memory theory that suggests language abilities are linked not only to processing functions in the brain, but also to memory. He refers to working memory as a system with limited capacity that is used for the storage and mental manipulation of information. The system consists of a central executive that controls and organizes communication and attention, a visuospatial sketchpad that deals with visual images, and a phonological loop that is responsible for storage and rehearsal of verbal speech. Verbal working memory is important for vocabulary acquisition, syntactic processing, and language and reading comprehension.

Research on language disorders in children suggests they have limited working memory capacities and demonstrate grave difficulties shifting attention which results in an inability to simultaneously process language and suppress irrelevant information. It is generally agreed upon that children with language disorders demonstrate delays in the speed of processing or producing information and this disrupts the child's ability to learn language. In effect, they have neural networks that are inefficient, and dysfunction in one part of the network (memory, attention, perception) can have a ripple effect on the entire network.

Children with language disorders not only have neuroprocessing differences, they also have neurostructural differences. These differences can affect their ability to discriminate, remember, and attend to linguistic stimuli. Brain imaging studies have shown that some children with language disorders demonstrate language processing in the right hemisphere (as a compensatory strategy), and delayed myelination.

Having a language disorder is part of the diagnostic criteria for autism. One neuroanatomical finding in children who have autism is that they exhibit a larger than typical brain. Brain imaging studies conducted by Martha Herbert and colleagues (2004) have reported that this brain volume increase appears to be related to abnormally large amounts of white matter as a result of early onset of myelination. It has been suggested that this abnormal myelin volume causes the brain to become rigid and lose plasticity. Recent brain imaging studies comparing autism to children with developmental language disorders showed similarities in myelin distribution suggesting that both disorders are on the same spectrum.

As the human brain in young children demonstrates great plasticity and as plasticity is experience driven, systematic intervention should ameliorate processing and production issues associated with language disorders. Instructional strategies should be functional and follow the developmental sequence.

Children acquire language primarily through imitation, play, real conversations with adults, and through interactive reading activities. During adult–child conversations, adults naturally make speech modifications that support language acquisition in children. These modifications, called parentese, include simplified utterances, exaggerated pitch, repetitions, linguistic simplicity, concrete vocabulary, contextual supports, and use of questions and directives. These strategies can also be used with children who have language disorders. Matching one's language level to the child's, or using language that is slightly more complex than the child's will promote acquisition of language content, form, and use. (This simplification of language is not baby-talk.) These parentese strategies help provide the child with a model that is easier to achieve than the adult-like model. Vary the length and complexity of your language model as the child's language acquisition increases.

Daily reading is an essential technique for supporting language acquisition. When reading to toddlers keep your language simple and use your finger to point to and then name pictures in the book. Once the child starts to imitate pointing you can name the pictures that the child is pointing to. As preschoolers, children benefit from books that have repetitive themes or phrases. Books that have themes such as rhyming words, promote phonological awareness, a skill necessary for reading.

Play is an important avenue for language acquisition. Children learn by doing. During play children can practice language forms and intentions that they have witnessed others (adults, siblings, etc.) using. During pretend play children learn and practice verbal problem-solving skills. When playing with children listen carefully to their conversations and narratives. Expand on what they say by either correcting their language form ("went" instead of "goed") or by adding additional new information to their discourse.

Children with language disorders commonly process or comprehend language at a slower rate than typical peers. These children may need "think time" to process the received message and then produce a response. Priming and pre-teaching techniques work well with these children. Pre-teach vocabulary that will be used in classroom discussions. Organize teaching of concepts into similar groups or categories.

Priming techniques are especially useful for teaching syntactic structures. Have the child imitate a sentence containing the specific syntactic structure being taught, and then present them with a picture that is semantically unrelated to the priming sentence, and ask them to describe the picture. Typically, the child is able to describe the picture using the correct syntactic structure. For instance, when teaching the child to use the word ending "ing," the child repeats the sentence "The boy is jumping, then show the child a picture of a girl eating ice cream and the child will be able to describe the picture as "the girl is eating." Priming techniques have been shown to speed up syntactic production.

Children who are disorganized or have severe language delays benefit from modifications made in the environment that provide structure and visual cues. Visual schedules and structured routines can help the child organize their thinking and to remember or recognize routines and behaviors. Many children with severe language disorders do not develop functional verbal skills. Language acquisition for these children may be at a pre-symbolic level. For these children, strategies to help promote language acquisition might include picture-based schedules, labels, and stories. Structure, visual cues, and gestures can also reinforce attending behaviors. Additionally, these children may need concrete reinforcement, choice-making activities, and verbal or nonverbal cues to help with regulating behavior ("I need a break" picture card, etc.). These children also need many opportunities to practice language skills in contextual settings. See also: **Autism Spectrum Disorders; Play.**

Further Readings

Baddeley, A.D. (1996). Exploring ther central executive. *Quarterly Journal of Experimental Psychology: A Human Experimental Psychology* 18, 5–28.

Bloom, L. and Lahey, M. (1978). Language Development and Language Disorders. New York: Wiley.

Herbert, M.R., Ziegler, D.A., Makris, N., Filipek, P.A., Kemper, T.L., Normandin, J.J., Sanders, H.A., Kennedy, D.N., Caviness, V.S. (2004). Localization of white matter volume increase in autism and developmental language disorder. *Annals of Neurology* 55(4):530–540.

Owens, R.E., Jr. (2005). *Language Development: An Introduction* (6th ed.). New York: Pearson Education, Inc.

Toppelberg, C.O., Shapiro, T. (February 2000). *Language Disorders: A 10-year Research Update Review*. Retrieved January 20, 2005 from http://0-gateway.ut.ovid.com.novacat.nova.edu/gw2/ovidweb.cgi

KAREN MAHAN, M.A.

Learning Cycle

The term "learning cycle" has become associated primarily with David Kolb's theory of experiential learning. It can be viewed as a description of the process used by people who are effective in learning from experience. The steps proceed in a cyclic fashion, with each element depending on the other. Concepts inherent in the cycle are described in early work (pre-1950) by Jean Piaget, John Dewey, and Kurt Lewin, but were assembled into the current model in the 1980s. The steps as defined by Kolb are as follows: (1) concrete experience, (2) reflective observation, (3) abstract hypothesis construction, and (4) active testing of hypotheses. The activity in step (4) generates new concrete experience, so the cycle continues. Kolb does not argue that the cycle must start with any particular stage, but rather that individual learners may prefer one or more of the steps, and thus develop a "learning style."

This cycle has now been shown to reflect four major aspects of neocortex function, particularly in the human brain. The following paragraphs show this parallel for each of the four stages.

Concrete Experience

Nervous systems are built on sensory elements that respond to concrete events in the environment; for example, physical encounters, movement, sound, light, color, smells, and tastes. The first impact of concrete experiences on the brain, then, come through the sensory system. For example, in the experience of meeting and conversing with a friend, sensing light reflections from the face of the friend provides sensory information about such things as smiles, concern, or a wink of the eye. Sound is the vehicle for language and the content of the conversation. Our friend may slap us on the back, triggering our pressure sensory system, and so forth. Thus, the specific sensory regions of the cortex are activated; for example, the occipital lobe for vision, the parietal lobe for touch, and the temporal lobe for sound.

Reflective Observation

Following sensory events, the brain integrates sensory data (which alone is meaningless) into clusters of associations that begin to give meaning to the experience. We may recognize the meaning instantly, or it may take time. For example, in the conversation with a friend, the language is composed of scripts and context that become associated with memories, and together reveal aspects such as a connection with an earlier experience, another friend, and so on. These association functions are mediated by a "post-sensory" region of the cortex, where such things as object recognition, categories, and spatial relationships are assembled. The post-sensory integrative cortex is located in the back regions of the cortex, adjacent to the sensory regions. Thus, flow from sensory to back association regions is the natural progression, dictated by brain structure. In learning, these associations can be extremely complex, and may take days or even years to be recognized. They are facilitated by reflection when the brain is freed of competing sensory and motor activities, such as occurs in "mindless" activities or day-dreaming. Recent research also confirms that the reflective, meaning-making, part of the learning cycle is facilitated by deep **sleep**. The association regions of the brain can be highly active during sleep, while motor and sensory cortex are quiescent.

Abstract Hypotheses

As various meanings and interpretations of experience are being assembled, the next aspect of the learning cycle is also initiated. The creation of specific theories and potential responses to the experience begins. This function deeply engages the frontal and prefrontal cortex. These regions are involved in decision making, problem-solving, creating plans for action, and other aspects of idea-generation. Their function is to plan the actions we will take in response to our experiences, and biologically, this function is essential for human survival. In our example of a conversation with a friend, as we begin to interpret the meaning and significance of the experience, we will recall particularly relevant aspects, make the decisions that are important, and begin to get ideas about how we might respond. For example, if the conversation was about a successful experience in resolving a conflict, we will place the specific aspects such as the nature of the conflict, the solution discovered by the friend, and our own situation, into working memory and begin to manipulate them into an idea for how we might solve a problem of our own. We develop our abstract theories of how we might respond to the specific meaning of our concrete experience. This idea-generation and decision-making function relies on sensory input and our personal interpretations of its meaning, and thus, data from the back regions of the cortex become the working material for these front regions.

Active Testing

The last stage of the learning cycle involves the active initiation of our abstract ideas. It engages the motor brain, which is responsible for direct control over the muscles of the body in ways that are designed to achieve a specific purpose. Action is the expression of thought and decision, when the learning cycle is fully engaged. In the case of our friend and conversation, we may decide to adapt her solution to her problem for our own purposes. We actively try it out. Such action is essential to the learning, as all the prior brain processes are receptive and abstract. Action, on the other hand, is aggressive, committed, and concrete. It turns our experience into useful new data, because it generates new *concrete* experience (emphasis on "concrete"). If our actions confirm our ideas, we may build on them and try them in different circumstances. If they do not confirm our ideas, we turn our attention to new interpretations and abstractions.

Learning Over Time

The brain parallels suggest that any learning that lasts and is of use to the learner must take place through these broad stages of the learning cycle. Even when we learn quickly, such as learning a new word, the four steps seem to occur. First, we encounter the word with our senses; second, we connect it with our existing knowledge; third, we speculate on its meaning; fourth, we test our speculation by asking an expert, or looking it up in the dictionary. Finally, the concrete experience of testing the meaning leads us in new directions that aid in further learning. The cycle does not stop, and it does not spin in place, rather it progresses endlessly toward deeper understanding. This progression may be smooth and quick, as with this example, but it may also be halting and extended. Sometimes it may consume a lifetime. We experience something in childhood that we reflect about for years, and possibly in later life we finally develop our theory about its meaning, and change our behaviors because of it. We then recognize the new concrete experiences that such change has generated, and begin the cycle over again.

Learning Styles

The learning cycle reveals specific essential elements of cognition, which fit with brain structure and signaling routes in the cortex. However, not all learners necessarily engage all aspects of the cycle. For example, some learners may not use or value the concrete elements, and may turn more to their abstract ideas for guidance in their actions. This leads to the division of the world into experimentalists and theorists. Some learners may not utilize the reflection elements of the cycle, and simply leap ahead to ideas and actions, while others are slow to act and analyze things carefully. Thus, we have the thinkers and the actors. These different responses to the learning cycle are primarily based on **emotion**. The approach to learning depends on how the different phases make the learner feel. If they are inclined to avoid interactions and experiences, preferring mental "activity," the reason for this inclination lies in their personal feelings, both fears and loves. Thus, the learning cycle provides an explanation of specific preferred styles of learning, engaging different "intelligences" with different individuals.

The emotional impact of the learning cycle, with each stage associated with specific feelings, is completely consistent with the known interactions of the emotions and cognition in the brain. All regions of the cortex are connected to the emotion systems of the brain, both by direct wiring, and by chemicals of emotion that flood all regions of the cortex.

Thus, although the learning cycle generates long-term memory and understanding, in part because it utilizes all the major regions of the cerebral cortex, its power is also related to engagement of multiple emotion systems in the brain. Each phase produces specific feelings and emotion. The concrete sensory phase produces feelings of recognition, confidence, and certainty, as it is related to things that are obvious and appear certain to the learner. The reflection phase produces feelings of discovery, concern, and hope, as the learner begins to develop insight into new connections, points of difficulty, and a sense of growing understanding. The creative phase leads to strong feelings of ownership, excitement, and motivation, as the learner manipulates and takes control of her knowledge. And the action phase requires commitment and energy, leading to feelings of completion, and pleasure with actual accomplishment, or frustration in actions that fail. This wide range of emotions produced by the learning cycle brings in modulators of synaptic strength such as epinephrine, serotonin, and dopamine, and the resulting change in synapses is the generator of cortical plasticity produced by experience. Biologically, this is learning.

Teaching

Despite the intrinsic preference for a style of learning, the learning cycle suggests that such preferences, while useful for initially engaging learners, should not be the only approach utilized when deeper learning is desired. Indeed, completion of the entire cycle is essential for such deep learning.

Probably the greatest challenge in modern education, then, is to find ways that lead to completion of the learning cycle by students. Rather than didactic and "delivery" methods, the learning cycle and its parallels with the human brain strongly suggest that interaction and problem-solving methods should be utilized and created by teachers. Development of concrete experiences that engage the learner and generate thought and idea construction is of greater importance for learning than are teacher explanations or stressing "paying attention."

While this may sound daunting and risky, the parallels of the learning cycle with the natural structure and function of the brain are encouraging. They suggest that the closer we come to such "natural learning" conditions, the more likely it is that learning will occur. Learning is what the human brain evolved to do.

See also: **Multiple Intelligences.**

Further Readings

Kolb, D.A. (1983). *Experiential Learning: Experience as the Source of Learning and Development.* New York, NY: Prentice Hall.

LeDoux, J. (2002). *Synaptic Self: How Our Brains Become Who We Are.* New York, NY: Viking Penguin.

Zull, J.E. (2002). *The Art of Changing the Brain: Enriching Teaching by Exploring the Biology of Learning.* Arlington, VA: Stylus.

JAMES E. ZULL, PH.D.

Learning Disabilities

Learning disabilities is a dysfunction of the central nervous system that affects a heterogeneous group of students in their ability to acquire proficiency in the areas of **reading, writing, math**, listening, speaking, a. d organizing. It is a lifelong disability.

The US Education Department reported in *The Condition of Education Report 2002*, that 2,513,977 students with specific learning disabilities (SLD) were taught in our regular education classes (Numbers generated by 1994–1995 school reports). We can statistically expect that at least 3.5 percent of students in each class have some level of specific learning disability. Depending on how SLD is defined, up to 30 percent of students may have some form of this neurological disorder. What does brain research tell us about the three areas of the brain that are affected? What strategies are most effective and what assistive technologies or smart tools can support them in our classrooms?

Brain scans revealed that the wiring system in the central nervous system of students with SLD is very different than it is in a non-SLD brain. These scans also demonstrated that for the same visual/auditory stimulus different areas of the brain light up at different times and in different areas for students with SLD. These scans document the heterogeneous nature of the students within this disability category.

The brain is a parallel processor. Information comes in through our sensory receptors shooting through the neural network at an amazing speed. Our brains develop strong synaptic paths to regions that help us interpret what we hear, feel, see, taste. We store relevant information into recallable categories and we prune out superfluous information. Much of this processing becomes automatic. As the central nervous system creates this strong automatic retrieval of information, our brains are freed-up to focus on new information and connect it to our prior knowledge. For the student with SLD this parallel processing does not function as designed. For this individual, what the ear hears and the brain interprets may not be the same thing.

This is where the faulty wiring comes into play. All information comes in through the ear to the thalamus, which then sends it on to the proper systems for processing. All of this happens simultaneously. For students with language processing issues, the messages may come in too quickly for their slower less effective central nervous system to handle. For examples, the teacher says, "Everyone, take out your math book, turn to page 25, use you calculators to finish problem 17, and raise your hand when you are finished." The student with central auditory processing disorders has heard "math book." The message goes from the thalamus to the auditory cortex to Wernickes and Brocas areas for language processing, to the cortex to check for math-related memories and the frontal lobes for information about math and stored information. By the time it takes the majority of the class to raise their hands, the student with SLD has the desk open, their hand on their math book and they are unable to remember the rest of the directions. It took that long to process the first five words of the directions. It is not that they have no memory; it is that they cannot get the information into their memory.

The student with SLD has difficulty with most language-based activities. Because of the heterogeneous nature of the population within this category, that difficulty may manifest itself in different subject areas. For some students it is remembering the steps in oral directions, for others it is deciphering the meaning in math story problems, focusing on the key elements in a trade book full of different colored fonts, charts, and captions or it may be working with print in unfamiliar reading activities that is problematic.

Dyslexia is a prevalent reading disability. It has been stated that 5–17 percent of the school age population may have Dyslexia. Harvard's Dr. Sally Shaywitz found that readers who had dyslexia showed less activation in posterior brain regions contrasted with relative over activation in anterior regions of the brain. A reader must first convert the visual features (the letters) of the word into the linguistic sounds (the phonemes) they symbolize and then locate its word meaning. Therefore, for this group of students, phonemic awareness instruction is critical. They require a longer processing time to join the sounds together, recognize the word, and retrieve its meaning. These students have average to above average cognitive abilities; they just cannot bridge their difficulty in processing written language to their higher order thinking skills.

Brain research has also assisted in developing computer-based software that increases the ability of the brain's auditory processing centers to recognize and speed up the process and sound out phonemes. Increases have been shown in left temporal-parietal cortex and left inferior frontal gyrus bringing brain activation in these regions closer to that seen in children with normal reading abilities. This approach may help children reset the timing structures and boost their ability to segment words into phonological pieces more efficiently.

Students with SLD expend an incredible amount of energy trying to take in information. Because of the language processing issues described above, they have difficulty placing information into working memory and long-term memory for later retrieval. They also have difficulty processing multiple sensory inputs, filtering out background noise from the spoken directions and filtering out important information from unimportant information.

As we gather information, our neural networks create strong synaptic connections for working with important information. At the same time, we purge ourselves of synaptic connections that carry less important information. This allows us to forget unimportant information and use our energies to focus **attention** on more useable information. Students with SLD are not able to do this purging of synaptic connections. They have difficulty focusing on the important and ignoring the unimportant. For example, they have a difficult time identifying an important fact when they are asked to choose one from a reading sample. They can spend an incredible amount of time trying to start a writing assignment. They have difficulty organizing their thoughts. Without instructional supports the students have difficulty getting any information to the automatic level of processing that allows them do two things at once. They are unable to take notes while they are listening to the information. This processing discrepancy affects how information is passed and processed in one or more of three different brain systems. Each system contains the neurological processing necessary for effectively storing and using information. These brain systems are referred to as: The Recognition System, Strategic System, and Affective System.

The Recognition System takes in all incoming information and pulls it apart into single elements (color, size, texture, and previous feelings about it). As it does this, it tries to put these items into categories that will be retrievable in a more efficient manner. This is an area in which students with SLD struggle. They have trouble due to their limited ability to process only the critical elements and ignore unimportant stimulus. They also have difficulty processing the language necessary to fully understand and utilize categories to speed recognition and utilize the parallel processing capabilities of the brain.

The Strategic System is the system that contains the categories and is capable of applying stored information. If information does not get into the recognition system, it cannot be used by the Strategic System. There are teaching strategies and assistive technology tools that support students with SLD in bridging this transfer of information.

The Affective System is an important and often neglected system in our schools. It is located in the amygdala. It not only connects the language centers, but it stores our feelings and memories. For memory to be stored it needs to move from the Recognition System to the Strategic System and then to the Affective System. Here is where we rearrange information into other meaningful uses. It is here that some students with SLD may remember what they learn not for the content, but for how badly they felt trying to learn the content. Teachers need to remember unpleasant learning experiences release stress hormones into the system, whose sole purpose is to purge the memory of content and get the students out of the difficult or stressful situation.

Students with SLD benefit from a multi-strategy approach to instruction. Thankfully, this brain-based approach is beneficial to the learning of all students. These strategies are: (1) Setting goals and providing feedback, which creates a mental framework for information, creating a neuro-network upon which the information may travel. (2) Providing nonlinguistic representations of instructional content, so they have a visual to reference for the **auditory** content. (3) Providing cues, questions, and advanced organizers. Again, this provides the framework they do not have and allows them a system to pattern and assist in the sorting and retrieving of relevant information. (4) Identifying similarities and differences. This demonstrates to them how we do the sorting by characteristics and provides a concrete model for categorization. (5) Summarizing and note taking. Teachers need to provide ongoing examples of how to do this as it is not apparent to these students what is important and what can be ignored. (6) Reinforcing effort and providing feedback. This is important for creating a sense of well being and limiting the stress hormones that are released during difficult tasks. (7) Home work and practice. These can be effective strategies if used appropriately. Students need practice with tools to place the tools in the automatic level freeing their brains for "hard thinking" tasks. This should not be done with new material. (8) Cooperative learning. This is an especially important strategy providing the opportunity for students to practice using their strengths in groups.

Constructing instruction that utilizes all of these approaches will go far to meet the processing needs of students with SLD. Most students will also need assistive technologies. These are tools that support them in reading, math, writing, organizing, and spelling. When these tools are used effectively, they can make all the difference to the student's development of independence and self-esteem.

Table1. Assistive Technology (AT) as a complementary or compensatory tools for brain compatible instructional strategies

Effective Teaching Strategies	Brain Systems Targeted	Teaching Strategies Described	Assistive technologies that may support students with Learning Disabilities
Setting Goals And providing Feedback	Recognition System Strategic System Affective System	Teachers can encourage the active learning by placing students in small groups. Have them discuss and write on a chart what they know and what they need to know and how they will demonstrate that. Provide immediate feedback on their process. Students require praise for work. Intrinsic learning does not fully develop in the frontal lobe until the mid twenties.	• Inspiration© • Kidspiration© • Rubric maker© • Electronic Portfolios • Video • Draft Builder©
Identify Similarities and differences	Recognition System	Breaking large concepts into smaller chunks of information based on relationships. May be teacher or student led. Research indicates a stronger learning impact when students identify and discuss similarities and differences in small groups.	• Kidspiration© • Inspiration© • Word templates with drop-down menus • Draft Builder© • Edmark Thinking Things • Intellimathics© • Graph Master©
Nonlinguistic Representation	Recognition System	Research indicates that information is stored in many areas of the brain. Adding a visual component allows the brain more opportunities to store and retrieve information.	• Picture supports-charts, models, posters/BoardMaker • Writing with Symbols 2000© • Picture It© Pix Write© • Inspiration©

(Continued)

Table1. (*Continued*)

Effective Teaching Strategies	Brain Systems Targeted	Teaching Strategies Described	Assistive Technologies that may support students with Learning Disabilities
		Picture support allows students with language/print disabilities another way to learn and remember information.	• Kidspiration© • Kids Works© Kids Pix© • Intellistudio© Buildability© • PowerPoint© • Hyper Studio© Kids Media Magic© • Scholastic Keys© • Clicker 4© • Some Edmark Laureate, and Soft Touch Software • Intellitools Classroom Suite©
Cooperative Learning	Strategic and Affective System	Allow students of various ability levels to work together, each working from their own strengths. Each student has a role. Teachers can facilitate the effectiveness of this model by providing cue sheets for each member of the team.	• Kidspiration© • Inspiration© • Kids Works© Kids Pix© • Intelli Classroom© Buildability© • PowerPoint© Hyper Studio© Kids Media Magic© • Lego© software, Blocks in Motion© • The Cruncher© • SOLO© by don Johnston • Scholastic Keys©
Generating And testing hypothesis	Strategic System	Begin a lesson by questioning what may happen if something is changed in the chosen topic. Have them predict. Give them some information to check their prediction. Revisit their prediction. Then predict, again, what resources or information will they need to better answer their original question.	• Inspiration© • Kidspiration© • Rubric maker© • Hyper Studio© • Hollywood High© • Intellikeys with overlays for writing

Strategy	System	Description	Tools
Cues, Questions and Advanced Organizers	Strategic and Recognition system	May use this after the initial question is asked. Then the teacher may foreshadow the lesson topic utilizing a story, bulletin board, picture, movie, or song. Then have them use this experience as a basis for the content they will be studying.	• Word walls, may be in electronic format • Specialized vocabulary lists • Color-coded systems • Franklin hand-helds • PDAs • Portable word processors • Judy Sweeney's Lottie kit • Electronic study sheets • WYNN© or Read and Write Gold© • SOLO© by Don Johnston • Intellikeys • On-screen keyboards with words/phrases
Summarizing and Note Taking	Strategic System	Note taking can be used effectively if the student has the following skills: 1. An awareness of basic writing formats (ex. intro, supporting information, summary) 2. The ability to substitute, delete and recognize key elements of a written selection 3. The ability to ask questions and predict what information will come next in the written text.	• Writing models • Kidspiration© • Inspiration© • Note-taking templates • Draft Builder© • Colored dots to mark designated points • Recorded notes with study guides • Provision of consistent study guide templates • Electronic or paper copy of teachers lecture notes • WYNN© teacher utilizes note pad or voice note feature to ask essential questions, Kurzweil© • Read and Write Gold© • Fill in the blank note taker skeleton • Bingo Generator • Amazing Writing Machine© • Scholastic Keys©

(Continued)

Table 1. (*Continued*)

Effective Teaching Strategies	Brain Systems Targeted	Teaching Strategies Described	Assistive Technologies that may support students with Learning Disabilities
Homework and Practice	Strategic System	Homework should be an opportunity to extend, or apply classroom knowledge. It should be appropriate to the grade level of the student. The purpose of the homework should be clear to the parent and the student. Parent involvement should be minimal. Homework is to practice already acquired skills, not to learn new information.	• Word walls, may be electronic • Specialized vocabulary lists • Color-coded systems • Franklin hand-helds • PDAs • Portable word processors • Judy Sweeney's Lottie Kit • Electronic study sheets

Jill Gierach, CESA 2. jgierach@cesa2.k12.wi.us.

It has been the law for over a decade that any student with an IEP, 504 plan or ADA accommodation plan must "be considered" for the use of assistive technology. Assistive technology (A.T.) is anything that may increase, maintain or improve functional capabilities of a student with a disability. That means the school must provide both the item the student might need and then the service or training to use that tool in the school setting. Students with SLD have difficulty with automaticity. Therefore, for the brain to be able to focus on the content, the student must be able to operate the A.T. without much conscious thought.

Assistive technology may be the answer to providing students with SLD a tool that provides a scaffold from their inefficient central nervous system to their higher level cognitive skills. In most cases, assistive technology also engages a motor component that helps focus attention on whatever task the student is engaged.

Assistive technology use is typically assessed by looking at an area of need and then looking at a tool that assists the student in being more independent in that area. In writing, we may use pencil grips, raised line paper, writing templates, talking word processing or word prediction software. In reading, we may look to adding picture supports to words, changing font size or color, utilizing a scanner, and text reading software to read text electronically. For spelling, we may provide word family cards or talking spell checkers. For math there are electronic hand-held math supports, math charts and software that helps teach problem alignment.

There are many available tools. These tools provide support to the student with SLD and bridge the gap between knowing and showing. The following chart lists the brain systems, teaching strategies, and some possible assistive technologies that support students with specific learning disabilities in the educational system.

See also: **ADD and ADHD; Cognitive Disabilities; Language Acquisition and Disorders; Mastery.**

Further Readings

Harvey, S., Goudvis, A. (2000). *Strategies that Work: Teaching Comprehension to Enhance Understanding.* Markham, Ontario: Stenhouse Publishers.

Temple, E., Deutsch, G.K., Poldrack, R.A., Miller, S.L., Tallal, P., Merzenich, M.M., Gabrieli, J.D. (2003). Neural deficits in children with dyslexia ameliorated by behavioral remediation: Evidence from functional MRI. *Proceedings of the National Academy of Sciences* 100(5):2860–2865.

Wolfe, P., Nevills, P. (2004). *Building the Reading Brain, PreK-3,* Thousand Oaks, CA., Corwin Press.

Brain Connection – a website owned by Scientific Learning makers of Fast Forward®. http://www.brainconnection.com

Support for students with learning disabilities, their families and those that support them. http://www.ldonline.org

Everything you wanted to know about assistive technology. http://www.wati.org

JILL GIERACH MSE ATP

Learning Styles

Even though all human beings use their senses of sight, hearing, smell touch, and taste to assimilate environmental stimuli, each sense does not contribute the same amount of information to each individual brain. People appear to have different ways of knowing—different learning preferences, styles, or modalities. History records a variety of learning style theories, some with accompanying profiles that individuals can complete to determine preferences. As far back as 450 BC, Hippocractes, a Greek physician, claimed that every person had four liquids in the body. Although those liquids were to be kept in balanced supplies, too much of any of the four liquids resulted in one of the following four personalities—phlegmatic, Sanguine, choleric, and melancholic.

In the 1900s, Swiss psychologist, Carl Jung, categorized these personalities as psychological types and attributed the differences in human behavior to a product of perception (how we take in information) and judgment (how to process the information we take in). These two cognitive functions, therefore, manifested themselves in the following four dimensions of personality: sensing, feeling, thinking, and intuition.

A 1984 program, called *True Colors,* takes Jung's dimensions and delineates them in terms of corresponding colors: *Gold* (sensing), *Blue* (feeling), *Green* (thinking), and Orange (intuition). By the time participants in a *True Colors* workshop have prioritized four character cards (one for each color), they have determined their preferred temperament and learning styles. This internationally recognized program created by Don Lowry, author and founder of True Colors not only advocates a balanced temperament but also differentiates those strategies that would be appropriate for each accompanying learning style or color.

Rita and Kenneth Dunn (1987) pioneers in learning styles, describe three styles of learning: auditory, visual, and tactile/kinesthetic and have designed an inventory that categorizes learners as analytic (auditory) or global (tactile/kinesthetic). Analytic (auditory) learners have little difficulty with traditional school tasks such as decoding sounds in words, following directions and class rules, and keeping their notebook organized. Global (tactile/kinesthetic) learners tend to view tasks randomly. They are divergent thinkers who need to see the entire picture before they recognize the parts.

Howard Gardner describes learning styles as **multiple intelligences** and advocates that while human beings tend to have preferences, we are all a combination of the intelligences in varying degrees. Verbal-linguistic and logical mathematical intelligences are most honored in traditional schools, however, there are at least six others that we all possess to varying degrees. Individuals who possess the additional six intelligences of visual/spatial, bodily/kinesthetic, musical/rhythmic, naturalist, interpersonal, and intrapersonal usually find their occupational niche in the real world but may experience difficulty in an educational system where a graduation exam or the SAT only assess verbal and mathematical abilities.

Robert Sternberg combines learning styles into three categories that he also refers to as intelligences. He delineates three types of knowing: practical, analytical, and creative.

While these theories all result in a preponderance of learning styles, no one style theory appears appropriate or consistent with what current brain research is telling us. Our brains are so multifaceted and complex that they simultaneously process a multitude of information. Neuro-scientific evidence, then, does not support an individual's ability to process information from a single sensory source but from multiple sources instead.

Providing a variety of learning experiences and giving learners a choice in selecting which experiences are most appropriate appears preferable. Although a teachers' own style of learning may preclude their ability to see the need for multi-modality instruction, teachers must design lessons that address all learning styles. Twenty instructional strategies will be discussed that address the four major learning modalities (visual, auditory, kinesthetic, and tactile), all eight multiple intelligences, and all three of Sternberg's practical intelligences. Their use is also consistent with the brain research regarding which strategies appear to work best for maximizing memory and minimizing forgetting. These twenty *ways of knowing* appear appropriate for offering all learners a variety of choices for taking in and processing information.

Visual Learning Style

As the eyes contain a majority of the body's sensory receptors, most individuals take in more information visually than through any one of the other senses. Many students are therefore strong in the visual modality. Visual learners assimilate information most effectively if they can read or see it. They tend to be more global or holistic thinkers and need to see the *big* picture before they are shown the parts. Visual learners will want to see the entire forest before naming the individual trees. Graphic organizers, technology, visualization, and the use of visuals all address this common modality.

The use of the graphic organizer, semantic map or word web not only engage all of the functions of the brain but also enable all learners to see the connections between ideas and the thinking involved in those connections. Both left and right hemispheres of the brain can benefit from this strategy. The left hemisphere enjoys the verbage while the right appreciates the depiction of those ideas.

When individuals work on the computer or research on the Internet, the visual modality is in full gear. Not only does the 1991 SCANS Report list technology as one of eight major competencies necessary for success in the actual world but a technology-based curriculum is more visual and global than many others.

Visualization is one of the most powerful strategies for all brains and is often used by coaches who ask their athletes to imagine themselves scoring the touchdown, or sinking the basket before the game even begins. This technique increases the likelihood that points will be scored once the game is underway.

The use of visuals is another strategy that can be used to address the visual learning style of all students. Visual learners prefer instruction accompanied by pictures, illustrations, maps, charts, and diagrams. They often want to connect verbal notes with images and symbols as that linkage strengthens the person's ability to store and later retrieve information.

Auditory Learning Style

People learn 90 percent of what they say or discuss as they complete an activity. Auditory learners prefer to talk about their learning. This act alone helps them process information. They tend to be analytical, logical, and very sequential thinkers and therefore, just right for a traditional classroom. Asking them to decode a word phonetically, follow a set of directions, or analyze the motive of a given storybook character is right in line with their preferred modality. The strategies of brainstorming, discussion, humor, music, reciprocal teaching, and cooperative learning all can be utilized to take advantage of the way this modality learns.

Brains are more alert when they are discussing class content or brainstorming ideas as oxygen is flowing to the brain. One person's idea can activate the neural networks that cause other people to have similar or contrasting ideas.

Music is such an important carrier of signals for activating long-term retention that almost any lyric put to music can be long remembered. Those same students who have difficulty recalling class content have no trouble recalling the lyrics of every song they enjoy from the radio.

The fact that we learn 90 percent of what we teach others supports the need for reciprocal teaching or cooperative learning. Having students re-teach a concept to a close partner or "make a date" with a fellow class member to discuss an assigned topic are two useful activities for this modality.

Kinesthetic Learning Style

Oftentimes, the most difficult learning modality to address in the classroom is the kinesthetic. Students who need to be bodily engaged in the learning may often be found drumming on their desk or perpetually moving in and out of their seat. While bodily kinesthetic intelligence is probably the most neglected in most traditional classrooms, it is one of the most important learning styles to the brain as these learners are at their best when involved in real-life, meaningful activities. When the body as well as the brain is engaged in the learning process, information gets placed in one of the strongest memory systems in the brain—**procedural memory.** This fact is the reason that a person never forgets how to drive a car or ride a bike once they learn these skills. It is also the reason that a person learning a new computer application usually does not retain their ability to perform the application unless they practice, practice, practice.

When students walk, stomp, clap, or jump as they learn or review class content, their procedural memory is strengthened. Having students role-play a scene from history or the definition of a vocabulary word almost ensures that learners will recall the information, not only for tests, but for long term. The ancient Chinese proverb appears timely. *Tell me, I forget; show me, I remember; involve me, I understand.*

Tactile Learning Style

The instructional strategies of drawing, games, manipulatives, experiments, labs, constructed models, writing, and journaling address the tactile modality. The connection between the hand and the brain is so pervasive that there is not a single theory that explains it. However, we do know that the most effective instructional techniques unite the mind and the body. For this reason, students often count on their concrete fingers before they are able to count abstractly. Many students, particularly male, can be found drawing impressive pictures of super heroes or cars; there is much in the curriculum that can be drawn. Others find it difficult to understand a science concept until they become engaged in an experiment or build a model of a concept being studied. The brain also tends to remember what is written. A grocery list can be written and then mistakenly left at home. Still, many of the things on the list will be recalled. Having students write key vocabulary or short chunks of information is important to memory. Those who have a tactile learning style can find success in the real world as an architect, engineer, graphic designer, surgeon, or sculptor.

While human beings have individual preferences for the way they take in and process information, each individual's learning is strengthened when a variety of strategies are used to address multiple learning styles. After all, if people don't learn the way we teach them, then we must teach them in the many ways they learn.

See also: **Auditory Development and Learning; Visual Brain.**

Further Readings

Dunn, R. & K (1987).Teaching elementary students through their individual learning styles:. Practical approaches for grades 3–6. Boston, MA: Allyn and Bacon.

Gardner, H. (1983). *Frames of Mind: The Theory of Multiple Intelligences.* New York: Basic Books.

Silver, H., Strong, R., Perini, M. (2000). *So Each May Learn: Integrating Learning Styles and Multiple Intelligences.* Alexandria, VA: Association for Supervision and Curriculum Development.

Sternberg, R.J., Grigorenko, E.L. (2000). *Teaching for Successful Intelligence: To Increase Student Learning and Achievement.* Arlington Heights, IL: Skylight.

Tate, M.L. (2003). *Worksheets Don't Grow Dendrites: 20 Instructional Strategies that Engage the Brain.* Thousand Oaks, CA: Corwin Press.

Center for Teaching Effectiveness, Learning Styles, http://cte.udel.edu/learnstyle.htm

MARCIA L. TATE, PH.D.

Legal Culpability and Correctional Facilities

On March 1, 2005, the United States became one of the last countries in the world to prohibit capital punishment for crimes committed by juveniles. When the Supreme Court handed down its decision in *Roper v. Simmons,* seventy-nine child offenders were sitting on death row in thirteen states across the United States. In *Roper v. Simmons,* the U.S. Supreme Court held that the execution of individuals for acts committed before their 18th birthday was a violation of the Constitution's prohibition of cruel and unusual punishment. In doing so, the Court referenced research findings submitted by the American Psychological Association and the American Medical Association regarding the development of the adolescent brain as it relates to criminal culpability. These findings echo what other researchers studying the cognitive development of the adolescent brain have recently learned.

The part of the brain perhaps most relevant in criminal culpability is the frontal lobe. The frontal lobe is the largest part of the brain and it is responsible for the brain's most advanced functions. The ability to prioritize thoughts, imagine, and think in the abstract are all controlled by the frontal lobe. More important for the purposes of legal culpability, the frontal lobe is in charge of anticipating consequences, controlling impulses, and modifying our actions and responses.

Functional magnetic resonance imaging (fMRI) scans reveal that the teenage brain relies more on the amygdala than the frontal lobe when reasoning or solving problems. The amygdala is a more primitive part of the brain responsible for gut reactions and aggressive behaviors. When an adolescent reaches age fifteen or sixteen, development of the frontal lobe becomes noticeable. Teens become more accurate in reading facial expressions and respond more appropriately in social situations. They are better able to control impulses, defuse anger, and delay gratification.

The frontal lobe undergoes dramatic changes during adolescence— more than at any other stage of life. Scientists have found that during adolescence the brain goes through an intense process where there is first an overproduction of gray matter, synaptic connections. This is followed by a period of pruning that involves discarding the gray matter at a rapid rate. These changes continue until adolescents reach their early twenties.

One way to measure cognitive development is by studying myelination. The rate of myelination is the main index of maturation. Myelination focuses and refines the operation of neural networks regulating behavior. A comparison of fMRI scans of young adults and teens show a substantial difference in the rate of maturation among brain regions.

For example, scans of parietal and temporal areas, which are responsible for spatial, sensory, auditory, and language functions, look similar in the young adult and teenage brain. This indicates that the teenage brain has reached maturity in these areas. However, there appears to be a significant difference in myelin rates of the frontal lobe, and the prefrontal cortex is viewed as the last to mature. This indicates a lack of maturation of cognitive processing and other executive functions in the teenage brain.

The lack of maturation in these areas is crucial to determining criminal culpability. Without the full development of the frontal lobe, an adolescent's ability to control impulsivity, foresee consequences, and plan for the future is hindered. In fact, recent evidence even implicates the frontal lobe in the processing of moral judgments.

This is evident when you examine the types of crimes juveniles commit. For example, crimes that tend to be the result of impulsive behavior such as theft and simple assault are among the most common crimes for which juveniles are arrested. Drug crimes also make up a large amount of juvenile arrests, reflecting the juvenile's inability to appropriately assess the long-term consequences of their actions. Other crimes that juveniles are likely to commit include arson, vandalism, and disorderly conduct. These crimes contain an element of the sort of rash decision-making and reactive violence that diminishes as the brain reaches maturation.

On the flip side of this, crimes that involve a greater amount of premeditation or malice are less prevalent among juveniles. In 1998, juveniles made up about 10 percent of the total U.S. population. In approximate accordance with this, arrests of juveniles accounted for about 15 percent of all arrests for violent crimes. However, juveniles were significantly overrepresented in arrests for property crimes, accounting for about 30 percent of all those arrests. Finally, many juvenile offenders "age out" of their criminal behavior; that is, they stop participating in criminal activities as they reach full adulthood. These statistics indicate that the higher incidents of crime among juveniles are at least partially explained by the lack of maturation of the adolescent brain.

Instructional Strategies for Juvenile Correction Programs

Once a juvenile has committed a crime they may find themselves out of the traditional classroom and in a correctional facilities' education program. The revolving door nature of the juvenile corrections classroom requires that the teacher in that classroom be patient, innovative, and flexible. The traditional public school classroom is far from the reality of juvenile corrections. Adjudicated teens serve disparate sentences, disparate both in length of time and time of year. They may serve only a matter of weeks, several months, or, in some cases, years depending on the particular student's offense, family history, living arrangements, and physical and emotional requirements. In addition, once the student enters the legal system, the public school calendar is often a moot issue and they may enter a placement at any time of the year.

To deal with this revolving door, the teacher should be cognizant of the fact that, for the most part, juvenile corrections students are not motivated by the traditional school motivators such as good grades, fear of failure, fear of repercussions at home, or failure to graduate from high school. It becomes necessary, then, for the teacher to find each student's motivator and to determine if the student can cope best with long-term or short-term goals. Once determined, the teacher must then become familiar with the student's educational situation, such as the IEP, particular behavioral or emotional problems, and level of ability. It is important to remember that grade-level appropriate may not be age-level appropriate. Consequently, finding subject matter that will keep the student interested is vital to student success. Generally, adjudicated teens have perfected a series of strategies to get them out of an assignment or, better yet, removed from the classroom. Because of this, the teacher and student will be better served when the teacher acts as a facilitator to keep the student engaged through relevant material in which the student perceives some value.

The question of textbooks will inevitably enter into any discussion of curriculum planning. In the juvenile corrections classroom, however, the consistency that is offered through the traditional use of a textbook, proceeding from chapter to chapter, is rendered ineffective because of the revolving door syndrome. Turning units into hands-on projects is a viable option that can be geared toward the many different ability levels and behaviors found in one classroom. Most often, adjudicated teens have not experienced many successes in their lives and traditional classroom assessment is difficult. Hands-on projects, therefore, offer many ways for incarcerated youth to express themselves, learn without the boundaries that a textbook presents, and experience some success as well.

Current events offer myriad opportunities for learning and can be incorporated not only into the core classes of math, English, reading, and writing, but can also be geared toward anger management, making better choices, and drug and alcohol problems, all issues that must be addressed in juvenile corrections. Newspapers offer many teaching opportunities and can be fine-tuned to fit the many grade levels found in this type of classroom. Word searches, math problems, geographical questions, writing opportunities, life-skills lessons, and cause-and-effect articles are only a few examples of the assignments that can be gleaned from a daily/weekly newspaper. Scavenger hunts offer fun and learning for the student and class discussions surrounding local, national, and international news provide occasions to connect to the larger world.

Teaching math in a juvenile corrections facility often provides many challenges, both to the student and the teacher, as well. As most of the students in correctional facilities have a long history of failure in the traditional school setting and because most possess few life and vocational skills, instruction in math can be approached in such a way as to offer realistic lessons in daily living. Banking and budgeting, paying bills, and grocery shopping are only a few examples of assignments that can be most helpful to the student struggling to obtain independence. Locating housing, purchasing a vehicle, loans, and insurance are additional topics in which incarcerated youth need instruction. Math teachers can offer a most functional curriculum aimed at the lack of knowledge in the life skills and problem-solving areas for adjudicated youth.

Educating youth in correctional facilities is challenging, but worthwhile work. A combination of the adolescent brain maturing and supportive adult guidance can help them become productive citizens.

See also: **At-Risk Behavior; Adolescent Cognitive Development; Adolescent Social and Emotional Development.**

Further Readings

National Institute of Mental Health (2001). *Teenage Brain: A Work in Progress.* Retrieved March 10, 2005 from www.nimh.nih.gov/publicat/teenbrain.cfm

Ortiz, A. (January, 2004). *Cruel and Unusual Punishment: The Juvenile Death Penalty: Adolescence, Brain Development and Legal Culpability.* Retrieved January 5, 2005 from www.abanet.org/crimjust/juvjus

Correctional Education Association http://www.ceanational.org

Juvenile Justice Educational Enhancement Program (JJEEP) http://www.jjeep.org

The National Center on Education, Disability and Juvenile Justice http://www.edjj.org

**JENNIFER FEINSTEIN, J.D. AND
CAROLE NAASZ, M.A.**

M

Mastery

Learning is the result of physiological changes in the brain and these changes take time and involvement of the body–brain learning partnership. Previous definitions of learning/mastery learning were not based in brain research; in hindsight, they made little impact on the everyday practice of classroom teachers. Now, however, brain research gives us a powerful definition of learning that provides practical guidance beginning with curriculum development through lesson design, selection of instructional strategies, and assessment.

Although we have only scratched the surface in our exploration of the brain, there is now sufficient information to provide a basis for defining learning and guiding school improvement efforts. Two concepts from brain research are especially important to a new working definition of mastery learning:

(1) Learning is the result of real physiological change in the brain.

Such changes occur as the result of sensory input that causes the brain to create new dendritic connections that become hardwired over time and thus readily available for future use. If physiological change in the brain does not occur, there is no long-term memory storage or mastery learning.

Unfortunately, the possible range of sensory input needed to create physiological change is far more extensive than that elicited by textbooks, worksheets, and lecture. Human beings have at least nineteen senses, not five, most of which cannot be activated inside the traditional classroom. Consequently, students need *being there* experiences, opportunities to experience what they are learning in real-world contexts; for example, walking a key section of a local watershed to track water flow, or going behind the scenes in a grocery store, aquarium, or mall to see a business in action. The greater the sensory input, the greater the physiological change in the brain. The greater the physiological change in the brain, the greater the likelihood that long-term memory/mastery learning will occur.

(2) Learning is a two-step process:

Step 1: Detecting and then understanding patterns—a process through which our brain creates meaning. This is the sensory input stage.

Step 2: Developing meaningful mental programs to use what is understood and to store it in long-term memory. This is the output stage—the capacity to use what is understood, first with assistance and then, when learning is complete, almost automatically. The importance of such near-automaticity is that old information and skills can then be used to help create new mental programs in response to new situations with new information and skills.

Toward a New, Brain-Based Definition of Learning

This two-step definition of learning contrasts sharply with definitions of learning inherent in current assessment practices. For example, in our multi-billion dollar standardized testing programs, responses to true/false and multiple choice are interpreted to mean learning has occurred. However, the typical multiple choice and true/false questions can be answered based on a faint ring of familiarity of one answer over another: "Choice B rings a bell." "Hmm, that statement doesn't sound familiar, so it must be false." The student does not even have to understand the content. And step two of this new definition of learning—being able to use what is understood and store it in long-term memory—is not even considered by test makers. Likewise in the classroom, 90 percent on a pop quiz does not necessarily mean that students understand and can use the knowledge or skills.

Step one of learning, the brain's ability to detect patterns—large or small, subtle or gross—is finely tuned. For example, the brain easily recognizes a capital H in size 3 font as well as on the hills of Hollywood. Subtle degrees of sadness can be detected, for example, melancholy, pensive, despondent, depressed. These similarities and differences are not academic; they are important because they tell us how to interact with someone in these emotional states. A pattern is any object (teapot, toothbrush), action (walking, running), procedure (getting dressed, driving a car), system (transportation, government), relationship (family, cause/effect), or situation (first day of school, meeting a stranger at a party) that we are capable of noticing and naming.

Pattern seeking is an innate capability of the brain. It is how we identify something and how we make connections between that new thing and previous understandings so that we emerge with larger understandings about our world, how it works, and our place in it. We do not need to teach students how to detect pattern, they are born with this capacity; it is quite simply how the brain works. It is our job as teachers to state curriculum in ways that enhance this pattern seeking and to select instructional strategies that invite students to explore these patterns until they are fully understood. As no two brains are alike, due to genetic predisposition and prior experiences, each brain goes about pattern seeking differently. Thus, the input one person perceives may not be what another picks up, yet both brains, given enough input, can come to a core understanding of our curriculum's concepts, significant knowledge, and skills through each person's unique pattern-seeking processes.

Recommendations: (1) State curriculum as conceptually as possible; eliminate factoids. Concepts are rich in patterns; factoids provide little for the brain to hang on to. (2) Give them a learning environment that is rich enough to provide multi-sensory input (different strokes for different folks). The fullest sensory experiences come through *being there* visits to locations that give real-world context to the concepts and skills students are studying. (3) Use low sensory-input tools, such as textbooks and lecture, to expand what students understand and can use; to introduce or re-teach, use high-sensory input.

Step two of this new definition of learning requires that students develop a mental program(s) for using the patterns they understand in real-world situations, not just the artificial environment of the classroom. The first phase of this process requires guided practice, with all its fits and starts, errors and approximations. The final step is the use of these programs with expert ease, almost automatically, which occurs as the brain hardwires the necessary connections into long-term memory.

Learning to drive a car is a good example of this two-step learning process. The patterns to be identified and understood include finding the right remote button to unlock the car door, fastening your seat belt, finding where the key goes and what the different positions are for, checking that the transmission is in park or neutral, turning the key the right number of clicks, pressing the brake pedal before shifting, and so forth, through a long list of steps that become a single program, selected and used daily as we drive our car.

Student drivers can understand all of this and pass the written driving test but can they drive the car to the grocery store? Learning to apply these patterns requires conscious attention to each step and lots of guided practice. Sometimes steps may be forgotten, sometimes done out of order. But a safe trip to the grocery store requires that these steps become virtually automatic so that the driver's attention can be given to the traffic ahead—cars, pedestrians, and the unexpected.

In the final phase of building a program for driving a car, the mechanics of driving become one large mental program, not a check list of individual tasks. To test this, ask yourself if you have ever driven somewhere and upon arrival realized that you do not recall a single thing about large portions of the journey. This expert level, near automaticity, is important because it frees our brain to attend to other things—how to use what we know and new learnings. It also indicates that the necessary connections in the brain have become hardwired into our long-term memory and available for use in the years to come, for example, the order of the alphabet when using a dictionary, typing, interdependence in a habitat, the algorithm for long division, punctuation rules for periods and commas, adding fractions in a recipe, and so forth.

What role does rote learning play in building programs? While rote learning has its place, it should be relegated primarily to those things that are necessary to remember but are not understandable (the things simply are what they are), for example, the order of the alphabet, state capitals, the multiplication tables (not the concept of multiplication), the location of keys on a keyboard, and so forth.

Recommendations: (1) Give students many and varying opportunities to use what they are learning in real-world situations. (2) Allow them time to practice using the concept or skill using all the multiple intelligences. (3) Ensure they get immediate feedback through the pattern-seeking and program-building stages of learning to ensure their understandings and applications are correct. (4) Require that students take action and use their bodies (the movement centers of the brain also sequence thought).

See also: **Patterns and Programs.**

Further Readings

Goldberg, E. (2001). *The Executive Brain: Frontal Lobes and the Civilized Mind*. Oxford: University Press.

Hart, L.A. (1999). *Human Brain and Human Learning*. Covington, WA: Books For Educators.

Kovalik, S.J., Olsen, K.D. (2002). *Exceeding Expectations: A User's Guide to Implementing Brain Research in the Classroom* (2nd ed.). Kent, WA: Susan Kovalik & Associates, Inc.

Ratey, J.J. (2001). *A User's Guide to the Brain: Perception, Attention, and the Four Theaters of the Brain*. New York: Pantheon Books.

KAREN D. OLSEN, ED.D.

Math

Mathematics is often viewed as a complex subject to teach and to learn. Historically, mathematics is a subject at which only a relatively select few people are able to excel and appreciate. As more is learned about how the human brain intakes, processes, stores, and recalls information, the accessibility of mathematics grows to encompass even those who tend to avoid the subject. The practical applications of this brain research have implications in many areas of mathematics instruction. These findings typically paint a starkly different picture of an effective mathematics classroom than a traditional one in which students simply view examples followed by time spent practicing in class and at home. Research strongly supports the mathematics classroom that is involved, movement oriented, filled with rich discussion, focused on complex problem-solving, low in threat, and geared for deep understanding as opposed to the memorizing of facts and figures. These positive characteristics are closely related and come together to form a classroom that is more congruent with how we understand the brain learns mathematics.

Involvement

Getting students involved and engaged, physically, socially, and mentally, in the acquisition of mathematical knowledge can take many forms and has many benefits. During a traditional mathematics lecture in which students watch the teacher solve several problems, only a small percentage of the brain is highly active. To maximize attention and retention, it is critical that the mathematics educator involve as many parts of the brain as possible. Involvement in the broadest sense may encompass simply activating the motor cortex as an additional active sector.

The concept of involvement includes the learners' level of engagement with the material, each other, and the teacher throughout the acquisition and processing of the material. Each of these areas will engage a larger percentage of the brain than is stimulated through lecture. Effective mathematics learning is social. A classroom, then, should involve communication between peers about the content as well as teacher–student communication. Through this communication, students will be able to make personal sense of the content and develop meaningful mathematical knowledge. This communication will also bridge into the students interacting with the content itself. This can begin to be accomplished by the teacher allowing the students to discuss with each other what the content *means* to them. In a more traditional classroom, the *teacher* assigns the meaning of the content. This shift in focus requires the teacher to become skilled at facilitating discussion to ensure the students are guided to a proper perspective with respect to the content.

Movement Oriented

Although movement is a helpful key to learning any content, it is especially helpful in the mathematics classroom. Much mathematical content can be viewed as quite abstract. In any classroom, the ability for the learners to process and retain abstract concepts varies greatly from one student to another. Research shows some learners will never be as good at this skill as others. To make mathematics accessible to a wider range of learners, then, procedures must be in place throughout the lesson to help make mathematics more concrete. Movement is a way to help this conversion take place.

Besides increasing the amount of blood, and therefore oxygen, in the brain, movement does several other things to increase the effectiveness of instruction. Kinesthetically involving students in a mathematics lesson can help to bring holistic, right brain, random thinkers into the world of understanding and appreciating the subject. If the teacher would like the students to practice twenty problems on a certain topic, those problems could be written, in pairs, on ten sheets of paper. The sheets of paper can then be hung around the room. In small groups, the students can take their papers from sheet to sheet solving the problems. In the experience of many educators, students, because they are active, complete the problems more quickly than if they were given a work-sheet with twenty similar problems. This is because the students are active, involved, and more awake. This can be done with practice problems, an assessment, as well as many other problem sets. A great benefit of this strategy is that it can be used with any level of mathematics.

Another powerful way to use movement to great effect in the mathematics classroom is to use what we know about **episodic** and **semantic memory**. These two memory pathways contrast and interact with each other. This is useful because it is common in mathematics to present a series of steps that the learners are asked to remember to recall them for future use and application. Focusing on the semantic memory pathway (used for memorizing facts and concepts) alone will not maximize the retention of such material. To engage the episodic memory in mathematics, try the following.

Consider a mathematical process that involves four steps. Begin by writing the four steps on large, separate sheets of paper and hang them in four distinct, physically separate areas of the room. When it comes time to present the steps to the learners ask them to stand and gather by the sheet that contains step number one. As the class gathers around sheet number one, the teacher can take time to explain the importance of the step, its pitfalls, its strengths, etc... When it is time to move on to step number two, simply ask the class to join you in another corner of the room. This process is repeated until the steps have all been described, the learners are creating memories of the movement and the event, not just the content. Later, when the students are asked to recall step number two, the teacher may even find students turning to look at the corner of the room in which it was previously placed. Rechecking their environment will likely give them clues to the content that was experienced there. This is a significant tool that can also be used to classify equations, organize equations, and many other common mathematical tasks. Again, this is a powerful strategy at any level.

Rich Discussion

Learners create meaning mainly through the process of social interaction and processing. This interaction involves the process of the construction and discovery of mathematical concepts, communicating mathematical ideas both written and verbally, supporting and defending mathematical ideas, scrutinizing approaches with supporting evidence of such scrutiny, and building formal and informal complex mathematical arguments. It is the rich discussion about mathematical concepts that leads to true understanding of the material. The antithesis of this point is to encourage the students to simply recall facts and figures. In the modern age of the internet and readily available information, the acquisition of facts is not difficult. The analysis and discussion of those facts often proves to hold the difficulty.

Fostering discussion about the above details gives the students the ability to acquire new mathematical knowledge more quickly because they are building a larger base of experience with the content. This *experience* with the content utilizes a different memory pathway in the brain than the recall of rote memorization. Utilizing these additional memory pathways has shown to increase the retention of material.

Complex Problem-Solving

The ability to solve problems on a worksheet is becoming less useful as society turns to rapidly changing technology, newly researched ideas, and ever changing job roles. Recalling the rules and procedures required to complete many worksheets do not serve a great purpose in terms of applying knowledge to a novel situation. In other words, focusing on obtaining the solution to problems is not as helpful as focusing the process involved to arrive at a solution. Mathematics educators must go beyond rote memorization of facts, figures, and equations to facilitate the learning of *mathematical thinking*. It is the rehearsal of logical thinking and problem-solving that makes mathematics useful in an ever changing world.

Including complex problem-solving can take different forms. An easy strategy is to solicit student ideas *how* to solve a particular real world problem that invites a specific approach. This can be utilized even before the desired problem-solving strategy is presented. With the right guidance, students will often be able to, through discussion and experimentation, formulate a plan similar to the strategy intended for the lesson.

Another form of complex problem-solving takes place in a prescribed environment, set up by the teacher, meant to solve a specific problem. These problems may not require a specific strategy to obtain a solution. It may be the discussion about the problem itself that accounts for complex problem-solving. In essence, including *complex problem-solving* is a gateway to foster many other mathematical skills. It is closely tied to the topics of rich discussion, deep understanding and requires a lower threat environment. Problem-solving is the best way to build a better brain, and it's the process not the product, that is the influential factor.

Lower Threat

Appropriate levels of challenge can certainly help provide an enriched environment capable of fostering mathematical understanding. High levels of threat, however, can quickly contribute to the large amount of anxiety toward the potentially daunting subject of mathematics. Threat comes in many forms and current research suggests that a threatened brain has trouble absorbing and retaining complex subjects such as mathematics. Anything an educator can do to reduce the threat in the math classroom will help increase participation, maximize attention, and increase retention.

If learners come into the mathematics classroom feeling threat, which is quite common, the teacher's first job is to reduce the stress and then teach the content. To tackle this we must first look at some of the causes of math anxiety. One source of anxiety comes from mathematics being presented as a process through which you must find the one answers. The answer, then, becomes the focal point of the energy spent. Students may get to a point where, if they believe they cannot reach the correct answer, they refuse to even attempt the first step of a problem. Another source of anxiety stems from the reality that learners at any given level vary greatly in mathematical ability. Students not proficient in a piece of the content may feel inferior to students with a higher proficiency, thus potentially stunting their future performance. A third source of high threat comes from the presentation of mathematics. If mathematics is only presented as a strict set of rules and procedures, less skilled learners can view mathematics as a nearly impossible task consisting of confusing, unrelated webs of steps and processes.

If these three sources of threat work as a beginning point for discussion, educators can attempt to tackle each source in turn. Many learners, either naturally or through conditioning, tend to get "obsessed" with the answers to a problem. This can happen to such a degree that the actual process involved in obtaining that answer can begin to seem irrelevant. This rears its ugly head in many classrooms in the following manner: A student takes an assessment and only puts the answers on the paper contrary to the directions to include supporting work and evidence of the answer. When the teacher does not give the student full credit, it may be met with a confused look and a response of, "why didn't I get full credit, I got the write answer?" This type of response is a clue that the student places heavy weight on the answer as opposed to the process itself. A strategy to help "rewire" this thinking is to write the problem, leave some white space, and provide the answer. The instruction then becomes, "please show me how to get from the start to the finish." This technique often can be used even when the topic is new. For instance, when teaching the order of operations [The "order of operations" is the prescribed order in which mathematical operations (addition, division, etc...) must be computed to obtain the correct answer. For instance, in the problem, "ten plus eight divided by two," the correct answer is fourteen. The division must be computed prior to the addition. If the addition is computed first, the answer would be nine, which is incorrect.], the students need not be told the prescribed order in advance. If provided several example problems with their answers included, groups of students can, relatively easily, create the rule themselves. This social activity of working in groups in conjunction of the reduction in the level of threat (because the answers are provided) will help the students construct the knowledge and, therefore, have a greater attachment to the content. Surprising to some, many students are able to create knowledge in this complex nature well into advanced mathematics.

The second source of high levels of anxiety toward mathematics, differing levels among peers, can vary greatly from class to class. Many experts spend time studying differences in "innate" mathematical ability among people. Both through nature and nurture, mathematical ability (or apparent inability) is developed early in life. The disparity of mathematical ability among peer groups is obvious even in the first grade and earlier. One way to reduce the threat in the teaching of mathematics is to keep learning social. The human brain is more likely to create meaning from mathematical content if there are social times to process, discuss, and evaluate. Varying the mode of presentation will also help in reaching learners who do not predominantly think "mathematically." For instance, an effective mathematics classroom has occasional hands-on manipulatives and, at other times, quiet practice time. This practice time is balanced by small and large group discussions and problem-solving.

The third source of anxiety toward math comes with some irony. In general, mathematics educators are people who are quite knowledgeable about their subject. This type of thinker tends to be a linear, logical, mathematical, left-brain thinker. If mathematics is presented predominantly in that manner, however, students who do not naturally process in that manner are at a disadvantage. The days of thinking that students should just, "try harder" are long past. We know now that different brains have different strengths. This is not to say that random, holistic, right-brain thinkers cannot excel at mathematics, quite the contrary. The secret lies in the presentation of the material to this type of learner. Mathematics can be presented as a language to explain the world around us. Setting students up to discover principles and rules allows them to create meaning instead of viewing mathematics as a prescribed set of rules. The strict hierarchical presentation of mathematics can greatly increase threat in students who do not have a dominant **learning style** that is congruent with such a presentation. To present mathematics in a manner congruent with the wide variety of learning styles, educators should actively include tasks, problems, activities, and assessments that also include the creative and artistic side of mathematics, thus reducing the level of threat in many students. At the same time, this causes the concepts to seem integrated and purposeful.

Deep Understanding

Many people who succeed at finding correct answers to math problems have trouble when asked for further explanation as to *why* that answer is correct. Any push to go beyond merely quoting a rule, principle, or algorithm (a given set of step-by-step procedures to find an answer to a problem…the pre-defined steps taken in long division, for example) as the supporting explanation causes many to pause and respond with, "because that is just how you do it." An individual who has a true understanding of the material would be able to explain the reason the particular rule exists and, therefore, be more likely to be able to apply that rule to a new and different situation.

For instance, consider the problem "4 1/3 divided by 1/3." Most people who have recently been involved in a mathematics course would be able to work out the answer of thirteen. Many students, however, would also be unable to give a description of *why* the answer is thirteen. If a student cannot explain the purpose of their chosen process, they are less likely to be able to adapt to novel mathematical situations that arise throughout their life. If a student focuses on the answers, those answers are paired with specific problems instead of growing the knowledge base in regards to the content in general. If a student spends their time learning the process, the answers will naturally follow and the specific numbers or organization of the problem in question do not have a crippling effect on the student's ability to obtain a solution.

If an educator, then, simply increases the number of "why?" questions the students are asked, they are moving toward a teaching model more compatible with what is known about retention. Once students get comfortable communicating with each other about the "why?" they will begin to develop the skills to begin answering questions such as, "what next?" Since we know mathematics is hierarchical, being able to connect new information to previous information as well as predict future occurrences is critical to deep understanding. Teaching for deep understanding lies in contrast to solely teaching for the rote memorization of facts, tables, and equations. Teaching for deep understanding is credited by the National Council of Teachers of Mathematics as a reason for increased math scores, according to the National Center for Education Statistics, in the United States.

See also: **Classroom Environment; Constructivism; Social Context of Learning Physical Movement; Processing Time.**

Further Readings

Allen, R.H. (2002). *Impact Teaching: Ideas and Strategies for Teachers to Maximize Student Learning.* Boston, MA: Allyn & Bacon.

Burke, M.J., Curcio, F.R. (Yearbook; 2000). *Learning Mathematics for a New Century.* Reston, VA: National Council of Teachers of Mathematics.

Cuoco, A.A., Curico, F.R. (Yearbook, 2001). *The Roles of Representation in School Mathematics.* Reston, VA: National Council of Teachers of Mathematics.

National Council of Teachers of Mathematics http://nctm.org

DUKE R. KELLY

Moral Development

Character education, values clarification, and moral education are terms that have all been used to describe the process of actively defining and teaching students about right and wrong as they make socially significant decisions. Even within our pluralistic society that draws its standards from a variety of sources, there is a broad spectrum of common values that help us to get along without harming self or others, treating each other with dignity and respect.

Moral behavior is dependent on the ability to predict potential outcomes of our own actions, take the perspective of another, and delay gratification. Some researchers believe that empathy is required to make moral decisions, while others have discovered that the ability to experience empathy does not guarantee that someone will use his or her understanding of another's feelings ethically. These abilities grow over time and with experience. Morality and moral identity are constructed through reflective interaction with others inside a particular social and cultural context. There are both spoken and unspoken rules that come to govern our relationships and there are consequences we experience when we violate them. We are able to use memory, emotion, reasoning, language, social feedback and finally choice to act with moral consistency.

Solving moral dilemmas involves multiple areas of the brain. The prefrontal cortex, sometimes called the executive brain, is actively involved in moral reasoning. Studies of people with early damage to this area indicate that these individuals do not develop effective connections between cause and effect, have trouble with impulse control and may not benefit from social correction. Damage to the prefrontal cortex at or before birth, however, when separated from intellectual functioning deficits, may not be as significant as damage done to the brain between one and two years of age.

A National Institute of Mental Health study that tracked healthy brain development with MRI technology concluded that the prefrontal cortex is not fully developed at age twenty-one, and may not be until the age of thirty. This has important implications for moral reasoning and behavior. Even young children can think with regard to others—babies in the nursery respond to the distress of other infants, and toddlers can act with compassion. Still, the human brain may not have the cognitive skills until well into adulthood to fully think through the impact of one's actions upon others and to control one's impulses accordingly.

Emotions associated with morally laden images or circumstances involve not only the frontal lobes, but the amygdala, the thalamus, and the upper midbrain. Malfunction in these areas may interfere with a person's ability to accurately "read" either the situation or the feedback he or she receives in response to the situation. For example, perceived threat may cause someone to misinterpret or ignore facial expressions or body positions that are usually interpreted and responded to without conscious thought. So moral reasoning develops within a process that involves both thinking and feeling what is right based on feedback and introspection.

The ability to make moral decisions and the development of conscience as an internal guide has been linked to early bonding and nurturing experiences, as well as inborn temperamental differences. **Trauma** and lack of predictable care can interfere with the establishment of the relational background necessary for connecting doing good with feeling good. Healthy children develop the ability to respect others and care about their needs as they themselves are respected and cared for. From a brain perspective, the complex neural networking that occurs in early childhood literally forms the moral fiber we draw on throughout life.

Moral instruction needs to be seamlessly integrated within the educational process and must be based in an understanding of developmental characteristics. In infancy and toddlerhood, the focus is on differentiation of the self and others and helping children to find commonalities between their experience and the experiences of others. The preschool years include an emphasis on learning self-control, interpreting the perspectives of others, and learning social behaviors that promote peace and fairness such as sharing and using appropriate language to express one's own needs. Elementary level moral instruction includes helping children to recognize their ability to influence others through their actions, and adolescent instruction might focus on helping students to self-identify their moral convictions and explore the history and implications of ethical philosophy. These developmentally based instructional goals should not be taught in "morals time," but should be entrenched within the curricular framework, as they are entrenched in life. Challenges that refine these basic skills are encountered throughout the life cycle, so in a sense our moral development is never complete.

Most researchers agree that foundational moral development requires experience with externally imposed rules that contribute to the development of personal habits and acculturation. These external rules are developed independent of the child, and help to insure justice. A child needs to see these rules as firm and consistently applied to come to view them as fair. At early stages of cognitive development, when children have limited capacity to reason for themselves, these rules—delivered by trustworthy, loving, caregivers—establish safe boundaries of behavior toward the self, others, and the environment. Limits and stated reasons for the limits from parents, teachers, and others granted authority in a child's life help to define what will eventually become self-imposed limits established by internal convictions.

Teachers can help to develop these internal convictions by having only a few memorable and unchanging rules that invite reflection and make the classroom a lab for moral reasoning experimentation. These rules must be based on the teacher's own core values because children seem to absorb more of the hidden agenda of authority figures than what is expressed. This may reflect back to the amygdala's unconscious voice in the moral reasoning process. Morally stimulating rules must be developed intentionally to be broad enough to generate dialog based upon moral values, and firm enough to be inviolable. For instance, the classroom rule, "safety first" can form the basis for discussions that inspire morally based reasoning about domains of safety (physical, emotional, environmental), prediction of outcomes, expression of feelings, elaboration of details in internal rule-making and risk-taking choices, and discussing mitigating circumstances within the rule (such as sacrificing the safety of one to secure the safety of others). The process of working out the rule with individuals, both teachers and students, who have different moral backgrounds and who are at different moral developmental levels thus becomes the tool for moral training, while the ethical absolute of safety within the community is reinforced.

One time-honored way to discuss moral issues is through literature. Students learn to pick out words that cue moral issues, behavior, and reasoning. As students are emotionally engaged with fictional or historical characters that are making moral decisions, they are personally invested in the decisions that are made. As there is emotional engagement, the brain work that is happening is more than just objective analysis. Students are actually practicing moral reasoning along with the character and they get to vicariously experience the consequences of the behavior that the characters choose. Students might be encouraged to imagine different choices that might be made by the character and what the outcomes might be, to imagine how another character in the story might have responded, or be asked how they would respond if they were faced with the same choices the character had. This helps to build a sense of moral consistency and identity. Stories can also be told from alternative points of view, such as is done in "The True Story of The Three Little Pigs" (told by A. Wolf) by Jon Scieszka to encourage an understanding of perspective-taking.

Also in the realm of literacy, students can be encouraged to discuss and discover the relevance of sayings, maxims, or significant quotes in small groups or to create their own wisdom sayings that synthesize their ideas about good living. These activities reinforce literacy skills with embedded moral content.

Service learning has been found to be effective when students engage in a learning project by choice and follow the experience with purposeful debriefing questions that help students to connect the what and why of the event. To plant trees for community service credit is nothing more than acting in self-interest to earn a reward, but to have the opportunity to reflect on the significance of those trees both now and in the future can help students to see the moral value of giving of themselves for the benefit of the community.

Similarly, problem-based learning that involves students in brainstorming and implementing solutions to real life conflicts or issues offers them the opportunity to experience the benefits of good actions.

Simulations and orchestrated experiences such as "If the world were a village," mock election debates, or model United Nations councils that help students to have a concrete experience of real-world social structures can provide rich material for perspective-taking. Establishing a classroom bank or corporation and introducing moral conflicts as part of the experience gives students the chance to explore the consequences of operating with or without an ethical system in place.

Teachers can help linear-thinking students design flow charts for decision making and self-assessment processes that include moral considerations and can include such tools in classroom use, encouraging the use of multiple cognitive domains in the moral reasoning process.

Moral development is nurtured through daily interactions in home, school, and society. Values are integrated as they are modeled indirectly and as they are taught intentionally. Sound moral reasoning involves critical thinking, choice making, and attention to the needs of both the self and others. To neglect teaching morals does not mean that moral development will not occur; only that it will occur with greater attention to the self than to others. Intentional integration of moral reasoning opportunities within the curriculum helps insure that kids grow up sensitive to the needs of others and able to make moral choices in the real world.

See also: Emotional Intelligence; Self-Esteem; Spirituality.

Further Readings

Borba, M. (2002). *Building Moral Intelligence: The Seven Essential Virtues that Teach Kids to Do the Right Thing.* San Francisco: Jossey-Bass.

Damasio, A. (2003). *Looking for Spinoza: Joy, Sorrow, and the Feeling Brain.* New York: Harcourt.

Sapolsky, R. (2003). "A Bozo of a Baboon: A Talk with Robert Sapolsky" http://www.edge.org/3rd_culture/saplsky03/sapolsky_print.html. Viewed online, 29 October, 2004.

Stilwell, B., Galvin, M., Kopta, S.M., Kopta, S. *Right Vs. Wrong: Raising a Child with Conscience.* Bloomington, IN: Indiana University Press.

New Horizons for Learning, Character Education http://www.newhorizons.org/strategies/character/front_character.htm

Studies in Moral Development and Education, http://tigger.uic.edu/~lnucci/MoralEd/

LORI NILES, M.A.

Motivation

Motivation is defined simply as the "why" of behavior. Psychologists refer to motivation as an organism's internal state that directs and instigates their behavior in persistence and energy. Understanding the factors that determine what makes some students engage in tasks or persuades other to avoid similar task is important to predicting academic outcomes. Motivation has been characterized by the intensity, direction, and duration of behavior, and studies have shown that heightened motivation increases effort, persistence, and responsiveness.

Motivation constructs include self-worth, attributions, self-regulation, and achievement goals. Especially important to educators are students' reasons for learning and the reinforcement of their locus of control. Intrinsic reward is associated with activities that are their own reward in contrast to an extrinsic reward that is created by external factors like rewards and punishments. Psychological studies with children and adults show that intrinsic motivation directs behavior more effectively than does externally administered rewards. Although educators know the benefits of intrinsic motivation, most school policies and methods use extrinsic rewards.

Educators often make judgments about which students appear to be "motivated" and those who are "unmotivated." These judgments may not always be supported by evidence, for example, a student in a math class may be considered to be unmotivated during class instruction but otherwise may eagerly count the money in her pocket. Effective teachers develop attitudes in students that contribute to a long-term commitment to learning. One example used is how homework affects motivation. One teacher grades all daily homework with letter grades counting 30 percent toward the final grade. Another teacher grades homework as satisfactory or unsatisfactory, lets students correct their work, and counts the homework for only 10 percent of the total grade. While the casual observer may think more stringent evaluation would increase student performance, research shows that the teacher who lets the students correct homework improves motivation.

Brain-based research broadens our understanding of motivation by analyzing the neurogenic causes of external and internal motivation, and causes of temporary and chronic demotivation. Neuroscience reveals that the brain rewards the cerebral cortex with natural opiates called endorphins through the hypothalamic reward system. This pleasure system rewards the cerebrum on a daily basis, although each person responds differently based on genetics, brain chemistry, and life experiences. Research has found that external rewards do not stimulate the brain's internal reward system in the same way. Learning is not dependent on promises of good grades and future employment; studies show that animals and humans will seek new experiences and behaviors without perceivable immediate gratification.

Using rewards as a teaching strategy is complicated. Behaviorism's stimulus–response approaches have only been effective with simple physical responses. Rewarding students for creative, critical, and higher level thinking actually impairs internal motivation. When teachers offer strategies to "motivate" students typically they rely upon external rewards by offering choice, time, food, and other privileges. These methods work for some students, but not others, especially for students who exhibit temporary apathetic states or characteristics of chronic demotivation or learned helplessness. Teachers must distinguish between these states to accurately diagnose and refocus students.

Students who come to class with an "apathetic glaze" may be temporarily unmotivated. Eric Jensen reports three reasons for temporary apathy. First, memory associations from a poor educational experience create a negative response. These associations are reported to be stored in the brain's amygdala, and when triggered, adrenaline, vasopressin, and adrenocorticotropic hormone (ACTH) are released by the adrenal glands into the bloodstream. Students who suffered a past embarrassment or failure with math can be retriggered by present sounds, smells, and visual cues. Sensory signals journey to the thalamus that serves as a relay station to the neocortex, the cognitive part of the brain, and the amygdala, which stores our emotions; the emotional brain reacts ahead of the thinking brain. This is why we often feel anger before understanding where it originates.

The second source of a temporary lack of motivation stems from the environmental factors that are formed from the patterns arising from those negative educational experiences. These factors include adverse learning styles, poor classroom environments, social problems such as prejudice, and **self-esteem** factors such as fear of exclusion and failure. Teachers routinely adapt their teaching methods according to students needs by using visual displays and reinforcing content with auditory supplements; however, solutions to social problems often lie outside the scope of a school's context. The third source for a temporary lack of motivation is the student's relationship with the future such as the ability of the student to define their goals. This source includes efficacy expectations where students believe that they can achieve tasks and perceive that the task has interest, attainment, and utility value. Positive beliefs trigger the release of chemicals such as dopamine and endorphins that are natural self-rewards that reinforce positive behaviors. Efficacy itself is situation specific; however, efficacy affects self-worth that is threatened when the task is important and when one's ability is questioned. In classrooms, all student effort can be made important through the use of external rewards and evaluation, and self-worth can be potentially threatened.

Teachers extensively use external motivators including telling students what to do, punishing them if they do not comply, and rewarding obedience. The problem with this reward–punishment approach is that it becomes more objectionable as the child matures. Jean Piaget and Lawrence Kohlberg believed that moral responsibility depends on cognitive growth. Piaget further believed that external rewards can lead to conformity, deceit, or revolt. Incentives in elementary and middle schools set students up to be dependent on reward rather than appropriate behavior. As these students become adolescents, the need for approval changes from teacher-based to peer-based as the students' reference group changes. Adolescents are motivated by social goals as much if not more than academic goals so that the adolescent culture creates their cognition. Adolescents' need for inclusion and avoidance of exclusion motivates their behavior toward school, activities, and learning. These principles dramatically alter how teachers motivate adolescents versus motivating younger students.

Unfortunately, grades and achievements are only incentives for students interested in those rewards. When a student asks, "Will this be graded?" The focus is not learning, but the external incentive, thus grades change motivation. In some situations, competition for grades can produce deceit and cheating which in reality is a systems problem, not a student problem. This paradox of external incentives creates an environment where the student cannot learn at the same time as being perfect. This competitive environment diminishes a student's tolerance for risk, and research shows that creativity declines with competition but not with collaboration.

Rewards and punishments teach students to make decisions based on other's reactions and are a short-term answer to disruptive behavior. Teachers use rewards because they create obedience through manipulation with M&Ms, games, free time, but after the rewards are gone, the students' attitudes are unchanged. After years of a stimulus–response psychology, students and teachers believe that rewards are necessary for learning. Teachers often believe that rewards such as flattery and grades build self-esteem; however, praise give transient good feelings that do not significantly change our self-perceptions. Even young students easily detect insincerity and manipulation, and a teacher's good intentions can be counterproductive; thus, coercion creates compliance, but not commitment. Thus, rewards actually punish when one student is praised and the other is not. The "good" student is embarrassed or disliked by their classmates, and the "bad" student senses rejection and manipulation—a no-win situation. Achievement itself brings self-acceptance and satisfaction.

Characteristics of chronic demotivation or learned helplessness are emotional responses such as anxiety, depression, a liking for hostile humor such as sarcasm. Learned helplessness is a belief that a student's outcomes are independent of a student's actions. Learned helplessness stems from a trauma of an uncontrollable event where the student does not have the skills to effectively deal with the circumstance. Bullying, household abuse, and humiliation in front of peers all qualify as trauma while pulling a student aside with a quiet reminder does not. The amygdala, the center of our fear response, sends neural impulses throughout the entire sympathetic system stimulating the release of adrenaline, vasopressin, and cortisol. These chemicals have an immediate effect on feelings and behaviors. Children who have had frequent exposure to threat have receptor sites adapted to survival-oriented behavior. These students fight for "rank" and territory and have difficulty maintaining attention because of fear of or preying upon others. While moderate amounts of stress enhance learning performance, a survival mode diminishes higher order learning and complex problem-solving. These threats initiate defense mechanisms and behaviors that work well for survival but are deficient for learning.

While conjecture might lead us to think that providing successful outcomes might alleviate learned helplessness, literature shows that success for these children is not sufficient to help them construct a belief that they can reverse failure. Training students to attribute their failures to effort rather than ability, and crediting success to ability rather than chance leads to persistence. These students need practice in using strategies to achieve short-term goals instead of focusing on outcomes. Students who suffer from chronic demotivation may need fifty (or more) positive reinforces before they can become mobilized again. Teachers who become frustrated with these students after a few positive attempts do not understand the nature of learned helplessness. A teacher's frustration may even result in reprimands or threats that further impede a student's progress. Research on intrinsic motivation recommends that these students need to have control in decision-making and personal choice to alleviate the symptoms of learned helplessness.

Human beings have three needs: relatedness, competence, and especially autonomy. Social psychology research suggests that intrinsic motivation is based on experiencing autonomy. If there is no experience with self-determination, the student only feels pressure and tension. They also suggest that activities that enhance perceived competence and are optimally challenging will enhance intrinsic motivation. Mastery goals develop competence and self-regulation and low avoidance behaviors. Teachers who communicate with failure statements imply incompetence and undermine intrinsic motivation. Deadlines, surveillance, and threats convey external control thus decreasing autonomy and inhibiting intrinsic motivation. Reward and control orient people toward wanting success, but not toward challenging tasks or risking failure. Thus, students who are more extrinsically motivated have more difficulty solving problems. Students who learned to teach others had greater conceptual learning and were more intrinsically motivated; the shift toward competition, toward cooperation, produced greater self-esteem and autonomy.

Jensen recommends several practical strategies for reducing **stress** in these students that include eliminating threats from outside the class, threats from other students, and internal threats within the students themselves. Although teachers cannot eliminate all environmental stress, they can create a safe classroom by setting clear expectations of behavior, setting realistic deadlines, and managing transitions within the class and in hallways. Allowing students physical activity is important because exercise releases brain-derived neurotropic factor (BDNF) that improves neural connectivity, elevates mood, and aids in long-term memory formation. Teachers need to allow students to stretch, dance, or walk during classroom transitions. Teaching students alternative ways to reframe failure can help them minimize negative self-talk; teaching them that they have choices and to see that there are connections between their actions and outcomes. For a chronically demotivated brain to rewire itself, teachers need to provide frequent, consistent, and positive replenishment into the student's environment.

Most students are intrinsically motivated for certain things. Students who will not read may spend hours learning a sophisticated video game. Modern society has a multiplicity of literacy that includes not only reading and writing, but multimodal texts that mix words and images through multimedia. Challenge, complexity, and uniqueness stimulate both hemispheres and result in more learning. Any discussion of intrinsic motivation must include the learners' construction of meaning that corresponds to their semiotic drives and beliefs. Natural neurotransmitters mediate intrinsic motivation. With mild cognitive motivation, increased levels of norepinephrine or dopamine manifest while more vigorous motivation escalates levels of peptide vasopressin or adrenaline.

Jensen suggested five strategies to aid students to uncover their own intrinsic motivation. The first and most important strategy is to eliminate threat that only inhibits intrinsic motivation for learning. Asking small groups of students to identify barriers that inhibit learning can facilitate their search for solutions as well as benefit classroom management. A second strategy is to allow students to participate and choose their goals for learning. This includes priming a student's interest and connection when introducing a topic. Allowing for construction of connections makes the material relevant and meaningful for students. A third strategy involves activating and engaging positive feelings and emotions. Effort at community building creates belongingness that instills cooperation. Building students' self-efficacy includes using affirmations, celebrations, win-win games, and creative activity through music, art, and theater. The fourth strategy is similar to the third in teaching students to manage their emotions through constructive means. Creating a positive environment through celebrations, rituals, optimizes relationship building. Increased feedback may enhance intrinsic motivation.

John Goodlad believed that learning was enhanced when students understand expectations, are recognized for their efforts, learn from their mistakes, and are guided to improve their performance. Today computers can create endless, self-managed feedback, although well-organized projects, cooperative learning, and other activities can do the same. Peer feedback is more motivating than teacher feedback and obtains greater long-term results. Using peers for feedback also has potential to create a cooperative classroom community and to assist teachers with classroom management.

Thus, using rewards to motivate students impairs their internal motivation. Teachers typically try solutions to "motivate" students who are disengaged. While these strategies may aid some students they may be unnecessary because the brain has natural opiates to daily reward the cerebrum that are not sustained by external rewards. Some students exhibit temporary apathetic states, others may display characteristics of chronic demotivation or learned helplessness. Teachers must distinguish between these states to accurately diagnose and to help students refocus. Learned helplessness stems from a trauma of an uncontrollable event where the student does not have the skills to effectively deal with the circumstance. Students who are not intrinsically motivated need to feel like they have control in decision-making to alleviate the symptoms of learned helplessness. Eric Jensen suggested five strategies for teachers to increase students' intrinsic motivation: (1) eliminate threat, (2) set goals involving students, (3) activate and engage positive emotions, (4) create a strong positive climate, and (5) increase feedback. Although some of these strategies have been known for a long time, researchers are gaining greater understanding of what motivates the brain. Teachers need this information to use the brain's internal mechanisms to naturally motivate students and create long-term results.

See also: **Behaviorism; Classroom Management; Social Context of Learning.**

Further Readings

Ames, C. (1999). Motivation: What teachers need to know. In A.C. Ornstein & L.S. Behar-Horenstein (Eds.), *Contemporary Issues in Curriculum* (pp. 135–144). (2nd ed.). Needham Heights, MA: Allyn & Bacon.

Dahl, R. (2003). *Emotional Learning: The Crucial Role of the Adolescent Brain in Developing Lifelong Motivation, Passion, and Drive.* Columbus, OH: McGraw-Hill.

Jensen, E. (1998). *Teaching with the Brain in Mind.* Alexandria, VA: Association for Supervision and Curriculum Development.

Marshall, M.L. (2001). *Discipline Without Stress.* Los Alamitos, CA: Piper Press.

Rogers, S. (2003). *Hot Topics: Key Connections: The Brain, Motivation, and Achievement.* San Diego, CA: The Brain Store, Inc.

CAROL A. ISAAC AND
LINDA S. BEHAR-HORENSTEIN, PH.D.

Mozart Effect

The Mozart Effect is popular terminology identifying the positive effects of music in health and education. French physician Alfred Tomatis in his book *Pourquoi Mozart* (1991) highlighted Mozart's music in his work to improve children's speech and communication disorders through auditory stimulation. Beginning in the 1950s, he used Mozart's music extensively because of its musical clarity, elements of form, and abundance of high frequency overtones.

In the 1990s, University of California-Irvine researchers Frances H. Rauscher, Gordon L. Shaw, and Katherine N. Ky explored music listening effects upon spatial-temporal reasoning using Mozart's music. The researchers suspected that Mozart, who began composing at age four, might have had extraordinary access to inherent spatial-temporal firing patterns. The research found that mental image rotation improved temporarily following brief listening exposure to Mozart's music. Controversy arose when the media inappropriately claimed that "Mozart Makes You Smarter" associating music listening with increased general intelligence. Ensuing studies to replicate the music listening results have been inconsistent perhaps due to methods and purpose variability.

Further research by Rauscher, Shaw, and others detected significant, long-term improvements in mental object rotation through music learning and practice. The theoretical explanation proposes that early exposure to music may support development of built-in cortical firing patterns and enhance the ability for spatial-temporal reasoning.

See also: **Music.**

Further Readings

Campbell, D. (1997). *The Mozart Effect*. New York, NY: Avon Press.

Rauscher, F.H., Shaw, G., Levine, L., Wright, E., Dennis, W., Newcomb, R. (1999). Music training causes long-term development of preschool children's spatial temporal reasoning. *Neurological Research* 19:2–8.

The Mozart Effect Resource Center http://www.mozarteffect.com/learn/read.html

Musica: The Music and Science Information Computer Archives http://www.musica.uci.edu

CHRIS BREWER-BOYD, M.A., FAMI

Multimedia Technology

Children and teenagers spend more time with media than with their parents. In fact, they spend more time with media than on any other activity except sleeping. Media technology is becoming more portable all the time, and it is delivering multimedia, the integration of text, graphics, audio, and animation. Concerned by the increasing availability of media at home and school, some parents and educators worry that media overload is incompatible with the brain's optimal learning conditions. There is no doubt, however, that multimedia technology, if used wisely, presents unparalleled opportunities to engage students' creativity and stimulate higher order thinking skills.

The manner in which information is communicated to students has become increasingly complex. Long ago, listening attentively was essential to learning, with teachers lecturing and students listening. Texts became available, pictures were added to lessons, then music or a recorded voice, radio, films, educational television, and video. As schools have added computers and connected them to the internet, multimedia technology has become more common in classrooms.

Computers are used for word processing, research, games, programming, social interactions, and artistic activities. The Internet provides access to increasingly complex combinations of text with graphics, sound, music, animation, and streaming video, and enables students to make connections across time and space with text messages or videoconferencing.

Although writing is still essential, students often do presentations incorporating pictures, animation, video, audio, objects, and graphs. Educators are aware of the need to reach as many learners as possible by teaching to the way they learn, and technology to do so is available. No longer do students have to choose whether to listen to an audio presentation, look at a visual, or read a text for information. They can do all three at once.

A landmark study by the Kaiser Family Foundation in 1999, called "Kids and Media @ The New Millenium," teaches us that the students of today are indeed "The Media Generation," with extended, mostly unsupervised, access to televisions, audio systems, print materials, and game systems in their own rooms, and increasing access to computers.

Researchers have questioned whether the characteristics of multimedia technology can be reconciled with what educators know of brain compatible environments. Some believe that before age twelve students should spend their time "doing" rather than "viewing," while others say total immersion in multimedia is the future of education. David Sousa and others contend that student brains of today are different from the brains of the past, as they have been exposed from an early age to multimedia and have adjusted their learning styles to this technology. We know much about how the brain learns, and what it needs to learn best, and we continue to learn more.

Many recent studies by neuroscientists, physicians, and educators, tell us important things about how the human brain works, how it learns, and what disrupts learning. We know that the brain naturally searches for meaning, creating patterns and solving problems, and that it is influenced both positively and negatively by **emotions**. If students are to be receptive to new information, intellectually engaged in the classroom, and able to retain and build on what they learn, they must be taught in ways that are brain compatible.

Many authors have applied the latest scientific findings about the brain to learning environments, and established elements needed to create the optical learning environment. Multimedia technology may be evaluated in relation to these elements necessary for a brain compatible classroom.

Absence of Threat

The brain notices first, and remembers longer, information that has a strong emotional component. Text, music, and pictures that evoke emotional responses will be remembered longer than others, but if **emotions** are too intense, such as anxiety or fear, learning is impeded. Mass media often bombards users with sound, rapid action, and color, and uses emotions to attract and keep the audience. Multimedia technology, including virtual reality, attempts to make the viewer feel the complete experience, and if that virtual reality is one of danger or anxiety, it may also impede learning. While an emotional "hook" works to get the immediate interest of a student, an ideal learning situation requires a feeling of trust and the absence of threat. Learners will take more intellectual risks in an environment that feels safe and non-threatening. The optimal condition for complex learning combines low threat and high challenge.

Choices

A brain-compatible environment offers choices, whenever possible, about how to learn, how to demonstrate learning has occurred, and how to receive **feedback**. Research has shown that each learner has a preferred method of learning, or a "learning style." According to Howard Gardner, of the Harvard School of Education, there are 8 1/2 different **learning styles**. An individual usually prefers one learning style, but often employs other styles too. Multimedia technology is available to create opportunities for all different types of minds to access knowledge, gain a fuller understanding, and demonstrate that understanding.

For example, the Verbal/Linguistic learner will enjoy e-books, interactive books, multimedia authoring, story creation software, and desktop publishing. The Logical/Mathematical learner will use the Internet to research, record, and analyze data, and will enjoy problem-solving software and Computer Assisted Design programs. Visual/Spatial learners like pictures, and can employ video and digital cameras, photo software, and graphic arts programs. Bodily/Kinesthetic learners will prefer robotics, dancing and filming the movement, claymation creation and recording. Musical/Rhythmic learners will favor using CDs and DVDs, video and audio recorders, music composition software, and music files. Intrapersonal learners like to use technology that helps them explore feelings and record their ideas, such as mind maps, multimedia portfolios, and problem-solving software. Interpersonal learners enjoy working with others. They will be enthusiastic about technology such as collaborative webquests, group Power Point presentations, and teleconferencing. The Naturalist learns through contact with nature. This student will be happy with a digital camera or videocamera recording outdoors, in a virtual nature setting, and with microscopes and projections of their views. The Existentialist (1/2 intelligence) asks philosophical questions about the world, and wonders about everything. Listservs, e-mail, and teleconferencing would enable this learner to contact other people.

Time

The brain learns by attaching new information to known information. To make connections and process new information, the brain requires adequate time to integrate, experiment, and reflect. Multimedia programs usually offer students a comfortable beginning level before the challenge of something more difficult. If the gap between the known and the new is too wide, the learner will be frustrated. Multimedia designed to be compatible with this element will run in real time, allowing opportunities to pause or change the pace, providing time for reflection. Students must also learn to use the technology in ways that are brain compatible, and not speed from one webpage to another without time for reflection. Individual differences among students dictate different lengths of time needed for learning, whether the learner is reading a book or using multimedia.

Regardless of the medium, learning requires repetition. Different types of rehearsal are necessary for different types of learning. Rote rehearsal is most effective for learning a skill or habit, and repetition will form the strong neural connections needed to insure that the skill is automatic. Elaborative rehearsal strategies help the learner bring additional meaning to the information. Elaborative rehearsals may include mnemonics, creating associations, and role playing or simulations.

Multimedia technology can include repetition of audio and visual components as well as requiring repeated responses from the users. Some programs elicit a certain number of correct repetitions before allowing students to progress to the next level. Gaming systems teach players that rote repetitions are necessary; and the faster the better. Rewind and replay buttons on many forms of technology assure the possibility of repetition, and allow additional time if needed, to master the learning. Virtual museums, CD-ROMs, and music videos, to name a few, all employ elaborative rehearsals.

Movement

Physical movement accompanying a song or rhyme increases the likelihood that the song will be remembered because another aspect of learning has been added. Physical movement aids memory, language acquisition, and learning. Multimedia technologies that include physical movement in any aspect, rather than prolonged periods of sitting still, are more brain compatible.

Enrichment

The brain is built to respond to novelty, complexity, and enrichment. Neurons and dendrites grow when surrounded by sensory stimuli, 3D resources, and real life applications. Multimedia allows the student to make new connections, changing presentations to add sound, color, light or motion to create an original project.

When using multimedia technology, as with all teaching, planning the assignment is important. The brain pays attention to one thing at a time. Without structure, it is easy for students to ignore content and focus on adding images, animation or music, endlessly reconsidering the font for the title page, or the right sound for one page of the Power Point presentation.

Another aspect of enrichment important in a brain compatible environment is optimizing the sensory input. Multimedia technologies regularly stimulate the senses of sight, hearing, and touch, and continue to experiment with smell, taste, balance, and the touch-related senses of heat and pressure to provide a richer experience.

Music is part of an enriched environment, and may also be used to help establish an atmosphere of calm and safety. Music can reduce stress, yet help the mind stay alert and ready to learn. Music affects the levels of several brain chemicals and triggers various **emotions**. Musical experiences can activate the motor, visual, cognitive, auditory, or affective system depending upon whether you are writing, reading, listening to or performing music.

Multimedia technologies use music as the main attraction and also to enhance programs. Most people have musical preferences, so technologies often have musical style choices available, whether you are designing a game, sending an e-card, or creating a presentation. Music must be used with caution in the classroom, because some students can relax with it in the background while others become distracted.

Collaboration

Working with others allows students to increase understanding by examining what is known and comparing it with new knowledge. Collaboration is effective when it allows students to experiment and compare or contrast information. Video- and computer-based learning programs, interactive computer programs, and videoconferencing all enable remote collaboration. Through multimedia, students can be connected with other students and with experts such as artists and scientists who enrich learning experiences and make deeper understanding possible.

Feedback

Effective feedback or assessment, a necessary component to learning must be timely, specific, and part of the learning process. Most educational software programs and computer games provide feedback for the user that is immediate, such as a flashing score, a sound, or advancement to the next level. Multimedia technology used incorrectly also provides immediate feedback. A Power Point presentation that does not buzz or change pages gives the student feedback. Immediate feedback can be incorporated in multimedia use through student projects with a peer-feedback component, employing instant messaging, teleconferencing, webcam, or e-mail feedback for distance collaboration.

Mastery

Mastery involves putting knowledge into long-term memory. The student should understand the concepts, be able to apply them to real life situations, and retrieve them when necessary. Many types of multimedia technology are available that enable students to demonstrate understanding and mastery. Multimedia is often best when used creatively to demonstrate knowledge.

Multimedia technology can, if used correctly, enhance the educational experience for any style of learner. When an assignment is meaningful and challenging, multimedia technology can be employed to help students make connections between the known and the new, create associations and make meaning, enhance communication, and foster collaboration. Multimedia technology offers a myriad of possibilities for learners to demonstrate mastery of information, and share what they know. Multimedia technology offers an opportunity for creativity and open-ended exploration. It helps students use **multiple intelligences**.

Multimedia technology is growing more conspicuous in every aspect of our lives, but it is still just one component of the big picture that is education. Having multimedia technology in the classroom or at home does not guarantee that learning will occur in greater depth or last longer. It does not guarantee that the learning will occur at all. Many parents and educators worry that students are spending too much time with electronic media and are missing other important experiences. Parents and teachers should establish clear and reasonable guidelines for usage, and students should have time for other activities and time to relate with friends and family members. Good teaching and learning occur, regardless of what technology is used, when meaningful activities are planned that require higher order thinking skills.

See also: **Challenge and Enrichment; Information Processing Model.**

Further Readings

Erlauer, L. (2003). *The Brain Compatible Classroom: Using What We Know about Learning to Improve Teaching.* Alexandria, VA: Association for Supervision and Curriculum Development.

Kaiser Family Foundation. (November, 1999). *Kids and Media @ The New Millenium.* Retrieved August 12, 2004 from http://www.kff.org/entmedia/1535-index.cfm

Lamb, A. (January, 2004). *Technology and multiple intelligences.* Retrieved August 18, 2004 from http://www.eduscapes.com/tap/topic68.htm

Veenema, S., Gardner, H. (November 1, 1996). *Multimedia and multiple intelligences/ The American Prospect.* Retrieved August 6, 2004 from http://www.prospect.org/print/V7/29/veenema-s.html

Wilson, D.K. (February 2, 2004). *Understanding how human brain works essential to good teaching and learning/Bridgewater State College News.* Retrieved August 3, 2004 from http://www.bridgew.edu/bridtoday/2004/feb/davidsousa.cfm

CHARLENE K. DOUGLASS, D.A.S.L.

Multiple Intelligences

The theory of multiple intelligences (also known as "MI theory"), was created by Dr. Howard Gardner, currently the John H. and Elizabeth H. Hobbs Professor of Cognition and Education at the Harvard Graduate School of Education in Cambridge, Massachusetts, in the course of his broad investigations in cognitive psychology, neuropsychology, developmental psychology, anthropology, and a number of other fields. The inauguration of the theory can probably best be marked by the publication in 1983 of his book *Frames of Mind: The Theory of Multiple Intelligences*. In this book, Dr. Gardner argued that the psychometric construct of "Intelligence Quotient" or "IQ" as originally developed in 1905 by Alfred Binet, and modified by a number of European and American psychologists (as evidenced by the subsequent development of other standardized IQ tests), was seriously flawed, and needed to be replaced by a new theory based upon the idea that there are many or "multiple" intelligences that constitute the core of human cognition.

In *Frames of Mind*, Gardner proposed seven candidates for these multiple intelligences. They are as follows: linguistic intelligence: the intelligence of the spoken and written word; logical-mathematical intelligence: the intelligence of numbers and reasoning; spatial intelligence: the intelligence of pictures and images; bodily-kinesthetic intelligence: the intelligence of the whole body and of the use of the hands; musical intelligence: the intelligence of rhythm, melody, and timbre; interpersonal intelligence: the intelligence of being able to make distinctions in the mood and intentions of other people; and intrapersonal intelligence: the intelligence of being able to access one's inner feelings, purposes, skills, and goals. In 1995, Gardner began writing about an eighth intelligence, the naturalist, which he describes as the intelligence of being able to discriminate among different plants or animals, or the ability to differentiate other features of the natural world such as clouds or mountains.

More recently, Gardner has considered the possibility of a ninth intelligence, which he calls the existential, and describes as the intelligence of concern with ultimate life issues (such as "what happens after we die?" "why do bad things happen to good people" and "what is the purpose of life?"). Thus far, he has declined to add it definitively to his list of intelligences because it does not meet all the criteria for an intelligence. Currently, Gardner speaks of there being "8 1/2 intelligences"—the 1/2 referring to the existential intelligences.

Perhaps the key feature of the theory of multiple intelligences, and one too often neglected by practitioners of MI theory, is the set of eight criteria used by Gardner to generate his list of intelligences. Gardner originally described these criteria in a chapter entitled "What Is An Intelligence?" in his book *Frames of Mind*; a chapter which should be required reading for anyone who wishes to go further in investigating MI theory. The first criterion that must be met for an intelligence to be included in his theory is that it must be able to be isolated by brain damage. In the course of Gardner's work at the Boston VA Hospital as a neuropsychologist, he noted how certain cognitive abilities could be wiped out by lesions in a specific area of the brain due to an illness or an accident, while leaving other cognitive abilities intact. Gardner suggests that a key prerequisite for the candidacy of "intelligence" in MI theory, is that one should be able to find evidence in the neuropsychological literature of a given intelligence being severely compromised as a result of specific brain damage, while leaving the other intelligences relatively unimpaired. For example, an individual with damage to linguistic areas of the brain might still be able to sing, relate to others non-verbally, dance, do logical problem-solving, and have insight into his or her own inner emotional life, because the areas of the brain required for these activities were unimpaired. Brain injury provides indisputable evidence of the existence of multiple intelligences.

A tentative, partial, and generalized list of areas of the brain specialized for the eight intelligences include: linguistic (left temporal and frontal lobes), logical-mathematical (left frontal and right parietal lobes), spatial (posterior regions of the right hemisphere), bodily-kinesthetic (cerebellum, basal ganglia, motor cortex), musical (right temporal lobe), interpersonal (frontal lobes, temporal lobes—especially right temporal lobe—and limbic system), intrapersonal (frontal lobes, parietal lobes, limbic system), and naturalist (areas of left parietal lobe important for discriminating "living" from "nonliving" things). It should be noted here that one of the reasons that Gardner has not included the existential intelligence as a definitive part of his theory is that he feels it does not fully meet this particular criterion.

A second, related, criterion, is that one should find instances of an intelligence working at a high level of competence in individuals that have come to be called "savants." This criterion, like the first one, is based on neuropsychology and an understanding of how brain dysfunction can create instances of individuals who, while possessing low levels of functioning in other intelligences, have gifts in one or more specific intelligence areas. Examples include individuals with low IQ scores who can sing opera in twenty-six different languages, or compute numbers and calendars rapidly in their minds, or paint with astonishing accuracy, or read encyclopedias at the age of three without understanding, or show a spectacular ability to mime or dramatize, or relate exceptionally well to others. In these cases, one sees a specific intelligence (or a component of a specific intelligence) working in isolation, demonstrating its relative autonomy from the other intelligences. In this sense, the second criterion is an instantiation of the first.

The third criterion is that each intelligence should have an identifiable core operation or set of operations. In other words, for example, one could conceivably break down or analyze the ability to perform a dance into a set of specific motor operations. It should be noted here that Gardner has held back on adding the existential intelligence fully to his model because he feels that it fails to fulfill this particular criterion as well as the first criterion. The fourth criterion is that each intelligence must have a distinctive developmental history and set of "end-state" performances. In other words, one should be able to chart the history of an individual proficient in an intelligence, say a musician, from her first infant experiences banging on a xylophone, to her "end-state" performance as a percussionist at Carnegie Hall. The fifth criterion is that each of the eight intelligences should have an evolutionary history and an evolutionary plausibility. That is, one should be able to see instances of each intelligence in earlier stages of human prehistory—as for example, in primitive musical instruments found at archeological sites—as well as in other species—as for example, in bird song.

The sixth criterion is that the existence of each intelligence should receive support from experimental psychological tasks. In particular, studies that show, for example, how the ability to dance does not make one a better mathematician, or that demonstrate how reading better does not necessarily make one a better salesman, may indicate the relative independence of each intelligence from one another. It should be noted that Gardner has acknowledged recent studies that suggest that early music training may facilitate mathematical or spatial ability, and has left room for a reevaluation of the validity of these intelligences in the light of future confirming studies along these lines. The seventh criterion is that the relative autonomy of each intelligence should receive support from psychometric findings. An examination of the subtests of an IQ test, for example, should reveal in at least certain individuals, an uneven profile among those subtests that assess different intelligences (picture completion, which requires spatial intelligence being much higher or lower, for example, than vocabulary, which draws upon linguistic intelligence).

The eighth criterion is that each intelligence must be capable of being encoded in a symbol system. This is seen in the different symbol systems used by practitioners highly skilled in working with a specific intelligence (writers using linguistic symbol systems like English, French or Russian, musicians using different musical notational systems, computer programmers using different computer languages and so on). Finally, it should be noted that while not included as a specific criterion, Gardner has written that each intelligence should represent the ability to solve problems and/or fashion products that are culturally valued. In other words, a person demonstrating an intelligence should show the ability to solve a real problem, such as fixing a broken machine, or fashion a culturally valued product such as a painting, a novel, or an invention. In this regard, one has to question whether the tasks required on typical standardized IQ tests really represent authentic culturally valued activities, or are instead artificial skills contrived for the purposes of furthering relatively obscure academic research.

In the two decades that have passed since its inception, the theory of multiple intelligences has grown from a relatively obscure concept embraced mainly by private schools for gifted children, to a mainstream concept in contemporary education. Hundreds of schools based upon multiple intelligences have developed in the United States and in scores of other countries around the world (e.g., the August 16–18, 2002 conference in Beijing, entitled the "International Conference on Pushing Forward the National Education and Improving Student's Quality: Research on the Development and Assessment of Multiple Intelligences," included nearly two hundred papers on multiple intelligences). Multiple intelligences have been woven into the staff development goals and instructional frameworks of many school districts worldwide. Hundreds of books and thousands of articles have been written about the theory of multiple intelligences and its educational applications in English and at least thirty other languages. The theory of multiple intelligences has been applied to virtually all levels of education, from infancy to adulthood, and to a wide variety of settings including vocational and career education, literacy, technology, special education, gifted education, substance abuse prevention programs, parochial education, outdoor education, arts education, bilingual and english for speakers of other languages (ESOL) education, and higher education, among other areas.

The variety of applications of multiple intelligences to educational settings has likewise been quite diverse. One criticism of traditional academic schooling, according to Gardner, is that only two intelligences are primarily emphasized: linguistic intelligence and logical-mathematical intelligence. On the broadest level, then, MI theory has helped educators see the value of content areas typically deemed of less value in the overall curriculum by traditional educators, including music programs, arts education, physical education, and the development of personal and social skills in students. MI theory has served as a major conceptual support to these programs in arguing for more funding and greater presence in school programs. In addition, many magnet schools specializing in one or more of these areas have received validation for their raison d'etre, and have used MI theory as a foundation for their goals.

On a more strategic level, the theory of multiple intelligences has been used in staff development programs to help teachers at all grade levels and in all content areas develop curricula, lesson plans, and instructional approaches that incorporate the eight intelligences over time into their teaching repertoire. Thus, for example, instead of simply giving a lecture on the Battle of Gettysburg in U.S. History, a teacher might show a movie or a slide show, involve the students in a re-enactment of the battle, engage the students in writing songs detailing the events of the battle, create time-lines or other cognitive organizers to help students master the material, or lead discussion groups, debates, or cooperative learning groups seeking to investigate the impact of the battle on the course of the

Civil War. This broader approach to instruction has had the effect of reaching students who had previously been unreachable in the classroom, due to their relative weaknesses in the academic intelligences (linguistic and logical-mathematical), and their relative strengths in intelligences typically not addressed in traditional lecture-based, textbook-based classrooms. In one study of forty schools using multiple intelligences conducted by researchers at Harvard Project Zero, a number of positive outcomes related to decreased dropout rates, improvement in students labeled "learning disabled," and standardized test scores were noted.

A related application of multiple intelligences to education consists in educating students about their own multiple intelligences profile. A variety of informal checklists and formal diagnostic activities exist for assessing multiple intelligences in students. Teaching students about their own multiple intelligences may be particularly helpful for those students who have had school difficulties, or received labels such as "learning disabled" or "attention deficit hyperactivity disorder." These students may discover that they possess gifts that when recognized and developed can serve to raise their self-esteem and that can provide a means of acquiring skills in areas of difficulty through strategies based on their most highly developed intelligences. These checklists or diagnostic approaches can also be helpful in counseling students as to their own career proclivities.

Another major application of MI theory to educational settings consists in its impact upon how students are tested concerning their mastery of material taught in the schools. Again, the typical academic approach has relied heavily upon linguistic and logical-mathematical intelligences, usually through paper-and-pencil tests. MI theory has supported the development of assessments in all content areas that include the eight intelligences, so that students might be assessed in their understanding of fractions, for example, not simply by taking a traditional test, but by solving hands-on problems using math manipulatives, or relating fractions to the musical scale, or writing an imaginative story based upon their understanding of fractions.

The theory of multiple intelligences, while popular among educators at all levels, is not without its critics. MI theory has found disfavor particularly in the field of psychology where academicians still hold tightly to the idea of IQ, or some other equivalent single generalized intelligence factor. Critics claim that MI theory is based primarily on intuition, and not quantitative measures. Some educators, likewise, have claimed that MI theory lacks good empirical evidence to back up its claims that using all eight intelligences in instruction boosts academic achievement. Such criticisms often come from those with a positivist orientation, that is, from those with a belief that knowledge, in order to be true, must be quantifiable. Such critics have difficulty with the qualitative aspects of MI theory and that it bases many of its knowledge claims upon findings from anthropology, autobiography, clinical psychology, and other non-quantitative sources.

Despite its critics, the theory of multiple intelligences has made a major impact upon the face of American education over the past twenty-one years. It has caused educators to think differently about how children learn and significantly contribute to a wave of school reform that has made academic institutions more interesting and lively places for students. In a sense, Gardner's work has initiated a kind of paradigm shift in contemporary education, by taking educators out of their myopic focus on splinter skills and narrow instructional objectives, and causing them to see a broader view of learning that encompasses not simply the 8 1/2 intelligences of his model, but that opens new questions about what is truly valued in schools and in culture at large, and what are the limits to human knowing and achievement. In this respect, the theory of multiple intelligences deserves credit for opening many people's eyes to a new vision of learning and teaching.

See also: **IQ.**

Further Readings

Armstrong, T. (1999). *7 Kinds of Smart: Identifying and Developing Your Multiple Intelligences.* New York: Plume.

Gardner, H. (1993). *Frames of Mind: The Theory of Multiple Intelligences.* New York: Basic Books.

Gardner, H. (2000). *Intelligence Reframed: Multiple Intelligences for the 21st Century.* New York: Basic Books.

Multiple Intelligences, www.thomasarmstrong.com

THOMAS ARMSTRONG, PH.D.

Music

We all have firsthand examples of the mental, emotional, and physical effects of music. Music triggers memories of images and feelings. We intuitively listen to music that helps us energize or relax. Science has verified these experiences and established that music alters multiple physiological and psychological parameters that impact cognition and emotions. Music affects the chemistry and rhythms of the brain and body, patterns and frequency of neural firing in the brain, and creates changes in emotional and physical states.

Music Instruction and Academics

Harvard psychologist Howard Gardner endorses music as a form of human intelligence speculating that it is the earliest of the **multiple intelligences** to emerge. The recognition of music as an innate human intelligence and the prominence of music as a universal mode of expression justify unconditional inclusion of music education in schools. Beyond the intrinsic value of music, there is evidence that music instruction strengthens skills necessary in academic endeavors. A 1980 survey of thirty six published and unpublished studies by James Hanshumaker established that learning and practicing music significantly enhance reading readiness, language acquisition, verbal skills, motor development, creativity, and personal and social growth. The survey noted greater student motivation and lower middle school truancy rates.

Norman M. Weinberger, professor of neurology and biology at the University of California-Irvine, identified skills acquired through music instruction that are basic to various academic domains. These include development of the sensory and perceptual systems (visual, auditory, kinesthetic and tactile); the symbolic and linguistic arenas of cognition; the movement planning, muscle action and physical coordination networks; feedback and evaluation systems; and motivation skills. Weinberger points out that music involves repeated practice, resulting in continual strengthening of synaptic connections between the networking brain cells that support these skills. When students learn and practice music they are reinforcing brain connections useful in many academic areas.

Neuroscience has discovered that synchronous neural firing in multiple areas of the brain is characteristic of higher thinking skills and is stimulated in music listening and performance. The fundamental music elements, such as pitch or rhythm, are processed by networked groups of neurons in different areas of the brain including the cerebellum and regions of the frontal, parietal, and temporal lobes. Both left and right hemispheres are involved. Music listening and performance activates these associated neural groups simultaneously. This neural firing across multiple brain sites is called *neural synchrony* and is believed to assist the brain with pattern recognition necessary in cognition and memory.

Prominent research has specifically correlated music instruction with language development and increased abilities in certain spatial-temporal reasoning tasks. The College Board reported in 1999 that students with one half-year of music instruction demonstrated an average 7- to 10-point increase in verbal and mathematics test scores, respectively, over students not exposed to music. The report shows these benefits improve over time. Four years of music instruction resulted in average gains of 58 points in verbal test scores and 39 points in math scores. Music lessons in early childhood that include keyboard instruction and singing have demonstrated significant increases in test scores, specifically mathematics and language comprehension. Improvements have been noted in mathematics even when music lessons reduced the amount of time spent on direct math instruction.

Music and Spatial Reasoning

Scientists have detected similarities in neural firing patterns between spatial-temporal reasoning skills and high-level brain functions including music, math, and chess. Physicist Gordon L. Shaw and mathematician Xiaodan Leng theorize the presence of cortical structures pre-disposed for development of specific firing patterns. They believe early music instruction accesses and reinforces the inherent firing patterns related to spatial-temporal reasoning. This strengthens pattern development within the specialized cortical building blocks designated for spatial skills and makes it easier to accomplish spatial tasks. In studies with preschool children Shaw and cognitive psychologist Frances H. Rauscher concluded that learning music keyboards in early childhood stimulates greater capability in the spatial task of mental object rotation, particularly important in understanding proportional math. Providing early music instruction may be a natural way of building the necessary cortical hardware for working with fractions, ratios, and other spatial math operations.

Music Instruction and Language

Scientists generally agree that music is an intrinsic human function that supports verbal communication. Hearing is the first sense to develop in the womb, establishing brain structures for processing sound. The idea that we are pre-wired for musical development is further suggested by the fact that even six-month-old infants recognize tunes and detect small changes in melody. Some researchers theorize that music is a pre-language communication.

Brain imaging has affirmed the link between music and language by confirming certain jointly shared processing structures. The part of the right hemisphere sensitive to musical pitch also reacts to pitch in speech. The left hemisphere section of Broca's area recognizing verbal incongruity responds to inappropriate sounds and chords in music. The same left brain region designated for split-second discrimination between sounds like "pa," "ba," or "da" is activated during music listening. When musicians read music the area in the right hemisphere responsible for reading text is stimulated.

Language text-reading and reading music notation involve very similar processes. Many of the skills developed for music are required for language and reading. Symbol decoding, phonemic awareness, sight identification, orthographic awareness, and cueing systems awareness are among the language abilities learned in music instruction. Pitch discrimination, a primary component in music education, stands out as an important common element between music and reading. The second stage in the reading acquisition model developed by cognitive psychologist Uta Frith requires readers to associate a letter with the corresponding sound or phoneme. Readers must be able to distinguish between pitches in this step. Beginning readers with strong ability to identify pitch differences have higher reading scores than readers who experience difficulty.

Educators can use the relationship between music and language to students' advantage. Pre-K children and beginning readers benefit from music education that builds rhythm, pitch, and melody skills. Rhymes, chants, songs, and rhythmic movement are highly effective music activities that can be integrated directly into language and reading programs. Academic benefits from these activities have also been noted in secondary language classes.

General classroom teachers can use content-oriented songs to help students remember important facts while strengthening language abilities. Student- or teacher-written songs using academic content for lyrics and set to familiar tunes help with recall. Chunking information into short, memorable verses with a repeated chorus of essential content assists with semantic memory. The melody acts as a carrier of the information and triggers recall. Student involvement in writing the lyrics motivates participation and further enhances memory.

Raps engage semantic memory and can also stimulate students' procedural knowledge. The rhythmic emphasis can trigger movement-oriented neural pathways. Raps have special appeal to secondary students. Student-written raps are often quite complex and include a great deal of content information.

Simple rhythmic raps using key terms can be chanted in basic musical meters. An example for a lesson on atomic particles is:

e-lec-tron-******-**neg**-a-tive-******

pro-******-tons-are—**pos**-i-tive-******

neu-******-trons-******-**neu**-******-tral-******

In this 4/4 meter example (four beats to a measure), the asterisks represent a half-beat rest. Bold syllables are accented to help hold the rhythm. This rap could be chanted in unison, as a round, or with groups of students chanting each line at the same time.

Music Education in Schools

Administrators are encouraged to prioritize music instruction as an academic essential. Maintaining or expanding existing programs with music education specialists can facilitate academic improvements in proportional math, reading, and higher thinking skills. Music education methods, like the Kodaly and Kindermusik systems, that emphasize singing and include concrete body involvement when teaching pitch, rhythm, and rhythmic patterning are most effective in building language skills. Music therapists have developed techniques to assist with specific populations and classroom challenges that offer unique strategies for facilitating reading and special education programs.

Programs demonstrating improved academic abilities through music study have incorporated music from two to five days per week. One year of instruction has not proven to offer substantial long-term results. While research has not provided definitive specifics on optimal years of music study or at what age music instruction should begin, results from SAT test scores correlated with instruction show the greatest advances occur after four years. Pre-school music instruction will provide special benefits in neural pattern development but music instruction at all age levels demonstrate benefits.

Music Listening and the Brain

Neuroscience has documented physiologic changes in the brain and body during music listening that impact **attention**, energy, and attitude. Music can be used as an effective teaching and classroom management tool for gaining and holding student attention, motivating student participation, increasing attention span, stimulating **creativity**, assisting in memory and recall, and building classroom community. All teachers, even those with no musical training, can play appropriate recorded music to enhance students' ability to learn, remember, and create.

Music listening has been attributed with enhancement of learning in a variety of ways. Brain imaging shows that certain music helps students attain a coherent brain and body state that increases focus on learning tasks. French physician Alfred A. Tomatis discovered that the higher frequencies in music overtones provide electrical stimulation to the brain that heightens attention and has effects throughout the body. Some music, including certain Mozart selections, activates a brain area used when working with short-term memory and is theorized to result in enhanced recall. It is also hypothesized that music stimulates firing in the 4 Hertz low frequency theta wave range essential for memory encoding by the hippocampus. Research does not support that listening to recorded music has the same degree of effect on cortical pattern development for spatial reasoning that is attributed to active music participation, but it is hypothesized that there is some strengthening of neural networks and firing patterns derived from music listening.

The use of recorded music for classroom management requires that teachers understand the effects of music, techniques for implementing music in the learning environment, and how to select music appropriate for desired results. Recorded music becomes less than effective if played indiscriminately or if inappropriately selected.

Basic physics laws are used in music therapy to understand how listening to live or recorded music affects the mind, body, and **emotions**. The principle of musical entrainment explains changes in physical and mental states. Derived from Latin, entrainment means *to bring along with* and accurately defines how the rhythm, tempo, and feel of music can bring us to different moods or energy levels.

Upbeat music prompts changes in body rhythms by engaging rhythmic entrainment to help students re-energize or maintain focus. The effect can alter neurochemistry through the release of adrenaline and cortisol. These hormones heighten attention levels in the brain and body and, in appropriate amounts, enhance learning tasks. Conversely, slow, calming music increases parasympathetic system activity and entrains listeners to a relaxed state. This music can also induce the release of the neurotransmitter acetylcholine, important in long-term memory formation and found in higher levels in the afternoon and during **sleep**.

Under stressful situations cortisol and adrenaline levels rise and can inhibit memory and learning and cause damage to physical systems. Chronic **stress** destroys brain cells in the hippocampus causing deterioration of declarative memory and hampering explicit memory. High adrenaline levels can inhibit activity in the left pre-frontal cortex, an area responsible for maintaining positive feelings. This shut-down results in development of negative expectations that discourage learning. Listening to music can lower cortisol and adrenaline levels, reducing stress effects. It can shift negative mood states to more positive moods that promote learning. College students ranked music third of twenty-one anxiety mood regulators indicating that students intuitively seek to reduce stress with music.

Gaining and holding student attention requires lesson-planning that considers daily mind and body rhythms. Playing music as students enter the classroom, during breaks, to cue transitions, or for project work, sets the mood for a positive, low-stress environment and reduces the negative effects of stress. During low-energy times of day or following long periods of academic focus, play upbeat music to re-energize mind and body for more effective learning. Novelty and change are recognized as important elements of attention regulation. Music is a fun classroom management tool for gaining student attention. Short snippets of music used for classroom transitions will cue students when it is time to leave, begin class, take a break, return to work, or for other tasks. For example, playing the theme from the Pink Panther movie can cue students to quietly line up for lunch while "Rock Around the Clock" lets students know when it is time to begin the next classroom activity. Background music played as students read, write, or study can extend attention span if not overused.

The principle of habituation is important to effective classroom music use. The brain determines if a stimulus is critical to survival and whether or not it deserves attention. When music is over-used and played continually for long periods of time habituation can occur as the brain decrees the sound insignificant and filters it out. Purposeful use of music at periodic intervals is more effective than constant sound.

Generally, music quickly shifts attention and mood but sometimes change does not occur immediately. The *iso principle,* referring to "equal" in Greek, explains why at times teachers may need to play music that matches an existing mood or attention level and gradually shift to music matching the desired state. For example, a first grade teacher wanting to calm students after recess can use the iso principle if students have difficulty slowing down. The teacher matches the high student energy with a short selection of upbeat music, sung or played as students enter the classroom. This is followed with somewhat slower music and concludes with a slow, relaxing selection. This gradual calming process helps students entrain to a focused attention state and need only take three or four minutes.

A successful technique using music to assist in teaching course information originates from the Accelerated Learning model, developed by Bulgarian doctor Georgi Lozanov as Suggestopedia in the 1970s. His lesson-planning design includes the use of content "concerts" of essential lesson information read over background instrumental music. The content may be formatted as vocabulary words and definitions, metaphorical stories, important text, short plays, quotes, or facts. These concerts generally involve only the basic information in concise presentation. Ensuing activities elaborate further.

The Accelerated Learning model uses two distinct concerts to access different information processing modes through brainwave state and attention level. An Active Concert initiates an active beta brainwave mode while the Passive establishes a calm alpha-theta brainwave state referred to as relaxed alertness. The concerts are presented during a lesson or unit when the learner will benefit most by accessing the information in the associated state. The Active Concert introduces content information at the beginning of a lesson to stimulate attention levels as a way of helping students establish neural connections for the new information. The Passive Concert is most often presented at the end of a lesson and serves as a review. Passive Concert music assists students by encouraging a relaxed state of internal focus that provides an opportunity for reinforcement of neural connections and networks established during previous learning experiences.

When selecting recorded music, consider the energy level needed for classroom activities, matching music to the desired level. Tempo, rhythm, and dynamics are key elements but mood is equally important. Is the music bright and happy, calm and reflective, energized and dynamic? Does the music make you want to move or be quiet? Generally, the way music makes you feel is how it will affect your student although individual mental associations can impact music experiences. Emotion provides a strong memory hook that can be beneficial in learning. Music with strong emotional context can be highly effective in helping students remember content, but if you do not want to initiate emotional reactions, use music with a more neutral emotional tone.

The majority of recorded music for classroom use is instrumental. Many musical styles are effective. Classical music is recommended for encouraging focus. Concerto and symphonic works of the Baroque era by composers like Bach and Handel and Classical-era music of Mozart is commonly used. These styles have predictable harmonies and consistent rhythms effective for regulating and holding attention. This music works well for setting a positive learning environment, welcoming students to class or playing during breaks, and as students are leaving. If energy levels are low use the faster movements from 100 to 150 beats per minute. During reflective activities, or when a quiet but attentive state is optimal, the slower movements are best, around 50 to 75 beats per minute. Slow movements are often named by tempo markings like largo, adagio, or lento. Moderato is a medium tempo while allegro and allegretto are fast. Romantic, Impressionistic and contemporary classical music varies greatly and may be especially useful in setting specific moods related to course content. For example, Gustav Holst's *The Planets* provides interest when studying astronomy.

New Age music offers a wide range of options for setting moods and facilitating relaxation. Solo piano is often reflective. Big Band and 50's music can be fun and upbeat. Incorporating music from different cultures is a positive way of incorporating diversity but cultural music has an array of effects. Celtic music is widely appreciated. Some selections are invigorating while others are reflective. Much of African music is energizing. Native American flute music is frequently calming. Using a mixture of music styles provides interest and options for energy and mood shifts. Music specialists can be invaluable in helping make appropriate selections. Recordings designed especially for classroom use are available.

Early childhood teachers have long used recorded songs to teach topics like counting, letters, and behavior. Teachers of secondary grades can use popular music, selecting songs that connect with content. For example, "The Wind Cries Mary" by Jimi Hendrix can be used to teach personification. Marvin Gaye's "Mercy, Mercy Me" relates to ecology. Contemporary music with uplifting, motivating words can be played for all grades during transitions or breaks for a change of pace and to build student rapport. Music can set an appropriate theme for a day or unit. "I Can See Clearly Now" emphasizes accomplishments while the "Mission Impossible" theme motivates when beginning a challenging lesson. Music with lyrics is generally not recommended as background to focused classroom tasks as it can be distracting. Students may be taught how to select music for learning as a way of helping them use music to assist in homework and independent learning.

See also: Classroom Management; Mozart Effect.

Further Readings

Blakeman, S.J. and Frith, U. (2005). *The Learning Brain: Lessons for Education.* Malden, MA:Blackwell Publications.

de l'Etoile, S.K. (2002). The effect of a musical mood induction procedure on mood state-dependent word retrieval. *Journal of Music Therapy* 39(2):145–160.

Hansen, D., Bernstorf, E. (2002). Linking music learning to reading instruction. *Music Educators Journal* 88(5):17–21.

Hanshumaker, J. (1992). *Music for every child.* Woodridge, CT: Schirmer Books.

Jensen, E. (2000). *Music with the Brain in Mind.* San Diego: The Brainstore, Inc.

Leng X, and Shaw, G.L. (1991). Toward a neural theory of higher brain function using music as a window. *Concepts in Neuroscience,* 2, 229.

Rauscher, F.H. (2002). Mozart and the mind: Factual and fictional effects of musical enrichment. In J. Aronson (Ed.), *Improving academic achievement: Impact of psychological factors on education* (pp. 269–278). New York : Academic Press.

Register, D. (2001). The effects of an early intervention music curriculum on prereading/writing. *Journal of Music Therapy* 38(3):239–248.

Shaw, G.L. (2000). *Keeping Mozart in Mind.* San Diego: Academic Press. http://www.mindinstitute.net

Tomatis, A. (2004). *The ear and the voice.* Lenham, MD: Rowman and Littlefield Publications, Inc.

Weinberger, N.M. (1998). Brain, behavior, biology, and music: Some research findings and their implications for educational policy. *Arts Education Policy Review,* 99, 28–36.

CHRIS BREWER-BOYD, M.A., FAMI

N

Nature of Knowledge

"What should students know and what do students really know?" These questions drive much of the debate, and expenditure, on education. They impact such issues as standards, instruction, and assessment. Yet, although frequently discussed by philosophers, psychologists and others, the nature of knowledge remains unsettled and a vexing question for educators. Nor is it always dealt with directly in the context of education because it is bound up or implied in questions about information, meaning, understanding, skill, curriculum, and more. In recent times neuroscience has been added to the mix of resources available to educators but even that has been a mixed blessing because neuroscience can be invoked and applied in many different ways and can be used to support opposing positions and points of view.

The approach taken here is based on a synthesis of ideas and research from psychology, the neurosciences, and other domains. There are three points of departure. First, the learner is not a blank slate. Every human being enters life with a repertoire of basic capacities and predispositions that are then influenced and expanded through a combination of nature and nurture. Second (and more controversial) is that although the brain "makes inner representations of reality" it is not simply a device that stores objectively true facts and categories. Rather, the brain is a patterning device so that, even if most people subscribe to a set of ideas or believe that some ways of looking at the world are "right," each individual brain must come to see the patterns and make sense of things itself. This approach is popularly called **constructivism**, though constructivism does have many faces. Third, no person is an island. Although each of us comes to know individually, it is also true that we are social creatures and that people have much in common and construct understandings and knowledge together, both directly and indirectly.

Thus there is a dance between what is sometimes called formal knowledge and the knowledge developed by individuals—what could be called personal knowledge. When educators and policy makers prescribe standards and spell out levels of accomplishment in different subject areas, they are working with formal knowledge. Yet, formal knowledge needs to be worked on and digested by learners if it is to become personal.

From Inert Knowledge to Dynamical or Performance Knowledge

Not everything that people learn is useful. In the term used by the philosopher A.N. Whitehead, much personal knowledge is "inert." It sits in the mind and is rarely called into play. Many students, for instance, can recite a math formula or describe some of the basic features of a democracy. Yet, many of those students who "learn" facts, concepts, and procedures are lost when faced with real world situations that call for the use of that knowledge. There is a wealth of evidence, for instance, that even college graduates well versed in physics fail to apply basic principles of physics to ordinary, everyday situations such as explaining what happens as a coin is tossed or in explaining the seasons. On the other hand, much that is learned is personalized in such a way that it can be used naturally and appropriately to solve problems and deal with unplanned situations in the everyday world. Geoffrey Caine and Renata Caine call this latter, useful type of knowledge dynamical or performance knowledge.

A valuable platform for discussing the limits of inert knowledge and the differences between inert knowledge and dynamical or performance knowledge can be found in the work of Howard Gardner, originator of the theory of Multiple Intelligences. He describes three types of learners:

- *The intuitive learner (or unschooled mind)* is superb at mastering a great deal of information and understanding. So, although the child's knowledge is immature or "naïve," it is used in the real world and hence is dynamical.

- *The traditional student* is one from whom educators expect memorization but no genuine understanding is guaranteed. Schooled knowledge is largely inert, surface knowledge. Surface knowledge consists of both rote remembered but relatively meaningless facts and procedures, and of concepts and procedures that are intellectually understood but which cannot be used naturally, another term for which is technical/scholastic knowledge.

- *The disciplinary expert or skilled person* is the person that understands information in a content area and can apply it. The expert's knowledge is dynamical, but within the domain of expertise it is more mature and more appropriate than the knowledge of a novice.

Note that memory researchers have long made a distinction between declarative and procedural memory. Declarative memory has to do with what can subsequently be expressed or articulated by the learner. **Procedural memory** has to do with skills and procedures that show up in performance. Educational psychologists translate this distinction into declarative and procedural knowledge. And educators, including those who refer to the neurosciences, often rely on these differences in making suggestions for instruction. In addition, several other memory systems have been identified.

The point is that none of these memory systems individually account for dynamical or performance knowledge. All memory systems work interactively in the real world of experience, even when rote memory is involved. When a math problem is being solved, for instance, a formula must be recalled—declarative knowledge, and applied—procedural knowledge. Performance knowledge is formed as a result of the interactive engagement of multiple memory systems. It is, therefore, not the same thing as procedural knowledge.

What, then, is the difference between inert knowledge and dynamical knowledge, other than the fact that one is useful in the real world and the other is not?

Dynamical Knowledge is Perceptual

Caine and Caine developed an approach to knowledge that corresponds to the distinction that Gardner and others have made. They suggest that the crucial similarity between the unschooled or naïve mind and the mind of the expert is that dynamical or performance knowledge is *perceptual* as much as *conceptual*. Appropriate action in new situations become possible because the learner has acquired new ways of seeing and perceiving the world. As performance knowledge is perceptual, it both reflects and guides the ways in which knowers internally structure and organize their worlds.

Even though young children may not grasp situations in the ways that adults do, their knowledge is being applied to whatever they experience. A cow may be called "doggie," for instance, because doggie is what the child thinks it sees. The child is developing categories and perceiving patterns, a process first described by Jean Piaget. The categories are still immature, which is why the child seems to "get it wrong" sometimes, but a child's naïve knowledge is still used for the purpose of navigating through the world.

Experts have also developed new categories and perceive additional patterns within their domain of expertise. Knowledge that is thoroughly processed and reorganized in the brain becomes perceptual, and so becomes the foundation for a way of seeing and doing. Rather than simply knowing some math, a person begins to think like a mathematician; rather than just taking photographs, a person begins to see like a photographer.

The need to grasp the inner essence of knowledge that is used in the world has prompted the examination of mental models. Mental models are the way we interpret the world, they are our assumptions and generalizations. According to organizational theorist Chris Argyris, people frequently do not behave congruently with what they say (their espoused theories) but they always behave congruently with their mental models (their theories-in-use). In short, espoused theories are part of a person's technical/scholastic knowledge because they do not actually guide or shape behavior. Mental models, on the other hand, are aspects of a person's dynamical or performance knowledge. They are perceptual in nature and guide the way that a person reads and responds to a situation.

The Feeling of Knowing

The word "knowledge" tends to be associated with the cognitive domain, as though knowing is a purely intellectual process. Nothing could be further from the truth. At the heart of expertise and skill and dynamical knowledge is what psychologist Eugene Gendlin called a felt sense or felt meaning. It is an appropriate feeling of knowing.

Everyday usage takes the feeling of knowing for granted. In story after story, in sports as diverse as baseball and billiards, there is talk of a "feel" for the game. But the term reaches into every discipline. For example, Nobel Laureate and biologist Barabara McClintock advocated getting a "feeling for the organism" that was being researched. And noted management consultant Peter Vail specifically invites people who wish to understand something in depth to get a felt meaning for it.

Caine and Caine have therefore suggested that one of the characteristics that marks a shift from inert knowledge to dynamical knowledge is whether or not a person has gained a feel for what is being learned. It is as though we come to know something with our whole body and mind. We get it "in our belly." In effect, really high intellectual standards, expertise, mastery and great skill always rely on the blending and integration of thought with a feel for what needs to be known. That integration is at the heart of the perceptual shift that must occur for performance knowledge to develop.

The notion of felt meaning helps to address the vexing question of why it has been so difficult to convert formal knowledge into dynamical knowledge, and why so much of what students learn in school remains inert. The way to gain a feel for concepts and processes, and to grasp the patterns of a domain of knowledge as they play out in reality, is through experience. Young children and experts are typically immersed in a great deal of experience in which the "stuff" to be learned is embedded and, often, examined and processed. Schools, typically, rely on the transmission of information with almost no relevant experience for learners. That is why most schools are what Marion Diamond calls "impoverished environments."

Finally, a word of caution is needed here. The feeling of knowing is complex, and by itself is never enough for the development of dynamical knowledge. First, the feeling of knowing occurs through the engagement of the entire system of body, brain, and mind, and is not simply an emotion. Second, a feeling can also be inappropriate because novices often feel that they know when it is clear that they don't. Third, an adequate felt sense develops in partnership with rigorous analysis and appropriate action. And fourth, even experts sometimes get it wrong.

Practical Implications

The distinction between inert and dynamical knowledge has significant implications for learning outcomes, approaches to instruction, assessment, and more.

Outcomes

The public needs to be clear about the type of knowledge that it wants students to have if the goal is to be dynamical or performance knowledge. As a minimum, standards need to be framed in terms of what students can do in authentic situations, and not just in terms of what they "know" and "understand." For example, rather than learning about or understanding democracy, students need to be able to function naturally and appropriately in a democracy; rather than mastering some rules of grammar, they need to be able to read and write and deal with text in both simple and complex ways in the real world.

Instruction

Technical/scholastic knowledge is an important step on the way to developing performance knowledge. So there are times when memorizing information and practicing skills and routines are essential building blocks along the way to genuine competence. However, if the desired outcome is performance knowledge, then students must also have multiple opportunities to learn from experience. Caine and Caine, therefore suggest that good instruction involves at least three interacting elements:

> Relaxed alertness, a combination of low threat and high challenge as the optimal state of mind in the leaner;

> The orchestrated immersion of the learner in complex experience in which the curriculum is embedded, with direct instruction being regarded as one element in the larger immersion; and

> The active processing of experience so that the learning is deep enough.

Assessment

Genuine understanding and performance knowledge cannot adequately reveal themselves on multiple choice tests or tests that call for written explanations. The key to knowing what students really know, therefore, is authentic assessment, a process that involves several different modes of performance to complement examinations and tests.

The nature of knowledge is a complex one, and has only been partially addressed here. Many additional questions can be asked ranging from the role of consciousness to the nature of other types of knowledge such as tacit knowledge. The essential point for educators is that a person's knowledge is not all of the same general quality. Some types of knowledge are more useful than other types of knowledge. Insofar as educators want students to be able to use what they learn in the real world, the objective needs to be the development, in the learner, of dynamical or performance knowledge—in all grades and in all subject areas.

See also: **Teaching Model for the Brain; Patterns and Programs.**

Further Readings

Caine, R., Caine, G., McClinitic, C., Klimek, K. (2005) *The 12 Brain Mind Learning Principles in Action: The Field Book to "Making Connections: Teaching and the Human Brain."* Thousand Oaks, CA: Corwin Press.

Fuster, J.M. (2003) *Cortex and Mind: Unifying Cognition.* New York: Oxford University Press.

Root-Bernstein, R., Root-Bernstein, M. (1999). *Sparks of Genius.* New York: Houghton Mifflin.

GEOFFREY CAINE, LL.M.

Nutrition

As you eat, so shall you think. Every day people make decisions about what to eat, and these foods have a direct impact on the quality of their lives. The brain needs certain amounts and specific types of nutrients daily to function properly. Too much or too little (deficiency) of any nutrient can affect the nervous system negatively.

For example, if a new mother is lacking the vitamin folic acid at conception, then spinal bifida, a nervous system disease, could occur and affect that child's entire life. Foods greatly impact which chemicals and how many chemicals are being manufactured in the brain. These chemicals control daily behaviors or states of mind.

Neurons or brain cells need the following two main fuels to function—oxygen and glucose. Neurons cannot store these fuels, rather they use them up readily. A constant supply of these fuels is required for the brain to function. This indicates that in addition to eating three balanced meals a day, the brain benefits from several small snacks so that there is a supply of glucose when needed.

The second fuel needed for brain cell functioning is glucose. Foods are broken down though the digestive process into various nutrients. Glucose is one of the key nutrients, and most foods can be converted into glucose. Scientists are learning how nutrients such as glucose alter the neural networks within the brain, and ultimately affect daily behaviors or states of mind. A person's behavior, learning, mood, intelligence, stress, sleep, disease/sickness, aging process, and energy levels have been proven to be impacted by diet.

How it Works: Nutrients to Neurotransmitters to States

After a food is eaten, it goes through a process that allows the nutrients to be used by the brain. After food is broken down within the stomach, it

Table 1. Nutrient-Neurotransmitter-State cycle how foods affect behavior

FOODS Digested	Broken Down into Nutrients Such As:	Create Neurotransmitters Such as:	Affect the Following:
	fatty acids	serotonin	memory
	sugars	acetylcholine	sleep
	amino acids	dopamine	stress
	vitamins	norepinephrine	moods
	minerals	endorphins	learning
	antioxidants	glutamate	disease/sickness
			age
			energy

These affect which foods you consume.

travels along the digestive tract where it is absorbed by the intestinal cells and then transported through blood vessels into the bloodstream. These foods are broken down into the following nutrients: fatty acids, sugars, amino acids, vitamins, minerals, and antioxidants. Now the nutrients need to reach the neurons within the nervous system by crossing over a semi-permeable membrane called the blood–brain barrier (BBB).

The BBB protects the brain by blocking harmful, toxic substances from entering the brain. The BBB allows for nutrients to pass through so neurons can utilize them, but not all nutrients make it through. This is another reason why it is so important to eat foods high in the needed nutrients so enough is available for the neurons. Once the nutrients pass through the BBB, they are available for the neurons to soak them in so that neurotransmitters, or brain chemicals, can be created within the nucleus of the neuron. There are over two hundred neurotransmitters, and at least seventy of those regulate nerve function. Some examples are: dopamine, serotonin, acetylcholine, and epinephrine. Neurotransmitters are stored in tiny sacs, called vesicles, within the axon terminal, just waiting to be released to transport a message throughout the brain and eventually throughout the body.

Neurotransmitter manufacturing can be disrupted when there is an insufficient nutrient supply. When this occurs with even just one neurotransmitter a host of cascading effects follow. The electrical message coming down the axon will not have sufficient amounts of the correct neurotransmitter at the terminal. Communication to the next neuron is disrupted and the flow of information stops. For example, if there is a deficiency of calcium then receptor sites (site on a cell membrane where neurotransmitter can bind) can be blocked so that neurotransmitters cannot make it to the next neuron. Calcium cleans out these receptor sites so strong messages can be sent.

Vitamins, minerals, proteins, and fatty acids all aid in or protect the manufacturing of the neurotransmitters. If a person's diet does not have the sufficient amounts of these helpers or protectors, then the certain neurotransmitters are not made or stored in the right amounts, decreasing optimal moods, thinking, learning, and other life functions.

In summary of the nutrient–neurotransmitter–states cycle, foods are broken down into nutrients such as fatty acids, sugars, amino acids, vitamins, minerals and antioxidants which in turn pass through the BBB to be transformed into neurotransmitters that greatly affect our everyday life functions or states of mind such as sleep, learning, thinking, aging, energy release, stress, moods, and disease/sickness.

Nutrient–Neurotransmitter–States Connections

Certain foods contain precursors or starting materials for some neurotransmitters. When a person's diet is deficient in certain precursors, the brain is not able to produce necessary neurotransmitters. All kinds of problems exist with the brain because of the imbalance of certain neurotransmitters. The manufacture of most neurotransmitters is controlled by the brain, but some are influenced by what a person eats. The manufacturing of the following neurotransmitters can be directly linked to diet: serotonin, dopamine, norepinephrine, and acetylcholine. Table 2 below shows how the foods we eat are digested into certain nutrients which are precursors for the manufacturing of neurotransmitters within the neurons. These neurotransmitters in turn create certain states of behavior.

Carbohydrates for Quick Energy

According to the current food pyramid, carbohydrates should be about 60 percent of a person's diet. Carbohydrates are not created equally. Carbohydrates are rated with glycemic index levels based on how quickly the food is broken down. Depending on the glycemic index, two categories of carbohydrates are created: simple carbohydrates or complex carbohydrates. The larger the grains in the carbohydrate, the longer it takes to break down, and therefore, the smaller is the glycemic index. Complex carbohydrates (low glycemic index foods) are better for the brain than the simple carbohydrates (high glycemic index foods).

Complex carbohydrates such as any whole grain food (100 percent whole wheat bread, brown rice, oats, whole wheat pasta, etc.) should be the "carbs of choice." A complex carbohydrate is broken down gradually giving a person a gradual rise in blood sugar and gradual lowering of blood sugar. A person feels full and can concentrate for a long period of time.

Foods that break down quickly, simple carbohydrates (such as white bread, cookies, and cakes) leave you feeling hungry, weak, sluggish, and irritable about thirty to forty-five minutes later. These foods give a person high energy because of the high blood sugar rush at first, then the

Table 2. Nutrient – Neurotransmitter – State

Foods Eaten	Nutrient (Precursor)	Neurotransmitter	States It May Bring About (The below states/conditions have many other causal factors)
Milk, turkey, complex carbohydrates	Tryptophan	Serotonin	*Just Right Balance:* calm, concentrate, relaxed
(whole wheat breads and cereal, brown rice and pasta), bananas, foods high in Omega-3s (salmon, walnuts, tuna, flaxseed)			*Unbalance of the Chemical:* Depression, insomnia, increase sensitivity to pain, drowsiness, low motivation
Protein foods (meats, tuna, cheese, eggs chicken, yogurt), almonds, beets, soybeans, dairy products	Phenylalanine Tyrosine	Dopamine which manufactures norepinephrine (also called noradrenaline)	*Just Right Balance:* Attentive, focused, decreased appetite, energized, joyful, anticipation, quick thinking
			Unbalance of the Chemical: Low motivation, depression, irritability, moodiness
Egg yolk, soybeans, nuts, whole wheat bread, lean pork, spinach, foods high in vitamin B,	Choline (member of B family)	Acetylcholine	*Just Right Balance:* Healthy brain functioning, alert, short-term memory enhanced
wheat germ, cauliflower, liver			*Unbalance of the Chemical:* Alzheimer's Disease, memory loss, dementia, reduced thinking ability

343

blood sugar drops rapidly leaving a person with less energy than when eating started. This is detrimental for learning and for the body. A small candy bar will increase energy levels for about thirty minutes, but a decrease in energy levels will follow for the next hour or two. If the person does not make an effort to eat more food to raise this blood sugar level, then the hypothalamus might signal the release of cortisol, a stress hormone, to raise energy. Cortisol in large amounts for long periods of time can kill neurons.

Proteins for an Optimally Functioning Brain

Proteins are needed to manufacture brain tissue, enzymes, and neurotransmitters that boost alertness. Carbohydrates provide quick energy, but proteins provide stamina. It is important to know how protein affects the body.

When the brain is rapidly using up its supply of dopamine and norepinephrine, it will use tyrosine supplied by the protein food to manufacture more of these two neurotransmitters. When that happens, the brain will help a person respond more quickly and with greater accuracy to mental challenges. A person will feel more alert, more motivated, more joyful, and more mentally energetic. When dopamine and norepinephrine levels drop, a person is more likely to feel depressed, irritable, and moody.

Proteins are ideal for all meals, but especially for breakfast and lunch when the brain needs extended energy to get through the rest of the day. Breakfast is the most important meal of the day. The body's glucose reserves have been relinquished because of the eight-hour fast from sleeping. To rev up those neurons, a good breakfast with several energy reserves is needed. The optimal breakfast for brain energy is to have the following: two servings of fruit or vegetable; one to two servings of high complex carbohydrate with high fiber, one serving of protein and a little bit of fat. Each one of these types of foods release energy at different times providing sustained energy release throughout the morning. To make sure that there is enough energy in the afternoon, make sure to include a protein at lunch time.

Antioxidants for Protecting the Brain

Throughout a person's life, all of the cells in the human body are bombarded by attacks from unstable chemicals called free radicals that are the result of breathing chemicals in the air around us, eating foods (notably fatty foods), and drinking water. These free radicals are formed when the mitochondria within each cell burn oxygen to make energy for the cells. Free radicals are the by-products. They accumulate over time and lead to accelerated aging and several chronic diseases.

The brain generates more free radicals than any other organ because it is comprised of 50 percent fat, and free radicals thrive on fat. The brain uses more oxygen because it is a constant hotbed of activity. The brain also contains the least amount of antioxidants, a chemical that neutralizes and kills free radicals. Free radical damage within neurons causes dendrites to retract, synapses to vanish, and can even kill neurons.

As a person ages, free radicals proliferate. Free radicals are more successful after the age of twenty-five as the antioxidants slow down their production. They can get out of control and corrupt the cell's genetic DNA causing a host of diseases like Parkinson's Disease, ALS (Lou Gehrig's disease), Alzheimer's, arthritis, cancer, heart disease, and other degenerative brain diseases. The strength of antioxidant defenses—or free radical fighters—will affect the amount of cumulative damage and potential intellectual decline.

The more antioxidants that are in the brain, the more they neutralize the destructive free radicals. Increasing intake of foods high in antioxidants has been shown to prevent and reverse memory loss in aged animals, and even retard the progression of Alzheimer's in humans. Antioxidants attack free radicals and slow the aging process of the entire body, save a body from susceptibility to genetic diseases, and save cells at all ages and in all circumstances. In fact, antioxidants repair at least 99 percent of the free radical damage to cells.

Antioxidants vary in their ability to combat free radicals. When one of them gets exhausted from destroying the free radicals, one of the other antioxidants will go in and donate an electron to help the other regain strength to finish the job. The strongest antioxidants are: Vitamin E, Vitamin C, glutathione, coenzyme Q10, and Lipoic Acid.

Antioxidants are highest in the most colorful fruits and vegetables, but most prevalent in fruits. Those people who consume a high amount of fruits and vegetables slash the risk of developing cancer in half. In the past several years, researchers have dissected fruits and vegetables to find the types and levels of antioxidants. Some of the more common antioxidants are: carotenoids, lycopene, lutein, and flavonoids. Foods highest in antioxidants include prunes, raisins, blueberries, blackberries, garlic, kale, cranberries, strawberries, spinach, raspberries, tea (black and green), red wine, and chocolate. People should strive to eat five to seven fruits and vegetables a day.

Foods not Created Equally

Not all foods are created equally. Each food has unique nutritional values. There are foods that have been proven to help prevent cardiovascular disease, type II diabetes, cancers, dementia, and hypertension. Because of the high levels of nutrients, fourteen foods were labeled as being powerful foods. They are: beans, blueberries, broccoli, oats, oranges, pumpkin, salmon, soy, spinach, tea, tomatoes, turkey, walnuts, and yogurt. Because of the BBB, we need to make sure the right amounts of nutrients are reaching the neurons. Eat foods that are highest in the essential nutrients to ensure that the nutrients make it to the brain.

Some foods are processed, changed in original form with several steps involved, and have very little nutritional value. Food additives or preservatives are added to foods to aid in appearance, taste, and shelf life. Monosodium glutamate (MSG) and tyramine (in aged cheese) were shown in research studies to greatly affect brain activity. Additives can do the following: block neurotransmitters so that the receiving neuron is unable to comprehend the message; can increase your cells' deliverance of neurotransmitters, or can affect the enzymes that normally regulate how many neurotransmitters remain in the gap between nerve cells. Eat whole, natural foods as much as possible, and little, if any processed foods.

Fats for Structuring the Brain

Dietary fats are broken down into fatty acids that the body uses for many purposes such as body metabolism and forming the outer membrane of every cell in the body, including those in the brain. In fact, the myelin sheath around the axon of the neuron is made from a waxy, fatty substance (See Table 1). It coats the axon just like a chord covers an electrical wire. This is formed from the fat that we ingest. The myelin sheath allows faster electrical transmissions throughout the brain and prevents cross communication among other neurons. It is very important that good fats are a part of every person's diet, especially younger children.

Of the many fatty acids the body uses, two are called "essential" because the body cannot manufacture them—they must be supplied by diet. Essential fatty acids (EFAs) are also called Vitamin F or polyunsaturated fats. They are found in high concentrations in the brain and a deficiency of EFAs can lead to an impaired ability to learn and recall information.

Not all fats are created equally either. There are good fats and bad fats. Unfortunately, people tend to ingest too much of the bad fat and not enough of the good fat. There are three main types of fats: saturated fats, unsaturated fats, and partially hydrogenated fats (type of saturated fat).

Saturated fats are solid fats and are found primarily in animal products. A high diet of these can impair student's ability to learn rules of a task and to remember how to apply them. Too many could raise chances of heart disease and raise blood cholesterol levels. Some examples are: steaks, butter, cheese, and the like.

Unsaturated fats are liquid fats that get thicker when chilled or stay liquid when chilled. These fats are considered "good" fats. There are two different categories of these fats: mono-unsaturated and poly-unsaturated. Mono-unsaturated fats are found mostly in vegetable and nut oils such as olive, peanut, and canola oil. These fats reduce the bad cholesterol (LDLs). These fats cannot be made by the body. Research indicates that high mono-unsaturated fat diets lower the risk of cardiovascular disease even more effectively than do the standard low-fat diets. Poly-unsaturated fat are called essential fatty acids and examples are corn oil, safflower oil, soybean oil, and omega-3 oil.

Research has come out about how little omega-3 fats people are consuming and how this deficiency affects people. Omega-3s increase the amount of acetylcholine. A Purdue University study found that hyperactive and attention deficit students had lower levels of omega-3. Omega-3 deficiencies have been tied to the following problems: violence, depression, memory problems, cancer, eczema, allergies, and more. Researchers believe that about 60 percent of Americans are deficient in omega-3.

There are two ways to ingest omega-3 fats. Plant-derived foods that are high in omega-3s are: flaxseeds, nuts (walnuts are highest), canola oil, flax oil, and olive oil. Marine-derived foods that are high in omega-3s are: salmon, mackerel, sardines, tuna, grouper, and herring.

The third and worst kind of fat is called partially hydrogenated fat or trans fatty acids. They are man-made and solid. These fats are found commonly in margarine, shortening, doughnuts, French fries, fried chicken, potato cheese, and imitation cheese. Excess amounts of this type of fat can impair neuron function and learning.

Vitamins are Vital

When the brain is not given enough vitamins and minerals, it can get the same damage caused by radiation. Brain cells lacking vitamins and minerals suffer DNA and mitochondrial damage. Multivitamins are highly recommended to ensure that the brain receives the proper nutrients. The following is some research that explains why taking multivitamins is vital.

1. Ten out of thirteen studies show that giving children multivitamins/mineral pills raises their non-verbal IQ scores as much as 30 percent, reports psychologist David Benton from Britain's University of Wales Swansea.

2. Taking multivitamins for a year boosted immune functioning and cut infections, such as the flu, 40 percent in diabetics and 50 percent in the elderly, compared with taking a placebo.

3. In a new Swedish study, men who took multivitamins had a 20 percent lower risk of heart attacks, and women had a 35 percent lower risk, than those not taking supplements.

4. Harvard studies show that taking multivitamins containing folic acid cut the risk of colon cancer by 50 percent in women with a family history of the disease.

5. Taking a multivitamin pill for more than ten years slashed the risk of clouded vision by 60 percent.

British psychologist David Benton did research that showed that a multivitamin could improve IQ scores. He gave thirty children (12 years old) a special vitamin-mineral supplement and thirty others a placebo pill for eight months. The students then took a standard intelligence test before and after these eight months. Scores on the "verbal" part of the test did not change, but scores of the vitamin-taker's "nonverbal" part soared an average of nine points compared with one point in non-supplemented kids. Vitamins did not raise verbal IQ scores because they measure achievement and reflect cultural, educational, and environmental factors. Nonverbal intelligence reflects brain potential. Benton contends the vitamins work because they correct substandard intellectual functioning due to marginal deficiencies caused by a poor diet. Brain cells starving for nutrients cannot function optimally. The conclusion drawn was that taking vitamin supplements does not push a kid's brain beyond normal capacity, but instead, the lack of the vitamins cause a youngster to perform below capacity. Since this study, there have been many other studies that support his findings.

See also: **Aroma and Learning; Beverages.**

Further Readings

Carper, J. (2000). *Your Miracle Brain*. New York, NY: HarperCollins Publishers.

Jensen, E. (2003). *Tools for Engagement: Managing Emotional States for Learner Success.* San Diego, CA: The Brain Store, Inc.

Somer, E. (1999). *Food & Mood*. New York, NY: Henry Holt and Co.

Wolfe, P. (2002). Healthy Brains for Healthy Educators. *The Health Educator.*

United States Department of Agriculture Food and Nutrition Services www.fns.usda.gov/nn/

LEANN NICKELSEN, M.ED.
WITH CONSULTATION OF RDLD DIETITIAN,
TERRI ANDERSON

O

Obesity

Today's children may be the first generation to live shorter lives than their parents, and much of this is due to physical problems associated with obesity. Obesity issues are pandemic and are affecting our children's mental and physical health. Diabetes, hypertension, and other obesity-related chronic diseases once only prevalent among adults, have now become more common in children. Today's youth are considered the most inactive generation in history caused in part by reductions in school physical education programs and unavailable or unsafe community recreational facilities. Metabolism, eating habits, exercise have all been chronicled as having a role in obesity; now with new technology we are able to examine the brain's role.

Overweight and Obesity Defined

- Overweight and obesity for children and adolescents are defined respectively in this fact sheet as being at or above the 85th and 95th percentile of body mass index (BMI).
- Some researchers refer to the 95th percentile as obesity. The centers for disease control and prevention (CDC), which provides national statistical data for weight status of American youth, avoids using the word "obesity," and identifies every child and adolescent above the 85th percentile as "overweight."
- The American obesity association (AOA) uses the 95th percentile as criteria for obesity because it corresponds to a BMI of thirty which is obesity in adults. The 85th percentile corresponds to a BMI of twenty-five, adult overweight.

Bad News for Brains

While studies have linked obesity to serious cardiovascular diseases including strokes and heart attacks, University of Toronto researchers have found that overindulging can damage overall health—from slower thinking to experiencing more pain. Figures from Statistics Canada's National Population Health Survey were used to analyze the overall welfare of Canadians from 1996 to 1997. Overweight and obese people reported slower cognitive abilities, increased pain, and limited mobility among other ailments.

Leptin is a hormone released from fat cells that signals the brain when the stomach is full. Normally it takes about ten minutes for the brain to receive the message and for the individual to stop eating. This is a strong argument for eating slowly. Regrettably obese people's brains have a difficult time interpreting leptin's message. It is unclear if this is due to the brain not receiving leptin or if it is unable to properly interpret the message. The reality is that obese people don't get the signal to stop eating, which leads to overeating. The problem then becomes cyclical. It is speculated that people go into an eating frenzy trying to get leptin to the brain. They eat more and more in an effort to get the signal that they are satiated.

The more obese a person becomes, the more they eat to get significant amounts of leptin into their brain. Research on rats and humans indicate that individuals are not born with this blockage, but instead the communication problem develops over time.

Preliminary studies show that individuals who have received leptin treatment not only had dramatic weight loss, but also experienced vivid changes in their brain. These changes occurred in the inferior parietal lobes and the cerebellum on the left side of the brain, and the anterior cingulate gyrus; all areas related to self-regulation behaviors. There was an increase in gray matter, overproduction of dendrites and synapses, in these areas. Of particular interest is the anterior cingulate gyrus, an area of the brain associated with cravings and **addiction**. The anterior cingulate gyrus and leptin may hold the key to understanding the craving for food, and drug addiction.

Dopamine and Obesity

Dopamine, a neurotransmitter that modulates motivation and reward circuits, is also likely to be involved in obesity. Dopamine receptor availability was significantly lower in obese individuals than in average weight people. Normally, eating causes the body to release dopamine. This causes the pleasurable feeling a person gets after eating a satisfying meal. The availability of dopamine receptors is decreased in obese individuals in proportion to their BMI. Dopamine and hence dopamine deficiency in obese individuals may perpetuate pathological eating as a means to compensate for decreased activation of these circuits. Strategies aimed at improving dopamine function may be beneficial in the treatment of obese individuals.

Obesity and Dementia in the Aging Brain

A study by the researchers from Kaiser Permanente and the University of California has revealed the links of obesity with risks of dementia in old age. The study found that fat people with a body mass index (BMI) of at least thirty have a 74 percent increased risk of developing degenerative brain diseases including Alzheimer's later in life. Among the overweight with a body-mass index over twenty-five the risk of dementia was increased by 35 percent. It may be possible to enhance the cognitive performance of even healthy elderly people through changes in diet and lifestyle. Recent data indicate that improved prenatal and perinatal care along with greater access to educational opportunities may result in a decreased incidence of dementia in future generations of older adults.

Impact in the Classroom

Exercise has a profound effect on weight and mood control. Studies have found that exercise influenced the activational state of synapses as well as serving as an anti-depressant. Exercise increases the release of endorphins and in turn leads to an increase in positive emotions. Studies have also shown that exercise increases a student's ability to concentrate on academic material and reduce stress. Increase exercise in the following ways:

- Use energizers in the classroom.
- Encourage students to walk to school.
- Provide physical education every day.
- Use physical activity as a reward.
- Role model good physical activity.
- Require recess at the elementary level at least once a day.

What we eat also impacts the brain. A diet high in total fat reduces hippocampal levels of brain-derived neurotrophic factor, a crucial modulator of synaptic plasticity and a predictor of learning efficacy. Eating healthy is the other important component to reducing obesity; the following are ways to facilitate this:

- Adopt a health curriculum.
- Establish healthy eating policies in the lunchroom and classroom.
- Start a school health team consisting of students, teachers, administrators, and parents.
- Eliminate vending machines with unhealthy food options and replace them with healthy choices.

See also: Anorexia; Beverages; Nutrition; Physical Movement; Pleasure and Love.

Further Readings

Gill, T. (2005). A matter of fat: Understanding and overcoming obesity in kids. *Nutrition & Dietetics: The Journal of the Dieticians Association of Australia.* 62(1):54.

Summerford, O. (2005). *Action Packed Classrooms. Strategies to Motivate and Invigorate the Learning Process.* San Diego, CA: The Brain Store Inc.

Adding an Hour a Day May Fight Childhood Obesity. http://www.azcentral.com/health/kids/articles/0907GirlsExercise07-ON.html

National Heart, Lung, and Blood Institute Obesity Education Initiative http://www.nhlbi.nih.gov/guidelines/obesity/practgde.html

Unsafe Areas and Kid's Obesity. http://www.azcentral.com/health/kids/articles/0914teenobesity0914.html

World Health Organization http://www.who.int/nut/obs.htm

CATHIE SUMMERFORD, M.S.

P

Patterns and Programs

Brain compatible learning came to the interest of the education world with the publication of several books by the late Leslie A. Hart. For educators, brain compatible learning simply means learning activities that are in sync with how the brain processes information. We know much more today about the brain's internal working through new imaging processes developed through neuroscience and the work of cognitive researchers.

The complexity of the brain challenges our imagination. The brain has hundred billion neurons and many million times more connections among the neurons, a network more complex than the entire telephone system of the world. We are still in the early stages of unraveling the mysteries of the brain. The brain appears to have two basic structures for organizing learning. It forms patterns and creates programs.

Patterns

Patterns can be described with the words: recognition, identification, and understandings. Patterns are structures in the brain for organizing information. We see this most clearly watching an infant learn. Given a stable, loving home an amazing amount of learning or understanding develops in the child's brain before school starts. By the age of five a child can distinguish between mother, sister, aunt, grandmother, woman, and friend. Interestingly, none of these concepts was taught in any formal sense. Through exposure, repetition, and endlessly varied circumstances, the **infant's brain** sorts this information into patterns readily available for use.

The brain continues on its unrelenting path of developing patterns for everything it encounters, even incidentally. If we see a table set with plates and silverware, our brains recognize it as a mealtime pattern. We have highly sophisticated patterns for faces, sounds, smells, tastes, and touches. We may recognize a face we haven't seen for five years in a crowded room because the brain connected the face to a pattern in its memory. One can only speculate how many billions of patterns or elements of patterns the brain holds.

The brain thrives on input. Amazingly, the input does not need to be highly organized and sequenced. The brain has an enormously powerful pattern detecting device. It sorts even random input into patterns if provided large quantities of details, variations of situations and ample opportunities to "play" with or manipulate material.

Patterns develop from experience. The more rich and stimulating the environment the more efficiently patterns are developed. They develop through large amounts of input to the brain. Schools must increase variety, experiences, activities, and stimulation enormously, even tenfold, for healthy brain development. Most parents know this instinctively and try to provide a great variety of experiences for their child. It also appears that the brain works most efficiently from complexity; it works better from a holistic view. Increasing age, meaningfulness and reality impact what we, that is, our brains attend to. These findings on the brain have major implications for schools.

Certainly not by design, but unfortunately, many traditional classroom practices might be described as brain antagonistic. The brain starves without massive amounts of varied, complex and meaningful input. Providing the brain with huge amounts of input is done by immersing students in issues that have meaning and emotional content for students, using real world projects, taking many field trips, hearing enlightening speakers, listening to stories and using various media—in short, what good teachers and progressive educators have advocated all along. Getting the brain's attention is what we in education call student **motivation.** The brain doesn't thrive on textbooks and worksheets. We require students to do them, but unfortunately, little enduring learning results.

Programs

The second building block in the brain is programs, which are the brain's instructional set or actions—whether to walk, read, button a shirt, or speak. Just to say the word "hot" in a whisper or a roar or to write it requires an enormous amount of different instructions for the muscles and vocal cords. Many of these programs in the brain run almost automatically once well-learned. Still, given damage to part of the brain from a stroke, the program for walking is impaired even though the muscles of the body are intact. Analogously, if a computer's program is damaged, it will not run.

Programs are learned largely through trial and error, with increasing refinement through practice and **feedback.** Humans develop and deepen thousands, perhaps millions, of programs through the reinforcement of carrying out activities many times in various ways. Think again to the formative years when a child learns to manage a spoon and to express needs through speech. The infant with constant practice comes to master these actions, thereby establishing an efficient program for each of these activities in the brain's structure.

Research has demonstrated that a more richly woven tapestry of neuronal connections for programs occurs from stimulating, active environments. Programs develop by doing, actions, projects, and practice. Schools must be experiential; a place where students invent, try their wings, build and exercise their thinking skills, talents, and abilities.

Sitting passively in straight rows kills motivation and creates discipline problems. The brain needs, indeed craves, challenges and opportunities to apply learning. In most school settings, students are like racecars at the starting line, energized and ready to go, but the flag never falls. So, they sit and sit and sit. Students must be given and assume reasonability, be encouraged to tackle new tasks, be involved in complex interdisciplinary projects and life-linked studies—in short, contextualized learning.

As an illustration of how patterns and programs interact, Leslie Hart pointed out that the three-year-old who says, "Mommy, Jimmy hitted me," demonstrates how the child's brain has extracted the past tense ending pattern though the word "hitted" has never been heard. This remarkable achievement of the brain, erroneous as it is for an irregular verb, is surpassed by an even more amazing event. The brain self-corrects the wrong pattern with only the mildest suggestion from mommy when she says, "You mean hit." A grammar lesson on the past tense would not be nearly as efficient and probably would sail over the head of the child. The child's new speaking program will soon be, "Jimmy hit me." Two other key features support the development of patterns and programs.

Safety and Security

It seems readily apparent that a student racked by anxiety, uncertainty, or fear will not be an attentive learner. Clearly, for relaxed learning, the brain requires a sense of well-being and safety. Leslie Hart created the colorful term "downshifting," to describe the brain's response to danger as one of involuntarily shifting to preparation for fight or flight rather than openness to higher levels of thinking. It now appears that the brain blocks or shunts incoming data that threatens the person's security.

This explains why the child needs to feel safe and secure to learn. Schools must accept the child as a precious and honored person and provide a kind, orderly, safe environment. The brain does not function as well for higher level learning under threat or danger. In such settings, children will accept huge challenges, but at their own pace. If the student senses lack of trust or belief in them by the teacher, less learning is the result. The brain learns best under conditions of safety and security; and, if possible, joy.

Feedback

Feedback is how the brain determines if it is successful or unsuccessful. Students, indeed all human beings, need to know if they understand or misunderstand information. Through observation and what others tell us we receive feedback on our performance. The brain refines its patterns and programs through feedback. Every coach knows the danger of practicing the wrong action and not realizing its incorrectness. That would reinforce the wrong pattern or program in the brain and make it harder to eradicate. This is, of course, true not only of physical actions but also of thinking patterns, responses, and habits.

Feedback is the mechanism for the perfection of patterns and programs. Feedback in a practical sense means suggestions and coaching at all stages of development. Even champions have coaches! The feedback must be immediate and helpful. Reflection is a powerful form of self-feedback. Most classrooms give too little time to showing students how to improve, limiting feedback to test scores and grades. Students need to be coached, given suggestions, receive peer reactions, and see the results of their efforts in important endeavors, such as teaching a younger child arithmetic. A tutor sees if a child is interested and is learning. The tutored child receives real time, real life feedback so that adjustments can be made.

Learning can be defined, therefore, as the acquisition of patterns and the development of useful programs. This constitutes learning inside the brain.

See also: **Challenges and Enrichment; Classroom Environment; Mastery; Teaching Model for the Brain.**

Further Readings

Caulfield, J., Jennings, W. (2002). *Inciting Learning: A Guide to Brain Compatible Instruction.* Reston, VA: National Association of Secondary School Principals.

Diamond, M., Hopson, J.L. (1998). *Magic Trees of the Mind: How to Nurture Your Child's Intelligence, Creativity and Healthy Emotions from Birth through Adolescence.* New York: E.P. Dutton.

International Brain Research Organization www.ibro.org

Science Daily, Brain Center Searches for Patterns, www.sciencedaily.com/

JOAN CAULFIELD, PH.D.
AND WAYNE B. JENNINGS, PH.D.

Pedagogy

Active brain imaging techniques, advances in understanding of biochemical messengers, and the ability to analyze the function of single cells are radically and rapidly transforming our understanding of brain structure and function. We can look at which parts of the brain are engaged as learners perform different tasks. As the methodology advances, increasingly we will be able to pinpoint sequences of brain structures and processes engaged while complex cognitive tasks are performed. We are on the threshold of undreamed discoveries: We are actually beginning to watch thinking!

Contrary to protestations that brain science has not advanced to a point far enough to inform educators which instructional practices to use, active brain imaging studies do provide enough information to allow us to conclude with relative certainty that some instructional strategies align well with how the brain best learns whereas others do not. Using brain-friendly instructional strategies is like swimming with the current—students learn more, and teaching and learning are more enjoyable. Using instructional strategies that are incompatible with how the brain naturally learns is like swimming against the current— teaching and learning are more of a chore and students retain less.

Principles of Brain-Friendly Instruction

Brain-friendly instruction maximizes brain engagement, creates the conditions for optimal brain functioning, and provides the learning material in ways the brain is most likely to attend to and retain. The most important principles of brain-friendly instruction can be outlined as follows:

    I. Creating Brain Engagement

    II. Optimizing Brain Function

        A. Nourishment

        B. Safety

        C. Emotion

    III. Providing Preferred Stimuli

        A. Social

        B. Novel

        C. Predictable, Meaningful

        D. Feedback

    IV. Respecting Multi-Modal Processing

        A. Multiple Intelligences

        B. Multiple Memory Systems

Books can be written about each of these principles, so the discussion here necessarily will be brief and suggestive rather than comprehensive. Further, there are many ways to implement each of these principles. The Kagan Structures and instructional methods are aligned with how the brain best learns. Structures are relatively simple step-by-step teaching/ learning sequences designed to structure the interaction of learners with the academic content, with the teacher, and with each other.

Creating Brain Engagement

If the brain is not attending to or processing the content, little learning will occur. As obvious as this is, it is the most important of all principles of brain-friendly instruction. Instructional strategies that increase engagement with the content will increase learning.

Many traditional instructional strategies ignore this basic principle. For example, the traditional teacher wishing to create active engagement asks a question of the class. Several hands go up. The teacher calls on one. That student responds. At that moment, Broca's area is engaged in the student who is responding as the student formulates her/his response, but the brains of all the other students in the class are relatively quiescent. Using a simple structure, *Timed Pair Share,* the teacher can make the same content more engaging for all learners. In a *Timed Pair Share,* students interact in pairs, one speaking and the other listening for a specified time, and then students switch roles. Using *Timed Pair Share,* in the same amount of time that the traditional teacher requires to call on and respond to two or at most three students, every student in the class has verbalized an answer. *Timed Pair Share* is one of over two hundred carefully designed cooperative learning and multiple intelligences structures designed to maximize engagement among learners.

Active brain engagement is probably responsible for much of the well-documented gains produced by cooperative learning. Cooperative learning has an enormous empirical research base and the outcomes have been very positive, including student gains in academic achievement, social skills, race relations, classroom climate, self-esteem, and empathy. Cooperative learning consistently produces powerful gains in part because it more actively engages more brains than the traditional sequential instructional strategies. But as we will see, it relates to each of the basic principles of brain-friendly instruction in different ways.

It is important to note that simply asking students to talk or work together in pairs or groups will not lead to brain engagement and gains for all students. Group work is not cooperative learning. During unstructured interaction (group work), one or a few students can do most or all the talking; there is nothing to prevent a student from disengaging and allowing their partner or group mates to do all the talking or work. Only by carefully structuring the interaction can we be sure of engagement of all students.

Optimizing Brain Function

A. Brains Need Nourishment. Brains are small—they weigh about three pounds and are approximately the size of two fists put together. Although they account for only about 2 percent of our body weight, they consume up to 25 percent of the body's oxygen and blood glucose. When brain oxygen and glucose levels drop, so does brain functioning. Increasing the supply of oxygen and blood to the brain of students in a classroom increases student alertness, sense of well-being, and learning.

Bodily/kinesthetic structures involve movement and so help nourish the brain. Cooperative learning structures include movement, interaction among students, and hands-on manipulatives. Class-building structures all have students get out of their seats and move in the classroom. There are a host of brain-breaks and energizers that take only a few minutes but dramatically increase students' energy levels. The movement and interaction integral to cooperative learning increases breathing rate and volume as well as heart rate; which in turn increases the supply of oxygenated blood to the brain. Increased blood supply to the brain also increases the delivery of glucose, the primary nourishment that fuels cognitive activity.

Take Off, Touch Down is one of the simplest of all Kagan Structures. In this structure, students stand when the instructor says something true of them and sit if it is not true. For example, an instructor wishes to poll the class to see how many agree with four alternative actions our country can take in response to terrorism. Traditionally, we would simply have students raise their hands to indicate agreement. Using *Take off, Touch Down* the instructor announces each action and students stand to express their agreement. Everything is exactly the same except now students are using a total physical response rather than just raising their hands. Why bother with something as apparently silly as *Take off, Touch Down?* My physiology friends say there is approximately 15 percent more blood and oxygen in the brain after standing and sitting twice compared to raising one's hand twice! Thus, through the structures we choose, we actually nourish or fail to nourish the brain!

B. Brains Seek Safety. Our brains have evolved to help us survive. The amygdala fires far more in response to strangers than friends, more in response to those of other races than our own race. When the amygdala fires, our adrenal glands release the peptide called cortisol, which in turn triggers a string of physical reactions including tensing of the large muscles and increased blood pressure. Heightened firing of the amygdala is associated also with the release of adrenalin and sympathetic nervous system arousal, which predisposes us to fight or flight. This fight or flight defense alarm reaction is associated with a narrowing of the perceptual field, inability to perceive subtle internal and external cues, and a general constricting cognition that makes concentration on academic content difficult or impossible. The optimal state for learning is relaxed alertness, which is accompanied by parasympathetic nervous system arousal. Parasympathetic and sympathetic nervous system arousal are mutually antagonistic, so in the face of threat we "shut down." As our bodies prepare to meet a threat, we become narrowly focused on potential threats and less able to think broadly, creatively.

The negative effects of stress are not just temporary: chronically high cortisol levels lead to the death of brain cells in the hippocampus, a structure essential for laying down new memories. The hippocampus of Vietnam veterans suffering from post-traumatic stress disorder atrophied from 8 to 24 percent and was associated with impaired ability to recall old memories and lay down new memories.

Team-building, class-building, and community-building structures and activities are designed explicitly to create social safety. The class-building and team-building structures allow students to know and support each other and to accept individual differences. Through team-building and class-building, students drop their fear of social rejection and their worry about social acceptance—they are freer to focus on the academic content. No longer fearing rejection of their ideas, students are more expressive, offering and receiving feedback essential for learning.

For example, during a team or class discussion the instructor might use *Paraphrase Passport*. The rule is simple: The right to speak is earned by accurately paraphrasing the opinion of the person who spoke just beforehand. Because of this structure, every student knows his/her ideas will be listened to and validated, creating a caring, safe context for the exchange of ideas. *Paraphrase Passport* reduces the risk students experience for sharing a new or contrary opinion. Each student knows his/her ideas will meet a sympathetic paraphrase rather than an argument or put-down. This reduction of fear frees the brain for higher level cerebral functioning. Safe students think more clearly and more deeply.

*C. Brains Retain **Emotion**-Linked Stimuli.* Brains are exquisitely designed to respond to and remember stimuli that elicit emotions. There are receptors on the cell walls of neurons that respond to ligands, neurotransmitters, steroids, and peptides. Each receptor is a single very large, complex amino acid chain molecule—some approach 3,000 times the size of a water molecule. Seventy types of receptors have been identified to date, and each responds to only one type of ligand. For example, some receptors respond to opiates (endorphins, morphine, and heroin, which make us feel euphoric), others respond to stress peptides (like cortisol, which makes us feel stressed and anxious). A neuron may have millions of receptors on its surface, different numbers of different types—perhaps 10,000 of one type of receptor and 100,000 of another. Thus, a particular neuron may be quite sensitive to one type of chemical, but relatively insensitive to another. Just as our eyes and ears sense different types of stimuli in the external world, through the receptor on their cell walls, neurons sense different types of stimuli in the internal world of our bodies—emotional stimuli. Our brains are constantly bathed in these ligands and every neuron is responding to their presence or absence. From moment to moment in the classroom, we are changing the chemical composition of brains, releasing more stress peptides by giving embarrassing public feedback or releasing more endorphins by having students do a supportive teambuilding structure.

Why is sensitivity to emotions so crucial to brain functioning? Emotions are the primitive signals that keep us alive by motivating us to flee from being bitten or eaten, care for and protect our progeny, and hunt for a tasty morsel. It is elegantly argued by Antonio Damasio that the very origin of consciousness resides in the brain's capacity for emotion. The brain naturally focuses on and remembers stimuli associated with emotions. The ability to respond to and remember what produces pain, fear, and pleasure keeps us alive. As a nation, we pay huge sums to keep our emotional reactions in tune, if only by exercising them vicariously through spectator movies, sports, and drama. That which makes us feel, is remembered.

To better understand the link between emotion and memory, we need to take a brief detour into the nature of short-term and long-term memory systems. There is very strong evidence that short- and long-term memories are based on completely independent processes. It does not surprise us to hear we can have short-term memory without long-term memory. What is shocking, though, is to learn that we can actually have long-term memory without short-term memory. Contrary to our phenomenological experience, short-term memory does not turn into long-term memory. We have independent short-term and long-term memory systems! The long-term memory system takes a longer time to consolidate (we recall better after sleeping on it). This feature is very adaptive because it allows us to give more weight to and better remember things that are *followed by* positive or negative consequences, even if those consequences occur well after the event. Injection of certain drugs *following* learning enhances long-term (but not short-term) memory, a process called retrograde memory enhancement. Retrograde memory enhancement is adaptive: if emotion follows an experience, the brain says, "This is something worth remembering." Retrograde memory enhancement has important implications for us as teachers, indicating the need to teach with emotion. *A brain-friendly classroom is one in which emotions are not avoided, but rather elicited in service of learning.* Various cooperative learning and **multiple intelligences** structures link emotions to the academic content and help students understand and deal effectively with their own emotions and those of others.

In *Agree-Disagree Line Ups,* for example, students learn to take a stance depending on their feelings about an issue, and to listen with respect to opinions of other students who hold different feelings about the issue. The instructor simply states an opinion and the students line up to indicate the degree of their agreement with the opinion, strongly agree at one end of the line and strongly disagree at the other. Students then talk to those nearest them in the line to reinforce their position and to gain fresh arguments in favor of their opinion. The line is then folded so the strongly agree and strongly disagree students interact, often using *Paraphrase Passport.* In the constructive controversy that results, students find the content more memorable, and also learn to understand better their own emotions and those of others. Anything that elicits and allows students to deal effectively with their own emotions and those of others promotes emotional literacy and emotional intelligence while making the academic content more memorable. Many cooperative learning and multiple intelligences structures elicit and help students deal with the emotional component of curriculum and so are compatible with the finding that brains selectively respond to and remember any stimuli associated with emotion.

Providing Preferred Stimuli

A. Brains Attend to Social Stimuli. In a remarkable book, *Friday's Footprint: How Society Shapes the Human Mind,* Leslie Brothers makes the case that our brains have evolved to selectively attend to social stimuli. For example, babies at nine minutes of age are much more likely to turn their heads and eyes to follow a black and white picture if the parts are arranged to resemble a human face than if the same parts are arranged randomly. Single neurons of primates respond selectively and preferentially to social stimuli. Some neurons do not respond to an inanimate object moving, but do respond to a person moving; others do not respond to a geometric form, but do respond to a form resembling a hand—and the more the form resembles a hand, the more they respond! In *Mapping the Mind,* Rita Carter displays results of active brain imaging studies that show brains are dramatically more active when learning in interaction with others than when alone, reading or listening to a lecture. Opiate-like substances are released in mammalian brains during care giving and play, explaining why these activities are so rewarding. Our brains, to a remarkable extent, are social organs.

If we naturally attend far more to social stimuli, and our brains are more active during social interaction, it makes sense to have students interact regularly over academic content—having them discuss, debate, and work together on the content. Cooperative learning and multiple intelligences structures do exactly that.

For example, if rather than answering questions alone, the instructor uses *Numbered Heads Together* to have students respond to questions, students are far more engaged. In *Numbered Heads Together* students usually sit in teams of four, each with a number: one, two, three, and four. The instructor first asks a question. The students then think, write their individual responses, and discuss their responses in their teams. This social interaction provides the kind of stimuli that brains crave.

B. Brains Seek and Attend to Novelty. The **attention** systems in the brain are activated when novel or unexpected stimuli appear. We become more alert. We attend more carefully. The evolutionary basis for this is obvious: Those animals that did not become more alert when novel or unexpected stimuli appeared, did not survive to pass along their genes! Infants become bored, habituate, when presented with the same stimuli over and over; they instantly become alert when new stimuli are presented. One of the greatest sources of novelty is other people. When we interact with others there is always new and unexpected stimuli. Part of the reason we find it so rewarding to interact with others is because we become more alert and engaged in the face of the novel stimuli they present.

Cooperative learning and multiple intelligences structures are compatible with the brain's need for novelty in two ways: First, by changing structures on an ongoing basis, the instructor is always creating novel stimuli in her/his classroom—quite in contrast to the instructor who always lectures or only uses any other single mode of instruction. Second, the structures involve interaction, and social interaction is a primary source of novel stimuli. The input and feedback of a peer is often unpredictable and so provides novel stimulation. Students are encouraged to use new and unexpected praise, and to use different gambits as they interact to keep the stimulation high. Students in classrooms in which the structures are used regularly report the classes to be more "fun." In technical terms students are telling us that structures respond to the brain's need for a regular flow of novel and unexpected stimuli!

C. Brains Seek Predictable Patterns and Meaning. Seeking patterns is one way we make sense of the world; it is related to our need for safety. For some students, a classroom is not safe unless there are predictable routines. At birth infants show a startle reaction to novel stimuli, but quickly habituate; they are seeking patterns and forming expectations. In a classic experiment babies are presented with a ball that rolls down an incline and hits a miniature bowling pin, making a loud noise as the pin falls over. The infants show a diffuse startle reaction for several trials but on subsequent trials they simply watch with little excitement. However, when the apparatus is rigged so the ball hits the pin and there is no loud noise, the babies once again show a startle reaction. The pattern is broken; the world is no longer predictable; the babies fixate, searching to make meaning of this novel set of events. We are meaning makers. With no instruction babies learn to make sense of these funny sounds we emit called words. They convert the buzzing confusion of visual stimuli into familiar objects and predictable relations among objects.

The structures respond to the need to establish patterns and make meaning in two ways: First, the structures themselves are a predictable sequence of events. Once the students know the steps of a structure like *Numbered Heads Together,* they feel secure because they know exactly what is coming next. Second, a number of structures are explicitly designed to help students discover patterns in stimuli. This of course, facilitates learning because facts learned in isolation are soon forgotten; facts that are part of a coherent whole, which have meaning, are retained. Making meaning goes beyond seeking patterns; it involves examining relationships, relating stimuli to other stimuli and categories of stimuli, and constructing conceptual models.

One of the many Kagan Structures designed explicitly to help students make meaning of the academic content is *Team Mind Mapping*. There are many forms of *Team Mind Mapping*, but a very simple form is to have students in teams, each working with a different colored marker, create one large Mind Map of the content. They begin by putting the main idea in the center of a piece of chart paper. They draw lines out from the main idea and write or symbolize core concepts. Supporting details are added to the core concepts. Use of colors, pictures, symbols, arrows, and other graphic elements offer more ways of organizing information and creating meaning than does the traditional outline. Further, in the process of negotiating agreement on how to construct the mind map, the students are more likely to discover patterns and construct meaning than if they were to work alone. Constructing meaning by processing and interacting over the content, revealing patterns and connections, makes the content memorable. This, in part, is why structures improve academic achievement. The structures are brain-compatible because they assist the brain in its natural search to construct meaning. Instruction that promotes identification of patterns and construction of meaning is brain-friendly instruction.

D. Brains Seek Feedback. The hundred billion neurons in the brain each fire not as a simple function of the amount of input they receive, but also as a function of how other neurons in the past have responded when they fired! There are feedback loops even at the neuronal level. Our brains are feedback hungry. The search for feedback is biologically rooted in our need to be an effective organism, to satisfy our needs, and to make a difference. A brain-compatible classroom is feedback rich.

The search for feedback is related also to the search for meaning. In our search for meaning, we try something and then check to see if it works. All of us are scientists from birth, conducting mini experiments to see which behavior produces which consequences.

Traditional individual worksheets or individual assignments are feedback poor. Students do not get feedback until the next day, or until after the instructor has graded the papers. But the brain seeks immediate feedback. Mastery structures like *RallyCoach* provide immediate peer feedback and are brain-compatible; they are aligned with the brain's need to receive frequent and immediate feedback.

RallyCoach is simple. Students work in pairs solving a series of problems or answering a series of questions. Student A in the pair solves or answers the first question, talking through the solution as they write it. Student B, watches and listens, and then either praises (if the answer is correct) or coaches (if A needs help). Then the students reverse roles. Student B solves or answers the second problem while A watches and listens, and then either coaches or praises. Students continue alternating roles as they work through the series of problems.

There are many advantages to *RallyCoach* over individual worksheet work, including immediate rather than delayed feedback, frequent rather than infrequent feedback, peer-based feedback, immediate and frequent reinforcement, and peer support and coaching. Students who might otherwise practice a whole worksheet wrong get immediate correction opportunities and have the opportunity to immediately practice the correct skill. Feedback-rich instruction and practice meets the basic need of all humans—to have what they do make a difference. We all need positive feedback.

Respecting Multi-Modal Processing

This last principle, respecting the ways brains process information, is the most complex. Brains are mini-modular and process different types of information with different subsystems. For example, when we engage in deductive reasoning, areas of the right hemisphere are engaged; when we engage in probabilistic reasoning, left hemisphere areas are more engaged. Further, there is almost no mutual engagement: One type of reasoning does not depend on another! To take another example, when we are asked to determine if one object is above or below another, we are categorizing objects with regard to where they are in space. This kind of categorical spatial reasoning is associated with left hemisphere activation. In contrast, when we are asked if the two objects are more or less than two feet apart, we engage in coordinate spatial reasoning that is performed in the right hemisphere. Single neurons respond to certain kinds of stimuli and not others; neuron groups are dedicated to different types of information processing. We recognize a table because of the functioning of our object recognition system; we recognize a face with face recognition neurons that are part of an entirely independent information processing system. As our understanding of brain structure and process increases, we discover the brain is incredibly differentiated, with different systems and subsystems responsible for processing different types of information. All consciousness and complex cognition is assembled.

Given the enormous complexity of the brain and the way it processes information, we might be tempted to say that inferences about the usefulness of classroom instructional strategies based on how the brain processes information are indeed "bridges too far." Nevertheless, there are a number of inferences that can be made with a great deal of certainty. The two we will examine here are the need to use multiple intelligences instructional strategies, and the need to address multiple memory systems.

A. *Multiple Intelligences.* Howard Gardner defined eight intelligences: verbal/linguistic; logical/mathematical; visual/spatial; musical/rhythmic; bodily/kinesthetic; interpersonal/social; and intrapersonal/introspective. Because engagement of each intelligence is associated with activity in different brain structures, we are actually developing different parts of the brain when we teach in ways that engage the various intelligences.

Brain plasticity can be summarized by the *use it or lose it* principle. The brain is constantly rewiring itself depending on which parts of the brain are frequently used and which fall into disuse. For example, when a blind person touches Braille dots, neurons in the *visual* cortex respond. As the visual cortex is not used, but touch is frequently used, the brain of the blind person rewires itself to make use of the unused parts of the brain. When a finger is amputated, within a few months neurons that received input from that finger are receiving input from surrounding fingers. Thus, it is not too much of a stretch to conclude that by using otherwise unused intelligences we are actually rewiring brains—developing parts of the brain that otherwise would be under-developed.

By engaging a range of intelligences through a range of multiple intelligences structures, we not only appeal to a far greater range of learners, we actually develop otherwise underdeveloped parts of the brain. Schools have implemented multiple intelligences theory in different ways and the academic and nonacademic outcomes have been extraordinary.

There are eighty-four established multiple intelligences structures, each designed to engage and develop different intelligences. For example, *Kinesthetic Symbols* is a simple structure in which learners use their hands to symbolize the content, often creating a sequence of hand movements to remember items in a sequence, like the steps of a math algorithm, the parts of a letter, or the steps in the scientific inquiry process. For example, when *Kinesthetic Symbols* are used, parts of the pre-motor and motor cortex are engaged in association with the content. This provides an alternative way to symbolize the content, makes the content more attractive and understandable to kinesthetic learners, and develops the kinesthetic intelligence.

B. Multiple Memory Systems. The brain remembers different types of information differently. For example, learning to ride a bike (**procedural memory**), remembering what we had for dinner last night (**episodic memory**), and remembering a list of unfamiliar vocabulary words (**semantic memory**), involve quite different memory systems. Procedures are usually learned by trial and error, with plenty of practice. Episodes are often remembered effortlessly, with little or no conscious intent, especially if they have an emotional component. Formal memory systems such as peg systems and other mnemonics can facilitate semantic memory. Semantic memory that is not related to a meaningful context can be quite difficult, but if semantic memory is embedded within memorable episodes, it can become effortless. Different structures are designed to address different memory systems. For examples, the *Flashcard Game* addresses semantic memory; *Simulations* address episodic memory; and *RallyCoach* addresses procedural memory.

Just as the brain processes different information differently, individuals process the same information differently and have preferences for how best to remember information. One student may remember information easily by using a memorable visual image, a second student might be more comfortable with a peg system, a third may need to draw the content, and yet another student may find making kinesthetic movements to be the most helpful. Because students have different preferred ways of processing information, using a range of structures is the approach most likely to reach the most students. As there are different brains in each classroom, we need a range of instructional strategies.

Toward a Brain-Based Pedagogy

As brain science continues to reveal how brains function, it will be increasingly clear which instructional strategies align with how the brain best learns and which do not. This in turn will allow us with increasing confidence to develop a brain-based pedagogy. Increasingly, we will align our instructional strategies with the findings of brain science and in the process transform how we teach and how students learn. At this point, however, we can say with confidence that teachers will be more successful with instructional strategies that include safety, movement, social interaction, emotion, novelty, predictable patterns, meaning, feedback, and with strategies that engage the multiple memory systems and the multiple intelligences. When we align our instruction with how the brain best learns, students not only learn more and learn more easily, they acquire a love of learning in the process.

See also: **Feedback; Patterns and Programs; Social Learning.**

Further Readings

Brothers, L. (1997). *Friday's Footprint. How Society Shapes the Human Mind.* New York: Oxford University Press.

Campbell, L., Campbell, B. (1999). *Multiple Intelligences and Student Achievement. Success Stories from Six Schools.* Alexandria, VA: Association for Supervision And Curriculum Development.

Gopnik, A., Meltzoff, A.N., Kuhl, P.K. (1999). *The Scientist in the Crib.* New York, NY: William Morrow.

Kagan, L., Kagan, M., Kagan, S. (1997). *Cooperative Learning Structures for Teambuilding.* San Clemente, CA. Kagan Publishing.

Kagan, S. (2000). *Silly Sports and Goofy Games.* San Clemente, CA: Kagan Publishing.

Kagan, S., Kagan, M. (1998). *Multiple Intelligences. The Complete MI Book.* San Clemente, CA: Kagan Publishing.

Marzano, R.J., Pickering, D.J., Pollock, J. E. (2001). *Classroom Instruction that Works. Research-Based Strategies for Increasing Student Achievement.* Alexandria, VA: Association for Supervision and Curriculum Development.

McGaugh, J.L. (2003). *Memory and Emotion. The Making of Lasting Memories.* New York: Columbia University Press.

SPENCER KAGAN, PH.D.

Physical Environment

The human brain is wired to be sensitive to the surrounding environment for signs of threat. When its attention is drawn to a perceived threat, the brain's ability to learn and remember new information may be minimized. In classrooms, real or imagined threats may be from a combination of social interactions, academic challenges, or physical elements. In the last thirty years neuroscientists have also shown that the brain's capabilities can be enhanced when it is exposed to novel, meaningful, interesting multi-sensory stimuli in a comfortable physical environment. Reducing student **stress** and creating enriched learning environments should be educators' first considerations.

Effects on the Brain

Physical survival and safety are the brain's primary goals so we are on constant alert and guard against possible harm. When we feel threatened, intimidated, not included, confused, incompetent and physically unsafe the brain shifts into survival mode. The brain sends chemical signals throughout the body and we go into the "fight or flight" reflex response. Even the anticipation of a stressful or dangerous situation can trigger the hypothalamus and amygdala to release an immediate overabundance of neurotransmitters such as cortisol and adrenaline. Heart rate, blood flow, breathing, and muscle strength increases, while the immune system, digestive systems, sex drive, and the ability to carefully process new information, diminishes. The brain focuses on immediate survival issues rather than on learning and storing new memories.

In addition to this rapid first response to threat, the brain also responds with a slower reflective response. We analyze the situation, connect the new stimuli to past, related experiences and plan appropriate responses. We try to detect recognizable patterns in the event. This can assist us in predicting what might happen next and determine an action we might take to avoid it if necessary. The greater the variety of effective problem-solving strategies we can draw upon, the more likely we are to override the stress reaction with reasonable solutions and thoughtful actions.

Students' interpretation of perceived threats in a classroom environment regulates their abilities to learn and think. While new learning often involves some stress caused by an element of risk and some degree of pressure, if the stress exists in an otherwise low threat environment learners can be motivated to try new and difficult tasks without ridicule or a lack of support. Memory is enhanced by an appropriate degree of stress and our ability to remember things may be interfered with if the stress is really intense and prolonged.

In addition to the potential negative effects of too much stress, educators can enhance learning by orchestrating a wide variety of multi-sensory experiences in an enriched environment. Neuroscientists have stated that by creating deliberate enrichment in the learning environment educators can promote brain growth and development. Studies reveal that input from the environment actually helps shape the human brain. Many studies suggest that by paying attention to the details of the physical learning environment educators can enhance learning and ultimately, students' success at school. When we learn, amazing changes take place in the brain. How a teacher goes about structuring learning experiences will affect the strength and duration of those changes. When assessing a physical environment for learning or play, one should consider the possible negative effects on the learner from physical elements, perceived social and emotional threats or restrictions. Orchestrating a developmentally appropriate enriched environment may include aesthetics, comfort, meeting basic needs, organization, and orchestrated experiences.

Potential Physical Harm and Distractions

A safe learning environment is largely influenced by physical attributes in the classroom. There can be negative effects on the learner's body from elements such as poor lighting, noise and acoustics, and air quality. Many other distractions can occur in classrooms such as inappropriately sized furniture, interruptions, and clutter.

Lighting

A learning environment with a lack of natural, full-spectrum lighting, and a dependence on fluorescent lights, has possible adverse effects on students' vision, general health, growth rates and concentration levels. In several studies fluorescent lights have been linked to triggering headaches, mild seizures, attention disorders, and hyperactivity. The flickering vibration of the light quality and the audible hum may contribute to the detrimental effects and add to distractibility. Research indicates providing full-spectrum bulbs can increase calcium absorption, lessen visual and physical fatigue, improve visual acuity, and decrease hyperactivity.

Carol Venolia, an architect interested in how buildings affect quality of life, emphasizes the need for people to get outside and be exposed to sunlight on a daily basis. Some people are particularly sensitive to the shortening of daylight in winter and suffer from SAD (Seasonal Affective Disorder). Symptoms include lethargy, carbohydrate cravings, being sedentary, weight gain, and avoiding social interactions. When we do not see the sunlight for extended periods of time we can become disoriented about the time of day and even lose a sense of direction. These same symptoms can be seen in people who have a lack of exposure to full-spectrum light.

First and foremost educators should utilize natural day lighting whenever possible. New buildings designed with the brain in mind should include windows on one or two walls, skylights, and provide overhangs or blinds to allow each teacher more control over the direct sunlight. Optimum lighting should include more ambient light produced from indirect sources (usually reflected off of the ceiling). This type of lighting is appropriate in classrooms using lots of technology and in commons areas. Task lighting and accent lighting can combat monotony, enliven spaces, and provide adequate light for specific activities and breakout areas.

Noise

Research studies on sound and noise in classrooms have determined that constant exposure to loud noises, "white" ambient noise, and a poor acoustical environment can hamper learning in a variety of ways. We rarely escape noise and the sound level is often physically harmful. High noise levels interfere with conversation, reading, thinking, or listening to music; just about everything that could contribute to our well-being. Sudden loud noises are registered by our bodies as warning signals and can trigger the reflex response. In addition, classrooms are often bombarded with constant white noise from air conditioning and heating systems, computer stations and monitors, overhead projectors, and light fixtures. Even students with normal tolerance levels and attention spans often have difficulty filtering out this ambient noise and complain of being fatigued, having headaches, and not being able to concentrate.

If unable to eliminate it, educators can try to mask background noise by playing soft music or introducing a small fountain or fish tank to produce some environmental sounds. Use area rugs on the floor and fabric or tapestries on walls to help soften as many hard surfaces in the classroom as possible to improve acoustics. Teachers should orchestrate a variety of times during the day for quiet reflection or silent reading and studying. Many schools emphasizing brain compatible strategies have also placed restrictions on intercom interruptions and when outdoor maintenance (such as leaf blowers) can be used around classrooms.

Air Quality and Temperature

A classroom that is either too hot or too cold may be uncomfortable to students and distract from learning. Students may be groggy or sleepy if the room is too stuffy. Good airflow and a constant room temperature of 68–72 degrees have been reported to enhance learning for most students. Consider using a room ionizer to enhance the air quality.

Aromas—Introduce some scents to make the classroom pleasant smelling. Using mild lavender, lemon, cinnamon, or peppermint aromas can reduce anxiety and encourage attention.

Visual Stimulation and Clutter—In some classrooms, teachers let the massive amount of materials, resources, and student examples become unorganized and overwhelming. There is a great concern for what the surrounding environment is teaching. While an enriched environment is conducive to learning, a cluttered classroom can harbor massive amounts of dust, mold, and even critters. The visual stimulation may be too distracting to many students. An interesting and challenging environment should not bombard young brains with too much of a good thing. Poor physical conditions in classrooms can have a negative effect on student learning and behavior and can promote absenteeism and vandalism. It is believed that approximately one-third of all public schools in the United States were in need of extensive repair. As we examine student success, and orchestrate high standards, the physical learning environment must become a greater priority.

Restrictions and Limitations

Being able to satisfy basic needs is a necessary survival strategy, and if not attended to in a timely manner, can disrupt the learning process. When students perceive that water, food, and even bathroom breaks will be limited, they may have anticipatory anxiety about when those survival needs can be met. Fresh water should be easily accessible. Scheduled times to eat healthy snacks should be consistent. Reasonable restroom breaks should be allowed.

The size of the physical classroom can have an influence on students' brains. When there is more space, teachers can design a variety of flexible areas. Smaller meeting and individualized work areas allow students to seek out comfortable safe places to work and get help. Different places for active and passive learning activities decreases rigidity and provides some choice for students. Physical activity is essential in promoting brain growth. Schools need less restrictive spacious areas where students can move. In addition to attending to form and function, the scale of the classroom design and furniture needs to be body compatible. When desks and chairs are not ergonomically correct it can affect health and cognitive functions.

Social and Emotional Threats

Bullies, "put downs," lack of inclusion, and confusion can all contribute to an insecure learning environment. Educators must attend to building a sense of belonging so that students feel supported and cared about within the classroom community of learners. Adult help and supervision should be highly visible. A high priority should be on the development of systems and procedures that alleviate ambiguity and confusion. When students know what the agenda is and what the expected behaviors are, they are able to attend to learning rather than worrying about what they should (or should not) be doing.

Enriched Environments

Brains are known to grow and develop when exposed to an enriched environment. In addition to basic needs being met and a steady source of positive emotional support, there are many qualities that teachers and parents can deliberately orchestrate. Children should have opportunities to choose from a variety of age-appropriate novel challenges. Adequate materials and resources need to be available that are appropriate to the developmental and language needs of the learner. Children should have experiences to develop mental, physical, aesthetic, and emotional skills as well as have many opportunities for social interactions. Perhaps most importantly, brain compatible classrooms should be environments that allow children to be active participants and promote exploration and the joy of learning. Enriched learning environments give children a chance to make mistakes without ridicule, assess their own results of their efforts, and to modify and try again. Deliberate enrichment includes activities that are fun, interesting, and exciting to a child. They provide challenge and stimulation and require active involvement.

Keeping kids, and their brains, feeling safe and secure has to be our first and foremost goal if we want to maximize learning. Professionals need to understand the difference between classrooms and brain-compatible learning spaces. Schools should be designed that meet the curriculum needs of students, as well as be "teacher friendly" schools. School planners should be concerned about safety and security, plenty of natural light, manageable circulation (movement) patterns, aesthetic designs, appropriate scale, access to the outside, and flexible spaces. These modifications can be made to the physical environment by providing low threat, comfortable settings where challenging tasks, curiosity, and engagement abound.

See also: At-Risk Behavior; Attention; Challenge and Enrichment; Classroom Environment; Emotion; Proactive Classroom Management. Teaching Model for the Brain.

Further Readings

Clayton, M.K., Forton, M.B. (2001). *Classroom Spaces That Work.* Northeast Foundation for Children, Greenfield, MA: Stenhouse Publishers.

Jensen, E., Dabney, M., Markowitz, K., Selso, K. (2003). *Environments for Learning.* San Diego, CA: The Brain Store.

Kaufeldt, M. (2005). *Teachers, Change Your Bait! Brain-Compatible Differentiated Instruction.* Norwalk, CT: Crown House Publishing.

Le Doux, J. (1996). *The Emotional Brain.* New York: Touchstone.

Sylwester, R. (2000). *A Biological Brain in a Cultural Classroom.* Thousand Oaks, CA: Corwin Press.

Wolfe, P. (2001). *Brain Matters: Translating Research into Classroom Practice.* Alexandria, VA: Association for Supervision and Curriculum Development.

Burch, L. (Architect and Vice President 3D/I). "Brain Compatible Learning Environments" www.3di.com

Diamond, M. Ph.D. (Neuroscientist UC Berkeley) Brain Connection www.brainconnection.com/topics/?main=conv/diamond

Fielding, R. (Educational planner and architect) "Lighting the Learning Environment." www.DesignShare.com

Lackney, J.A. (Professor, University of Wisconsin-Madison, architect)
www.engr.wisc.edu/epd/faculty/lackney_jeffery.html
Tanner, C.K. Ph.D. School Design & Planning Laboratory, The University of Georgia
www.coe.uga.edu/sdpl/sdpl.html

MARTHA KAUFELDT, M.A.

Physical Movement

Neuroscience supports the link of physical movement to learning. Important aspects of physical movement increase learning: preparing and developing the brain for learning, being physically fit to learn, and reinforcing cognition using movement designed to rehearse and anchor learning. The physical condition of the body and the way the body moves affects the way the brain thinks. The brain and body connect to navigate the environment by predicting, planning, and executing physical movements. The brain uses this framework to sequence, order, practice, and rehearse cognition. Being physically active prepares the brain for learning by increasing oxygen and glucose to feed the brain nutrients and by integrating, organizing, and energizing key components of brain function through physical activity. Learning academic concepts kinesthetically through physical movements using games, activities, and lessons reinforces memory and retrieval and allows the student to rehearse the learning in a non-threatening environment.

Physical Movement and Brain Development

Brain development corresponds to and depends on physical movement as body and brain systems connect from infancy to adulthood preparing the brain for cognition. Proper functioning, enrichment, and remediation of these systems are critical to a child's ability to learn.

Physical movement activities are designed to develop necessary components that enhance whole brain learning and to access the parts of the brain that may be otherwise underdeveloped. Each component is important to build the framework for learning. These components are described in the following passages.

Vestibular Activation and Spatial Awareness

The vestibular and cerebellum systems (inner ear and motor activity) are the first systems to mature. These two systems work closely with the reticular activation system (RAS system) located at the top of the brain stem and is critical to our attentional system. These systems interact to balance, turn thinking into action, and coordinate moves. Physical movement activities like rolling, jumping, and spinning stimulate inner ear motion. These movements aid the brain in putting numbers or letters in sequence, discriminating different sounds, placing letters and words on a page, and writing letters in proper proportion. For example, a series of vestibular balance exercises similar to those found on a typical playground during recess helped dyslexic students to improve reading skills at a greater rate. The results were said to be the closest thing to a cure yet.

Cross Lateral Movement

Crossing the midline of the brain and body facilitates neural activation allowing the brain to process information efficiently. Information in the brain travels back to front across the motor cortex, side to side across the corpus callosum, and up and down from the brain stem to the top of the frontal lobe. The action of crossing the midlines lays the framework for learning. Mastering crossing the midline can facilitate the ability to see words and letters on the page, track and trace letters and words, group like objects and organize thoughts.

Motor Skill Development

The brain uses its motor skills as a framework for learning. Motor skills enable the brain to put patterns into sequence. There are three basic human motor movements: walking (crawling is the prerequisite), rolling, and jumping. These basic motor skills simulate the way the information flows in the brain: walking sends information back to front, rolling sends information side to side, and jumping sends information up and down in the brain. When motor skills are mastered, the brain has the ability to put letters into words, numbers in sequence and groups. The motor skill of skipping signals reading readiness, indicating that the brain has mastered putting mature motor patterns into a complicated, coordinated sequence.

The cerebellum is the part of the brain instrumental in physical movement and motor skills. It is the brain region that controls balance, coordination, and agility and is also instrumental in the reading process. The cerebellum has one-half of the brain's neurons even though it is only one tenth of the brain's volume. Brain imaging shows that most of the energy from the cerebellum is output and not input. Physical movement and motor activity initiated in the cerebellum is preceded by quick thought that problem-solves, plans, and executes the movement. This ability of the brain to put patterns into an ordered sequence builds the framework for the brain to puts patterns like letters or numbers into an ordered sequence. Physical movement connects the brain and body to rehearse tasks needed for cognition.

Sensory Integration

The physical movement skills of spinning and rolling and jumping integrate the visual, auditory, and kinesthetic systems. The senses are enhanced and coordinated as students move through space at different levels, speeds, and positions. The central nervous system matures from the center of the body out to the extremities. Joint compression while jumping activates and develops the nerves along the extremities as students bounce on a hoppity hop or jump and land. This coordination of bodily systems prepares the brain to coordinate, and organize thoughts.

Eye Tracking, Ocular Fitness Exercise, and Peripheral Vision Development

Vision is affected in early brain development when physical movement is impaired causing inadequate peripheral vision function. A critical period of vision development is in the first six months of life. Some infants are kept in baby carriers or car seats for long periods of time and not given equal time to lie on their stomachs. This inhibits the ability of the infant to lift his/her head to look around to develop muscles needed for vision development.

The lack of eye fitness affects the ability to read. The average American child watches a TV or computer screen on an average of three hours a day. The prolonged staring locks the eyes into a state of constant distant vision and the muscles that control eye movement may begin to weaken. Physical movement provides an avenue for specifically strengthening eye muscles. Tracking exercises, manipulatives, navigation activities, and target games exercise the eye muscles making the eyes fit to read.

Physical Movement and Physical Activity

When humans exercise, the body/brain goes into a homeostatic state, balancing brain chemicals, hormones, electricity, and system functions. When the body/brain is out of balance because of poor nutrition and lack of physical activity, the student is not in a good learning state. Movement, physical activity, and exercise change the learning state increasing one's ability to retain or retrieve memory. The beneficial effects of physical activity may last for a thirty to sixty minute period depending on the student.

Neuroscientists recognize that students who exercise do better in school, lifelong fitness boosts brain function, movement anchors learning as more of the senses are involved, and that which makes us move is also what makes us think. Numerous studies support the link of movement and physical activity to cognition.

Exercise Grows New Brain Cells

Running and other aerobic activity promotes brain cell regeneration (neurogenesis) in the hippocampus learning and memory center. A Japanese study suggested that daily exercise can increase memory retention because exercise strengthens secondary dendritic branching, the brain's mechanism to remember details.

Exercise Boosts Brain Function

Exercise triggers the release of a brain derived neurotropic factor (BDNF) that enables one neuron to communicate with another. Students who sit for longer than twenty minutes experience a decrease in the flow of BDNF. Educators should provide physical movement opportunities during the school day for a brain break, for consolidation and review of concepts, and to motivate students to learn.

Exercise Reduces Stress

Mental stress and anxiety can rob the brain and body of adequate oxygen by interrupting normal breathing patterns. However, studies also indicate that exercise can enhance oxygen flow, thereby reducing heart rate and anxiety. Aerobic activity releases endorphins—the class of neurotransmitters that relax us into a state of cortical alertness and reduce the symptoms of depression.

Vigorous Exercise Helps ADHD

Vigorous exercise helps students with ADHD to focus attention longer and self monitor behavior. Exercise puts the brain into optimal function and its positive effects lasted thirty to sixty minutes depending on the student.

Lifelong Fitness Makes the Young and Aging Brain More Resilient

Physical movement in the form of aerobic exercise actually slows the decline of brain density in white and gray matter areas of the brain as we age. Among older adults, aerobic exercise (activities such as walking, jogging, running in place and jumping jacks) helps preserve white and gray matter density in the brains frontal, temporal, and parietal cortexes, areas vital to higher-order thinking.

Fitness Levels Correlate with Student Achievement Levels on Standardized Tests

A 2002 California study shows that physically active kids perform better academically. The statewide study provides compelling evidence that the physical well-being of students has a direct impact on their ability to achieve academically. The results indicate that students achieve best when they are physically fit.

Proper Nutrition Improves Performance

Participation in school breakfast programs is associated with significant improvements in academic functioning. Missing breakfast may be associated with reduced cognitive performance. Schools with proportionately large numbers of students who engage in weekly physical activity and who ate nutritiously have higher Academic Performance Index scores. Good physical health improves grades, school attendance, and school success.

Investing in the health needs of early childhood students has profound effects on school readiness and early learning. Secondary students who reported recurrent health problems also reported school failures.

Recess/Play Can Increase Attention

The brain needs recess. The brain shifts its attention and focus about every ninety minutes. Even a short break from focused concentration allows the brain to consolidate information for better retention and retrieval of memory. Using physical movement in the classroom gives the brain that opportunity.

The play process uses methods of observation, visualization, communication, imagination, creativity, cause and effect, and problem-solving. Play helps to create mental pictures using different perceptions that will aid in reading and writing concepts. In play situations children often operate beyond their average age mentality or behavior. Social skills are increased among players. Using physical movement in play creates a healthy, imaginative non-threatening environment to try out higher level thinking processes.

Physical Movmement and Learning

If students learn through movement, then how does that translate to classroom practice? Teachers can incorporate activity and physical movement by using kinesthetic teaching strategies to teach academic concepts. Some of the activities may be short brain breaks that increase blood flow to the brain, while others reinforce concepts without breaking the flow of the lesson. In the same way that classroom teachers use movement to anchor learning in the classroom, physical educators integrate academic content using physical education concepts to put learning into action in the gym. Students find meaning and purpose in the learning as teachers build bridges from the classroom to the gymnasium and vice versa. For example, as the physical educator works on motor skill development, the teacher may see improvement in reading or spelling.

An example of a kinesthetic activity is "Action Punctuation" used to reinforce punctuation concepts in a fun way. Students work cooperatively to create an action and a sound for each punctuation mark. As the teacher reads a story, the students use the whole body to act out the punctuation marks.

Another example is reviewing geography map skills. Students use body mind mapping to represent a globe. They raise the right hand to represent North America, touch the nose to represent Europe, raise the left hand to represent Asia, touch the waist to represent Africa, touch the right knee for South America, touch the left knee for Australia, and waddle like a penguin to represent Antarctica singing the continents to the tune of "Are You Sleeping?"

The physical and cognitive systems interact to anchor learning. Physically fit students are more receptive to learning and physically fit students who move to learn have an advantage in learning. When healthy active students use physical movement to understand concepts, the concepts are better learned and remembered because they are processed using the whole body and the whole brain. Activity time in the classroom and reinforcement of academics in the gym involves the whole child in the learning process and does not sacrifice precious instructional time. Accordingly, schools should provide time during the school day for exercise, physical activity and movement by providing recess and physical education and add time for kinesthetic activities in the classroom. The evidence is clear. Exercise helps the brain to grow and learn and a large majority of students learn best kinesthetically.

See also: **Early Childhood Brain; Physical Environment.**

Further Readings

Ayres, J. (1996). *Sensory Integration and the Child.* CA: WPS Publishing.

Blaydes Madigan, J. (2000). *Thinking on Your Feet.* Murphy, TX: Action Based Learning.

Dennison, P., Dennison G. (1986). *Brain Gym* (Teacher's Edition). Ventura, CA: EDU-K Publishing.

Jensen, E. (2005). *Teaching with the Brain in Mind* (2nd ed.) Alexandria, VA: ASCD publishing.

Action Based Learning www.actionbasedlearning.com

JEAN BLAYDES MADIGAN

Play

One of the most intriguing questions in the study of the brain is how the play of children affects their brain development. It is well known that young animals of many species engage in play, including human young. Indeed, play is such a pervasive characteristic of children that it is the topic of many books and education texts, and its many forms have been observed in numerous research studies. While play decreases with maturity in many animal species, in humans, play extends throughout life in various forms. Researchers have seen both animal and human play as adaptive for the species; thus, the brain must be involved in this behavior. Exactly what the connections are between play and the brain is only beginning to be explored.

Many psychology theorists (e.g., Piaget; Vygotsky) have speculated on the value of play for children's development and have described ways play seems essential not only for physical development but also for the development of cognition, language, social skills, emotional regulation, and creativity. Conversely, in the formal educational system, play has often been considered an unimportant or even meaningless activity, and it is rarely included in the curriculum of the school. Recently, however, neuropsychological researchers are speculating that youthful play may be a major enhancer of brain development. Although some studies of human brain development are beginning to focus on the relationship between play and the brain, the majority of current neuropsychological research connecting play and brain development has focused on non-human animal play.

For example, animal researchers have noted that the proportionate size of the brain (in relation to an animal's overall size) is related to the amount of playful behavior observed in various species. The greater the proportion of the body devoted to the brain, the more extensive and long lasting is play in that animal species. The human animal plays more extensively, longer, and in more complex ways than do the other playful species, and of course, the proportion of overall size taken up by the brain in humans is extremely high in childhood and even in adulthood. Neuropsychological research on play now being conducted with animals suggests that during rough and tumble play (the typical play of many animals) neurochemicals associated with pleasure and excitement in humans are increased. These researchers are speculating that play may activate many parts of the animal brain and stimulate the growth of nerve cells. Play may be especially important in fostering the development of the frontal lobe. In brain imaging studies of children diagnosed with ADHD, there appear to be delays in the development of frontal lobe areas that are involved in inhibition of action, planning, and conceptualization of complex tasks. One researcher has hypothesized that these children's active behavior may be signaling a need for a longer period of rough and tumble play and that when children are given drugs that inhibit this activity the development of their frontal lobe may be further inhibited. Another type of evidence for the connection between active play and brain functioning is found in the studies of effects of school recess on children's ability to attend to school work. This body of research indicates that having an active play period at recess enhances later attention to school tasks.

Although neuroimaging studies have not yet demonstrated the specific neurological connections between play development and brain development, a comparison of these two areas of development certainly suggests that they are related. For example, in infancy the neurons of the brain are only beginning to be connected in networks. The connecting process (synaptogenesis) proceeds rapidly during the first year in the sensorimotor area of the brain. This is also the age period when sensorimotor (practice) play is most extensive. Infants explore textures and sounds, manipulate objects, and perform increasingly elaborated actions in their play. By six to eight months, when frontal lobe development begins, social games such as "peek-a-boo" become a major form of play. As frontal lobe synaptogenesis increases, children's play becomes more diverse and involves social interactions. Other areas of the brain that are developing during the toddler age include the language areas (Broca/Weirnicke), and as these areas develop, play with the sounds and symbols of language becomes extensive. The areas of the brain that are active sites of emotions (amygdala/limbic system) also gain more connections with the frontal lobe, and at this time, toddlers begin to exhibit pretense in caregiving behaviors, such as "feeding" a doll. In early childhood (age three to eight), which is the fastest growth period for the frontal lobe networks, a corresponding ability to think logically in concrete ways is observed. Children at this age engage in extensive and very complex pretend play, taking varied roles and wearing elaborate costumes to play out extended scripts for "superman" or "doctor's office" or "school." Through their play they demonstrate how elaborate their symbolic thought processes have become and they show their ability to self-regulate and work cooperatively with others. As the maturation of the brain continues during middle childhood and adolescence and pruning occurs, speed and efficiency of thought increases, planning and problem-solving skills increase, and scientific reasoning and metacognition are achieved. Play during this age period becomes increasingly sophisticated and symbolic, with pretense themes continuing for extended periods, symbolic board games and computer games becoming popular, and play that has elaborate rule systems being preferred. One view of why play continues to be an activity throughout life is that play serves to keep the frontal lobe networks active when survival-related problem-solving is not needed. That is, the rich networks in the frontal lobe are designed to deal with crises that might affect survival. In a society where such crises are less evident, play serves as a way to create challenges that keep humans prepared for action of more serious types. Older children and adults engage in symbolic games such as Monopoly, sports-related play such as golf or mountain-climbing, and socially acceptable forms of pretense through use of computer-aided virtual realties or actual role-taking in little theater. With maturity, play may still have an important role in keeping the brain active and preventing deterioration of the neuronal networks. Some studies of senior citizens are beginning to show that maintenance of brain functioning can also be enhanced through playful activities and thinking games (e.g., crossword puzzles).

Although understanding of the specific ways that play aids brain development await more neuropsychological research, and because play development and brain development seem to have many parallels, enhancing children's play skills and giving many opportunities for play is likely to be useful in helping the brain develop well. At present, there is no research that points to specific play or creative activities, such as listening to Mozart, as being especially useful to the brain. However, there are many aspects of play that are likely to enhance brain development. The most important role that play has is to help children to be physically and mentally active, to have control and choices, to solve problems, and to practice actions to mastery. Until more is known about how specific types of play might enhance particular brain structures or functions, a variety of play experiences in a wide variety of content areas is probably warranted because these will be important for the development of a complex and integrated brain. Play that links sensorimotor, cognitive, and social-emotional experiences together really provides an ideal setting for brain development. Here are some suggestions for extending play's role in enhancing children's brain development.

For infants and toddlers, the play environment should provide many safe and easily manipulated toys and other objects that are accessible to the child. Objects that encourage development of the sensorimotor areas of the brain are especially important. For example, toys with an interesting variety of sounds, shapes, sizes, colors, and textures will give young children motivation to be active and this will involve activity also in the brain. Often the best play objects for young children are adults and older children, who initiate social play, demonstrate ways to use these objects, and encourage variation and elaboration of object play. Having a variety of objects that activate sensorimotor and language areas of the brain and increasing the complexity level of toys as children grow older, will enhance the synaptogenesis process. Similarly, language, social, and emotional interactions with other people in play will help activate the brain centers related to these capabilities.

During the preschool and early elementary years, the time of greatest pretend play, having many opportunities to engage in pretense is especially likely to enhance development in higher brain centers. Providing adult models of symbolic actions and pretend roles while labeling those actions and emotions can help children expand the variety of their pretense. In peer play, provision of the time, space, and materials needed for complex and extended scripts and roles is likely to promote the development of the higher brain centers. Synapses in the frontal lobe are likely to be activated when children follow self-designed scripts and take roles that require self-regulation and problem-solving abilities. As children's pretend play skills increase, their pretense can be enhanced with books, writing, and other symbolic materials, which will be incorporated in their play.

As pruning of synapses in the brain becomes more extensive during later childhood, the pruning process may be affected by the types of play in which children most frequently engage. Playing games with rules that require higher order thinking processes, involve negotiation and problem solving, and promote self-regulation skills are important as brain processes become more efficient. Children's processing will be slower than adults because pruning and myelination of neuronal networks are still occurring. One of the types of play that extends from childhood into adulthood is play involving symbolic games, and often it is evident how such play promotes the capability of using the control processes of the frontal lobe. In early adolescence, children's choices of play activities become more focused and intense; this may be a result of the pruning activity of the brain.

While at one time it was believed that neuronal and synaptic development ended in adulthood, some studies indicate that the brain is capable of developing new networks and strengthening existing networks throughout life. Such activity may be highly related to new and enjoyable experiences—that is, play. Thus, opportunities for play should continue throughout life to preserve creativity and innovative thought. There are now many creators of games and other play activities for adults, some of them utilizing computers and some promoting interaction through board games. There are a number of recent games specifically promoted for enhancing or maintaining effective brain activity during adulthood. In sum, play and brain functioning are related throughout life.

See also: **Early Childhood Brain.**

Further Readings

Bergen. D. (2003) *Play's Role in Brain Development.* Olney, MD: ACEI.

Bergen, D. (2002). The role of pretend play in children's cognitive development. *Early Childhood Research & Practice [Online], 4*(1). Available: http//ecrp.uiuc.edu/v4n2/bergen.html

Panksepp, J. (1998). Attention deficit hyperactivity disorders, psychostimulants, and intolerance of childhood playfulness: A tragedy in the making? Current Directions in Psychological Science, 7(3):91–98.

Pellegrini, A., Bjorklund, D.F. (1996). The place of recess in school: Issues in the role of recess in children's education and development (Introduction to theme issue, J. Johnson, Theme Coordinator.) *Journal of Research in Childhood Education* 11(1): 5–13.

Siviy, S.M. (1998) Neurobiological substrates of play behavior: Glimpses into the structure and function of mammalian playfulness. In M. Bekoff, J. Byers (Eds.), *Animal play: Evolutionary, Comparative, and Ecological Perspectives.* New York: Cambridge University Press.

http://www.cranium.com (board game for adult play)

DORIS BERGEN, PH.D.

Pleasure and Love

It is becoming increasingly clear that early sensory experiences and environments have a definite impact in determining the foundational organization and capabilities of the brain. How we experience pleasure and love plays a key role in the brain's response to its environment as well as how the brain will interpret future interactions and relationships. These early experiences define and lay the foundation for motivation, energy, and joy throughout life.

The areas of the brain that are responsible for pleasure and love will be examined. In addition, we will discuss what factors trigger the pleasure pathway of the brain as well as the implications for school success.

The Limbic System and The Pleasure Pathway

The brain's pleasure pathway was discovered in the 1950s by James Olds. He inserted electrodes into the limbic system of rat brains. The electrodes were connected to a bar that sent a small charge of electricity to stimulate the pleasure pathways of the rat brains. The research showed that the rats would push the bar nonstop. So often in fact (up to 5,000 times an hour) the rats went without food, water, and sex until they collapsed from exhaustion.

Every brain has an area that responds to pleasure. The pleasure pathway, located in the limbic system, makes us repeat behaviors by giving us charges of emotional energy that range from powerful highs and satisfaction for doing a good job to powerful lows that cause depression, anxiety, and impulsiveness.

The limbic system is the emotional seat of the brain and responsible for our social world. It is where we learn to make friends, bond with our primary caregivers and handle our anger. The limbic system is located in the center of the brain and is about the size of a walnut. This area of the brain is also thought to store extremely charged emotional memories. The brain makes associations from a specific event and generalizes that event to other situations. Hearing the growling of a saber tooth tiger and its association with danger should only take one experience. However, the generalization from the embarrassment caused by one teacher is stored and processed over numerous years. This experience then provides the context for that student to feel anxious in all or many learning environments. An experience in the classroom can trigger a strong emotional response to the past experience, thereby causing the student to re-live that past experience of being embarrassed by a teacher. This process of association and generalization literally can alter the way future experiences are perceived and processed.

The pleasure pathway is fueled by neurotransmitters and endorphins with dopamine playing a key factor. When a human experiences pleasure, these neurotransmitters and endorphins are released into the pleasure pathway of the brain and our emotions take over.

Powerpacked with functions critical to human behavior and survival, the limbic system's functions include the capacity for problem-solving, planning, organization, and rational thought. These functions correlate directly to the early sensory experiences that define what gives us pleasure, passion and the emotional desire to complete a task. It is largely developed by the age of four years and is dependent upon our early experiences with primary caregivers. It is in these experiences that we define pleasure.

The pathway is involved in movement, cognition, **emotion, motivation,** and **addiction.** There is a direct link between the brain chemicals and the physical and emotional sensations of the body for example, the experience of different states of euphoria through praise, finding a dollar, sex, laughter, alcohol, and drugs, and even the chemicals found in chocolate.

Research has suggested that if these pleasure pathways are not stimulated or do not receive differing amounts of pleasure, we can become depressed, bored, function poorly, or die. The brain needs positive interactions to function appropriately. Activities that stimulate the pleasure pathways can be both positive and negative and include eating, drinking, sex, drugs, and anything else that gratifies us. For example studies show that animal and human babies who do not receive appropriate amounts of nurturing and physical touch after birth have stunted growth and may even die.

The brain develops through sensory experiences: touch, taste, smell, sight, and sound. Whether it is pleasurable or not, we learn through our experiences and interactions. Imagine how the loving touch of our primary caregiver translates to the desire and passion to do well on a spelling test. It is the pleasure of external feedback that translates to internal motivation. We have to have pleasure and stimulation from daily activities put into our bodies to power our brains to think, interact, and engage with others. Without these experiences the brain experiences a pleasure deficit that translates to depression and a lack of drive to complete a task, learn, or engage with others.

The brain wires itself in the context of relationships. These relationships build the neuronal networks that interpret how we will interface, connect with, and relate to others. We are pleasure-seeking creatures that need the joy, touch, and love of others to sustain both our physical and mental health.

Experiencing love outside the family and learning mating rituals is considered a normal part of adolescence. Some neuroscientists and educational psychologists hypothesize that the teenage years are the **critical period** for learning these skill. Typically, boys and girls experience their first puppy love at age ten and it is thought the brain, not hormones, initiates this happening.

Further evidence of the brain's role in love can be seen by research conducted at University College London. Scientists performed neuroimaging on the brains of young adults who were in love. Pictures of boyfriends or girlfriends were shown to participants while their brain was being scanned. At the sight of their love interest four regions of the brain lit up—the medial insula, associated with emotions, the anterior cingulated gyrus, involved in feeling good, and the putamen and the caudate nucleus related to positive experiences and addiction.

As was mentioned earlier, dopamine plays an important role in feeling pleasure, so it is no surprise it is involved in love. When an individual falls in love dopamine is released, and a person feels satisfaction, contentment, and joy. The brain interprets these positive emotions associated with love as a reward and wants the feelings to persist so it pursues the stimuli, love.

Love is only one of many strong emotions students experience. A teacher's praise, the classroom bully, or the smell of crayons can elicit a strong emotional response. The pleasure pathway in the limbic system provides the filter through which we interpret the events of the day. Sensory stimulation is the nutrient that is essential for normal growth, development, and brain functioning. Positive experiences matter; they define and frame what will drive and motivate us, and ultimately what we find pleasurable.

Humans do not learn only with their minds. Some psychologists believe as much as 80 percent of human learning is unconscious and registered through sensory and emotional neural pathways. The brain relies upon specific learning behaviors and possesses specific beliefs regarding learning, challenges, problem-solving, and motivation based on the surrounding sensory experiences.

Implications

Experiencing pleasure is key in motivating children to learn. Experiences such as hunger, lack of appropriate feedback, the wrong temperature, uncomfortable seating, unsuitable learning styles, and flickering lights cause students to lack feelings of pleasure, thus creating an environment not conducive to learning. The learning environment must meet the needs of every student and provide experiences that elicit pleasure.

Reward is another component that should be considered when discussing pleasure and learning. As discussed previously, the brain produces its own internal rewards. Because the brain does produce its own rewards, it raises the question of the effectiveness of external rewards. Educators have observed that external rewards are effective with some students and ineffective with others. Every student responds differently to external rewards based on genetics, life experiences and brain make-up. Research has demonstrated that students who receive external rewards for a job well done will expect an increasingly valuable reward every time they do a good job. Therefore, external rewards withhold lasting pleasure for the student.

To provide an environment that elicits pleasure, experiences need to be nurturing, comfortable both emotionally and physically, nonthreatening, and intrinsically motivated. As educators, it is imperative that we treat students with respect and encourage them to discover the pleasure and intrinsic rewards of learning. Teachers have the opportunity and the responsibility to provide students with the fuel to seek pleasure in learning by motivating, praising, and recognizing students as the individuals their brains have defined them to be.

See also: **Emotion; Emotional Intelligence; Depression; Stress.**

Further Readings

Kotulak, P. (1997). *Inside the Brain: Revolutionary Discoveries of How the Mind Works.* Kansas City, MO: Andrews McMeel Publishing.

Ratey, John J. (2001). *A User's Guide to the Brain: Perception, Attention, and the Four Theaters of the Brain.* New York, NY: Pantheon Books.

Corante Brain Waves http://www.corante.com/brainwaves

International Brain Research Organization www.ibro.org

LYNETTE POOLMAN AND
LAURA CRAWFORD, MA.

Poverty

Poverty affects millions of students each day in the United States. It is a risk factor impacting one in five children, making it a serious and pervasive school issue. Poverty is defined as an income below $19,350 in 2005 for a family of four. This economic status has a high incidence of unemployment, violence and neglect, substance abuse, and homelessness. The culture of poverty impacts school success in a variety of ways, academically and behaviorally. Educating children of poverty requires meeting basic needs first and then tending to educational requirements.

The Brain and Poverty

Babies are born with approximately hundred billion brain cells. During the first year of life the human brain develops quickly and is eager to learn. The hardware, neurons, is present at birth, but the software, massive dendrite production and synaptic connections, is yet to be developed. Experiences, both positive and negative are the primary influence in creating these neural networks. Poverty undermines the quality and number of experiences an individual has and so impedes brain development. Medical care, safety, nutrition, maternal depression, stress, substance abuse, and violence are additional remnants of poverty that impact the brain throughout the lifespan.

Educators and child care providers have long been aware of the importance of early language activities and rich experiences in developing cognitive skills and thinking patterns. Now neuroscience is providing insights that confirm this viewpoint. Unfortunately, an impoverished environment is not conducive for growing dendrites and making synaptic connections. Children born into poverty are immediately at a disadvantage; their mothers tend to have less prenatal care, putting them at risk for birth complications. The expense of medical care continues to haunt them into adulthood, as they are frequently not able to afford proper medical attention. Not only is their physical well-being problematic, but the emotional setting is complicated. These infants' and children's mothers are often dealing with depression. The children of depressed mothers have more stress hormones and receive little stimulation. The lack of interaction between infant and mother inhibits cognitive growth as does the activation of stress hormones.

In addition, parents living in poverty tend to be less equipped with parenting skills. This results in reduced social interaction between parent and child, which limits language growth. The intermittent language the children are exposed to tends to be simply structured and does not exhibit higher order thinking skills such as critical thinking, problem-solving, and synthesis. Homes are often not equipped with computers. Visiting science museums, parks, and libraries are a rarity. The majority of preschoolers in poverty do not attend preschool and quality child care is lacking. All of these experiences have the potential to add to cognitive growth. The lack of initial neural networking makes academic readiness an issue. The less you know, the more difficult it is to learn new information. In other words, the more dendritic branching and synaptic connections an individual possesses, the easier it is to produce more.

The amygdala and hippocampus work together to store memories. The aymgdala is the emotional center of the brain and the hippocampus plays a major role in storing memory. The hippocampus identifies the person or event and the amygdala interprets how we feel about it. The involvement of the amygdala allows emotional experiences, good and bad, to easily be stored in long-term memory.

Unfortunately, the primary emotions children in poverty experience are fear and stress. When the brain is under intense stress it is more difficult to pay attention, learn, and retrieve information. The person feels helpless and takes no academic risks, all creativity is hindered. When individuals are under chronic stress cortisol is released into the system. One of the effects of cortisol is a reduced immune system, making not only the cognitive system shutdown, but also the physical.

Dopamine is the neurotransmitter that helps us feel happy, motivated, and attentive. The body releases it when we feel good about something such as winning the race, seeing a good friend, or eating a delicious meal. Unfortunately, fear of failure, isolation and trauma, often present in poor children, causes dopamine to be converted into norephinephrine. Norephinephrine energizes an individual and under adverse conditions results in aggression and agitation. This makes it difficult for the individual to tolerate frustration and stress. Students may become belligerent or apathetic. In school this is the student that flies into a rage over a simple comment such as, "Where's your homework?" or falls asleep during class.

Serotonin, a calming agent, is naturally produced in the body. Low levels are associated with depression and low self-esteem and conversely high levels are associated with tranquility and positive self-esteem. Poverty has been correlated with depression and low self-esteem. Researchers have found that individuals in poverty have less serotonin in their bodies, contributing to feelings of unrest and agitation.

Nutrition goes first to vital organs, then to muscle and skeletal growth, and finally to cognition. The more poverty an individual faces, the lower the nutritional value in their food. Nutrition delivers a two-fisted punch to the brain. First, people in poverty are not receiving the necessary nutrients to support cognitive growth. Second, chronic stress, frequently found in poverty, prevents the body from properly absorbing the nutrients which then inhibits the growth of dendrites and synaptic connections.

Basic Needs

Resources most people take for granted are not present in an impoverished environment. Basic needs such as food, physical and emotional safety, and community connections are all in jeopardy. The theorist Abraham Maslow's groundbreaking research brought to the forefront the understanding that basic needs must first be met before learning can take place.

Too often children in poverty come to school hungry. To counter this, federal hot lunch/breakfast programs provide free and reduced meals for low-income families. Teachers may act as facilitators, encouraging and assisting families in receiving and filling out the necessary forms for these benefits. Food feeds the brain and gives the students the edge they need for optimum learning. But it is not just the physical that needs to be tended to in the lunchroom. Creating a pleasant atmosphere by greeting students and letting them know their absence is missed conveys the message that you care about their mental as well as their physical well-being.

The homes and communities where poor children sleep are not always safe environments. School may be their one safe haven. Feeling threatened can produce emotions of depression and anger. Teachers need to be attentive to these emotions and help students press through or diffuse these feelings so the focus can be on education.

Teachers need to provide a community in which all children can learn. Living in poverty can isolate a family and student. Nurturing a class where everyone feels like they have a place and purpose gives courage to students. A sense of belonging is created by using competition carefully and promoting noncompetitive group activities, offering academic support outside the classroom, and getting to know each individual and their interests. Realizing that many students need added support outside the school, teachers can act as a liaison with community and school services. Community health and dental clinics are available in most counties, cities, and states. Bringing in the school nurse to share hygiene and good health practices can influence the home life for children.

Some students are parents themselves, trying to raise a child of their own. Connecting them to the Special Supplemental Nutrition Program for Women, Infants, and Children, better known as WIC, can provide necessary nutrition for the entire family. School in-house daycare may make the difference between teenage moms dropping out of school or continuing their education. Keeping the parent and the child close together and available for nursing and noon-time meals create an incentive to stay in school.

Finally, the dream for higher education often seems impossible for students of poverty. Teachers can connect their students with career counselors and college representatives. Oftentimes students who have nothing expect nothing. They are unaware of how to navigate the post-secondary scene. Knowing how to apply for technical schools or four-year colleges and availability of student loans and grants is outside their radar screen. A high school diploma is no longer sufficient to support a family of four. A high school dropout is expected to make $16,000 annually, a GED $18,000, and a high school diploma recipient $20,000; all incomes at or below the poverty line. The reality is that in this age of information students need an advanced degree. A one year post-high school program acts like an economic rocket, propelling an individual above the poverty line.

Educational Needs

Families in poverty are often transient; frequently moving from place to place. Children are enrolled and re-enrolled in different schools throughout the course of their K-12 education. Each move creates a learning gap. For instance, one school may be in the midst of teaching long division while the next has already completed this unit. Therefore, the child has missed a fundamental concept. Teachers can not make assumptions about the academic background of a student that has frequently moved. Identifying where the student is and then providing ample opportunities to learn and practice missed skills is necessary. Regular review of all major concepts provides an educational framework that is beneficial for all students. At the same time a curriculum totally based on repetition and drill will quickly lose interest for students and motivation to learn will cease. A balance must be found.

Poverty creates absenteeism. For example, the car breaks down, younger siblings need to be watched or parent(s) or guardian may need to appear in court. Teachers need to be prepared for the academic inconsistencies this presents by having the day's assignments available and attainable. Be flexible whenever possible; explore alternative ways for assignments to be completed that will be practical for the students' erratic lifestyles. When dealing with at-risk students, understanding is important, but pity is misdirected. This is a time to assist and support their success. Hold all students accountable and provide clear guidelines for absences.

Common knowledge, prior knowledge, and background knowledge is often lacking for poverty students. Language and literacy-rich classrooms provide an academic setting for learning. Real vocabulary, not just lists of words to be defined, boosts their academic foundation. Crossword puzzles, sharing current events and numerous field trips will bolster background knowledge which is the springboard for continued learning.

One of the best practices for meeting the needs of all students is differentiated instruction. This consists of giving students multiple options for learning and showing their academic progress. Differentiated instruction provides students with curriculum that best meets their ability to grasp the concepts being learned. Most lessons can be adapted to meet the specific learning level of all students in the classroom. Because of the gaps in education and the need to scaffold the learning of students born and living in poverty, differentiated instruction can provide the necessary elements in the learning cycle: instruction, content, and product.

Meeting basic needs first and then meeting educational needs will nurture and encourage students disadvantaged by poverty. Teachers can then provide an equal and fair chance at an education that may break the cycle of poverty. Poverty is not destiny.

See also: **At-Risk Behavior; Beverages; Nutrition.**

Further Readings

Banks, J.A. (2006). *Cultural Diversity and Education* (5th ed.). Boston, MA: Allyn and Bacon.
Kozol, J. (2005). *The Shame of the Nation.* New York, NY: Crown Publishers.
Payne, R. (2005). *Framework for Understanding Poverty.* Highlands, TX: aha! Process, Inc.
Poverty and Race Action Research Council http://www.prrac.org

**SHERYL FEINSTEIN, ED.D. AND
EVIE J. BROUWER, M.A.**

Prenatal Brain

The prenatal brain develops in three basic ways: the expanding basic structure of brain regions, multiplication and pruning of individual neurons available for synaptic connections, and finally, the wrapping of an insulating myelin sheath around the axons allowing transmission of electrochemical signals that produce abilities and functions.

The sensory pathways available for systematic stimulation are limited in utero, but are demonstrably effective according to scientific studies. Stimulation effects during the prenatal period can be profound (a result of nature plus nurture, rather than Nature vs. Nurture). For example, Wolfgang Amadeus Mozart grew up in the home of the premier music teacher in all of Europe where lessons were given and live music was performed daily during his prenatal period. Mozart had both musical genes and a musical environment from conception, along with a loving mother and an eight-year-old big sister who practiced the keyboard daily. The prenatal brain is plastic and is fashioned by the environment either accidentally or intentionally.

Growth and Development

Prenatal care, including examination and supplemental nutrition are essential. The building blocks of the brain are protein for essential amino acids, beneficial fats (Omega-3) for fatty acids and myelin, carbohydrates for glucose, and oxygen. Enzymes and neuro-growth factors guide these basic brain-building nutrients, along with vitamins and minerals, to specific construction sites. Nutritional deficiencies cause the body to take nutrients from the mother's body tissue to supply fetal needs.

Neuronal growth increases at phenomenal rates to more than 100,000 cells per minute in the ninth month. Cells are overproduced and then pruned, with about one-third of the cells trimmed in the final weeks prior to birth. Certain cells physically migrate up to a millimeter in the cerebral hemispheres unless disturbed by alcohol, at which time organization and symmetry of cell formations are scrambled and disconnected. By contrast, babies born to mothers addicted to crack cocaine have normally constructed brains but with extreme oversensitivity to environmental stimuli.

The prenatal brain is plastic and subject to influences beyond merely adding growth weight. Prenatal stimulation studies were conducted by Brent Logan, and Rene Van de Carr, and Marc Lehrer, beginning in the 1980s. The processes are simple and somewhat mechanical. The impact of repeated stimuli over days and weeks has immediate and long-term implications for cell organization and later preferences, abilities, and behavior. Principles of prenatal stimulation are those universally applied in childhood: systematically increase the frequency (how often), intensity (how loud, how fast, how strong), and duration (at least twenty seconds or longer). Soothing stimulation shuts down cell activity while arousing stimulation increases electrical activity at an exciting level to produce growth and development. Regular, daily, systematic stimulation establishes and maintains connections and expectations. Stimulation should always be at pleasant (but exciting and challenging) levels.

Insulation of neuronal axons in the spinal cord begins in the fifth month with the process of upward myelinization. The myelin sheath allows cells to conduct electro-chemical activity through axons to dendrites, producing the first reflexive physical movements in response to sensory stimuli. The myelin (Schwann cell) is a beneficial form of cholesterol that wraps around the axon, becoming thicker with increased stimulation to facilitate faster and more efficient transmission. The spinal cord and axons are fully covered by an initial myelin wrap at birth and the visible functions of a newborn derive from the extent of the progression of myelin. The medulla is also myelinated to some extent at birth.

Fetal brain functions at eleven weeks involve only slight movements of arms and legs, and some slight abdominal reflex. With the beginning of spinal cord myelinization, by eighteen weeks the functions include differential movement of arms and legs easily felt by the mother, thumb sucking and face scratching, motions of crying, reception of sounds, opening and closing of hands, and movement of lips and tongue. By twenty-eight weeks, survival of premature birth is possible because the spinal cord is myelinated sufficiently to produce function and reflexes, including extensive physical movement and reactions, sucking, grasping, sound startle, and opening and shutting of eyelids. Prenatal stimulation is possible through vestibular, auditory, and vibratory senses. At full term of thirty-eight weeks the spinal cord is fully myelinized, producing light, sound startle, grasp, foot Babinski, sneeze, Moro, and asymmetrical tonic neck reflexes.

Once myelinization has begun in the spinal cord, reception of stimuli and motor responses become evident with kicking reflexes in response to sound and movement. Mothers have reported that the fetus can habituate to a time schedule in which movement is expected at certain times of the day and kicking can indicate desire for stimulation.

Primitive reflexes are established in the spinal cord prenatally and are available and visible at birth, including the Moro, sound startle, asymmetrical tonic neck reflex (ATNR) (fencer arm extension), Babinski big toe extension, grasp reflex, rooting reflex, pupillary reflex, sucking reflex, and many more. The fetal position is a flexor position and reflex actions are extensor reactions. The newborn is a bundle of primitive reflexes at birth as only the spinal cord and medulla are myelinated and operational. The ATNR is considered to assist in the movement through the birth canal. The Apgar rating at one and five minutes following birth includes the nasal sneeze irritability for tactile sensitivity, cry for respiration effort, pink skin color for circulation, and active motion of all limbs.

Systematic procedures for prenatal nurture of brain development are well-known and accepted for active stimulation by parents. Interoceptors are the physical/biochemical emotional senses of fear, anger and joy; proprioceptors are internal bodily sensors of balance and vestibular swinging/spinning movements, and exteroceptors include the prenatal sound and touch senses.

Biochemical nurture is produced through aerobic physical activity by the mother that increases oxygen supply to the fetal brain; wholesome nutrition provides nutrients, including calcium for bone-building and neuronal synapses, a variety of proteins for amino acid production and healthy fats for production of myelin; spring water rather than caffeine and sugar drinks for hydration and evacuation of toxins; the joyful and secure mother habituates the desirable happy parasympathetic acetylcholine biochemical state in the fetus.

Sensory nurture utilizes the myelinized and available exteroceptors by playing pleasant loud music in the environment or through earphones on the mother's abdomen, loud talking and reading to the fetus, playing tapes of foreign languages, dancing/moving to loud music, swinging, twirling, singing to the fetus, and touching the foot as it kicks. The sounds heard by the fetus are similar to those heard while swimming under water so the speech must be louder and intentionally pleasantly lilting, happy, and playful. The sound of the mother's heartbeat is a constant rhythmic stimulus. Recognition of specific parent and sibling voices has been observed at birth by the newborn turning the head toward the familiar voice. Quieting of crying has been observed when familiar prenatal music is played. A variety of auditory stimuli are produced, including those produced by the preferences of the mother including singing, humming, talking, talking on the telephone, environmental sounds (ticking clock, animals, traffic), music, songs, reading to the fetus, birds, instruments during music lessons or practice. Movement choices include spinning, dancing, swaying, swinging, sliding, upward/downward, acceleration, deceleration, and vigorous rocking. Effects of stimulation are noticeable in the infant and produce enthusiasm for nurture in parents and siblings.

Threats to the Fetus

At conception, the developing brain is dependent on the health of the egg and sperm, influenced by the prior **nutrition** of each parent and limited exposure to toxins and/or other substances, including medications, radiation, and allergies. The presence of genetic threats from family heredity, toxic exposure, aging mother, and Rx factor (blood type incompatibility) suggests seeking genetic counseling to determine the probability of a positive pregnancy. Toxic threats include alcohol, nicotine, drugs, tobacco smoke, exposure to toxins from building materials and home chemicals, ambient tobacco smoke, caffeine from chocolate, coffee, and tea, and the obvious heavy metals such as mercury and lead. Agricultural pesticides and herbicides, plastics (vinyl), wood treatments, construction and carpet installation compounds, radon and fuel gasses, traffic fumes are also possible threats to the fetus.

Following conception, the neural tube forms during the first weeks, eventually becoming the spinal cord and complex brain levels and regions. The placenta acts as a barrier for some toxins, and as the brain develops, the blood–brain barrier increases defense against toxins. The brain is vulnerable in spite of these barriers, however, including threats of alcohol, rubella, toxoplasmosis parasite from cats, tobacco, and nutritional deficiencies such as folic acid/folate (causing spina bifida). Natural chemical threats include negative maternal emotions precipitating habitual sympathetic autonomic nervous system stressors of fear and anger/frustration (high epinephrine and norepinephrine states) and estrogen effects on males. Negative effects of anesthesia, ultrasound, and radiation have been noted. Avoidance of biochemical and emotional stress at birth is accomplished by using spinal block in place of anesthesia and low-stress birthing such as Lamaze, LeBoyer, water birthing, and a pleasant delivery room,

Premature birth (low birth weight) is implicated in numerous difficulties, including learning problems, cerebral palsy, health problems, dyscoordination and impaired intellectual development. Diet and supplementation are especially important; lack of omega-3 fats (canola, fish, flaxseed, olive oils) have recently been linked to prematurity. The effects of poverty on pregnancy and delivery result from convergence of several variables producing increased proportions of prematurity. African American premature births, for example, are at twice the rate of premature births in Africa because of the high American poverty rate and malnutrition. In the United States about 8 percent of births are premature with more than 15 percent of low birth weight births being African American children. Miscarriages, at 30 percent of conceptions, are much more common than previously thought, and indicate chromosomal abnormalities in half the cases.

The prenatal brain has plasticity and is eager to learn. We have a unique opportunity to begin creating an active and responsive brain before birth.

See also: Beverages; Fetal Alcohol Syndrome; Gender Differences; Infant Brain; Music.

Further Readings

Fleming, A.S., O'Day, D.H., Kraemer, G.W. (1999). Neurobiology of mother-infant interactions: Experience and central nervous system plasticity across development and generations. *Neuroscience Behavioral Review* 23(5):673–685.

Jefferis, B., Power, C., Hertzman, C. (2002). Birthweight, childhood socio-economic environment and cognitive development in the 1958 British birth cohort. *British Medical Journal* 325:305–308.

Logan, B. (1992). Prelearning; trials and trends. *International Journal of Prenatal and Perinatal Studies* 4:67–69.

http://www.asoundbeginning.com
http://www.ecobaby.com
http://www.thesmartbaby.com

LYELLE L. PALMER, PH.D.

Proactive Classroom Management Strategies

Fear, apprehension, discomfort, lack of understanding, and loneliness: just a few of the emotions students battle daily when entering the classroom/school. Consciously or unconsciously, our emotional reactions determine our behavior, our health, our learning, and our memory of past experiences. Emotions literally drive attention, learning, memory, and how we go about the day: emotion is the gatekeeper to learning and performance. Creating a brain-compatible classroom and school is within our reach Providing a safe and predictable environment, consistency and continuity, adults as role models, common expectations of personal interactions, and a commitment to meaningful curriculum that leads to responsible citizenship will make a difference in the lives of our students.

The past twenty-five years of research into the physiology of the human brain have provided an abundance of vital information relevant to educators. A most consistent message is the enormous and all-encompassing power our emotions have in every aspect of our lives. This information is critically important to educators as they facilitate and orchestrate effective learning communities. Creating a positive and productive emotional tone in our schools and classrooms is a number one priority for academic achievement. Both the physical space of the school/classroom and the personal interactions within that space contribute to the overall emotional tone.

Creating the Space for Learning

The effects of space on our emotional wiring can be illustrated by the difference between walking through Disneyland, a space uniquely orchestrated for enjoyment and efficiency; and walking through a carnival midway with people yelling for our attention and a cacophony of sounds coming from many directions. Our bodies respond to each space differently. The goal in a school is to create an academic learning space that is safe and predictable, both in the design of the classroom and in the interaction of all those in the building.

The emotional and visual appeal of a learning community begins when parents and students approach the building. The outside of the school provides the invitation and the school entryway reflects what we think of our clientele. We all have had the experience (feeling) of knowing ahead of the actual experience that something was good or bad. You never get a second chance to make a first impression. A school should welcome and invite students and their parents into the building. Adequate signage directing students and parents to their destination alleviates worry and confusion. Evidence of the mission of the school in language that is understandable and specific provides confidence that the educators in the building are committed to the task of educating the students in their charge. The academic content goals and the social skills necessary to accomplish these goals, clearly displayed, allow a measure of confidence for those who enter, stating that a successful and productive learning experience is expected here and that the educators have the necessary knowledge and skills to reach that goal.

Solid academic achievement can be orchestrated when all adults in the building recognize the power of a safe and predictable environment and work toward establishing consistency and continuity for all students, thus allowing the brain to stay focused on the learning at hand. The teacher sets the tone at the classroom door by greeting students and calling their attention to the entry procedures. Being well planned and organized allows students to have confidence in their teachers as they direct their attention to the learning goals of the day. It is clear to the students the decisions for which they are responsible. Decision-making, both personally and within the group, leads to independence and a sense of authonomy, important in building positive self-esteem.

Creating the Climate for Working Together

A classroom, by design, illustrates the expectation for the year, both socially and instructionally. A productive learning environment provides physical and emotional space for learning to occur. It is free of clutter, toxins have been removed, it is well ventilated, well lit, has ambient temperature, and the furniture is appropriate for the age of the students. A healthful and aesthetically pleasing setting contributes to a relaxed and positive learning environment. The room must reflect a conscious intent for collaboration. Furniture is arranged in clusters so students can interact in learning groups and have a support group. Their materials are within close reach so they do not have the distraction of having to leave their desks. Group procedures clearly state the expectations of how to best work together in a variety of situations. Written procedures provide detailed guidelines about how to go about daily activities. They are used to describe what to do when you enter the room, go to the library, the restroom, recess, what to do when you have finished your work, how to head your paper, and how to work in a group. A copy of the procedures is placed within each cluster, freeing the teacher from answering the same questions countless times, while building confidence and responsibility in the students, thereby providing another level of consistency.

To assist students in mentally preparing for their day, a daily agenda is clearly visible for all students to read. A daily agenda defines the flow of the day and the personal responsibilities of the students and the teacher. A yearlong curriculum theme posted in a prominent location indicates the curriculum content for the year. Meaningful curriculum includes activities that are emotionally engaging, academically challenging, community based, and that lead to responsible citizenship. By implementing agendas and themes, students need not worry about the direction of their learning as they can readily see the big picture of how all aspects of the classroom come together to create a meaningful learning experience.

Creating Classroom Behaviors for Learning

In orchestrating a brain-compatible environment there must be agreed-upon behaviors valued by all; thereby allowing students the freedom to learn. Creating the emotional safety necessary requires agreement on how people, students and staff alike, treat one another. Behavior modeled by adults within a school should be of the same quality expected from students. In contrast to a punitive model of discipline, which depends upon fear and threat, a brain-compatible environment is built upon civility and respect. Especially challenging today is exposure to extreme behaviors modeled in our visual world of television and the computer and their influence in the everyday behaviors of children. In a flash of images children view content that is negative and regularly focusing on survival at any cost. Often these scenarios spill over into the school and classroom. The result of these constant visual messages is costly to the learner. These negative images can create dysfunctional circuits within our emotional wiring. Students must understand cause and effect to comprehend the differences between the surreal actions they are watching and the real life they are living.

Implementing a Positive Model of Behavior

The Lifelong Guidelines and LIFESKILLS, as coined by the integrated thematic instruction model (ITI), identify character behaviors needed for a solid working relationship between friends, spouses, employees, teachers, and students. The Lifelong Guidelines are the foundation for what makes a community work and the LIFESKILLS are the specific actions we should expect from our peers within the community. The Lifelong Guidelines include: Trustworthiness, Truthfulness, Active Listening, No Put-Downs, and Personal Best. When presenting these Guidelines to students, the following questions help form a deeper understanding: What is it? Why practice it? How do you practice it? What does it look, sound, and feel like in the world beyond the classroom? How do you know when you are successful?

A learning community is only as strong as the everyday behaviors all people within the building routinely demonstrate. LIFESKILLS are consciously taught to provide students with the social and character behaviors that will support their cognitive development. We cannot separate cognition from emotion, as each influences the other. Emotions are the glue that hold us together; whether good, bad, or indifferent, we become part of the emotional tone of the school. The eighteen LIFESKILLS are easily recognizable daily behaviors that enhance our ability to work together. They include: Caring, Common Sense, Cooperation, Courage, Curiosity, Effort, Flexibility, Friendship, Initiative, Integrity, Organization, Patience, Perseverance, Pride, Problem-Solving, Resourcefulness, Responsibility, and Sense of Humor.

Throughout the day, all activities have the potential to illustrate a necessary or missing LIFESKILL. The broad use of these skills begins first thing in the morning as students select and record in their journal the LIFESKILL they personally want to work on. Additionally, each learning group chooses a LIFESKILL they will practice during the week. The LIFESKILL or lack thereof can describe characters in a story, the newspaper, or a television show. LIFESKILLS can set the parameters for working on a project, having a guest speaker, attending a performance, or having lunch in the cafeteria. Beginning in the faculty room, the use and practice of the Lifelong Guidelines and LIFESKILLS form the basis of school and classroom interaction and are the foundation for orchestrating a brain-compatible learning environment.

In the coming years we will learn more of how the brain learns; in the meantime we have enough to begin creating a proactive brain-compatible learning environment that acknowledges the importance of emotion in all that we do. Aristotle said, "We are what we repeatedly do. Excellence then, is not an act, but a habit." We will continue to learn more each year about the physiology of learning and to build on what is known of the powerful effect emotions have on all we do.

See also: **Classroom Management; Handling Specific Problems in Classroom Management; Pleasure and Love, Social Context of Learning; Visuals and Classroom Management.**

Further Readings

Damasio, A. (1994). *"Thinking about Emotion," Descartes' Error: Emotion, Reason, and the Human Brain.* New York: Grosset/Putnam Sons.

Kovalik, S.J., Karen D.O. (2002). *Exceeding Expectations: A User's Guide to Implementing Brain Research in the Classroom* (2nd ed.). Kent, WA: Susan Kovalik & Associates, Inc.

LeDoux, J. (1996). *The Emotional Brain.* New York: Simon and Schuster.

Pearson, S. (2000). *Tools for Citizenship & Life: Using the Lifelong Guidelines & LIFESKILLS in Your Classroom.* Kent, WA: Susan Kovalik & Associates, Inc.

Ratey, J. (2001). *A User's Guide to the Brain.* New York: Pantheon Books.

Sylwester, R. (1995). *A Celebration of Neurons.* Alexandria, VA: ASCD.

Thompson, J.G. (1998). *Discipline Survival Kit for the Secondary Teacher.* Hoboken, NJ: Jossey-Bass.

Education World www.educationworld.com

SUSAN J. KOVALIK

Procedural Memory

Once a child learns how to ride a bike, it is highly unlikely that he would have to relearn it. This is because of procedural memory. Procedural memory is remembering how to do things. Virtually every subject in school can use this type of memory: music, orchestra, athletic programs, science, social studies, language arts, math, driver's education, and more. Procedural memory strategies are easy to use, easy to master, and are an enjoyable way to learn.

What Is It?

Procedural memory is often called muscle memory, body memory, motor memory, or kinesthetic learning. This memory lane stores habits, learned skills, and how to do something. It stores processes that the body does and remembers involuntarily and automatically. Some examples of information that you might store within this memory lane would be: riding a bike, rollerblading, driving a car, reading, following lab procedures, writing a letter, cheerleading, and more.

Neuroscientist Larry Squire found that amnesic patients, who had temporal lobe damage, would succeed or fail on a word retrieval task depending on the specific instructions given. The patients performed poorly when asked to list words after given some time to review the words. They performed better when given a cue and then asked to say the word. The conclusion of this piece of research was that the ability to recall something depended on which pathway the person used to retrieve the information. The information was within the brain, but the research participants just donít know it (procedural/automatic memory lane). Educators need to aid students in storing information in the strongest memory lanes so retrieval will be successful.

Brain Location

Procedural memory is stored within the cerebellum, the back part of the brain that controls movement and balance. The cerebellum has many neurons within it. It helps with memory formation. Automatic memories that are not associated with muscles are also stored within the cerebellum. For example, multiplication tables and the alphabet are stored within the cerebellum. Kinesthetic information is temporarily stored in the motor cortex (top portion of head) and then when the information is mastered; it is permanently stored within the cerebellum. In other words, once a procedure becomes a routine or habit, then it is stored within the cerebellum.

Declarative vs. Nondeclarative

Memory can be categorized as declarative (explicit) or nondeclarative (implicit). Declarative memories, or conscious memories, can be recalled and reported. They contain two types of memory: **semantic**, or word memory; and **episodic**, or location memory. These explicit memory lanes take effort and much practice to get information into them. Explicit information is first stored within the hippocampus.

Declarative knowledge must precede procedural knowledge. A learner needs to know the steps of how to do the procedure. For example, to read fluently and automatically, the student needs to know several sight words quickly. This requires accessing decoding skills that use the semantic memory lane. The more words that students know automatically, the more the brain can be free to comprehend or think about the text or words as a whole. Students that have difficulty decoding words, use all their working memory space just to decode words and are unable to use memory for comprehension. If an unknown word is come upon while reading, automatic processing is disrupted while the reader tries to decode the word. The processing within the brain goes from reflective to reflexive or automatic.

Pros and Cons

There are pros and cons when learning information that is stored within any of the memory lanes. One huge benefit of storing information within the procedural memory lane is that it gives students the ability to essentially do two things at once. Motor neurons may become so used to being activated in a particular sequence that they fire automatically with little or no conscious processing. For example, holding a conversation and driving can be done simultaneously because these two functions activate two different areas within the brain. They do not compete with each other. Doing two things at the same time is different from consciously processing two inputs at the same time. A person can do two things at the same time if one of them is stored in the automatic or procedural memory lanes. Driving a car and holding a conversation at the same time is fine for adults who have been driving for quite some time, but not for an adolescent who is still learning these motor skills.

Classroom teachers can help students make procedures more routine so that the information can be recalled automatically, freeing the brain to think and focus on something else. For example, while students are in their morning routines (putting homework in bins, hanging up coats, etc.), the teacher could have a question written on the chalkboard that the students are thinking about.

Procedures and routines decrease stress and allow the mind to more actively focus on conscious learning. The more automatic learning is for students, the more they free up their working memories to focus on deeper, higher-level tasks. Working memory overload can cause great stress, and could make learning very challenging. Think of the stress involved with a student who is doing long division and has not put the multiplication facts within her procedural or automatic memory lane.

Procedural memory skills are so memorable that they are the most often used methods for early childhood learning. A child's life is filled with standing, running, playing, building, and riding. All of these actions create a more complex and over-all greater source of sensory input to the brain than just cognitive activity. Unfortunately, this memory lane is used less as students proceed to higher grades. This continues to happen even while there is a host of research out there that says that procedural knowledge is easier to master, more easily remembered, and full of fun memories of the learning episode.

A con of the procedural memory lane is that it takes much practice and effort to ingrain the information into the memory lane, but once it is learned, it is in that brain for a long time. Distributed practice is the key when it comes to strengthening the connections between the neurons. For example, while learning vocabulary words by attaching a body movement to represent the meaning of the word, students should review these words and their definitions right after the lesson. A second review should take place twenty-four hours later since about 90 percent of information is forgotten within twenty-four hours, and a third review seven days later as the hippocampus (brain part with the role of cataloguing memories and transferring them to long-term storage sites) makes a decision to keep or discard the information. While reviewing this pattern of numbers (10-24-7), students should use the body movements associated with the sequence so they are stored in both the semantic and procedural memory lanes.

Another con of procedural memory is that the information takes time (anywhere from Four to six hours) for the learning to consolidate. Researchers at the Massachusetts Institute of Technology Department of Brain and Cognitive Sciences have observed that learning a motor skill sets in motion neural processes that continue to evolve even after practice has ended. When subjects learned a second, different motor skill immediately after a first skill was learned, the consolidation of the first motor skill was disrupted. However, if four hours elapsed between learning the first and second skills, this disruption did not occur. Researchers suggest that motor skill consolidation relies on the same structures in the medial temporal lobe that are necessary for the consolidation of explicit memory tasks. When teaching a procedural movement skill, it is important not to teach a new and different skill immediately following the initial skill taught. Teachers should give the initial skill time to consolidate.

Accessing the Procedural Memory Lane

There are two ways that will help students access the information from their procedural memory lanes. One way is to have students perform or use the information enough so that it becomes a procedure. With enough repetition and practice, the procedure can be stored permanently so it can be accessed with a cue. This is why schools have fire drills and tornado drills—so that these procedures can be performed automatically under stress when the fire alarm sounds, a time in which thinking is much challenged.

A second way to help students access the information from procedural memory lane is to invent procedures with the students so that the subject area is cemented with a movement into this memory lane. Connect the content to be remembered to movements. Some examples are: role-playings, simulations, school plays, dances, debates, puppet shows, hands-on manipulatives, choral reading, and games. Tying movements with vocabulary words can be very useful and memorable. For example, when the word "noun" is said, all of the students jump out of their chairs and point to objects in the classroom and chant, "A person (point), a place (point), a thing (point) or idea (palm out by brain)." The word "noun" is the cue for the body and brain to define it.

How to Teach Procedural Knowledge

There is a process for teaching procedural knowledge. In the early stages of procedural learning, there are three brain parts that are involved in forming the new pathway. The prefrontal cortex, parietal cortex, and cerebellum allow a person to pay attention to the tasks and ensure correct movements. This is why perfect practice needs to be a priority. How a person practices is how the information will be remembered. The bottomline for storing information into this lane is the amount and type of skill practice. As students practice skills, the memories become more efficient and can be performed with little conscious thought or recall. Eventually after lots of distributed practice, all of these brain areas show less activity. In other words, as a skill is mastered, there is less activity within the brain.

For procedural knowledge to become part of long-term memory, there are several processes or steps that must be present in the lesson. First, the teacher should model the process by talking through the process aloud so that students can visualize it. For instance, while reading aloud, the teacher might come across an unknown word. The teacher would think aloud the steps to solving this context clue mystery. She might say: "I have never heard or seen this word before. I wonder what it means. I'm going to reread the paragraph before the unknown word to see if there are any clues for this unknown word." The teacher takes the time to model and talk through how to find context clues. Students are more apt to visualize the process in this situation.

Second, the teacher should provide a written set of steps for the procedure so that students can see and review the steps. For example, there are four steps that aid students in finding context clues:

1. Box-in the unknown word.

2. List words or phrases that are clues to the meaning of the unknown word.

3. Mentally think about what the unknown word might mean.

4. Guess the meaning of the unknown word. Check in the dictionary if the guess is correct.

Teachers should take the time to teach the students to talk through the process. Teachers should make time for guided practice and independent practice. For example, the teacher could provide time for students to pair up and talk through finding context clues.

Finally, teachers should provide time for students to practice enough so that the steps are mentally rehearsed. Encourage students to mentally rehearse the steps involved within the process so that eventually, the process becomes automatic. Eventually, each step will no longer be a separate step, instead, the brain will be able to complete the process quickly, automatically, and unconsciously while looking at it all as one whole process.

Once the procedural knowledge is automatic, it is extremely challenging to consciously express the skill while performing it. If this is tried, the performance may be impaired. For example, once a piano song is learned automatically or by memory and the pianist tries reading the song by looking at each note, the song will sound slow and may not be played the same way at all.

Procedural memory lane is a fun, valuable, and highly memorable lane to use in all subject areas.

See also: **Information Processing Model; Mastery.**

Further Reading

Jensen, E. (1998). *Teaching with the Brain in Mind.* Alexandria, VA: ASCD.

Sprenger, M. (1999). *Learning and Memory: The Brain in Action.* Alexandria, VA: ASCD.

Squire, L., Kandel, E. (2000). *Memory: From Mind to Molecules.* New York: Scientific American Library.

Walker Tileston, D. (2004). *What Every Teacher Should Know About Learning, Memory, and the Brain.* Thousand Oaks, CA: Corwin Press.

LEANN NICKELSEN, M.ED.

Processing Time

The time required for the brain to neurologically process and encode newly acquired information is often referred to as *processing time.* This critical aspect of the learning process allows new ideas to settle into memory and become easily retrievable. Brain research even reports that perhaps the most significant period of learning frequently occurs not when learners are paying attention to external stimuli, but in fact when they are allowed time to mentally process new information. Educators who handle these moments correctly can allow learners to encode and understand new content, and create a strong foundation upon which to build further related concepts.

Simply stated, to "learn" new information the brain needs to build connections between brain cells. This occurs when the dendrites of one brain cell approach the axon of another brain cell. They get close, yet don't quite touch. The dendrites then secrete chemicals—neurotransmitters—which the axon of another brain cell detects. If the information being passed is sufficiently "interesting" to the receiving brain cell, it will pass it along to yet another brain cell nearby. This process continues extremely rapidly, between millions of brain cells nearly simultaneously. Connections are made between brain cells as incoming information is sorted, organized, and stored for later recall.

For these connections to be strong, myelination must also occur. This is the process by which fatty tissue forms around the axons being used most often. This layer of tissue functions much like rubber insulation on electrical cords. The result of myelination on these axons is the more rapid and reliable transmission of electrical impulses, thus creating better communication between and among neurons. Perhaps this description of how the brain biologically learns can be summarized by saying it is a *bio-chemical process stimulated by electricity.*

Brain researchers will recognize this as a fairly simplistic explanation of a vastly complex process, one they are learning more about every day. However, for the purposes of this discussion it is more than adequate because for educators the key lies not in understanding the technical terms, nor even in fully grasping how the processes actually happen. Rather the most important aspect of this description to a practitioner— someone who plans on *using* this information in a classroom—lies simply in that fact that encoding new information is a *process.* For this process to be effective, it must have sufficient time to work. Essentially, for learning to effectively occur, these processes—as well as many more complex yet related biological ones—must be given an appropriate amount of time to accomplish the tasks for which they were biologically designed by nature.

Interfering with the process, whether through an overload of information or by competing stimuli, causes the process to either never finish as energy in the brain moves on to a new task, or in some cases simply abort. The result is a series of incomplete connections between brain cells, causing learners to develop hazy memories of new information. Consequently, little or no learning will have actually occurred. Building further upon this ill-constructed foundation only complicates the multiple problems that have already been created.

Understanding this critical need to allow the brain to complete building these neural connections naturally leads to the question of how educators should handle facilitation of the learning process. However, the optimum learning sequence can be stated in a fairly simple manner. New content should be presented in brief bursts, possibly between ten to fifteen minutes, followed by a period of time allowing learners to process the newly acquired information.

How long an educator chooses to allow for processing will depend on a wide variety of factors. If the recently presented information is entirely new to the learners, the necessary processing time may be significantly greater than if what was just taught was closely related to previous material, or even a straightforward review. The length of time may also be influenced by the depth of the new information. If the content is dense with important facts, critical concepts, and possibly even new terminology, learners may need a lengthy amount of time to fully encode and store the information. On the other hand, if the content section was somewhat lighter, the processing time required might be significantly less. In general, however, after ten to fifteen minutes of presenting new information, educators can expect to allow from two to five minutes for processing, and then adjust the time appropriately given these various factors.

In addition to deciding how long to allow for processing, educators must also make another critical choice regarding what learners will actually be doing during their processing time. One way to process the information verbally might be to have learners form dyads or small groups, and simply discuss their reactions to the material in an open-ended manner. At the conclusion of the processing time, they could even be invited to share their thoughts, ideas, and insights. Educators might also allow more directed verbal processing time by providing each dyad or group with a pointed question that they will respond to, again based on their reactions to the material.

Another direction educators might pursue could be to allow learners to process the material in some written manner. Perhaps they are given time to review the notes they have already taken and make clarifying notes to themselves. Perhaps they are directed to write on a piece of paper at least three questions from their notes regarding any aspect of the presentation where they would like further clarification. Another choice might be to again form groups, and this time each group must generate a paragraph that summarizes the key aspects of the information.

There is even a wide range of highly creative choices that an open-minded educator might choose to explore. For example, perhaps small groups of learners could each be given one key aspect of the new information. Their assignment would then be to present this idea to the rest of the class in a nonverbal manner, perhaps by acting it out, by telling a story about it, or maybe even drawing a picture of it. A further choice related to drawing might be to have all learners review their notes, and then allow them a specified number of minutes to add creative doodles around their notes. For many students, the related visual stimuli will provide a more powerful memory clue to the content than the written words.

These are only a few of the many ways in which an educator might chose to allow for processing time. Given that there is usually a wide variety of preferred **learning styles** in most classes, the best classrooms frequently allow for a mixture of these strategies. Any of these options would allow the brain to continue to build and solidify connections between brain cells without the adverse effect of competing stimuli.

This idea connects directly to one of the most dangerous phrases in education, "Time On Task." Brain research clearly indicates educators should not want learners to always be "on task." Consider a situation in which the task given to the students was to process new information by discussing the material in groups, and then drawing images in their notebooks. This clearly might be valuable processing time for some learners. However, an outside observer might view this activity as frivolous and "off task," when in fact learners are doing exactly what they should be doing to fully understand and remember the information.

Many word pairs could possibly be used to express the strategy discussed here, where new information is presented followed immediately by processing time. It might be referred to as "ebb and flow," or "focus and diffuse," or "press and release." All of these are indeed appropriate descriptions of how the brain processes information and its need for adequate processing time. A final metaphor to consider might be the manner in which bread is baked. After the dough has been prepared, it must be allowed to sit for a period of time while it rises due to the reaction of the yeast. Baking dough too soon creates a "flat" result. The same situation applies as the brain attempts to process new information. After it has taken in a certain amount of information, the "dough" has been created, and the chemical processes in the brain must be allowed to act upon the content, just as the yeast acts upon the dough, so the information is processed and stored correctly. When educators provide learners with appropriate periods of processing time, they are essentially using the correct recipe for creating solid learning.

See also: **Attention; Learning Cycle; Information Processing Model; Learning in a Social Context.**

Further Readings

Allen, R. (2002). *Impact Teaching: Ideas and Strategies for Teachers to Maximize Student Learning.* Boston, MA: Allyn and Bacon.

Hart, L. (1999). *Human Brain and Human Learning.* Kent, Washington: Books for Educators, Inc.

Philp, R. (2005). *The Engaged Brain.* San Diego, CA: The Brain Store, Inc.

Sapulsky, R. (1999). *Why Zebras Don't Get Ulcers.* (4th ed.) New York: W. H. Freeman.

Sylwester, R. (2000). *A Biological Brain in a Cultural Classroom.* Thousand Oaks, CA: Corwin Press.

RICHARD H. ALLEN, PH.D.

R

Reading and Comprehension

That reading happens in the brain is obvious. However, how this occurs has been a focus of scientific investigation for over hundred years. What do we really know about how the brain learns to read? We know that whereas speaking is natural, reading is not. Children do not automatically read. They have to learn how to do it. Reading in its simplest form is a process of decoding and comprehension. The ultimate goal of reading is for children to become sufficiently fluent to understand what they read. Reading begins when someone unlocks the code of a written language system. And the "someone" to be a reader needs to know how this system works. Where does this knowledge reside? It resides in the brain. However, the neuroscience of reading is much more complex than this simplistic view. Reading is an elaborate process that involves decoding abstract symbols into sounds, then into words that generate meaning.

In particular, the past decade has experienced amazing progress in our understanding of the brain and its impact on reading and comprehension. Never before have neuroscientific studies and classroom instruction been so closely linked. Educators can now refer to carefully designed research studies to determine the most effective ways to teach reading. What does this evidence tell us? Several studies have found that reading originates in and relies on the brain systems for spoken language. The major findings of the National Reading Panel indicate that in order to read, children need to be taught alphabetics (phonemic awareness and phonics); reading fluency; vocabulary; and strategies for reading comprehension. These components of the reading process need to be taught comprehensively, systematically, and explicitly.

Another important question about recent research findings is whether teachers can implement these findings in their classrooms. The connection between theory and practice remains paramount in the minds of educators concerned with the issue of reading and comprehension. Reading is very likely the one area of the school curriculum where neuroscience has made its greatest impact. Educators have been well aware of the difficulties involved in learning to read and have long debated the best methods to teach beginning reading. Reading proficiency depends on expert teaching so that the reader learns how to access print accurately and fluently.

Brain researchers have developed new technologies for looking inside the brain and analyzing functions and process. These technologies fall into two major categories: those that examine brain function and those that focus on brain structure. Different technologies are utilized to look at how the brain works. These procedures can be used to isolate and identify the areas of the brain where distinct levels of activity are occurring. Using these technologies, researchers have been able to determine how different brains function when conducting certain activities, including reading. Some of these discoveries include:

- Novice readers use different neural pathways while reading than skilled readers.
- Individuals with reading difficulties access different brain regions to decode text than proficient readers.
- The brains of people with reading difficulties are working harder than those of skilled readers.
- With proper instructional intervention, the brains of young, struggling readers can be rewired to use different cerebral areas that more closely align with those of typical readers.

Clearly, we have a lot to learn. Investigators and researchers have worked hard to understand reading and now with the ability of new technology to observe the brain in action, they have a place to focus their research.

The ultimate goal of reading is for children to become sufficiently fluent to understand what they read. Reading comprehension depends heavily on spoken language comprehension. Reading comprehension is a complex cognitive process that relies on several components to be successful. To comprehend a printed word, we first need to decode it. However, much more is involved. To develop these comprehension skills, students need to interact with text to derive meaning and develop vocabulary and linguistic knowledge.

An area of the brain that primarily has to do with this meaning-making process is the temporal lobe of the brain. The temporal lobes are located on each side of the brain just behind the ears. Looking through this new focus on brain imaging, we can see how some children experience greater challenge and struggle in becoming readers. It is important to look at appropriate interventions for these children. Some students can read and not understand a word, and yet others seem to understand everything but struggle with decoding the words. Because of this discrepancy, educators are vitally interested in information and strategies that are brain-based and can assist them in reaching all students and engaging them in the reading process.

From this research, applications for instructional practices that are brain-compatible have been developed. These strategies also take into consideration how to build the reading brain and how to differentiate instruction.

Understanding Text

How do good readers derive meaning from text? Good readers are constantly monitoring their own comprehension and are thinking what they need to do to understand the text. They are metacognitive and aware of their own comprehension. Text comprehension occurs when the brain's frontal lobe is able to derive meaning by processing the visual and auditory input with the reader's prior knowledge.

What do good readers do when they read?

- Good readers are active readers.
- They have clear goals in their mind as they read and constantly evaluate while reading the text.
- Good readers skim the text to preview before reading, noting structure and format.
- Good readers make predictions as they read.
- They read selectively—making decisions about their reading—what to read carefully, what to skim quickly, what to re-read, etc.
- Good readers construct, revise, and question as they read.
- They draw upon, compare, and integrate their prior knowledge with the material in the text.
- They think about the author's craft—their style, beliefs, intentions, etc.
- They monitor their understanding of the text, making adjustments of their reading as necessary.
- Good readers try to determine the meaning of unfamiliar words and concepts in the text.
- They evaluate the text's quality and value and react to the text in a range of ways.
- Good readers read different kinds of text differently, using distinct approaches for narrative and expository text.
- For good readers, comprehension is a consuming, continuous, and complex activity that is both satisfying and productive.

Explicit instruction is important for all learners as they engage in the meaning-making process interacting with text. Some tested, brain-compatible and research-validated strategies include:

Predicting—Preview the title, pictures, headings, connecting student experiences to story themes or topics of informational text. Have students make "informed guesses." Help "fill in the gaps" in their prior knowledge. This stage is critical for students to construct meaning.

Questioning—Have the students ask and answer questions. Use higher order thinking strategies for questions based on Bloom's Taxonomy (application, analysis, synthesis, and evaluation). Teach students to generate good questions. This process helps set a purpose for reading: to read, discuss, and investigate.

Clarifying—It is important to note the big ideas and to assist students with comparing and contrasting their understandings. Establish the common base of understanding and fill in the gaps.

Summarizing—It is necessary to assist the students to synthesize the big ideas, key events, and critical themes. They can write their summary or share it verbally with a partner.

Imagery—Help students form pictures in their minds, making "mental movies." Assist them in techniques to visualize the action.

Teachers need to keep in mind some specific components that are important to build comprehension strategies in students. These strategies are best taught through "reciprocal dialogue." Dialogue moves from teacher-directed to student-directed. An explicit description of the strategy and when and how it should be used needs to be shared. Teachers should model the strategy in action with specific examples. The use of mental modeling and thinking aloud provides a "window on the thinking" for the student. Collaborative use of the strategy in action should follow, so that students are able to cooperatively share their application of the technique. Practice and feedback within an interactive social setting is essential. This should be followed by guided practice using the strategy with gradual release of responsibility. The final stage should be independent use of the strategy on the part of the learner.

Think Aloud Strategy

Specific approaches to comprehension instruction that are brain-compatible involve teaching multiple strategies simultaneously. A technique that teachers can use to help all students become more metacognitive is the Think Aloud strategy. Comprehension strategies to model during Think Alouds include: activating prior knowledge; building vocabulary; determining importance; questioning and clarifying; inferring; synthesizing; summarizing.

When a teacher introduces Think Aloud, some techniques need to be considered. Before reading the book to the class, decide which strategy will be the focus of the session. Preview the text to determine appropriate places to pause for personal commentary related to the focus strategy. Plan how you will demonstrate the use of that strategy. When introducing the book, explain that you will be stopping to share your thoughts. During various think alouds focus on different strategies. If focusing on background knowledge, select parts of the story or text that connect with your personal experiences (text-to-self connections), that connect with other literacy works (text-to-text connection), and that connect with events and life in general (text-to-world connection). Pause at chosen spots and share with the students. When the reading is complete, invite the students to share their thoughts. When the students are engaged in their own independent reading, guide them to use these strategies that have been modeled for them.

Visualization

Proficient readers create images in their brains as they read. Visualization is a natural part of reading for them. Struggling readers, for various reasons, are not able to connect to the text in this way. They have not learned to make "movies in their mind." To help students visualize as they read, start with a simple sentence and ask the students questions that help create images.

Guiding students with detailed questions that lead to open-ended answers helps them create their own visual interpretation of the sentence. It transforms a simple image into a complete setting. This activity not only encourages students to create imagery, but also encourages them to think about questioning and generate questions themselves.

Graphic Organizers

Graphic and cognitive organizers can help students to consolidate and elaborate their understanding of what has been read. These strategies are usually best done in small collaborative teams using the principles of cooperative learning. The goal is to get students to process the information at a deeper and more meaningful level. This in turn will facilitate increased retention and recall of information.

Scaffolding instruction with cognitive organizers is important. The teacher needs to model the filling out of the diagram during the lesson. The student follows along. Then the teacher fills out only the first part of the diagram and the students work in pairs to complete the rest, using their notes and texts. Then the teacher hands out blank diagrams for the students to complete. The final stage is when the students create their own diagram, map, or graphic and complete it based on the reading.

Graphic organizers are brain-compatible tools for comprehension and help students gather data, organize, and categorize information and create points of comparison. Graphic organizers appeal to various learning styles and help students learn concepts because they are able to order the information in a pattern for the brain to make the information more memorable.

Reciprocal Teaching

Reciprocal Teaching is a research-validated intervention strategy designed to assist less capable readers in developing powerful reading comprehension strategies as they gain more control over their reading. This technique helps students focus and monitor their reading to achieve higher comprehension. The process involves structured dialogue in which the teacher begins by being the leader, modeling the strategies, guiding student responses, and taking care to "think aloud" during modeling. The students then move into guided practice in four areas: predict, question, clarify, and summarize.

As students take on the roles in Reciprocal Teaching, they predict content, question and clarify their understanding of the content, and then summarize what they have learned.

Directed Reading-Thinking Activity

Directed reading-thinking activity (DRTA) has many facets that support and extend the student's reading and thinking. The components that support comprehension include: activating prior knowledge through brainstorming and providing an anticipatory set of questions to create a need to know, predicting the content that will be covered in the reading using a cloze procedure so that students will make appropriate predictions around key concepts of the story utilizing syntactic and semantic cues; reading and revisiting predictions to compare and contrast with the actual events of the story or chapter.

This is a powerful brain-compatible strategy to help students activate prior knowledge as they brainstorm words and phrases they associate with the topic. At the predicting stage, students are establishing their own purposes for reading. When they select appropriate words and phrases for the cloze procedure of a passage from the text, they are building their word bank and anticipation of the actual content. Finally, when students are given the opportunity to reflect, collaborate, confirm, and revise predictions after the reading, they are practicing active engaging strategies for comprehension.

In conclusion, reading and comprehending well is an instructional imperative in our schools. Certainly, there is more to developing better comprehension than just memory. Research on how the brain reads has produced impressive progress. There is still a lot to be learned about how the brain implements the cognitive processes of reading. Teachers need to provide an enriched brain-compatible environment to foster the meaning-making process. It is important to display learning resources throughout the room. Provide opportunities for interaction among students, because the human brain is a social communicative brain. Guide students, through brain-based practices, to help them master important skills and strategies.

See also: **Reading and Fluency; Content Area Literacy.**

Further Readings

Jensen, E. (1998). *Teaching with the Brain in Mind.* Alexandria, VA: ASCD.

Shaywitz, S., Shaywitz, B. (2004). False claims about literacy development. *Educational Leadership* 60:6–11.

Sousa, D. (2005). *How the Brain Learns to Read.* Thousand Oaks, CA: Corwin Press, Inc.

Wolfe, P., Nevills, P. (2004). *Building the Reading Brain, Pre k-3*. Thousand Oaks, CA: Corwin Press, Inc.

The Brain Store (Eric Jensen): www.brainstore.com

KATHERINE D. PEREZ, ED.D.

Reading and Fluency

According to the 2000 National Reading Panel report fluency is acknowledged as one of the five basic components of a good reading program with the others being phonemic awareness, phonics, vocabulary, and comprehension. Traditionally the fluency piece of the reading puzzle has been left to develop on its own or as a side effect of the oral reading component associated with phonics and vocabulary. A clearer definition of fluency leads to a better understanding of how students acquire fluency.

Fluency is the ability to read text automatically, accurately, and with expression. When fluent readers read, it sounds as though they are speaking. The reading is fluid and accurate, with appropriate speed, appropriate phrasing, and correct intonation. Fluency becomes the puzzle piece placed between word recognition and comprehension. In independent leveled text and with practice, word recognition and comprehension occur simultaneously. With rereading and good strategies, readers are able to develop a sense of knowing how and when to pause within sentences and at the ends of sentences, and when to change tone and emphasis within sentences.

Accurate Letter and Word Decoding

Reading fluency has three important stages that lead to full comprehension of text. The first stage of fluency is accurate letter and word decoding. This group of readers is putting the phonics puzzle pieces together to sound out the words in a text with minimal errors. Although sometimes fluency and automaticity are used interchangeably, they are not the same thing. Automaticity is the fast and accurate recall of words and phrases. This begins to occur when students' brains are establishing the visual patterns within written language. Students first recognize high frequency words and then process other words that may be less familiar by following known patterns. The more times that students see words separately and within text, the better chance that they will be able to read those words accurately, automatically, and fluidly. Rehearsal is a critical component in transferring new information from working memory to long-term storage in their brains. It is important to devote adequate time to the practice and to make sure that the rehearsal is positive. The **feedback** that the students get during this learning stage must be specific, quick, and supportive. The structure of the fluency puzzle piece is teaching the predictable patterns in the written system to give the readers the code necessary to learn to read.

Automatic Processing

The second stage of fluency uses automatic processing. In this stage readers are more ready to consolidate and automate basic decoding skills and give more attention to making sense and meaning of the text. Fluency is that bridge between word recognition and comprehension. Because fluent readers do not need to spend so much time laboring over decoding words, they can focus on the sense and meaning of the text.

Using strategies that good readers employ for comprehension purposes, students have a head start in making sense of the text through strategies such as previewing the book to see what it is about and connecting the topic to what they know in their own lives. Then regardless of the strategy chosen by the teacher to instruct fluency, the students have a head start in understanding the text.

Reading requires the brain to perform in many areas for readers to be successful. The visual cortex is involved in recognizing the visual pattern of the word and the angular gyrus translates the written word into sounds. Wernicke's Area and Broca's Area are located in the left hemisphere and are the two language processing centers of the brain. Wernicke's is involved in the comprehension of words, while Broca's is involved in the processing of syntax, which is the area that helps us understand language. If the spoken sentence structure is complex, more areas of the brain are activated, including areas in the right hemisphere. Reading is complex and not linear and singular. Many processes including decoding, word identification, vocabulary, reasoning, concept formation, and sense/meaning are going on at the same time.

Automatic processing can be increased through strategies that use guided, modeled, and repeated oral reading. There are many structures for teaching fluency, but all include using a "perfect" model for the student. In one instructional model students hear the text read aloud by a teacher first. The second time the teacher reads the text again with the students joining in when they can. After the second reading the teacher and the students discuss any words that are unfamiliar or patterns that might be troublesome. The passage can be reread a third time. The following day the same passage is read first by the teacher and then followed by reading by the student or students with the teacher fading the voice until only the students' voices are heard. Passages can then be practiced with a reading partner, read silently, and read alone to the teacher to get a scoring on rate or accuracy.

Flashcards with irregular words or familiar regular high-frequency words that students have mastered can be used in games that encourage them to read as many words as possible in thirty seconds. Words that are correct are placed in one stack, while words missed are placed in a second stack. Obviously, feedback for both students playing should be provided to increase the accuracy, but their mission is to improve their own goals.

Letter naming is included in fluency activities and can be addressed through activities that involve students using plastic letters or letter tiles randomly drawn out of a bag. Place the five or ten tiles on the table top and model naming the letters (or sounds of the letters.) Rapid automatic naming of objects is shown to be a precursor to reading with fluency. The brain can use the practice in naming familiar objects such as colors, numbers, animals, household objects, or toys within a given time. The brain is working at developing connections to identify items rapidly, disengaging from that category, and moving to a new category then identifying the new set. Flashcards with pictures categorized in groups can be used to encourage accuracy and speed.

Prosody

The third stage of fluency has readers sounding the way "good readers" sound. In this stage the reader reads with "prosody," a term that describes reading with accuracy, speed, and expression. Readers, who read with the same intonation on each word, who pay little or no attention to surface punctuation, and who stop and start at inappropriate times throughout the text, will have little understanding of the meaning of the piece of text.

Inefficient word recognition and poor decoding skills lead to a slow, halting pace, poor phrasing, careless mistakes, and little expression. This lack of skill affects comprehension as well as the ability for the readers to self-monitor and self-correct their own reading.

Students benefit from appropriate texts and activities that have been structured to allow for success and enjoyment. Many of our struggling students who are pulled out for the flashcard repetitive activities often miss the fluency activities that include the Readers' Theater, the choral reading, the partner reading, and other activities that are more passion-filled, theater-like, "why-we-read" parts of the class.

Fluency can be developed through instruction. When students are working alone or with peers on activities to foster reading with expression, they should be working with independent level texts. If working with teachers, then instructional level texts are appropriate to use, however frustration level text should not be used to develop prosody. For the purpose of developing fluency, students should read and reread text that they have already read as they are trying to improve speed, accuracy, intonation, and expression.

To sound like good readers, students need to hear what good reading sounds like. In its simplest form, teachers must provide various models of good reading. Teachers reading picture books aloud, guest readers reading favorite books, books read on tape, and teachers sharing chapter books are all examples of modeling good reading. Teachers who partner together to model Readers' Theater for groups of students are wonderful examples of enthusiasm for reading. The key to making this component of fluency work is repetition. The students need the opportunities to experience the same text multiple times. Too often we present them with new material and rush them through the work without providing them the time necessary to manipulate the rhythm, the tone, the expression, and to dig into the deeper meanings of the work.

Fluency at Work

Using appropriately leveled text that is of high interest to the reader will assure success with building fluency skills. Students need guided, repeated oral reading that has been modeled along with independent silent reading at their appropriate levels. There are many reading strategies that can improve fluency. Echo Reading allows the students to listen to the teacher read part of a text while following along, and then "echo reading" the same text, trying to repeat the teacher's rate and expression. The teacher begins by reading only two or three sentences of the text fluently. In echo reading the text can be available to each student individually, or can be shown on an overhead or chart paper. Text can be from a story, a poem, or even a song.

With Choral Reading students again use a variety of text either individually or as a class, but in this format the reading is done a little differently. The teacher models the task by reading the first part of the text out loud, setting the pace and reading with proper phrasing, rate, and expression. On the second reading, the students read along with the teacher trying to match the pace, phrasing, rate, and expression of the teacher. With each following reading, the teacher begins to lessen the support until the students sound more in control. On subsequent days for most of these strategies, the teacher can assess small groups or individual students for pace, phrasing, rate, and expression.

Partner Reading has several variations but is often used in pairing a higher performing student with a lower performing reader for fluency practice. Each pair of students has texts at the lower performing reader's instructional-reading level. Partner A being the stronger reader reads the text aloud modeling fluent reading for one minute. Partner B follows along while A reads. Then Partner B reads for one minute. Partner Reading needs to be modeled for the entire class several times before everyone begins the process. Students are not told that Partner A is the stronger reader.

Readers' Theater is one of the most enjoyable fluency activities for students. Students are given a reading passage in script format. This passage often comes from a favorite book that the class has read and that the teacher has adapted or a text that has been commercially adapted. Copies of the text are given to each student depending on the number of characters in the script. The text for each character is highlighted, and parts are modeled and practiced. This type of production is performed for an audience; however it does not require students to memorize their parts as reading is the key. Costumes and props are not necessary, but a set day and time for the reading performance is important.

Through brain compatible instructional strategies this piece of the puzzle can be taught and facilitate reading comprehension.

See also: **Patterns and Programs; Reading and Comprehension; Reading Vocabulary and Word Recognition.**

Further Readings

Lyons, C., Clay, M.M. (2003). *Teaching Struggling Readers: How to Use Brain-Based Research to Maximize Learning.* Portsmouth, N.H.: Heinemann. (2000). *Report of the National Reading Panel: Teaching Children to Read.* Washington, D.C.

Rhodes, L. (1996). *Readers and Writers with a Difference.* Portsmouth, NH: Heinemann.

Sousa, D. (2004). *How the Brain Learns to Read.* Thousand Oaks, CA: Corwin Press.

Vaughn, S., Linan-Thompson, S. (2004). *Research-Based Methods of Reading Instruction Grades K-3.* Alexandria, VA: ASCD.

Wolfe, P., Nevills, P. (2004). *Building the Reading Brain, PreK-3.* Thousand Oaks, CA: Corwin Press.

LINDA G. ALLEN, M.ED.

Reading in the Content Area

Content Area Reading is the use of language—reading, writing, speaking, and listening—to learn subject matter. Teachers of content who embrace this concept understand how students learn and reflect this in their instruction. They not only teach content, they teach students how to read, write, speak, and listen in the language of the content area in their efforts to help students become independent, lifelong learners.

Recent research with the use of functional magnetic resonance imaging (fMRI) has led to a better understanding of the reading process. No one area of the brain specializes in reading, rather, various areas of the brain work together to make sense of and construct meaning from text. Being able to read and make sense of what we read is predicated on our knowledge of previously acquired spoken language. Our brain must first "know" its abc's so that the brain can connect letters to sounds or phonemes. Children who have already been successfully using spoken language, a natural development, must now learn to read, an unnatural activity . Our language is a complex one and letters and groups of letters often represent different sounds. For example, the "a" sound in water differs from the "a" sound in cake. While some come by this naturally, most will have to be taught how to read and make meaning of text.

During the reading process, text is processed by the brain's right hemisphere where the visual cortex of the brain first "sees" the word. This information is then transferred to the brain's left hemisphere where the brain's language areas help to sound out words and make meaning from text. In the Angular Gyrus, the word is phonetically decoded as this area breaks the word down into its basic sounds or phonemes. This sounding out process activates Broca's area of the brain where the word is identified. Finally, through the brain's higher level functions of reasoning and concept formation in Wernicke's area, we are able to think about and understand what the word means or represents.

The brain is a pattern seeking device and this quality is fundamental in teaching reading in the content areas. As the student reads content in science, math, or social studies it is seeking patterns to connect it with stored knowledge. Every area of the content has its own distinctive patterns of information. The brain must find the pathway to the prior knowledge to make sense of the reading text.

Neuroscientists discovered through positron emission tomography (PET) scans that the brain stores related words together. Verbs are in one area, nouns in another, and then further desegregation of nouns between tools and animals. Proximity between bits of information enables them to quickly activate each other aiding in retrieval and storage. For instance, biology investigates cells and mitosis; this information is stored near each other.

When reading a passage, students must be able to hold one paragraph in their memory and associate it with the next. Working memory must link paragraphs together so that the main ideas can be understood at the end of a reading. Text comprehension occurs when the brain's frontal lobe is able to derive meaning by processing the visual and auditory input that resulted from the reader's prior knowledge.

During elementary school, reading instruction focuses on narrative text rather than informational text, and tends to be fiction rather than nonfiction. In addition, the typical textbook for the high school level classroom is much more sophisticated and complex than the type of texts students encounter during elementary school. Secondary students are expected, all of a sudden, and in most cases without instruction, to be able to read and understand vast amounts of complex material. However, reading is much more than simply sounding out or being able to pronounce words. Being able to read difficult text material requires advanced reading skills. In addition, reading tasks vary and do not always require the same types of thinking skills. Reading a chapter from a physics text requires a different approach to reading than one would use when reading a short story, for example. According to the national assessment of education progress (NAEP) 60 percent of secondary readers are able to read at a basic level but only 5 percent of these same readers can interpret what they read. In other words, while most secondary students may be able to decode written text, the vast majority of them are not able to make sense of what they read. Perhaps more alarming is the fact that this statistic has remained constant over the past twenty years.

We know what characterizes good, active readers. Good readers are able to construct meaning from what they read. They know how to monitor and adjust their reading and when done, to reflect upon what was read. Good readers take time before reading to set a purpose for reading, to preview and make predictions. During reading, good readers stay focused and know how to monitor and regulate understanding, to ask and answer questions, to stop, slow down, or re-read. Good readers strive to make connections, to consider how new information fits with what is already known. After reading, good readers take time to summarize and reflect upon what was read, to revisit predictions, and make adjustments to their understanding of subject matter. Good readers will often seek out additional information beyond what was just read.

Poor readers, on the other hand, are passive. They are often overwhelmed and plunge into a reading task without any thought from beginning to end. Easily distracted, poor readers make no effort to monitor their reading, and when finished, are often not sure what they just read. Most often, they are relieved to have finished the assignment.

Good readers, then, are strategic. They are deliberate and thoughtful in their approach to a particular learning task. These readers are able to apply strategies to construct meaning as they read. Somewhere along the way good readers acquire the tools to enable them to make meaning of what they are reading. Although some students seem to intuitively figure out how to be strategic, most of our students need to be explicitly taught how to be strategic. Eventually, applying the strategies becomes automatic but not until we, as content area teachers, model for our students how to read, learn, and be strategic in meaningful, authentic ways. Secondary teachers should provide students with the tools to strategically approach reading tasks. Content area teachers can be more effective when they purposefully incorporate strategies into their instruction.

The National Reading Panel reports that most secondary teachers do not use content area strategies in their instruction. Many teachers feel they do not have the time or expertise to teach their students how to read. They view their role as that of content area specialist, not reading teacher, and feel that the teaching of reading is something that elementary school teachers were supposed to have done. Reading instruction should, however, continue after elementary school and be integrated with the teaching of content. As today's secondary teacher often feels pressured to cover content and teach a prescribed set of standards, many secondary content area classrooms continue to be characterized by the assign and tell method. These students, having spent hours in these classrooms, are rarely actively involved in their learning. In fact, they are quite comfortable being told what, not how, to think by their teachers. It is time for a change and a shift from teaching students how to read to teaching students how to use reading as a tool to learn.

If our students are to be strategic in their learning, we must be strategic in our teaching. Content area teachers should adhere to an instructional framework, a guide or outline, to facilitate the teaching of lessons. The instructional framework reflects what we know about good readers: they prepare to read, they are actively engaged while they read, and they take time to reflect upon what they have read when they are finished. If we utilize a consistent approach to instruction in our classrooms, our students will be more likely to internalize it and apply it in their own learning.

Strategies can be plugged into the stages of the instructional framework to provide students with the tools they need to be good readers. As teachers, we need to model strategic reading and teach our students strategies with the same deliberateness and passion as we teach our content. In addition, we must deliberately and purposefully inform students what the strategy is and why they are engaging in it so that students have an understanding behind the strategy and when it can be useful. Finally, we need to incorporate a variety of strategies so that students are able to select the strategy that works best for them and for a particular academic task. Content area teachers can play a vital role in teaching their students how to read to learn by incorporating strategies in a purposeful, meaningful manner. It is essential that teachers take time to inform students what the strategy is, why they are engaging in it, and to model the strategy for students.

In the first phase of the instructional framework, the pre-reading phase, the teacher's job is to prepare the students for learning. During this phase teaching goals include determining and building upon students' background knowledge, setting a purpose for reading, getting students motivated or curious about the reading, and creating a need to know. This pre-reading phase is perhaps the most critical as research has shown that the strongest factor in learning new information is the ability to connect it to existing knowledge. Schema theory explains how prior knowledge plays a role in comprehending new information. As we present our students with new information, we must create ways for them to connect the new ideas with their prior knowledge. Tapping into students' background knowledge is a key aspect of comprehension and helps students to be prepared for the reading ahead.

Consider having students engage in the following types of activities to facilitate the pre-reading phase of the instructional framework and to make an initial connection to the topic being studied:

- Describe in writing or share with the class what they know or think they know about the topic and what they want to know about the topic (KWL).
- Incorporate **writing** to learn and have students respond to a specific teacher-created prompt related to the topic (Quick Write, Admit Slip).
- Show a video clip, take a field trip, or visit web sites to spark students' curiosity about the topic or simply write a question on the board to get students thinking about the lesson.
- Share key vocabulary words students will encounter in the reading, ask students to decide if they know the word, have heard of the word, or have no idea about the word (Knowledge Rating Scale).
- Have the class generate a list of ideas related to the topic, record on the board or overhead (Brainstorming, Factstorming).

- Share visuals related to the topic, have students record their thoughts in writing or share with a partner or the class (Journal, Log).
- Fill in a Graphic Organizer as a class to help students see relationships and connections among ideas related to the topic.
- Have students agree or disagree with teacher-created statements related to the reading (Anticipation Guide).
- Preview the text, have students look for its organizational features such as headings and bolded terms (Text Preview, Skim Away).
- Generate a list of questions by turning section headings into questions (SQ3R).

In the second phase of the instructional framework, the teacher's job is to support the students while they are engaged in the reading process and facilitate student comprehension of text. One of the most effective ways teachers can do this is by demonstrating or modeling their own thought processes by thinking aloud for their students. Teachers can walk students through the thought process of figuring out an unfamiliar word or verbalize how to use a graph or read a chart. The during-reading phase of the instructional framework is directly related to a student's ability to be strategic while reading, to monitor understanding of what is being read, to be megacognitively aware. Megacognitively aware readers are able to monitor their understanding by asking questions to determine if what they are reading is making sense. These readers have self-knowledge of how they learn and they know how to regulate their understanding.

Consider having students engage in the following types of activities to facilitate the during-reading phase of the instructional framework as they work to understand ideas and concepts:

- Teach students to stop, think, and ask questions while they read, such as: Do I understand what I am reading? What is the main idea of what I am reading? Or create questions starting with Who? What? When? Where? How? and have students record answers as they read (Self-Questioning).
- Take turns posing questions to your students and having them pose questions to you while reading; model the types of higher level thinking questions they should be asking themselves (ReQuest).
- Ask students to think of personal experiences they have had that help them connect to what they are reading, have them close their eyes and try to get a visual image as they read (Visualization, Imagery).
- Create statements for students to respond to on the literal, interpretive, and applied levels of thinking (3-Level Reading Guide).

- Incorporate writing to learn and have students stop from time to time while reading to take notes or record questions they are having or thoughts that come to mind (Journal, Log).
- Have students keep running lists of new or confusing vocabulary as they read (Vocabulary Self-Collection).
- Create data charts or information tables and have students fill them in with information as they read (Jot Chart, Story Map, Think Sheet).
- Working in partners, have students take turns reading aloud and questioning one another about the reading (Paired Reading).
- Have students use post-it notes to mark areas in the text they agree with, disagree with, question, or do not understand OR create a system of symbols to correspond with categories of information such as "!" Significant Information "?" Unclear Information and "=" Information I Can Connect With; have students use the symbols to mark text as they read (X Marks the Spot, SMART/Self-Monitored Approach to Reading and Thinking).
- Add to the Graphic Organizer started prior to reading.

In the third phase of the instructional framework, the teacher's job is to determine comprehension by helping students to summarize, reflect, and evaluate, in essence, to think critically about what was read. Consider having students engage in the following types of activities to facilitate the post-reading phase of the instructional framework and to act upon or apply what they have just read about:

- Incorporate writing to learn and have students write a summary, in their own words, to reflect their understanding of what they just read (Summary Microtheme, One-Sentence Summary); have students write a letter to the editor of the school newspaper to express their opinion related to the reading or write a patterned poem to reflect their understanding of the reading (Cinquain, BioPoem).
- Students could further explore the topic area by completing a research paper or project and presenting the findings to the class (Research Paper).
- Have students participate in a discussion about what was read, use the questions generated prior to reading to get the discussion going (Reaction Guide).
- Revisit the statements students reacted to prior to reading to see if thoughts have changed and discuss why or why not (Making Predictions).
- Have students discuss both sides of an issue, identify rationale points for each, and take a stance (Discussion Web).

- Incorporate writing to learn and have students complete a ticket out of class where they indicate what they learned or what they are still unsure about, collect and use to start the next day's lesson (Exit Slip).
- Finalize the Graphic Organizer.

There is perhaps no other skill that pervades our daily lives as much as our ability to read. Most of us could not get through our day without being able to make sense of the written word. Reading is a continuously developing skill, requiring constant practice, development and refinement, much as one learns to play a musical instrument or excel in a particular sport. It is learned through and improves with practice. As teachers of content, we can be a tremendous resource and model to our students for how to use reading to learn.

See also: **Patterns and Programs; Reading and Comprehension; Visual Brain; Writing.**

Further Readings

Lenski, S.D., Wham, M.A., Johns, J.L. (2003). *Reading and Learning Strategies Middle Through High School.* Dubuque, IA: Kendall/Hunt Publishing Company.

Manzo, A.V., Manzo, U.C., Thomas, M.M. (2005). *Content Area Literacy Strategic Teaching for Strategic Learners.* Hoboken, NJ: John Wiley & Sons, Inc.

Meyer, A., Rose, D.H. (August 21, 2000). *Learning to Read in the Computer Age.* retrieved June 28, 2004 from http://www.cast.org/udl/index.cfm?i=18.

NAEP 1998 reading report card for the nation and states (NCES 1999500). (1999). Washington, DC: National Center for Educational Statistics, U.S. Department of Education.

National Reading Panel (NRP). (2000). Teaching children to read: An evidence-based assessment of the scientific research literature on reading and its implications for reading instruction. Washington, DC: National Institute of Child Health and Human Development.

Sousa, D.A. (2001). *How the Brain Learns.* Thousand Oaks, CA: Corwin Press.

Stephens, E.C., Brown, J.E. (2000). *A Handbook of Content Literacy Strategies: 75 Practical Reading and Writing Ideas.* Norwood, MA: Christopher-Gordon Publishers, Inc.

Tovani, C. (2000). *I Read it but I Don't Get it. Comprehension Strategies for Adolescent Readers.* Portland, ME: Stenhouse Publishers.

SHARON E. ANDREWS, ED.D.

Reading Vocabulary and Word Recognition

Having reading class perceived as not only pleasurable but also as appropriately challenging or strenuous ensures continual growth and independent application of literacy skills. Viewing reading and literacy as a contact sport calls on students to become engaged and actively participate as they develop the capacity to use reading as a multifaceted tool for learning. Teachers are called on to design instructional days based on student need, content standards/benchmarks, and the current research regarding best-practice, brain-compatible learning.

Research about how the brain learns to read is informing teacher decisions with respect to meeting student needs, materials used, and teaching strategies employed. The classroom teacher using a balanced approach takes the best from several philosophic or program models and develops learning experiences that are an optimal match for students as they journey toward literacy.

Current brain imaging studies indicate that effective reading instruction not only improves reading skills but also changes the processing in the brain that in turn makes the task of reading easier. Data now supports the assertion that teaching matters and good teaching prompts changes in the brain that can increase learning. Scientists studying the brains of poor readers who participate in intensive reading programs have documented increased brain activity in the areas used by good readers. After the intervention of strong phonemic awareness lessons, words are recognized instantly, and this is evident in brain-imaging studies. Their newly developed ability to recognize words without decoding or reinventing them each time they appear in a text allows for increased fluency, comprehension, and accuracy.

The beginning reader uses a portion of the brain that involves both the parietal lobes, involved in information processing, spatial orientation, and visual perception, and the temporal lobes, linked to emotional responses, hearing, memory, and speech. These two areas are put to work to identify new words. Broca's area, involved in speech and understanding language, also plays an important role in making word/sound association. With repetition the beginning reader begins to identify patterns between the sounds of spoken language and the letters of the alphabet. They learn to read one letter at a time, just as they learn to utter one sound at a time. As they blend phonemes they begin to decode words. For instance, when a child sees the word "dog" they first connect it to the spoken da-au-gu. As the reader sounds out the word the information then goes to the occipital area where a mental image of a dog develops. This is time consuming, hard work, exasperated by the fact that often the word must be read and reread multiple times before all the associations are made.

As a reader becomes more skilled, a different pathway in the brain is used for reading. In the proficient reader the occipital lobes and the temporal lobes store word forms. Identifying the form of the word facilitates quick recognition; the word no longer needs to be analyzed bit by bit. The form of the word is not the only information stored in these two areas of the brain. An abundance of information about each word is warehoused, including meaning and pronunciation, making it very efficient for the brain to identify the word. Broca's area, that played a key function in the beginning reader identifying words, now has a nominal role. The ability to decode words cannot be underestimated; research shows that decoding abilities are the best predictor of reading comprehension. In addition the skilled reader is able to identify words without any conscious effort, aiding in fluency.

How vocabulary and word recognition/identification are taught has changed drastically. Teachers are asked to consider how students learn new information, how they retain it, and how they can apply these skills to the larger job of being literate. An important part of a quality literacy program is the students' work with vocabulary and word recognition/identification as both have a longlasting impact on their success with literacy. Students with larger vocabularies are more capable readers and they use more strategies to determine unknown words. Word recognition/identification includes all the strategies students employ to decode words, including phonemic analysis, analogies, analysis of syllables, sight word mastery, and analysis of morphemes.

Educators know that retention rates after twenty-four hours for a Lecture mode class= 5 percent, Reading about a topic= 10 percent, an A.V. presentation= 20 percent, Demonstration= 30 percent, A Discussion Group= 50 percent, Practice by Doing= 75 percent, and Teaching Others= 90 percent. This dictates that teachers move away from the lecture or *look it up in the dictionary* methods for vocabulary instruction. Meaningful vocabulary instruction calls for teachers to be aware that connecting to past schema or prior experiences is critical as students store new information by similarities but retrieve it by differences. Good vocabulary and word recognition instruction then will group words to teach by similarities (i.e., vocabulary words to talk about your siblings). This also means that assessments for vocabulary and word recognition/identification need to test distinctly different groups of words not similar groups of words.

Vocabulary and Word Recognition/Identification instruction needs to ask learners to do something significant with their newly learned data or their brain will discard the information within eighteen seconds of processing it. Learning activities need to be purposeful, specific and integrate reading, writing, speaking, listening, and viewing. Reader's Theatre, visual pictures to trigger understanding, pantomime, and paraphrasing are examples of doing something significant with new words or vocabulary. Eight to ten repetitions are necessary for most students to recognize words automatically and the instruction needs to be more than just writing the definition. Knowing the etymology, synonyms, antonyms, multiple meanings, and making a personal connection to the word ensures carryover. New vocabulary should be reviewed in centers, posted on word walls, and used frequently by the teacher in a supported context if we want students to "own" them. By pairing a new, harder word with a known word the teacher can stretch the students without straying from the focus of the lesson. For example, narcissistic could be paired with thinking too much of themselves to let students infer what the hard term means as it relates to a known concept.

Programs of vocabulary and word recognition/identification should provide formative assessments so that students can correct their misconceptions. Summative evaluations come too late in the learning process to inform student learning and a teacher's instructional decision-making. Conversely, immediate or timely feedback helps students and teachers identify strengths and areas needing growth.

If reading is a tool for learning, a process skill and not a content area in and of itself then our instruction needs to mirror this belief by structuring activities and materials so students will not only learn to read but simultaneously read to learn. Consequently, instruction of vocabulary and word recognition/identification needs to occur in the context of real books and authentic printed materials. Isolated, before reading, vocabulary lists are rarely effective. Implanting vocabulary as the class previews a chapter or a new text is more meaningful and more likely to be remembered and used while reading.

Effective literacy teachers provide many, many demonstrations of how to do reading, writing, speaking, listening, and viewing. They design multi-sensory experiences with real books and authentic tasks, maintain a classroom atmosphere that is intense but not pressured, and provide timely and meaningful feedback. Meaningful challenges and an optimal match between readiness and curricular materials and methods allow every student to grow and develop as lifelong readers.

See also: **Challenge and Enrichment; Reading and Comprehension; Reading and Fluency; Content Area Literacy.**

Further Readings

Fountas, I., Pinnell, G. (2000). *Guiding Readers & Writers 3–6*. Portsmouth, NH: Heinemann.

Shaywitz, S.E., Shaywitz, B.A. (2003). Brain scans show dyslexics read better with alternative strategies. *Biological Psychiatry* 54:25–33.

Tompkins, G. (2005). *Literacy for the 21st Century: A balanced approach* (4th ed.), NJ: Prentice Hall.

National Reading Panel 2000. Teaching Students to Read. www.ncrel. org/rf/sbrr/five.htm

LAURIE WENGER, ED.D.

S

Schizophrenia

Schizophrenia is a disease of the brain that affects approximately 2.2 million Americans. Symptoms usually begin between ages sixteen and thirty and include hearing voices (auditory hallucinations), delusions, and disordered thought patterns. In the past two decades, there has been an outpouring of research on the brains of individuals who have schizophrenia showing that such brains have abnormalities in both structure and function. This has conclusively proven that schizophrenia is a brain disease in the same way that multiple sclerosis, Parkinson's disease, and Alzheimer's disease are brain diseases.

Abnormalities of Brain Structure

Research on the structure of brains of people with schizophrenia is done using imaging techniques (e.g., magnetic resonance imaging, MRI) on living individuals and also by studying the brains of individuals with schizophrenia after they have died. At first glance, such brains appear to be normal except for slight shrinkage in some cases. On closer examination, however, a number of structural abnormalities become apparent. These abnormalities can best be measured on individuals with schizophrenia who have not been treated with antipsychotic medications, commonly used to treat schizophrenia, because these medications themselves may cause some structural brain changes, thus creating confusion regarding which changes are disease-related and which are medication-related.

The most consistently replicated structural brain change in schizophrenia is enlargement of the brain ventricles, the fluid-filled spaces in the middle of each half of the brain. This is illustrated by identical twins, one of whom has schizophrenia and has enlarged brain ventricles and the other of whom does not have schizophrenia and has normal ventricles. It is thought that the enlargement of the brain ventricles is caused by a disease-related loss of brain tissue in the brain areas immediately adjacent to the ventricles.

In addition to the enlarged brain ventricles, abnormalities in never-treated individuals with schizophrenia have been reported for a variety of brain structures thought to be involved in schizophrenia. These include the hippocampus, amygdala, cingulate, frontal cortex, temporal cortex, thalamus, and cerebellum. The hippocampus is thought to be especially important in schizophrenia and has been more carefully studied than any other brain area. In addition to having a slight reduction in its overall volume in individuals with schizophrenia, the hippocampus has also been reported to have subtle disease-related differences in its shape.

Abnormalities of Brain Function

The types of brain functions that have been most extensively studied in schizophrenia are the neurological, neuropsychological, and electrophysiological functions and brain metabolism. In each of these, there are well-documented abnormalities in individuals with schizophrenia who have never been treated with antipsychotic medication.

Neurologically, individuals with schizophrenia may have abnormalities in spontaneous movements called dyskinesias. For example, they may show sudden involuntary movements of their tongue, facial muscles, shoulders, or arms. Such movements may also be a side effect of antipsychotic medication, but at least eleven studies have demonstrated that these movements also occur more often in never-treated patients than in normal controls.

Seven recent studies have also shown that individuals with schizophrenia who have never been treated with antipsychotic medication may have more rigidity, tremor, and slowing of their movements, similar to what is seen in individuals with Parkinson's disease. These symptoms may also occur as side effects of antipsychotics used to treat schizophrenia.

A third type of neurological abnormality found in some individuals with schizophrenia is what is commonly referred to as neurological soft signs. These include activities such as being able to identify the type of coin put in your hand while your eyes are closed. Neurological soft signs involve impairments in the integration and coordination of complex sensory functions. At least seven studies have reported more neurological soft signs in individuals with schizophrenia who have never been treated with antipsychotic medication compared to normal controls. Taking antipsychotic medications, in fact, appears to decrease the neurological soft signs and improve the person's neurological function.

Still another type of neurological dysfunction found in some individuals with schizophrenia is decreased perception of pain. This occurs in only a small subset of patients, but when it does occur, it can be very dramatic. There are reports, for example, of individuals with schizophrenia undergoing surgery, such as the removal of their appendix, without requiring any anesthesia and claiming that they felt no pain. The brain abnormality in such cases almost certainly involves the thalamus, which is the part of the brain that plays a major role in the perception of pain. Multiple studies have suggested that the thalamus is involved in schizophrenia.

The second major type of brain dysfunction commonly found in individuals with schizophrenia is neuropsychological dysfunction, especially verbal memory, attention, and planning (also called executive function). Verbal memory, for example, is tested by reading a list of objects to the individual and then asking them to repeat the list. Planning (executive function) may be tested by asking the person to match colors and shapes of objects in a test in which the rules for matching are constantly changing (the Wisconsin Card Sort test).

In the past two decades, over two hundred studies have been published reporting neuropsychological abnormalities in individuals with schizophrenia; in eight of these studies, the individuals had never been treated with antipsychotic medications when tested, but the outcome of these studies showed just as many abnormalities as in the studies in which the individuals had been treated.

One particular type of neuropsychological abnormality commonly found in individuals with schizophrenia has drawn much attention in recent years. This is self-perception, the ability of the person to step back and objectively look at him or herself. The ability to do this reflects complex brain functions that involve the frontal and parietal lobes as well as other areas. Neurologically impaired individuals, especially those who have had strokes involving the right side of the brain, are sometimes observed to lose this ability to perceive themselves. For example, people with a stroke-caused paralysis of their left leg will sometimes adamantly deny that anything is wrong with their leg.

This is not merely denial, a psychological stratagem we all use occasionally. This is instead an anatomically based loss of self-perception and is technically called anosognosia. In recent years, research has demonstrated that approximately half of all individuals with schizophrenia have partial or complete anosognosia, meaning that they do not realize that anything is wrong with them. They therefore commonly refuse to take medication, and a disproportionate of these untreated individuals end up among the homeless population.

The third major type of brain dysfunction seen in individuals with schizophrenia is electrophysiological abnormalities. Electrical impulses are one way that neurons and other brain cells communicate with each other. One means of measuring electrical impulses in the brain is by electroencephalogram (EEG), commonly used to detect abnormalities in brain diseases such as epilepsy. EEG studies of individuals with schizophrenia also have shown abnormalities, although these are much more subtle than those seen in epilepsy.

Another technique used to measure electrophysiological function is called evoked potentials. A loud sound, for example, elicits a brain electrical impulse (the evoked potential) that is then measured. Many studies, including some done on patients who have never been treated with antipsychotic medications, have demonstrated electrophysiological abnormalities in individuals with schizophrenia.

The final major type of brain dysfunction seen in individuals with schizophrenia is abnormalities of brain metabolism. These studies are typically done using advanced imaging techniques for studying the brain, including positron emission tomography (PET) and functional magnetic resonance imaging (fMRI). As it is known that antipsychotic medications can affect these tests, it is important to use never-treated individuals whenever possible.

Since 1991, more than twenty studies have measured brain metabolism in individuals with schizophrenia who have never been treated; all except one of them found more abnormalities of brain metabolism in the individuals with schizophrenia compared to normal controls.

Evidence has accumulated in recent decades that the brains of individuals with schizophrenia have abnormalities in brain structure and function. Studies done on patients who have never been treated with antipsychotic medications have proven that these brain abnormalities are disease-related and are not a consequence of having been treated with antipsychotic medications.

It should be cautioned, however, that these abnormalities of brain structure and function are nonspecific, that is, none of them are specifically diagnostic for schizophrenia. In other words, abnormalities such as enlarged brain ventricles, neurological soft signs, and electrophysiological abnormalities may also be found in many other brain diseases and occasionally in people who are otherwise normal. All of these abnormalities, however, occur statistically more commonly in individuals with schizophrenia than in individuals who do not have schizophrenia and, as such, provide the basis for categorizing schizophrenia as a brain disease.

With regard to what causes schizophrenia, a definitive answer to this question is not yet known. There are many theories and much research is taking place. It is widely assumed that genes play some role, although probably as predisposing genes rather than directly causative genes. It is also known that brain neurochemicals are involved, including the chemicals that transmit messages from neuron to neuron (neurotransmitters), such as dopamine, glutamate and GABA. Many of the medications used to treat schizophrenia target these neurotransmitters, and that is thought to be one of the reasons why they are effective in improving symptoms. Another current research approach is examining the possibility that infectious agents, such as viruses and protozoa, play a role in causing the disease; this research appears promising.

Instructional Strategies

The following strategies have been found to be effective with schizophrenic high school and college students:

- Spend extra time with the student as needed
- Teach study skills and time management
- Give direct instruction on target behaviors
- Clearly define expected behaviors, requirements, and assignments
- Allow students to tape-record lectures
- Make available a note-taker
- Provide hard copies of notes, and assignments for later reference
- Create an absence of background noise

- Allow them to work on computers and on-line from home when possible (reduces stress)
- Be aware of emotionally sensitive course material and discuss it privately prior to class
- Establish a behavior management program that includes positive behavior supports, immediate consequences, consistency, and a cool-down area.
- Give extra time on exams
- Be flexible
- Don't single them out
- Ask them what they need from you to concentrate and be productive.

See also: Adolescent Cognition Development; Adolescent Social and Emotional Development.

Further Readings

Deveson, A. (1992). *Tell Me I'm Here.* New York: Penguin Books.
Sheehan, S. (1982). *Is There No Place on Earth for Me?* Boston: Houghton, Mifflin.
Torrey, E.F. (2002). Studies of individuals with schizophrenia never treated with antipsychotic medications: a review. *Schizophrenia Research* 58:101–115.
Torrey, E.F. (2006). *Surviving Schizophrenia: A Manual for Families, Consumers, and Providers* (5th ed.). New York: Harper Collins.

E. FULLER TORREY, M.D. AND
MICHAEL B. KNABLE, D.O.

Self-Efficacy

Much has been said, in the last century, about the need for students to have a positive self-image. How we feel about ourselves is paramount to how we tackle problems, how we persevere, and to our own mental well-being. While a positive self-image is important, self-efficacy may be even more crucial to academic and social success. It is thought to be the gatekeeper to **motivation** and it has a significant impact on our **self-esteem**. In reality an individual may not be able to sustain positive self-esteem over time without self efficacy.

Self-efficacy differs from self-esteem. Self-efficacy is built on fact: "I know that I can be successful in this subject, class, or endeavor because I have been successful before." Self-esteem is built on "I think and I feel," not necessarily on fact. While self-esteem is a judgment of self-worth based on how I feel about myself in comparison to the value put on my perceived abilities; self-efficacy is a judgment of my ability to succeed based on past experience. This is one of the reasons that it is so important to provide students with the opportunity to be successful: success really does breed success.

A meta-analysis study, conducted through the Mid-continent Regional Educational Laboratory, found self-efficacy to have one of the highest effect sizes on student learning. When teachers reinforced self-efficacy in students (as opposed to control groups in which self-efficacy was not addressed), there was an effect size of eighty, which translates to a percentile gain of 29 points. This means that a class average at the 50th percentile where self-efficacy is properly incorporated can increase to the 79th percentile in learning.

Origins of Self-Efficacy

The basis for the idea of self-efficacy came from a Stanford psychologist, Albert Bandura, in the 1950s who believed in a social learning theory that was an extension of the classical behaviorist principles related to modeling, imitation, and reinforcement. Bandura published *Social Foundations of Thought and Action* in 1986 in which he outlined his belief that self-efficacy was critical to human behavior and motivation. Bandura would later comment that self-reflection is the most distinctively human characteristic. Self-reflective judgments include perceptions of self-efficacy—the beliefs that we hold about our capability to organize and execute a course of action required to manage prospective situations. In essence, self-efficacy is the confidence that we have in our own abilities. Without positive self-efficacy, people tend to have a low locus of control and a feeling of helplessness. For students with inner-city **poverty** characteristics, being able to tap into the self-system of the brain, and in particular, self-efficacy is a positive start in changing defeatist behavior.

Connection to Brain Research

An individual's positive or negative self-efficacy is determined by the storage of long-term memories created by past experiences. The self-system of the brain houses the memories of what constitutes our self-efficacy. This is not a singular place but is composed of the attitudes, emotions and beliefs that are at the heart of self-efficacy. An area in the left hemisphere of the brain manages the inner sense of self, while the right hemisphere controls the outer impressions of the environment.

Memories are initially stored in working memory and then may or may not be moved into our long-term memory (LTM). Working memory connections between neurons are temporary and wear off in minutes or hours. The hippocampus, Greek for seahorse because of its shape, stores temporary memories and then decides which information will be turned into long-term memory. LTM storage is influenced by information that is repeated, meaningful, or filled with emotion.

Long-term memory (LTM) storage is relatively permanent and anatomically changes the brain. LTM requires the synthesis of new proteins. CREB, a protein, becomes active with LTM storage; it signals other proteins that aid in assisting the growth of new synaptic connections between neurons. For instance, students that are learning to read new words are growing dendrites and making new synaptic connections with each bit of learning. In reverse, if CREB is not activated it stops production of other proteins and actually prohibits long-term memories from being formed. Once synaptic connections have been formed (evidence that you have learned something new) you no longer possess the same brain.

It is the self-system that engages the brain in what must be attended to in all facets of the learning process and then becomes dedicated to the work at hand. Self-efficacy, how we feel about the learning and the personal relevance of the learning, determines our willingness to engage.

Instructional Strategies that Enhance Self-Efficacy

First and probably the most common way that students establish self-efficacy is through positive mastery experience. Strong personal performance that is positive and satisfying leads to a belief in one's abilities to be successful again. Teachers should provide opportunities for all students to be successful. Begin with simple tasks and questions and build to more complex tasks and questions.

Self-efficacy is greatly influenced by the **feedback** that we get from others, especially teachers and other influential individuals in our lives. Feedback should be both positive and prescriptive and it should be deserved. Just saying, "good job" is not what is meant by feedback. Students need to know specifics: how they are doing; what they are doing right; what needs work; and how to make adjustments. Writing personal goals for learning and then revisiting those goals allows students to see their progress. Never give praise that is undeserved; students quickly see through this and will learn not to trust what you say.

Provide ample wait time after questions. There is a tendency in all of us to move on too quickly when we fear that the student does not know the answer. Allowing sufficient wait time conveys confidence in your student's abilities. Other ways to communicate positive teacher expectations are by giving cues and prompts, monitor your nonverbal communication (smiling, tone of voice, proximity), flexible grouping strategies, believe all your students can learn and deserve to be challenged.

From the works of Bandura on the effects of self-efficacy beliefs we can conclude that consciously or unconsciously students do make choices based on their self-efficacy beliefs. They will take part in those tasks in which they feel confident and will avoid those in which they lack confidence. Once students begin a task, their willingness to complete the task is based, in part, on self-efficacy. Students with a low sense of efficacy will acquiesce when they confront obstacles to the work. As we all know, stress and anxiety are increased when we lack the confidence to engage and complete a task.

See Also: **Information Processing Model.**

Further Readings

Bandura, A. (1994). Self-efficacy. In V.S. Ramachandran (Ed.). *Encyclopedia of Human Behavior* (4), pp. 71–81. New York: Academic Press.

Marzano, R.J. (2001). *Designing a New Taxonomy of Educational Objectives*. Thousand Oaks, CA: Corwin Press.

Tileston, D.W. (2000). *What Every Teacher Should Know About Motivation*. Thousand Oaks, CA: Corwin Press.

Belief and Brain Research, www.control-z.com/pages/bbr.html

DONNA WALKER TILESTON, ED.D.

Self-Esteem

Self-esteem is one of the most misused, misunderstood psychological terms in today's world. The self-esteem industry has made millions promoting the quick fix, all the while supporting superficial and shallow self-esteem. Countless people have been led to believe that the memorization of *"I'm Special"* and *"Yes I can"* poems and similar incantations will lead to inner security and strength, and a new life.

On the other hand, *authentic self-esteem* results when people reach an emotional–cognitive balance that allows them to feel honestly good about themselves and be quietly confident in taking these "selves" to the outer world. They enjoy who they are, are willing to take calculated risks, able to acknowledge their large and small successes, willing to accept responsibility, able to give themselves to others without fear of loss, and while they appreciate honest feedback they are not dependent upon the applause of others.

It is critical that we understand that our self-esteem is a developed emotional–cognitive interaction that exists between the limbic areas and frontal cortices of our brain. The word "emotional" is placed before cognitive because authentic self-esteem is highly dependent on one's emotional neural networks and corresponding memories. These networks and memories are normally influenced by controlling messaging from the cognitive, prefrontal cortex. This desired emotional–cognitive balance may be more difficult to achieve if the developing brain has been negatively impacted by excessive stress or trauma.

There are a number of brain facts that should be understood. First of all, material that is memorized in rote format tends to be stored only as language in the left frontal cortex. Unless efforts are made to apply the message within the language to gain increased understanding or to process it in other ways the material will remain as language. In other words, for this material to become useful more neural connections and neural integration *must* be formed. The impact of most motivational speeches tends to be short-lived unless the person makes an immediate, concerted effort to enhance their own skill set using this information.

The limbic area, primarily the amygdala, continually focuses on our survival and unless the frontal cortices are able to generate stable plans and send soothing messages to this area, the amygdala, overcome by fear, will inhibit or even sabotage the growth of self-esteem. The amygdala does not have the capacity to form or reframe memories based on language alone as emotional memories tend to be episodic in nature. Some of these memories may have reference values, "right and wrong," empathy, success, and community. For example, if a person has a fear of not being accepted by others, it is necessary to provide safe environments and activities where that person can, over time, gain certain social skills and learn how to read the actions of others. Activity is critical.

The cognitive neural networks associated with self-esteem are built over time through language, reflection, building on previous learning, and again activity. The ability to process is critical. This may include processing data, thinking in conceptual terms, projecting in an abstract manner, and being emotionally committed to the activity. The person who learns that he or she can be self-dependent, has the capacity to make choices, can take calculated risks, care, and can take a position that may be inconsistent with that of their peers.

Through practice and supportive experiences the brain becomes increasingly comfortable in sharing this state of mind with the community at large. Although we cannot give a person self-esteem, we can coach the person to reach this state. This coaching must include teaching, modeling, and evaluation.

Characteristics of People with High Self-Esteem

- Act with integrity including acting responsibly, with psychological harmony, sincerity and consistency, possessing inner delight, being trustworthy and able to stand tall.
- Are most likely to have emotional bonds with one or more adults and possess "memory banks" full of positive affirmation experiences.
- Have an increased sense of purpose.
- Are accepting of others.
- Have the capability to laugh at themselves and have a healthy sense of humor.
- Are willing to seek out help from experts or colleagues.
- Perform better academically.
- Are more motivated in school.
- Have fewer classroom management problems.
- Get along better with teachers and peers.

Characteristics of People with Shallow Self-Esteem

- Place great reliance upon material possessions.
- Denigrate others for their own personal gain.
- Cling to fashion statements, social or cultural status for self-definition.
- Rely on "quick fixes" or applause.
- Are excessively focused on instant gratification or egocentrism.
- Develop an artificial persona or try continually to "play a role."
- Use chemical substances to enhance feelings of self.
- Are more at-risk of dropping out of school.
- Experience more depression.

The primary purpose of our brain is to keep us alive. However, "staying alive" also includes the maintenance of a positive sense of self. We all want to be somebody and hopefully this can be accomplished in a profound, honest manner, rich in value and emotional security.

The Problems of Shallow Self-Esteem

Many people base their self-identity on their car, clothes, holidays, brand of alcohol, work, office size, parking spot, physical size or shape, power over people, snow board, family status, children's accomplishments and the size of their bank accounts. Maintaining this sense of self requires a constant struggle to "keep up appearances."

The hyper vigilance of shallow self-esteem leaves the bully prone to acts of violence, disrespect toward authority, extreme sensitivity to criticism, and other negative behaviors. Their emotional memories tend to be those of fear, failure, and helplessness. Many bully to bolster their own self-esteem.

Shallow self-esteem leaves individuals vulnerable to be used and abused by others. I think of Jack, the overweight outsider who gained a group of friends when his Dad let him bring the family car to school. His "new buddies" were happy to have Jack drive them all over town. Jack told me, "I didn't used to have any friends but now I have lots of friends."

Disparity within a school usually leads to the forming of informal clusters of students. In addition, subtle differences occur within each of the subgroups as individuals vie for status. Special shoes or clothes often become the currency to "buy" their self-esteem. It is extremely difficult for most adolescents to say "I don't need special shoes to allow me to feel good about myself."

Behavior can be a self-esteem item. Some students take a perverse pride and gain self-esteem by being an "active slacker." They are generally afraid to put forth an effort and their self-esteem rests with being successfully unsuccessful. Other students act outside of the rules to get applause. This feedback re-enforces their behavior and it satisfies their need to feel good right here, right now.

Teenage self-esteem is often shaped by the intense marketing and media imaging that is fostered and supported by teen magazines, electronic media, advertisements, TV sitcoms, teen music, and associated peer pressure. This superficial approach to character development leaves these teens vulnerable to incredible self-obsession and poor decision-making that can have serious short and long-term effects on themselves and others.

Some people have suggested that children who are successful "car thieves" or "drug dealers" are held in high regard in their "communities" and may have good self-esteem. While these individuals may feel a momentary sense of pride they constantly need to have "criminal hits" to maintain that feeling. This also applies to seemingly "popular" students who harass others.

Even under normal conditions teenagers may feel "they're not good enough" or "smart enough" and that they have failed. They are likely to feel they have failed yet again when they are unable to meet the artificial expectations of today's pressure-ridden teenage world. Teenagers are extremely vulnerable to **depression**. Authentic self-esteem will not prevent a person from becoming depressed but it is likely to help the person regain good mental health.

The power of positive thinking (POPT) is largely a left brain activity. Readers of POPT literature are often left feeling empty, perhaps even failures, when they are unable to convert POPT messages into reality. In fact, authentic self-esteem is the outcome of the integration of many brain areas and a multitude of cognitive and emotional memories.

Cautionary Points

Sociopaths, psychopaths, and persons with antisocial personality disorder usually present a strong sense of self. This pattern of behavior is, however, devoid of most emotions such as fear, empathy, and social conscience. Blatant egocentric behavior should not be confused with authentic self-esteem. Such behavior is sometimes exhibited by one-dimensional star athletes who are overidolized both inside the school and the community at large.

See also: **Addiction; Adolescent Social and Emotional Development; Emotion; Episodic Memory; Trauma; Processing Time.**

Further Readings

Branden, N. (1995). *Six Pillars of Self Esteem* (1st ed.). New York, NY: Bantam Books.

Dacine, R.N., Caine, G. (1997). *Unleashing the Power of Perceptual Change: The Potential of Brain-Based Teaching.* Alexandria, VA: ASCD.

DeMoulin, D.F. (2000). I Like Me!: Enhancing Self Concept in Kindergarten-age Children Through Active School/Business Partnerships, *NASP Commu. ique* 27(8).

Reasoner, R. (2000). *Self-esteem and Youth: What Research Has To Say About It.* e-book on International Council, www.self-esteem-international.org

DAVID HALSTEAD, M.ED.

Semantic Memory

In 1972, the psychologist, Endel Tulving, used the term semantic memory to describe this memory for organized world knowledge. Semantic memory is considered one of the Explicit, or Declarative, memory capacities. These memories can be consciously retrieved and can be "declared" or put into words. It is the long-term memory for facts and includes words, symbols for words, meanings, rules, formulas, and general knowledge. Much of this information is organized into categories, such as: Fido is a sheepdog, sheepdogs are dogs, dogs are animals. This factual information is stored through a structure in the brain called the hippocampus, which is found in the medial temporal lobe. If incoming sensory information contains facts, it will trigger the hippocampus to search its files for matching information. This information will then be brought into temporary storage areas to be examined. The brain will try to make connections between previously stored facts and new information. In this way, new long-term memories can be made.

The hippocampus is essential to the storage and the retrieval of semantic memories. The memory itself is distributed in various brain areas, but the hippocampus keeps track of it and pulls it back together. A person who has recently seen a movie stores visual memories of the faces and objects in the temporal lobe; landscapes and patterns in the parietal lobe; and social interaction is stored in the frontal lobes. As the movie is reflected upon, the components of the memory are pulled together by the hippocampus. The memory is reconstructed, so therefore, it may not be completely accurate. To recall memories without the hippocampus, a process that neuroscientist Daniel Siegel refers to as "cortical consolidation" must occur. It is believed that memories become self-sufficient after multiple repetitions of the memory. At that time, the memory becomes independent of the hippocampus. This process, however, can take years. The evidence of this presents itself in individuals who have hippocampal injuries due to an accident. The damage prevents them from storing new memories, but many memories prior to the accident are retrievable.

It was through surgery on a young man known only by his initials, H.M., that much was discovered about memory and the hippocampus. H.M. suffered a fall as a child and many years later began to have seizures. Medication could not control them, and eventually they became so severe that surgery was suggested. On August 23, 1953, Dr. William Scoville performed a bilateral resection of the medial temporal lobe, in hopes that it would alleviate H.M.'s seizures. After the surgery, the seizures had decreased significantly; however, so did H.M.'s ability to form new memories. His doctor had to reintroduce herself to him each day. Sadly, if she stepped out of the room for mere minutes, upon her return he did not remember ever having met her. Even though his I.Q. remained normal, his recall ability was absent.

Semantic memory is used extensively in school. The difficulty lies in the processes the brain must use to store these memories. Semantic information must go through short-term memory processes. Information is received into sensory memory. If it is attended to, it begins the immediate memory process. This fleeting memory lasts only four to twenty seconds. The information must then be rehearsed in the process called active working memory. This memory can hold information for extended periods of time, but it will remain a temporary memory until connections are made. When a student "crams" for an exam, information is stored in working memory and is quickly forgotten after the test.

Using either recognition or recall usually tests semantic information. Authentic assessment may be used, but most standardized tests rely on these two types of assessment. Recognition tests include multiple choice questions, matching, and true – false. Recall tests are essay questions that involve retrieving information from long-term memory, manipulating it in working memory, and producing written answers. Recall tests are thought to utilize more brainpower because only one cue is given to trigger the memory. Recognition tests offer at least two cues. For instance, a recall question might be "Describe the main character." For a recognition test, the question could be multiple choice as in "The main character has the following characteristics: (A) charming, kind, and patient; (B) hostile, angry, and sullen; (C) kind, patient, good-natured. The answer selections in the multiple-choice question provide more cues to trigger the memory.

Researcher Howard Eichenbaum refers to the commonly held belief that our semantic memories are born out of our **episodic memories**. Our lives are a series of experiences or episodes. The brain takes the repeated bits of information out of the experiences, and those become our semantic memories. As an example, consider what you might know about apples: (1) they are different colors including red and green, (2) they grow on trees, (3) they are a fruit, (4) they are somewhat round and can roll, (5) most smell sweet, (6) some grandmas make apple pies, apple crisp, and apple cider. Even this limited information was probably derived from many "apple" experiences. The experiences themselves may have escaped our memories so that we no longer know the time and the place that these events occurred, but the distinguishing characteristics of apples stay with us due to the repetition of those features. Hence, the episodes contained some repetitive information that eventually became facts that are stored in long-term semantic memory.

Multiple rehearsals are necessary for semantic information to be stored in long-term memory. The more varied these rehearsals are, the more brain areas will have access to the memory. Each rehearsal helps to organize the information for later retrieval.

Instructional Strategies to Make Semantic Memories

As semantic memory for facts and concepts is most often assessed in school, it behooves educators to have a toolbox of strategies for processing new information. Keep in mind that information is more easily remembered if it can be attached to prior knowledge.

Graphic organizers help students access previously learned information. They help form a picture of information for the students to remember. One popular example for accessing prior knowledge is a K-W-L chart. Three columns are drawn on a paper with one initial in each. The K is for what the students already Know about the topic. This information is brainstormed by the class or in small groups. Then the W column is utilized, which stands for What you want to know. Students discuss this. Then the subject is researched or taught. The final column, L, allows the students to determine what they have Learned. Other graphic organizers include concept maps, mind maps, and webs.

Comparisons, examples, and associations often activate semantic information. Identifying the similarities and differences in a topic may be helpful. This scientifically based research strategy includes metaphors, similes, and analogies. Allowing students to create their own metaphors, like "The brain is a motorcycle," encourages the student to examine the attributes of each and determine how this statement is true. In so doing, the student learns about the brain and connects that information to previously stored motorcycle knowledge. Higher level thinking skills are used when identifying similarities and differences.

Semantic strategies include emotional situations such as debate and role-playing. Defending one's stance in a debate demands that the participant know the information well. Role-playing adds the dimension of movement and emotion. Students who participate in role-playing often remember information through their bodies and through the feelings they experienced.

Repetition is essential for some semantic learning. For students to learn the multiplication tables, they must be rehearsed extensively. This repetition strengthens the connections being formed in the brain. Although this type of repetition may be rote rehearsal, applying the facts and making them meaningful is a way to elaborate. Elaboration provides more meaning to the content.

A powerful semantic memory strategy is teaching. Research suggests that teaching allows us to store and recall more information than simply seeing it or hearing about it. For students to teach concepts and facts, they must first understand them. A useful practice is to pair students and have them take turns teaching each other the concepts just covered.

Questioning sessions may emphasize significant pieces of semantic information. Asking open-ended questions that begin with How? or Why? often permits students to think seriously about the question and access prior knowledge to answer it. Eventually the goal is to have the students asking and answering their own questions. Applying questions from the various levels of Bloom's Taxonomy can increase critical thinking about the topic and aid in creating long-term semantic memories.

Outlining, summarizing, creating timelines, and giving practice tests may all encourage the formation of semantic memories. As most state assessments are paper and pencil tests, practice tests may help transfer information to the semantic test format.

See also: **Episodic Memory; Forgetting; Information Processing Model.**

Further Readings

Eichenbaum, H. (2003). Speaker. *The Neurobiology of Learning and Memory*. *Learning and the Brain Conference*. Cambridge, MA.

Siegel, D. (1999). *The Developing Mind*. New York: The Guildford Press.

Sprenger, M. (2005). *How to Teach So Students Remember*. Alexandria, VA: ASCD.

Squire, L., E. Kandel. (1999). *Memory, From Mind to Molecules*. New York: Scientific American Library.

MARILEE SPRENGER

Sexual Learning

A common understanding of sex education is that it reveals the secret of how babies are conceived and then born into the world. In the past, boys and girls would be separated for a short lecture on physiological changes during puberty; and then exposed to this big secret. But the domain of sexuality is broader and more pervasive than the mechanics of reproduction. Sexual development during puberty is nothing less than a complete transformation of the biological, hormonal, emotional, cognitive, and social being. It is much more than being male or a female. Sexuality is at the heart of our identity as a person.

The neural map of masculinity and femininity is constructed in the womb. The moment of conception begins the initial trajectory of gender but this differentiation is not evident until the sixth week. The basic ground plan of the fetus is female and it continues to grow as a female unless the chromosomes produce the primitive gonads that release high levels of testosterone and another hormone that impedes the growth of the female reproductive system. Testosterone not only animates the development of the male reproductive system, but it "masculinizes" the neurological system and begins to form the male brain.

By adulthood the male brain is about 10 percent larger than the female's, but the female brain contains about 10 percent more brain cells in the cortical layers. Research suggests that the corpus collosum, which facilitates communication between hemispheres of the brain, is larger with more connections in women. This may in part explain why women are more adept at processing feelings and recognizing feelings in others. The male brain has more fluid and fat, which seems to speed communication, while the female brain has larger structures to impede aggressive impulses. **Gender differences** are evident in sensory acuity, brain size, and specific cognitive abilities.

Masculinity and femininity develop out of an interplay of both genetics and experience. It is difficult to single out one or the other as a cause. However, neuroscience is giving us added insight into sexuality.

Puberty

During puberty, the process of sexual differentiation that began in the womb is completed. Neuroscientists believe that the brain is actually what triggers puberty. It is speculated that the massive pruning of dendrites and synapse during puberty prompts the maturation of the hypothalamus that initiates a carefully orchestrated set of neurological and hormonal growth patterns.

Androgens in males, in particular testosterone, and estrogen in females are released at higher levels. Once it was believed these hormones only impacted the hypothalamus, however, researchers recently discovered androgens and estrogen were sprinkled all over the brain, including the cortex and cerebellum. They set into motion the development of the primary sexual characteristics, the testes and ovaries, and the secondary sexual characteristics, lowered voices in males, pubic hair and breast development.

During puberty testosterone levels in young males are the highest they will ever be. They are ten to twenty times higher than females and one thousand percent higher than levels during childhood. Testosterone is associated with dynamic, impulsive, and aggressive behavior, along with an increased sexual appetite.

Estrogen levels in females are ten times as high as in males. The hormone patterns of females take them through monthly fluctuations that can spawn depressed and irritable moods. Norepinephrine (energizes), serotonin (soothes), and dopamine (pleasure), are neurotransmitters normally found in the body. Beginning with puberty they are mixed with fluctuations of estrogen causing girls to feel lonely and sad one moment and gregarious and happy the next.

While it is possible to measure physiological growth during puberty in terms of inches and pounds, the impact on the personality and psychological profile of young people is difficult to quantify. Puberty launches the child on a journey of self-discovery that moves toward autonomy and self-sufficiency. The transition from childhood to adulthood requires mastery of a complex set of cognitive, emotional, and social competencies.

Gender or biological sex: There is no single biological parameter that makes one male or female. Gender is determined by the interaction of chromosomes, hormones, and the growth of internal and external genitalia. In approximately one out of one hundred births, physiological differences deviate from the standard male or female with regards to chromosomes, hormones, genitalia and/or reproductive ability. This condition of gender ambiguity is known as inter-sex.

One variable is the hormonal environment of the womb. A genetic female exposed to high levels of androgens in the womb may have female reproductive organs yet appear male externally. Conversely, a male who is underexposed to androgens may not develop a penis. In other words, the gender that becomes hardwired in the brain may be different than the genitalia that develop. Every year, about one in four thousand children are born whose gender is ambiguous. Typically, prompt surgery has been used to assign a gender along with hormone therapy to "masculinize" or "feminize" the brain. Currently, the trend is to wait until the child reaches puberty to allow the individual to develop an internal sense of being male or female before determining gender.

Gender identity: Gender identity is the subjective aspect of sexuality, a distinct feeling of being male or female. Awareness of gender seems to begin at a very early age and develops over a lifetime. With the rapid physiological and sexual growth during puberty, the internal sense of being male or female comes into sharp focus. There is a sense of urgency in the hormonal rush of young boys, a growing awareness of sexual power. A young girl realizes that her developing figure generates new and unfamiliar attention from men. These new feelings mus` be negotiated and integrated into the personality. For most people gender identity is consistent with their biological sex. The further away from the cultural norm of masculinity and femininity a youth finds him/herself, the more difficult the challenge.

Gender roles: These describe the acceptable roles and behaviors assigned to females and males by a particular culture. They are the learned behaviors and attitudes about how men and women are expected to act. The manner in which a culture defines acceptable male or female behavior changes over time. In the past century, the parameters that define gender roles have shifted. There are more options for the type of career choice, acceptable modes of parenting, and how men and women relate. Much of the learning of attitudes about gender roles comes from modeling and is not always taught overtly. This learning is a process that begins at birth and continues throughout a lifetime.

Gender Expression: This refers to the way a person's sense of maleness or femaleness is expressed through behavior, manner of dress, hair style, and mannerisms. Gender expression may conform to socially sanctioned gender roles, deviate somewhat or deviate to a marked degree. Youth may choose to defy accepted gender expression as a way to rebel or establish independence. The use of jewelry; earrings; short, long or colored hair; tight, baggy or revealing clothing; tattoos and body piercing; are popular ways to flaunt accepted gender expression or establish a unique look or identity.

Sexual orientation: This describes the pattern of romantic, emotional and sexual attraction. Sexual orientation can be a predominant attraction to the same sex (lesbian, gay), a relatively equal attraction to both sexes (bi-sexual) or to the opposite sex (heterosexual). Sexual orientation seems to be influenced by a variety of genetic, hormonal, and environmental influences. Sexual orientation defines the nature of sexual relationships. Adolescents sometimes struggle with the acceptance of sexual orientation and periods of experimentation are not unusual.

Though the dynamics are not clearly understood, sexual orientation seems to be well established by the age of five. Recent evidence demonstrates a difference in the size of the hypothalamus in gay men as compared to heterosexual men. Sensitivity in the inner ear in lesbian women is closer to that of men than women and seems to result from higher levels of testosterone in the womb. These differences are examples of increasing evidence that sexual orientation is a predisposition that is hardwired into the brain.

Transgender. When someone's internal sense of being male or female (gender identity) does not match their biological genitalia, this condition is referred to as transgender. Such a discrepancy is frequently accompanied by distress as a person tries to establish a healthy sexual identity in a culture that only officially recognizes male and female expressions that match biological sex. For some children, this awareness manifests as a feeling of "being different" from same-sexed peers. Some transgender individuals choose to undergo a process of hormone therapy and sex reassignment surgery to have their biological sex match their gender identity. The shifts are referred to as male to female (MTF) or female to male (FTM).

Adolescents must navigate all of these domains of gender to develop a healthy sense of self. There are many permutations of gender roles, gender identity, gender expression, and sexual orientation. They are an essential part of the adolescent quest for determining "who am I?" Just knowing that one is male or female is only the beginning.

Sexual Behavior

Adolescents live in a culture that exposes them to highly sexualized images on a regular basis. Of all industrialized nations, the United States has the highest rate of teen pregnancy and sexually transmitted diseases (STD). This is still true even though teen pregnancy declined 28 percent between 1990 and 2000. Nearly four out of every five teen males and females have had sex by age twenty. By this time, those who are sexually active have had two or more sexual partners. Teen sexual activity can be sporadic. While approximately half of high school students have had sexual intercourse, at any one time 66 percent are abstinent, that is, not having had sex in the past three months. Each year, one out of four sexually active teens will get a STD with half of all new HIV infections occurring in youth under the age of twenty-four.

The average age of marriage in the western world hovers around twenty-five. This means that there is a thirteen year span between the onset of puberty and the typical age of marriage. This is also a period of dramatic personal and social growth. There is no cultural consensus as to the guidelines for sexual behaviors and relationships that guide young men and women through this period. Perspectives range from complete abstinence until marriage to the view that what does not harm oneself or another is acceptable.

Social/Emotional

Fulfillment in life cannot be measured by money, career status, or the number of possessions. The biggest predictor of happiness and fulfillment is the quality of emotional well-being and personal relationships. Adolescents must learn to develop a set of emotional and social competencies that are essential for the broad range of relationships that adulthood requires. Some relationships will be intimate and sexual, while others will be familial, professional, or based on friendship.

The growth spurt of puberty is accompanied by a growth in the emotional life. The surge of hormones creates a range of new feelings that must be managed and integrated into the personality. Emotional intensification is the natural companion to physical awkwardness. Managing the flow of powerful sexual feelings and impulses can be challenging for young adolescents due to a lack of experience with such feelings.

Children are taught to share toys, make friends, play nice, and get along. These relationship competencies are sufficient until sexuality enters the picture and complicates the arena of human relationships. Simply distinguishing between the flush of infatuation and an enduring love is challenging even for adults. Cultivating a range of healthy relationships requires a new set of skills.

The social and emotional competencies that adolescents must master include the ability to develop a healthy body image, identify a broad range of feelings, delay gratification, and manage sexual impulses, identify with the feelings of others (empathy and compassion), and manage conflicting emotions. Skills needed for establishing healthy relationships include the ability to communicate feelings appropriately, set clear and appropriate boundaries, manage and negotiate interpersonal conflicts, and be open to feedback from others.

Experimentation and Risk Taking

The brain undergoes a period of remodeling during the teen years. New neural connections are formed while other connections are pruned away. The prefrontal cortex continues to grow but will not be fully developed until the mid-twenties. When it comes to social and emotional responses, the reactive and sometimes impulsive amygdala continues to overshadow the well-planned thinking of the cortex. Rather than well-formed rational thought, the adolescent struggles with planned decision-making. A mindset focused on the present moment makes it difficult to predict consequences and plan for the future.

The growth and restructuring of the brain during adolescence makes this an ideal time to form new attitudes. The brain is poised and ready for this period of profound learning and adaptation. There is a shift from concrete to abstract thinking. Rather than complying with the guidance of parents and other adults, the adolescent is learning to make independent moral and ethical judgments. There is a fresh optimism and idealism that animates attitudes and thinking.

Two hallmarks of adolescence—experimentation and risk-taking—are the way in which adolescents accomplish the developmental tasks that they face. Creating an independent life and autonomous identity requires trying on new attitudes and behaviors, braving new challenges, and learning from mistakes. The successful mastery of the competencies related to sexuality requires active learning, and pushing outward beyond the comfort zone of safety. Experimentation involves not just physical intimacy, but exploring the boundaries of emotional intimacy.

There is a dark side to adolescent experimentation. Real and permanent harm is the ever-present companion to risk-taking, particularly when combined with the adolescent's penchant for feeling invulnerable to consequences. The effects of STDs and unwanted pregnancy are not the only dangers. The impact of sexual violence or abusive relationships on the emotional life can be equally damaging. Adolescents must be mentored to experiment and take risks within a protective environment that will minimize consequences. The best medicine is to prepare adolescents to face the developmental challenges well in advance, engage in active decision-making, take calculated risks, and generalize from baby steps.

Sex Education

Adolescents learn about sex from many sources: parents, teachers, peers, and the media. The physiology of adolescents is no different than it was thousands of years ago, but the world they will grow into is highly sexualized. The span of time between the onset of puberty and settling into enduring relationships (thirteen years) makes this an especially vulnerable period. Preparing adolescents to navigate these growth challenges must be a deliberate and comprehensive effort.

Research repeatedly demonstrates that a comprehensive approach to the sexual education of youth does not increase sexual behavior. In fact, comprehensive education is associated with postponement of initiation of sexual behavior, lower rates of unwanted pregnancy and STDs. Parents of adolescents in the United States overwhelmingly support sex education in schools although there remains some disagreement about the topics that should be addressed.

The traditional approach to educating adolescents about human sexuality is cognitive, imparting the information necessary to understand sexual development, anatomy and physiology, and reproductive health. Learning contraceptive methods and those that reduce the risk of infection are important to preventing unwanted pregnancy and STDs. Sex education should be more than preventing disasters or reducing the risk of harm, but about the creation of healthy and fulfilling intimate relationships of all kinds. This means addressing the many social and emotional competencies that adolescents must master. Learning these competencies requires skill development and practice.

Sex education for adolescents is everyone's responsibility. Parents exert a major influence over the sexual attitudes and behavior of their children and remain their primary sex educator. To adequately address all of the domains of sexual learning and prepare adolescents for the challenge of being healthy sexual adults, the partnership of schools and the larger community are essential. This will ensure that the healthy sexual learning necessary for adulthood is not an accident.

See also: **Adolescent Social and Emotional Development; Emotional Intelligence; Prenatal Brain; Self-Esteem.**

Further Readings

Allgeier, E.R., Albert R. (2000). *Sexual Interactions*. Boston, MA: Houghton Mifflin Company.

Gay Lesbian Straight Education Network (GLSEN), (2004). *Safe Space Training Materials*. www.glsen.org.

Kaiser Family Foundation, U.S. Teen Sexual Activity, January, 2005, www.kff.org.

Sexuality Information and Education Council of the United States www.siecus.org

JOHN ELFERS

Sleep

The function of sleep is not known, though it has been a target of sleep research for decades. For example, Allan Rechtschaffen of the University of Chicago began studying the function of sleep in the 1970s. His research was driven by his conclusion that sleep was a vital biological function. The evolutionary conservation of sleep in virtually every animal species—despite costs associated with prolonged intervals in an unresponsive and vulnerable state—suggests that sleep indeed serves a critical adaptive function. One such possible function of sleep is to facilitate learning, an idea fostered by many anecdotal reports of discoveries or insights gained during sleep. For example, Friedrich Kekule's discovery of the ring-like structure of benzene was said to have appeared to him during a dream about six serpents chasing one another in a circle.

Before discussing the association of sleep and learning, let us first clarify the meaning of both terms. As noted below, sleep can be defined by behavioral and electrophysiological criteria that establish it as a defined state, distinct from rest or waking. Different types of task-dependent learning (i.e., spatial, motor, perceptual) may be enhanced by different types, or stages, of sleep.

Definitions of Sleep

To study sleep in animals that are very small or difficult to monitor, behavioral requirements are necessary. Irene Tobler is a Swiss scientist who studies common lab animals, and she has also studied such animals as cockroaches, scorpions, and elephants. Tobler uses a set of behavioral criteria to determine if an animal sleeps. These criteria include having a (1) specific sleeping site (e.g., cave or bed), (2) typical body posture (e.g., lying down), (3) physical quiescence (e.g., lying still and quiet), (4) elevated arousal threshold (e.g., not responsive to soft noises), (5) rapid state reversibility (wakes up quickly from a big enough stimulus, unlike coma or hibernation), and (6) regulatory capacity demonstrated by compensation after deprivation (i.e. sleeping more after a time when sleep is prevented). When these criteria are used to evaluate sleep-like behavior, all must be met to classify the behavior as sleep. Yet, this system cannot make finer distinctions about the type of sleep occurring at a specific moment.

Specificity of sleep states and stages is defined based on electrophysiological criteria from recording brain waves, eye movements, and muscle tone, chiefly for birds and mammals. The transition from wake to sleep is accompanied by brain wave changes from irregular, low-voltage fast waves seen with waking to higher-voltage and slower waves characteristic of sleep. The sleep state with high-voltage slow waves is called non-rapid eye movement (NREM) sleep or slow wave sleep (SWS). The other sleep state, REM (rapid eye movement) sleep, is characterized by irregular, low-voltage, fast frequency brain waves, in conjunction with muscle paralysis and bursts of rapid eye movements. These two sleep states alternate cyclically during an animal's sleep, with NREM typically accounting for three to six times more of sleep than REM sleep.

In summary, sleep can be defined based on electrophysiological criteria providing state distinction (NREM/REM), or sleep can be determined more generally based on behavioral criteria without distinguishing states. Both sets of criteria have been used in the study of sleep and learning.

Learning Facilitated by Sleep

Many experiments have shown that sleep in general or specific states of sleep appear to improve learning in animals and humans. Types of learning that seem to be most affected involve basic brain changes after exposure to enriched environments, visual perceptual tasks, motor tasks, spatial tasks, and more complex types of learning including acquisition of bird songs and attainment of "insight." Evidence for the role of sleep in each type of learning is summarized below.

Basic Brain Changes

A fundamental requirement for learning is for the brain to undergo changes reflecting plasticity in neural structure and function. NREM and REM sleep may play roles in the neurological processes and brain changes underlying learning. One demonstration of sleep directly affecting neuronal structure was a study of how the brain's visual system grows when kittens are denied sleep and undergo monocular visual deprivation. Monocular deprivation, when one eye is covered to prevent visual input, causes a rapid remodeling of the visual cortex during the critical period of development (a time of enhanced brain change). Varying sleep in kittens undergoing monocular deprivation (some were kept awake in the dark, others were allowed to sleep in the dark, and others were kept awake in the light), demonstrated that sleep enhanced the brain changes in ocular columns that occur after monocular deprivation. Although not strictly speaking a study of learning, one interpretation of the study was that sleep and sleep loss modify experience-dependent neuronal changes. The brain changes were correlated with the amount of NREM sleep that occurred in the animals allowed to sleep, arguing against the possibility that the stress of sleep-deprivation might have inhibited development rather than sleep enhancing the process.

Evidence for the involvement of REM sleep with basic brain changes underlying learning comes from examining rats living in enriched environments. Brains of such rats show increases in the numbers and sizes of neural connections compared to rats living in impoverished environments. These brain changes are required to process and learn about the new environment. When sleep states are examined in these animals, those in an enriched environment show an increase in the amount of REM sleep, perhaps because REM sleep contributes to neural changes that underlie learning.

Perceptual Learning

Additional studies on visual processing and learning have been done with visual perceptual task learning. For example, a visual discrimination task has been used to assess a type of perceptual skill acquisition thought to rely on neural changes in the visual cortex. This task requires subjects to report if either a "T" or "L" appears in the foreground and if horizontal or vertical bars appears in the background of the screen. Human performance on this visual discrimination task improves after sleep, specifically due to the amount of deep NREM sleep in the first part of the night in combination with the amount of REM sleep in the second part, and does not improve simply with the passage of time. This research indicates that the progression of NREM to REM sleep across the night (not just one or the other) is necessary for the neurological processes underlying the visual perceptual task learning to occur.

Motor Task Learning

Motor task learning may require other processes than are needed for visual or perceptual processing, and NREM sleep has been implicated in enhancing motor task learning. Finger-tapping tasks have been used in humans to assess the effect of sleep on the acquisition of a motor skill that relies mainly on primary motor cortex plasticity. Participants trained on the task either in the morning or evening showed improvement after a night of sleep and no improvement after twelve hours of wakefulness. In this study, the amount of a particular type of NREM sleep (stage 2) was correlated with the amount of improvement, which may mean that stage 2 sleep is important in facilitating motor learning.

Spatial Learning

In addition to facilitating visual and motor learning, sleep has been implicated in spatial learning based on recordings from the hippocampus in rats during waking and sleep. During waking, "place cells" in the hippocampus fire together when the rat is in certain locations in its environment. These cells that fired together when the animal was in specific locations while awake were more likely to fire together during subsequent sleep. In addition, cells that did not actively fire while the rat was awake did not show an increase in firing during sleep. These findings provide evidence that experience or information acquired while awake may be repeated during sleep, perhaps as part of a consolidation process.

Song Learning

Such sleep-related replaying of waking brain activity during sleep for spatial memory consolidation is similar to that seen in a very different type of task: bird song learning. Firing patterns of neurons in sleeping birds closely parallel waking patterns, indicating birds spontaneously replay fragments of songs while asleep.

Neuronal replay demonstrated by bird song neuronal firing during wake (mot.), are replayed during sleep (spon.). For each spontaneous sample, a corresponding sample of the waking neuronal activity, indicated by "mot" is given, both under a color spectrograph of the song the bird sang. Both neurons simultaneously fire during sleep, with complex firing structures that match waking activity.

One interpretation of this result is that birds' songs experienced during the day are consolidated during sleep when the neuron firing activity mimics waking activity associated with the song. This avian research did not identify sleep stages, thus it is not clear if the replay activity occurs during NREM or REM sleep, and studies using electrophysiological techniques to identify sleep-stages are necessary for further clarity.

Insight and Creativity

Evidence for sleep facilitating learning comes not only from studies on basic brain mechanisms and simple motor and perceptual skills, but also from more complex tasks requiring higher level thinking. In one experiment, the role of sleep and insight was examined by having participants perform a cognitive task that required them to learn stimulus–response sequences. Their performance improved either gradually or came abruptly, when they gained "insight" into a hidden abstract rule. At retest, greater than twice as many subjects gained insight into the hidden rule following a night of sleep than after a night of sleep deprivation or after normal daytime wakefulness. Thus, sleep may facilitate extraction of factual knowledge and insightful behavior.

Criticisms

Other scientists have criticized research on sleep and learning for several faults. In the first place, they say that the stress and emotional effects of sleep deprivation may interfere with the learning process rather than sleep facilitating it. Second, some scientists believe that the theory of sleep and learning predicts that humans with greater intelligence or more intelligent animals sleep more than others, but this is not the case. In addition, humans taking medications that inhibit REM sleep do not have learning deficits as might be predicted. The inconsistency of findings from one experiment to another also warrants concern. The final question is whether sleep is necessary or simply advantageous for learning.

Strategies

When choosing strategies, educators should consider two things: (1) lack of sleep may interfere with acquisition of new material and (2) lack of sleep may hinder consolidation. The studies described in this article were all performed with humans or other animals where sleep was normal before they were exposed to the new material. Many other studies show that not getting adequate sleep, that is, having a "sleep debt," will interfere with acquiring new information. Sleep loss impairs alertness and attention, hindering a student's ability to learn while in the classroom. Thus, sleep not only affects learning consolidation during sleep, but also has consequences on daytime functioning and alertness. In some cases, the learning process is compromised simply because the student cannot stay awake and pay attention. In addition, emotional consequences of inadequate sleep, such as decreased behavioral inhibition and increased irritability and emotional instability, may cause classroom behavior problems that interfere with information acquisition.

To promote optimal acquisition of new material, students need to know the importance of getting a full night's sleep to help them study better and to help the information they study to "stick." Then, of course, they need to sleep. Students worried about not having enough time to finish homework if they sleep more, may be reassured to know their concentration and focus are much better with adequate sleep. They may also learn more efficiently, taking full advantage of sleep's facilitating power.

Data from a number of studies also indicate that, while pulling "all-nighters" may be sufficient for short-term memorization and regurgitation, the information will not be retained long-term. Finally, students with inadequate sleep find it difficult to pull together the facts into comprehensive themes, and therefore their papers and essays may suffer.

In summary, students who have a regular sleep pattern that allows plenty of sleep, have a learning advantage over those with poor sleep habits.

See also: **Adolescent Social and Emotional Development; Animal Studies.**

Further Readings

Carskadon, M.A. (2002). *Adolescent Sleep Patterns: Biological, Social, and Psychological Influences.* Cambridge, NY: Cambridge University Press.

Dave, A.S., Margoliash, D. (2000). Song replay during sleep and computational rules for sensorimotor vocal learning. *Science* 290(5492):812–816.

Frank, M.G., Issa, N.P., Stryker M.P. (2001). Sleep enhances plasticity in the developing visual cortex. *Neuron* 30(1):275–287.

Rechtschaffen, A., Kleitman, N., & Dement, W. (1961–1986). Association for the Psychophysiological Study of Sleep Records, *Psychophysiology* 6, 68–69.

Siegel, J.M. (2001). The REM sleep-memory consolidation hypothesis. *Science* 294(5544):1058–1063.

Vyazovskiy, V., Borbely, A.A., & Tobler, I. (2000). Fast track: Unilateral vibrissae stimulation during waking induces intermispheric ##G asymmetry during subsequent sleep in the rat. *Journal of Sleep Research.* (9)4 367–376.

Wagner, U., Gais, S., Haider, H., Verleger R., Born, J. (2004). Sleep inspires insight. *Nature* 427(6972):352–355.

Walker, M.P., Brakefield, T., Morgan, A., Hobson, J.A., Stickgold, R. (2002). Practice with sleep makes perfect: Sleep-dependent motor skill learning. *Neuron* 35(1):205–211.

Wilson, M.A., McNaughton, B.L. (1994). Reactivation of hippocampal ensemble memories during sleep. *Science* 265(5172):676–679.

Stanford University Center for Human Sleep Research, med.stanford.edu/school/psychiatry/humansleep/

TRACY L. RUPP, M.S. AND
MARY A. CARSKADON, PH.D.

Social Context of Learning

The common perception is that learning is something that one does privately, inside his or her own head. While there's a good deal of common sense to that, another question arises, "What *other* factors influence the learning going on inside the head?" Social cognition is the processing of information, which leads to the accurate processing of the dispositions and intentions of others. It is quite plausible that it was the development of complex social hierarchies, not our intellect that contributed to the rapid increase in the size of the human brain. As humans must learn to survive, it is likely the social brain is designed to handle some kind of social learning. A burgeoning new field, social neuroscience, has revealed an astonishing array of multilevel influences that social contact has on the brain. Areas of the brain dedicated to social structure are extensive and have been identified as the anterior prefrontal lobe, anterior cingulate, frontal gyrus, amygdala, fusiform gyrus, and posterior temporal lobe. To process social information, we use areas of the prefrontal cortex, somasensory cortex and amygdaloid complex.

Social Experience is Powerful

Many believe that the process begins at birth. Studies have shown that newborns, even as early as the first hours and days of life, preferentially look toward simple face-like patterns. This early tendency to fixate on faces might be to establish bonding with adult caregivers and to bias the visual input toward likely support. But the social systems that develop are much more complex than "eye contact with mom." A systems analysis suggests events at one level of an organism (molecular, DNA, cellular, nervous system, organs, immune, behavioral, social, etc.) can profoundly influence events at other levels. A social event is not isolated from the rest of our mind and body—and we ought to pay closer attention to the nature of social contacts at school.

We cannot think of ourselves and our social contacts as fragmented. Social events at one level of an organism (molecular, DNA, cellular, nervous system, organs, immune, behavioral, social, etc.) can profoundly influence events at other levels. If you fall in love one afternoon, you can be assured that you have a different biological makeup by evening! Naturally, if your sweetheart dumps you, your whole mind, body, and emotions are affected. This suggests that social contact at school may have a much more widespread influence than researchers earlier thought. We are strongly influenced by others in the social learning process through many ways including, but not limited to:

- explicit reinforcers given by others
- peer acceptance
- influences on decision-making
- risk of social disapproval
- role of emotions in decisions
- peer cognitive support.

If students do not feel socially accepted, comfortable, safe, or included, they run serious health and academic risks. Healthy social contact improves immune activity and social stress weakens immune systems. As the classroom and the school experiences take in over 13,000 hours in a child's K-12 schooling, the brain of students will be altered by those experiences. There are many types of social structures for learning including the school campus itself, lunch areas, clubs, teams, and cooperative learning in the classroom. Each elicits a different set of responses from us socially.

Learning with Many or Few?

Student class size changes how we behave. In bigger groups, the students may feel more lost, but there is less accountability. In smaller groups, the reverse is true. Class size matters to teachers, administrators, taxpayers, and students. More numbers create greater social opportunities (friends, potential mates, etc.) but also may expose greater risks (cliques, gangs, less attention, etc.). The evidence is somewhat mixed on this matter, but there is a general positive correlation between smaller class size and student learning but only at the primary level. This means the actual class size effect is negative on student achievement. To make any kind of an impact on student learning, class size has got to be at about a fifteen to one ratio. Children in smaller classes often perform better on literacy skills. The exceptions are where students are in ESL, special needs classes, or English composition. This may be a result of the type of teaching that is done or needs to be done as much as any other factor. For example, greater use of cooperative learning and other engaging strategies can mitigate the negative achievement effects of a larger class size.

Learning with Peers – Or Not?

Understandably, parents want their own children in groups that are either equal to or above the ability *level of the other students.* In general, this notion is supported by a decade of research. Ability grouping is highly controversial because of the potential implications for academic and life status. One study found that students of all ability levels could benefit from ability grouping when contrasted with a heterogeneous grouping. The student groups that benefit the most are those with low ability—they do better when placed in multi-ability groups.

Yet tracking, as you might suspect, can reduce the positive peer effect, says a Rand Corporation study. After all, students often, but not always, live up to the class norms. But mixed ability groups often learn other skills that may have more lasting value than a slightly higher grade. Many researchers have found positive social skills to be part of the results. The take-home message here is that ability grouping by itself may be helpful if done well. The greater issue is *how* grouping is done and the corresponding teacher affect. Some effective teaching strategies may ameliorate the negative social impact tracking may have on self-esteem.

To Cooperate or Compete?

Some social structures are less structured, such as context-dependent friendships or a temporary class partner for an activity. Others are more structured, such as ability grouping or cooperative learning groups. Cooperative learning pioneers Roger and David Johnson, have a distinct model for cooperative learning, which defines one of the key elements as positive interdependency. Putting students together in a relevant social structure can be highly effective. In fact, the evidence suggests that if you compare students who are in cooperative groups against those doing the tasks individually and competing individually, the collaborative social strategy works better. That is a key factor because positive time with peers can reduce **stress**. Excess cortisol can be a highly negative factor in learning. In rodents, after peer separation, cortisol levels for both males and females soar 18–87 percent higher than those housed with friendly established social groups.

Research on cooperative learning suggests that it produces better learning when compared to students competing against each other individually. Other studies corroborate this effect, showing that a quality cooperative learning strategy will outperform random grouping or individual learning. The perception among those interviewed, who are using cooperative social support, is that the academic challenges are more achievable. In fact, students do achieve more; even if the increase is not always robust, other social values are typically improved. The effects of social variables cannot be either isolated or underestimated. Part of the value of positive social experiences is that it generates peer acceptance and approval. That boost in self-esteem creates hope and optimism that influences brain chemistry and capability assessments.

Learning without Peers

Is there a negative side to social grouping? Students who dislike working with others cooperatively should be listened to, but not catered to exclusively. Provide some variety and some choice and ultimately students will feel included. This is not a case of saying that "All increased social contact is better!" The fact is, some students like working by themselves and may do better solo than with forced social contact. Their dislike or underperformance may actually skew the overall statistics, meaning that the rest of the *students may be doing even better* than earlier reported. Many students find intense or prolonged social contact to be more, not less, stressful. To those students, you have a message: "School is not always a democracy and you don't have to like everything, all the time."

Keep in mind, some students don't like technology, others don't like visual arts or physical education, and still others eschew music. We should respect, but not necessarily cave in to their wishes. It is still important to (1) explain WHY we are asking them to do something they don't wish to and (2) provide some variety so that no student has to spend 100 percent of their time in an uncomfortable, stressed social structure. But they ought to try it, even if they are not comfortable with it. One study among sixth graders randomly assigned them to work in either triads or individually on computer-based problems. After the initial assignment was over, the ones who had worked in triads outperformed (as individuals) the other individuals who had no exposure to the cooperative group. While some students may not be comfortable working with others, some cognitive and social benefits may persist.

Why Status Matters to Students

Sometimes adults are amused that schoolage students seem so obsessed with status in the classroom. But there may be a biological reason for the concern. Changes in social status influence an important neurotransmitter in our brain. Moderate levels are highly implicated with attention, mood, and memory, all factors that can drive achievement. In addition, lower serotonin levels are also correlated inflexible behaviors. Given these effects, it should come as little surprise that social status, serotonin, and academic achievement are all correlated. In another study of 345 children over two years, peer rejection assessed as early as kindergarten and social rejection that is stable across the two years are highly correlated with deficits in first and second-grade academic achievement and work habits. But for those who received stable social acceptance, their achievement was higher and this pattern remains significant even after the study authors controlled for initial kindergarten academic competence. Social status matters; and there is little doubt in the researchers' minds.

Part of the role of schools is to create a citizenry for tomorrow that has the ability to cooperate as well as compete. Some of our students may end up being better at competition and others better at cooperation. But all of them ought to be able to get along with others.

We can say there are significant and broad-based effects of positive social contact. It should not be left to random forces, but rather orchestrated and nurtured. The new field of social neuroscience suggests that educators be very purposeful in fostering positive, interdependent social contact. This does not mean that every single social grouping in school must be meaningfully engineered to nurture lasting emotional and social skills. But it does mean that every social contact a student has will either reinforce their positive capabilities, mood and self-concept, or undermine them. Consider every school contact we orchestrate as an opportunity to do just that.

See also: Adolescent Social and Emotional Development; Emotions; Motivation.

Further Readings

Feinstein, S. (2004). *Secrets of the Teenage Brain*. Thousand Oaks, CA: Corwin Press.

Jensen, E. (2003). *Tools for Engagement*. San Diego, CA: The Brain Store.

Johnson, D., Johnson, R. (1999). *Learning Together and Alone: Cooperative, Competitive and Individualistic Learning*. Boston, MA: Allyn & Bacon.

Lupien, S.J., Lepage, M. (2001, December). Stress, memory, and the hippocampus: Can't live with it, can't live without it. *Behavioural Brain Research* 127(1–2):137–158.

ERIC JENSEN

Spirituality

The concept of spirituality is defined differently among cultural groups. The common characteristics of spirituality across cultures, however, include a sense of transcendence and connection to something greater than the self, forming a framework from which to make sense of potentially chaotic experiences. Religion is a codified expression of spirituality shared by a particular people group. The observation of religious expression in rituals related to life and death practices throughout history and across cultures has led researchers to search for underlying structural and functional characteristics of the brain to help explain the similarity and universality of such behaviors.

This study is controversial because it touches on some of our most cherished ideas and beliefs. Some researchers approach the data from a reductionist perspective, defining spiritual experience as merely a chemical-electrical brain-based event, non-dependent on any cosmic force. Others point to the fact that all human experiences elicit chemical-electrical responses. Thus, the human brain would register and record an encounter with a "cosmic other" in the same manner it records an encounter with any other, neither proving nor disproving the reality of a divine source of spiritual experience. The emerging science attempting to bring neurological research, psychology, philosophy, and religion into dialog is called neurotheology. Neurotheology does not seek to prove the existence of God or to evaluate a particular religion, but rati. ̴r to understand how humans perceive and relate to the concept of God or supernatural forces.

There are four primary arenas in which the relationship between spirituality and the brain has been studied: through experiments that attempt to cause a spiritual perception through brain stimulation; through fMRI scans of those who are willing to use meditative practices to induce perceptions of a mystical experience; through reports of those who have had near-death experiences they define as spiritual; and through correlative studies of spiritual temperament inventories with measures of serotonin uptake activity in the brain.

Through these studies researchers have identified sites in the prefrontal cortex that correlate with a sense of an unseen presence, a sense of being aware yet detached from physical limits or boundaries, and even sensory perceptions such as voices or visions. Other studies indicate that a meditative state activates the limbic system, forming powerful emotional connections to perceived spiritual experiences that can often be paradigm-shifting and thus life-changing. D'Aquilli and Newberg have specifically postulated a chemically based explanation for the sense of being at one with the universe that occurs when both the sympathetic and parasympathetic systems are operating at maximum levels simultaneously, and at least one study indicates that individuals with a spiritually sensitive temperament have a particular way of processing serotonin.

These kinds of spiritual experiences, though they can be physiologically documented, are often described as mystical and "beyond expression." Mystical experience is not the only understanding of spirituality, however. Non-mystical spiritual experiences are harder to study, though, because they cannot be predicted or induced on command. They are often linked to practices of a particular spiritual or cultural tradition, but engagement in the practice may produce inconsistent outcomes. When the practice does yield an identified non-mystical outcome, it generally results in a sense of personal or ultimate meaning, well-being, or purposefulness and can be expressed through language or by means of a story communicable through words or another art form. Such spiritual practices are usually intentionally engaged, cognitively mediated, and involve all components of learning including **motivation**, rehearsal, social reinforcement, memory, and transference. As such, these practices are usually passed from generation to generation through some form of religious or cultural education or indoctrination.

Some of the most commonly cited expressions of spirituality in practice include prayer; creativity; aesthetic appreciation or expression through design and music; ethical reasoning; virtuous behavior; ritualistic practice that is either deeply personal or highly traditional; altruistic service; philanthropic giving; caring for the weak or less fortunate; investing in intimate relationships; community-building; conscious suffering, birthing and/or dying; caring for the natural world and ecological system; generativity (leaving a legacy); and "mindfulness" (attending to both physical and emotional details of everyday experiences). Ultimately, the pursuit of any of these spiritual expressions flow from individual values and preferences that may be expressions of **multiple intelligences**, developmental levels, personality traits, or physiological states in an intricate web of cause and effect.

Each expression of spirituality is subjectively based, even though many people who practice particular forms of spiritual expression believe that they are operating in harmony with objective truths. The key to addressing spirituality in the classroom is to plan opportunities to allow for activities based on subjective engagement. Teachers can ask questions that require affective answers and structure assignments so that students can choose alternate modes of expression as well as draw from alternate sources of authority. The wise teacher recognizes that not all aspects of learning can be quantified or measured, but some learning can instead be observed along a continuum of growth. Children who fear or are intimidated by a measurement system lose their natural ability to wonder freely.

Opportunities for cooperative, collaborative, non-competitive, community-based service learning appeal to students who value corporate or social expressions of spirituality. Times of directive and non-directive silence, opportunities to discuss ethical implications of curricular material, and space to explore both materials and concepts independently will all help the intuitive child to pursue common ground between the spiritual and the intellectual agenda of the classroom. While all classrooms should allow for **creativity**, introducing elements of daily or weekly ritual can also help to anchor the spiritually sensitive child to the learning environment. In general, the younger the child, the stronger the need for ritualized practices in the classroom; yet students of all ages can be powerfully impacted by the establishment of unique classroom traditions.

Respect for differences and appreciation of cultural and religious diversity are important to the developing child because spirituality is interwoven with both family practices and personal experiences. An anti-bias curriculum can help to develop a classroom climate in which children of varying spiritual and/or religious traditions can flourish. A simple way of keeping students open to differences in perspective is periodically to invite them to spend three to five minutes writing down everything they observe in the classroom. At the end of that time, students can compare lists to take note of the differences of perspective represented by their observations. While each thing on both lists can be concretely identified, it is unlikely that students will have noticed exactly the same things as anyone else in the classroom.

If spirituality is about noticing and meaning-making, adequate time and opportunity for reflection and open dialog in a context of respect are essential to student processing. A playful, exploratory environment and attention to the aesthetic sensitivities of individual children can also contribute to the learning climate of the classroom.

Spiritually sensitive teaching techniques are educationally sound because they open opportunities for depth of knowledge rooted in self-awareness and personal application. A spiritually sensitive framework need not be religious in nature and does not violate any principles of separation of church and state.

There is very little doubt from the research perspective that the brain can and does become "spiritually activated." The source of that activation, its interpretation, and the effective outcome of it remain for the study of the theologian, the sociologist, and the philosopher. Still, the classroom practitioner can focus on utilizing teaching practices and encouraging a classroom culture that do not hinder a child's ability to engage in personal meaning-making and ongoing spiritual formation in the context of a content-driven curriculum.

See also: **Emotion and Self-Esteem.**

Further Readings

D'Aquili, E., Newberg, A., Rause, V. (2001). *Why God Won't Go Away: Science and the Biology of Belief.* New York: Ballentine.

Joseph, R. (2002). *Neurotheology: Brain, Science, Spirituality, Religious Experience.* San Jose, CA: University Press.

Lantieri, L. (2001). *Schools with Spirit: Nurturing the Inner Lives of Children and Teachers.* Boston: Beacon Press.

LORI NILES, M.A.

Stress

A salesman, stressed about being late for work, can't remember where he left his car keys. A student, worried that she just failed her final exam, forgets to stop at the store for groceries on her way home from school.

A doctor, troubled about a sick patient, forgets to drop off his infant son at daycare on his way to the office. Later that day, the boy, still in the backseat of his father's car, dies of heat exposure as his father is immersed in his work. These examples illustrate stress-related memory impairments and some of their consequences. In most cases, episodes of failed memory are relatively benign and may even be amusing, as when a harried commuter drives off to fight the morning traffic, oblivious to the coffee mug he left on the roof of his car. In other cases, stress-related memory failures can have tragic outcomes, such as when children are left in cars by otherwise loving and attentive parents; the death of a child forgotten in an overheated car is a memory lapse these parents will never forget. Stress-induced forgetting, which in it's most intense form is referred to as *traumatic amnesia,* is an important area of research by neuroscientists who are interested in studying how strong emotions can cause the brain's memory systems to go awry.

Neuroscientists think of the neurobiology of memory in terms of the interactions of brain structures, with each structure providing a different contribution to how information is processed. The entire limbic system, which includes the hypothalamus, amygdala, and the hippocampus, is involved in stress. This chapter will focus on one of the primary structures involved in memory–stress interactions, the hypothalamus which is also one of the most primitive of all brain structures. The hypothalamus controls the expression of our primal emotions, such as fear, anger, and our craving for food and sex. The hypothalamus is also the interface through which the brain communicates our feelings of being stressed to the rest of the body. When the hypothalamus is activated in times of fear, anger, frustration, or more generally, being stressed out, it responds as if your very survival is in doubt. To help you deal with a real or perceived threat the hypothalamus releases a chemical known as corticotropin releasing factor (CRF). CRF, in conjunction with epinephrine and cortisol (two stress hormones released from the adrenal glands), activate physiological responses that enhance the likelihood of survival in the event of an attack. For example, CRF, epinephrine, and cortisol increase blood glucose levels to enable you to have sufficient energy to escape or fight an aggressor. These hormones also stimulate the immune system to help you to ward off infections that could be caused by wounds inflicted by a predator.

The hypothalamus, in a primitive manner, takes a sledge-hammer approach to ensure that we pay attention to what is causing us to feel stressed. Hypothalamic CRF, in conjunction with epinephrine, cortisol and other neurochemicals, all intensify our attentional faculties to focus on the arousing stimulus. However, the hypothalamus has difficulty distinguishing between a real threat, such as the fear you feel if someone threatens you with a knife, from stressful experiences that are aggravating, but not life threatening, such as being afraid of failing an exam or when you get angry at someone for cutting you off in traffic. This intensification and focusing of attention at times of strong emotionality is called "perceptual narrowing." A common example of perceptual narrowing is when people experience an actual threat to their lives, such as being caught in the middle of a bank robbery. People tend to report that they have little or no recollection of the details of this kind of terrifying experience except that the image of the robber's weapon is forever "burned" into their memory. This phenomenon, called "weapon focus," is the bane of the prosecutor trying to convict a bank robber because witnesses may have accurate and vivid memories of the gun pointed at their faces, but only vague and flawed memories of the details of the criminal's face.

How does hypothalamic activation induced by stressful experiences get transformed into forgetfulness? The hypothalamus, itself, is the engine that drives emotions and helps to intensify attention. It is essential for the expression of emotions, but it doesn't have the internal circuitry to process specific memories. The actual memory storage and retrieval machinery is in other structures deep within the brain. One of these structures is the hippocampus, which enables us to store facts, details, and the events of our lives. Neuroscientists unintentionally learned about how the hippocampus has an essential role in memory in 1953, after a surgery was performed on a twenty-three year-old man suffering from uncontrollable epileptic seizures. This patient, referred to in the literature as "HM," had his hippocampus surgically removed because the neurosurgeons believed that his hippocampus was the source of his seizure activity. Indeed, the surgery was successful in that regard because it resulted in a reduction of his seizure activity. However, the negative side effects were so damaging to HM's ability to function that the surgery has not been conducted again on any other patient. HM is now seventy-four years of age, is fully capable of carrying on a conversation, and he can reminisce about the first twenty-three years of his life. The last five decades, however, are only a hazy fog of lost memories. Since 1953, all of the new experiences of HM's life, the mundane and the significant, have been forgotten almost immediately. For example, each time he is told of the death of his mother he expresses sadness and grief, as if he had never learned of her death before. He forgets that his mother died years ago and that he has expressed the same feelings of grief upon learning of the loss of his mother on dozens of previous occasions. Each time he is told of her death his awareness of her passing fades and is lost in a matter of minutes. The Vietnam War, Watergate, the destruction of the Berlin Wall and the terrorist attacks on 9/11/2001 all trigger strong memories in those who experienced these events; HM has no recollection of these events because they all occurred after he lost the ability to form new memories. As a result of work with HM and similar findings in other people and animals with brain damage, we have learned that the hippocampus is required for the storage and retrieval of new information, but is not necessary for the retrieval of remote (old) memories.

The connection between the hippocampus and memory is revealed by manipulations far more subtle than brain surgery. Neurochemical studies have shown that of all the structures in the brain, the hippocampus is the primary target of stress hormones. These hormones, including CRF, cortisol, and norepinephrine (a form of epinephrine), produce a profound disturbance of hippocampal electrical and chemical activity. Moreover, chronic stress, the kind that produces cardiovascular disorders and gastric ulcers, has a detrimental effect on the physical structure of the hippocampus. Prolonged periods of stress can cause parts of hippocampal neurons (another term for brain cells) to wither, in a manner similar to the way a tree loses its leaves in the winter. As a tree may die as a result of an extremely cold winter, the constant bathing of the hippocampus in stress hormones can bring about the death of its neurons. The debilitating effects of stress on the hippocampus have been documented in people with extreme stress and anxiety, such as in those who develop post-traumatic stress disorder (PTSD) as a result of suffering through a traumatic experience, and in people with Major Depressive Disorder. Brain imaging studies have shown that people with these types of anxiety disorders have a shrinkage (atrophy) of their hippocampus and profound memory deficits.

As gloomy as this story is about how a hyperactive hypothalamus in stressed people can lead to cell death and damage to the hippocampus, there is cause for optimism. The hippocampus shows great resiliency in response to stress. Animal and human studies have shown that with the termination of either chronic stress or with drug therapy, hippocampal neurons can regrow their withered connections, much as a tree recovers its foliage in the spring. Even more dramatic findings of growth and recovery come from work showing that the hippocampus, unlike virtually all other brain structures, can grow new neurons that help the hippocampus in its learning and memory functions, even in elderly individuals.

The latest research has led to a new generation of antidepressants and anxiety reduction drugs that help to improve memory performance in individuals under stress by blocking the stress-related chemical reactions that interfere with hippocampal functioning.

Neuroscience research over the past five decades has given us a good understanding of how and why stress exerts such a profound influence on our memory. Stress activates primitive brain structures, such as the hypothalamus, which increases production of stress hormones and shifts the brain into survival mode. This strategy is effective for animals attempting to escape from a predator, but is not an effective strategy in our highly technological society where a stressor is more likely to be a bill collector than a predator. Excessive production of stress hormones impairs memory and can trigger the development of anxiety disorders, all of which involve damage to the hippocampus. The next stage of progress is the application of our knowledge of how stress damages the brain to develop medication that will improve memory and provide life-long protection of the hippocampus from damage by stress.

The following strategies can reduce stress in the classroom:

1. Provide academic scaffolding. Students need the background knowledge necessary to accomplish assignments, along with clear expectations and fair consequences.

2. Offer homework helpers and tutoring.

3. Use competition carefully. Every student should have a chance for success.

4. Allow some choice in content, instructional strategies, or assessment.

5. Teach time management, study skills, and test-taking strategies to students that need the support.

6. Schedule special student–teacher meetings to enhance communication and convey that you care about them.

7. Have students rate and chart their stress on a scale of one to ten. This puts the stress level in perspective and is often preferred by students that enjoy logical/mathematical thinking. If the stress level is too high, refer them to a professional counselor.

8. Provide opportunities for students to journal or talk about stress in their lives.

9. Show role models of individuals that handled stress well.

10. Set a calm soothing tone through music.

See also: Animal Studies; Classroom Environment; Depression; Music Teaching Model for the Brain.

Further Readings

Bremner, J.D. (2002). *Does Stress Damage the Brain?: Understanding Trauma-Related Disorders From a Neurological Perspective*. New York N.Y.: W. W. Norton & Company.

Kim, J., Diamond, D. (2002). The stressed hippocampus, synaptic plasticity and lost memories. *Nature Reviews Neuroscience* 3(6): 453–462.

LeDoux, J. (1998). *The Emotional Brain: The Mysterious Underpinnings of Emotional Life*. New York, NY: Simon & Schuster.

McEwen, B., Lasley, E.N., Lasley, E. (2002). *The End of Stress As We Know It*. Washington, D.C.: National Academies Press.

DAVID M. DIAMOND, PH.D.;
COLLIN R. PARK, PH.D.;
ADAM M. CAMPBELL PH.D., AND
JAMES C. WOODSON, PH.D.

Suggestopedia (Accelerated Learning)

Researchers, teachers, and students are looking for ways to accelerate the learning process. Accelerated Learning integrates current research on how people learn into a teaching process and a curriculum design template. The goal of Accelerated Learning is to empower students to tap into their potential, overcome the often unconscious limiting beliefs they have, and apply knowledge and skills effectively in their lives.

Accelerated Learning developed from *Suggestopedia,* a methodology tested in Bulgaria in the 1960s by Dr. Georgi Lozanov. The name *Suggestopedia* derives from two words—*Suggestion* and *Pedagogy.* The method's main concern is the influence of *Suggestion* in teaching/facilitating. Lozanov describes *Suggestion* as the underlying messages people take in on both a conscious and unconscious level. The interpretation of those messages lead to both limiting and empowering beliefs. Neuroscience now confirms the power of our beliefs. Students who perceive themselves and their possibilities negatively do so because of their embedded memories of negative and significant emotional events that have now become part of their cognitive belief system and self-concept. The emotionality sets a process in motion that imprints the memory with all its related stimuli into the brain. Any of those stimuli can trigger the memory and the resulting stress. Accelerated Learning asks several questions in preparation for teaching: What will the classroom, the seating arrangement, the teaching methods, and the verbal and nonverbal communication suggest to, or trigger in, the student? What are the *Suggestions* that students bring into the learning environment about themselves and about learning? How can teachers help students move beyond their limiting beliefs and tap into their potential? The answers guide teachers in planning their lessons, in designing the classroom, and in preparing themselves mentally, emotionally, and physically to teach.

Neuroscience research shows the importance of positive emotions to both memory and learning. In fact, many researchers and educators say *there is no learning without* **emotion**. Positive emotional experiences reinforce learning by promoting the likelihood that memory will be stored immediately in the locale, spatial memory involving multiple regions of the brain. If the learning experience is stimulus rich, and the student is actively engaged in the process, there will also be many potential triggers to support retrieval when needed. Any stimulus can act as an anchor to recall the entire experience. Anchoring is sometimes called state dependence. It is the theory that recall of learning can depend on the state or other situations that existed when the learning took place. Neural networks connect the two, the content learned with the place, mood, smell, and physical condition. The richer the learning experience, the more possible connections can be made and used to retrieve information. Accelerated Learning creates multiple opportunities for students to experience positive emotional experiences that can significantly change how they see themselves. Classroom spaces, tone of voice, music, and certain ritualized events in the classroom act as anchors to support learning and a shift in perspective. The teacher also provides learning activities that are multi-sensory to both appeal to various learning styles and provide stimuli-rich learning to act as an anchor for later retrieval.

Extensive research also demonstrates the negative effects of **stress** on learning. The brain produces cortisol and other stress hormones, and activity in the neo-cortex slows down or stops completely. There is a downshifting to the lower regions of the brain, the so-called R-Complex or reptilian brain consisting of the brain stem and cerebellum. Accelerated Learning creates a safe environment for students. The teacher supports cooperation and team learning. When the students play learning games, there are only winners. No one is singled out as a loser. Mistakes are applauded as steps to mastering the material. Accelerated Learning also uses various relaxation techniques, guided imageries, and focusing activities to support students in their learning. Neuroscience research shows that relaxation response produces serotonin, a chemical in the brain that promotes sleep, relaxation, and positive self-concept.

Accelerated Learning orchestrates learning to appeal to both the conscious mind and the para-conscious, or things outside of consciousness at the moment. Research shows the ability of the brain to take in information at a conscious and unconscious level and store it for later retrieval. The brain also automatically registers the familiar and constantly searches for novel stimuli as part of the survival instinct. As the brain responds to everything within the sensory context of the classroom, everything in the classroom teaches and becomes part of the student's learning. Lozanov looked closely at the role of the environment in learning. The Accelerated Learning classroom uses peripherals to teach, to inspire, and to create a positive and engaging learning environment. Teachers learn the importance of voice, language, non-verbal communication and their attitudes to the success of their students. Everything in the classroom is orchestrated to support learning. The physical environment provides the needed light, oxygen, water, as well as the variety of stimuli the brain needs. The emotional environment supports students in moving beyond their limiting beliefs and opening up to possibilities. The design of the lesson facilitates students' meaningful interaction with the material, with one another, and with the teacher.

The brain is constantly searching for meaning. To make sense of an experience, the brain perceives and generates patterns. It resists meaningless patterns such as isolated and irrelevant bits of information. In Accelerated Learning, carefully designed learning activities offer opportunities for significant and positive emotional experiences that can shift students' perspectives. The lesson plan provides variety and novelty within enough structure to provide a roadmap for learners while they navigate through the learning materials creatively. Accelerated Learning encourages students to experience learning with the mind, body, and emotions. Students find personal meaning and importance in the subject matter and stay actively involved throughout the process. They create their own patterns and personal meaning in what they learn. Both interaction with others and self-reflection play a role in helping students connect the content with their lives in a profound way. The pace moves from more active phases to more reflective ones. The change in methods and pace reinforce the brain's need for rest and change to function optimally.

Accelerated Learning offers a philosophy, a teaching process, and a design template for lesson plans and the curriculum. The philosophy is based on the research of Lozanov into the effect of *suggestion* on learning and his theories on how teachers can help students *de-suggest* their limiting beliefs through carefully designed classroom activities. The teaching process integrates current thinking on the brain and learning and human development. The Accelerated Learning Cycle provides a template to create successful lesson plans and guide teachers in creating an optimal learning environment.

The Accelerated Learning Philosophy

Accelerated Learning operates on the theory that each person has innate but hidden capacity and talent that Lozanov calls the reserve capacities of the mind. Neuroscience today shows the enormous capacity of the human brain for learning and retention. As each student has untapped reserve capacities of the mind, the teacher's main task is to create opportunities for each person to tap into their potential. The task of a teacher is to support students in developing more empowering beliefs about themselves and their world. Robert Rosenthal's, of Harvard University, work on the Pygmalian Effect shows that what a teacher thinks of students translates into what a student achieves. Lozanov's research into the effects of *suggestion,* or the underlying messages in every type of communication, supports Rosenthal's research. The teacher's role becomes more important in light of their research. Accelerated Learning teachers carefully monitor their thoughts about students to make sure they are supporting and not hindering someone's learning. They pay attention to their verbal and nonverbal communication because they both contribute greatly to student success or failure. Teachers develop their sensory acuity or ability to recognize subtle cues from learners. Based on their observations, an Accelerated Learning teacher uses language, story, and ritual to help students widen their perspective and embrace possibilities. Teachers frame learning positively at all times. They help students reframe negatively perceived experiences to emphasize the positive.

The Accelerated Learning Process

Much of what Lozanov proposed in the 1960s has been confirmed by researchers today who have access to sophisticated equipment to study the brain—the importance of emotions to learning, the need for a wide variety of interaction with the learning materials, with other students, and with the teacher to support learning, the importance of both the physical and the emotional environment to learning, and the ability of the brain to process and create patterns in parallel. His emphasis on the learning environment, his belief in sensory overload to bypass the conscious brain, and his use of music, the arts and game-like activities to engage the student are in keeping with what we know about the brain and learning.

The Accelerated Learning process provides students with a variety of multi-sensory input based on the premise that the more senses involved in learning, the more neural pathways will be developed and strengthened. The more stimuli used in the initial learning phase, the easier it will be to recall the information later. Teachers include learning activities to appeal to all learning styles and build strengths in areas that are less developed in students. Accelerated Learning emphasizes the role of the learning environment. Add artwork and other peripherals that support learning and *de-suggest,* or enable a shift of perspective, in the student to your classroom. Use the space intentionally to create powerful visuals. Include posters with key learning concepts, positive suggestions in the form of sayings or proverbs, and graphics and colors that reinforce the key concepts. Provide a seating arrangement to support interaction, either using a circle of chairs and tables behind the circle for group activities for a small group or if the room is large enough, several round tables for groups of five to six students scattered around the room for groups of any size. Ensure full spectrum lighting if at all possible, and provide plenty of water to drink and fruit to eat. Place green plants around the room. The lecture-style seating, gray bare walls, and sterile atmosphere that act as negative anchors from the traditional school classroom suggest that learning is sterile, the teacher is the knower, and the students are passive receivers of knowledge. The pleasant physical environment replaces those underlying negative suggestions with more empowering ones. Learning becomes an interactive process involving all the senses. The seating arrangement places the student at the center and not the teacher. The interaction with the environment, the content, and the other students become equally important to the teacher–student interaction. The physical environment becomes a positive suggestive factor and not one that inhibits on both the conscious and unconscious level. Play **music** to support a positive internal state and to reinforce learning.

Neuroscience has looked at the impact of music on learning and retention. The right music creates and maintains an optimal state for learning. Lozanov also describes music as one of the most powerful suggestive factors in learning. Accelerated Learning uses music in a multitude of ways, to help students focus and center themselves, to add drama to the presentation of materials. Use music to support group work, facilitate creativity, and as an anchor to signal certain events. Play one type of music when it is time to change groups, another type to end the break, and a different piece of music to help students focus. Choose instrumental music to support learning. For breaks and energizers or to change groups or activities, select songs with a positive message and one that supports the learning or the activity. Use pop music to celebrate certain events. Play *One Moment in Time* by Whitney Houston when students are preparing for an important test or event. Choose *We are the Champions* to celebrate student success. Use the theme for *Mission Impossible* or *Pink Panther* to signal a detective-type activity. Play Baroque largos and adagios to review material or while students are doing individual work or reading.

Ritual also plays a key role in Accelerated Learning. The oldest part of our brain, the reptilian brain or R-complex thrives on ritual. You can use certain spaces in the room for certain types of learning or teaching. Use one part of the classroom for questions and answers. Designate other parts of the room as a creativity space, a reflection space, or a place to present new materials. Ritualize the beginning and ending of each day by playing a certain piece of music to begin and another to end the day. Create a special process to begin the day. Ask students to reflect on a quote, tell a story, or do a series of brain-gym exercises. Use music as part of the ritual when appropriate.

Accelerated Learning Design Template and Strategies

The Accelerated Learning cycle provides teachers with a foolproof design template. The cycle consists of a Learner Preparation Phase, a Connection Phase, a Creative Presentation Phase, an Activation Phase consisting of three parts, and an Integration Phase.

The Learner Preparation Phase includes an overview of the learning content and desired outcomes that answer the questions why, what, how, and what if. It also prepares the student emotionally, mentally, and physically to learn. In the overview, the *why* addresses the bigger picture of how the learning will impact the students' lives. It may include solutions to their perceived problems or ways to achieve their personal goals. The *what* offers a short description of the basis of the work to be done, gives an overview of the process, the timing, and the steps to achieve success. The *how* informs students of the ways in which they will learn and lets them see that the diverse methods will support each of them. Finally, *what if* demonstrates the potential impact of learning the content or process for them, and invites them to imagine their success, to experiment with possibilities, and discover for themselves how they will use the learning.

The second stage of the Learner Preparation Phase allows students to focus on the here and now, center themselves, and calm their minds. The process of *centering* or focusing their thoughts, relaxing their bodies, and freeing themselves of self-talk or distracting images prepares the student for the learning experience. To help students center and focus, allow them to listen to a few minutes of reflective music and think about a saying that relates to the day. Guide them through a short guided imagery that encourages them to remember a positive learning experience, and then connect the experience to the present. Walk students through a short relaxation exercise to prepare them for learning. Do brain-gym activities to coordinate and balance their bodies, minds, and emotions.

The Connection Phase provides activities that help students connect emotionally to the subject matter. They may include experiments, mini-simulations, guided-imageries, personal "burning" questions on the subject, drawing, or metaphorical activities. The activities allow students to find meaning in what they are learning and engage their minds, emotions, bodies, and spirit. Have students collect everything they know about a given subject on large pieces of paper using words or symbols. Lead a guided imagery that takes students to a period of history, through the process of photosynthesis, or on a tour of the digestive track or circulatory system. Involve students in an experiment that simulates reality and invite them to offer their hypothesis about what happened and why. Show a part of a movie that dramatizes something you will be teaching, and then elicit their feelings and thoughts.

The Creative Presentation Phase "teaches" the subject matter or process. Depending on the content, the needs of the learning group, and the timeframe, this phase may include any of the following: a simulation in which students experience all the key concepts, an experiment in which the students formulate questions, experiment to find the answers, then teach the concepts back to the rest of the class, a creative presentation that involves three-dimensional mindmaps, skits, panel discussions, game show formats, or interactive lectures. Foreign language teachers present the new dialogues in the form of *concert readings*. The dialogues are written in the form of a movie script. They are rich in imagery and natural language without the artificial grammar progression found in traditional foreign language texts. The story is dramatic and contains plot points, twists and turns and a dramatic and positive ending. The *Active Concert* is a dramatic reading of the foreign language text to music of the pre-romantic phase of classical music (Beethoven, Mozart, Haydn, Tchaikovsky). While the students listen, they repeat the sentences in the foreign language silently and read along. The *Active Concert* is followed by a *Passive Concert*. The *Passive Concert* begins with a short guided imagery to induce a relaxed state in the students. The students then listen to the dialogue to slow movements of Baroque music (largos and adagios, by composers like Vivaldi, Telemann, Albinoni, and others) and imagine they are in the scene.

The Creative Presentation Phase involves students in the process of teaching, allowing them to discover the key concepts, problem-solve, create, and interact with the material and one another. The students become familiar with the material at a basic level and their involvement in the teaching process creates a sense of ownership for the learning. Get students' bodies involved and use body, muscle memory to support the retention of the concepts. Personify parts of the body, parts of a sentence, and the like. Give them characteristics similar to their "role" in reality and tell a story to introduce key concepts. Have students play the parts of a process, use themselves to model it, move around, and make connections. Give students texts and other resources on a given subject. In groups, have them create a newspaper with a special section on the topic as if it had just happened. Ask students to create a boardgame that includes all relevant information from their textbooks on a certain subject, then let everyone play the various games in class. By deciding on the pertinent information, creating the game themselves, then playing it, they will master the material better than when someone teaches it. Have each person "become" a famous person from an area you are teaching. After studying their character and the role they have in history, science, economics, or any other subject area, invite everyone to a party and allow them to mingle and get to know one another in character. Keep the communication going by asking important questions and generating rich discussion. By identifying with key figures, students will retain more of the important information.

The Activation Phase consists of three parts and moves from more teacher-guided activities to more student-directed ones. The *Elaboration Phase* offers a series of structured game-like activities that allow students to practice the material enough to begin to master it. The activities promote the self-concept of the students by promoting win-win situations in which cooperation instead of competition is emphasized. Potentially difficult concepts and ideas are embedded in activities that engage the whole person and make it easier to learn concepts that, on their own, might seem daunting. Board games, card games, memory, dominoes, and other adaptations of children's games, as well as rhythm and movement, story and song can be used in this first activation phase. Create a board game and include a variety of question types—closed, one answer questions, open-ended ones that may have multiple right answers, and thought provoking questions that stimulate higher thinking skills. Add various surprise cards to spice up the game. Include sayings and proverbs to de-suggest or contribute ideas related to the subject. Create prize or activity cards to add variety to the game. Include cards to keep the game interesting like ones that read, *If you were born in the Spring, move two spaces forward.* Toy stores and game shows are a great resource for ideas on how you can make content fun and easy to master.

The Assimilation Phase uses many of the same generic types of activities, but encourages students to synthesize, use the material in new and novel ways and tap into their own creativity. The teacher's role is to observe, offer support when needed, maintain a positive environment, and encourage the involvement of each person. Have students develop a skit or role-play that includes the relevant information. Play game shows that require students to answer questions, give their opinions, and explain processes randomly.

The Implementation Phase provides an opportunity for students to demonstrate what they know. It can be a group skit, a collage, a story, or role-plays to demonstrate competency in a real-life situation. The Implementation Phase gives students an opportunity to experience how much they have learned and demonstrate their expertise in novel and creative ways. Ask groups to think about all the key concepts they have been practicing and create a documentary for younger students. Have them perform, and then allow the other students to ask the performers questions as if they were the actual audience for the documentary. Allow students to participate in a panel discussion as experts on the subject. Give students a complex task to solve that encourages them to manipulate the material and make connections between the various elements they have mastered.

The Integration Phase completes the Accelerated Learning Cycle by providing an opportunity for reflection. It brings closure to a learning module or class period. Conduct a guided-imagery that walks students through the day or module. Play music and give students time to journal or answer some key questions. Show a PowerPoint presentation that includes photos, images, the key concepts of the content, and some motivational phrases to close. Give students time to synthesize their learning in the form of a poem, a story, a work of art, or by creating a commercial, giving a speech, or writing an article. By taking time at the end the day or a learning module to reflect on what they've learned and experienced, students realize how far they have come, how much they have been able to master in a short period of time.

Even if time is short, take a few minutes and walk through the key concepts and invite students to reflect on what was important to them and how it will support them. Pause after each concept for students to contemplate its relevance. Play reflective music as you speak and match your voice to the music. Keep eye contact with everyone and point to relevant posters and other anchors for the group's shared learning experience. Mention any humorous or meaningful moments the students have shared in addition to simply summarizing content or process.

See also: **Aroma and Learning; Classroom Environment; Emotion; Multiple Intelligences; Music; Self-Esteem.**

Further Readings

Heidenhain, G. (Ed.) (2003). *Learning Beyond Boundaries. Fundamental Experiences Using Accelerated Learning*. Lawrenceville, Georgia: International Alliance for Learning Publication.

LeHecka, C. (2003). *Historical Review of Accelerated Learning Research: A Monograph.* Theoretical Implications and Practical Applications. Lawrenceville, Georgia: International Alliance for Learning Publication. www.IALearn.org, professional organization for Accelerated Learning. www.accelerated-learning.info

GAIL HEIDENHAIN

T

Teaching Model for the Brain

During the past decade the neurological and cognitive sciences have produced a vast frontier of knowledge on how the brain processes, stores, and retrieves information. As educators have increasingly recognized their role as consumers of this emerging knowledge, translating brain research into classroom instruction often becomes a challenge for the typical educational practitioner.

In an era of high-stakes accountability for student performance, many teachers feel pressured to prepare students to meet proficiency levels on standardized tests. At the same time, they are often required to implement a plethora of ever-changing educational initiatives and reforms handed to them by well-meaning school district supervisors. In this climate, it would not be surprising for new teachers to feel overwhelmed and seasoned teachers to view any educational initiative, including research in the neurosciences, as merely a fad that will soon be replaced by yet another new initiative. Perhaps this thinking accounts for the fact that educational research is largely ignored by practitioners; as a result little actual change has occurred in our nation's classrooms during the last several decades.

For any research, especially current brain research, to become readily accessible to teachers, fragmented initiatives must be integrated into a cohesive model of instruction. The brain-targeted teaching model described in this chapter is designed to meet this need. It provides teachers with a format for using research in the neurosciences as well as research-based effective instructional practices to guide them in planning, implementing, and assessing a sound program of instruction. The model also assists administrators, supervisors, and professionals supporting instruction as they guide teachers in implementing research-based effective teaching strategies.

First, it might be wise to address those critics who scoff at the term *brain based learning*. Some, for example, might contend that the term has no meaning since all learning is brain-based. "After all," they may say, "we don't think with our feet!" We know, of course, that all learning involves the brain. Yet, we also know that not all teaching results in learning. Thus, while all *learning* is "brain-based," all *teaching* is not. Unfortunately, many teaching practices that regularly occur in our schools defy what neuroscience tells us about the brain's natural learning systems. The model presented here, therefore, does not refer to *brain-based learning* but rather to *brain-targeted teaching*.

BRAIN-TARGETED TEACHING
LEARING UNIT

Teacher: Dates:

Unit Topic:/Title   Grand Level:

Standard(s):

Brain Target #1
Emotional Connection:

Brain Target #2
Physical Environment:

Brain Target #3
Concept Map/
Advanced Organizer:

Learing Goals:

Introductory "Big Picture" Activity/Assessment of Prior Knowledge

---

The Brain-Targeted Teaching Model © Mariale M. Hardiman

Brain Target #4
Activities for Teaching Declarative/Procedural Knowledge

Brain Target #5
Activities for Extension and Application of Knowledge

Brain Target #6
Evaluating Learning

Materials:

The Brain-Targeted Teaching Model © Mariale M. Hardiman

The brain-targeted teaching model presents six stages, or "brain targets" of the teaching and learning process and describes brain research that supports each stage. While each brain target is presented separately, the components are interrelated. For example, Brain-Target One describes the importance of establishing a positive emotional climate to foster high levels of learning; these strategies are applied throughout the entire model. At the same time, evaluating learning, Brain-Target Six, is an integral part of each component of the model.

Brain-Target One: Setting the Emotional Climate for Learning

Neuroscientists have recently described the intricate interactions between the **emotional** and cognitive brain systems. Research has shown that the brain's limbic system, located just above the brain stem at the base of the brain, is responsible for our emotional responses. This system, which includes the thalamus, hypothalamus, hippocampus, and amygdala, is also the first to process sensory stimuli. Visual signals travel from the retina to the thalamus, which sorts the information and sends it to the neocortex, the thinking center, to be processed for meaning. The thalamus also sends the information to a small almond-shaped structure, the amygdala, which determines the emotional relevance of the information. This signal, sent simultaneously to both the cognitive and emotional centers, travels first through a "quick and dirty" route to the amygdala, arriving there about fourty milliseconds before it reaches the neocortex. If the amygdala senses threat, it triggers the hypothalamus to activate hormones, mainly cortisol, which elevates blood pressure, increases heart rate, and contracts muscles—all in preparation for an immediate emotional reaction. As the heart rate elevates, blood is directed away from the cortex to the muscles for quick movement, thus diminishing cognitive processing. This "downshifting" prepares the organism for fight or flight, allowing the limbic system to activate and process information before it is analyzed in our cognitive system. As a result, information is processed first in the emotional center before being processed in the thinking center.

Once released into the bloodstream, cortisol can remain in the system for hours. While cortisol levels are high, we may become more easily distracted and lose efficiency of working memory. Unfortunately, chronic high levels of cortisol can have troubling effects. Studies have shown a shrinkage of the hippocampus, a center for memory, when an organism is exposed to long-term stress.

The effects of stress and threat on learning have clear implications for educators. While we may be unable to control all the factors of stress in the lives of our students, the adept teacher can minimize threat-causing practices within the classroom. For example, teachers should liberally praise positive student performance and eliminate practices that cause a child to become embarrassed or disenfranchised within the classroom. At the same time, the teacher should maximize strategies that promote positive emotion. Research has shown that while threats impede learning, positive emotional experiences, during which the brain produces the neurotransmitter serotonin, can contribute to long-term memory. The more intense the arousal of our amygdala the stronger the memory imprint, which, in turn, enhances long-term learning.

Teachers are encouraged to deliberately plan for positive emotional connections within the framework of a specific unit of study. Such connections include specific activities that will connect the students emotionally to the content. For example, within a history lesson students could assume the role of a historical figure and describe feelings and attitudes associated with a particular historic event. When studying literature, students' creative thinking could be encouraged by having them engage in activities to role play various characters in a story or rewrite the story's ending. The infusion of the visual and performing arts is an effective way to tap into children's emotional response systems to enhance learning and should be included within the activities of every learning unit.

Brain-Target Two: Creating the Physical Learning Environment

While the first strategy focused on establishing a positive emotional climate and using emotional responses to enhance learning, Brain-Target Two fosters the careful planning of the physical learning environment. We know that our eyes register about 36,000 visual images per hour, with about 90 percent of the brain's sensory input coming from visual stimuli. The retina supplies about 40 percent of all nerve fibers that are connected to the brain. With this vast visual capacity, the active brain constantly scans the environment seeking visual stimuli.

Researchers tell us that the brain's visual attending mechanism is strongly influenced by *novelty* in the environment. Studies by Sydney Zentall (1983) compared the effects of bland, unchanging environments on the learning habits of children. Such environments were compared with classrooms that provided students with stimulation through frequently adjusting and changing classroom displays. Findings revealed that children were off task more often in settings that lacked novelty. In bland environments, students tended to seek out their own stimulation through movement, off-task talking, or disruptive behaviors.

Sound, lighting, and scent also appear to have an effect on learning. Soft background music can help to relax students although, while performing tasks that demand high levels of concentration, a quiet environment appears to be most effective. Lighting also seems to have an effect on student performance. Researchers have demonstrated up to an 18 percent increase in achievement levels of students who were taught in classrooms with the most natural and full spectrum lighting compared to classrooms with cool-white fluorescent lights. Scent can also be used to enhance the memory system. As we have learned, most stimuli is sorted first by the thalamus, then sent to various structures within the brain for processing. Olfactory input, however, is the exception as it bypasses the thalamus and moves directly into the brain's limbic and memory systems. This may account for the vivid memories that certain scents seem to produce such as the smell of our mother's favorite recipe or the cologne of a friend.

Carefully plan the physical learning environment by providing novelty within each learning unit. In preparation for a new learning unit, teachers are encouraged to create flexible seating arrangements, recreate bulletin boards and other classroom displays, add content-specific artifacts, soften harsh lights with lamps, use natural lighting when possible, organize horizontal and vertical spaces to add color and beauty, and use scents such as peppermint to promote alertness or lavender for calm.

Brain-Target Three: Designing the Learning Experience

Brain-Target Three encourages teachers to design the learning experience in a way that is compatible with the brain's natural learning systems. While it may seem natural for teachers to write lesson plans that present information to students in sequential order until all of the content has been covered, this approach may in fact impede learning. Neuroscientists tell us that the brain categorizes new stimuli into concepts that are either familiar or novel, then combines these concepts to create new patterns of thinking and understanding—a concept referred to as *patterning*. The brain filters new information through the lens of prior experience and prior knowledge to create new meaning. New information, then, becomes integrated into a holistic pattern of cognition.

Imagine completing a jigsaw puzzle without ever having seen the overall image that the puzzle displays. Without giving students "big picture concepts" of the content that they will learn in a unit of study, students are often learning disconnected bits of information that too often never come together into an overarching concept or pattern. Lack of conceptual understanding typically results in loss of retention of the disjointed facts and details.

Use content standards and curriculum guidelines to design overarching goals and concepts, then display these learning goals in non-linguistic representations such as concept maps or graphic organizers. Activities are then designed to allow students to understand how the objectives they will learn during the unit relate to the big picture concept. As they continue through the content, students are referred back to the concept map to reinforce the relevance of each learning activity.

Brain-Target Four: Teaching for Declarative and Procedural Knowledge

The next stage of the Brain-Targeted Teaching Model is to engage students in activities that will enable them to demonstrate mastery of skills, content, and concepts. Brain-Target Four promotes mastery of learning goals and objectives by planning multiple activities to activate the brain's memory systems.

In teaching for declarative and procedural knowledge, teachers must provide students with learning activities to create and sustain new *engrams,* or memory patterns. Cognitive scientists have identified three types of memory systems: short-term, working, and long-term memory. Short-term and working memory systems provide a form of temporary storage; short-term memory allows us to retain information for a few seconds or minutes, while working memory serves as a "desk top" for retrieval of information when it is in immediate use. Once the brain determines that the information in our working memories is no longer needed, it is partially or totally forgotten. Unfortunately, too often what is presented in our classrooms is designed for students' working memories—students learn information so they can retrieve it on a test or quiz then quickly forget much of it as they move on to the next topic.

Clearly the goal of teaching and learning is for students to acquire knowledge, processes, and skills that they can use to build new knowledge, a process that requires the use of long-term memory systems. Leading researcher on memory, Larry Squire (Squire and Kandel, 2000), tells us that the most important factor in determining how well we remember information is the degree to which we rehearse and repeat that information. Based on the method and frequency of presentation, memories consolidate as the brain reorganizes, modifies, and strengthens synaptic connections among neurons. During tasks that involve only working memory, the brain uses proteins that currently exist in brain synapses. When information moves, however, from working to long-term memory systems, new proteins are created. Effective teaching can result in biochemical changes in the brain!

Planning for repeated rehearsals of content, skills, and concepts ensures that the information becomes part of students' long-term memory systems. Such repetition would be terribly boring for students (and teachers too) if the same activities were presented multiple times in the same way. Instead, teachers are encouraged to plan varied experiences so that students can manipulate information within a variety of modalities. For example, students could demonstrate understanding of a concept by designing a graphic organizer, preparing a power-point summary, designing a lesson to be taught to students in a lower grade, preparing an oral debate depicting multiple points of view, preparing a dramatization, or representing the concept in a visual display. By providing students with multiple ways to manipulate content, skills, and concepts, teachers are not only promoting long-term memory but are providing the opportunity to differentiate instruction based on students' needs, abilities, and learning styles.

Brain-Target Five: Teaching for Extension and Application of Knowledge

The acquisition of knowledge is only the beginning of a sound instructional program. Brain research supports what educators know to be the hallmark of effective instruction—lifelong learning best occurs when students are able to apply content, skills, and processes to tasks that require them to engage in higher-order thinking and problem-solving skills. Using knowledge meaningfully requires students to extend thinking by examining concepts in deeper, more analytical ways, thus requiring the brain to use multiple and complex systems of retrieval and integration. Brain researchers have used the concept of the *modular brain* to describe differentiated functions of brain regions. Modules from one part of the brain connect to other modules when we perform complex tasks. Research has demonstrated, for example, that the motor cortex, originally thought only to control motor functions, becomes activated when the brain engages in problem-solving that includes such cognitive components as memory, language, emotion, and active learning.

Utilize performance-based instructional activities within each learning unit. Such activities require students to engage in inductive and deductive thinking, analysis, and problem-solving skills. It allows students to apply what they have learned in tasks that have real-world application. Activities include conducting investigations, designing experiments, creating metaphors and analogies, examining cause and effect patterns, analyzing perspective, and engaging in creative thinking through the visual and performing arts. For example, a third-grade teacher integrates science and mathematic objectives by having students measure a plot of ground, then design and plant a flower and vegetable garden. Sixth-grade students study immigration patterns by researching archives at Ellis Island, then designing a map that depicts the settlement of various ethnic groups throughout the United States. Seventh graders build a model of a human cell and write a skit in which each character assumes the role of a different cell structure. Eighth graders rewrite a novel into a children's book including illustrations and present the book to a younger child.

Brain-Target Six: Evaluating Learning

While Brain-Target Six is the last stage, each stage of the model includes evaluation activities. The goal of evaluation is to provide students with relevant **feedback** about their performance so that the student can adjust learning habits and the teacher can make sound instructional decisions. Cognitive science supports what teachers know by experience: Immediate feedback strengthens learning and memory patterns. In addition to traditional grading methods (quizzes, tests, essays, etc.) evaluation measures should also employ a combination of tools including scoring rubrics, grading keys, and self-grading tools (e.g., the KWL chart

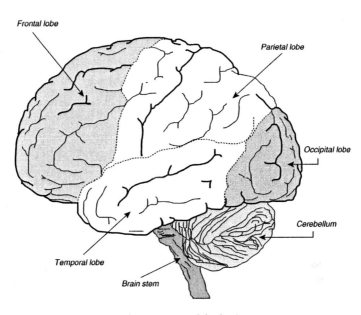

The structure of the brain

in which students indicate what they know in the K column, what they want to learn in the W column, and what they learned in the L column).

By using the following format teachers can be assured that they are implementing research-based effective teaching strategies as well as implementing what the neurological and cognitive sciences tell us about how the brain thinks and learns. Teaching and learning not only becomes more effective, it becomes more fun!

See also: **Aroma and Learning; Drama; Music; Physcial Environment; Visuals and Classroom Management.**

Further Readings

Hardiman, M. (2001). Connecting brain research with dimensions of learning. *Educational Leadership* 59(3):52–55.

Hardiman, M. (2003). *Connecting Brain Research with Effective Teaching: The Brain-Targeted Teaching Model.* Landam, MD: Scarecrow Press, Inc.

LeDoux, J. (1996). *The Emotional Brain: The Mysterious Underpinnings of Emotional Life.* New York: Touchtone Books.

Marzano, R.J., Pinkering, D.J., Pollock, J.E. (2001). *Classroom Instruction That Works.* Alexandria, VA: Association for Supervision and Curriculum Development.

Sylwester, R. (1994). How emotions affect learning. *Educational Leadership* 52(2):28–32.

BrainConnection: The Brain and Learning, http://www.brainconnection.com

MARIALE M. HARDIMAN

Transfer

Transfer is the process of using knowledge from previous experiences in novel situations. Most formal education aspires to promote transfer, because the context of learning usually differs from the contexts in which the learning will be applied. However, research has shown that transfer does not inevitably occur. For example, a lack of transfer is evident when we see students get an "A" in math class, but are not able to apply their math skills to balance a checkbook. Why is it so difficult to take what we know and put it to purposeful use in a new context? To discover the key to answering that question, let's consider transfer in a bit more depth.

What are the neurobiological underpinnings of transfer? While the specific phenomenon of transfer has not been explicitly explored, research in three major areas—cognitive neuroscience, system-level neuroscience, and molecular neuroscience—has contributed to our understanding of some forms of learning and memory, which form the basis for transfer. At the molecular level, we know that biochemical changes accompany memory and learning. As long ago as the late 1800s, Santiago Ramon y Cajal proposed that increased connections between neurons resulted from learning and led to better communication and stronger memories. This proposal has been confirmed by extensive experiments in simple nervous systems like those of the marine snail Aplysia and the fruit fly Drosophila, enabling the modeling of both non-associative (habituation and sensitization) and associative (classical conditioning, operant conditioning, and extinction) learning at the cellular level.

Research at the molecular level continues to provide ever finer grained resolution of the state and condition of specific single neurons or subcellular components. For example, it has been found that RNA content is altered and new proteins are created and deposited at synapses involved in long-term potentiation (LTP). Additionally, researchers are now able to explore the genetic basis of learning and memory through gene knockout in mice.

While there is a certain delight and authority in being able to explain the basis for learning and memory at such fine levels of resolution, the degree to which this can or should inform our educational practice is uncertain and negligible. With the pervasive notion of brain-based education, we are unreasonably forced to justify what we do in our classrooms not in terms of what experience has shown works, but in terms of what is learned in the neuroscientist's laboratory. This is a worthy long-term goal but one that requires carefully balanced and honest collaboration between scientists, psychologists, and educators. At this point, it is feckless and counterproductive to elaborate an explanation of cognitive behavior in terms of subcellular components. In one instance, James Byrnes (2001) pointed out that some authors have erroneously indicated learning is more effective with increased synapse formation and that this can be accomplished via divergent thinking as part of a lesson. There is no sensible bridge that can span the enormous conceptual distance between the single synapse and human behavior, and there are currently no experimental paradigms available that would prove or disprove such an assertion.

Much more intuitively resonant, though perhaps not so seductively and fashionably "cutting edge," are the findings generated from the fields of cognitive neuroscience (which incorporates cognitive psychology and overtly recognizes that the brain is the seat of all behavior), and systems level neuroscience. From these fields, which generally study human or higher primate learning and memory in conditions that come to some degree closer to what we do as educators, have come increasingly useful constructs of learning and especially memory. These are the fields from which the techniques outlined above have emerged. We expect that these fields are the ones that will come closest to providing guidance to educational practice, if educators continue to hold researchers to such a goal.

Most of what is known about memory at the systems and cognitive neuroscience levels can be summarized in three principles: (1) Storage of memory occurs in stages and is constantly changing; (2) the hippocampus, responsible for short-term memory, plays a unique role in memory processing; and (3) memory traces—chemical or structural changes encoding memory—are found throughout the brain. We know different structures of the brain are critical in short-term vs long-term memory, and there are multiple memory systems distributed throughout the central nervous system. Important structures for declarative memory (e.g., of facts, dates, etc.) are the hippocampus (part of the limbic system), diencephalon (including parts of the thalamus and hypothalamus), ventromedial prefrontal cortex, and the basal forebrain. The prefrontal cortex appears to function as the structure that excites or inhibits other brain regions, the hippocampus is essential for the learning and memory of spatial relationships, and the amygdala has a special role in memory of emotional content. The basal ganglia and cerebellum have roles in motor skill learning and habit formation, and much of the cerebral cortex is important in long-term storage of memory. It is likely that in the foreseeable future, research at the systems and cognitive levels, using powerful imaging techniques and with enhanced collaboration between scientists and educators, will provide answers to questions about the parts of the brain that are important in transfer and how educators can structure learning environments to efficiently activate those parts to ensure that transfer occurs. Given the high cognitive demands of transfer it would not be surprising if all the known areas participate to a greater or lesser degree when transfer occurs.

Transfer encompasses many subtleties. Transfer can be positive when the application of knowledge to a new problem results in new and strengthened learning, or it can be negative, interfering with new learning. Negative transfer is a short-term condition. When learning a new language, for example, the learner's native tongue may encourage use of grammar rules not applicable in the new language. With appropriate feedback, the learner adjusts to rules of the new language, rendering negative transfer harmless in the long term.

When positive transfer occurs, the benefits of learning are fully realized: one's knowledge is successfully leveraged. Some authors distinguish between "high-road" and "low-road" transfer. "Low-road transfer," or "near transfer," occurs when the new learning situation closely resembles the original situation. This kind of transfer holds for situations where the learning is task specific, or routine and consistent, and for mastery of procedural objectives, those that involve a series of steps. If in the original learning context there is ample practice, such that the learning becomes almost "reflexive," near transfer occurs when a new stimulus evokes almost automatic application of the previously learned strategy. For example, in a health education class, high school students learn steps in the process of negotiation. They practice these steps repeatedly. In a similar situation, at home or on the job, if students use the steps of negotiation successfully, they have experienced "low-road" or "near" transfer.

At the other end of the continuum, "high-road" or "far" transfer occurs when one's existing knowledge is applied to situations that vary from the initial learning situation. The variation can be relatively benign or quite profound, but a key feature of far transfer is that it involves judgment about how the knowledge is to be applied. Consider a student who has learned how to write an essay, and now needs to create a policy paper for government officials responsible for determining the level of state funding for mental health needs. The essay writing skills need to be applied in a different context, one with much higher stakes and one requiring critical judgment skills, sensitive to the needs of a specialized audience in a particular situation. This specific "essay" had not been practiced previously.

Before we explore ways to encourage transfer, we need to clarify the relationships that link learning, knowledge, memory, and transfer. Learning means that we had an experience that left us with more knowledge than we had previously. Knowledge can be facts: an art teacher indicated the primary colors are red, yellow, and blue. It can be information perceived or inferred from the environment: it is a cloudy day, so there's a chance of rain. It can be confidence in content: knowing times tables from one through twelve. Or, it can be acquisition of a new skill: performing cardiopulmonary resuscitation (CPR). Memory refers to the storage of knowledge that can be retrieved at will. For transfer to occur, learning needs facilitation by strategies that support memory storage and retrieval.

Madeleine Hunter identified four factors that impact transfer: similarity, critical attributes, association, and the context and degree of first learning. The following example of driving a car illustrates these factors at work:

1. Similarity refers to the degree to which a new learning experience resembles a past one. Similarity from one vehicle to the next—location of ignition, brake, accelerator—increases the likelihood of skill transfer. There is some tension in the concept of similarity—negative transfer can occur when the new environment is too similar (or perhaps only superficially similar) to the past situation.

2. Critical attributes, the unique characteristics that distinguish a task or situation from others like it, impact transfer because identifying them allows for appropriate allocation of attention to the novelty. If you drive a car with automatic transmission, and subsequently need to drive a car with manual transmission, identifying the presence of a clutch allows you to devote most of your attention to training the previously uninvolved left foot in a new motor pattern. Critical attributes and similarity are two sides of one coin.

3. Association is demonstrated as follows: If you learned to drive while listening to Beethoven's Moonlight Sonata, hearing the song while you attempt to drive a new car may help resurrect previously learned skills for tasks common to driving both cars. Things learned together are recalled together even if they are not similar. One evokes the other in the same way trademark logos and advertising jingles bring products to mind.

4. Finally, the context and degree of the original learning lead to transfer if the original learning emphasized the range of contexts where you use this information and provided you with ample practice (repetition, feedback, guided practice, etc.). The deep, thorough learning resulting from diverse practice before one is able to get one's license enhances the probability that even in a different car you will easily transfer motor skills and driving strategies.

To the extent that transfer is not inevitable because we tend to overlook it in instructional design and delivery, adopting these strategies should enhance transfer. The techniques relate to planning, delivery, and future instruction. At the planning level, teachers need to assess the degree to which a new topic or situation is similar to one just taught. If near transfer is desirable, one might plan to employ hugging, a technique that depends heavily on similarities, especially involving the use of skills, or a series of steps, and builds on them. Examples are: simulation games for practice in diverse situations, mental practice to review applications of new knowledge, and contingency learning for challenging students to seek out additional information needed to solve problems. If there is a risk of the similarity interfering with transfer, or causing negative transfer it is desirable to teach similar concepts at different times, or at least take special care to emphasize and teach the differences before addressing the similarities.

In the delivery stage of instruction it is essential to (1) identify what students already know and (2) "bridge" or help them to see the differences and similarities between what they already know and the new material. Asking students to write short stories or songs, to interview other students, use graphic organizers, or make murals, collages or models are all strategies that serve the dual purposes of helping a teacher assess current knowledge and of helping students retrieve and activate their past learning, a first step in transfer. Bridging can be achieved with activities like brainstorming (identification of other ways to apply new learning), analogies (comparisons of the new learning to something else, allowing for identification of critical attributes), and metacognition (thinking about solving problems, and evaluating the success of the solution as well as alternative strategies for the future).

Emphasis on critical attributes throughout all stages is a key technique in facilitating transfer. The teacher identifies critical attributes, illustrates them with simple examples, further illustrates with conceptually richer examples, provides students with opportunities to create their own examples and finally, teaches the student the limits of the critical attributes; helping them to recognize the times the rules don't apply. In a parallel fashion, West, Farmer and Wolff recommend the use of metaphors to enhance transfer, proposing a sequence that runs like this: select a metaphor that fits, emphasize it consistently through the lessons, establish a context for its use, provide instructions to benefit from the imagery, emphasize similarities and differences, and provide opportunities for rehearsal.

To ensure that the *new* learning transfers well to *future* learning, teachers need to foster deep learning. Ample practice of a new skill in different contexts, engaging in abstraction highlighting the importance of principles underlying the new learning, active self-monitoring, and arousing the level of mindfulness to the environment rather than simply being passive participants in it, are all techniques that set the stage for positive transfer in future learning situations. Use journal writing as a reflective tool at the end of a lesson to help students identify what they learned, how it relates to what they already know, and how it can be used in the future.

Over the last few years the traditional construct of transfer has been criticized as limited, and a new focus on the role of attentional processes in explaining how transfer occurs is emerging. The bottom line though, is that to facilitate transfer, teachers need to be ever mindful of design and delivery of instruction, and learners need to be provided with the tools that will allow them to reap benefits.

This brief introduction gives a sampling of the ways transfer can be enhanced based on psychological models and a summary of what is known about the neurobiological basis for learning and memory. With an understanding of the strategies and conditions that facilitate transfer, educators as well as learners can capitalize on this knowledge, ensuring that learning will be a productive venture. Further exploration through additional reading of historical and contemporary research, and careful application of the principles and concepts discovered, will yield satisfying and efficient learning experiences.

See also: **Constructivism, Mastery, Nature of Knowledge.**

Further Readings

Bransford, J.D., Schwartz, D.L. (1999). Rethinking transfer: a simple proposal with multiple implications. *Review of Research in Education* 24:61–100.
Shank, P. (2004). Can they do it in the real world? Designing for transfer of learning. *The eLearning Developers' Journal, September 7, 2004.* Retrieved August 15, 2005, from http://www.learningpeaks.com/pshank_Transfer.pdf
Sousa, D. (2001). *How the Brain Learns: A Classroom Teacher's Guide* (2nd ed.). California: Corwin Press, Inc.
Squire, L.R., Kandel, E.R. (2000). *Memory: From Mind to Molecules.* New York: Scientific American Library.
Dana Foundation www.dana.org

**TREZ BUCKLAND, M.A. AND
KATHLEEN A. MULLIGAN, PH.D.**

Trauma

The effects of trauma are linked to such far-reaching and long-term consequences as difficulty thinking and concentrating, persistent and recurring memories of the traumatic event, and social detachment. When traumatic experiences invade the landscape of the developing child, the effects form patterns of adaptation that predispose a child to live in a heightened state of **stress** and fear, undermining the child's normal developmental processes. Both the structural and the neurochemical systems of the brain can be permanently altered by trauma. In the classroom, this can affect a child's attention, behavior, emotions, social function, and ultimately the ability to learn.

In general, the earlier trauma is experienced, the greater the effect on the developing brain. As the brain grows from the brainstem to the neocortex in an orderly manner beginning before birth, the least conscious areas of the brain are organized earliest. When those areas of the brain are organized in response to the chemical flood engendered by fear, chaos, or threat, the unconscious functions of the brain come to "expect" danger and are set up to function accordingly. This may cause the traumatized child to experience altered and poorly regulated neurological functioning with increased levels of stress hormones and associated physical responses such as anxiety, impulsivity, sleep problems, and hyperactivity. In short, the traumatized child may be in a perpetual state of "fight or flight" and this state is not subject to the logic or reason of later developing areas of the brain. A traumatized child does not know why he or she experiences the physiological responses of this state, nor does the child perceive the state as abnormal.

Studies of adult survivors of childhood abuse show a statistically significantly smaller hippocampus than that of non-traumatized adults. Decreased functioning of the hippocampus may result in dysfunctions of remembering and forgetting and in hyper-responsiveness to environmental conditions.

Not all children who experience a traumatic experience suffer lasting effects, but specialists estimate that of the four million who experience trauma in the U.S. each year, half will exhibit symptoms related to the event in the form of behavior disorders, anxiety, **depression**, or phobias.

Some researchers have indicated that the predictability of persistent low-level stress can be less damaging than chaotic, unpredictable trauma because in some way the dysfunction creates its own normative pattern. When a child never knows what to expect, he or she maintains a hypervigilance in case there is a need for a defensive response. While this may be a useful state in a high-threat environment, it undermines the child's ability to function successfully in a safe environment. Children who are wired to "survive" have a difficult time responding to situations in which there is potential to thrive, because their energy is being sucked up at a level of brain function beneath that of conscious thought and reasoning. For example, these children often have a deep sensitivity to the environment and to nonverbal cues that interfere with their ability to attend to language. In the classroom, traumatized children may be waiting anxiously for signs that a threat is about to appear and have little attention left over to engage in planning for the accomplishment of a learning task that requires a state of relaxed alertness.

Different children respond differently to the same stressor based on a number of factors including age, family history, and previous experience with trauma. Bruce Perry and his colleagues have linked specific stress responses to gender. Young males are likely to respond to perceived threat with aggression, while females are more likely to have an internalized response, indicated by physical signs such as a lowered heart rate during questioning about a traumatic experience. Thus, females, as well as very young children, may be more prone to dissociative symptoms such as avoidance, compliance, and physical illness, than to active aggression in response to perceived danger. While males are likely to pick a fight with a peer, be resistant or defiant of authority, females are more likely to suppress aggression unless it can be expressed against someone they consider weaker. However, impulsivity, cognitive distortion, hyper-reactivity, and intimacy avoidance are common characteristics of any traumatized child and may be expressed in either a hyper-aroused or dissociated manner. For example, rugged individualism and intense loneliness are both expressions of intimacy avoidance.

Some researchers have postulated that both experienced violence and images of violence can have an impact on the developing brain. Violence and threat need not be physical to cause a fear response. However, intensity and frequency of the occurrence of threat, as well as the developmental stage at which the threat occurs, influence the degree to which a child's brain functioning will be affected by trauma. Supportive individuals and systems can mitigate the impact of trauma upon the child, and the sooner a fear-reducing intervention is introduced, the lesser the degree of impact on the child's brain organization.

Children who are traumatized by sudden unpredictable events such as sexual abuse or irrational physical violence may pursue behaviors that help them to establish a sense of control over the abuse. This is the mechanism behind provocative or seductive behavior in the victimized child, as well what motivates a victim of violence to become a perpetrator.

Children who experience trauma may be subject to later disease in adulthood. These include increased incidence of high blood pressure and other cardiovascular conditions, neuroimmunological, gastrointestinal, and psychiatric conditions for which they have familial or genetic predisposition. Children who experience violence are more likely to exhibit violent behavior in adulthood.

The classroom teacher's goal must be to provide a learning environment that is safe and comfortable for the traumatized child. Just as experiences formed the traumatized child's view of the world, new experiences can help to alter the child's view of the world. Repetitive and patterned activities that emphasize respect and healthy boundaries can be helpful. Even such simple classroom rituals as observing manners (saying "please," "thank you," and "may I?") can contribute to learning appropriate social interactions. Don't expect a traumatized or maltreated child to engage in socially acceptable behavior without modeling, discussing, and practicing your expectations.

A child will not learn to react differently to threat situations simply by changing the environment or by taking an abstract thinking approach to behavior management. The traumatized child must build an experiential base of consistent responses that are different from those which initially influenced his or her inappropriate adaptation. As a child relates to an adult authority who does not overreact to him or her, the child will be able gradually to try out different responses. As a child role-plays a different way of reacting to stress with a peer, he or she builds a range of responses that can be used instead of relying on those that are instinctual.

A teacher can best help student performance by being a caring, non-anxious presence who gradually increases expectations as a child's fear-state subsides over time. If you know about a specific traumatic event in a child's life, don't be afraid to talk to the child about it, but don't force **conversation** about it either. Wait until a student creates an opening to talk and allow the student to decide how much to reveal through conversation, art, or writing opportunities.

Offer a classroom environment that is predictable through scheduling and clearly defined rules and policies. Make plenty of room for choice-making within reasonable limits. This will help create an external structure that focuses a chaotic internal state without demanding unreasonable rigidity. Be responsive to a child's need for physical reassurance rather than initiating physical contact that may be uncomfortable for a traumatized child.

Observe and record the student's reactions to specific activities and don't be afraid to modify expectations based on the child's emotional responses to activities or lesson content. Be especially careful to watch for withdrawal behaviors that are sometimes harder to spot than extroverted behaviors that can sometimes be obviously irritating.

Remember that a traumatized child's ability to cope with stressors will vary and learning new ways of approaching social and relational situations such as those required in school will take time to develop.

See also: **At-Risk Behavior.**

Further Readings

Perry, B.D. (August 1999). Post-traumatic stress disorders in children and adolescents. *Current Opinions in Pediatrics,* (11)4.

Soloman, M.F., Siegel, D.J. (Ed.). *Healing Trauma: Attachment, Mind, Body, and Brain.* New York, NY: W.W. Norton & Co.

Stein, P.T., Kendall, J.C. (2004). *Psychological Trauma and the Developing Brain: Neurologically Based Interventions for Troubled Children.* Binghamton, NY: Haworth Press, Inc.

The ChildTrauma Academy http://childtrauma.org

International Society for Traumatic Stress Study (ISTSS) http://www.istss.org

http://www.trauma-pages.com/vanderk4.htm

LORI NILES

V

Visual Brain

The visual sense is arguably the most powerful way that the brain gathers information about the environment, and the processing of visual data and its resulting images is intimately and essentially linked to learning and cognition. It seems impossible to discuss learning without reference to vision and images. We see, we imagine, we develop insight, and we "get the picture."

The following paragraphs, then, do not purport to be complete or profound. Rather they touch briefly on the key topics of the process of vision in the eye, the way the cortex maps and responds to signals from the eye, the use of visual information for cognition, and other important topics related to vision and learning such as **critical periods** and **learning styles**.

The Eye

To understand the role of vision and images in learning, it is helpful to first identify the nature of information about the environment that is gathered by the visual organ, the eye. Visual information can be divided into distinct categories such as contrast, color, and location. Contrast depends on the existence of different intensities of reflected light emanating from objects, and this information is first gathered by *rod* cells in the retina of the eye that respond *differently to lights of varying intensity. Cone* cells in the retina respond to light of different wave-length (colors,) and cellular networks in the retina are the first to analyze signals from rods and cones with regard to motion.

The physical structure of the eye also allows for faithful mapping of the *location* of objects in the visual field. Thus, light reflected from objects in the visual space to the left, impinges most directly on the right half of the retina for both eyes, and vice versa for light reflected from the right. This is a direct result of the fact that the retina follows the curvature of the back of the eyeball, so light entering the eye strikes the retina most directly (i.e., perpendicular to the retinal surface) on the opposite side of its origin, while only glancing off the retina on the same side as its origin. The reader can envision this phenomenon by holding up the index finger of the left hand off to the left of the visual field. Following the straight line from the finger to the eyes, it becomes apparent that the light impinges most directly on the retinal tissue to the right side of each eye. Likewise, light coming from above the height of the eye impinges most directly on the bottom half of the retina, and light from below the height of the eye impinges with the top half of the retina. Thus, the retina of the eye makes a faithful spatial map of the contrast, color, and location of objects in the visual field. The environment is mapped on the retina of the eye.

Visual Cortex

The eye itself thus records information about both the nature of objects and their location. This information is then passed on to the visual regions of the brain, where, remarkably, it is literally mapped on the brain surface layer of cells, the *visual cortex*. Thus signals from any particular part of the retina always send information to a specific and fixed region of the visual cortex.

The first region of the cortex to receive signals from the eyes is called the *primary* vision cortex, or V1. Located at the very back of the cerebral cortex, V1 then simply contains information about shapes, colors, movement, and location. However, this information is not yet in a form that identifies intact objects, or comprehension of relationships. It is still just bits of data.

The strength of firing of neurons in each specific subregion of the cortex depends on contrast generated by edges of objects and the color of these objects, while the physical location of the different active neurons over the surface of the V1 cortex maps their location in space. Thus, the brain begins to separate form and location.

The flow of information from V1 to deeper regions of the cortex is required for perception of intact objects and establishing spatial relationships. These processes occur in integrative regions of the cortex, which are still considered visual cortex, but are identified as V2, V3, V4, and so on. As bits of perceived information flow into these regions, the separation of form and location is preserved, with information about form taking a physically lower route toward the temporal lobe of the brain, and information about location taking an upper route toward the parietal lobe. These two pathways are often called the *what* (lower) pathway, and the *where* (upper) pathway.

Ultimately, information in the *what* regions of the cortex is used to establish categories of objects (e.g., tables, cars, faces) with similar features, and also images of individual objects in categories, such as individual faces, or specific tables or cars. Thus, in this region of the cortex we find the so-called "face" cells, where specific neurons fire only when an intact and specific face is seen.

Information in the *where* regions is used to establish spatial location, and by extension, relationships in general. Thus, it has also been found that this region is active when we are required to estimate significance (which is derived from relationship—things of less significance are in a smaller, or less important, space from those of great significance,) relative positions such as number lines, and even relative value of objects or experiences. Thus, a great deal of cognitive information relies on the spatial relationship analysis capability of the *where* visual pathway.

In addition to this integrative process, visual information is also sent directly from V1 to regions of the brain in the frontal lobes. This route often has been found to lead to a region called the anterior cingulate, which is central in decision-making. Thus, even as we analyze the nature and location of what we see, we are also making judgments about whether we should act on it, and what the nature of such actions should be. This route is fast and can bypass the integrative processes above. We may act on what we see before we fully understand it.

All these pathways are thought to be bi-directional. That is, signals can also flow from anterior cingulate back to the visual integrative cortical regions, or from the integrative regions back to V1. The direct receipt of visual data from the environment described thus far, is sometimes called the "bottom up" processing, whereas the internal activation of the visual regions initiated by the anterior cingulate through conscious choice, is called "top down" processing. We can get the same image either by directly experiencing it or by recalling it from memory. And the *what* and *where* regions of integrative cortex are activated though either route. Whether seen directly or recalled from memory, the same neurons fire in the same patters when we sense a particular image.

The Image

What, then, is an image? The neuroscience answer to this question is that an image is the firing of collections of neurons together in a pattern that depends on the physical form, color, and location of objects in the world. The image is the *primary* product of perception. This can be contrasted to language, which consists of symbols for images. That is, language is the *secondary* product of perception. Language is represented by patterns of neuron firing also, but those patterns are only meaningful if they trigger firing of the primary patterns for the image itself.

Given their primary nature, and the fact that large regions of back integrative cortex are dedicated to processing of visual information, it is perhaps not surprising that memory of images seems almost unlimited. Humans can recall having seen hundreds of pictures even days later, and can sort out pictures that they have not seen before with remarkable accuracy. We "picture" our lives through recall of meaningful images, and to the extent that we can recall what has occurred throughout our life, we can say that we remember literally millions of images. The *what* region of the visual cortex also surrounds the hippocampus, and interacts with other nearby cortical regions important in the formation of long-term memory (and short term, to some extent.) In part this may account for the great capacity for memory of images noted above.

The vast flexibility and variability of images most likely results from the repeated use of *parts* of firing patterns. Thus, the image of a window consists of parts that can be repeatedly used for images of non-window objects. For example, the corner in a window is part of the image, but there are countless objects that can use the "corner network." It seems very likely that recall of images is primarily triggered through cues that consist of such image fragments. That is, firing of the pattern for a cue triggers firing of a larger pattern for an object that includes the cue. The human brain seems to be particularly adept at picking up these cues, and reconstructing an image from bits and pieces.

Images and the Non-Visual Senses

The other senses (auditory, touch, olfactory, and gustatory) are variously limited with regard to sensing shapes, colors, distances, movement, and physical attributes of objects, but vision gives us detailed information about all these and others as well. Vision is generally more precise and faster than the other senses. Indeed, the other senses sometimes channel information into the visual cortex for analysis and perception, or alternatively, are modified and regulated by input from vision.

The primacy of the visual sense is also indicated by the fact that, the data from the other senses is subject to modification and interpretation by interaction with the visual system. Recent research has shown that the sense of touch enhances perception of visual images through neuron pathways that run from the primary somatosensory (touch) cortex to the visual cortex. Further, research with owls demonstrated that the visual pathways can gain entry to the auditory pathways, thus correcting or adjusting auditory spatial maps so they correspond to visual spatial maps. This influence of the visual on the auditory is normally inhibited, but that inhibition breaks down when the two sensory maps do not correspond, leading to learning and correction of the non-correspondence.

The senses of smell, taste, and sound do not generate images directly, but they do evoke neuronal pathways that are linked to images, thereby enhancing memory of images. For example, we cannot smell the shape of a rose, but we can visualize its shape when triggered by smell. We can also use these "non-image" senses to create maps of space, by remembering the intensity of smell, taste, or sound in different locations of the space around us. But again, the maps generated in this fashion only become meaningful when we visualize them—when we trigger firing of a primary pattern that is derived from or part of a visual image.

Images in Cognition and Learning

The neurological explanation of images provides insight into many aspects of cognition and learning including **creativity**, estimating, theorizing, and problem-solving. Some examples of this are found in the following paragraphs.

Creativity seems heavily dependent on front regions of the cortex that are responsible for working memory and decision-making. It is this region of the brain that initiates the "top-down" functions mentioned above. Through such top-down instructions, working memory space in the front cortex is loaded with a small number of images, or parts of images, to generate new combinations that represent potential solutions to problems, or novel arrangements—new images! For example, Salvador Dali's painting, *The Persistence of Memory*, shows images of clocks, home furniture, and desert assembled in novel ways that trigger many new ideas—new images—for the viewer. The clocks drooping over tree branches or table edges, and this image of melted time in a desert environment, may trigger thought about our own life in which we recall moments where time seemed warped, or the pressures were great. Thus assembly of new images from parts of others is the foundation of creativity. The number of images triggered by great **art** is virtually unlimited and varied between different individuals.

Estimation in **mathematics** engages the *where* region of the visual cortex. This is also a brain region activated when we judge the relative value of objects or experiences. These approximations and judgments seem to be based on the spatial information in a number line, which progresses from small to large numbers; things of high value are analogous to the large numbers, or the first number (the most important ones). We mentally place things in relationships relative to each other, which provide the basis for estimation. We may estimate the size of a dog by visualizing it between other dogs of larger and smaller size, or by mentally comparing it to a measuring instrument marked off in feet or inches. Value, then, seems to be judged in this same physical way, through physically estimating *where* on some value scale a particular object lies.

Theories, ideas, and hypotheses also heavily engage the visual brain. We imagine (note *image* root of imagine) the outcomes of a series of actions, by picturing the sequence and its natural results. For example, we develop strategies for games, business, or war by picturing a sequence of actions with predictable outcomes, and linking those outcomes to an image of goal achievement. We imagine overcoming an opponent by a "pincers" action of two objects or forces, leading to the image of entrapment, and overpowering.

The assembly of a collection of specific features of objects by the *what* pathway in visual integrative cortex leads to generalizations and categories, which in turn allow us to predict behaviors and results in future actions. We picture some objects as similar to others in their form, or their force, or other physical properties, and we put them together in categories. This allows us to predict the properties and behaviors of new objects, and to solve problems based on known behaviors of members of the group. For example, we characterize some mathematical equations as "quadratic" and that allows us to proceed in our analysis and methods appropriate for this type of equation. Or, we place new chemical structures in the category of "nucleophile" and thus we can visualize how this chemical will behave when it is combined with others of the same, or different, category. In all such cases, we "see" the nature of things, and then, we visualize the result of specific interactions between things of a different, or the same, category.

In sum, the visual brain gives us information about relationships and categories, which are the tools of cognition. This applies to objects, but also to stories, people, and principles, encompassing virtually all thought and creativity. Learning, then, is enhanced by paying attention to relationships and categories in *every* problem and challenge, rather than relying on the limited and specific information provided by recall of individual images and experiences.

Study of the details of specific images can, however, be of great value in developing deeper understanding. For example, in language, it is powerful to use the "image test" when choosing words or phrases. Asking, "is this the image I want?" will lead to greater clarity in language expression, which in turn leads to deeper learning. Creating and reproducing images with attention to details of form and spatial relationships, requires deeper and specific use of front parts of the cortex and the motor cortex. This engagement of more parts of the cortex in analysis, creation, and utilization of images in all steps of the **learning cycle** will produce exceptionally powerful learning experiences.

Emotion

The amygdala, an emotion center of the brain, also is heavily connected to the visual brain. The connections appear to be primarily to the *what* region and the primary visual cortex. The specific meaning of these connections for learning is a matter for speculation, but combined with the visual-anterior cingulate interactions mentioned above, they support the idea that visualization and interpretation of images depend on emotion. Thus, what we see and how we act on what we see is subjective, so that one learner may see danger in an image, and another learner may see opportunity. Thus, visual images are subjective, pointing to the centrality of emotion in learning and interpretation.

Laterality and Attention

There seems to be little difference between V1 in the right and left hemisphere. However, damage to the visual integrative regions, for example, the right spatial cortex (*where* region) can lead to what is called the "neglect syndrome," in which the left visual space may be ignored, literally remaining unperceived. Thus, the *where* region of visual cortex, then, is strongly implicated in attention. Commonly, this function is attributed to the right hemisphere, but some research also indicates a role for the left *where* region of attention is directed to objects by drawing a circle around them, or by otherwise delineating a limited region of space for visual examination. These results lend support to the belief that the right cortex functions in a more global manner, whereas the left cortex functions on the fine details within a limited space. This further suggests that learning may be enhanced by challenging learners to attend both to the detailed aspects, and the global aspects of visualized material.

Development and Critical Periods

The development of the V1 region in newborn animals and humans is strongly dependent on visual experience. If one eye is covered or otherwise closed immediately after birth, such as can occur in newborn humans who have cataracts, the wiring of the V1 region develops improperly, and if sensory input is not restored in a relatively short time period (weeks to a few months in humans) it can lead to permanent blindness in the covered eye. This is not due to malfunction of the eye itself but rather to inadequate or incorrect wiring in this region of the visual cortex. Experiments of this sort were the first to directly demonstrate the impact of experience on the physical structure of the brain, and have been central to the now accepted proposal that the process of learning depends on physical change in neuron networks. Also, the idea that certain experiences must occur within a limited timeframe for the brain to develop normal wiring, is the basis for the belief in "critical periods" for learning particular things. In the case of visual learning, this period can be quite short, but in a different sensory experience, the development of language, may be years.

Learning Styles

Finally, we briefly address the concept of learning style and images. It is common to identify different learners as having a visual or an auditory learning style. However, the way that images and language are produced in the brain suggests that these two learning styles are not equivalent, and that serious efforts should be made to assure that *all* learners develop visual images of the world and their experiences. The basis for this contention is that image is primary, and language secondary. We cannot create an image with all its rich content of category and relationship, based on auditory experience in isolation. We may remember a great deal of what we hear, but still have no image for it. The argument leads to the suggestion that learners who claim an auditory learning style already have good visual images, and are simply using auditory experience to recall them. Alternatively, they may actually believe that memory of the language is real learning. However, we contend that no amount of auditory input can substitute for lack of visual images.

See also: **Blindness; Visuals and Classroom Management.**

Further Readings

Gangwer, T. (2005). *Visual Impact, Visual Teaching.* San Diego, CA: The Brain Store, Inc.

Mathew, W., Zeki, S. (2005). The integration of colour and motion by the human visual brain. *Cerebral Cortex* 15:1270–1279.

Posner, M.J., Raichle, M.E. (1997). *Images of Mind*. New York, NY: Scientific American Library.

Silverman, L.K., Jones, B. (2002). *Upside-Down Brilliance: The Visual-Spatial Learner*. Glendale, CO: DeLeon Publishing, Inc.

Zeki, S. (1999). *Inner Vision: An Exploration of Art and the Brain*, New York, NY: Oxford University Press Inc.

Visual/spatial Learning Study Guides & Strategies http://www.studygs.net/visual.htm

JAMES E. ZULL, PH.D.

Visuals and Classroom Management

Many teachers complain that effective classroom management skills are primarily invisible—the teachers can't see what to do to get their students on track and focused. Indeed, unless one knows what to look for, it's often hard to see what works. And this can cause hardship for teachers trying to succeed at their craft. Without effective classroom management, content won't easily follow.

One way to make management more visible, to students and to teachers, is to increase the use of visuals, particularly when teaching classroom procedures to students. Recent brain research is corroborating what teachers already know intuitively—that visuals in the classroom help students learn.

The brain is built to do imagery quickly and efficiently. When a visual is presented the retina perceives the representation and launches it on its journey to the visual cortex. The visual cortex, located in the occipital lobe, or lower rear portion, of the brain's hemispheres, is continually adapting and interpreting information. It is highly specialized for processing information and pattern recognition. For instance, when one meets someone, one's brain first identifies "human" and then differentiates between friend and stranger.

A common belief is that vision is primarily deciphered in the right hemisphere, while language is located in the left hemisphere. Neuroimaging sheds light on this issue; vision and language are both too complex to be delegated to one hemisphere of the brain. The complex deciphering of images and language requires interaction between both hemispheres.

A study by the Institute for the Advancement of Research in Education found that graphic organizers improved student learning and retention across grade levels and content areas. A number of educational research studies support these findings, suggesting that using visuals in teaching results in a greater degree of learning. Indeed, many in the field suggest that over half of what we learn is from visual images. This increased focus on using visuals for classroom content ought to be mirrored in an increased use of visuals for classroom procedures.

Visual Rubrics for Procedures

Most teachers are familiar with rubrics for content, but very few are familiar with rubrics for procedures. For example, for many elementary teachers, one of the toughest procedures to teach is getting kids to line up. To use visual cues, teachers can have their students form five separate lines, and number them from one to five. A one is a poorly structured line, a five is a perfect line. Now the students have a common language, and they'll tend to self-correct: "C'mon guys we look like a three – let's go!" To close the deal, teachers can take pictures of their students in their five lines and number the pictures one through five. They can then be put above the door where the students exit the classroom. The teacher stands in the doorway, waiting for the kids to line up. Then she uses the fingers on one hand to signal what "caliber" line they have. When she holds up all five fingers, they can start to walk.

Another example centers on "classroom dismissal formation." Teachers often tell their students "I'm not dismissing the class until the desks are clean, lined up, organized, and everyone is seated." Unfortunately, students have different definitions of those words. Some are out of their seats in "sprinters position," ready to race out the door. In addition, many students put their packs on before the bell rings to end class. One solution is to have five pictures of "dismissal readiness" up on the wall above the board. In number four, the desks are clean and lined up and everyone is seated, but two students have their packs on. The teacher doesn't have to say a word. She simply holds up four fingers and waits. The kids see the fingers, look at the pictures, and look around the room. Within seconds they yell out to their neighbors "hey- your pack! Take your pack off!" The packs fly off, the teacher breaks into a big smile, raises a fifth finger, and points to the door, signaling that the students can leave.

Pictures for Procedures

Teachers don't need to use rubrics—just pictures. With a digital camera they can take a picture of the kids in their "dismissal formation." The photograph can then be run through a computer onto an overhead. The teacher simply places the picture on the overhead screen. The students will quickly get the desks clean and lined up and ready to go, using the overhead photo as their guide. No longer does the teacher need to say "okay class it's time to clean up and get ready to go." She can simply turn the overhead on with the picture, and watch the magic happen.

This works for just about every possible classroom procedure. Setting up labs in science provides a clear example. The teacher can take an aerial photo of the lab table with all the items where they are supposed to be. She then can put it onto an overhead and turn it on, announcing "Okay. You have thirty-nine seconds to form your teams around your lab tables, set up like this. Go."

This works as well for putting things away, such as books on the bookshelf, physical education supplies in the closet, and art supplies in their trays. Teachers take photos of what the supplies are supposed to look like, put the photos next to where the supplies live, and the students will tend to put things away according to the photographs.

This works for parents at home. A declaration parents often make to their kids is: "You're not going out until your room is clean." After the declaration, there is often a full-scale debate about characteristics of a clean room. The solution? Parents can take a photo of their child's clean room, and put the photo on the wall. The child will tend to clean the room according to the photo. Inside the child's sock drawer is a photograph of a clean sock drawer! One parent confesses that her three-year-old daughter can't read, but loves to clean: "Can we play clean up again mommy?" It's a game to her—and she plays it well!

There is no limit to how teachers can use pictures to communicate clarity of procedures. Photographs aren't necessary. Diagrams and drawings work just as well. The students can be put in small groups and each group given a procedure for which to generate an appropriate picture.

This works wonderfully for substitute teachers. The classroom teacher can take photographs of her class or classes while the students are sitting in their assigned seats. Then, the name of each student can be written next to his or her face. When the substitute teacher starts class, she will know the names of all the students and where they are supposed to sit. One substitute teacher claims: "Personally, I would never sub again, unless I brought my digital camera to class: "You two are making mischief"– Click!" One doesn't need batteries or film—just the camera. The kids see the camera and are suddenly transformed into angels.

Other classroom procedure examples include setting up centers, keyboarding posture, proper listening body language, desk cleanliness, headings on papers, test taking readiness, and what the computer desktop should look like when students log off. Pictures work for schoolwide issues and procedures such as school dress code, sitting during assemblies, and clean cafeteria tables.

Airplane safety direction cards no longer use words—just pictures and diagrams. Passengers see images of a seat belt being fastened, oxygen masks being used, people evacuating the plane. This is true as well for directions for how to put together a computer system or bookshelf. Companies have discovered that for safety and increased customer satisfaction, visuals communicate clearly and quickly. This same approach works wonderfully in our classrooms. Neuroscientists are echoing what teachers have known for a long time—visuals are highly brain-compatible. We need to translate this not only into teaching content, but also into teaching classroom procedures to our students.

Step-By-Step Visuals for Content

Additionally, visuals can also be used to teach content. I taught a woodshop class for several years. I took photographs of finished projects, laminated them, and put them on the wall to inspire kids' choices of projects. Then I learned to take a series of photos of the works in progress—five or seven photos. The students would then use the photos as a teaching tool to see what their next steps were in the process. Rather than ask me what the next step was, they would simply go over to the picture wall for a visual consultation. I was out of a job!

Students often do such great projects in class that they take them home and they're never seen again. Why not take pictures of the finished projects to use as inspiration for next year's students?

As teachers increase the use of visuals for procedures and content in their classrooms, they realize the profound benefits. Management is easier, students are more focused, and the learning environment is enhanced.

See also: Classroom Management; Visual Brain.

Further Readings

Hyerle, D. (2004). *Student Successes With Thinking Maps : School-Based Research, Results, and Models for Achievement Using Visual Tools.* Thousand Oaks, CA: Sage Publishing.

Smith, R. (2004). *Conscious Classroom Management: Unlocking the Secrets of Great Teaching.* Fairfax, CA: www.consciousteaching.com

Wolfe, P. (2001). *Brain Matters: Translating Research Into Classroom Practice.* Alexandria, VA: ASCD.

RICK SMITH

W

Writing

Mental activity occurs when the billions of tiny neurons of the brain communicate information using small electrical signals. The point of contact between neurons is called the synapse. Synaptic connections tend to be reinforced by repetition over time, thus reinforcing learning. As cognitive and sensorimotor skill connections develop, alphabetic letters become words, then sentences. Eventually, writing emerges as a skill that provides a virtual window into cognitive thought patterns. Writing documents the brains' sensory experiences, thoughts, ideas, beliefs, and opinions.

One of the first brain activity imaging studies conducted in 2001 examined how the brain processes information. It was discovered that listening to a sentence affects cortical activation pathways different from those affected by reading a sentence. As spoken language is fleeting, information must be immediately processed or stored to make sense of it. Writing acts like an external hard drive facsimile that provides permanent records.

With the stroke of a pencil, pen, or keystroke, writers express real or imagined sights, sounds, tastes, touches, and smells. Writing is a dynamic manifestation of **creative** and **critical thinking** skills. Both a sensorimotor and cognitive process, writing serves all of Howard Gardner's **multiple intelligences** not just verbal-linguistic. Writing serves the *music* intelligence when maestros share their genius through written composition. Writing serves *bodily-kinesthetic* intelligence when athletic coaches write strategic plays that athletes execute. It services *logical-mathematical* intelligence when scientists write proofs to theories and *interpersonal* and *intrapersonal* intelligences when people become everything from speechwriters to novelists and philosophers.

Writing is active, reflective, spontaneous, fluid, erratic, exhilarating, or frustrating. It can be a pleasant experience, the tool by which ideas and memories spill onto pages and computer screens. It can also be a painful experience that blocks and stalls ideas and memories, causing student writers to feel frustrated and ignorant, because the brain must feel safe to sustain the **motivation** necessary to master the writing process.

Brain translator Robert Slywester explains that neurons thrive in environments that are emotionally safe and intellectually stimulating. Learners must therefore experience emotional and physical safety to be fully engaged in learning, especially learning about writing, which easily intimidates students to believe they "can't do it." Help students remain motivated by creating writing process settings within safe, supportive environments that promote productive cognitive thinking.

Writing helps the brain organize and reflect. Writing enables students to make sense of complex, multifaceted pieces of information. Journaling and other note-taking forms provide written records for review and reflection that enhance both immediate and long-term recall ability. Reflective journaling can also help the emotional brain.

A two-part study on the effects of expressive writing on the working memory conducted by Klein and Boals revealed that individuals who wrote reflective narratives about negative experiences experienced a decline in dissonant, avoidance thinking related to the events. Such findings suggest that writing provides a healthy and productive way to improve memory and in fact, deal with trauma, offering tremendous opportunity as a life skill and also a life-coping skill.

Kinds of Writing

Writing can be expressive, descriptive, narrative, expository, or persuasive. It can involve untimed *process writing*, which includes brainstorming, drafting, conferencing, revising, editing, and finalizing. Writing can also be a timed process often called *demand writing*, whereby writing is timed and prompt-specific, that is, writing that answers an essay question. Writing that is completed within test environments is an example of demand writing, which, as a result, is more stress-laden than process writing. Grooming students to be proficient in both types of writing requires a safe and enriched learning environment.

Planning

To help the brain make connections that lead to writing mastery, a strategic plan must be in place that helps to develop the strengths of young writers. The plan must attend to the challenges inherent in each type of writing. Begin the school year with more expressive types of writing, description and narration, which readily tap into existing **episodic memories** and sensory experiences. Within the safety of their own memories and creative thoughts, students write with relative willingness.

Jean Piaget suggested that when introducing experiences that initially may produce some struggle, students need tools to resolve their cognitive difficulties. Provide students with examples of topics from which they might choose and help them remember episodes from their past by inviting students to recall experiences that made them happy, sad, embarrassed, and the like. Encourage them during the drafting stages. Use student writing to provide proof that students do indeed have something to write about. Empower and instill students with confidence to move on to the more challenging forms of writing, exposition and persuasion, which require higher order thinking skills. Provide them with writing activities that are both challenging and engaging. Ask them to argue a controversial topic using a "Letter to the Editor" format. Invite them to write cover letters that persuade employers to hire them. Allow them to express their feelings through poetry.

No matter what students are writing, allow them to compose freely. Unimpeded by analytical cognitive processes that monitor mechanical skills, for example, frees students' cognitive thought processes to more readily tap into memories, ideas, and opinions. Researcher and educator, Frank Smith describes a study conducted by two leaders in writing pedagogy, Donald Graves and Lucy Calkins whereby third grade students were encouraged to write using their own punctuation. By the year's end, the children who had no formal training demonstrated a greater command of punctuation and its function than those who had had typical skill and drill training.

Employ patience while observing student errors in early drafts. Holding students to high expectations regarding mechanical skills stifles the spirit to experiment and succeed that fledgling writers show when they are left free to write. This freedom helps students view writing, not as a laborious or boring school requirement, but a tool by which they can truly express themselves.

By emphasizing creative versus critical thinking during the early stages of writing instruction empowers students with the confidence that they can write. Learn how to use textbooks as resources and guides. Have faith in authentic writing processes whereby quantity, generated in safe yet rigorous environments, produces quality.

Modeling

Social cognitive theorist, Albert Bandura, has emphasized that learners are motivated to learn when their own levels of competence and self-efficacy are high, and when they perceive activities as meaningful. There is no better way to promote the self-efficacy levels of students and to make the writing process more meaningful than for teachers to act as coaches who take part in that process, sharing their abilities with their fledgling writers.

Writing becomes more meaningful and less threatening for students when they identify their teachers as fellow writers who brainstorm topics, compose drafts, discuss experiences, share frustrations and ultimately produce final products. Model for students how real writers write—and rewrite. Enhance writing environments with frequent feedback, peer and teacher interaction, and stimulating and meaningful writing opportunities.

Make sure that peer model samples are also plentiful to help students of all age levels and abilities learn from others in their own age groups. Samples of work of various qualities from weak to strong provide opportunities for students to strengthen their evaluation and **assessment** skills that they can apply to their own and their peers' writing.

Strategic Flexibility

An understanding of Piaget's stages of cognitive theory of development enables writing coaches to understand that moving from young child to adolescent stages means moving from concrete to more imaginative and abstract thought. For the youngest group of writers, help students by scribing for them when they may excitedly recount memories faster than they can write them down themselves. Prepare handouts containing a series of *I remember* blanks to help youngsters identify their memories. Prepare engaging writing assignments that invite students to incorporate their interests into editorials, screenplays, or commercials for their favorite products.

Encourage thinking and groom proficient writers by learning more about the differences in the behavioral and cognitive stages of various age groups. Even coaches of adult writers, senior citizens in a creative writing class at an adult center for example, must understand the nature of their learning audience. Encouraging memory writing for example would be particularly useful (and perhaps vital) for the senior age group not just because narration readily taps into episodic memories as with young children, rather, reflecting on the meaning of their lives in a safe learning environment can help seniors process through difficult memories they might otherwise keep private, causing cognitive or emotional discord or despair.

Cognitive Freedom

Just as real writers do not produce all kinds of writing, they also do not always follow rules, schedules, or stages of a writing process. When such rule-breaking writers are students, they are often labeled as problematic or weak writers. Provide writers the cognitive freedom to demonstrate ability in their own way. If students struggle with expository essays, encourage them to change their products (and consequently their audiences) to newspaper articles or letters. Provide writers flexibility and opportunity to demonstrate *their* ability, guiding them beyond what Piaget called *disequilibrium*, cognitive conflict, to self-confidence and discovery. Their tools: reassurance, encouragement, and empowerment.

Sequence each day's activities carefully. Move students through the writing process by following the lead of each writer's needs. Writing coaches must know their craft well to prepare effective lessons and activities for whole, group, and individual instructional settings, again dependent on student and process needs. Diagnoses of students' needs gathered from their writing, drives the direction of what Nancy Atwell calls *minilessons* that instruct students on, for example, topic choice, dialogue, paragraphing, correcting fragments or run ons, and the like.

Editing

While evidence like the Graves and Calkins study suggests that even the youngest students acquire mastery skills when left unfettered by *skill and drill* approaches, at some point, conventions and mechanics instruction becomes very important to students who ultimately must be able to effectively communicate in both oral and written modes.

Help students care about *how* they write what they write, that is, conventions and mechanics. Using student products that contain authentic mistakes to teach mechanical skills captures the enthusiasm of students who are typically bored by traditional grammar lessons. Student engagement is high when game-like, *solve the* (grammar) *problem* activities rely on genuine mechanical problems from student writing, not textbooks. Students routinely challenged to identify mechanical errors within anonymous peer models become proficient at identifying increasingly more subtle errors. Freed from meaningless textbook grammar activities, mechanical skills improve, because students, empowered by continuing successes, routinely attend more critically to their own mechanics.

Educator and researcher Frank Smith, reminiscent of Dewey, wisely argues that students can be trusted to learn as long as they are provided meaningful learning environments that encourage thinking. The brain-compatible editing process, which uses student work to illustrate examples of conventions and mechanical miscues, provides just such a personalized and meaningful environment in which students can learn.

Assessment

Students must learn to think critically about their writing so that they become literate and successful adults. Use of rubrics and criteria may be the single most effective way to empower students with a real understanding of what proficient and superior writing looks like. Ideally used as guiding, not grading tools, rubrics enable students to evaluate and assess their writing as well as their peers', leading them to mastery. It is important therefore that students learn the language of rubrics so that they can receive and offer worthwhile **feedback**. Research findings, for example, of D. A. Rogers suggest that verbal feedback during and after a learning task is critical in the error-connection process. Let students know what they are doing well and ask probing questions that stimulate them to challenge what they have written.

Never give students a grade without feedback. Learners always need to know if they are on track; using the language of rubrics is one way of ensuring their learning. Writing coaches will first need to learn their state's rubric and scoring system before they can help their students understand them.

Demand Writing

Writing exams—prime examples of demand writing—can produce anxiety and **stress**, which inhibit the cognitive processes essential to writing prowess. Some stress is beneficial, releasing adrenaline that makes students mentally alert. Harness *good* stress in ways similar to athletic coaches who pump their players up for the big game.

Demand writing requires a synthesis of the creative and analytical skills of student writers who must, within a specific amount of time, read and interpret an essay prompt, then apply and demonstrate their writing skills in finished products that demonstrate writing proficiency. Proficiency will not be obtained without first providing students the strategies that will keep cognitive thinking optimal and interfering stress signals minimal.

No matter what a prompt asks, students will succeed if they learn to follow their brain's natural inclination to organize. It was the organizational genius of the **pattern**-seeking brains of NASA engineers that transformed a seeming pile of junk into an air filter that safely returned the Apollo thirteen astronauts to Earth. Engineers saw beyond the random items strewn before them to their potential functionality, which they harnessed under an unimaginable amount of anxiety and stress to create a life-saving filter. How much less stressful to organize random thoughts into proficient essays!

Train students to analyze and organize carefully, but swiftly, the components of specific essay prompts. Train students to master the rubric of organization. Careful analysis of essay prompts produces word and phrase maps that establish their exact requirements. Entering stressful testing environments armed with organizational writing strategies and confidence is the gift that brain compatible writing coaches give their students.

A Celebration of Writing

To appreciate themselves as writers, students must celebrate themselves as writers. Without celebration, there is no evidence that working to become a stronger writer has value. Making time at the end of each quarter or at least each semester, for students to share their writing validates students as writers.

Brain researcher and educator, Robert Sylwester, suggested in the title of his book, *Celebration of Neurons*, that there is something worth celebrating in learning about the brain. Einstein believed that imagination is more important than knowledge. As writing miraculously transcribes imagination into words, perhaps learning about the brain's expression of itself is cause for the celebration of *writing*.

See also: **Classroom Environment.**

Further Readings

Alexandria, VA: Association for Supervision and Curriculum Development.

Hanson, A. (2001). *Visual Writing.* New York: Learning Express.

Hanson, A. (2002). *Write Brain Write.* San Diego: The Brain Store.

Michael, E., Keller, T., Carpenter, P., Just, M. (2001). FMRI investigation of sentence comprehension by eye and by ear: Modality fingerprints on cognitive processes. *Human Brain Mapping* 13(4):239–252.

Rogers, D.A. (1998). Computer-assisted learning versus a lecture and feedback seminar for teaching a basic surgical technical skill. *American Journal of Surgery* 175(6):508 –510.

Slywester, R. (1995). *The Celebration of Neurons. An Educator's Guide to the Human Brain. Explorations in Learning & Instruction:* The Theory into Practice (TIP) Database. (2004). As stated at their site, "TIP is a tool intended to make learning and instructional theory more accessible to educators. The database contains brief summaries of 50 major theories of learning and instruction. Available at: http://tip.psychology.org/

North West Regional Educational Laboratory 6 + 1 Trait Writing – Training, http://www.nwrel.org/assessment/trainings

ANNE M. HANSON, M.A.

Glossary
of
Brain Terms

ACTH – Adrenocorticotropic hormone is secreted by the pituitary gland. It acts directly on the adrenal glands to increase the secretion of cortisol and other hormones.

Adrenal Glands – They are adjacent to the kidneys and responsible for the secretion of various hormones from the body; particularly cortisol and adrenaline.

Amygdala – The amygdala is an almond-shaped structure located in the base of the brain. It is involved in emotions such as anger, fear, and pleasure. It is part of what is sometimes referred to as the limbic system.

Androgens – The general class of male hormones, with the main one being testosterone. Testosterone is responsible for primary and secondary sex characteristics such as pubic hair and lowered voice.

Axon – A long extension of a nerve cell that takes information away from one neuron to another neuron.

Basal Ganglia – Loosely grouped collection of large neurons within each cerebral hemisphere. It plays an important role in motor control and learning.

Brain Cells – Neurons and glial cells are the two main types of cells found in the brain.

Brain Stem – The brain stem plays a vital role in basic attention, arousal, and consciousness. All information passes through the brain stem on its way to and from the brain.

Broca's Area – This area of the brain is located in the frontal lobes and controls speech production and language understanding. It is connected to Wernicke's area by a neural pathway.

Cerebellum – Located at the base of the brain, it is two peach-sized mounds. It is in charge of coordinating movement, balance, and posture. Mental activities are also coordinated in the cerebellum; it is involved in thinking and memory.

Cerebral Cortex – It is the outer layer of the cerebrum. It consists of deep folds of gray matter. It determines intelligence, personality, sensory impulses, motor function, planning, and organization.

Cerebral Hemispheres – They are the right and left portions of the brain.

Cerebrum – This area of the brain controls sensory interpretation, thinking, and memory. In the cerebrum, there are up to one hundred thousand neurons. The cerebrum is divided into two hemispheres, the right and left hemispheres.

Corpus Callosum – The corpus callosum is a network of fibers connecting the cerebral hemispheres. It facilitates communication between the two hemispheres.

Cortisol – This hormone is released from the adrenal glands when the body is under stress. It increases blood pressure and heart rate and lowers the immune system.

CT scan – Computerized tomography, formerly referred to as a CAT scan. This technology utilizes x-ray pictures to examine the structure of the brain.

Dendrite – A dendrite is part of a neuron, it brings information to the cell body. One neuron may have as many as 100,000 dendrites.

Dopamine – Dopamine is a chemical substance (neurotransmitter) manufactured in the brain involved in feeling pleasure and pleasure-seeking behavior.

Endorphins – Endorphins are naturally occurring painkillers in the brain.

Pleasurable activities cause the release of endorphins and a sense of well-being is created.

Estrogen – A female sex hormone produced primarily by the ovaries; and in smaller amounts by the adrenal cortex. In women, levels of estrogen fluctuate with their menstrual cycle. It is involved in the development of secondary sex characteristics, including breasts, menstruation, and preparation for pregnancy.

fMRI – Functional Magnetic Resonance Imaging (fMRI) is a brain imaging technology that shows the increased blood flow to areas activated in the brain. It is used to examine the functions of the brain.

Frontal Lobes – They are located in the front of the brain and are considered the higher-level thinking center, emotional control site, and locus of personality. The frontal lobes are involved in problem solving, memory, language, decision-making, and social and sexual behavior.

Glial Cells – They make up 90 percent of the brain's cells. Glial means glue, they are involved in digestion of dead neurons, manufacturing myelin, and provide physical and nutritional support for neurons.

Gray Matter – It consists of the neurons that make up the cerebral cortex. Gray matter consists of dendrites and synapse.

Hemispheres – The brain is often illustrated as being divided into two sections (hemispheres) that are connected by the corpus callosum. The two hemispheres are symmetrical in design and divided into four lobes: frontal, parietal, temporal, and occipital. See Left Brain Hemisphere and Right Brain Hemisphere.

Hippocampus – The hippocampus is a horseshoe shaped set of neurons located within the temporal lobes and adjacent to the amygdala. It is associated with working memory, emotions, and visual-spatial perception.

Hormones – Chemicals produced by glands in the body that circulate in the bloodstream. Hormones control the actions of certain cells and organs.

Hypothalamus – The hypothalamus is located below the thalamus. It controls the pituitary glad. Its functions include emotions, homeostasis, pain, pleasure, hunger and thirst, sleep wake cycle, and sexual desires.

Lateralization – Different functions are handled mainly by one hemisphere of the brain. For most people, speech primarily resides in the left hemisphere of the brain, and visual-spatial on the right.

Left Brain Hemisphere – Psychologists often associate the left hemisphere with language skills (both Broca and Wernicke's areas are located in the left hemisphere), logic, and sequential skills.

Leptin - A hormone synthesized by fat cells and thought to be involved in the regulation of hunger and eating.

Limbic System – The system of areas in the brain that control emotions, hormonal secretions, motivation, pain, and pleasure. The structures included in the Limbic System are: amygdala, cingulated gyrus, fornix, hippocampus, hypothalamus, olfactory cortex, and thalamus.

Medulla Oblangata – It is the lowest part of the brain stem, regulating involuntary behaviors such as breathing and heartbeat.

Melatonin – A hormone involved in regulating daily sleep-awake cycle. Nature's sleeping pill.

Myelin – Coats and insulates the neuron, increasing speed and efficiency in communication between neurons, making thinking quicker.

Neurons – The brain cells that send and receive signals to and from the brain and nervous system. Individuals have about 100 billion neurons in the brain. They consist of a cell body, dendrites, and an axon.

Neuroscience – Neuroscience is the study of the brain and the nervous system.

Neurotransmitters – Chemicals that are released from one neuron and transmit the signal to the next neuron. Neurotransmitters include: norepinephrine, serotonin, dopamine, and adrenaline.

Occipital Lobe – Located toward the back of the cerebral cortex, this area of the brain controls vision and color recognition.

Parietal Lobe – It is located above the occipital lobes and behind the frontal lobes. The parietal lobe is associated with sensory information such as touch, temperature, and pain.

PET scan – Positron emission tomography, gives a three-dimensional view of the functions occurring in the brain.

Pituitary Gland – The pituitary gland is located at the base of the hypothalamus. It produces growth hormones and other hormones in response to signals from the hypothalamus.

Plasticity – Plasticity, or neuroplasticity, is the lifelong ability of the brain to learn new information.

Pons – They are located on the brainstem and involved in arousal, sleep, and some speculate dreaming. They relay sensory information between the cerebrum and cerebellum.

Pruning – A term used to describe the elimination of dendrites and synaptic connections.

Reptilian Brain – The brain stem is the oldest and smallest region in the human brain. It evolved hundreds of millions of years ago and is more like the entire brain of present day reptiles, hence its name. It regulates breathing and heartbeat. Basic emotions of love, anger, fear, and lust are lodged in this area of the brain.

Reticular Formation – It is located in the brain stem and is associated with sleep and wake cycle.

Right Brain Hemisphere – Psychologists often associate the right hemisphere with creativity, random thought, and intuitiveness.

Serotonin – A neurotransmitter that modulates mood, emotion, sleep, and appetite. It creates a sense of calm.

Synapse – Information from one neuron flows to another neuron across a synapse. The synapse is a small gap separating neurons. This process enables neurons to communicate with each other.

Temporal Lobe – Part of the cerebrum, it is involved in hearing and memory.

Testosterone – Testosterone is a hormone produced by the testes and adrenal glands. It is required for sperm production, the development of the male reproductive organs, and the male secondary sexual characteristics, such as lowered voice and beard growth.

Thalamus – The thalamus is located at the top of the brain stem, in the middle of the brain. It receives auditory and visual sensory signals and sends selected sensory information to the cerebral cortex.

Wernicke's Area –Wernicke's area is located in the left hemisphere of the brain in the temporal lobe. It is instrumental in language understanding and comprehension.

White Matter –White matter refers to the myelin coated areas under the cerebrum's gray matter.

Bibliography

A study reveals link to obesity with dementia in old age. (2005, April). [On-line]. Retrieved October 25, 2005, from: *http://www.money-plans.net/frontend2verify–6240.html.*

Allen, R. H. (2001). *Impact teaching: Ideas and strategies for teachers to maximize student learning.* Boston: Allyn & Bacon.

Allgeier, E.R., & Albert, R. (2000). *Sexual interactions.* New York: Houghton Mifflin.

Allman, J. (1999). *Evolving brains.* New York: Scientific American Library.

Amabile, T. (1989). *Growing up creative.* New York: Crown.

Amen, D. (1999). *Change your brain, change your life: The breakthrough program for conquering anxiety, depression, obsessiveness, anger, and impulsiveness.* San Diego, CA: Three Rivers Press.

Amen, D. G. (2002). *Healing ADD: The breakthrough program that allows you to see and heal the six types of attention deficit disorder.* New York: G. P. Putnam's Sons.

Ames, C. (1999). Motivation: What teachers need to know. In A. C. Ornstein & L. S. Behar Horenstein (Eds.), *Contemporary Issues in Curriculum* (2nd ed., pp. 135–144). Boston: Allyn & Bacon.

American Psychological Association. *Just like us: Chimpanzee brains are asymmetrical in key areas and their handedness reflects it* [On–line]. Retrieved June 25, 2005, from *http://www.apa.org/releases/chimp-brains.html.*

Andersen, C. (2002). Thinking as and thinking about: Cognitive and metacognitive processes in drama. In B. Rasmussen & A. Østern (Eds.), *Playing betwixt and between: The IDEA dialogues 2001* (pp. 265–270). Oslo, NOR: Landslaget Drama i Skolen.

Andersen, C. (2004). Throwing out the baby with the bathwater?: A psychologist's view of "brain-based drama." *Drama, 11*(2), 29–30.

Anderson, J. R., Reder, L. M., & Simon, H. A. (1996). Situated learning and education. *Educational Researcher, 25*(4), 5–11.

Anderson, O., Marsh, N., & Harvey, A. (1999). *Learn with the classics: Using music to study smart at any age.* San Francisco: Lind Institute.

Apps, J. W. (1988). *Higher education in a learning society.* San Francisco: Jossey-Bass.

Armstrong, T. (1999). *7 kinds of smart: Identifying and developing your multiple intelligences.* New York: Plume.

Armstrong, T. (2000). Multiple intelligences in the classroom. Alexandria, VA: Association for Supervision and Curriculum Development.

Attwood, T. (1997). Asperger's syndrome: A guide for parents and professionals. London: Jessica Kingsley Publishers.

Atwell, N. (1990). *In the middle: Writing, reading, and learning with adolescents.* Portsmouth, NH: Heinemann.

Ayres, J. (1996). *Sensory integration and the child.* Los Angeles, CA: WPS Publishing.

Bailey, B. A. (1994). *There's gotta be a better way: Discipline that works!.* Oviedo, FL: Loving Guidance.

Bailey, B. A. (2000). *Easy to love, difficult to discipline.* New York: Perennial Currents. *I love you rituals.* New York: Perennial Currents.

Bailey, B. A. (2001). *Conscious discipline: 7 basic skills for brain smart classroom management.* Oviedo, FL: Loving Guidance.

Baird, A. A., et al. (1999). Functional magnetic resonance imaging of facial affect recognition in children and adolescents. *Journal of the American Academy of Child and Adolescent Psychiatry, 38*(2), 195–199.

Baker, Colin. (1993). *Foundations of bilingual education and bilingualism*. Clevedon, ENG: Multilingual Matters.

Bandura, A. (1994). Self-efficacy. In V.S. Ramachaudran (Ed.), *Encyclopedia of human behavior* (Vol. 4, pp. 71–81). New York: Academic Press.

Barlow, D.H., & Durand, V.M. (2005). *Essentials of abnormal psychology* (5th ed.). New York: Wadsworth.

Bar-On, R. (1997). *EQ-I: Bar-on emotional quotient inventory*. Toronto, ON: Multi-health Systems.

Barron, B. (2000). Problem solving in video-based microworlds: Collaborative and individual outcomes of high-achieving sixth-grade students. *Journal of Educational Psychology, 92*(2), 391–398.

Barry, L. M., & Messer, J. J. (2003). A practical application of self-management for students diagnosed with attention-deficit/hyperactivity disorder [Electronic Version]. *Journal of Positive Behavior Interventions, 5*(4), 238–248. Retrieved January 17, 2005, from EBSCOhost Academic Search Premier Database.

Baverstock, A. C., & Finlay, F. (2003). Who manages the care of students with attention deficit hyperactivity disorder (ADHD) in higher education? [Electronic Version]. *Child: Care, Health, & Development, 29*(3), 163–166. Retrieved January 17, 2005, from EBSCOhost Academic Search Premier Database.

Bebko, J. M. (1998). Learning, language, memory, and reading: The role of language automatization and its impact on complex cognitive activities. *Journal of Deaf Studies and Deaf Education, 3*(1), 4–14.

Beck, A.T., Rush, A.J., Shaw, B.F., & Emery, G. (1979). *Cognitive therapy of depression*. New York: Guildford Press.

Bereiter, C., & Scardamalia, M. (1993). *Surpassing ourselves: An inquiry into the nature and implications of expertise*. Chicago: Open Court.

Berenbaum, S. A. (2000). Psychological outcome in congenital adrenal hyperplasia. In B. Stabler & B. B. Bercu (Eds.), *Therapeutic outcome of endocrine disorders* (pp. 186–199). New York: Springer-Verlag.

Bergen, D. (2002). The role of pretend play in children's cognitive development [Electronic Version]. *Early Childhood Research & Practice, 4*(1). Retrieved June 25, 2005, from *http://ecrp.uiuc.edu/v4n1/bergen.html.*

Bergen, D. (2003). *Play's role in brain development*. Olney, MD: Association for Childhood Education International.

Bergen, D., & Coscia, J. (2001). *Brain research and childhood education: Implications for educators*. Olney, MD: Association for Childhood Education International.

Berne, R.M., & Levy, M.N. (Eds.). (1998). *Physiology* (4th ed.). St. Louis, MO.: Mosby.

Bialystok, E. (Ed.). (1991). *Language processing in bilingual children*. Cambridge, ENG: Cambridge University Press.

Biklen, D., & Cardinal, D. (Eds.). (1997). *Contested Words, Contested Science: Unraveling the Facilitated Communication Controversy*. New York: Teachers College Press.

Bloom, F. E., Beal, M. F., & Kupfer, D. J. (2003). *The Dana guide to brain health*. New York: Free Press.

Boesch, C., & Boesch-Achermann, H. (2002). *The chimpanzees of the Tai Forest: Behavioral ecology and evolution*. Cambridge, UK: Oxford University Press.

Bondy, A., & Frost, L. (2001). *A Picture's Worth: PECS and Other Visual Communication Strategies in Autism*. Bethesda, MA: Woodbine House.

Boozer, M., & Rouse, C. (2001). Intraschool variation in class size: Patterns and implications. *Journal of Urban Economics, 50*(1), 163–189.

Borba, M. (2002). *Building moral intelligence: The seven essential virtues that teach kids to do the right thing.* San Francisco: Jossey-Bass.

Bourtchouladze, R. (2002). *Memories are made of this.* London: Columbia University Press.

Bransford, J.D., & Schwartz, D.L. (1999). Rethinking transfer: a simple proposal with multiple implications. *Review of Research in Education, 24,* 61–100.

Bremner, J. D. (2005). *Does stress damage the brain?: Understanding trauma-related disorders from a neurological perspective.* New York: W. W. Norton & Co.

Brendtro, L. Brokenleg, M., & VanBockern, S. (2002). *Reclaiming youth at risk.* Bloomington, IN: National Educational Service.

Brendtro, L., & Shahbazian, M. (2004). *Troubled children and youth: Turning problems into opportunity.* Champaign, IL: Research Press.

Brewer, C. B., & Campbell, D. G. (1991). *Rhythms of learning.* Tucson, AZ: Zephyr Press.

Brockman, J. (2003). A bozo of a baboon: A talk with Robert Sapolsky. [On-line]. Retrieved June 24, 2005, from *http://www.edge.org/ 3rd_culture/sapolsky03/sapolsky_index.html.*

Brody, B. A., Kinney, H. C., Kloman, A. S., & Gilles, F. H. (1987). Sequence of central nervous system myelination in human infancy. *Journal of Neuropathology and Experimental Neurology, 46,* 283–301.

Brooks, J. G., & Brooks, M. G. (1999). *In search of understanding: The case for constructivist classrooms.* Alexandria, VA: Association for Supervision and Curriculum Development.

Brooks, R. (1994). Children at risk: Fostering resilience and hope. *American Journal of Orthopsychiatry, 64,* 266–278.

Brothers, L. (1990). The neural basis of primate social communication. *Motivation & Emotion, 14,* 81 81.

Brothers, L. (1997). *Friday's footprint: How society shapes the human mind.* New York: Oxford University Press.

Brothers, L. (2002). Neurophysiology in a new domain. In J. Cacioppo, et al. (Eds.), *Foundations of Social Neuroscience* (pp. 367–385). Cambridge, MA: MIT Press.

Burke, M. J., & Curcio, F. R. (2000). *Learning mathematics for a new century: Yearbook.* Reston, VA: National Council of Teachers of Mathematics.

Burns, D. D. (1980). *Feeling good: The new mood therapy.* New York: Avon.

Burton, J., Horowitz, R., & Abeles, H. (1999). Learning in and through the arts: Curriculum implications. In E. Fiske (Ed.), *Champions of change: The impact of the arts on learning.* [On–line]. Retrieved June 19, 2005, from *http://www.artsedge.kennedycenter.org/champions/.*

Byrne, R. W., & Whiten, A. (Eds.). (1988). *Machiavellian intelligence: Social expertise and the evolution of intellect in monkeys, apes and humans.* Cambridge: Oxford University Press.

Byrnes, J.P. (2001). *Minds, brains and learning: Understanding the psychological and educational relevance of neuroscientific research.* New York: The Guilford Press.

Cabeza, R. (2001). Cognitive neuroscience of aging: Contributions of functional neuroimaging. *Scandinavian Journal of Psychology, 42,* 277–286.

Cacioppo, J., et al. (Eds.). (2002). *Foundations of Social Neuroscience.* Cambridge, MA: MIT Press.

Caine, G., & Caine, R. (2001). *The brain, education and the competitive edge.* Lanham, MD: Scarecrow Press.

Caine, R., & Caine, G. (1994). *Making connections: Teaching and the human brain.* Menlo Park, CA: Addison Wesley Longman.

Caine, R., & Caine, G. (1997). *Education on the edge of possibility.* Alexandria, VA: Association for Supervision and Curriculum Development.

Caine, R., Caine, G., McClinitic, C., & Klimek, K. (2005). *The 12 brain mind learning principles* inaction: The field book to "Making Connections: Teaching and the Human Brain." Thousand Oaks, CA: Corwin Press.

Calvin, W. (1996). How brains think: Evolving intelligence, then and now. London: Weidenfeld & Nicolson.

Carbone, E. (2001). Arranging the classroom with an eye (and ear) to students with ADHD [Electronic Version]. Teaching Exceptional Children, 34(2), 72–81. Retrieved October 17, 2004, from EBSCOhost Academic Search Premier Database.

Cardinal, R. N., & Everitt, B. J. (2004). Neural and psychological mechanisms underlying appetitive learning: Links to drug addiction. Current Opinion in Neurobioogy, 14, 156–162.

Carter, R. (1998). Mapping the mind. Berkeley, CA: University of California Press.

Caulfield, J., Kidd, S., & Kocher, T. (2000). Brain-based instruction in action. Educational Leadership, 58(3), 62–65.

Childhood Bilingualism: Current Status and Future Directions. [On-line Report]. (2005). Retrieved July 2, 2005, from http://www.nichd.nih.gov/crmc/cdb/Childhood-Bilingualism_2005.pdf.

Clark, D. A., Beck, A. T., & Alford, B. A. (1999). Scientific foundations of cognitive theory and therapy of depression. New York: John Wiley & Sons, Inc.

Clarke, H. F., Dalley, J. W., Crofts, H. S., Robbins, T. W., & Roberts, A. C. (2004). Cognitive inflexibility after prefrontal serotonin depletion. Science, 304(5672), 878–880.

Claxton, G. (1997). Hare brain, tortoise mind: How intelligence increases when you think less. New York: Ecco Press.

Clement, J. (1983). A conceptual model discussed by Galileo and used intuitively by physics students. In D. Gentner & A. Stevens, (Eds.), Mental models (pp. 325–340). Hillsdale, NJ: Laurence Erlbaum Associates, Inc.

Corina, D. P. (1998). Studies of neural processing in deaf signers: Toward a neurocognitive model of language processing in the deaf. Journal of Deaf Studies and Deaf Education, 3(1), 35–48.

Cornet, C. (2003). Creating meaning through literature and the arts. Upper Saddle River, NJ: Merrill Prentice Hall.

Corsini, R. J. (1999). The dictionary of psychology. Philadelphia: Taylor & Francis.

Cowan, N. (2001). The magical number 4 in short-term memory: A reconsideration of mental storage capacity. Behavior Brain Science, 24, 87–185.

Craik, F. I. M., & Salthouse, T. A. (Eds.). (2000). The handbook of aging and cognition. Hillsdale, NJ: Lawrence Erlbaum Associates, Inc.

Cummins, J. (1986). Empowering minority students: A framework for intervention. Harvard Educational Review, 56, 18–36.

Cummins, J. (1987). Bilingualism, language proficiency, and metalinguistic developments. In P. Homel, M. Paliz, & D. Aaronson (Eds.), Childhood bilingualism: Aspects of linguistic, cognitive, and social development. Hillsdale, NJ: Lawrence Erlbaum Associates, Inc.

Cuoco, A. A., & Curico, F. R. (2001). The roles of representation in school mathematics: Yearbook. Reston, VA: National Council of Teachers of Mathematics.

Damasio, A. R. (1994). Descartes' error: Emotion, reason and the human brain. New York: Avon Books.

Damasio, A. R. (1999). The feeling of what happens: Body and emotion in the making of consciousness. New York: Harcourt.

Damasio, A. R. (2003). Looking for Spinoza: Joy, sorrow, and the feeling brain. New York: Harcourt.

D'Arcangelo, M. (2000). How does the brain develop?: A conversation with Steven Peterson Educational Leadership, 58(3), 68–71.

D'Arcangelo, M. (2000). The scientist in the crib: A conversation with Andrew Meltzoff. Educational Leadership, 58(3), 8–13.

Davatzikos, C., & Resnick, S. M. (1998). Sex differences in anatomic measures of interhemispheric connectivity: Correlations with cognition in women but not men. Cerebral Cortex, 8, 635–640.

Dave, A. S., & Margoliash, D. (2000). Song replay during sleep and computational rules for sensorimotor vocal learning. *Science, 290*(5492), 812–816.

Deci, E., Vallerand, E. R., Pelletier, L. G., & Ryan, R. M. (1991). Motivation and education: The self-determination perspective. *Educational Psychologist, 26*(3–4), 325–346.

Delfos, M.F. (2004). *Children and behavioural problems: Anxiety, aggression, depression ADHD – A biopsychological model with guidelines for diagnostics and treatment.* London: Jessica Kingsley Publishers.

Dennison, P., & Dennison, G. (1986). *Brain gym.* Ventura, CA: Edukinesthetics.

DePorter, B., Reardon, M., & Singer-Nourie, S. (1999). *Quantum teaching: Orchestrating student success.* Boston: Allyn & Bacon.

Diamond, A., & Goldman-Rakic, P. S. (1989). Comparison of human infant and rhesus monkeys of Piaget's AB task: Evidence for dependence on dorsolateral prefrontal cortex. *Experimental Brain Research, 74,* 24–40.

Diamond, M. (1967). Extensive cortical depth measurements and neuron size increases in the cortex of environmentally enriched rats. *Journal of Comparative Neurology, 131,* 357–364.

Diamond, M. (1988). Enriching heredity: The impact of the environment on the anatomy of the brain. New York: The Free Press.

Diamond, M., & Hopson, J. (1998). *Magic trees of the mind: Nurturing your child.* New York: Penguin.

Druckman, D., & Sweets, J. A. (1988). *Enhancing human performance: Issues, theories, and techniques.* Washington, DC: National Academy Press.

Durkin, K. (1995). *Developmental social psychology: From infancy to old age.* Oxford, UK: Blackwell Publishers.

Ekman, P., Levenson, R.W., & Friesen, W. V. (1983). Autonomic nervous system activity distinguishes among emotions. *Science, 221*(4616), 1208–1210.

Eliot, L. (2000). *What's going on in there? How the brain and mind develop in the first five years of life.* New York: Bantam.

Erlauer, L. (2003). *The brain-compatible classroom: using what we know about learning to improve teaching.* Alexandria, VA: Association for Supervision and Curriculum Development.

Esman, M. J. (1987). Ethnic politics and economic power. *Comparative Politics, 19,* 295 417.

Fairburn, C.G., & Harrison, P.J. (2003). Eating disorders. *The Lancet, 361,* 407–416.

Feingold, A. (1996). Cognitive gender differences: Where are they and why are they there?. *Learning & Individual Differences, 8,* 25–32.

Feinstein, S. (2004). *Secrets of the teenage brain: Research-based strategies for reaching and teaching today's adolescents.* San Diego, CA: The Brain Store.

Ferguson, E. D. (1996). Motivation. In R. J. Corsini & A. J. Auerbach (Eds.), *Concise encyclopedia of psychology* (pp. 578–580). New York: John Wiley & Sons, Inc.

Fischer, K. W., & Rose, S. P. (1998). Growth cycles of brain and mind. *Educational Leadership, 56*(3), 56–60.

Fiske, E. (Ed.). (1999). *Champions of change: The impact of the arts on learning.* [On-line]. Retrieved June 19, 2005, from *http://www.artsedge.kennedy-center.org/champions/.*

Flippen Group. (2003). *Capturing kids' hearts.* College Station, TX: The Flippen Group.

Ford, M. (1992). *Motivating humans.* Newbury Park, CA: Sage Publications.

Fountas, I., & Pinnell, G. (2001). *Guiding readers and writers (Grades 3–6): Teaching comprehension, genre, and content literacy.* Portsmouth, NH: Heinemann.

Frank, M. G., Issa, N. P., & Stryker, M. P. (2001). Sleep enhances plasticity in the developing visual cortex. *Neuron, 30*(1), 275–287.

Freeman, H. D., Cantalupo, C., & Hopkins, W. D. (2004). Asymmetries in the hippocampus and amygdala of chimpanzees (Pah troglodytes), *Behavioral Neuroscience, 118*(6), 1460–1465.

Frith, C. & Frith, U. (1999) Interacting minds-biological basis. *Science, 286,* 1692–1695.

Funk, A. (1992, November 8). Art integral part of learning. *The Topeka Capital-Journal*, p. C2.

Fuster, J. M. (2003). *Cortex and mind: Unifying cognition.* New York: Oxford University Press.

Gardiner, M. (1996). Learning improved by arts training. *Nature, 381*(580), 284.

Gardner, A. (2004). Fast food linked to obesity, insulin problems. *HealthDayNews* [On-line]. Retrieved October 25, 2005, from: *http://www.healthfinder. gov/news/newsstory.asp?docID=523168.*

Gardner, H. (1991). *The unschooled mind: How children think and how schools should teach.* New York: Basic Books.

Gardner, H. (1993). *Frames of mind: The theory of multiple intelligences.* New York: Basic Books.

Gardner, H. (2000). *Intelligence reframed: Multiple intelligences for the 21st century.* New York: Basic Books.

Garrick-Duhaney, L. M. (2003). A practical approach to managing the behaviors of students with ADD. [Electronic Version]. *Intervention in School & Clinic, 38*(5). Retrieved January 17, 2005, from EBSCOhost Academic Search Premier Database.

Gazzaniga, M. S., Ivry, R. B., & Mangun, G. R. (1998). *Cognitive neuroscience: Biology of the mind.* New York: W. W. Norton & Co.

Gee, J. P. (2003). *What video games have to teach us about learning and literacy.* New York: Palgrave Macmillan.

Genesee, F. (1981). A comparison of early and late second language learning. *Modern Language Review, 12,* 115–128.

Genesee, F. (1987). *Learning through two languages: Studies of immersion and bilingual education.* Cambridge, MA: Newbury House.

Genesee, F. (2001). Portrait of the bilingual child. In: V. Cook (Ed.) *Portraits of the second language user.* Clevedon, ENG: Multilingual Matters.

Giedd, J. N., et al. (1999). Development of the human corpus callosum during childhood and adolescence: A longitudinal MRI study. *Progress in Neuro-Psychopharmacology & Biological Psychiatry, 23*(4), 571–588.

Goodall, J. (1986). *Chimpanzees of Gombe.* Cambridge, MA: The Belknap Press.

Goodall, J. (2000). *In the shadow of man* (Rev. ed.). New York: Houghton Mifflin.

Goodenow, C. (1992). Strengthening the links between educational psychology and the study of social contexts. *Educational Psychologist, 27*(2), 177–196.

Goodlad, J. I. (1984). *A place called school: Prospects for the future.* New York: McGraw Hill.

Gendlin, E. T. (1982). *Focusing.* New York: Bantam.

Ghaith, G. (2002). The relationship between cooperative learning, perception of social support, and academic achievement. *System, 30*(3), 263–273.

Gillies, R., & Ashman, A. (1998). Behavior and interactions of children in cooperative groups in lower and middle elementary grades. *Journal of Educational Psychology, 90*(4), 746–757.

Goldberg, E. (2002). *The executive brain: Frontal lobes and the civilized mind.* New York: Oxford University Press.

Goldberg, M. (2004). The Test Mess. *Phi Delta Kappan, 85*(3), 361–366.

Goleman, D. (1995). *Emotional intelligence: Why it can matter more than IQ.* New York: Bantam.

Goleman, D. (1998). Working with emotional intelligence. New York: Bantam.

Goleman, D. (2002). *Primal Leadership: Realizing the power of emotional intelligence.* Boston: Harvard Business School Publishing.

Gopnik, A., Meltsoff, A. N., & Kuhl, P. (1999). The scientist in the crib: Minds, brains, and how children learn. New York: William Morrow.

Gore, A. (1996). The metaphor of distributed intelligence. *Science, 272,* 177–180.

Grandin, T. (1996). *Thinking in pictures: And other reports from my life with autism.* New York: Random House.

Greene, R. (2001). *The explosive child: A new approach for understanding and parenting easily frustrated, chronically inflexible children.* New York: HarperCollins Publishers.

Gutstein, S., & Rachelle, S. (2002). *Relationship development intervention with children, adolescents and adults*. London: Jessica Kingsley Publishers.

Hanson, A. (2001). *Visual writing*. New York: Learning Express.

Hanson, A. (2002). *Write brain write*. San Diego, CA: The Brain Store.

Haskell, R.E. (2001). *Transfer of learning: Cognition, instruction, and reasoning*. London, Eng.: Academic Press, Inc.

Harlow, H. F. (1965). Sexual behavior in the rhesus monkey. In F. A. Beach (Ed.), *Sex and behavior* (pp.234–265). New York: John Wiley & Sons, Inc.

Hart, L. A. (1999). *Human brain and human learning*. Covington, WA: Books for Educators.

Harvey, S., & Goudvis, A. (2000). *Strategies that work: Teaching comprehension to enhance understanding*. Markham, ON: Stenhouse Publishers.

Hawkins, J. (2004). *On Intelligence*. New York: Henry Holt.

Hayes, S.C., & Smith, S. (2005). *Get out of your mind and into your life: The new acceptance and commitment therapy guide*. Oakland, CA: New Harbinger Publications.

Healy, J. (1987). *Your child's growing mind*. Garden City, NY: Doubleday.

Heffner, M., & Eifert, G.H. (2004). *The anorexia workbook: How to accept yourself, heal suffering, and reclaim your life*. Oakland, CA: New Harbinger Publications.

Heidenhain, G. (2003). *Learning beyond boundaries: Fundamental experiences using accelerated learning*. Colorado Springs, CO: An International Alliance for Learning Publication.

Helmuth, L. (2001). ADDICTION: Beyond the pleasure principle. *Science, 294,* 983–984.

Hodgdon, L. (1995) *Visual strategies for improving communication: Practical supports for school & home*. Troy, MI: Quirk Roberts Publishing.

Hoerr, T. (2003). Distributed intelligence and why schools need to foster it. *Independent School, 63*(1), 76–83.

Holloway, J. H. (2000). How does the brain learn science? *Educational Leadership, 58*(3), 85–86.

Howard, P. J. (2000). *The owner's manual for the brain*. Austin, TX: Bard Press.

Huang, S. C., Tsai, S. J., & Chang, J. C. (2004). Fluoxetine-induced memory impairment in four family members. *Journal of Psychiatric Medicine, 34*(2), 197–200.

Hughes, D. (2003). *Behavioral neurogenetics: A complementary strategy to understanding neuropsychiatric disorders* [Electronic Version]. Retrieved June 24, 2005, from *http://neuropsychiatryreviews.com/apr03/npr_apr03_neurogenetics.html*.

Huttenlocher, P. R. (1990). Morphometric study of human cerebral cortex development. *Neuropsychologia, 28,* 517–527.

Izard, C. E. (1971). *The face of emotion*. New York: Appleton-Century-Crofts.

Jacobs, B., Schall, M., & Scheibel, A. B. (1993). A quantitative dendritic analysis of Wernicke's area in humans. II. Gender, hemispheric, and environmental factors. *Journal of Comparative Neurology, 327,* 97–111.

Jamieson, J. R. (1995). Interactions between mothers and children who are deaf. *Journal of Early Intervention, 19*(2), 108–117.

Janzen, J. E. (1996). *Understanding the nature of autism: A practical guide*. San Antonio, TX: Therapy Skill Builders.

Jensen, E. (2000). Learning smarter: The new science of teaching and training. San Diego, CA: The Brain Store.

Jensen, E. (2001). *Arts with the brain in mind*. Alexandria, VA: Association for Supervision and Curriculum Development.

Jensen, E. (2003). *Tools for engagement: Managing emotional states for learner success*. San Diego, CA: The Brain Store.

Jensen, E. (2005). *Teaching with the brain in mind (2nd ed.)*. Alexandria, VA: Association for Supervision and Curriculum Development.

Johnson, D., & Johnson, R. (1999). *Learning together and alone: Cooperative, competitive and individualistic learning*. Boston: Allyn & Bacon.

Johnson, D., Maruyama, G., Johnson, R., Nelson, D., & Skon, L. (1981). Effects of cooperative, competitive, and individualistic goal structures on achievement: A meta-analysis. *Psychological Bulletin, 89*(1), 47–62.

Johnson, S. (2004). Antonio Damasio's theory of thinking faster and faster. *Discover, 25*(5), 44–49.

Johnson-Laird, P. (1983). *Mental models.* Cambridge, MA: Harvard University Press.

Johnston, V. (1999). *Why we feel: The science of human emotions.* Cambridge, UK: Perseus.

Katchadourian, H. A. (1990). The biological aspects of human sexuality. Austin, TX: Holt, Rinehart, and Winston, Inc.

Kauchak, D. P., & Eggen, P. D. (1998). *Learning and teaching: Research-based methods.* Boston: Allyn & Bacon.

Kaufeldt, M. (1999). *Begin with the brain: Orchestrating the learner-centered classroom.* San Diego, CA: The Brain Store.

Khilnani, S., Field, T., Hernandez-Reif, M., & Schanberg, S. (2003). Massage therapy improves mood and behavior of students with Attention-Deficit/Hyperactivity Disorder [Electronic Version]. *Adolescence, 38*(152). Retrieved January 17, 2005, from EBSCOhost Academic Search Premier Database.

Kilander, L., Nyman, H., Boberg, M., & Lithell, H. (1997). *Cognitive function, vascular risk factors and education: A cross-sectional study based on a cohort of 70-year-old men. Internal Medicine, 242*(4): 313–321.

Kim, J., & Diamond, D. (2002). The stressed hippocampus, synaptic plasticity and lost memories. *Nature Reviews Neuroscience, 3*(6), 453–462.

Kimura D. (2002) Sex hormones influence human cognitive pattern. *Neuroendocrinology Letters, 23*(4), 67–77.

Kinoshita, J. (1997). Nourishing thoughts: The surprising role of "Neurotrophins" in memory [Electronic Version]. *Brainwork: The Neuroscience Newsletter, 7*(1). Retrieved June 25, 2005, from *http://www.dana.org/articles/bwn_0297.cf* #contents.

Klosko, J. S., & Sanderson, W. C. (1999). *Cognitive-behavioral treatment of depression.* New York: Aronson.

Kluth, P. (2003). *You're going to love this kid: Teaching students with autism in the inclusive classroom.* Baltimore, MD: Paul H. Brookes Publishing Co.

Knowles, M. (1980). *The modern practice of adult education.* (Rev. ed.). Chicago: Follet Co.

Kotulak, R. (1996). *Inside the brain: Revolutionary discoveries of how the mind works.* Kansas City, MO: Andrews McMeel Publishing.

Kovalik, S. J., & Olsen, K. D. (2002). *Exceeding expectations: A user's guide to implementing brain research in the classroom* (2nd ed.). Covington, WA: Books for Educators.

Kranowicz, C. S. (1998). *The out-of-sync child: Recognizing and coping with sensory integration dysfunction.* New York: Berkley Publishing Group.

Lambert, L., et al. (2002). *The constructivist leader* (2nd ed.). New York: Teachers College Press.

Lambert, W. E., & Taylor, D. M. (1990). *Coping with cultural and racial diversity in urban America.* New York: Praeger.

Lambert, W. E., & Tucker, G. R. (1972). *Bilingual education of children: The St. Lambert experience.* Rowley, MA: Newbury House.

Laumann, E. O., et al. (2000). The organization of sexuality: Sexual practices in the United States. Chicago: The University of Chicago Press.

Lazaer, D. (2004). *Higher order thinking the multiple intelligence way.* Chicago: Zephyr Press.

LeDoux, J. (1996). *The emotional brain: The mysterious underpinnings of emotional life.* New York: Simon and Schuster.

LeDoux, J. (2002). *Synaptic self* (1st ed.). Toronto, ON: Viking-Penguin Books.

Leary, M. R., & Downs, D. L. (Eds.). (1995). *Efficacy, agency, and self-esteem.* New York: Plenium Press.

Lerner, R., & Benson, P. (Eds.). (2003). *Developmental assets and asset-building communities: Implications for research, policy, and practice*. Minneapolis, MN: Search Institute.

Lipsey, M., & Wilson, D. (1993). The efficacy of psychological, educational and behavioral treatment. *American Psychologist, 48*(12), 1181–1209.

Lock, R. H., Church, K., Gottschalk, C. M., & Leddy, J. (2003). Enhance social and friendship skills. [Electronic Version]. *Intervention in School & Clinic, 38*(5). Retrieved January 17, 2005, from EBSCOhost Academic Search Premier Database.

Lonsdorf, E. (2004).Sex differences in learning in chimpanzees, *Nature, 428,* 715.

Lopes, P. N., Brackett, M. A., Nezlek, J., Schutz, A., Sellin, I., & Salovey, P. (in press). Emotional intelligence and social interaction. *Personality and Social Psychology Bulletin.*

Lou, Y., Abrami, P., Spence, J., Paulsen, C., Chambers, B., & d'Apollonio, S. (1996). Within-class grouping: A meta-analysis. *Review of Educational Research, 66*(4), 423–458.

Lupien, S. J., & Lepage, M. (2001). Stress, memory, and the hippocampus: Can't live with it, can't live without it. *Behavioural Brain Research, 127*(1–2):137–158.

Lurie, K. (2005). ADHD brain scan [Online]. Retrieved June 25, 2005, from *http://www.sciencentral.com/articles/view. php3?language=english&type=& article_id =218392460.*

MacDonald, A. (2003). Imaging studies bring ADHD into sharper focus [Electronic Version]. *Brainwork: The Neuroscience Newsletter, 13*(2). Retrieved June 25, 2005, from, *http://www.dana.org/pdf/periodicals/brainwork_0403.pdf.*

Maddux, J. (1999). Expectancies and the social-cognitive perspective: Basic principles, processes, and variables. In I. Kirsch (Ed.), *How expectancies shape experience* (pp. 17–39). Washington, DC: American Psychological Association.

Mann, V. A., Sasanuma, S., Sakuma, N., & Masaki S. (1990). Sex differences in cognitive abilities: A cross-cultural perspective. *Neuropsychologia, 28,* 1063–1077.

Marieb, E.N. (1995). *Human anatomy and physiology* (3rd ed.). Redwood City, CA.:

The Benjamin Cummings Publishing Company, Inc.

Marschark, M., Lang, H. G., & Albertini, J. A. (2002). *Educating Deaf Students: From research to practice.* New York: Oxford University Press.

Marshall, M. L. (2001). *Discipline without stress.* Los Alamitos, CA: Piper Press.

Marton, F. & Saljo, R. (1976). On qualitative differences in learning-II: Outcome as a function of the learner's conception of the task. *British Journal of Educational Psychology, 46,* 115–127.

Marzano, R.J. (2001). *Designing a new taxonomy of educational objectives.* Thousand Oaks, CA: Corwin Press.

Marzano, R. J. (2003). *Classroom management that works: Research-based strategies for* Development.

Marzano, R. J., Pickering, D. J., & Pollock, J. E. (2001). *Classroom instruction that works.* Alexandra, VA: Association for Supervision and Curriculum Development.

Matsuzawa, T. (2001). Reproductive memory processes in chimpanzees: Homologous approaches to research on human working memory. *Primate Origins of Human Cognition and Behavior.* Tokyo: Springer-Verlag.

Mayberry, R. I., & Eichen, E. B. (1991). The long-lasting advantage of learning sign language in childhood: Another look at the critical period for language acquisition. *Journal of Memory and Language, 30*(4), 486–512.

Mayer, J.D., Caruso, D., & Salovey, P. (1997). The Multifactor Emotional Intelligence Scale: Emotional intelligence a key to success. Simsbuy, CT: Charles J. Wolfe Associates, LLC Publisher.

Mayer, J. D., Salovey, P., Caruso, D. R., & Sigarenios, G. (2001). Emotional intelligence as a standard intelligence. *Emotion, 1,* 232–242.

Mayer, J. D., & Salovey, P. (1997). What is emotional intelligence? In P. Salovey & D. Sluyter (Eds.), *Emotional development and emotional intelligence: Educational implications* (pp. 3–31). New York: Basic Books.

Mayer, J. D., Salovey, P., & Caruso, D. R. (2002). Mayer-Salovey-Caruso Emotional

Intelligence Test. Toronto, ON: Multi-Health Systems, Inc.

McClannahan, L. E., & Krantz, P. J. (1998). *Activity schedules for children with autism: Teaching independent behavior*. Bethesda, MD: Woodbine House.

McEwen, B., Lasley, E. N., & Lasley, E. (2002). *The end of stress as we know it*. Washington, DC: National Academies Press.

Mendez-Sanchez, N., Ponciano-Rodrigoez, G., Chavez-Tapia, N., & Uribe, M. (2005). *Effects of leptin on biliary lipids: Potential consequences for gallstone formation and therapy in obesity*. *Curr Drug Targets Immune Endocr Metab Disord, 5(2)*, 203–8.

Michael, E., Keller, T., Carpenter, P., & Just, M. (2001). fMRI investigation of sentence comprehension by eye and by ear: Modality fingerprints on cognitive processes. *Human Brain Mapping 13(4)*, 239–252.

Miller, P. (2002). Another look at the STM capacity of prelingually deafened individuals and its relation to reading comprehension. *American Annals of the Deaf, 147(5)*, 56–69.

Molteni, R., Wu, A., Vaynman, S., Ying, Z., Barnard, R. J., & Gomez-Pinilla, F. (2004). Exercise reverses the harmful effects of consumption of a high-fat diet on synaptic and behavioral plasticity associated to the action of brain-derived neurotrophic factor. *Neuroscience, 123(2)*, 429–440.

Moore, B., & Caldwell, H. (1993). Drama and drawing for narrative writing in primary grades. *Journal of Educational Research, 8(2)*, 100–110.

Mukhopadhyay, T. R. (2000). *Beyond the silence: My life, the world and autism*. London: The National Autism Society.

Myles, B. (2001). *Asperger syndrome and adolescence: Practical solutions for school success*. Shawnee Mission, KS: Autism Asperger Publishing Company.

Nakamura, K. (1993). A theory of cerebral learning regulated by the reward system. *Biological Cybernetics, 68(6)*, 491–498.

National Reading Panel. (2000). *Teaching Children to Read* [On-line]. Retrieved Oct. 24, 2005, from: *http://www.nationalreadingpanel.org/Publications/publications.htm*.

Nelson, C. A., & Carver, L. (1998). The effects of stress and trauma on brain and memory: A view from developmental cognitive neuroscience. *Development and Psychopathology, 10(4)*, 793–809.

Nemoto, S., & Finkel, T. (2004). Ageing and the mystery at Arles. *Nature, 429, 149–152*.

Nestler, E. J., & Malenka, R. C. (2004). The addicted brain. *Scientific American, 290(3)*, 78–85.

Niehoff, D. (1999). *The biology of violence: How understanding the brain, behavior, and environment can break the vicious circle of aggression*. New York: The Free Press.

Nolan, K. A., & Blass, J.P. (1992). Preventing cognitive decline. *Clinics in Geriatric Medicine, 8(1)*, 19–34.

Novak, J. D. (1998). *Learning, creating, and using knowledge*. Hillsdale, NJ: Lawrence Erlbaum Associates, Inc.

Novak, J. D., & Gowin, D. B. (1984). *Learning how to learn*. New York: University Press.

O'Neil, R., Welsh, M., Parke, R. D., Wang, S., & Strand, C. (1997). A longitudinal assessment of the academic correlates of early peer acceptance and rejection. *Journal of Clinical Child Psychology, 26(3)*, 290–303.

Paddison, S. (1998). *The hidden power of the heart: Discovering an unlimited source of intelligence*. Boulder Creek, CA: Planetary Publications.

Padgett, D., Sheridan, J., Dorne, J., Berntson, G.., Candelora, J., & Glaser, R. (1998). Social stress and the reactivation of latent herpes simplex virus type 1. *Proceedings of the National Academy of Sciences, 95(12)*, 7231–7235.

Panksepp, J. (1998). Attention deficit hyperactivity disorders, psychostimulants, and intolerance of childhood playfulness: A tragedy in the making? *Current Directions in Psychological Science, 7(3)*, 91–98.

Papalos, D., & Papalos, J. (2002). *The bipolar child: The definitive and reassuring guide to childhood's most misunderstood disorder* (2nd ed.). New York: Broadway Books.

Paradis, M. (2004). *A neurolinguistic theory of bilingualism*. Philadelphia: John Benjamins.

Parr, A. (2001). Cognitive and physiological markers of emotional awareness in chimpanzees (Pan troglodytes), *Animal Cognition, 4*, 223–229.

Pearson, S. (2000). *Tools for citizenship and life: Using the ITI lifelong guidelines and lifeskills in your classroom.* Kent, WA: Susan Kovalik & Associates.

Pellegrini, A., & Bjorklund, D. F. (1996). The place of recess in school: Issues in the role of recess in children's education and development. *Journal of Research in Childhood Education, 11*(1), 5–13.

Perachio, A. A. (1978). Hypothalamic regulation of behavioral and hormonal aspects of aggression and sexual performance. In D. C. Chivers, & J. Herbert (Eds.), *Recent advances in primatology* (Vol. 1, pp. 549–566).

Perkins, D.N., & Salomon, G. (1992). Transfer of learning. In Husen, T., & Postlethwaite, T.N. (Eds.), *International Encyclopedia of Education* (2nd ed.). Oxford, ENG: Pergamon Press. Retrieved also Oct. 24, 2005, from: *http://learnweb.harvard.edu/alps/thinking/docs/traencyn.htm.*

Pert, C. (1997). *Molecules of emotion.* New York: Scribner.

Peterson, C., Maier, S., & Seligman, M. (1993). *Learned helplessness.* New York: Oxford University Press.

Phelps, E., et al. (2002). Performance on indirect measures of race evaluation predicts Amygdala activation. In J. Cacioppo, et. al. (Eds.), *Foundations of social neuroscience,* (pp. 615–627). Cambridge, MA: MIT Press.

Phillips, P. E. M., Stuber, G. D., Heien, M. L. A. V., Wightman, R. M., & Carell, R. M. (2003). Subsecond dopamine release promotes cocaine seeking. *Nature, 422,* 614–618.

Piaget, J. (1976). *To understand is to invent: The future of education.* New York: Penguin.

Piaget, J. & Inhelder, B. (1969). *The psychology of the child.* New York: Basic Books.

Pinker, S. (1997). *How the mind works.* New York: W. W. Norton, Inc.

Pinker, S. (2002). *The blank slate: The modern denial of human nature.* New York: Viking.

Polanyi, M. (1958). *Personal knowledge: Towards a post–critical philosophy.* London: Routledge and Kegan Paul.

Popham, J. (2001). *The truth about testing: An educator's call to action.* Alexandria, VA: Association for Supervision and Curriculum Development.

Popham, J. (2002). *Classroom assessment: What teachers need to know* (3rd ed). Boston: Allyn & Bacon.

Preston, S. D., & deWaal, F. B. M. (2002). Empathy: Its ultimate and proximate bases. *Behavioral and Brain Sciences, 25*(1), 1–71.

Preuschoft, S., & vanHooff, J. A. R. A. M. (1995). Homologizing primate facial displays: A critical review of methods. *Folia Primatologica, 65,* 121–137.

Prietula, M. J., & Simon, H. A. (1989). The Experts in your midst. *Harvard Business Review, 1,* 120.

Prior, M., Smart, D., Sanson, A., & Oberklaid, F. (1993). Sex differences in psychological adjustment from infancy to 8 years. *Journal of the American Academy of Child and Adolescent Psychiatry, 32,* 281–304.

Project Zero. (2000). The arts and academic improvement: What the evidence shows [On-line]. Retrieved June 24, 2005, from *http://www.pz.harvard.edu/Research/Reap/REAPExecSum.htm.*

Public Broadcasting Station. (2002) *Frontline: Interviews inside the teenage brain [On-line]. Retrieved July 6, 2005, from* http://www.pbs.org/wgbh/pages/frontline/shows/teenbrain/.

Ratey, J. J. (2001). *A user's guide to the brain: Perception, attention and the four theaters of the brain. New York:* Vintage Books.

Reid, R. (1999). Attention deficit hyperactivity disorder: Effective methods for the classroom [Electronic Version]. *Focus on Exceptional Children, 32*(4). Retrieved January 17, 2005, from EBSCOhost Academic Search Premier Database.

Restak, R. (1995). *Brainscapes.* New York: Hyperion.

Restak, R. (2003). *The new brain.* New York: Rodale.

Rhodes, L. (1996). *Readers and writers with a difference.* Portsmouth, NH: Heinemann.

Richards, R. G. (2001). *The source for learning and memory.* East Moline, IL: Lingui-Systems.

Rogers, D. A. (1998). Computer-assisted learning versus a lecture and feedback seminar for teaching a basic surgical technical skill. *American Journal of Surgery, 175*(6), 508–510.

Rogers, K. (1986). Do the gifted think differently? *Journal for the Education of the Gifted, 100,* 17–39.

Rogers, K. (2002). *Re-forming gifted education.* Scottsdale, AZ: Great Potential Press.

Ronis, D. (2000). *Brain-compatible assessments.* Glenview, IL: Skylight Professional Development.

Root-Bernstein, R., & Root-Bernstein, M. (1999). *Sparks of genius.* New York: Houghton Mifflin.

Rothenberg, J., McDermott, P., & Martin, G. (1998). Changes in pedagogy: A qualitative result of teaching heterogeneous classes. *Teaching and Teacher Education, 14*(6), 633–642.

Rothschild, B. (2000). *The body remembers: The psychophysiology of trauma and trauma treatment.* New York: W. W. Norton & Co.

Ryan, R. M., Connell, J. P., & Deci, E. L. (1985). A motivational analysis of self determination and self-regulation in education. In C. Ames & R. Ames (Eds.), *Research on motivation in education: The classroom milieu* (Vol. 2, pp. 13–51). New York: Academic Press, Inc.

Sackett, G. P. (1966). Monkeys reared in isolation with pictures as visual input: Evidence for an innate releasing mechanism, *Science, 154*(3755), 1468+1471–1473.

Salend, S. J., Elhoweris, H., & Van Garderen, D. (2003). Educational interventions for students with ADD [Electronic Version]. *Intervention in School & Clinic, 38*(5). Retrieved January 17, 2005, from EBSCOhost Academic Search Premier Database.

Salend, S. J., & Rohena, E. (2003). Students with attention deficit disorders: An overview [Electronic Version]. *Intervention in School & Clinic, 38*(5). Retrieved January 17, 2005, from EBSCOhost Academic Search Premier Database.

Salomon, G., & Perkins, D. N. (1988). Individual and social aspects of learning. In P. D. Pearson & A. Iran-Nejad (Eds.), *Review of Research in Education, 23,* 1–24.

Salomon, G., Brown, J. S., & Pea, R. (1996). *Distributed cognitions.* Cambridge, UK: Cambridge University Press.

Salovey, P. & Mayer, J. D. (1990). Emotional intelligence. *Imagination, Cognition, and Personality, 9,* 185–211.

Schick, B., de Villiers, J., de Villiers, P., & Hoffmeister, B. (2002). Theory of mind: Language and cognition in deaf children [On-line]. Retrieved August 20, 2004, from *http://www.asha.org/about/publications/leader-online/archives/2002/q4/f021203.htm.*

Schewe, P. F., & Stein, B. (February 10, 2005). Chain reactions in neuron firing might be used to store information [Electronic Version]. *The American Institute of Physics Bulletin of Physics News, 719.* Retrieved June 29, 2005, from *http://physics.about.com/od/biophysics/a/MemoryAvalanche_p.htm.*

Schunk, D. H. (2004) *Learning theories: An educational perspective* (4th ed.). Boston: Pearson.

Schutte, N. S., et al. (1998). Development and validation of a measure of emotional intelligence. *Personality and Individual Differences, 25,* 167–177.

Schwartz, J. M., & Begley, S. (2003). *The mind and the brain: Neuroplasticity and the power of mental force.* New York: Regan Books.

Schwiebert, V. L., Sealander, K. A., & Dennison, J. L. (2002). Strategies for counselors working with high school students with attention-deficit/hyperactivity disorder [Electronic Version]. *Journal of Counseling & Development, 80*(1). Retrieved January 17, 2005, from EBSCOhost Academic Search Premier Database.

Science A Go Go. (2001). *Stress and aggression reinforce each other* [Electronic Version]. Retrieved July 2, 2005, from *http://www.scienceagogo.com/news/20040903231503data_trunc_sys.shtml.*

Senge, P. M. (1990). *The fifth discipline: The art and practice of the learning organization.* New York: Doubleday.

Sergiovanni, T. J. J. (1996). *Moral leadership: Getting to the heart of school improvement.* New York: John Wiley & Sons, Inc.

Sexuality Information and Education Council of the United States. (2004). *Guidelines for comprehensive sexuality education: Kindergarten through 12th grade* (3rd ed.) [Online Report]. Retrieved July 2, 2005, from *http://www.siecus.org/pubs/guidelines/guidelines.pdf.*

Shank, P. (2004, September 7). Can they do it in the real world? Designing for transfer of learning. *The Learning Developers' Journal.* [On–line]. Retrieved Oct. 24, 2005, from *http://www.learningpeaks.com/pshank_Transfer.pdf.*

Shaywitz, B., et al. (2000). The neurobiology of reading and reading disability (dyslexia). In M. Kamil, P. Mosenthal, P. Pearson, & R. Barr (Eds.), *Handbook of reading research (Vol. III, pp. 229–249).* Hillsdale, NJ: Lawrence Erlbaum Associates, Inc.

Shonkoff, J. P. & Phillips, D. A. (Eds.). (2000). *From neurons to neighborhoods.* Washington, DC: National Academies Press.

Shore, S. (2001). *Beyond the wall: Personal experiences with autism and Asperger syndrome.* Shawnee Mission, KS: Autism Asperger Publishing Company.

Siegel, D. (1999). *The developing mind: Toward a neurobiology of interpersonal experience.* New York: Guilford Press.

Siegel, J. M. (2001). The REM sleep-memory consolidation hypothesis. *Science, 294*(5544), 1058–1063.

Silverman, L.K. (1993). The gifted individual. In L.K. Silverman (Ed.). *Counseling the gifted and talented* (pp. 3–28). Denver, CO: Love Publishing.

Simos, P. G., et al. (2001). Mapping of receptive language cortex in bilingual volunteers by using magnetic source imaging. *Journal of Neurosurgery, 95,* 76–81.

Siviy, S. M. (1998). Neurobiological substrates of play behavior: Glimpses into the structure and function of mammalian playfulness. In M. Bekoff & J. Byers (Eds.), *Animal play: Evolutionary, comparative, and ecological perspectives.* New York: Cambridge University Press.

Slavkin, M. (2002). Brain science in the classroom. *Principal Leadership, 2*(8), 21–23.

Smilkstein, R. (2003). *We're born to learn: Using the brain's natural learning process to create today's curriculum.* Thousand Oaks, CA: Corwin Press.

Smith, D. D. (2003). *Introduction to special education: Teaching in an age of opportunity* (5th ed.). Boston: Pearson.

Smith, F. (1990). *To think. New York: Teachers College Press.*

Sousa, D. (2001). *How the brain learns* (2nd ed.). Thousand Oaks, CA: Corwin Press.

Sousa, D. (2004). *How the brain learns to read.* Thousand Oaks, CA: Corwin Press.

Squire, L. R., & Kandel, E. R. (2000). *Memory: From mind to molecules.* New York: W. H. Freeman.

Squire, L. R. & Zola, S. M. (1996). Structure and function of declarative and nondeclarative memory systems. *Proceedings of the National Academy of Sciences,* 93: 13515–13522.

Stengle, J. (2004, December 4) *Obesity is rising sharply among U.S. preschoolers.* Associated Press, n. pag.

Stiggins, R. (2002). Assessment crisis: The absence of assessment for learning. *Phi Delta Kappan, 83*(10), 758–765.

Stilwell, B., Galvin, M., Kopta, S. M., & Kopta, S. *Right vs. wrong: Raising a child with a conscience.* Bloomington, IN: Indiana University Press.

Strauch, B. (2004). *The primal teen: What the new discoveries about the teenage brain tell us about our kids.* New York: Bantam Doubleday.

Summers, C. H., et al. (2004). Dynamics and mechanics of social rank reversal. *Journal of Comparative Physiology. A, Neuroethology, Sensory, Neural, and Behavioral Physiology, 191:* 241–252.

Suomi, S. (1999). Attachment in rhesus monkeys. In J. Cassidy & P. Shaver (Eds.), *Handbook of attachment* (pp. 181–197). New York, NY: Guildford Press.

Surowiecki, J. (2004). *The wisdom of crowds.* New York: Bantam Doubleday.

Swain, M., & Lapkin, S. (1982). *Evaluating bilingual education: A case study*. Clevedon, ENG: Multilingual Matters.

Sylwester, R. (1995). *A celebration of neurons*. Alexandria, VA: Association for Supervision and Curriculum Development.

Sylwester, R. (1998). Art for the brain's sake. *Educational Leadership, 56*(3), 31–35.

Temple, E., et al. (2003). Neural deficits in children with dyslexia ameliorated by behavioral remediation: Evidence from functional MRI. *Proceedings of the National Academy of Sciences, 100*(5), 2860–2865.

Terrazas, A., & McNaughton, B. (2000) Brain growth and the cognitive map. *Proceedings of the National Academy of Sciences, 97*(9), 4414–4416.

Thatcher, R.W., Lyon, G.R., Rumsby, G., & Krasnegor, K. (Eds.). (1996). *Developmental neuroimaging: Mapping the development of brain and behavior*. San Diego, CA: Academic Press, Inc.

Tileston, D.W. (2000). *What every teacher should know about motivation*. Thousand Oaks, CA: Corwin Press.

Tobin, M., Nelson, J., & Castellanos, F. (1999). Development of the human corpus callosum during childhood and adolescence: A longitudinal MRI study. *Progress in Neuro-Psychopharmacology & Biological Psychiatry, 23*, 557–588.

Tomlinson, C. (1996). Differentiating instruction in mixed ability classrooms. Alexandria, VA: Association for Supervision and Curriculum Development.

Tompkins, G. (2005). *Literacy for the 21st-Century: A Balanced Approach*. Upper Saddle River, NJ: Prentice Hall.

Toye, S. (2001). *Study shows obesity bad for the mind, too* [On-line]. Retrieved June 24, 2005, from *http:// www.sciencedaily.com /releases/ 2001/05/010529071515.htm*.

U. S. Office of Special Education Programs. (2003). Identifying and treating attention deficit hyperactivity disorder: A resource for school and home [Electronic Version]. Retrieved June 24, 2005, from *http:// www.ed.gov/teachers/needs/speced/adhd/adh d–resource–pt1.doc*.

Vail, P. B. (1996). *Learning as a way of being*. San Francisco, CA: Jossey-Bass.

Vaughn, S., & Linan-Thompson, S. (2004). *Research-based methods of reading instruction grades K-3*. Alexandria, VA: Association for Supervision and Curriculum Development.

Wagner, U., Gais, S., Haider, H., Verleger, R., & Born, J. (2004). Sleep inspires insight. *Nature, 427*(6972), 352–355.

Walberg, H. (1999) Productive teaching. In H. C. Waxman & H. Walberg (Eds.), *New directions for teaching practice and research* (pp. 75–104). Berkeley, CA: McCutchen Publishing Corp.

Walker, M. P., Brakefield, T., Morgan, A., Hobson, J. A., & Stickgold, R. (2002). Practice with sleep makes perfect: Sleep-dependent motor skill learning. *Neuron, 35*(1), 205–211.

Walsh, D. (2004). *Why do they act that way?: A survival guide to the adolescent brain for you and your teen*. New York: Free Press.

Walsh, P. (2000). A hands-on approach to understanding the brain. *Educational Leadership, 58*(3), 76–78.

Wang, G.J., et al. (2001). Brain dopamine and obesity. *Lancet, 357*(9253), 354–357.

Wang, M. C., Haertel, G. D., & Walberg, H. J. (1993). Toward a knowledge base for learning. *Review of Educational Research, 63*(3), 249–294.

Weber, E. (1998). Marks of brain-based assessment: A practical checklist. *National Association of Secondary School Principals Bulletin, 82*(598), 63–72.

Wentzel, K. R., & Wigfield, A. (1998). Academic and social motivational influences on students' academic performance. *Educational Psychology Review, 10*(2), 155–175.

West, R. L. (1996). An application of prefrontal cortex function theory to cognitive aging. *Psychological Bulletin, 120*, 272–292.

Whitehead, A. N., Griffin, D. R., & Sherburne, D. W. (1978). *Process and reality: An essay in cosmology*. New York: Free Press.

Wilkinson, I., & Fung, I. (2002). Small-group composition and peer effects. *International Journal of Educational Research, 37*(5), 483–504.

Willey, L. H. (1999). *Pretending to be normal: Living with Asperger's syndrome*. London: Jessica Kingsley Publishers.

Williams, D. (2003). *Exposure anxiety–the invisible cage: An exploration of self-protection responses in the autism spectrum and beyond.* London: Jessica Kingsley Publishers.

Wilson, M. A., & McNaughton, B. L. (1994). Reactivation of hippocampal ensemble memories during sleep. *Science, 265*(5172), 676–679.

Wlodkowski, R. (1985). *Enhancing adult motivation to learn.* San Francisco: Jossey–Bass.

Wolfberg, P. J. (1999). *Play and imagination in children with autism.* New York: Teachers College Press.

Wolfe, P. (2001). *Brain matters: Translating research into classroom practice.* Alexandria, VA: Association for Supervision and Curriculum Development.

Wolfe, P., & Nevills, P. (2004). *Building the reading brain, PreK-3.* Thousand Oaks, CA: Corwin Press.

Wood, D. (1991). Communication and cognition: How the communication styles of hearing adults may hinder-rather than help-deaf learners. *American Annals of the Deaf, 136*(3), 247–251.

Wurtman, J. (1988). *Managing your mind and mood through food.* New York: Harper Collins.

Young, J. E., Beck, A. T., & Weinberger, A. (1993). Depression. In D. H. Barlow (Ed.), *Clinical handbook of psychological disorders: A step-by-step treatment manual* (2nd ed). New York: Guildford Press.

Zentall, S. S. (1983). Learning environments: A review of physical and temporal factors. *Exceptional Education Quarterly, 4,* 90–115.

Zimmer, R. (2003) A new twist in the educational tracking debate. *Economics of Education Review, 22*(3), 307–315.

Zull, J. E. (2002). *The art of changing the brain: Enriching teaching by exploring the biology of learning.* Herndon, VA: Stylus.

HTTP On-line Sources

ADHD. *http://www.adhd.com/index.jsp.* Retrieved July 6, 2005.

The Amen Clinics. *http://www.brainplace.com.* Retrieved June 25, 2005.

American Dietetic Association. *http: //www. eatright.org/Public.* Retrieved June 25, 2005.

Americans for the Arts. *http://ww3.artsusa.org.* Retrieved June 25, 2005.

Born to Explore! The Other Side of ADD. *http://www.borntoexplore.org/index.html.* Retrieved June 25, 2005.

BrainConnection. *http://www.brainconnection.com.* Retrieved June 25, 2005.

BrainStore. *http://www.brainstore.com/brainstore.cfm?pin=1.* Retrieved June 25, 2005.

BrainWonders. *http://www.zerotothree.org/brainwonders/index.html.* Retrieved July 2, 2005.

Center for Applied Special Technology. *http://www.cast.org.* Retrieved June 25, 2005.

The ChildTrauma Academy. *http://www.childtrauma.org.* Retrieved June 25, 2005.

CollegeBoard *http://www.collegeboard.com/splash.* Retrieved June 25, 2005.

The DANA Foundation. *http://www.dana.org.* Retrieved June 25, 2005.

Drug Rehabilitation. *http:// www.usnodrugs.com.* Retrieved June 25, 2005.

EduScapes. *http://www.eduscapes.com.* Retrieved June 25, 2005.

Gay, Lesbian, Straight Education Network. http://www.glsen.org/cgi-bin/iowa/home.html. Retrieved July 2, 2005.

The Henry J. Kaiser Family Foundation. *http://www.kff.org.* Retrieved June 25, 2005.

Intersex Society of North America. *http://www. isna.org.* Retrieved July 2, 2005.

Learning Disabilities. *http://www.ldonline.org.* Retrieved June 25, 2005.

Learning Enrichment. *www.learningenrichment.org.* Retrieved July 6, 2005.

LifeSounds. *http://www. musicandlearning.com.* Retrieved June 25, 2005.

National Council of Teachers of Mathematics. *http://nctm.org.* Retrieved June 25, 2005.

New Horizons for Learning. http://www.newhorizons.org/index.html. Retrieved June 25, 2005.

Neuroscience for Kids. *http://faculty.washington.edu/chudler/neurok.html.* Retrieved June 25, 2005.

The Office for Studies in Moral Development and Education. *http://tigger.uic.edu/~lnucci/MoralEd/office.html.* Retrieved June 25, 2005.

Reclaiming Youth Network. *http://www.reclaiming.com.* Retrieved June 25, 2005.

Sexuality Information and Education Council of the United States. *http:// www.siecus.org.* Retrieved October 25, 2005.

Science A Go Go. *http:// www.scienceagogo.com.* Retrieved June 25, 2005.

Science Direct. *http://www.sciencedirect.com.* Retrieved July 2, 2005.

Starr Commonwealth. *http:// www. starr.org/site/PageServer.* Retrieved June 25, 2005.

U.S. Department of Education. *http:// www.ed.gov/index.jhtml.* Retrieved July 6, 2005.

U.S. National Institutes of Health: National Institute on Aging. *http://www.nia.nih.gov.* Retrieved June 25, 2005.

U.S. National Institutes of Health: National Institute on Drug Abuse. *http: //www. nida.nih.gov.* Retrieved June 25, 2005.

Wisconsin Assistive Technology Initiative. *http://www.wati.org.* Retrieved June 25, 2005.

About the Contributors

Linda G. Allen, M.Ed., is President and CEO, Apple Tree Consulting, Inc., LaGrange, KY and Strategies Consultant with the Exceptional Children Services at Ohio Valley Educational Cooperative, Shelbyville, KY. She is the coauthor of Karp, Karen, Brown, Todd, Allen, Linda G. (1998). *Feisty Females: Inspiring Girls to Think Mathematically* and contributing author of *Assessment for Third Grade Textbook.*

Richard H. Allen, Ph.D., is a world renowned facilitator, teacher, and author and holds a Ph.D. in educational psychology from Arizona State University. He is currently president of Impact Learning, Inc. and author of *Impact Teaching: Ideas and Strategies to Maximize Student Learning* and *Train Smart: Perfect Trainings Every Time.*

Christopher Andersen is Assistant Professor in the School of Teaching and Learning at Ohio State University. His research and teaching focus on the translation of psychological theory into classroom practice.

Sharon E. Andrews, Ed.D., is Chairperson of the Education Department at Augustana College in Sioux Falls, South Dakota; her areas of interest include reading and writing in the content area classroom.

Thomas Armstrong, Ph.D., is an award-winning author and speaker with over thirty years of teaching experience from the primary through the doctoral level, and over one million copies of his books in print on issues related to learning and human development. He is the author of eleven books including *Multiple Intelligences in the Classroom, In Their Own Way, Awakening Your Child's Natural Genius, 7 Kinds of Smart, The Myth of the A.D.D. Child, ADD/ADHD Alternatives in the Classroom,* and *Awakening Genius in the Classroom.*

Kevin D. Arnold, Ph.D., ABPP, is the Director of The Center for Cognitive & Behavioral Therapy of Greater Columbus, and serves as a clinical faculty member at The Ohio State University Department of Psychiatry. He is the author of many scholarly and practice-oriented works, recently publishing the Integrated Functional Behavior Analysis Protocol assessment manual. He has also authored chapters on self-help for adolescents to manage test anxiety and improve academic study skills.

Becky A. Bailey, Ph.D., is an award-winning author, renowned teacher, and internationally recognized expert in childhood education and developmental psychology. She is the originator of the Conscious Discipline program, and founder and co-owner of Loving Guidance, Inc.

Sandy Baumann, M.S., is Program Manager at the Center for Lifelong Learning, Henry Ford Community College, in Dearborn Heights, Michigan. As a biochemist with eighteen years experience in health promotion, she is the author of *Feed Your Brain for Learning Feed Your Bones Naturally* and *Feed Your Brain for Memory*.

Linda S. Behar-Horenstein, Ph.D., is Professor of Educational Leadership, Policy, and Foundations at the University of Florida, Gainesville. She has published four books and over forty book chapters and refereed articles. She is on the Editorial Board of the *Journal of Professional Studies* in Canada and *World Studies in Education* in Australia. Dr. Behar-Horenstein is a member of the Professors of Curriculum, a national group of distinguished professors elected for their contributions to research and teaching in curriculum studies.

Doris Bergen, Ph.D., is Professor of Educational Psychology at Miami University in Oxford, Ohio. She has published six books, including three on play development and two on infant/toddler assessment and curriculum. Her most recent book is *Brain Research and Childhood Education: Implications for Educators* (coauthored with Juliet Coscia). In 2000, she received the NAECTE/Allyn-Bacon award as Outstanding Early Childhood Teacher Educator and was also recognized as a Miami University Distinguished Scholar.

Charlotte A. Boettiger is Assistant Research Scientist at the Ernest Gallo Clinic and Research Center, a part of the University of California, San Francisco Department of Neurology devoted to the study of drug and alcohol addiction. Her research focuses on investigating executive control and decision-making processes that may be impaired in the context of addiction. Dr. Boettiger was awarded the Hugh O Connor Memorial Fellowship by the Wheeler Center for the Neurobiology of Addiction in 2002.

Larry K. Brendtro, Ph.D., is the founder and president of Reclaiming Youth International, a non-profit research and training institute. He is the former president of Starr Commonwealth, Albion, Michigan, and continues to serve as dean of Starr Commonwealth's International Research Council. Dr. Brendtro has forty years experience as an educator and psychologist, specializing in troubled children and youth, and has taught at the University of Michigan, the University of Illinois, The Ohio State University, and Augustana College. He co-edits the journal *Reclaiming Children and Youth* and is the author of ten books on troubled youth.

Chris Brewer-Boyd, M.A., FAMI, teaches educators about the integration of music into education and brain-based learning methods through university programs and as a consultant. She is fellow in the Bonny Method of Guided Imagery and Music, a psychotherapeutic method of using music, and is certified in the MARI© mandala art assessment. Chris has written extensively on the use of music in education and about medical applications of vibroacoustic music. She is coauthor of *Rhythms of Learning* and author of *Soundtracks for Learning*.

Evie J. Brouwer, M.A., is Assistant Professor of Education at Augustana College, Sioux Falls, SD. She has worked with at-risk youth for seven years. She has presented at various conferences particularly on the subject of reading comprehension strategies. Brouwer is experienced in educating all levels of learners from kindergarten through adults.

Trez Buckland, M.A., has his Masters in Counseling and is currently the Site Coordinator at the School of Nursing at the University of Washington, Seattle, WA. He is the 2001 recipient of the Washington State Recognition Award for National Alliance for the Mentally Ill.

Martha S. Burns, Ph.D., CCC-SLP, has been a practicing speech language pathologist in the Chicago area for thirty-five years. She serves on the Faculty of Northwestern University, department of communication sciences and disorders, and on the medical staff of Evanston-Northwestern Hospital, both in Evanston, Illinois. Dr. Burns has received honors from Northwestern University, Evanston Hospital Corporation, the American Speech Language Hearing Foundation and St. Xavier University. Doody's Rating Service selected her book on Right Hemisphere Dysfunction published through Aspen Press as one of the best health sciences books of 1997. In addition to that book, Dr. Burns is the author of a book on aphasia and the test *Burns Brief Inventory of Communication and Cognition* published by The Psychological Corporation.

Geoffrey Caine, LL.M., is the Executive Director of the Caine Learning Institute. He has published extensively. His work includes *Making Connections: Teaching and the Human Brain, Education on the Edge of Possibility, Unleashing the Power of Perceptual Change: The Promise of Brain Based Learning, Mindshifts, The ReEnchantment of Learning, The Brain and the Competitive Edge,* and *The 12 Brain/Mind Learning Principles in Action.*

Adam M. Campbell, Ph.D., recently completed his doctoral work at USF on stress, memory, and antidepressant actions on the brain. He is in the Department of Psychology, University of South Florida, Tampa, Florida and Medical Research Service, Veterans Hospital, Tampa, FL.

Mary A. Carskadon, Ph.D., is Professor of Psychiatry and Human Behavior at Brown Medical School and Director of Chronobiology and Sleep Research at E.P. Bradley Hospital. She has studied sleep and circadian rhythms in children and adolescents and is editor of *Adolescent Sleep Patterns: Biological, Social, and Psychological Influences* she is recipient of the National Sleep Foundation Lifetime Achievement Award.

Susan Catapano, Ed.D., is an Assistant Professor of Early Childhood Education at the University of Missouri St. Louis. She is the former owner and operator of two state licensed, nationally accredited early care and education programs that served 400 children and their families in St. Louis City and County. She is a principle investigator on a US Department of Education Teacher Quality Enhancement Grant ($3.2 million) that supports new teachers and student teachers learning to teach in urban settings.

Joan Caulfield, Ph.D., is the president of The Brain Incorporated and is a former teacher, principal, associate superintendent, and professor. She is the co-facilitator of the Brain Compatible Learning Network sponsored by the

Association for Supervision and Curriculum Development. She is co-publisher of the *Brain Compatible Learning Networker* newsletter and the author of numerous articles and books.

Tammy Chung, Ph.D., is Assistant Professor of Psychiatry at University of Pittsburgh, Pennsylvania. She conducts research on the assessment, diagnosis, and course of substance-related problems in adolescents.

Susan Clayton is a private consultant, former teacher, teacher counselor, and staff developer. Research interests: planning and teaching for understanding, the role of conversation in the learning process, and teacher study groups.

John J. Clementson, Ph.D., is Professor and Chair of Education at Gustavus Adolphus College in St. Peter, Minnesota. His expertise is with the middle-school learner.

Suzanne Corkin, Ph.D., is Professor of Behavioral Neuroscience in the Department of Brain and Cognitive Sciences at the Massachusetts Institute of Technology. Her research focuses on human memory systems and memory in aging. She has written extensively on these topics.

Kimberly Cornia, M.A. (MFT), graduated from the marriage and family therapy (MFT) program at Chapman University in August, 2005. She also worked as a therapist trainee in the Chapman University Community Clinic as part of her graduate studies.

Laura Crawford, M.A., is the Community Education Coordinator for HOME-FRONT, a collaboration of more than fifty agencies throughout the Kansas City metropolitan area that work together to provide resources to support and encourage the positive development of children, parents, and families. In addition, Laura is a trained ACT Facilitator.

Craig A. Davis, M.Ed., is a doctoral student in the Department of Educational Leadership, Policy, and Foundations, of the University of Florida's College of Education. His research interests include qualitative theory and methodology, educational sociology, and curriculum studies.

Mark D'Esposito is Professor of Neuroscience and Psychology, and Director of the Henry H. Wheeler, Jr. Brain Imaging Center at the Helen Wills Neuroscience Institute at the University of California, Berkeley. His research spans the disciplines of neurology, psychology, and neuroscience specifically focusing on investigating the role of prefrontal cortex in working memory and executive control processes. Dr. D'Esposito was awarded the Norman Geschwind Prize in Behavioral Neurology from the American Academy of Neurology in 1999 and is currently the Editor-In-Chief of the *Journal of Cognitive Neuroscience.*

Gloria Dey, Ph.D., is an Associate Professor in the Education Department at Washburn University in Topeka, Kansas. Her writing and speaking interests include learning disabilities, multicultural education, and the Comer School Development Program.

David M. Diamond, Ph.D., is a Professor in the Departments of Psychology and Pharmacology at the University of South Florida and is a Research Biologist in the Medical Research Service Division of the Tampa Veterans Hospital. He has been studying the neurobiology of stress and memory for the past 25 years.

Charlene K. Douglass, D.A.S.L., is affiliated with the Hillbrook School, Los Gatos, California. Her research interests include learning styles, child growth and development, and technology in education. She is the recipient of the ALSC Frederic G. Melcher Scholarship and Beta Phi Mu Award.

Georg H. Eifert, Ph.D., is Professor and Chair of the Department of Psychology at Chapman University in Orange, CA. He was ranked in the top thirty of Researchers in Behavior Analysis and Therapy in the 1990s and has authored over 100 publications on psychological causes and treatments of anxiety and other emotional disorders. He is a clinical fellow of the Behavior Therapy and Research Society, a member of numerous national and international psychological associations, and serves on several editorial boards of leading clinical psychology journals. He also is a licensed clinical psychologist. He is the author of *The Anorexia Workbook, Acceptance and Commitment Therapy for Anxiety Disorders,* and *ACT on Life, Not on Anger.*

John Elfers is a sex educator and marriage family therapist specializing in sexuality education and HIV/STD prevention with adolescents. He has written curricula for peer educators and is a trainer for teachers and persons living with HIV.

Lise Eliot, Ph.D., is Assistant Professor of Neuroscience at Rosalind Franklin University of Medicine and Science/the Chicago Medical School. She is author of *What's Going On in There? How the Brain and Mind Develop in the First Five Years of Life* and a forthcoming book on sex differences in children's brains and learning styles. She also serves as Neuroscience Consultant for the Erikson Institute in Chicago.

Sue Elliott is a teacher, teacher counselor, and staff developer. Research interests include: planning and teaching for understanding, the role of conversation in the learning process, and teacher study groups.

Laura Erlauer is an author, national consultant, and school principal at Brookfield Elementary School in Brookfield, Wisconsin. She is the author of *The Brain-Compatible Classroom: Using What We Know About Learning to Improve Teaching,* and several professional articles on the topic.

Jennifer Feinstein, J.D., received her law degree at George Mason University in Fairfax, Va. She is currently an attorney with Lewis Brisbois Bisgaard & Smith, LLP in New York.

Sheryl Feinstein, Ed.D., is an Associate Professor at Augustana College in Sioux Falls, SD. She is the author of the book, *Secrets of the Teenage Brain.* Her research interests include secondary education, middle school after-school programs, and at-risk adolescents. She presents nationally and internationally on the Adolescent Brain.

Susan Gibbons, M.A., has a bachelor's degree in psychology and a master's degree in Health Services Administration. She is currently pursuing a doctoral degree in Adult Education. She is the author of, *"I Can Sign My ABC's"* and has had a lifetime interest in animal studies.

Jill Gierach, M.S.E., ATP, is a special education teacher with over eighteen years of classroom experience. She currently is a regional consultant for seventy-five school districts in the area of assistive technology. She has been with the wisconsin assistive technology initiative (WATI) since its inception and holds national certification as an assistive technology practitioner (ATP) from RESNA (rehabilitation engineering and assistive technology society of north america).

Daisy Grewal, M.S., is a doctoral candidate in social psychology at Yale University. Her master's thesis investigated the relationship between emotional intelligence and creativity. Her other research interests currently include gender and emotion.

David Halstead, M.Ed., is a career educator with extensive classroom and counseling experience at the secondary and post secondary levels plus national and international (Caribbean, West Africa and Asia) student services administrative experience. He currently develops and delivers professional development programs for educators based on those applications of neuroscience that have application in the areas of teaching, learning, and classroom management. His publications include *Putting the Brain into the Classroom - 39 Brain Facts and 231 Teaching Strategies* and *Career Focus.*

Anne M. Hanson, M.A., is a National Board Certified Teacher in Early Adolescence/English Language Arts. She has lectured and written extensively on writing and the brain and is the author of *Write Brain Write* and *Visual Writing* as well as *Thin Veils* a young adult novel dealing with anorexia. Anne, whose honors include Fulbright Memorial Fund Scholar, Scottsdale Middle School Teacher of the Year, and Arizona Teacher of the Year finalist is currently working on her doctoral degree in Educational Leadership.

Mariale M. Hardiman is the principal of Roland Park Elementary/Middle School in Baltimore City. During her more than 30 years with the Baltimore City Public School System, Dr. Hardiman has served as a school administrator, staff developer, and teacher. Under her leadership, Roland Park Elementary/Middle School received numerous awards for continuous student achievement gains as well as its designation as a Blue Ribbon School of Excellence. Dr. Hardiman also serves as adjunct instructor at The Johns Hopkins University in Baltimore, MD. Her book, *Connecting Brain Research with Effective Teaching: The Brain Targeted Teaching Model* and article, "Connecting Brain Research with Dimensions of Learning" have generated widespread interest from educators worldwide.

Gail Heidenhain is an expert in Accelerated Learning and she has facilitated in the training of thousands of teachers. She serves as President of Delphin, Inc. and President of International Alliance for Learning.

Thomas R. Hoerr, Ph.D., is the head of the New City School in St. Louis, MO. The faculty has been implementing the theory of multiple intelligences (MI) since 1988. Hoerr has written more than forty articles and one book (*Becoming A Multiple Intelligences School*, ASCD Press, 2000) about how MI can be used in schools. His new book, written for school leaders, *Leadership That Respects the Art of Teaching* will be published in fall 2005.

Jack Huhtala, M.A., is an educational consultant (www.CoachingTheBrain.com) and Adjunct Professor of Education at Pacific University, Forest Grove, Oregon. He has published on Group Investigation and facilitating classroom inquiry discussion.

Carol A. Isaac is a Ph.D. candidate in the Department of Educational Leadership at the University of Florida.

Lisa M. Jackson, Ph.D., is the Agency Accountability Specialists at the Arizona Schools for the Deaf and the Blind, Tucson, Arizona. She specializes in assessment of students who are visually impaired and students who are deaf and hard of hearing. Her dissertation was titled *"The Effects of Testing Adaptations on Students' Standardized Test Scores for Students with Visual Impairments in Arizona"*

Wayne B. Jennings, Ph.D., is the Director of The Institute for Learning and Teaching and is a former teacher, principal, superintendent, and professor. He is the co-facilitator of the Brain Compatible Learning Network sponsored by the Association for Supervision and Curriculum Development. He is co-publisher of the *Brain Compatible Learning Networker* newsletter and the author of numerous articles and books.

Eric Jensen is one of the leaders in educational neuroscience. He has taught at three universities and authored twenty-six books on the brain and learning. He is a longtime member of the Society for Neuroscience and conducts research and staff development worldwide.

Susan J. Jones, M.A., is an Independent Education Consultant. Adjunct faculty member: Aurora University IL, Central Michigan University, Chapman University CA; Flagler College, FL. Regional Director and '02–'03 President of Florida Association for Supervision and Curriculum, former member Board of Directors of ASCD. She is the author of numerous books including *Blueprint for Student Success: A Guide to Research-Based Teaching Practice K-12* and *Backstage Pass for Trainers, Facilitators and Public Speakers.*

Spencer Kagan, Ph.D., is a former clinical psychologist and Professor of Pschology and Education, University of California. Kagan and co-workers created over 200 structures — simple instructional strategies. His books, *Cooperative Learning, Multiple Intelligences, Win-Win Discipline,* and *Silly Sports and Goofy Games* have been translated into many languages and are used worldwide in teacher education programs.

Martha Kaufeldt, M.A., is a full time trainer and consultant with an extensive background in brain compatible teaching and learning theory. She was a K-12 classroom teacher for over 20 years. She is the author of *Begin with the Brain: Orchestrating the Learner-Centered Classroom* and *Teachers, Change Your Bait! Brain Compatible Differentiated Instruction.*

Duke R. Kelly is president of Calculated Success, Inc., a staff development, training, and research company specializing in making instruction congruent with how the brain learns. Duke travels worldwide coaching and observing classrooms of all types.

Doreen Kimura, Ph.D., is Visiting Professor at Simon Fraser University, Burnaby, British Columbia, Canada. She has written extensively on biological influences on cognition, including individual differences. She is a Fellow of the Royal Society of Canada, and has received honorary degrees from Simon Fraser and Queen's universities. She has also received the Distinguished Scientist award from the Canadian Psychological Association, and in 2005 received the Hebb award for distinguished contributions from the canadian society for brain, behavior and cognitive sciences (CSBBCS). Her most recent book, *Sex and Cognition* has been translated into several languages.

Michael B. Knable, D.O., is Executive Director of the Stanley Medical Research Institute. He is also an Assistant Clinical Professor of Psychiatry at George Washington University and an Adjunct Professor of Psychiatry at the Uniformed Services University of the Health Sciences.

Susan J. Kovalik, classroom teacher and curriculum innovator for over thirty-five years, has spent the past twenty-three years developing a model for curriculum and instruction based on brain research. She developed the (integrated thematic instruction) ITI Model. In 1998, Susan was nominated a NASA Woman of the Year. She is the author of a number of books, her new newest book is *Exceeding Expectations: A User's Guide to Implementing Brain Research in the Classroom.*

James E. Longhurst, Ed.D., is vice president of Clinical and Psychological Services at Starr Commonwealth of Albion, Michigan, where he has been involved in various professional and leadership roles for over thirty years. He helped develop Starr's No Disposable Kids® Program, which focuses on creating positive school climates. He is a lead facilitator of the Institute for the Healing of Racism, a national trainer in Life Space Crisis Intervention, and an adjunct professor in psychology at Albion College. He is a licensed psychologist and a member of the American Psychological Association.

Jean Blaydes Madigan is an internationally known educational consultant for Action Based Learning in Dallas, Texas. She has thirty years teaching experience in classroom and physical education. She is the author of *Thinking on Your Feet* and co-creator of the Action Based Learning Lab. She has won numerous awards including one of six National Physical Educators of the Year and most recently the PE4LIFE National Advocacy Award.

Karen Mahan, M.A., is an Assistant Professor of Communication Disorders at Augustana College in Sioux Falls, South Dakota. Her research interests include the study of joint attention in children who have autism, and the effects of early joint attention on language development. She has presented on functional skills curriculum at CSUN and at local and state conferences.

Michael E. Martinez, Ph.D., is an Associate Professor of Education at the University of California, Irvine. His research centers on the nature of intelligence as a learnable ability, and on the cognitive, linguistic, semiotic, and biological foundations of intelligence.

Laurie Materna, Ph.D., RN is a nursing professor at Milwaukee Area Technical College. Her interest in adult learning has led to the development of a wide variety of brain-compatible teaching methodologies that she offers to students as well as faculty though workshops and seminars. She is currently writing a resource book, *Jump Start Your Brain: Creative Learning Strategies for Adults.* After examining the impact between nutrition and learning, Dr. Materna developed a nutritional snack alternative, Brain Fuel Energy Snack.

Allison Maxwell is a senior high school science teacher and curriculum mentor. She is a Professional Development Specialist in emotional intelligence and research-driven teaching and learning. She is a trainer associated with Mind Matters.

Judith Lynne McConnell, Ed.D., is a Professor of Education at Washburn University, Topeka, Kansas. Dr. McConnell is a previous preschool and elementary school teacher. She has spoken at more than a hundred conference presentations, published a book, *Teaching Renewal: Professional Issues, Personal Choices,* and has numerous article and chapter publications. Dr. McConnell is a faculty member of People to People International and led delegations of early childhood professionals to the Peoples Republic of China, Cuba, The Czech Republic, Russia, and Spain. During the past two years she has co-directed the *Oxford Round Table,* Manchester Campus, Oxford, England.

Cristal L. McGill, Ph.D., is an Adjunct Professor of Curriculum and Instruction at Arizona State University. Tempe Arizona. At the University and during *Educational Professional Development Seminars* she is known for delivering powerful, upbeat, interactive, and creative experiences for teachers, and youth.

Kathleen A. Mulligan, Ph.D., is in the Department of Biological Structure at the University of Washington in Seattle, WA. She has worked in neuroscience research in visual system and is the coauthor of over a dozen research publications. Currently, she teaches gross anatomy and neuroscience to health professionals at UW, and co-teaches in an online certificate program called "brain research in education." She is the proud recipient of the students' "Teacher of the Year" award three times.

Carole Naasz, M.A., taught in the public school setting in South Dakota for three years before moving into a Minnesota juvenile corrections classroom five years ago. Ms. Naasz has a Bachelors Degree in Social Sciences from Dakota Wesleyan University and a Masters Degree in Education Administration from South Dakota State University.

LeAnn Nickelsen, M.Ed., delivers presentations nationally on brain research topics, reading strategies, and vocabulary strategies, all based on the latest research. She is the author of the following teacher resource books published by Scholastic, Inc.: *Quick Activities to Build a Very Voluminous Vocabulary Teaching Elaboration & Word Choice Comprehension-Building Activities for Reading in Social Studies & Science* Four book Mini-Comprehension Reading series: *Inferences & Cause/Effect; Sequencing & Context Clues; Point of View & Fact/Opinion, Main Idea & Summarizing* (2004), and *Memorizing Strategies & Other Brain-Based Activities.*

Lori Niles, M.A., is completing her doctoral work in Educational Foundations and Leadership at George Fox University. She is an adjunct instructor at George Fox University. She has written a number of teacher resource and curriculum books including *Touching Hearts, Changing Lives: Becoming a Treasured Teacher* coauthored with Jody Capehart, and *The Warm and Wonderful Church Nursery,* coauthored with Kim Sikes.

Karen D. Olsen, Ed.D., worked for the California State Department of Education for twelve years. She was one of the original founders of the California Institute of School Improvement. She is the author of the definitive mentor book, *California Mentor Teacher.* She has been author and co-author of numerous books on the integrated technology Instruction (ITI) model.

Lyelle L. Palmer, B.M., M.M., Ph.D., is Professor Emeritus of Special Education (Learning Disabilities) at Winona State University, Minnesota. He is co-founder of the SMART early brain stimulation program and research scientist at the Minnesota Learning Resource Center in Minneapolis. He is editor of the *Journal of Accelerated Learning and Teaching* (www.ialearn.org) and is coauthor *of Bright Brain: Neuro-stimulators in Early Childhood.*

Collin R. Park, Ph.D., is a research Assistant Professor in the Department of Psychology at the University of South Florida and is a Research Biologist in the Medical Research Service Division of the Tampa Veterans Hospital.

Katherine D. Perez, Ed.D., is a Professor of Education at Saint Mary's College in Moraga, California. She is an international consultant on brain-based teaching and differentiating instruction; has published several articles and was awarded a Rotary International Fellowship Award.

Raleigh Philp is an Adjunct Professor of Education at Pepperdine University in Los Angeles, CA. He has studied neuroscience applications to education and is the author of a new book on primary neuroscience for secondary teachers. He received the Presidential Award for Teaching Science and the Outstanding Biology Teacher for California.

Rae Pica is a children's physical activity specialist and founder of Moving & Learning. She is the author of fourteen books, including the text *Experiences in Movement,* the *Moving & Learning Series,* and *Your Active Child.* Rae is nationally known for her workshops and keynotes and has shared her expertise with such groups as the *Sesame Street* Research Department, the Head Start Bureau,

Centers for Disease Control, and numerous state health departments throughout the country.

Olivier Piguet, Ph.D., is a postdoctoral fellow in the Department of Brain and Cognitive Sciences at the Massachusetts Institute of Technology, currently supported by a National Health & Medical Research Council Neil Hamilton Fairley fellowship (222909). His research interests include normal and pathological cognitive aging in very old individuals. His particular interest is memory and executive functions.

Lynette Poolman has completed Certification through the University of Florida's Carnegie Foundations Starting Points initiative on Brain Development. Since 1999 Lynette has worked for The Family Conservancy as the Director of HOMEFRONT. Her commitment to children and families has driven the HOMEFRONT partnership to identify initiatives and collaborations that enhance and support parents in their most important role; "raising children." Lynette is a National Trainer for the ACT Against Violence Program and has received a Presidential Commendation from the American Psychological Association for her dedication to violence prevention and young children.

Linda H. Rammler, M.Ed., Ph.D., is an educational consultant in private practice with Rammler & Wood, Consultants, LLC. She is a nationally renowned presenter on autism spectrum disorders and behavioral/emotional challenges focusing on brain research, positive behavior supports, and inclusion.

Linda Reimond, M.S., has been the director of the Lawrence Arts Center Arts-Based Preschool, in Lawrence, Kansas, since it began in 1985. She has taught kindergarten and preschool. She has been a presenter at early childhood conferences at the state, regional, and national levels. Linda has been an adjunct instructor at Washburn University. In January 2004, Linda received the Mayor's Award for Excellence in Teaching and in November 2004 received the Phoenix Award from the Lawrence Arts Commission for Arts Educator.

Regina G. Richards, M.A., an educational therapist in Riverside California, is Founder and Director of Richards Educational Therapy Center & former Director of Big Springs School, agencies that provide multidisciplinary evaluations and treatment programs for students with language learning disabilities. She has authored a variety of journal articles and books on reading, dyslexia, dysgraphia, and visual development. She is currently President of her local Inland Empire Branch of the International Dyslexia Association and presents workshops and keynotes at school districts and conferences nationally. She is President of RET Center Press

Diane Ronis, Ph.D., is Associate Professor of Education at Southern Connecticut State University. She has written extensively on instruction and assessment and is the author of *Clustering Standards in Integrated Units Critical Thinking in Math Problem-based Learning for Math & Science: Integrating Inquiry & the Internet, Brain-compatible Assessments* and *Brain-compatible Mathematics* She has presented at numerous conferences and workshops throughout the country.

Tracy L. Rupp, M.S., is a graduate student in experimental psychology at Brown University.

Peter Salovey, Ph.D., The Chris Argyris Professor of Psychology, Peter Salovey was appointed Dean of Yale College in 2004. Dr. Salovey is also Professor of Management and Professor of Epidemiology and Public Health. He directs the Health, Emotion and Behavior Laboratory and is deputy director of the Yale Center for Interdisciplinary Research on AIDS. With John D. Mayer, he developed a broad framework, coined "emotional intelligence," to describe how people understand, manage, and use their emotions. Salovey has published more than 200 articles and chapters, and he has authored, coauthored, or edited thirteen books including *Peer Counseling: Skills and Perspectives; Reasoning, Inference, and Judgment in Clinical Psychology; The Psychology of Jealousy and Envy; Psychology; The Remembered Self: Emotion and Memory in Personality; Peer Counseling: Skills, Ethics, and Perspectives; Emotional Development and Emotional Intelligence; At Play in the Fields of Consciousness; mayer-salovey-caruso emotional intelligence Test (MSCEIT): User's Manual; The Wisdom in Feeling: Psychological Processes in Emotional Intelligence; Key Readings in the Social Psychology of Health,* and *The Emotionally Intelligent Manager.*

Linda Weisbaum Seltzer, Ph.D., of Seltzer Educational and Behavioral Consultants has presented nationally on the current brain research and its implications to school climate, learning, and behavior. She has been the supervisor and principal of alternative education programs and Lee School in the public schools in Springfield, Illinois.

Rita Smilkstein, Ph.D., is Professor Emerita (English), North Seattle Community College, and teaches at Western Washington University's Woodring College of Education, Seattle Urban Campus. She has received a number of teaching awards, including two Excellence Awards from the National Institute for Staff and Organizational Development. A frequent speaker nationally and internationally, her publications include textbooks for constructivist teaching of study skills and grammar as well as articles on how to apply the brain's natural learning process to curriculum development and instructional methods across the disciplines. Her book, *We're Born to Learn: Using the Brain's Natural Learning Process to Create Today's Curriculum* won the Delta Kappa Gamma Society International's Educator's Award for 2004.

Dwayne Smith, Ph.D., has over twenty years of professional experience in higher education. He is currently an assistant vice-president for academic affairs at Avila University. Some of his awards include, Who's Who in America, Who's Who in American Education, The ACCESS Award from the Introspect Organization, and a Truman State University Alumnus of the Year Award.

Rick Smith is an international education consultant and national presenter, focusing on classroom management, brain compatible ways to motivate students, and strategies for mentor teachers. He has taught students in San Rafael, CA for over fifteen years (with a primary focus on students at-risk), and been a Mentor and Mentor Coordinator for many years. He has trained American Peace Corps Volunteer Teachers in Ghana, West Africa. He was awarded the Golden Bell Award for Outstanding Teaching, Marin County California, 1999 and is the author of *Conscious Classroom Management: Unlocking the Secrets of Great Teaching.*

Monica Soukup, Ed.D., is Assistant Professor of Education at Augustana College in Sioux Falls, South Dakota. She teaches courses in Deaf Education at Augustana College and has presented on topics related to effective communication strategies with deaf students, learning disabilities and deaf students, and creating environments that address all needs of deaf children.

David A. Sousa is an international educational consultant and the author of five books and numerous articles on the applications of brain research to educational practice. A former science teacher, school superintendent, and adjunct professor, he has been interviewed on the NBC *Today* show and received awards and an honorary degree for his contributions to education.

Marilee Sprenger is a professional development consultant and adjunct professor at Aurora University. She began her teaching career in 1971 and has taught primary, middle, high school, and college students. She speaks at state and national conferences as well as internationally. As a member of the American Academy of Neurology and the Cognitive Neuroscience Society, she remains current on brain research. She has written several books on brain-based teaching and memory including: *Learning and Memory – The Brain in Action, Becoming a Wiz at Brain-based Teaching,* and *Differentiation through Learning Styles and Memory.*

Donna Starr is Director of Starr Educational Services and an adjunct faculty member at Seattle Pacific University, Seattle. She was a classroom teacher in grades Kindergarten through eight and taught Reading Recovery and Math Intervention for thirty-six years. She is the author of *Current Brain Research and its Implications for Classroom Instruction.*

Thomas M. Stephens is Professor Emeritus, College of Education, the Ohio State University. He has written extensively on various applications of behavior modification and was an early advocate of direct instruction of social behavior in schools. He has authored twelve textbooks and over hundred journal articles. He is currently the Executive Director of the School Study Council of Ohio.

Jean Seville Suffield spent almost all of her career in education on the South Shore of Montréal, the home of the early immersion model. Jean holds a Master Certification Diploma in brain-based learning through the Jensen Learning Corporation. She is a senior faculty member of The William Glasser Institute and the founder of Choice-Makers, an international training and consulting service. Jean has authored several books for classroom use and is the recipient of the Lieutenant Governor Medal for Academic Excellence.

Cathie Summerford, M S , is the author of *Action-Packed Classrooms;* she also authored *PE-4-ME: Teaching Lifelong Health and Fitness* and is completing her third book *Obesity's Impact on the BodyBrain: A Guidebook for Parents, Teachers and All-Concerned.* As an Educational Consultant and President of Fit 4 Learning, Cathie has been recognized as a California Teacher of the Year, (NASPE) Southwest National Teacher of the Year, and california school boards association (CSBA) Golden Bell award-winning author. On top of it, she is an IRON-MAN Triathlon finisher!

Susan Tapert, Ph.D., is Assistant Professor of Psychiatry at University of California, San Diego. She directs the Substance Abuse Mental Illness program at the

VA San Diego Healthcare System, and her research focuses on the relationships between brain functioning and substance use in adolescents and young adults.

Marcia L. Tate, Ph.D., is an Educational Consultant and CEO of *Developing Minds Inc.* She is the author of the bestseller, *Worksheets Don't Grow Dendrites: 20 Instructional Strategies that Engage the Brain* and two subsequent books, *Sit & Get Won't Grow Dendrites: 20 Professional Learning Strategies that Engage the Adult Brain* and *Reading and Language Arts Worksheets Don't Grow Dendrites: 20 Literacy Strategies that Engage the Brain.* She was a former classroom teacher, reading specialist, language arts coordinator and the Georgia 2002 Staff Developer of the Year.

Donna Walker Tileston, Ed.D., has served education as a leader in teaching, administration, research, writing, software development, and national consulting for the past thirty years. Her administrative responsibilities have included curriculum development, management, technology, finance, grants management, public relations, and drug abuse prevention programs. For the past twenty years Dr. Tileston has been actively involved in brain research and the factors that inhibit learning or increase the brain's ability to put information into long-term memory. Dr. Tileston's research has been published through Corwin Press under the titles: *Strategies for Teaching Differently* and *Ten Best Teaching Practices: How Brain Research, Learning Styles and Standards Define Teaching Competencies* which has been on Corwin's Best Seller List since its first year of print.

E. Fuller Torrey, M.D., is Associate Director for Laboratory Research, Stanley Medical Research Institute, Bethesda, Maryland. He is also the President of the Treatment Advocacy Center (www.psychlaws.org), a Professor of Psychiatry at the Uniformed Services University of the Health Sciences, and the author or coauthor of nineteen books.

Dianna Townsend is a doctoral candidate in Educational Leadership at the University of California, Irvine. Her research interests include vocabulary development and the relationship between language and intelligence.

Laurie Wenger, Ed.D., is a Professor of Education at Augustana College in Sioux Falls, SD, serves as a trainer/speaker for Reclaiming Youth International and also directs the gifted program for an area school district.

Doris Señor Woltman, Ed.S. is the Superintendent at the Arizona Schools for the Deaf and the Blind, Tucson, Arizona. Ms. Woltman has worked in the field of visual impairment and blindness since 1980. Her specialties include community-based instruction and mental health issues for individuals with sensory impairment. Ms. Woltman is a Member of the Governor's Council for the Blind and Visually Impaired and a Commissioner for the Arizona Council for the Deaf and Hard of Hearing.

James C. Woodson, Ph.D., is an Assistant Professor in the Department of Psychology at the University of Tampa, Tampa, Florida.

James E. Zull, Ph.D., is Professor of Biology at Case Western Reserve University in Cleveland Ohio. He is a biochemist with over 100 publications. He has received many grants in support of his biochemistry research, including a Research Career Development Award from the National Institutes of Health. He is the Founding Director of the Center for Learning and Teaching (UCITE) at Case Western Reserve, and the author of the first book on the connection between the biology of learning and teaching written by a scientist: *The Art of Changing the Brain; Enriching Teaching by Exploring the Biology of Learning.*

INDEX